Best Companions

Women's Diaries and Letters of the South

CAROL BLESER, SERIES EDITOR

Best Companions

Letters of Eliza Middleton Fisher and
Her Mother, Mary Hering Middleton,
from Charleston, Philadelphia,
and Newport, 1839–1846

EDITED BY

ELIZA COPE HARRISON

UNIVERSITY OF SOUTH CAROLINA PRESS

UNIVERSITY OF SOUTH CAROLINA *BICENTENNIAL*

© 2001 University of South Carolina

Published in Columbia, South Carolina, by the
University of South Carolina Press

Manufactured in the United States of America

05 04 03 02 01   5 4 3 2 1

Library of Congress Cataloging-in-Publication Data

Fisher, Eliza Middleton, 1815–1890.
   Best companions : letters of Eliza Middleton Fisher and her mother, Mary Hering
Middleton, from Charleston, Philadelphia, and Newport, 1839–1846 / edited by
Eliza Cope Harrison.
      p.   cm. — (Women's diaries and letters of the South)
   Includes bibliographical references and index.
   ISBN 1-57003-375-7
   1. Fisher, Eliza Middleton, 1815–1890—Correspondence.   2. Middleton, Mary
Hering—Correspondence.   3. Mothers and daughters—South Carolina—
Charleston Region—Correspondence.   4. Women—South Carolina—Charleston
Region—Correspondence.   5. Mothers and daughters—Pennsylvania—
Philadelphia—Correspondence.   6. Women—Pennsylvania—
Philadelphia—Correspondence.   7. Charleston Region (S.C.)—Biography.
8. Philadelphia (Pa.)—Biography.   I. Middleton, Mary Hering.
II. Harrison, Eliza Cope.   III. Title.   IV. Series.
CT275.F5598 A4   2001
974.8'1103'0922—dc21   00-011420

Contents

Illustrations and Maps

Series Editor's Preface

Best Companions: Letters of Eliza Middleton Fisher and Her Mother, Mary Hering Middleton, from Charleston, Philadelphia, and Newport, 1839–1846 is the eleventh in what had been the Women's Diaries and Letters of the Nineteenth-Century South series. This series has been redefined and is now titled Women's Diaries and Letters of the South, enabling us to include some remarkably fine works from the twentieth century. This series includes a number of never-before-published diaries, some collections of unpublished correspondence, and a few reprints of published diaries—a potpourri of nineteenth-century and, now, twentieth-century Southern women's writings.

The series enables women to speak for themselves, providing readers with a rarely opened window into Southern society before, during, and after the American Civil War and into the twentieth century. The significance of these letters and journals lies not only in the personal revelations and the writing talent of these women authors but also in the range and versatility of the documents' contents. Taken together, these publications will tell us much about the heyday and the fall of the Cotton Kingdom, the mature years of the "peculiar institution," the war years, the adjustment of the South to a new social order following the defeat of the Confederacy, and the New South of the twentieth century. Through these writings, the reader will also be presented with first-hand accounts of everyday life and social events, courtships and marriages, family life and travels, religion and education, and the life-and-death matters that made up the ordinary and extraordinary world of the American South.

The Middleton Family of Middleton Place on the Ashley River is par excellence a representative of antebellum American aristocracy. Their family papers are among the largest existing archives of the history of South Carolina from the eighteenth to the twentieth century. *Best Companions* is drawn from three collections of Middleton papers, one of which has been in private hands and unappreciated until it was brought to light by Eliza Cope Harrison. Her discovery provided the key to her bringing together in this book as a coherent whole, three disparate collections of letters. The material in this volume is exciting, important, and new. It is particularly revealing in exploring the ties that bound together a family that extended across the Mason-Dixon Line, a significant but little explored aspect of our national experience.

Carol Bleser

Preface

Within two days of setting out from Charleston, South Carolina, for Philadelphia, her new husband's home, Eliza Middleton Fisher wrote a letter to her mother, Mary Helen Hering Middleton. Describing the first stage of her trip northward, that letter, written in the spring of 1839, began a seven-year-long correspondence in which the two Middleton women wrote to each other almost every week (except, of course, when they happened to be in the same place). Their regular correspondence ended in 1846 when Eliza's father, Henry Middleton—a prominent rice planter, politician, and diplomat—died and her widowed mother moved to Philadelphia. Mary Middleton and her daughter wrote because they were separated for long periods, but—being lively and articulate, well-educated, and widely traveled women—they created a treasure for later generations. Their letters, published now for the first time, are wide-ranging in subject matter and add, in several important areas, to currently available material about the lives and attitudes of cultivated and well-to-do southern women and their families, as well as to American social history generally, in the decades before the Civil War.

None of this was known when I started to look through Eliza Fisher's letters several years ago. She was my grandmother's grandmother and almost 175 of her letters to her mother—valued, if never read, by her descendants—had come to rest in a file drawer in my parents' home in Massachusetts. As I read them, it became clear that Eliza's weekly descriptions of what she did and thought, or rejoiced and worried about, were only one-half of an extended conversation by mail she and her mother were having. Unfortunately, Mrs. Middleton's half of the correspondence, tantalizingly echoed in Eliza's half, was not in the file drawer. I wondered: If Eliza's letters had been so carefully kept, was it possible that her mother's had also been saved, but somewhere else?

The search for her letters took me to Philadelphia. There, in the manuscript catalog of the Historical Society of Pennsylvania, I found a card which read "Middleton, Mary Helen (Hering) . . . [Letters] to her daughter, Mrs. J. Francis Fisher. Family and social matters and other interests." One hundred and sixty-one of her letters were there!

A third group of letters from both Mrs. Middleton and Eliza was waiting to be noticed in the South Carolina Historical Society in Charleston. In the three collections combined, there are 376 letters.[1] They form an unusually long and continuous correspondence which is of particular interest because it is the record of a mother and daughter who enjoyed a remarkably strong relationship.

Mary Hering Middleton and Eliza Middleton Fisher belonged to one of the South's most conspicuous families, but as neither spent her entire life in the South, they were, in many respects, more than southern. Mrs. Middleton, though she lived in South Carolina for almost forty years, grew up in England and spent a decade in Russia (1820–1830) while her husband was the U.S. minister. Eliza was intensely loyal to her southern roots but spent ten of her first fifteen years in Europe and then lived in Philadelphia for half a century. The two women's opinions and viewpoints therefore draw attention to an important group of cosmopolitan South Carolinians who continued to be at home both in, and beyond, the south during the antebellum decades.

Because they realized that other family members and friends would often read, or listen to at least parts of their letters, Eliza and her mother planned and composed them to make them interesting and entertaining. They succeeded so well that their letters came to serve as newsletters for a rather large group in Charleston, Philadelphia, and Newport, in which they sent messages back and forth, discussed political news as well as music, literature, and religion, and described family events. Concurrently with this "public" level, Mrs. Middleton and Eliza also wrote on an intensely personal and private level as a mother and daughter who loved and depended on each other. They shared worries, joys, and frustrations and talked about nursing babies, pregnancy, too many children, a strong-minded mother-in-law, and an uncommunicative husband, new daughters-in-law, their friends' romances, and marital troubles. Taking into account the number of people likely to see, or hear, their letters, and con-

---

1. Eliza and Mrs. Middleton must have written a total of about 450 letters in the seven-year period between May 1839 and May 1846. This figure is arrived at by estimating the number of letters which would have been written during periods from which no letters have survived and adding to this the number of letters which are mentioned but now missing.

sidering that Eliza's father and brothers frequently opened her letters in Charleston before they were delivered to her mother at Middleton Place, the intimacy which Eliza and her mother maintained is remarkable.

In writing about their family, Mrs. Middleton and Eliza covered the affairs of three generations of Middletons—that of Mary Hering Middleton and her husband, Henry; next, their children's generation, including Eliza and her husband, J. Francis Fisher; and third, that of an ever-increasing number of Middleton grandchildren. Their letters sometimes looked backward to the senior Middletons' youth in the later eighteenth and early nineteenth centuries, and they set the stage for the younger generation, many of whom lived into the twentieth century. The letters' main focus, however, is the extended Middleton family during the 1830s and 1840s. They provide considerable detail about the Middletons and other wealthy, influential, and often-related South Carolina Lowcountry families of that period and, among other things, highlight the continuation of social links between South Carolina and Philadelphia, which had often started in the previous century.[2]

The correspondence also provides firsthand accounts of Philadelphia in the first half of the nineteenth century. Eliza married Joshua Francis Fisher when Philadelphia was being transformed from a small city, where walking brought one to almost any corner, into a huge industrial metropolis of great wealth, appalling poverty, disturbing levels of civil unrest, and a rich base of cultural resources. Her letters reflect these conditions. Her descriptions of Philadelphia's musical life in the 1830s and 1840s are especially interesting because she wrote about both her own musical activities and her patronage of professional musicians.

The Fishers moved among distinguished lawyers and doctors, political leaders of both parties, visiting literary figures, and European dignitaries. Eliza knew many of the people her husband's cousin, Sidney Fisher, wrote about in

2. No similar contemporary account of the Middletons and related families in the 1830s and 1840s is in print. Covering an earlier period, however, Mrs. Charles Cotesworth Pinckney described the newly wed Henry Middletons in Paris in the 1790s in letters published in *Letterbook of Mrs. Mary Stead Pinckney*, edited by Charles F. McComb (New York: Grolier Club, 1946). Many in the Middletons' circle, including Henry Middleton's brother, John Izard Middleton, are also mentioned in *The Diary of Harriet Manigault, 1813–1816* (Rockland, Maine: Colonial Dames of America, 1976).

Two accounts, written later by people who knew the Henry Middletons' mid-nineteenth-century surroundings and lifestyle, are Alicia H. Middleton's *Life in Carolina and New England during the Nineteenth Century* (Bristol, R.I.; privately printed, 1929) and Mrs. St. Julien Ravenel's *Charleston: The Place and the People* (New York: Macmillan, 1906).

his diary, but, as a young bride and mother, she saw them from a different perspective and wrote generally without the pretensions or the eye to posterity which marked Sidney Fisher's comments.[3]

The third geographic focus of this correspondence is Newport, Rhode Island, where the Henry Middletons spent the summers throughout most of the 1830s and 1840s. Many of their friends—from Boston, New York, and Philadelphia, as well as from Charleston, Baltimore, and Savannah—did the same, and Mrs. Middleton's and Eliza's letters suggest Newport played a key role in fostering and maintaining friendships between southerners and northerners in that period.

Cumulatively, their letters reveal a good deal about the attitudes and circumstances which shaped their lives over the course of two generations, but in the end, Eliza and her mother were not writing a history of their lives or of their times. They were writing for each other, and they wrote about what was important and interesting to them; they wrote selectively without bothering to explain what they both knew.

As a result, neither everything nor everyone is presented equally or fully. For example, Henry Middleton, obviously a most important personality, remains a shadowy figure whose defects are perhaps overemphasized by his wife. The letters therefore give rise to questions—about the Middleton and Fisher families, about Charleston and Philadelphia and Newport, about American society and thought, customs and attitudes—which they do not answer. By provoking such questions, the letters will, I hope, invite readers to use them as the base for further exploration.

From Manuscript to Printed Page
Editorial Guidelines

Of the 376 located letters written by Mary Hering Middleton and Eliza Middleton Fisher between May 1839 and May 1846, 175, or nearly half, are in this

---

3. *A Philadelphia Perspective: The Diary of Sidney George Fisher Covering the Years 1834–1871,* ed. Nicholas Wainwright (Philadelphia: Historical Society of Pennsylvania, 1967), is much relied on as one of a small number of published primary sources about the social history of Philadelphia's upper class in the pre–Civil War decades. Some of the same people are mentioned in "Samuel Breck's Diary," ed. Nicholas Wainwright, *Pennsylvania Magazine of History and Biography* (October 1978 and January 1979). Eliza's husband provided considerable information about this group but concentrated on the eighteenth and early nineteenth centuries in *The Recollections of Joshua Francis Fisher, Written in 1864,* arranged by Sophia Cadwalader (Boston: privately printed, 1929).

volume. These have been selected to give continuity to the story of the Middletons and Fishers as it unfolded, keeping a balance as far as possible between Eliza's and Mrs. Middleton's letters, and to provide a representative sample of the subjects and people mentioned in the correspondence. Many exciting, amusing or thought-provoking letters have been left out only because of limitations to the size of this volume.

The letters are printed in their entirety and virtually as Mrs. Middleton and Eliza put them on paper, the dull and repetitious along with the dramatic and exciting,[4] so they will be a reliable source for present and future scholars. At the same time, to make the letters enjoyable and understandable for interested readers regardless of how familiar they are with American history, I have provided as much information as possible about the surroundings—people, places, and ideas—that Mrs. Middleton, Eliza, and their families took for granted.

In addition to the introduction to the collection, which presents the Middleton and Fisher families as they were in 1839, there is also a brief introduction preceding the letters for each year. Explanatory comments are added, when needed, before a particular letter or group of letters. People mentioned in the letters (except for a small group who have not been located) are identified at the end of the letter in which they are first mentioned. A group of family charts show the relationships between members of the extended Middleton and Fisher families.

Books, music, important events, and other items are also identified when first mentioned. Well-known public figures, such as presidents of the United States and major authors, are not identified.

Changes and symbols in the text:

- The original spelling has been kept. *Sic* is *not* used to confirm that a word was actually written as it is printed.
- The original punctuation, or lack thereof, is usually retained, but some punctuation is added or changed for clarity: periods are added to some sentences; dashes are often omitted.
- Paragraphs are added or changed rather freely. Closing phrases, such as "love to all I am Y^{r} most affectionate Daughter Eliza," are always run as part of the body of the letter whether or not they were written that way in the original.

---

4. The only exception to this is that some passages referring to Mrs. Middleton's relatives and friends in England have been omitted without notice. Even though they were extremely important to her, Mary Middleton's relatives are not central to the story of the Henry Middletons in America.

- When part of a word or phrase is missing from the letter, but the meaning is obvious (for example, where the paper was torn as the letter was opened), the missing word or letters are added. *Probable* answers to what is missing, however, are put in brackets; for example, [probably]. Editorial explanations which are added to the text are italicized in brackets; for example, [*her sister*]. Similarly, when a word is either illegible or missing and cannot be figured out, the explanation is italicized in brackets; for example, [*illegible*] or [*missing*].

- Where Eliza wrote "Mama" with a line over the second "m" to indicate a double letter, this is routinely changed to "Mamma." Careless errors, such as writing the same word twice or leaving out a letter, are corrected.

- Words which Eliza or Mrs. Middleton crossed out (there are surprisingly few) are omitted unless they show a change of meaning. Words or phrases which were interlined or added somewhere else on the page are put on the appropriate line.

- Many of the French words and phrases in the letters are found in English dictionaries such as Merriam *Webster's Collegiate Dictionary,* 10th ed., and have not been translated. Less common French and Italian phrases are translated and italicized in brackets; for example, parure [*ornament*].

- Abbreviated names are frequently completed, particularly when the person is first mentioned—for example, Mrs. T[homas] M[iddleton]—and some abbreviated words are extended for clarity—for example, "comp[limen]ts." In both cases, the added letters are in square brackets. When all or part of a date is missing at the head of a letter, it is supplied in brackets.

Each letter is preceded by the name of the person to whom it was written and the place to which it was sent. When Philadelphia only is given, the letter was sent to the Fishers' house at 170 Chestnut Street; when Charleston only is given, the letter went to the Middletons' house on Boundary Street. The original addresses, forwarding instructions, postal marks, dates of receipt or of answers, and occasional notes and figures on the outside of letters are usually omitted.

All the original letters are in manuscript form and signed by either Mrs. Middleton or Eliza Fisher; this is therefore not noted on individual letters. The collection in which the letter is found is indicated at the end of each letter. (See *Abbreviations.*)

Acknowledgments

So many people have given me encouragement and good advice since the start of this project that I am both exhilarated and embarrassed by their generosity. Barbara Doyle, historian and research consultant at Middleton Place Foundation, has shared her encyclopedic knowledge of Middleton family history and the intricacies of Lowcountry familial relationships, provided documents and illustrations, corrected my errors, and commented on more than one version of the manuscript. Timothy Harrison, the book's and my staunchest supporter, makes all things possible.

Elise Pinckney gave me wise counsel as well as encouragement and made sure I knew about people and places in the Charleston area I would otherwise have missed. Robert Leath, formerly at Historic Charleston Foundation, alerted me to important letters of Margaret Izard Manigault and made two helpful trips through the manuscript. Sarah Lytle, former director of Middleton Place Foundation, suggested (correctly, of course) that Mary Hering Middleton's half of the correspondence might be at the Historical Society of Pennsylvania. Beth Luey of Arizona State University and Richard Leffler of the University of Wisconsin, faculty members at the 1997 Institute for the Editing of Historical Documents in Madison, Wisconsin, have been particularly generous with their advice.

Assistance has come from every direction. Translations of the French passages came from Emmanuèle and Claude Maupas in Rouen, France, and answers to esoteric questions of British history from Richard Himsworth in Cambridge, England; Jocelyn Mason translated the Italian phrases in Washington, D.C., while in New York John D'Arms' careful reading helped improve the introduction. Helen Hill, in Ann Arbor, Michigan, willingly made more versions of the family charts than I care to contemplate. Mary Anne Hines helped with the research about Philadelphia; Kathryn Meehan did the same for Charleston. Sarah Jackson researched many of the Bostonians and New Yorkers mentioned in the letters. I am truly grateful to them all.

I thank the staffs of the many libraries and historical societies I visited. I particularly appreciate the help of the reference librarians of the Haverford College Library; Linda Stanley, formerly at the Historical Society of Pennsylvania; Jenny Ambrose at the Library Company of Philadelphia; Edith Willoughby at the Overbrook School for the Blind, Philadelphia; Bertram Lippincott and Joan Youngken at the Newport Historical Society; Maris Humphreys at the Redwood Library, Newport; David Percy and C. Patton Hash at the South Carolina Historical Society; and Allen Stokes and Beth Bilderback at the South Caroliniana Library, University of South Carolina.

Many members of the Middleton and Fisher families entered enthusiastically into the search for manuscripts and portraits for this book. Sandwith Drinker, Sophia Cadwalader Hayes, and Edward Middleton Rea allowed me to look at manuscripts in their possession. The following helped locate and examine important portraits and other potential illustrations, some of which are reproduced in this book: Frances Aub Bloomfield; Phyllis and Thomas F. Cadwalader, Jr.; Benjamin C. Chapman; Joan Ingersoll Coale; Sandwith, Edward, and John Drinker; Mary Drinker Elek; Nancy Aub Gleason; Sarah Barringer Gordon; Francis Fisher Hart; George Harrison Hart; Mary Anne Hart Minemier; Henry B. Middleton; Eliza Middleton Cope Nolan; Edward Middleton Rea; and Elizabeth Francis Aub Reid.

By their reading, critiquing, research, advice, or irrational enthusiasm, the following friends have contributed more than they may imagine to this book: Irene and Richard Brown, University of Connecticut; Robert DeN. Cope, Woodsville, New Hampshire; Charles H. P. Duell, president, Middleton Place Foundation; Lori Ginzberg, University of Pennsylvania; Abigail Harrison, Mtubatuba, South Africa; Emily Harrison, Burlington, Vermont; John Himsworth, Manchester, England; Hillary Johnson, New York City; David Moltke-Hansen, Historical Society of Pennsylvania; Jan Barney Newman, Ann Arbor, Michigan; Tacy R. Paul, Washington, D.C.; Martin Pernick, University of Michigan; Robert C. Reid, Cambridge, Massachusetts; David Sobel, New York City; Mary Edna Sullivan, curator at Middleton Place; Kirsten Swinth, Fordham University; and Richmond Williams, Wilmington, Delaware.

Finally, let me thank Director Catherine Fry, Alexander Moore, Barbara Brannon, Christine Copeland, Catherine McGrady, and Gretchen Sauer at the

University of South Carolina Press, whose support and interest have made *Best Companions* a reality. Alex Moore, from the start, understood the unusual interest of the Middleton-Fisher correspondence, and his sound editorial judgment has helped shape the letters into an exciting and interesting book for scholars and general readers alike.

Abbreviations and Identifications

INDIVIDUALS

EM   Eliza Middleton (before her marriage in 1839)
EMF   Eliza Middleton Fisher
EHS   Emma Huger Smith
GH   George Harrison
HM   Henry Middleton
JFF   Joshua Francis Fisher
J. Izard Middleton   Eliza's uncle John Izard Middleton
John I. Middleton   Eliza's brother John
MHM   Mary Hering Middleton

INSTITUTIONS AND COLLECTIONS

MPlFdn   Middleton Place Foundation
PHi   Historical Society of Pennsylvania
BrC   Brinton Coxe Collection
C/F   Cadwalader Collection, Fisher Section
FFP   Fisher Family Papers, 1681–1955
ScHi   South Carolina Historical Society

Frequently Cited Sources (See bibliography for complete citations)

JFF *Recollections* *Recollections of Joshua Francis Fisher Written in 1864*
Phila. GCI *Philadelphia Gazette and Commercial Intelligencer*
RSahr, OrStU Robert Sahr, Oregon State University (conversion factors for dollar values)
Wainwright, *Phila. Perspective* Nicholas Wainwright, ed., *A Philadelphia Perspective: The Diary of Sidney George Fisher*

Family Charts of Principal Families

CHARLESTON AND PHILADELPHIA

Family of Henry Middleton I

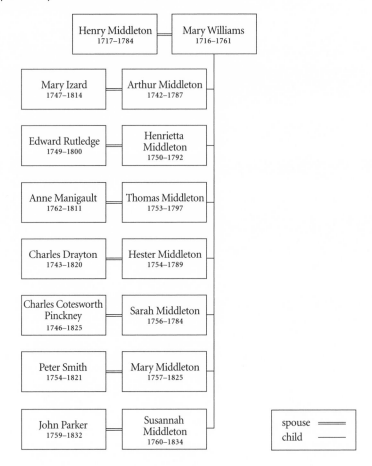

Henry Middleton 1717–1784	Mary Williams 1716–1761
Mary Izard 1747–1814	Arthur Middleton 1742–1787
Edward Rutledge 1749–1800	Henrietta Middleton 1750–1792
Anne Manigault 1762–1811	Thomas Middleton 1753–1797
Charles Drayton 1743–1820	Hester Middleton 1754–1789
Charles Cotesworth Pinckney 1746–1825	Sarah Middleton 1756–1784
Peter Smith 1754–1821	Mary Middleton 1757–1825
John Parker 1759–1832	Susannah Middleton 1760–1834

spouse ═══
child ───

This genealogical chart includes only persons mentioned in the Middleton-Fisher letters and their immediate families.

Family of Arthur Middleton

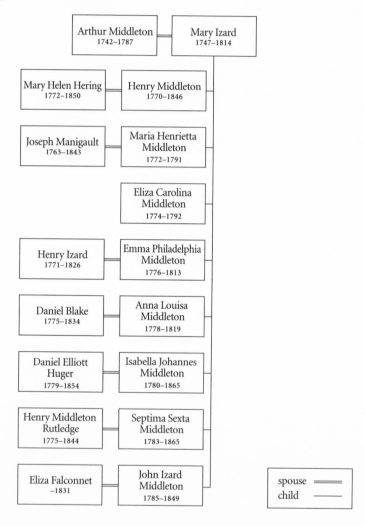

This genealogical chart includes only persons mentioned in the Middleton-Fisher letters and their immediate families.

Family of Edward Rutledge

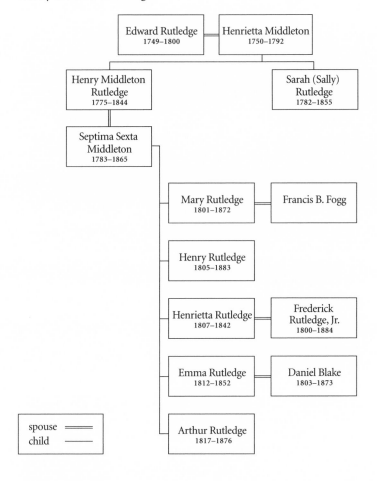

This genealogical chart includes only persons mentioned in the Middleton-Fisher letters and their immediate families.

Family of Thomas Middleton

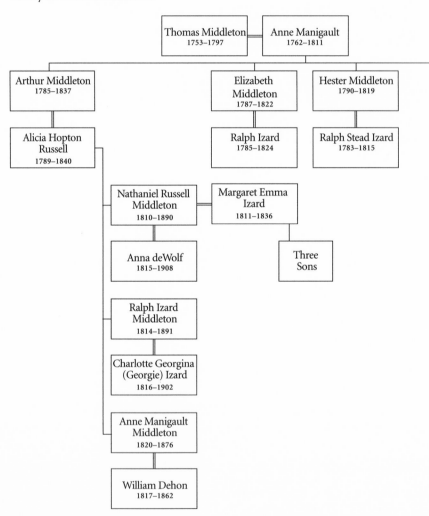

This genealogical chart includes only persons mentioned in the Middleton-Fisher letters and their immediate families.

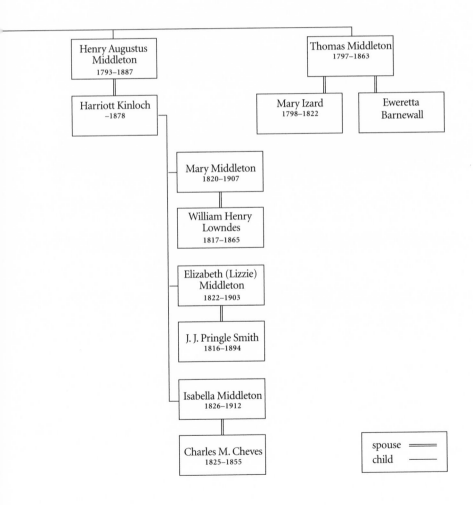

Henry Augustus
Middleton
1793–1887

Thomas Middleton
1797–1863

Harriott Kinloch
–1878

Mary Izard
1798–1822

Eweretta
Barnewall

Mary Middleton
1820–1907

William Henry
Lowndes
1817–1865

Elizabeth (Lizzie)
Middleton
1822–1903

J. J. Pringle Smith
1816–1894

Isabella Middleton
1826–1912

Charles M. Cheves
1825–1855

spouse ═══
child ───

Family of Charles Drayton

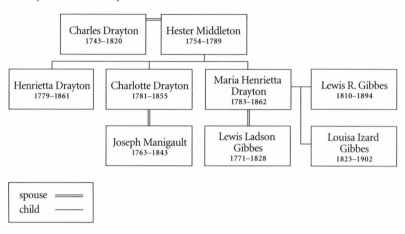

Family of Charles Pinckney

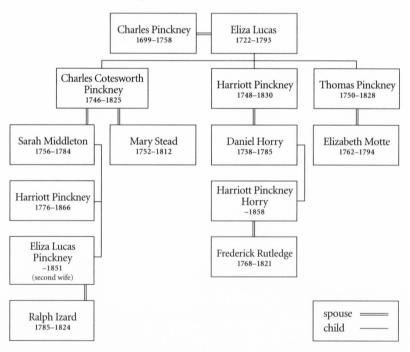

These genealogical charts include only persons mentioned in the Middleton-Fisher letters and their immediate families.

Family of Daniel Elliott Huger

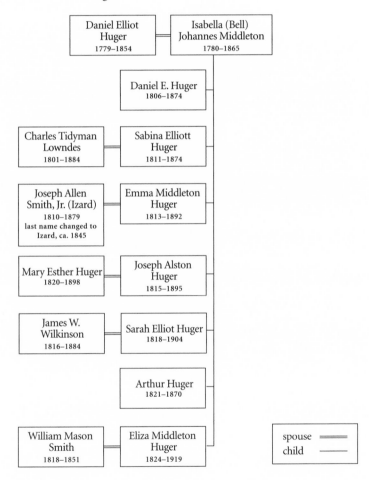

This genealogical chart includes only persons mentioned in the Middleton-Fisher letters and their immediate families.

Family of Ralph Izard

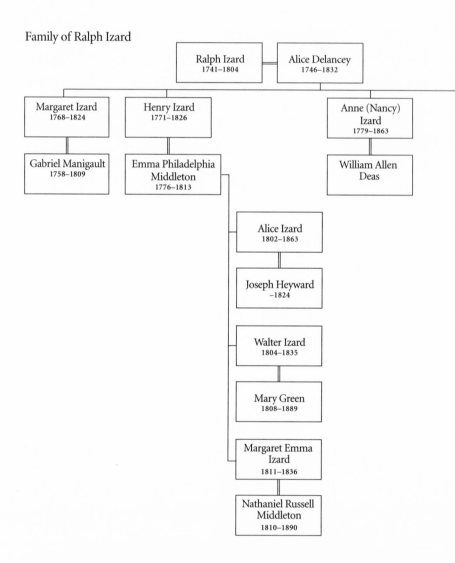

This genealogical chart includes only persons mentioned in the Middleton-Fisher letters and their immediate families.

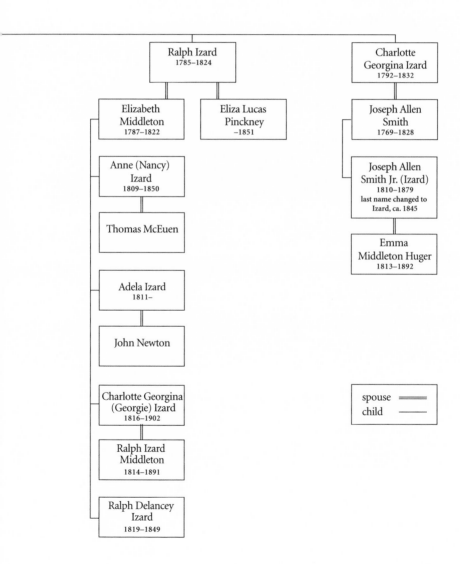

Ralph Izard
1785–1824

Charlotte
Georgina Izard
1792–1832

Elizabeth
Middleton
1787–1822

Eliza Lucas
Pinckney
–1851

Joseph Allen
Smith
1769–1828

Anne (Nancy)
Izard
1809–1850

Joseph Allen
Smith Jr. (Izard)
1810–1879
last name changed to
Izard, ca. 1845

Thomas McEuen

Emma
Middleton Huger
1813–1892

Adela Izard
1811–

John Newton

Charlotte Georgina
(Georgie) Izard
1816–1902

Ralph Izard
Middleton
1814–1891

Ralph Delancey
Izard
1819–1849

spouse ═══

child ────

Family of Charles Willing

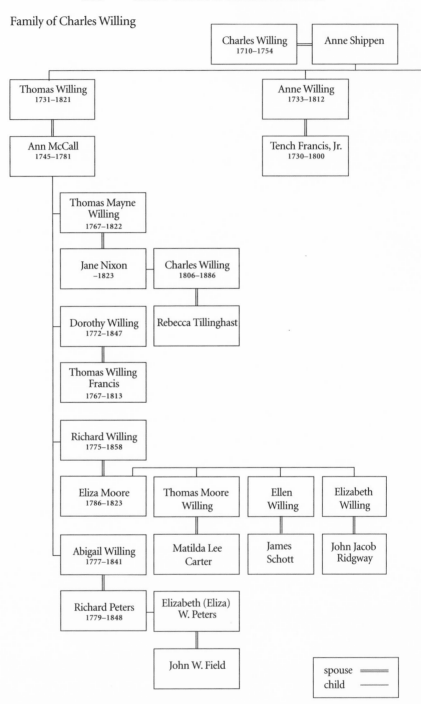

Charles Willing
1710–1754

Anne Shippen

Thomas Willing
1731–1821

Ann McCall
1745–1781

Anne Willing
1733–1812

Tench Francis, Jr.
1730–1800

Thomas Mayne
Willing
1767–1822

Jane Nixon
–1823

Charles Willing
1806–1886

Dorothy Willing
1772–1847

Rebecca Tillinghast

Thomas Willing
Francis
1767–1813

Richard Willing
1775–1858

Eliza Moore
1786–1823

Thomas Moore
Willing

Ellen
Willing

Elizabeth
Willing

Abigail Willing
1777–1841

Matilda Lee
Carter

James
Schott

John Jacob
Ridgway

Richard Peters
1779–1848

Elizabeth (Eliza)
W. Peters

John W. Field

spouse ═══
child ───

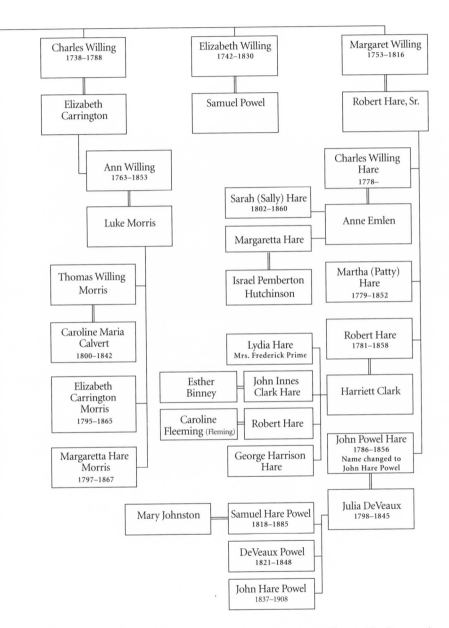

This genealogical chart includes only persons mentioned in the Middleton-Fisher letters and their immediate families.

Family of Tench Francis, Jr.

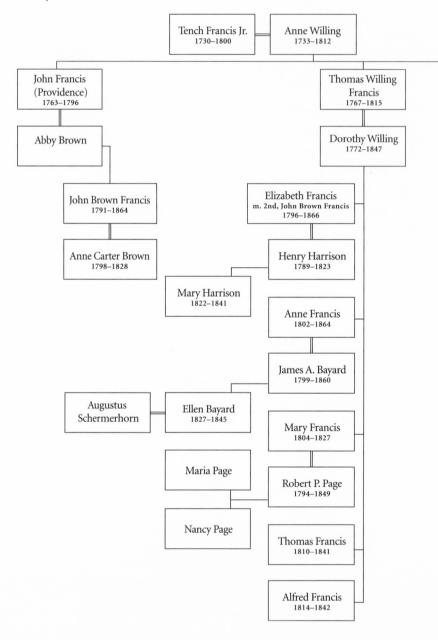

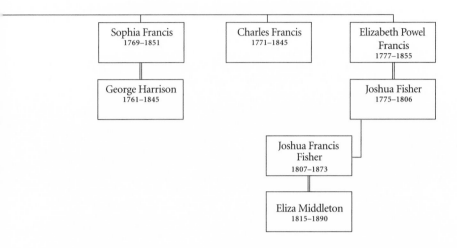

This genealogical chart includes only persons mentioned in the Middleton-Fisher letters and their immediate families.

Family of Thomas Fisher

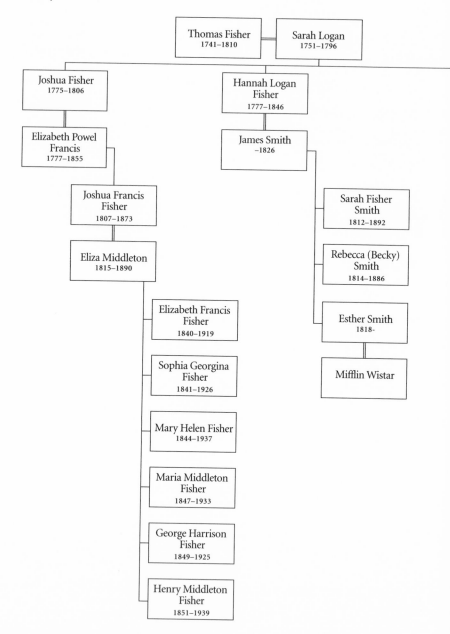

This genealogical chart includes only persons mentioned in the Middleton-Fisher letters and their immediate families.

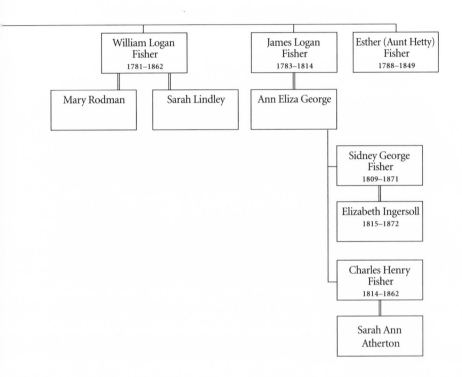

| William Logan Fisher 1781–1862 | James Logan Fisher 1783–1814 | Esther (Aunt Hetty) Fisher 1788–1849 |

| Mary Rodman | Sarah Lindley | Ann Eliza George |

Sidney George Fisher 1809–1871

Elizabeth Ingersoll 1815–1872

Charles Henry Fisher 1814–1862

Sarah Ann Atherton

| spouse ═══ |
| child ─── |

Cast of Characters

THE MIDDLETON, FISHER, AND HERING FAMILIES

ELIZA'S PARENTS

Henry Middleton (1770–1846). Born in London; brought to the United States by his parents, Arthur and Mary Izard Middleton, in 1772. In England and France during 1790s; married Mary Helen Hering at Bath, England, November 1794. Returned to South Carolina; state legislator and governor of South Carolina, 1801–1812. Congressman, 1815–1819; minister plenipotentiary to Russia (1820–1830). Strong Unionist during the nullification controversy in early 1830s. Owned Middleton Place, three rice plantations on Combahee River, several hundred slaves, a house in Newport. Primary income from rice.

Mary Helen Hering Middleton (1772–1850). Born in Jamaica; grew up in England. Daughter of Capt. Julines Hering and Mary Inglis Hering, who was from Philadelphia. Married Henry Middleton, 1794; lived in the United States, 1799–1850, except 1820–1830, when in St. Petersburg.

Ten children (six sons, four daughters) grew to adulthood. Two daughters died before 1839: Eleanor in St. Petersburg, 1827; Maria (Mrs. Edward Pringle) in explosion of steamship *Pulaski*, 1838.

ELIZA'S SIBLINGS

Arthur (1795–1853). Born in England; graduated from Harvard, 1814; trained as lawyer. Married (1) Ann Van Ness of Washington, D.C., 1821 (d. 1822). U.S. legation in Madrid, 1830s. Married (2) Paolina Bentivoglio (d. 1883) in

Rome, 1841; returned to United States with her. Two children: Henry Bentivoglio Van Ness (Benti), Angelina.

Henry (Harry) (1797–1876). Born in Paris; graduated from West Point in 1815 but soon resigned from army; studied at Litchfield (Connecticut) law school and in Edinburgh. Wrote about political theory. Interested in literature. In Europe 1835–1839. Married Ellen Goggin in England, 1858; no children.

Oliver Hering (1790–1892). Born in England; studied at South Carolina College; U.S. Navy 1817–1823. Planted cotton on Edisto Island land inherited by his wife, Susan Chisolm (d. 1865), daughter of Dr. and Mrs. Robert Trail Chisolm. Six children: Mary Julia, Susan Matilda, Eleanor Maria, Olivia, Emma Middleton, Oliver Hering, Jr.

John Izard (1800–1877). Born in Charleston; graduated from Princeton, 1819; secretary to U.S. legation in St. Petersburg, early 1820s; returned to United States and helped manage the Middleton rice plantations while his father was still in Russia. Rice planter (eventually successful) on Waccamaw River, near Georgetown. South Carolina state legislature, 1839–1858. Signed Ordinance of Secession, 1860.

Married Sally (Sarah McPherson) Alston (d. 1878), daughter of John Ashe and Sarah McPherson Alston. Six children: Henry (Hal or Harry); Sarah McPherson; John Izard; Thomas Alston; Mary Helen; Maria Henrietta.

Note: Identified in this correspondence as *John I. Middleton* to distinguish him from his uncle of the same name, who is identified as *J. Izard Middleton*.

Williams (1809–1883). Born near Charleston; educated in London and Paris, 1820–1827; attaché to American Legation in St. Petersburg, 1827–1830. After 1830 helped his father manage rice plantations on Combahee River. Signed Ordinance of Secession. Married Susan Pringle Smith (d. 1900), daughter of Robert and Elizabeth Mary Pringle Smith, in 1849. Two children.

Note: Although his given name was *Williams,* Mrs. Middleton and Eliza refer to him, almost without exception, as William. He is therefore also referred to as *William* in the notes throughout this volume. Starting in approximately 1847, however (after the end of this correspondence), everyone, including his mother and sister, consistently called him Williams.

Edward (1810–1883). Born in Charleston; educated in London and Paris, 1820–1827; entered U.S. Navy 1828; promoted to lieutenant 1841; served in Mediterranean, South America, etc. Remained in U.S. Navy during Civil War; retired as rear admiral 1876. Married (1) Edwardina de Normann in 1845; one child (b. 1847) died as infant; divorced in 1850s. Married (2) Ellida Davison in 1865; two children.

Catherine (Kitty) (1812–1894). Born near Charleston; educated with Eliza in London, 1820–1827; in St. Petersburg, 1827–1830. Became mentally disturbed when a teenager; lived with her parents until 1846. Lived in Philadelphia after her father's death.

Eliza (1815–1890). Always called Eliza, although her given name was Elizabeth Izard. See Fisher's Family.

FISHER'S FAMILY

His father, Joshua Fisher (1775–1806). Born in Philadelphia, son of Quakers, Thomas and Sarah Logan Fisher. Started as merchant in East India trade. Married Elizabeth Powel Francis in 1806 but died a few months afterward, before Fisher was born.

His mother, Elizabeth Powel Francis Fisher (Betsey) (1777–1855). Daughter of Philadelphians Anne Willing and Tench Francis, Jr. Lived at 170 Chestnut Street, Philadelphia. Widow of Joshua Fisher; her son, J. Francis Fisher, born after her husband's death.

His aunt and uncle, the Harrisons. Sophia Francis Harrison (Aunt Harrison) (1769–1851). Sister of Elizabeth Francis Fisher; wife of **George Harrison (Uncle Harrison) (1761–1845).** Wealthy merchant, retired from the Madeira wine trade. Lived at 156 Chestnut Street, Philadelphia. No children; helped bring up their nephew, Joshua Francis Fisher; paid for his education, trip to Europe. Left large fortune to Fisher.

An uncle, Charles Francis (Uncle Charles) (1771–1845). Brother of Elizabeth Francis Fisher and of Sophia Francis Harrison. Unmarried; Fisher inherited most of his estate.

Joshua Francis Fisher (Fisher) (1807–1873). Only son of Elizabeth Francis Fisher and Joshua Fisher (d. 1806). Born in Philadelphia; brought up by uncle and aunt, George and Sophia Francis Harrison, as well as by his mother. Harvard, 1825; literary, historical, and philanthropic interests. Primary income: wealth inherited from his uncles Charles Francis and George Harrison. Married Eliza Middleton at Middleton Place, near Charleston, South Carolina, March 12, 1839.

Eliza Middleton Fisher (1815–1890). Born in Charleston; youngest child of Henry and Mary Hering Middleton. Went to school in England, 1820–1827; in St. Petersburg until her family's return to the United States, 1830. Highly accomplished pianist and musician. Lived in Philadelphia, in her mother-in-law's house, from marriage in 1839 to Mrs. Fisher's death, 1855. Six children reached adulthood.

FISHER CHILDREN MENTIONED IN THE LETTERS

Elizabeth Francis (Lizzie/Lily): born 1840; married Robert Patterson Kane.

Sophia Georgina (Sophie): born 1841; married Eckley B. Coxe.

Mary Helen (Helen): born 1844; married John Cadwalader.

BORN AFTER END OF CORRESPONDENCE

George Harrison: born 1846; died as infant.

Maria Middleton: born 1847; married Brinton Coxe.

George Harrison: born 1849; married Betsey Riddle.

Henry Middleton (Harry): born 1851; married Mary Elwyn Wharton.

MARY HERING MIDDLETON'S SIBLINGS IN ENGLAND, THE CHILDREN OF JULINES HERING (1732–1797) AND MARY INGLIS HERING (1742–1818)

Catherine (1763–1840) married John Gordon; lived in Bristol.

Anna Maria (1766–1850) married Hon. Jno. Lumley, later seventh earl of Scarbrough.

Oliver (b. 1768) married Mary Ross. No children; guardian of four youngest Middleton children, 1820–1827. In 1820s lived at Heybridge Hall, Maldon, Essex; in 1840s lived in Southampton.

Eleanor (1777–1819) married Capt. John Milbank, later Sir John, seventh baronet.

Best Companions

The Middletons and the Fishers in 1839

An Introduction

Queen Victoria was newly crowned. Samuel Morse had developed an electric telegraph. Philadelphia's Pennsylvania Hall had been burned after an antislavery meeting. Martin Van Buren was hoping for a second term in the White House, and Congressman John Quincy Adams was about to propose a constitutional amendment ending slavery in the United States. All of these events were in the news as 1839 began, but at Middleton Place on the Ashley River, near Charleston, South Carolina, no one was thinking much about the world outside. The Middletons were preparing for a wedding, and the bride, Eliza Middleton, lay hovering near death with a virulent case of scarlet fever.

She survived leeches, bleeding, and nauseous drugs, as well as ulcers in her throat, and on the evening of March 12, the day set for her wedding, she was able to enter the second-floor drawing room, dressed in a simple white dress, her red hair in ringlets around her face. Her fiancé, Francis Fisher,[1] who had sailed six hundred miles from Philadelphia through freezing winter storms to marry her, had arrived shortly before from Charleston, driven by the Middletons' coachman, attired, as befitted the occasion, in the family livery of black velvet cuffs and collar on a brown coat.[2]

1. Although he was christened Joshua Francis Fisher, he did not use the name Joshua. Eliza, his close friends, and even his aunt and uncle called him Fisher.
2. One of the Middleton cousins described the coat as "drab," which could have been one of several shades of brown. EHS to EMF, November 10, 1840.

Although Eliza was still so weak she could hardly do more than whisper the wedding vows, she and Fisher were married while family and friends rejoiced at this happy conclusion to their romance. Eliza was almost twenty-four; Fisher was thirty-two.

The Middletons and Middleton Place

The Middletons, a well-known and prominent family in South Carolina, were among the earliest arrivals in the colony at the end of the seventeenth century. By the time Eliza was married in 1839, Middleton Place had been the home base of her branch of the family for a century, her great grandfather, Henry Middleton, having received it along with his bride, Mary Williams, in 1741. The brick mansion at Middleton Place, built in the early eighteenth century, was now one of the oldest in the South Carolina Lowcountry. It was beautifully sited on high ground, from which one looked eastward over terraced gardens that descended to the Ashley River. Neighbors landed at the foot of these gardens when they came to visit, and the plantation schooner moored there when it came to load or unload supplies or bring mail from town.

Visitors who arrived by land from Charleston, as Fisher did, usually came by ferry across the Ashley River and ten miles up the sandy river road to the Middleton Place gate. Turning in, they followed the drive across an open green where sheep kept the grass cut and around a circle to the west front of the house. Even if they had never been there before, they would have expected the "towering oaks" and elms and acres of gardens laid out "in a style of superior elegance"[3] on their left; if they came in winter, they would have hoped to see hundreds of camellia flowers along the paths, for these, along with the Middletons' library and the artworks decorating the house, had long since made Middleton Place famous.

The Middletons' elegant lifestyle was made possible by the profits from growing rice, South Carolina's principal, and immensely lucrative, staple crop. Large landholders from the start, the Middletons used slave labor to plant rice, first on plantations near Charleston and, as the eighteenth century progressed, on very fertile drained swamplands along the Combahee River, two days' journey to the south. Long before the Revolution, rice put the Middletons at the top of a small group of extremely wealthy families in a colony whose overall

3. *Charleston Courier*, March 7, 1840.

wealth far exceeded that of any of the other colonies.[4] In 1839 rice was still the Middletons' main source of income.

Wealth and political prominence went hand in hand. Members of the Middleton family served continuously in the colonial government until the Revolution, and since the Revolution three generations had had a role in the new nation's government. Eliza's great-grandfather, Henry (1717–1784), represented South Carolina in the First Continental Congress.[5] Her grandfather, Arthur (1742–1787), was a member of the Continental Congress, too, and signed the Declaration of Independence, as did his brother-in-law, Edward Rutledge.[6]

Eliza's father, a second Henry (1770–1846), carried his family's tradition of public service into the nineteenth century. As he welcomed the wedding guests to Middleton Place on that March day in 1839, he was nearing his seventieth birthday and had spent most of his adult life as a politician and diplomat. Serving first in the South Carolina legislature, he was elected governor (1810–1812) and then was twice elected to Congress (1815–1819). His final post was as U.S. minister to Russia. Taking his family abroad with him, he remained in St. Petersburg for ten years (1820–1830).

ELIZA'S PARENTS
Henry Middleton and Mary Helen Hering

From the start, the American Revolution shaped Henry Middleton's life. In 1776, at the age of six, he shared the excitement of being in Philadelphia while

4. As an example of the amount of land held by leading Carolina families, Henry Middleton, when he died in 1784, left his son, Arthur, nearly four thousand acres. This was in addition to land he had given Arthur previously and an equivalent amount he gave to his other son.

By mid-eighteenth century, rice accounted for more than 50 percent of South Carolina's exports. Actual production increased until, between 1768 and 1772, an average of more than 66 million pounds of rice were exported annually from South Carolina. This represented approximately one-quarter of the value of all exports from *all* thirteen colonies. George Winston Lane, Jr., "The Middletons of Eighteenth Century South Carolina: A Colonial Dynasty, 1678–1787 (Ph.D. diss., Emory University, 1990), 682; Peter A. Coclanis, *The Shadow of a Dream, Economic Life and Death in the South Carolina Low Country, 1670–1920* (New York: Oxford University Press, 1989), 76 ff.

5. He was elected president for the final days of the Congress in October 1774, when Peyton Randolph was ill.

6. Edward Rutledge married Arthur Middleton's sister Henrietta (1750–1792). Another sister, Sarah (1756–1784), married Charles Cotesworth Pinckney.

his father, Arthur, attended the Continental Congress. He also lived through the turmoil and devastation of war when the British army occupied Charleston in 1780. His father, marked as one of the most prominent patriots, was imprisoned in St. Augustine, Florida, and was therefore absent from his family for long periods, either in Florida or as a member of Congress in Philadelphia.

Henry's mother, Mary Izard Middleton,[7] was left with the burden of fending off marauders from both the British and American armies and trying to find food to keep her family together at Middleton Place. She managed to find a French tutor to teach the regular academic subjects to her older children, but Hal (as Henry was called) had to teach himself when it came to music and drawing.

Had the Revolution not intervened, his parents would almost certainly have sent him to England to be educated, and as an adult Henry Middleton felt he was not as well educated as he would have liked. His education was indeed informal if he compared himself with his father, who spent several years in England studying at Westminster School and Cambridge, or with the many other South Carolinians, including relatives in the Izard, Drayton, Rutledge, and Pinckney families, who went to Cambridge and Oxford or studied law at the Inns of Court in London. But Henry Middleton's opinion of his own deficiencies was not shared by others, including his son-in-law, Francis Fisher. They knew him as an accomplished scholar who had taken full advantage of alternate opportunities for education which travel and independent study had given him.[8]

Just as some normality was returning to the family after the Revolution, Arthur Middleton died.[9] Young Hal, an appealing boy with "a sweet agreeable countenance, [and] a very sensible ardent look,"[10] was only sixteen. Three years later, his mother, with the advice of his uncles, Edward Rutledge and Charles Cotesworth Pinckney, sent him northward with letters of introduction to eminent friends, including Thomas Jefferson, so he would be "acquainted with his own country and his own Countrymen."[11] He went abroad in 1792 and, during

7. Mary Izard (1747–1814) was the daughter of Elizabeth (Gibbes) and Walter Izard, one of the wealthiest Carolina planters. She grew up at Cedar Grove, a plantation across the Ashley River from Middleton Place, and married Arthur Middleton in 1764.

8. Benjamin F. Perry to JFF, October 3, 1866, private collection.

9. He died on January 1, 1787, probably of malaria.

10. Aedanus Burke to Arthur Middleton, July 6, 1782. Quoted in Lane, "The Middletons," 630.

11. Edward Rutledge to Thomas Jefferson, June 20, 1790. In Julian P. Boyd, ed., *The Papers of Thomas Jefferson* (Princeton: Princeton University Press, 1961), 16:544.

seven years in England and France, had an extraordinary opportunity to observe society and politics in the aftermath of the French Revolution. He also found a wife.

Mary Helen Hering was born in Jamaica in 1772, where her father, Julines Hering, an officer in the British army, owned sugar plantations and slaves. Her mother, Mary Inglis, grew up in Philadelphia, the daughter of a Scots merchant who had settled there. She married Julines Hering while he was stationed in the North American colonies in the 1760s. Though Captain Hering originally intended to bring up his own family in Philadelphia, he changed his mind when the colonial troubles broke out in the 1770s and took his wife and children back to England. His daughter, Mary Helen, therefore considered herself English, although she was really more a product of the wider English-speaking Atlantic world that existed before the American Revolution.

When Henry Middleton entered her life, probably in late 1793 or early 1794, Mary Hering was living with her mother at Bath. She was lively and charming, intelligent, and loved and admired by her friends.[12] She read widely, played the harp, and had a real love of music. Not surprisingly, she had suitors, but when her brother, Oliver, heard about Henry Middleton, he advised her to reject the others since "the Carolinian by your description seems better qualified to make you happy . . . notwithstanding his cold platonic Disposition and pretended indifference to your Charms." He suggested she "take him who has the ability to place you in a state of independence and prosperity, in case he should declare himself your humble servant."[13]

He did, and they were married at Bath on November 13, 1794. He was twenty-four; Mary, twenty-two.[14]

The young Middletons lived first in England and then, in the summer of 1796, went to Paris for a year. Henry's uncle, Charles Cotesworth Pinckney, had been sent to Paris as the American Minister, and he and his wife saw the

12. One of her English friends said that "whenever [she] heard of anything near perfection," she thought of Mary Hering. M. M. Evers to MHM, August 16, 1796, PHi, C/F.

13. Oliver Hering to Mary Helen Hering, June 15, 1794, ScHi.

14. Alice Delancey (Mrs. Ralph) Izard wrote her son, Ralph: "Mr. Middleton is really engaged to Miss Hering and only waiting to receive his Mother's consent in order to be married. She has given it, and seems now pleased with the match, as she has heard very pleasing accounts of the Lady." Since Henry was old enough to marry without parental consent, his request may have been a courtesy to his mother, but there may also have been questions of inheritance for which his mother's approval was needed. Mrs. Ralph Izard to Ralph Izard, Jr., December 4, 1794, Izard Family Papers, South Caroliniana Library, University of South Carolina.

Middletons frequently. Mrs. Pinckney[15] described Henry as "modest without reserve and polite without affectation. I think if I were a mother," she wrote, "I should wish for just such a son." Europe, she thought, had "neither made him foppish nor assuming."[16]

Mrs. Pinckney described Mary Middleton as "sweet-temper'd and agreeable," a charming woman. Her figure was "very pretty and the dress she wears very well calculated to shew it to advantage,"[17] and she was an amusing companion as they explored Paris. Mary shared Henry's French lessons and took music lessons as well, but much of her time was spent caring for her "little brats."[18] They began arriving in quick succession: Arthur was born in England in 1795; Harry (Henry) in Paris in 1797; and Oliver in 1798 in England.

The following year, the Middletons and their three boys sailed from England for the United States, arriving in Charleston at the end of September 1799, after a tedious three-month voyage. Henry's mother and sisters welcomed them warmly. "Thank God," Mary wrote Mrs. Pinckney, "I am among those who seem disposed to supply the place of those relations I have left, and nothing shall be wanting on *my* part, to show them how sensible I am to their attentions."[19] She liked Henry's sisters: Emma Philadelphia, who had married Henry Izard in 1795; Anne, soon to marry Daniel Blake; and Isabella ("Bell"), who eloped with Daniel Elliott Huger a year later. She became especially close to Henry's youngest sister, Septima Sexta, who was engaged to their cousin, Henry Middleton Rutledge.

Culture shock, however, existed long before our century gave it a name, and it is clear that adjusting to South Carolina was not always easy for Mary Middleton. She hated the climate. She thought the house at Middleton Place was rundown and dirty when they moved in (though she conceded that the "situation" of the house was delightful) and was apparently critical of her husband for not having had it fixed up beforehand. She told her mother, perhaps after visiting the Combahee River plantations, that she was "disgusted" by the plantation and the negroes.[20] On top of these irritants, her fourth child, John

15. Mrs. Pinckney, the former Mary Stead, was Pinckney's second wife. His first wife, Sally Middleton, died in 1784.

16. Charles F. McComb, ed., *Letter-book of Mary Stead Pinckney* (New York: Grolier Club, 1946), 26, 31.

17. Ibid., 31.

18. MHM to Mary Stead Pinckney, April 17, [1797,] ScHi

19. MHM to Mary Stead Pinckney, October 1, 1799, ScHi.

20. Mrs. Middleton's letters to her mother have not been found, but what she wrote is usually reflected in Mrs. Hering's replies. In this case, it is not clear whether she explained why she disliked the plantation. However, both the isolation of the place and the presence of several hundred slaves would have been unfamiliar and possibly

Izard, was born just four months after they reached South Carolina and was not a strong infant. A fifth, born the next year, soon died. Small wonder that she was homesick and sometimes "low in spirits."[21]

Her happy nature and sense of humor nevertheless usually won out. Settling into the Carolina rhythm, she and Henry interspersed the fall and spring seasons in the country with winter months in Charleston, where they enjoyed the city's extensive social life.[22] In the summer, they moved to cooler spots such as Greenville, in the South Carolina upcountry, or to northern resorts like Ballston Spa in New York and Newport, Rhode Island. Wherever she was, Mary Middleton was always liked and respected, and she soon had many friends. "I am sure you will have a good neighbour in Mrs M," Henrietta Drayton was told by a cousin who met her just after she arrived from England. "She appears very sociable pleasing amiable & agreeable—& pretty too."[23]

This assessment of Mary Middleton proved accurate. It did not, however, do her justice. She had been given a good, basic education and was widely read. She could describe William's state of mind by quoting a seventeenth-century poem ("Why so dull and mute . . . ?")[24] as easily as she could refer to characters in Shakespeare's or Sheridan's plays. She was as well acquainted with the musical repertoire of the time as with English literature, and though she gave up playing the harp, she was still able in her old age to coach her teenage granddaughter's singing with the assurance of an experienced singer.[25]

Mary Middleton was an excellent mother who, although she was helped by servants and governesses, took primary responsibility for bringing up her own children.[26] Both she and her husband adored their children and were

---

frightening to her. There is no evidence that she disapproved of slavery. MHM to Mary Stead Pinckney, November 25, [1799,] ScHi; Mrs. Hering to MHM, January 13, 1800, and April 21, 1801, ScHi.

21. Mrs. Hering to MHM, October 13, 1801, ScHi.

22. Henry Middleton bought a house in Charleston, soon after he and Mary returned to South Carolina.

23. Elizabeth Izard to Henrietta Drayton, October 13, 1799, MPlFdn.

24. The poem of Sir John Suckling (1609–1642) "Why So Pale and Wan, Fond Lover?" is in *The Oxford Book of Seventeenth Century Verse,* ed. Sir Herbert Grierson and G. Bullough (London: Oxford University Press, 1958), 560.

25. She urged Eleanor Middleton not to strain her voice, which was still maturing, by trying to reach a very high note, suggesting rather that she play the note on the piano for the time being. She also taught Eleanor Italian so she could sing arias from Italian operas. MHM to EMF, February 7, 1844.

26. Margaret Izard Manigault, who admired Mary Middleton very much, emphasized this, which suggests that she did not consider it the norm among women she knew. M. I. Manigault to Josephine duPont, September 28, 1808, Margaret Izard Manigault Collection, Hagley Museum and Library, Wilmington, Del.

closely involved in their education. Careful not to show favoritism, she was sensitive to each child's needs and special character.[27] She displayed the same attentiveness to her grandchildren thirty and forty years later.

She was also tough. In 1813 she traveled by herself with eight of her children, including ten-month-old Catherine, far into the still-unsettled South Carolina upcountry to meet her husband, who was a member of the commission to settle the boundary with North Carolina. "You have travelled in the back parts of the State," she told a friend, "therefore I pass over the fatigue of the journey, the filth & starvation of the Taverns, but you had not a Carriage full of roaring Children." It took nine days to go 240 miles.[28]

WASHINGTON AND ST. PETERSBURG
1816–1830

Henry Middleton was elected to Congress in 1815 and again in 1817. During the first session of the Fourteenth Congress, from December 1815 to April 1816, he lived in a Washington boardinghouse, as most congressmen did at the time. Among his fellow boarders were Henry Clay of Kentucky and John C. Calhoun from South Carolina. The next winter, the whole family went to Washington, where they rented a house in Georgetown and took an active part in the capital's social life. Arthur, who graduated from Harvard in 1814, and Harry, who graduated from West Point the following year, were both regular figures at their parents' and their friends' gatherings.[29]

The elder Middletons' own charm and good hospitality were also appreciated, however. Congressman Middleton, "a gentleman of elegant manners and cultivated mind,"[30] was an intelligent conversationalist and a "munificent" host.[31] His wife was friendly and fun with a wry sense of humor: when waltzing was new and considered an "indecorous exhibition" (because young women were held so closely by their partners), she commented to Harrison Gray Otis

27. The Middletons had ten living children. Maria followed four boys (Arthur, Harry, Oliver, and John) in 1802; a second daughter, Eleanor, was born in 1804. After two infants died, William was born in 1809, Edward in 1810, and Catherine in 1812. Eliza, the youngest, was born in 1815.

28. Presumably she was accompanied by a coachman and someone to help with the children. MHM to Margaret Izard Manigault, July 11, [1813,] PHi.

29. Oliver, who went into the navy in 1817, and John, who graduated from Princeton in 1819, were at home less often.

30. *Charleston Courier*, June 16, 1846.

31. "The Death of Hon. Henry Middleton" [circa June 20, 1846,] from unidentified newspaper, PHi, Collection #1858.

that the dance was popular—"to the dismay of all mothers."[32] Mrs. Otis considered Mrs. Middleton's "the most genteel and comfortable establishment in this part of the world,"[33] while Mrs. John Quincy Adams thought the family was "the pleasantest in Washington."[34] These seem to have been particularly happy years for the Middletons, during which they made lasting friendships among congressional colleagues and cabinet members, politicians, and diplomats.

In 1820 President Monroe offered Henry Middleton the post of minister to Russia. He was a good choice. He was fluent in French, the language of international diplomacy, and "conversant with fashionable European manners." His wife was willing to go to St. Petersburg, and, furthermore, since American diplomatic salaries were notoriously low, his personal wealth would permit him to "live as a Minister should live in Russia."[35] Finally, since Czar Alexander I had agreed to arbitrate the dispute between the United States and England over slaves taken by the English during the War of 1812, it was thought that a southerner, and a slaveholder, would best be able to represent slave owners' interests in the forthcoming negotiations.

By June 1820 the Middletons, with most of their children, were en route to England, where for the first time in twenty years Mrs. Middleton was able to see her own family. They left the four youngest children in England in the care of Mrs. Middleton's brother, Oliver Hering. Catherine and Eliza, who was only five years old, were placed in one school and Edward and William in another near London. In the ensuing years, they spent school holidays with their uncle and aunt.

Their parents then set off overland from Calais through northern Europe and, racing the winter, reached St. Petersburg in November 1820. Maria, Eleanor, and at least one of their sons were with them. They originally expected to be in Russia for two or three years, but as Middleton proved to be an able and popular diplomat[36] and the whole family enjoyed the social life of the impe-

32. Harrison Gray Otis to Sophia Otis Ritchie, November 23, 1818, quoted in Samuel Eliot Morison, *The Life and Letters of Harrison Gray Otis, Federalist: 1765–1848* (Boston: Houghton Mifflin, 1913), 2:212.

33. Sally Foster Otis to Sophia Otis Ritchie, March 19, 1818, Harrison Gray Otis Papers, Massachusetts Historical Society.

34. Norman E. Saul, *Distant Friends: The United States and Russia, 1763–1867* (Lawrence: University Press of Kansas, 1991), 94.

35. Louisa Catherine Adams to John Adams, April 17, 1820, quoted in Harold E. Berquist, Jr., "Russian-American Relations, 1820–1830: The Diplomacy of Henry Middleton, American Minister at St. Petersburg" (PhD. diss., Boston University, 1970), 65.

36. This is a central point of Harold Berquist's, "Russian-American Relations." For example, see pp. 683 ff. and 714–15.

rial court and diplomatic corps, their stay stretched to five, then seven, and ultimately ten years.[37]

It is not entirely clear why they stayed so long, although Henry Middleton may have stayed in St. Petersburg hoping he would be transferred from there to another post in Europe.[38] In any case, it was not until the fall of 1827, seven years after they had been left in England, that Eliza, Catherine, and the two boys finally joined their parents in Russia.

At first, Eliza was considered too young to "go into public," but she had every opportunity to absorb European culture and the details of diplomatic life by observing her parents and siblings as they made the rounds of balls, plays, concerts, dinners, and masquerades. She and Catherine continued their studies, and as their mother described it, Edward heard their "English lessons in the eveng (for their mornings are taken up entirely with French & Music) & [keeps] up their Arithmetic for me, as I am ashamed to confess I am too igno-rant to do it myself. I make a great point of their not forgetting their own Language, while so much of French is going on & the Dictionary lesson is always repeated after dinner." She added, "Eliza, to be sure is in no danger of forgetting her Mother tongue, for there never was a greater chatterbox."[39] She "was so desirous of learning German that her Governess is teaching her that language," Mrs. Middleton said, and somehow catching the essence of her youngest child, she judged that "with the desire she evinces to improve herself she cannot fail of making a rapid progress."[40]

Music was very much a part of the Middletons' life. Both Eliza's parents attended concerts, had music at home, and counted musicians among their friends. They encouraged Eliza and Catherine to continue playing the piano, and Eliza began to sing as well.

Return to the United States
1830

After President Jackson took office in 1829, he recalled Middleton from St. Petersburg and replaced him with John Randolph of Roanoke, one of his politi-

---

37. There was a long tradition among South Carolinians of means of lengthy stays abroad; Middleton himself had been born in London during his parents' several years' sojourn in Europe. He left his affairs in the hands of his factor, lawyer, and banker. His son, John, supervised the plantations during the final six years.

38. Mrs. Middleton told Arthur, "I am almost sure that [your father] will not quit this country before he is named to another & of that there seems no probability. . . . It is too bad to pass over your Father again." MHM to Arthur Middleton, February 7, 1828, PHi, FFP.

39. MHM to Arthur Middleton, October 27, 1827, PHi, FFP.

40. MHM to Arthur Middleton, February 7, 1828, PHi, FFP.

cal supporters. The Middletons left Russia in the summer of 1830 and arrived in the United States in December.

Financially, Henry Middleton's return to the United States was prudent. At the Russian court, which was well known for the costly social demands put on diplomats, Middleton certainly had met the expectations of how a minister should live. He kept a coach and four matched horses[41] and offered his share of "great dinners,"[42] but in the process he easily outspent his income. John Middleton, who was supervising his father's rice plantations, told one of his brothers that "Father's unmerciful drafts have created a debt that it will require years to pay off; years of economy and management."[43]

In subsequent years, this burden was doubtless increased by downward swings in the price of rice and poor harvests, general economic depression, and, possibly, difficulty changing a lifestyle which had developed over several generations. Consequently, though he may have wished he could be free from such cares when he returned to the United States, Henry Middleton continued actively to manage the rice plantations on the Combahee River until he died in 1846 at the age of seventy-five.

He was also drawn back into politics. Having left in the middle of the bitter debate over allowing Missouri to enter the Union as a slave state, Middleton returned to a country which was once again deeply divided. This time the quarrel was over protective tariffs, which the southern states believed unfairly raised the cost of their imports. Middleton strongly disagreed with his old colleague John C. Calhoun and others who were claiming that a state had the right to "nullify," or set aside, a federal law, and he was distressed when he realized that at least one of his own sons initially leaned toward the nullifiers. Believing that nullification was both unconstitutional and unwise, he was a leader of South Carolina's Unionists, the party opposed to nullification and to the implied possibility of secession, until the eventual settlement of the issue in 1833.

FROM CHARLESTON TO NEWPORT

Being part of a comparatively small group of cosmopolitan Americans who could afford to travel extensively, the Middletons went to the north every summer. They normally lived at Middleton Place about half the year, from early December until late May, but then left to avoid the terrible Carolina heat and

41. Benjamin F. Perry, *Reminiscences of Public Men* (Spartanburg, S.C.: Reprint Company, 1980), 3:111.
42. MHM to Arthur Middleton, February 7, 1828, PHi, FFP.
43. John I. Middleton to Arthur Middleton, January 10, 1831, MPlFdn.

the danger of malaria. They usually spent part of June in Charleston, seeing friends and shopping, and then went north by boat, or sometimes by train once railroads were built in the 1830s. They returned to Charleston in the late fall, after the first heavy frost put an end, so it was believed, to the malaria season.

Every year, starting in 1833 and continuing through the 1840s, the Middletons went to Newport. The island had been well known in the eighteenth century for its healthy climate and had attracted many southerners, but after the Revolution, summer visitors had tended to go elsewhere. By the 1830s, however, when steamboats made it easier than previously to get to the island, the cool sea breezes and beautiful surroundings of Narragansett Bay were once again making Newport a popular summer resort. Southerners as well as northerners went there in increasing numbers, usually staying in unpretentious boardinghouses. In 1835 Henry Middleton was among the first summer visitors who altered this pattern by buying a house where his whole family could gather each summer. Once they had the house, the Middletons regularly spent nearly four months in Newport, arriving in early July and staying until the end of October.

The Middletons had longstanding social connections with families up and down the East coast, and their trips north from Charleston in the spring and southward again in the fall gave them the opportunity to visit in New York, Baltimore, and Philadelphia. But by the mid-1830s, many of their friends—the Harpers and Calverts from Baltimore, the Joneses from Savannah, the Hares from Philadelphia, and the Thorndikes from Boston—were, like the Middletons, spending at least part of the summer in Newport. The town thus became a central meeting place where people could count on seeing their friends.

Newport also helped the Middleton children make or strengthen friendships in a wider world beyond Middleton Place and Charleston. Eliza's closest friends during this period, aside from her cousin Emma Huger from Charleston,[44] were two young women whose families also spent the summer in Newport. One was Julia Ward of New York;[45] the other, Sophia Thorndike of Boston.[46]

44. Emma was the daughter of Henry Middleton's sister, Isabella (Middleton) and Judge Daniel Elliott Huger. (See note following Eliza's letter of May 28, 1839.)

45. Julia Ward (1819–1910) (later Julia Ward Howe, noted abolitionist and author of "The Battle Hymn of the Republic") was the daughter of New York banker Samuel Ward. Although her papers apparently no longer contain any reference to her friendship with either Eliza or William Middleton, there is considerable evidence of their closeness in the Middleton-Fisher correspondence. (See note preceding Mrs. Middleton's letter of October 11, 1839.)

46. Sophia Thorndike was the daughter and granddaughter, respectively, of prominent Bostonians Israel Thorndike, Jr., and Harrison Gray Otis. (See note following Mrs. Middleton's letter of May 17, 1839.)

It was not at all surprising either that Eliza and Francis Fisher met at Newport.[47] Fisher went there regularly in the 1830s, and his family and the Middletons had several mutual friends.

The Fishers, the Francises, and the Harrisons

Fisher's background differed noticeably from Eliza's. Whereas the Middletons were southerners whose wealth was derived from plantations worked by slaves, the families from whom Fisher descended were all from Philadelphia, with roots in the mercantile community of that great colonial port.

The Fishers were Quakers who came to Pennsylvania with William Penn in the 1680s. Fisher's great-grandfather Joshua (1707–1783) was a prosperous merchant at the head of a family enterprise, Joshua Fisher and Sons, in which his sons and a son-in-law were employed. When the Revolution started, Joshua Fisher stuck to his Quaker pacifist principles, refusing either to participate or to aid either side in any way. His loyalty to the patriot cause, like that of many Quakers, was therefore suspect, and—as some measure of his prominence—he and several other leading Quakers were rounded up in 1777 by the wartime government of Pennsylvania and exiled for eight months to Winchester, Virginia, under very harsh conditions.

Joshua Fisher's grandson, however, also named Joshua (1775–1806), would have none of the Quaker tradition which was so important to his family. Not only did he disavow the Quakers' longstanding opposition to war by serving in the military during the Whiskey Rebellion, but he also developed tastes—he loved to drive fast horses, for example—which were too worldly for the Quaker community of his time. As a result, his uncles disapproved of him and he started his own trading business rather than joining the Fisher family firm. By 1806 he felt financially secure enough to marry Elizabeth Powel Francis (1777–1855).

Betsey Francis, as she was called, was the daughter of Tench Francis, Jr., and the former Ann Willing. Her parents represented two of Philadelphia's wealthy, respected, and decidedly not Quaker families who were joined in business as well as marriage: the firm of Willing and Francis was a leader in Philadelphia's European and East India trade after the Revolution. Both the Willings and Francises were part of a large connection of proud and fashionable families which included the Powels, Binghams, McCalls, Hares, and Shippens in Philadelphia and extended to the Byrds in Virginia and the Browns of Providence as well as the Barings in England.

47. Judging from comments in various letters, they must have met at least by 1836.

Throughout the eighteenth century they accepted their share of civic responsibility: Tench Francis, Sr., served as attorney general of Pennsylvania before the Revolution, while Charles Willing, Ann's grandfather, was mayor of Philadelphia; her brother, Thomas (though he was not in favor of the Declaration of Independence), was the founding president of the First Bank of the United States. By the mid-nineteenth century, however, they were no longer among Philadelphia's economic or political leaders.

Betsey Francis Fisher did not have especially broad interests, and her education had been only routine, but she was intelligent and practical. Her marriage to Joshua Fisher started very happily, but he unfortunately died only a few months after their wedding. At about the same time, a firm with whom he did business in the East Indies went bankrupt, causing him a large loss. Thus he left his widow not only pregnant but poor.

Their son, whom she named Joshua Francis Fisher, was born in February 1807, and though his grandfather left money in his will to provide for the boy, Fisher's uncles delayed paying it for many years.[48] Fortunately for her, Betsey Fisher's sister, Sophia, and Sophia's husband, George Harrison, were nearby to give her loving support and financial assistance.

The Harrisons, who had no children of their own, lived on Chestnut Street one block (or "square," as the Philadelphians said) from Independence Hall in what Fisher remembered as a "delightful residence," with two parlors opening onto a large garden. As a child, he could run in from his play to "partake of dessert or be fondled by the ladies in the Drawing-room."[49] Harrison bought a house for Mrs. Fisher and her son in the next block, so the two households were in constant contact.

George Harrison (1761–1845) was a key figure in this family group from the start. He was seventy-eight in 1839 when Eliza and Fisher were married, approaching the end of a life of "unostentatious generosity" and kindness.[50] Whether acting as an executor, as he did for his friend Joshua Fisher, or simply helping someone in need, he was both persistent and shrewd. He was often

---

48. Fisher believed that this was the result of their disapproval of his mother because she was not a Quaker, and he supposed that she, in turn, "had not conciliated her new Quaker relations." The disagreement over his inheritance contributed to Fisher's pronounced dislike of Quakers in general, even though he was fond of some of his relatives and other individual Quakers. *Recollections of Joshua Francis Fisher Written in 1864*, arranged by Sophia Cadwalader (Boston: privately printed, 1929), 30. Hereafter cited as JFF, *Recollections*.
49. JFF, *Recollections*, 191.
50. JFF, *Recollections*, 234.

asked to help the widows or unmarried daughters of his friends, for example, and Fisher knew that his uncle would "make the most advantageous . . . investments; if they had claims in any quarter, prosecute them with indefatigable zeal, till he had secured a competence . . . & in the end [make] it appear it was no more than their inheritance."[51] He had quietly managed his sister-in-law's financial affairs so well over the years that in 1839 she had an annual income of about $4,000,[52] more than enough to meet her needs. As Fisher said of him, "If ever there was a man whom the blessings of the Widow and the Orphan wafted to Heaven, it was my Uncle."[53]

When he was a young man just starting out in business, Harrison sailed to China in 1787 as the supercargo on the ship *Alliance,* which belonged to the merchant-financier Robert Morris.[54] The ship returned with a cargo of tea worth $100,000, and in the succeeding years, Harrison, as Morris's protégé, made himself quite wealthy. But in the wake of Morris's bankruptcy in the 1790s, he lost virtually everything he had except the house on Chestnut Street, which had been bought in his wife's name. Harrison was still only in his thirties, though, and made a second (and sizable) fortune in the Madeira wine trade in the early nineteenth century.[55] By then he had learned his lesson and thereafter invested only in "well-selected mortgages"[56] and low-risk loans augmented by a few carefully chosen stocks in banks, canals, and insurance companies.

Uncle Harrison, as Fisher (and later Eliza) called him, became a substitute father for Fisher, who always regarded him as his "kindest & best counsellor & friend."[57] His uncle watched carefully over every aspect not only of Fisher's

51. JFF, *Recollections,* 236.

52. This was equivalent to approximately $57,000 in 1999 dollars. Conversion factors for calculating the present value of a dollar amount provided by Robert Sahr, Political Science Department, Oregon State University, Corvallis. Hereafter cited as RSahr, OrStU.

53. JFF, *Recollections,* 236.

54. Robert Morris (1734–1806) signed the Declaration of Independence and was superintendent of finance for the Continental Congress in the early 1780s. Successful in business at a very young age, he became a partner of Thomas Willing's in 1754 and later won respect and gratitude because he advanced his own money to finance the American army during the Revolution. Once the war was over, however, he went bankrupt after huge speculations in western lands and thereby also ruined many other people who had trusted him with their money.

55. George Harrison's estate was valued at approximately $470,000 when he died in 1845, the equivalent of nearly $9.5 million in 1999 dollars. Conversion factor from RSahr, OrStU.

56. JFF, *Recollections,* 237.

57. JFF to Sophia Harrison, July 22, 1839, PHi, BrC.

education but also of the development of his character and manners as well. He was very precise in showing him how to manage his money and once, when Fisher was at college and had apparently been lax in some unexplained instance, Uncle Harrison admonished him to remember that "regular habits are necessary to your future comfort & prosperity, & you cannot too much cherish them."[58]

Uncle Harrison, who was known for his own supremely good manners, also drilled Fisher on the importance of the social graces and once inquired of his college-age nephew, "Do you occasionally practice an Entrée into a Drawing Room? I recommend your attending to this." Fisher recalled his uncle's arranging the chairs to show him how to greet the host and hostess first before saluting the other guests.[59] In short, from the time Fisher was a small boy, his uncle taught him to be "a finished Gentleman, an ornament to Society." He was to be considerate and helpful and, above all, a comfort to his mother to whom he was indebted for everything.[60]

Freighted with such expectations and his family's belief that he would easily qualify himself at least for the "Attorneyship of the US" as well as the "Honors & emoluments" of his country,[61] Fisher went off to Harvard College in 1822, when he was not yet sixteen. Although neither his mother nor the Harrisons were at all intellectually inclined, Fisher at some point developed a strong appreciation for literature and for history, and it seems quite likely that Harvard gave him the opportunity to exercise this. He felt, as he later told a classmate, he had not completely wasted his time at Harvard. He valued the close and lasting friendships he made and looked back at his three years at college as one of the happiest periods of his life.[62]

Having graduated in the Class of 1825, Fisher studied law with Joseph R. Ingersoll, one of Philadelphia's leading lawyers, and was admitted to the

58. GH to JFF, November 4, 1824, PHi, C/F.

59. GH to JFF, November 4, 1824, PHi, C/F; JFF, *Recollections*, 185.

60. GH to JFF, February 10, 1816, PHi, BrC.

61. GH to JFF, August 21, 1821, PHi, BrC.

62. Paul Trapier, who was from Charleston, remembered that students from anywhere south of New England were called southerners, and they "kept company with each other in an aristocratic exclusiveness, into which only a few exceptional Yankees of families of high distinction were admitted." One of those Yankees was Allyne Otis from Boston. He, along with Fisher's cousin Charles Willing from Philadelphia, and Trapier were Fisher's close friends and remained so after college. JFF to C. K. Dillaway, November 19, 1864, Harvard University Archives; Paul Trapier, *Autobiography of the Rev. Paul Trapier* (Charleston: Dalcho Historical Society, 1952), 9–10.

Pennsylvania bar in 1829. Then in the fall of 1830 his Uncle Harrison sent him to Europe to travel and study in England and on the Continent. He spent a good deal of his time in Paris and served for some time as an attaché to the American legation when William Cabell Rives was U.S. minister.

By the time Fisher returned to Philadelphia late in 1832, it had been clear to him for a long time that he had no interest whatsoever in practicing law or in going into business. He later told Henry Middleton that he lacked "the activity and enterprise necessary to manage an estate or improve a fortune."[63] He simply wanted to be able to "cultivate his tastes for reading and study" and fulfill "his duties in the station in which he [was] placed,"[64] by which he probably meant he expected to take part in the kind of community and charitable works which befitted a gentleman and which he had seen his uncle perform so well. Whether there was any connection between Fisher's inclination and his health is not known. However, as early as 1829 he was bothered by severe headaches and at some point during the 1830s, if not before, he began to have trouble with his eyesight.

Before Fisher went to Europe, the Quaker philanthropist Roberts Vaux asked him to help plan a school for the blind in Philadelphia. There was no one in the community "better qualified than thyself to render this service," Vaux told him. "I pray thee, give this suggestion a serious reflection." Vaux asked him to investigate European techniques for teaching the blind and to "bring with thee home all the knowledge to be had on the subject."[65] Fisher responded with estimates of costs and suggestions for sending future teachers to Europe to be trained and also sent books and apparatus from France for the new school.[66] On his return to the United States, he became a member of the original Board of Managers of the Pennsylvania Institution for the Instruction of the Blind and remained on the board for the rest of his life, the school being one of his principal interests.

Similarly, very soon after he finished college, his interest in history led him to become one of the first members of the Historical Society of Pennsylvania. This too became a lifelong commitment. He understood the importance of collecting documents about the country's early history before they were lost and, among other items, acquired for the society's collections William Penn's

63. Draft of JFF to HM, [September 20, 1838,] PHi, C/F.
64. EM to JFF, January 9, 1839, PHi, FFP.
65. Roberts Vaux to JFF, 6th month [June] 1829, Roberts Vaux to JFF, n.d., 1830, Overbrook School for the Blind.
66. JFF to Roberts Vaux, January 29, 1832, Overbrook School for the Blind.

original instructions to his commissioners who preceded him to Pennsylvania in 1681.[67]

ENGAGEMENT AND MARRIAGE

In all the large number of letters Fisher and Eliza saved, almost nothing is said about their courtship; perhaps they destroyed the evidence. In particular, Fisher gives no indication of what made him decide in the summer of 1838 that the moment had come for them to be engaged. It is certain, though, that at the end of August 1838 Fisher took the boat to Newport where Eliza was with her family; that he proposed to her during a moonlight ride on the beach; and that she accepted.

Neither their friends nor Eliza's family seem to have been surprised when they got engaged.[68] Fisher was already a "favorite" with the Middletons,[69] who must surely have long since made inquiries about his character and his financial situation through friends who knew the Fishers and Harrisons. Among these would have been John Sergeant in Philadelphia, Henry Middleton's former congressional colleague. The engagement was soon known and it was agreed to hold the wedding at Middleton Place early in 1839.

Interestingly, when Fisher asked Eliza to marry him, he did not have enough money of his own to support her. Though he knew he would eventually inherit a substantial fortune from his Uncle Harrison, he was, as he phrased it to Eliza's father, still "in a dependant situation."[70] Furthermore, he had not told either his mother or the Harrisons about Eliza.[71]

---

67. Anna Wharton Smith, *Genealogy of the Fisher Family, 1682–1896* (Philadelphia, 1896), 95.

68. Fisher's cousin, Sidney, wrote in his diary, "he told me of his intentions in the matter, & I knew very well that she would not refuse." Nicholas B. Wainwright, ed., *A Philadelphia Perspective: The Diary of Sidney George Fisher Covering the Years 1834–1871* (Philadelphia: Historical Society of Pennsylvania, 1967), September 12, 1838, 59. Hereafter cited as Wainwright, *Phila. Perspective.*

69. Mrs. Middleton's brother wrote, "This Mr. Fisher is already become such a Favorite, from Eliza's description, as well as yours, that I long to be personally acquainted with him." Henry Middleton's sister wrote, "I truly rejoice to find that my Dear Niece's choice so entirely meets yr approbation." Oliver Hering to MHM, October 20, 1838, PHi, BrC; Septima Sexta Rutledge to MHM, December 12, 1838, PHi, C/F.

70. Draft of JFF to Henry Middleton, [September 20, 1838,] PHi, C/F.

71. Fisher had tried to tell his aunt about Eliza some months before, but for reasons that are not at all clear, she told him she did not wish to "converse" on the subject. Sophia Harrison to JFF, September 1, 1838, PHi, BrC. Ellen K. Rothman, *Hands and Hearts: A History of Courtship in America* (New York: Basic Books, 1984), 116 ff., dis-

Fisher wrote to the Harrisons first. Even though they had apparently made it clear that they expected to give him money whenever he did marry, it was "a matter of no small delicacy,"[72] as Fisher told Henry Middleton, to raise the question without appearing to demand money from them. Having recovered from their initial surprise, the Harrisons responded generously. They not only promised to give Fisher $1,500 annually from their own income, but also persuaded Fisher's bachelor uncle, Charles Francis, to do the same. Further, Uncle Harrison proposed to give Fisher the house in which his mother and he lived, so Fisher would receive the annual rent of $600. This, combined with Fisher's own small income and extra money his frugal mother did not spend, would amount to a total annual income of about $8,600. "A pretty good begining for a Young man," his uncle snorted. "If you cannot all get on with this- you ought to stick in the mud."[73]

In addition, Henry Middleton, as would be expected from a man of his wealth and status, indicated that he would make some financial provision for Eliza. Ultimately, he chose to give her $1,800 annually, which was the equivalent of 6 percent interest on $30,000.[74] Eliza was to receive the full $30,000 at some point in the future.

It was much more difficult for Fisher to convince his mother to accept his marriage than it was to arrange his income. Aunt Harrison knew her sister well and warned Fisher that his mother would "be thrown into [a state]" by the news of his engagement,[75] and she was right. Mrs. Fisher, who for nearly thirty-two years had devoted all her attention, love, and energy to her only child, was now terrified she was going to lose him and did not take to the idea of his marriage at all.

Playing a role which was evidently not new to them, the Harrisons undertook to "soothe & comfort"[76] Fisher's mother. Then in November, Fisher took his mother to New York to meet Eliza and the Middletons as they traveled back to Charleston from Newport. Eliza concluded, "she is a most excellent old lady

---

cusses similar situations of men not telling their mothers about their plans for marriage when there was a close mother-son relationship.

72. Draft of JFF to Henry Middleton, [September 20, 1838,] PHi, C/F.
73. GH to JFF, September 14, 1838, PHi, BrC. In 1999 dollars, an income of $8,600 would be approximately $123,000 per year with no income tax to be paid. Conversion factor from RSahr, OrStU.
74. In 1999 dollars, $1,800 would be in the range of $26,000. This put their annual combined income at nearly $150,000 (estimated) in 1999 dollars. Conversion factor from RSahr, OrStU.
75. Sophia Harrison to JFF, September 1, 1838, PHi, BrC.
76. Ibid.

and I am already quite attached to her."[77] Fisher, however, was furious: he thought his mother had not shown sufficient interest in Eliza and worried that she might have been rude to Mr. Middleton when he passed through Philadelphia on his way to Washington. "I believe it would almost be agreeable to her that the match should be broken," he fumed to his uncle, but "she should know that my affections are as irrevocably fixed as my honour. I love Miss Middleton, as I did not believe it in my nature to love any one."[78]

Uncle Harrison wisely saw that Mrs. Fisher would come round. No matter who Fisher decided to marry, he told Fisher, "we should have the same excitement- and you must not construe it in the remotest manner as disapproving, be calm on this subject & receive my assurance that after the first tumult of parting with her Child subsides- everything will be as you could wish."

He also advised Fisher and Eliza to move into 170 Chestnut Street with Mrs. Fisher rather than taking a house of their own. "One household," he suggested, "for the present at least . . . would be, situated as you will be, most for the happiness of all."[79] To make this possible, he offered to add a wing onto Mrs. Fisher's small house so all three of them could be comfortable.

Eliza agreed to this proposal, and Fisher reported to the Harrisons that she "is sure she shall be much happier besides a thousand times more comfortable with my Mother at the head of the Establishment- for of course a northern Household would be a difficult thing to undertake at once." Doubtless for Mrs. Fisher's benefit, Fisher continued, saying Eliza had "every desire to be with my Mother that she might be the more sure of conciliating her affections, as well as to profit by her example & instructions."[80]

Then, as if answering questions that the Harrisons and Mrs. Fisher had raised, Fisher shifted to Eliza's southern upbringing. Knowing very well that the Harrisons objected to slavery, he assured them that Eliza "has none of the habits of a Southern woman- & I understand from those who know the family at home that they are utterly free from that indolent helplessness & languid carelessness which is usually the Characteristic of women bred up among slaves."[81]

Fisher was genuinely devoted to his mother and in the following months tried hard to convince her that by adding Eliza to his life he would not be

77. EM and MHM to Harry Middleton, November 19, 1838, PHi, C/F.
78. JFF to GH, November 15, 1838, PHi, BrC.
79. GH to JFF, September 8, 1838, PHi, BrC.
80. JFF to the Harrisons, September 21, 1838, PHi, BrC.
81. Ibid. Mrs. Fisher's view of slavery is not known.

subtracting her.[82] The Harrisons helped, and gradually, just as Uncle Harrison had predicted, Mrs. Fisher began to accept the idea of Fisher's marriage and even to look forward to having a daughter-in-law. In the beginning of March, when Fisher left Philadelphia to go to Charleston, Mrs. Fisher sent Eliza a diamond brooch. Along with it went a note which said, "Believe me, I shall exert every energy to win your love."[83]

Eliza had her own hesitations about getting married. Despite her conviction that Fisher would do everything in his power to make her happy,[84] she worried about tying herself to another person by "the irrevocable words" of the "important ceremony which is to decide my fate."[85] This was by no means a dramatic overstatement, but rather a realistic concern for any woman at the time, since the law still generally held that married women, and their property, were subject to their husbands' control.[86] While Eliza had been brought up to expect such control,[87] she nevertheless had a very independent spirit, and, if nothing else did, knowing her mother had to ask permission even to go to Charleston would have convinced her she did not want such a situation for herself.

It was logical therefore that Eliza should think about obedience. "There are some men perhaps who would require it," she wrote to Fisher, "but I flatter myself you are not of those, and even that you do not consider it indecorous in a woman to express an opinion when it differs from her liege lord's." Or must she, she asked only half-joking, resign herself "to entire submission, and

---

82. In writing to thank his aunt and uncle for the "kind & affectionate reception & treatment" he knew they would give Eliza, Fisher made a direct contrast with his mother. "You at least do not fear that my love for her will in any way interfere with my attachment to you," he wrote, "but on the contrary think what I am sure will be verified, that in my happiness I shall augment that of my dearest friends- and in gaining the affections of this charming lady, I have won for you also a source of joy & pleasure." JFF to the Harrisons, April 1, 1839, PHi, C/F.

83. Elizabeth P. Fisher to EM, [circa March 1, 1839,] ScHi.

84. EM to Harry Middleton, November 19, 1838, PHi, C/F.

85. EM to Harry Middleton, February 23, 1839, PHi, C/F. For a discussion of similar reactions from other women, see Rothman, *Hands and Hearts,* 61 ff.

86. State laws governing women's property rights were only beginning to be changed at this time. See Marylynn Salmon, *Women and the Law of Property in Early America* (Chapel Hill: University of North Carolina Press, 1986), 81 ff. and passim.

87. Mrs. Middleton had once written to Catherine and Eliza, "not only children but young Women [require control,] & it is what they will certainly experience when they marry, so that it is better they should become accustomed to it betimes." MHM to Catherine and Eliza, December 5, 1826, ScHi.

become a complete non-entity without a voice on any subject under discussion?"[88]

Marriage was a risky business for other reasons as well. Eliza knew she was likely to be pregnant within months after her marriage and that she might die in childbirth. Her mother survived the births of fourteen children in twenty-two years,[89] but Eliza was well aware that having too many children had ruined the health of her two sisters-in-law. So it is not surprising that, once home in South Carolina, where she was preparing for the wedding, she wrote to Fisher, "I cannot say in truth that I as ardently long for that <u>awful</u> day [*as you do*] altho' since our separation I am become more reconciled to the idea of the dreaded ceremony which is to join us forever. I still contend however that if you could always remain near me & with me without it, I should prefer an <u>eternal engagement</u>."[90]

Though her worries about the disadvantages of marriage were real, Eliza's decision to marry Fisher was not in doubt. Fisher's "good understanding and sound sense," she knew, were united with "the most affectionate disposition, the best temper & warmest <u>heart</u>."[91] Furthermore, she knew Fisher respected her for herself, as she was—talented, vigorous, articulate, and outspoken. He was not interested in the Philadelphia women he knew who lacked "good sense, education & taste,"[92] and he deliberately chose a wife who could be his respected companion—which may well reflect the influence of his Aunt and Uncle Harrison who were, as both Fisher and Eliza recognized, the "best examples of conjugal happiness."[93]

All hopes and plans for the future were abruptly put aside, however, when Eliza came down with scarlet fever in February 1839. For a worrisome week, she was so sick it seemed quite possible that she would die. She thought so herself and told Fisher, "it <u>was</u> a bitter thought that I might soon be called upon to . . . resign my life when just beginning to enjoy it, with happiness greater than I had ever allowed myself to hope would be my lot."[94] Once it was clear, though, that she would live, plans for the wedding were put back on track.

Mrs. Fisher and the Harrisons were too old to travel, but Fisher asked his

88. EM to JFF, January 23, 1839, PHi, FFP.
89. Four died as infants.
90. EM to JFF, December 25, 1838, MPlFdn.
91. EM to Harry Middleton, November 19, 1838, PHi, C/F.
92. EMF to MHM, May 28, 1839, private collection.
93. EMF to MHM, May 16, 1845, private collection.
94. EM to JFF, February 17, 1839, MPlFdn.

old friends Charles Willing and Allyne Otis to go with him to Charleston. Arriving a week before the wedding as first-time visitors to the South, they were probably surprised, as Sophia Thorndike was, by the number of black faces and the "untidy air of the habitations."[95] But they must have been correspondingly charmed by the sight of magnolia trees as tall as buildings and by the two-storied porches—piazzas, they would soon have learned to call them—running the length of many handsome houses. Fisher declared the city, with its newly finished public garden overlooking the harbor and elegant public buildings, "beyond [his] expectations." Middleton Place, with its extensive "pleasure grounds," he told the Harrisons, had "more of the signs of civilization than any thing I have seen in America."[96]

Guests began arriving some days before the wedding day, and Eliza had to reassure her apprehensive fiancé that there would not be "an alarming number" of her "innumerable" cousins, only as many "as the old House will hold."[97] At last, the twelfth of March came and, with Sophia Thorndike and two young Middleton cousins as bridesmaids and Charles Willing and Allyne Otis as groomsmen,[98] Eliza and Fisher were married by Paul Trapier, the third of Fisher's special Harvard friends.

LEAVING HOME

Eliza's decision to leave South Carolina was not entirely simple. On the one hand, being familiar with Philadelphia, as well as with Boston and New York, she shared her family's view that Charleston was less interesting and varied than those cities, and by some gauges this was true. From having been the fourth largest American city in 1790, Charleston had slipped to ninth place and by 1839 trailed the northern cities not only in population and commercial activity but in the breadth of its cultural life. Still, to Eliza, Charleston was her "dear dull dirty native city,"[99] and she was well aware that she would not be

95. Sophia spent the winter with the Middletons. Close to 60 percent of Charleston's 29,261 inhabitants in 1840 were black; the great majority of these were slaves. EM to JFF, December 11, 1838, PHi, FFP; Coclanis, *The Shadow of a Dream*, 115.

96. JFF to the Harrisons, March 6, 1839, PHi, C/F.

97. EM to JFF, December 11, 1838, PHi, FFP; EM to JFF, February 17, 1839, MPlFdn.

98. That Otis and Willing were groomsmen is only an assumption, since the letter Mrs. Middleton wrote describing the wedding to Eliza's brother, Harry, has not been found. EM to Harry Middleton, April 14, 1839, PHi, C/F.

99. EM to JFF, December 11, 1838, PHi, FFP.

able to go back there very often once she was married. By moving away, she would become an exception—almost all her close relatives were in South Carolina, and she would miss them.

Though she complained about the isolation and boredom of plantation life, she nevertheless realized how attached she was to the special routines and pleasures of her "old and happy" home[100] at Middleton Place—playing the piano for her father and brothers in the evening, walking in the gardens or horseback riding, conversing at the dinner table "on subjects worth talking about,"[101] reading aloud or enjoying a quiet game of piquet with Mrs. Middleton. She would be leaving these as well as her brothers and their families, her sister and her parents. So, even though the Middletons were well satisfied that her marriage would be a good one in every respect, Eliza's move to Philadelphia brought not only major changes in her life, but a "breakup," as her brothers called it,[102] of their closely knit family.

The separation was hardest of all on Eliza's mother. As she approached seventy, her health was failing and family tragedies had taken their toll on her: Eleanor, her second daughter, had died in St. Petersburg in 1827; Catherine had become mentally ill, imposing an especially heavy burden of care on her mother; and in the spring of 1838, the Middletons' oldest daughter, Maria Pringle, had drowned with her husband and children when the steamship *Pulaski* exploded on its way to New York. Now Mrs. Middleton was about to be deprived of her dearest, lively, and loving Eliza, the daughter who was, as Fisher put it, her "best companion & chief comfort."[103]

Fortunately, Eliza and her mother could look forward to being with each other in Newport for two or three months each summer; Fisher had specifically agreed to this when they were engaged. Mrs. Middleton could also hope to visit Eliza in Philadelphia, on the way south in the fall and perhaps on the way to Newport in the spring, but it was all too clear that for the remaining seven or eight months of each year they would not see each other at all. To stay in close touch, they agreed that once Eliza went to Philadelphia each would write to the other every week if possible.

Mrs. Middleton's talent for letter writing was well established. In the forty-five years since her own marriage, she had maintained correspondences with several friends and with her brother, Oliver. Her son, Arthur, had recognized

---

100. EM to Harry Middleton, April 14, 1839, PHi, C/F.
101. JFF to GH, November 15, 1838, PHi, BrC.
102. EM to Harry Middleton, December 31, 1838, PHi, C/F.
103. JFF to GH, May 1, 1839, PHi, C/F.

years before not only that she was "one of the best as well as most faithful of correspondents," but that she enjoyed the occupation.[104] Happily, Eliza soon showed that she was her mother's own daughter in this area. Writing her first letter before she had been gone two days on the journey to Philadelphia, she started the correspondence that both she and her mother came to rely on for comfort and support during the long periods they were separated.

104. Arthur Middleton to MHM, October 3, 1833, MPlFdn.

1839

*[I] very much prefer the rational amusements furnished in my
own drawing room by my books & piano to all the dull
trivialities I hear discussed elsewhere.*

After their wedding on March 12, Eliza and Francis Fisher stayed at Middleton Place for several weeks before setting out for Philadelphia so Eliza would have more time to recover from the scarlet fever. Her voice and eyes were still weak, and she was bothered by numbness in her legs and hands. Even though he was impatient to get home and introduce Eliza to his family and friends, Fisher was willing to delay their departure because he knew that Eliza's "separation from her mother must be such a heartbreaking affair to both," especially as the first anniversary of Maria Middleton Pringle's death in the *Pulaski* approached.[1]

Finally, however, knowing they would see Eliza's family again in Newport later in the summer, the Fishers set out at the end of April on a carefully planned journey of sightseeing and visits. Traveling first by boat from Charleston to Wilmington, North Carolina, they continued north by railroad and carriage, through North Carolina and on to Charlottesville, Virginia. There they visited Mr. and Mrs. William Cabell Rives, whom Fisher had known in Paris in the early 1830s when Rives was U.S. minister to France.

Eliza's first letters to her mother included not only an account of visiting Monticello but also fresh and lively descriptions of the Natural Bridge in Virginia and the Blue Ridge Mountains, places which were not yet on a well-trod tourist path. Her mention of their trip on the newly opened Petersburg to Richmond railroad is an early account of a still novel and exciting mode of transport.[2]

As she and Fisher neared the end of their trip and were on their way to Philadelphia from Baltimore, Eliza told her mother she didn't know whether to be glad or sorry. "I shall certainly be content to enjoy a little quiet after jolting over the roughest roads I ever was on in my life," she wrote, but "I cannot help regretting that our pleasant day's drive, and cosy evening readings, tho' by tallow candles in the meanest Taverns, are to give place to a routine of town visitors, and irksome tea drinkings. This is of course entre nous for I would not have the good old people suspect that I do not look forward with much delight to the society of which I am to become a part & I am sure it will be my own fault if I am not happy among them– [Mrs. Fisher] has written most kindly welcoming me home as her daughter, & says enough to convince me that she has my future welfare & happiness deeply at heart."[3]

Eliza's reference to town visits and irksome tea drinking suggests that Fisher wanted to keep her expectations low so she would not be disappointed with his family and friends or with his native city. In reality, the life she could look forward to in Philadelphia was far from dull. It was a "great, beautiful, rich and, self-complacent city," said an observant New Yorker.[4] Compared to Philadelphia, Charleston was but a small town.

By 1839 industry had become the city's leading source of wealth, surpassing the commercial activities which earlier enriched families like the Fishers and Francises. Locomotives rolled from the Baldwin works; fire engines and boilers from the Southwark foundry; textiles from mills along the Schuylkill River. With workers moving in from the countryside to look for jobs and thousands of immigrants arriving each year from Europe, the city's population grew at an unprecedented rate. By 1840 there were close to 260,000 people in Philadelphia County, nearly twice the number of twenty years before, and the number continued to increase in the following decade. Buildings were going up everywhere, it seemed, and new houses pushed the edge of the city westward, way beyond the Fishers' house at Eighth Street, into once open fields.

Philadelphia had ceded its place as the nation's financial center to New York by 1839, but it was second to none as a cultural center. In one of the several newspapers that flourished in the city, Eliza would be able to read, on any given day, announcements of lectures sponsored by the Mercantile Library or the Athenian Institute and of plays and operas at the Walnut and Chestnut Street theaters. Whether she walked on the tree-lined and straight streets for which Philadelphia was so famous or took a drive to the beautiful new Laurel Hill Cemetery, she would pass buildings designed by renowned architects. She would be able to have Thomas Sully paint her portrait, as he had her mother's some years before, or choose among several other artists. She would have her choice of visiting the Peales' Museum just around the corner from the Fishers' house, Nathan Dunn's Chinese Collection, or the Academy of Fine Arts. Probably most interesting to her, she could look forward to hearing first class musicians perform in concerts throughout the year.

At the time Eliza and Fisher were married, however, Philadelphia was suffering from a nationwide economic depression that had started in 1837 and continued into the 1840s. After President Jackson vetoed the bill to recharter the Bank of the United States in 1832, there was no longer any central control over banking practices. Hundreds of new banks sprang up and gave credit much too easily, and this, combined with wild speculation in public lands, which President Jackson attempted to stop by requiring payments in specie rather than paper money, all contributed to a financial panic in 1837. Banks failed and businesses went bankrupt, leading to widespread hardship and unemployment almost everywhere. Various comments in Mrs. Middleton's and Eliza's letters, as well as other family correspondence, indicate that the Middletons and Fishers lost some money through bank failures and low rice prices in the early 1840s but emerged relatively unscathed compared to many of their friends.

1. JFF to George and Sophia Harrison, April 1, 1839, PHi, C/F.

2. For a more dramatic account of a railroad journey, see MHM to EMF, December 21, 1839, PHi.

3. EMF to MHM, May 15, [1839,] private collection.

4. *Hazard's Register* 6 (1830), quoted in Russell F. Weigley, ed., *Philadelphia: A 300-Year History* (New York: W. W. Norton & Co., 1982), 275.

To Mrs. Middleton, Middleton Place

Powhattan House, Richmond May 1$\underline{st}$ 1839

I wrote you a few hurried lines from Wilmington [*North Carolina,*] dearest Mamma, just to tell you that we had got thro' what I consider the worst part of our expedition in safety– I can now have the pleasure of speaking of the dangers of the RailRoad and Stages also in the past tense– which is no small one I assure you, and no little comfort to find oneself quietly resting in a very good Hotel, & writing at a window commanding an extremely pretty view of the surrounding country, of our quickly & really pleasantly performed journey– I will not 'begin by the beginning' but preface my account of our adventures by telling you how much better I am already, which you will easily believe when I say that I was up at 5 this morning, and walked for nearly an hour before breakfast, admiring the State House and other Public Buildings, and many private residences which would stand a comparison with the best in New York & Phila$\underline{d}$ and have the advantage over them in situation & prospect– Indeed I am quite delighted with the whole appearance of the Place, and as far as I can judge of the environs, particularly the banks of the James River, which is a romantic looking stream, with some fine country Seats, deserving that appelation on either side– I should willingly describe the scenery which refreshed our eyes, after the N.C$\underline{a}$ swamps, all the way from Stony Creek, yesterday, particularly Petersburg and its immediate vicinity which pleased me the more as I was agreeably surprised to find the ugly sounding Appomattox river so beautiful– But I know that you do not care much to have descriptions which I should be apt to make diffuse, and would rather hear of the accomodations of the cars stages & Taverns.

To return then to where I took leave of you, we started from Wilmg$^{\underline{n}}$ at 8 o'clock Sunday Morng in very well finished & furnished Cars, and were whisked along to Waynesboro' at the rate of 13 or 14 miles an hour, stopping there an hour to dine & rest, and getting into the most comfortable Stage coach I ever was in some after 3– I need not stop to tell you anything of the country between Wilmington and Enfield, for it is all barren & uninteresting as possible except that I saw wild flowers enough to amuse me along the way side, one which I mean hereafter to describe to Papa, who no doubt knows it, was very singular & pretty and grows in great profusion. But without further digression, we took possession of an Extra,[1] which as I said was an exceedingly comfortable one and quite new, & remained in it, going at the rate of 6 miles an hour, until about 9 o'clk in the eveng when we reached M$^{\underline{r}}$ Vicks' nice looking House and were very tolerably accomodated for the night. The road thus far was good, and we were not much fatigued– notwithstanding we had been about 110 miles by RailRoad & Stage– I believe I should not have felt the least fatigue if the weather had been more moderate for we were not at all jolted, and could change our position and walk while they changed the horses, but the Thermometer was at 82 during the greater part of the day, but in the afternoon a thunder shower & gust cooled the air sufficiently to allow us to sleep soundly after getting rid of the Feather beds which would have suffocated us. The next day's ride was a very easy one indeed– I mean short– only 32 miles to Enfield– which we divided into 2 parts. Driving 22 miles to M$^{\underline{r}}$ Hilliard's, where we dined, & merely taking an afternoon airing, or as the Coachman found it wetting to Enfield which we reached in 2 hours– Both these Houses, Hilliard's and Southwell's are clean and well attended by willing handmaidens of sooty hue, who did all I required cheerfully, & gratefully accepted the quarter or half dollars distributed at our departure– so that I have not been in need of a body servant of my own– But as I hear bad accounts of the Inns on the other side of Charlottesville, and we shall no longer have M$^{\underline{r}}$ Putnam's[2] man to look after our baggage, I am going to engage a mulatto woman here for a fortnight, and send her back from Baltimore. It was rather warm again on Monday Morng & instead of taking the cool of the day for our ride we set out at half past 9– However there was a pleasant breeze stirring in the Pine woods altho' the sun was rather oppressive, and we rested nearly 3 hours at Hilliard's, and an hour after we left it the "parched & thirsty earth" received a plentiful supply of the dew of Heaven which fell in torrents, accompanied by sheets of lightning and peels of Thunder which appeared to burst just over our heads– I did not shew any signs of alarm altho' I confess that my heart fluttered a little, & beat faster for joy when we came in sight of our resting place. With an Umbrella over my head & Mrs Putnam's India Rubbers on my feet, I escaped all injury from the rain in getting from the Stage to the House, and I cannot say that my slumbers were much disturbed by the roaring and rattling of the Thunder which I am told was incessant during the night– The loudest clap awoke me at 1/2 past 4 and soon after I rose to be in readiness for breakfast and a start immediately after in the Rail road for Weldon– where we changed cars & proceeded two miles further to Gary'sburg, where we again changed and established ourselves very comfortably in the Petersburg cars, I reclining on one side and Mrs Putnam on the other shawled & cloaked up to the chin, and her husband's over coat over her besides poor Soul– She is in very delicate health, afflicted with Neuralgia and Rheumatism, & always kept all the curtains and windows down on her side– But altho' the dust was stifling for the first day, and even the second until the glorious Thunderstorm, I was obliged to let it in, as I preferred the alternative of being well powdered with sand to gasping for breath by excluding the air altogether.

Even in this respect however we agreed very well, for you know I detest a draught, and she always obligingly took the sunny side and put down the curtains, and I had all the benefit of the cool air that could be found. We shall part from her with regret, for she is a most amiable and intelligent person, and converses very sensibly & unaffectedly– Unfortunately her Boston Twang is very decided, and rather lessens my pleasure in her society, but I do not undervalue her good & agreeable qualities as a companion on that account– As for her husband, he is Yankee all over, and very inferior to her in every respect but a good sort of creature. He was a college companion of [Eliza's brother] Arthur's, after whom he made some enquiry and remembered with pleasure.

I must conclude my account of our journey hither by saying that after passing the N^o C^a boundary the country began to improve, and became very pretty some miles on the other side of Petersburg– It is an inconsiderable town, but altho' much more humble in its style of architecture than its great Russian namesake, in situation and climate it has much the advantage– I felt very much disposed to linger there a day or two and explore the banks of the Appomattox, but as Richmond offered more attractions, & our time is limited we left it after resting a couple of hours, and dining at the R. R^d Hotel, where instead of Bacon & salt fish which was the fare we had seen the previous days, they gave us very good fresh fish, Veal &c & Pancakes and Pound cake with tumblers of milk before the removal of the meat! Everything was good & fresh however, & we were glad to find ourselves once more on the verge of civilization if not at its very center– We started again in the afternoon for Richmond in very convenient cars in which we were entirely protected from another Thunderstorm the most severe of all which lasted until we were almost within sight of this Town.

N. B. Fisher is obliged to acknowledge that the <u>beautiful</u> cloak he thought <u>absolutely necessary</u>, has not been found so at all– [Stages] & Cars being so weatherproof, that my blanket shawl has been & <u>is</u> quite a sufficient protection– In candour & justice however <u>I</u> will add, that on one account it was useful Viz. in keeping the sparks from my dress, for not liking to make my entrée here in rags, I covered my gown with it after having several large holes burnt thro' my apron. Indeed I much regret having worn so good a silk, when a calico w<u>d</u> have been more serviceable & could have been <u>washed</u> at least– After beating brushing & spunging the illfated garment, it is somewhat more presentable, but can never be restored to its "pristine lustre" and will make rather a shabby figure at the ex-minister [*Mr. Rives*]'s,[3] whither we wend our way tomorrow morng–

Upon enquiring for the Wirts[4] I found they are all still in Florida and as it w<u>d</u> have been rather a bore to dress up & go & see them for a <u>very</u> short visit this afternoon, I do not so much regret their absence. Fisher found here a cousin of his who however went this morng. back into the country without having time (I hope) to inform some more of his acquaintances of our arrival. I am very well today, but had rather take another walk in this pretty town than be detained at home by visitors this afternoon. My fingers are not quite so numb, but are still enough so to excuse my scrawling in this style– My feet are much less so and not nearly so much swollen– I hope to find a letter in Winchester on the 13<u>th</u> but that is a long time to look forward to. If you do not hear from me within a fortnight, do not be uneasy– But if I can I will write from M<u>rs</u> Rives's or perhaps from Staunton, but certainly from Baltimore. I have just time to prepare for dinner & F. is waiting to put it in the P.O. so adieu dearest Mamma. With best love to all around you of whom I hope to have very particular accounts, I am as ever, Y<u>r</u> most affect<u>e</u> Daughter Eliza

Tell me <u>everything</u> when you write

PHi

1. A specially hired carriage.
2. The Fishers had met Mr. and Mrs. Samuel R. Putnam in Charleston. Mary (Lowell) Putnam (1810–1898) was "well-educated, sensible and genteel" and became a novelist and linguist; James Russell Lowell, poet and editor of the *Atlantic Monthly*, was her brother. JFF to GH, May 1, 1839, PHi, C/F.

3. William Cabell Rives (1793–1868) studied law with Jefferson and was appointed minister to France in 1829 by Andrew Jackson. Fisher served as an attaché to the American legation in Paris in the early 1830s. Rives became a U.S. senator and, at the end of the 1830s was one of the few southern politicians who still spoke publicly of slavery as an evil. He opposed nullification in the 1830s and secession in the 1860s. His wife, Judith (Page) Walker, inherited "Castle Hill," their house near Charlottesville.

4. The William Wirts had been friends of the Middletons in Washington, D.C., where Wirt (1772–1834) was attorney general from 1817 to 1829. After he died, his widow (the former Elizabeth Gamble of Richmond) managed lands in Florida he had bought in the 1820s.

⌒

To Mrs. Fisher, 170 Chestnut Street, Philadelphia

M.P. May 8th 1839

Not until yesterday my dearest Eliza did both your letters reach me– they were indeed a great comfort on a day which brought with it such painful recollections– Sally[1] & I read them together by turns. I am delighted to find that your numbness is decreasing & that the fatigue you suffered was not extreme– Upon the whole your sufferings must have been trifling compared to those of a sea voyage– How thankful I felt (when on reading the newspaper after finishing your letter) that you had gone when you did! the <u>next</u> Saturday night, the N. Carolina Steamer & the Vanderbilt struck against each other & were greatly injured– had you been on board what might have happened! It will be very provoking if your Father after reading the favourable account you give of your journey, does not consent to adopt that mode of travelling– it seems unaccountable that any one should prefer the horrors of a voyage. He was quite well when he returned last Monday & on the 4th inst went with Wm to Combahee–[2] They brought news of Susan's accouchement which surprised me as it did you of course, when you arrived in Charleston– I grieve however to inform you that she had two days after a severe attack of fever, from which she was recovering when they left town– but yesterday a note came from Oliver saying that she had had another attack & was at the time he wrote rather better. This is very trying to a person of her delicate constitution. I pray that the accounts I shall receive by the return of the messenger may be favourable!

9th You mention violent thunder storms– they have not reached this part of the country, except in the night after your voyage, when I rejoiced that you were not at sea– Since that, the weather became hot & yesterday & today the rain has been almost incessant. Every thing is going on as usual, so that there is nothing to tell you worth knowing– Mrs R[obert] Smith[3] & Anna called a few days since & your message was delivered to the latter– The reason Mrs S. gave for not coming sooner was that her Father had been so ill, she could not leave him. he was then better, & they intended to go to Charleston about the end of this week. We neither of us could touch upon the afflicting subject which engrossed our thoughts during the time of her visit. Your fellow traveller seems to have improved on further acquaintance– in the first letter you appeared to consider her anything but agreeable. What beautiful cloak can you refer to? both the purple ones are in the Entry, & I know of no other except y^r new one– that, I presume you mean– it was indeed lucky, that it served to conceal your tattered gown. You may remember my advising you not to travel in it. As I did not receive y^r first letter until the day before yesterday I could not comply with the request you made in it to write & direct to Winchester– You once mentioned that perhaps the excursion to the natural bridge might not be made; so that I take the chance of your arriving earlier at Philad^a & despatch this tomorrow particularly as there may not be another opportunity for some days to come.

Your Father said he intended to return on the 11th or 12th that, I suppose will be the 18th or 19th at which period John [*Eliza's brother*] will probably arrive. I have had another letter from Miss Moore–[4] The Professor [*Nathaniel Moore*] is meditating a journey in the East & in Egypt– she observes "Were I a second Mrs Haight, I sh^d most certainly go with him, but being no equestrian, I must forego the pleasure of accompanying him." He talks also of visiting S^t. Petersburg.

I am sorry to say we have no reading aloud in the Even^{gs} from Cath^e [*Eliza's sister*]. I wrote to Beile[5] for books, & Kinney[6] brought back the note, having forgotten to deliver it. Sally seems better than she was– she desires to be affectionately remembered to you– Pray offer my best regards to Mr Fisher, with best Compliments to Mrs F. & M^r & Mrs Harrison & believe me my dearest Eliza y^r Affect^{te} Mother M. H. M.

Do not forget y^r promise to write once a week 10th all well here– I am just sending Isaac to Charleston–

ScHi

1. Sally was John Middleton's wife. Everyone, including her mother-in-law, consistently commented on her affectionate and sweet nature. When Fisher first met her, he said her face had "the madonna beauty" and her character "every charm." It is not clear what "painful recollections" she and Mrs. Middleton were thinking of. JFF to Sophia Harrison, April 11, 1839, PHi, C/F.

Susan, mentioned later in the paragraph, was Oliver Middleton's wife. Their fourth daughter, Olivia, was born on April 25, 1839.

Catherine, mentioned in the final paragraph, was Eliza's sister; her nickname was Kitty.

2. Throughout the letters, Combahee refers to the area along the west side of the Combahee River, south of Charleston, where the Middletons owned three rice plantations: Nieuport (Newport), Old Combahee, and Hobonny. There was a small house at Hobonny, in which Henry Middleton, William, and others stayed when they were at Combahee.

3. Mrs. Robert Smith was the former Elizabeth Pringle (1791–1873), daughter of John Julius and Susannah (Reid) Pringle. Anna (1820–1840) was her daughter. Mrs. Smith's brother, Edward J. Pringle, married the Middletons' oldest daughter, Maria; they and their two children had died a year before when the steamship *Pulaski* exploded at sea on its way to New York on June 14, 1838.

The accident, as an acquaintance in Newport described it, "carried to their Watery Grave 50 or 60 who were Bound directly here. . . . I feel much Grieved at the loss of . . . the Pringles too, formerly Miss Middleton." At Trinity Church, she reported, people "are mostly in Black, it has cast a Gloom around every circle. 80 from Charlestown Saild in the morning & at 11 that Night were all drowned." Catharine Engs Dennis, "My Much Loved Friend," *Newport History* (winter 1984): 24.

4. Sarah Moore lived in New York. A few years earlier she had traveled in Europe with her brother, Nathaniel, a classicist who became president of Columbia College in 1842. Mr. and Mrs. Richard Haight of New York were among the earliest Americans to visit Egypt; Mrs. Haight's book, *Letters from the Old World by a Lady of New York,* appeared in 1840.

5. John P. Beile was a bookseller and stationer at 280 King Street, Charleston.

6. Kinney and Isaac, mentioned in the postscript, were slaves at Middleton Place.

⁓

To Mrs. Middleton, Middleton Place

Greenville V͟a͟ – 8ᵗʰ May 1839

As we stop here an hour to rest ourselves & our <u>cattle</u>, I cannot better employ it than by writing an account of our last week's adventures to my dearest Mamma. I shall make it as brief and succinct as possible, my time today being limited, and another opportunity not being likely to present itself until we reach Baltimore this day week. The one just past has been delightfully spent. We left Richmond, as we intended, on Thursday Morng before 6 and were <u>puffed</u> on to within 18 miles of M͟ʳ͟s Rives' by railroad. Her carriage was in readiness and conveyed us thro' a beautiful country, when we first caught a glimpse of the mountains, to a comfortable farm house 10 miles from her house, where we dined and then proceeded to Castle Hill where we arrived at sunset and were most warmly welcomed by our very agreeable Host & Hostess, who were all kindness & hospitality, and made us pass three days very pleasantly in their society– She is really a very nice little woman and he is quite charming– and I parted from them with much more regret than one usually feels after so short an acquaintance– They accompanied us as far as Charlottesville, where we took leave of them yesterday morng– expressing many regrets at the shortness of our stay, and often renewing their invitation to us to return & pay them a longer visit on our way to the South– I shall have much pleasure in so doing, for the little I have seen of them only makes me wish to see more & they are just the people to improve on further & more intimate acquaintance.

For the first time in my life I ascended a real mountain at Mrs Rives's– This important event took place on Saturday, between the hours of 10 & 3. Fortunately we had a cool & clear day & I enjoyed it exceedingly, & was amply repaid for the trouble of climbing up three miles, one of the roughest & rockiest roads I ever saw– do not suppose that I have suddenly regained the use of my limbs & footed it all the way– Indeed I consider it quite an achievement to have performed such a feat on horseback, & then to have walked down the greater part of the way– Altho' my steed was considered very surefooted, M^{rs} R's was not, & I confess I was rather glad of an excuse to dismount & bear her company, relying much more on my own legs than those of the safest beast in the possession of four. Altho' they were not in the most active condition, & often appeared to be giving way under me, at the steepest descent, I was in such a state of enthusiastic excitement, at the beautiful & extensive prospect around me, which seemed to vary at every step I took, that I managed to make them support me, notwithstanding their numbness (which was however much diminished, and has now nearly disappeared) until we arrived at a tolerably smooth path, where we remounted, and soon reached the House without much fatigue. I thought to refresh myself by a nap before dinner, but excitement kept slumber far from me, and when at night she did visit my eyelids, I dreamt only of climbing up craggy places & falling suddenly down. The following day I had completely recovered from the fatigues of scaling Peter's Mountain, which is after all but a molehill to some I have since seen; it is about 2000 feet above the sea, but not more than 12 or 15 hundred above the surrounding country– On Sunday we walked beyond Mr Rives' gate into the woods, and had a very pretty view of his farm & grounds from an adjoining hill– It is a sweet place– The variety "hill & valley, mountain & green shade" is beyond anything I ever witnessed.

On Monday we went to Monticello, from whence there is a magnificent prospect– not so extensive perhaps as the view from Peter's moun^{n} but richer &

more cultivated. The Rivanna river winding thro' the valley below, the University & the village of Charlottesville, adding so many features which were wanting in the other landscape– We went all over the curious old house, which is most singularly planned, & rather striking, but not having much veneration for the memory of the "great apostle of democracy",[1] I preferred the panorama which lay stretched out beneath me from the Portico to anything within the walls. Bidding a reluctant adieu to this beautiful spot, we drove to Mr Alex^r Rives' (brother of our host) where our admiration was again called forth by the superb view from his cottage windows– It is by some preferred to that from the summit, but I found both so fine that I could not decide between them. We dined there, & in the afternoon proceeded to Charlottesville where we made our arrangements for our 8 days expedition to the Natural Bridge, Weyer's cave &c. We have a very comfortable 4 placed stage, perfectly new, with four good horses & a very careful driver, who is to stop when & where we please and take us 30 miles a day on an average– For all which we pay 10$ and 75^c per diem, not including the Tavern bills which altogether bring up our daily expenses to about 15$. Fisher was a little cheated in his bargain he thinks, not that he expected to make a cheaper one, but the man insisted on making [us] pay 40 dollars extra for the return of the vehicle from Winchester (where we take the railroad for Baltimore) whereas 30 w^d have been ample as he will no doubt perform the journey back in less than 3 days. This is a trifle however, and we consider ourselves very lucky to have enjoyed so good a conveyance, and to be able to make such easy stages– The farm houses are always better & more comfortable than the Taverns in the Towns– but everywhere we get excellent bread & butter, fresh eggs & delightful cream– and the people are very civil & obliging. The woman I hired at Richmond is a capital femme de chambre [*chamber maid*] & I rejoice that I did not bring the Irish girl from Charleston for she w^d have been decidedly de trop & I sh^d always have had the pleasure of her company at meals–

Lexington V^a I was hurried off from Greenville yesterday, and thought it best to finish this here where I shall despatch it before my departure for the Bridge this morng– We came 23 miles after dinner, fearing it might rain today & wishing to take advantage of the fair weather– There is not much appearance of it however, & I hope we shall be able to walk about a great deal when we get there, as the sun is obscured & the heat much less oppressive than it has been for some days past– I have told you nothing of our first day's journey from Charlottesville across the Blue Ridge & I believe I shall not attempt to describe what so far exceeds my powers of description– My whole vocabulary of words of admiration was exhausted– and beautiful, superb, grand, magnificent, sublime, burst from my lips in rapid succession when we were crossing the Ridge & looking back upon the valleys extending as far as the eye could reach to what appeared to be the ocean in the distance, we suddenly turned round and came in view of a sea of mountains <u>entassées</u> [*piled up*] one upon the other, until they faded into the "blue serene". This view, from the Rock fish gap is said to be one of the finest in America, & I should think was little inferior to anything in any other part of the world– A few ruined Towers and a lake or River, would certainly be a great improvement, but everything else is perfect. The forests are as fine as possible, abounding in noble Oaks, Elms, Poplars, and almost every variety of Trees, and the valleys as rich in verdure & cultivation as any in England– Much as I admired the scenery on Tuesday, I was even more enchanted yesterday coming from Greenville– for we were nearly surrounded by mountains. The blue ridge on one side, and the chain of North Mountains on the other & in front the House mountain, the most elevated we have yet seen– We had been wishing for a water prospect, and as we approached this town our eyes were gladdened by the sight of a most romantic stream flowing at the foot of a Hill which rose almost perpendicularly above it about 3 hundred feet high. We crossed it, at sunset, and nothing could be finer than the effect of light & shadow reflected from the mountain at the head of the stream into the dark waters, and the bold & rugged sides of the Hill, lit up by the last rays of the departing sun– Don't laugh at my feeble description– I wish I could find words to describe all I feel. But I could not give you any idea of the emotions of wonder and admiration which filled my mind, during the greater part of yesterday & the days before– and now the stage is waiting at the door & Fisher at my elbow ready to seal up & send this scrawl– I have already kept him half an hour, and cannot in conscience detain him any longer– Wherefore adieu my dearest Mamma. I look forward with delight to my arrival at Winchester on Tuesday when I expect to hear of you all– Best love all round and believe me as ever Y^r most affectionate Daughter Eliza

F. begs me to add his kindest & most respectful remembrances.

Private Collection

1. Eliza's comment may reflect her new husband's views more than her family's. Fisher, who was intensely antidemocratic, later referred to Jefferson as "that Democratic serpent, . . . who, like his prototype, the one in the Garden of Eden, whispered his devilish lies about human equality into the ear of our people." JFF, *Recollections*, 241.

∽

To Mrs. Fisher, Philadelphia

M.P. May 17<u>th</u> 1839

My dearest Eliza,

Supposing you must be anxious to hear news of Susan, I write chiefly to remove your apprehensions which my letter may have created– The messenger returned from town with a note from little Mary[1] informing me that her Mama had no return of fever, and was sitting up, and that her Father had gone the day previous to Edisto, which he certainly would not have done, unless Susan had been much better. Since that time no news has reached me– I make sure however of receiving your promised letters from Stanton and Baltimore by the return of Isaac whom I shall send off tomorrow, unless your Father should arrive this eve<u>g</u>. The Liverpool must have arrived, and I am not a little anxious to learn whether Harry is at N. York–[2]

This is the day you expected to reach Philad<u>a</u>– a happy one no doubt for all parties concerned! You are by this time I trust cured of all your unpleasant symptoms, and are enjoying the kindness lavished upon you by your Friends– I expect soon to have a full account of your new mode of life and of all that concerns you. M<u>r</u> Beile sent me M<u>rs</u> Ellis's 'Women of England'[3] it is very well written and gives excellent advice, which if attended to, will no doubt improve the morals and manners of <u>all</u> Women. When you write to Miss [Sophia] Thorndike[4] tell her that when reading p.p. 87, & 8, & 182 & 3 of the 1<u>st</u> vol. her image rose before me exercising her kind attentions towards you on your bed of sickness, so exactly is her amiable conduct depicted in M<u>rs</u> E's description of what women <u>ought</u> to be! I hope her health has not suffered by her removal to Newport– On the subject of health, Sallys I think is better than when you left us. We have had very pleasant weather since I last wrote– cooler than I have ever known in Carolina at this season–

18<u>th</u> Here is a roasting day! I have just come in from walking before breakfast, for the sun is too powerful at 9 o'clock– Your Father did not come yesterday, so that I shall send a good supply of strawberries to Susan, and have my letters tomorrow. Cath<u>e</u> has lately become an early riser and reads often to herself though not much to <u>me</u>. I am sending for some novels which I hope will tempt her to do so– John is expected here on the 20<u>th</u>. when Sally is to go to Aiken,[5] is not yet decided I believe, but must be soon. You must not expect to receive any but dull letters from me, & it is time to release you from this– Remember me kindly to M<u>r</u> F. & offer my best Comp<u>ts</u> to M<u>rs</u> F. & M<u>r</u> & M<u>rs</u> Harrison– Sally desires her best love to you & I am my dearest Eliza y<u>r</u> Affect<u>te</u> Mother M. H. M.

PHi

1. Mary (b. 1828) was Susan and Oliver Middleton's oldest child. The Oliver Middletons lived on Edisto Island, south of Charleston, but like many planters also had a house in town.

2. The whole family was anxiously waiting for Eliza's brother, Harry (1797–1876), to come home after four years in Europe. Eliza knew by this time that he was not onboard the *Liverpool* and was now hoping that he would come on the *Great Western*, a new steamship which, on its maiden voyage in April 1838, had stunned the world by crossing from Liverpool to New York in only fifteen days.

3. Mrs. Sarah (Stickney) Ellis was an English missionary, reformer, and author. In *Women of England: Their Social Duties and Domestic Habits* she urged that young women be given practical education in the domestic sphere. Mrs. Middleton referred to the sections where Mrs. Ellis stressed the importance of knowing how to be a good nurse, because Sophia Thorndike had nursed Eliza, literally day and night, when she had scarlet fever.

4. Sophia Thorndike (1815–1885) spent the winter of 1838–39 with the Middletons in South Carolina and was Eliza's bridesmaid. She was the daughter of Bostonian Israel Thorndike, Jr. (1795–1867), and his first wife, Sally Otis (d. 1819). Her family had a house in Newport.

The friendship between the families went back to Sophia Thorndike's grandparents, Harrison Gray Otis (1765–1848) and his wife, Sally (Foster) Otis (1770–1836), who had known the Middletons at least since 1817, when Otis and Henry Middleton served together in Congress. Otis, one of Boston's most eminent citizens and former mayor, was a successful lawyer and an early developer of Beacon Hill real estate as well as former congressman and senator from Massachusetts.

Fisher, as well as Eliza, was a friend of Sophie's because the Otises had also been close friends of the George Harrisons since the 1790s.

5. Sally was pregnant with her seventh child in eleven years. Aiken, a popular new resort town in the cool South Carolina upcountry, was on the railroad line running from Charleston to Hamburg, across from Augusta, Georgia, on the Savannah River.

～

While her son was in South Carolina, Mrs. Fisher had been occupied in supervising work on the new wing that Uncle Harrison had offered to add to her house. Although no description of either the addition or the entire house has been found, a letter from the Harrisons to Fisher indicates that they were installing that relatively modern convenience, a bathroom: Fisher had to choose between a wooden or tin bathtub so that the pipes could be installed.[1] Eliza's bedroom and at least one adjoining room, which was later used as a baby's room, were probably also in the addition. With Mrs. Fisher "directing the removal of each snuff of dust,"[2] the building went smoothly and, complete with a "richly and elegantly furnished"[3] drawing room, was ready when Eliza and Fisher arrived in Philadelphia.

1. The Harrisons to JFF, March 13, 1839, PHi, BrC.
2. Ibid.
3. Wainwright, *Phila. Perspective* (November 21, 1839): 89.

To Mrs. Middleton, Middleton Place

Philadelphia May 23$\underline{rd}$ 1839

I found your first letter of the 8$\underline{th}$ & 10$\underline{th}$ awaiting me here, my dearest Mamma, and need not tell you with how much delight I received it. The pleasure it gave me was a little damped by the accounts of poor Susan's illness, and I was, as you justly supposed, quite uneasy about her until this eveng, when y$\underline{r}$ second letter, containing the good news of her recovery, relieved me from my anxiety. I was also rejoiced to learn that dear Sally continued better and that you were all going on so well– But I must beg you, dearest Mamma to take a larger sheet and fill it up next time, for really I am by no means satisfied with a mere note without even a line in the corners– I send you immense budgets, which are indeed much spun out but that you know is the fault of my style, which lacks brevity and every other attribute of wit–

To continue my journal– We left Baltimore at 9 o'clock on Friday & arrived here at 1/2 past three having come from Wilmington (Del) by Steamer up the Delaware– I recollected many views from the riverside which we had passed 8 years before altho' there is nothing very pretty after you leave the banks of the Susquehanna, & all the scenery in Maryland appeared tame in comparison to what we had left in V$\underline{a}$. We met M$\underline{rs}$ [Nathaniel] Chapman[1] in the cars, who was placed under Fisher's care– rather a pleasant person and intelligent in conversation. She saw that I was getting nervous as we approached the city and tried to cheer me up and encourage me by speaking of the amiability of my new relations, with whom she is intimate, but I could not help dreading a little the first rencontre [*meeting*]– altho' I found that I had alarmed myself very needlessly, for their reception of me was the very kindest possible, and I felt almost immediately at home among them. M$\underline{r}$ Harrison was at the Wharf waiting for us with his carriage to take us home, and his greetings were so cordial that I was soon at my ease with him– It was really a most unexpected piece of gallantry on the part of the old gentleman, for we knew that he had been confined to his chamber for some days previous. He reminds me of Uncle Oliver [Hering][2] in many things, and this is a very agreeable remembrance you may be sure– He begs me to say that he is delighted to see your daughter,[3] and both he & M$\underline{rs}$ H[arrison] add many kind and flattering things on my own account. Indeed they are all as affectionate as I could desire and more so than

I deserve, and M<u>rs</u> F– treats me as if I were her own daughter, and will spoil me before long I fear– All the Cousins and Aunts too are all attention and kindness, and everybody seems determined to give me the warmest welcome– The first eveng– of our arrival we had many visitors & several bouquets of flowers, and yesterday (being <u>reception eveng</u>) when I first made my regular début as M<u>rs</u> <u>Francis Fisher</u> they (the <u>flowers</u>) showered upon me from all quarters and our pretty little drawing room was adorned all round with a profusion of the most beautiful bunches of roses, pinks & a variety of fine plants.

I was in a complete <u>quandary</u> for the first 5 or 6 days that I was here. None of my Charleston Baggage had arrived, and not until yesterday morning, had I any intelligence of it– At last we heard of a Schooner below and early after breakfast Fisher returned with the acceptable news of its arrival– It was got out about 2 hours before our company came, and I had just time to unpack a few necessary articles of apparel, & make my appearance in the Bridal Veil, very becomingly arranged by a little french Coiffeuse. I know that 2 months after the ceremony I had little right to adopt the "costume de mariée" [*bridal dress*] but the dates were not particularly referred to, and everything went off admirably– I did not wear the Wedding dress itself, but one which I had had made here, in despair of being able to wear the original. The substitute was however extremely pretty, & by common consent thought becoming, and I submitted to the scrutiny of my future friends with remarkable self possession, altho' I felt almost as much alarmed at first as if I was about to undergo the awful ceremony for the second time. The weather was very unfavorable, but notwithstanding the incessant torrents of rain our room was much crowded and warm enough to prevent the change in my dress from giving me cold– Many kind & particular enquiries were made about you and Papa and hopes expressed that you would make Phil<u>a</u> your future residence. I could only answer that there was every prospect of it, and I will not allow myself to believe it can be otherwise– You would be so comfortable next door at Miss Hare's lodgings–[4] There are two very nice drawing rooms communicating– one of which is used as a bedchamber & above very excellent rooms and plenty of them– and there would be nothing to do but to walk down our 3 steps & into the very next door adjoining ours– Oh! I <u>will</u> hope and trust that you will be as near me as that– and when I feel that you are almost under the same roof (would it were <u>quite</u>) I shall be perfectly happy–

I found Edward[5] still here, and saw him constantly during the 3 days he spent with us– On Monday afternoon he was obliged to return to N.Y. promising to drop in on Wednesday Eveng if he could get leave of absence after repre-

senting the case to the Captain– He did not however make his appearance &
I fear found a surly or disobliging commander who detained him on . . .[6]

Private Collection

1. Rebecca (Biddle) Chapman was a Philadelphian, the daughter of Clement Biddle. Her husband, Dr. Nathaniel Chapman (1780–1853) was a prominent professor at
the University of Pennsylvania Medical School and physician to many wealthy Philadelphians, including the Fishers.
2. Oliver Hering was Mrs. Middleton's brother in England. He and his wife, Mary
(Ross) Hering, took care of the four youngest Middleton children, including Eliza, from
1820 until 1827, when they joined their parents in Russia. At that time, they lived at
Heybridge Hall near Maldon in Essex; by 1839 they had moved to Southampton.
3. Although the Harrisons had known the Middletons many years before, the two
families do not seem to have seen each other since before the Middletons went to Russia.
4. Martha (Cousin Patty) Hare (1779–1852) was a cousin of Fisher's through the
Willing family and particularly fond of him. Her brother, Robert Hare (1781–1858), was
a distinguished chemist and professor of chemistry at the University of Pennsylvania.
5. Eliza's brother, Edward (1810–1883), was a midshipman in the navy. He had
recently been assigned to the sloop *Marion* of the Brazil squadron after serving in the
Mediterranean from 1835 to 1838.
6. The rest of this letter is missing.

Eliza's uncle John Izard Middleton (1785–1849) lived in Paris and had agreed
to buy her trousseau for her. Provided with money for the purpose by Eliza's father,
he made the rounds of the Paris shops and dressmakers and wrote Eliza amusing
letters about the ever-changing French fashions. " 'Mantelets' are no longer
worn," he told her, "but square Shawls (such as you will receive) of black silk for
Summer, & black Cashmiere for winter. . . . The difficulty [with the linen] was to
steer clear of what you might judge parsimony on the one hand or Extravagance
on the other hand—and this was no easy matter for me when, in the single article
of Handkerchiefs, I had to chuse from F10.00 to F200 & 300 each. . . . Here is
(I beg you to believe) the longest article 'on Fashion' I was ever author of!"[1]
Uncle Izard, as he was called, was the youngest of Arthur and Mary (Izard)
Middletons' children and, growing up after the American Revolution, had gone
abroad to study at Cambridge, as his brother, Henry, had not had the chance to
do. A talented artist, he was among the first to recognize that accurate drawings
and paintings of Greek and Roman ruins were important to scientific understanding of them.[2] In 1810 he married Eliza Falconnet, the half-American daughter of
a banker in Naples and his wife, Anna Hunter, of Newport, Rhode Island; she
died in 1831. He lived in Europe for most of his adult life.

1. J. Izard Middleton to EMF, April 26, 1839, PHi, C/F.
2. He wrote *Grecian Remains in Italy: A Description of Cyclopian Walls and of Roman Antiquities, with Topographical and Picturesque Views of Ancient Lathium* (London, 1812).

To Mrs. Middleton, Middleton Place

Philadelphia, May 28ᵗʰ 1839

My dearest Mamma,

I was delighted to receive even the few lines you wrote by Col. Clive,[1] who sent them over on Friday Afternoon, and came himself by Fisher's invitation the following day. He had not much to tell me of you all, but as you may suppose I questioned him pretty closely about everything and everybody he saw at M. Place– He is rather a pleasant person I think– but as for Mʳ Bridges– he is the greatest <u>forlornity</u> I have beheld for a long time, and has evidently none of the "usage du monde" [*knowledge of what to do and say in society*]– indeed he looked so much alarmed when I asked him to take a seat by me on the Sofa, that I was led to suspect he never could have been similarly honored in society. We gave them an invitation to a Tea Party at Miss Hare's next door on Saturday, but they spent the day in the country and returned too late to avail themselves of it– Last evening, being Mʳˢ <u>Fisher's Sunday</u> [*to receive friends,*] we had them here, and asked several agreeable people to meet them and I daresay the Col. found it pleasant enough, for Mʳˢ Tom Willing[2] devoted herself exclusively to his amusement– Joe Carter tried to make something of his companion, but gave him up in despair after languishing and ogling at him in vain for some time– They went off this morng to Canada, refusing to stay and dine with us today as the Col. was under orders– I had this morng a letter of the 7ᵗʰ April from Harry which I see Wᵐ forwarded from Charleston to me. He speaks of coming out in the beginning of May in the "British Queen".[3] I would rather he should have adhered to his former project of taking his passage in the Gᵗ Western for besides the risk of trying a new Vessel on her first trip across, there seems to me less probability of his returning whilst he so constantly changes his plans.

I was interrupted and not able to write more yesterday. Today (Tuesday) I was to have returned some of my 150 visits in Mʳˢ Harrison's carriage,[4] but it looked so much like rain that I sent to beg her to let me postpone the undertaking until tomorrow, and am very glad of the reprieve. Altho' it poured last evening I was obliged to go to a teaparty at Mʳˢ Mifflin's[5] (not our NewPort friend) as it was made expressly for me, & she wᵈ have been highly offended if I had absented myself on the plea of bad weather. Many did however, but the few who braved the pelting storm were agreeable, & all very polite & kind to me. M‍ᶦˢ Willing was the life of the company– she makes tender enquiries after Papa & William [*Eliza's brother,*] and is very anxious to see them again. She is really a very bewitching creature– I cannot help admiring her talent and being charmed by her sprightliness, altho' I disapprove of her manners, & familiarity with the male sex– I heard of two engagements which seem to give general satisfaction– Anna Walsh's[6] to a M‍ʳ Lafin of Savannah, and Margaret Sergeant's to a M‍ʳ Mead–[7] younger than herself, and not remarkable for anything I believe but for being the son of a very handsome & clever woman, and not inheriting much of her talent & certainly none of her beauty– He is said to be very good tho', and M‍ᶦˢ S[ergeant] appears well satisfied & the young lady herself quite happy– so of course nobody else ought to find fault– They seem (the Sergeants) to be a little hurt at my accepting 2 or 3 invitations for this week after refusing their's for last Friday– but the fact is I am obliged to go to some of M‍ᶦˢ Fisher's most intimate & oldest friends, & could not now give the plea of fatigue after my journey, which at first stood me in good stead. For the future I have a still better excuse, for D‍ʳ Chapman, who came to see me by Fisher's request, <u>agrees with me</u> that the late hours are very bad for me and forbids me to go out in the evening after this week, so that I shall decline all the parties in prospect, & have already firmly the entreaties of one or two ladies who I really believe are disappointed at my <u>obstinacy</u>. But when I know that early hours are important to my health, and wish to take exercise before breakfast, I cannot think of disobeying orders, but am delighted to follow D‍ʳ C's advice, and defer all dissipation until the Autumn when I hope I shall be better able to enjoy the gaiety, my new friends are so anxious for me to mix in. Indeed, at present, it is too great an exertion, morally & physically speaking, to enter again into society, and I rejoice that I may now be able to enjoy a little quiet at home, & wait until my nerves are stronger, and my health perfectly restored, before I am called upon to make what I consider a great sacrifice– for I have not the least relish for what I formerly found so pleasant, & very much prefer the rational amusements furnished in my own drawing room by my books & Piano to all the dull trivialities I hear discussed elsewhere. Some of [my] new acquaintances I like much, but I confess by far the greater part of them, are wofully deficient not only in good sense, but in education & taste, for everything besides dress, wh as Fisher warned me, is the sole and engrossing subject of their thoughts.

A propos I heard this morng from Uncle Izard [Middleton] who was to dispatch my cases by the Packet of the 8ᵗʰ, so that I may soon expect them.

He writes very kindly, & seems to have done his best in the purchases– But has somewhat exceeded my orders– particularly in regard to the <u>embroideries</u>, which he says are the <u>mania</u> of the day– & has reserved only 12 hundred francs, out of the 5000, after paying all expenses of packing &c, for the jewelry, which Papa suggested the remainder of the remittance should be laid out in & which he begs me to tell him how to dispose of– There will be time enough to give directions on that subject, as I should probably have no use for any "parure" before next winter, if then– Pray thank W$^{\underline{m}}$ with my love for attending so exactly to my request about the baggage f$^{\underline{m}}$ Charleston. It is fortunate that he had a second cover put on the box of books, for the inner one had all given way– Everything arrived perfectly safe, and the Miniatures now grace my pretty writing Table, where they are extremely admired–[8] Judge [Joseph] Hopkinson,[9] who pretends to be a great connaisseur, shewed me his Pictures this morng (Wednesday) & wants me to go to the Academy of Fine Arts, of which he is President– He has himself some pretty Pictures, given to him by C[ount] Survilliers,[10] particularly a Vernet, I think Papa w$^{\underline{d}}$ admire. We are invited out to spend the day at M$^{\underline{rs}}$ N[icholas] Biddle's in the country,[11] and I hope shall soon be able to go and see her grapery & flowers, which are celebrated. I hope Fanny Butler[12] will visit me, for clever people are scarce, and I am very anxious to make her acquaintance– I believe everybody else has been here– even M$^{\underline{rs}}$ [William] Camac[13] & the Markoes to my astonishment– Miss H[enrietta] Drayton[14] called the very morning that I was occupied unpacking, and M$^{\underline{rs}}$ Gibson[15] also– I have received the whole town now I believe– M$^{\underline{rs}}$ [William] Drayton[16] came on Wednesday last, and as I was to be <u>at home</u> in the eveng– & did not expect anyone in the morng– she was refused– which I regretted very much–

Thursday 30$^{\underline{th}}$ I hope to have another letter from you today my dearest Mamma– and that it will be longer than the last– I trust that the time of y$^{\underline{r}}$ departure will have been decided upon, & that I shall know when to expect you– I have been longing to see you comfortably established next door in Miss Hare's apartments, which she is soon to quit. They w$^{\underline{d}}$ suit you exactly, and are so airy and convenient, & to be had at so reasonable a rate, that I feel sure Papa w$^{\underline{d}}$ approve of them. Their vicinity to the Squares is a great recommendation also, particularly on Kitty's account– I am sure you w$^{\underline{d}}$ like to walk in the shady avenues of Independence Square, where you meet very few people besides nurses & children. I myself prefer them to the crowded streets, & intend after this week to take regular exercise there, until Fisher can procure me a horse– He is trying hard to do so, and making enquiries of all the good judges in town– but hitherto without success– D$^{\underline{r}}$ Chapman recommended me strongly to ride daily, and if possible morning & eveng as much as <u>twenty</u> <u>miles</u>– if I can only canter half that distance I shall soon be perfectly well. He says that there is nothing now to be done for me by <u>dosing</u>– but insists upon the necessity of exercise on horseback and early hours–

I paid 100 of my 150 visits yesterday, and found more cards on the table on my return home– Today the weather is so delightfully cool, that I am going on foot to get rid of the rest of this troublesome job. Fortunately we are seldom admitted, or I sh<u>d</u> find it an interminable business– We went to Miss Waln's[17] last evening, & I enjoyed myself a good deal, altho' there were few people there.

I heard that M<u>r</u> Calderon was appointed Ambassador to Mexico, much to poor Fanny [Inglis Calderon]'s[18] distress, to whom the separation from her family will be very trying– I have written to beg her to let me know all about it. This will be the last letter addressed to M. Place. I suppose you will be leaving it in a very few days now. Pray give my love to Emma [Huger Smith][19] & say that I shall write to her in a day or two, which I consider a <u>magnanimous</u> message and resolution, considering her utter neglect of me– Best love to Susan & Sally, their sposi [*husbands*] & children and to Papa, W<u>m</u> & Kitty– Give me detailed accounts of all you know I love to hear of and believe me my dearest Mamma, y<u>r</u> most affectionate Daughter Eliza

Y<u>r</u> old Bath friend M<u>rs</u> Griffiths who was Miss Patterson, enquired very particularly after you yesterday– Many people recollect you here with much affection and will welcome you warmly.

Private Collection

1. Colonel Clive was a British army officer traveling in America with a friend, Egerton Brydges. Miss Moore, in New York, gave him a letter of introduction to the Middletons.

2. Matilda Lee Carter of Virginia, who was a talented harpist, married Fisher's cousin, Thomas M. Willing, in 1831. Mrs. Fisher said at the time that "she [cared] not a fig for him," and the marriage was not a happy one. Josephine Carter was Matilda Willing's sister. Mrs. Fisher, Sr., to JFF, Aug. 10, [ca. 1831,] PHi, C/F.

3. The steamship *British Queen* was one of the steamships making the transatlantic passage on a regular schedule.

4. Eliza would have been expected to return the visits of the many people who called on her when she first arrived in Philadelphia. This was often done by presenting a calling card at an individual's house without expecting to be invited in.

5. Probably Mrs. Samuel Mifflin, whose husband (d. 1829) was a relative of Fisher's through the Francis family. However, there was more than one Mrs. Mifflin in Philadelphia at this time.

6. Anna Walsh was the daughter of Robert Walsh (1784–1859), founder and edi-

tor of the *National Gazette*, a member of the American Philosophical Society, and well-known Catholic intellectual. Both Anna and her brother, Robert Walsh, Jr., were friends of Fisher's.

7. Margaret Sergeant was a daughter of Margaretta (Watmough) and John Sergeant (1779–1852), who was one of Philadelphia's most distinguished lawyers. Sergeant had been chief advisor to the Second Bank of the United States, a state legislator, a member of Congress with Henry Middleton, and again a member at this time.

Margaret's fiancé was George Gordon Meade (1815–1872), future general of the U.S. Army. In 1839 he was assigned to surveying the northeast boundary between the United States and Canada.

8. Four trunks and three boxes were shipped from Charleston to Philadelphia. In addition to books, they contained china and pictures for the Fishers' house. JFF to GH, May 1, 1839, PHi, C/F.

9. Joseph Hopkinson (1770–1842), judge of the U.S. Court for the Eastern District of Pennsylvania, was also a prominent member of the American Philosophical Society, a founder of the Academy of Fine Arts, and author of the patriotic song "Hail Columbia." He served in Congress with Henry Middleton.

10. This was Joseph Bonaparte, Napoleon's brother, who, after Napoleon's defeat at Waterloo, lived near Philadelphia for many years. Many Americans were introduced to European art and taste through the large art collection which he brought with him.

11. Nicholas Biddle (1786–1844) and his wife, the former Jane Craig, lived at Andalusia, a Greek revival house on the Delaware River north of Philadelphia.

From 1822 until 1836, Biddle was president of the Second Bank of the United States, which was headquartered in Philadelphia. During this time, he put the bank on a sound footing and developed it as a central bank, which, by forcing local banks to keep a certain amount of specie on hand, was able to stabilize the value of the many different bank notes in circulation. After President Jackson vetoed the recharter of the bank in 1832, it continued as the Bank of the United States of Pennsylvania. Although Biddle continued as president until 1839, his reputation was tarnished by his battle with President Jackson to preserve the bank and by his efforts to keep it going after the financial panic in 1837.

12. Fanny (Frances Anne Kemble) Butler (b. 1809) was known to be interesting but unconventional in thought, behavior, and dress. She came from a famous family of English actors and was wildly successful as an actress when she came to the United States in 1832 with her father, Charles Kemble. She left the stage in 1834 to marry Pierce Butler (1810–1867), a Philadelphian who changed his last name from Mease to Butler in order to inherit his grandfather Pierce Butler's estate. Butler's wealth came principally from rice-growing plantations on the Altamaha River in Georgia.

13. Mrs. Camac was the former Elizabeth Markoe (1807–1886); she was widowed in 1842.

14. Henrietta Drayton (1779–1861) was Henry Middleton's first cousin: her mother, Hester Middleton (Mrs. Charles) Drayton and Henry Middleton's father, Arthur, were brother and sister.

15. Mrs. James Gibson was the former Elizabeth Bordley (1777–1863), a girlhood friend of Mrs. Fisher's.

16. Maria (Heyward) Drayton was the second wife of Col. William Drayton (1776–1846). Drayton, a former congressman from South Carolina and, like Henry

Middleton, a strong Unionist, moved to Philadelphia from Charleston after the nullification crisis in the early 1830s. In 1841 he became the last president of the Second Bank of the United States and was responsible for winding up its affairs.

The Fishers' servant probably told Mrs. Drayton that Mrs. Fisher was "not at home." This was accepted practice except when the caller was a close friend or special person, as Mrs. Drayton was.

17. Probably Sally Waln (1806–1886), daughter of William (d. 1826) and Mary (Wilcocks) Waln. She became one of Eliza's good friends, but Eliza may not have known her well enough at the time to refer to her by her first name.

18. Fanny Inglis Calderon was a relative of the Inglises, Mrs. Middleton's mother's family. Her husband, Angel Calderon de la Barca, was a Spanish diplomat who served as minister to Mexico and later to the United States.

19. Emma (Huger) Smith (1813–1892) was the daughter of Henry Middleton's sister Isabella (Middleton) and Daniel Elliott Huger (1779–1854). Always a very close friend of Eliza's, Emma was witty, direct, and affectionate. Described as "handsome [and] high-bred," even "imperial," she was "said to be the greatest belle ever known in Charleston." She married Joseph Allen Smith, Jr., in 1838.

Allen Smith (1810–1879) was the son of Joseph Allen and Charlotte Georgina [Izard] Smith. An 1829 graduate of West Point and former army officer, he was now a rice planter, owning Recess Plantation on the Savannah River. (In the mid-1840s he began to use Izard as his last name to avoid confusion with other Smiths.)

Emma's father, Judge Huger, a lawyer, circuit judge, and U.S. senator in the 1840s, was one of Charleston's most eminent citizens. Dinner parties at the Huger house on Meeting Street, "where every public question was ably discussed," were famous. Like his brother-in-law Henry Middleton, he was a strong Unionist during the nullification controversy in the 1830s. Beverly Scafidel, "The Letters of William Elliott" (Ph.D. diss., University of South Carolina, 1978), 361; Mrs. St. Julien Ravenel, *Charleston: The Place and the People* (New York: Macmillan, 1906), 469, 472.

～

To Mrs. Middleton, Boundary Street, Charleston[1]

Philadelphia June 5th 1839

I began to be quite uneasy at not hearing for ten days, when your letter of the 30th arrived to dispel my fears, my dearest Mamma– Thank you for writing me such a nice long one, and giving me such good news of all, except of Emma [Huger Smith,] whose change of plans for the summer, I had not learnt & which distressed me beyond measure– I immediately sat down and wrote her a long reproachful letter, complaining of her (or Allen's) want of faith– but I can hardly hope that my prayers and entreaties will produce the desired effect, and make her return to her first determination of going to New Port– It is indeed a bitter disappointment to me to lose her society during the whole summer and following winter also– and I feel half inclined to quarrel with Allen, whose fault I am sure it must be. As to Harry, I now give him up altogether, and shall never believe he is coming until he actually arrives in N.Y.

6$\underline{th}$ I should have written further yesterday, dear Mamma, but after finishing my letter to Emma, I was <u>so cold</u> that I got up & played at Battledore & Shuttlecock for an hour to warm myself. In the afternoon I walked with Sarah Sergeant[2] all the way to Schuylkill[3] and back to [*the Sergeants' house on*] Fourth S$\underline{t}$, altogether 3 miles & a half, without much fatigue, and spent the eveng at M$\underline{rs}$ H[arrison]'s where we go 4 nights out the 7– and generally meet some pleasant people– I am now steadfast in my resolution to make my escape before ten o'c$\underline{k}$– and find early hours much better for my health which is certainly improving without the aid of any physick, regular exercise being the best remedy. The numbness has disappeared from my hands, & almost entirely from my feet, and altho' I am still occasionally hoarse, I have no soreness in my throat– This morning I rode for the first time for 6 weeks, and enjoyed it exceedingly– but intending to drive out to M$\underline{rs}$ [Thomas] Rotch's[4] in the country this afternoon I returned in an hour and a half, & had only time to go out 2 miles beyond the town– riding very slowly over the Pavements. The pony is a very nice little creature, with a pleasant gait & perfectly gentle, which Fisher has hired for me until he can find a good horse without vices of any sort, [Legnen?][5] is assisting him in his researches, and he could not have a better adviser in this respect– Sidney & Henry Fisher[6] are also on the look out, & taking a vast deal of trouble in trying horses for me, and if a good one is to be had, he will certainly fall to my share–

On my return home today I found a very kind note from Miss Fisher[7] (an old quaker Aunt of F's) and a most beautiful India work table, which she begs me to accept– I was of course very happy to do so, and wrote a properly grateful answer of thanks– The present is one of the prettiest and most complete things I ever saw, filled with carved <u>implements</u> of Ivory of all descriptions, for every notable purpose, & is a very ornamental addition to my nicely furnished apartment. The sister of the <u>donor</u> is M$\underline{rs}$ Smith, the <u>Preacher</u>, who presented me the other day with a curious book, a compilation of her own, published at her expense, of obituary notices & biographical sketches of some of <u>our distinguished</u> relations on the Quaker side, but I merely glanced thro' the pages, for Fisher snatched it away, & refuses positively to let me read it, and expose the weakness of mind of his old Aunt– She has been a beautiful woman, but has lost both beauty and Intellect by severe Illnesses–

I paid a long visit of an hour to Miss Henrietta Drayton the other day and had to listen to her usual chapter of disasters & ailments– none of which, except a severe Toothache, I could understand– She spoke of you affectionately, &

begged to be remembered particularly when I wrote. I promised to call for her and take her to drive some eveng– & must try to do so soon. I have also seen Miss Gadsden[8] & Mrs Gibson, who both send you kind messages. I called upon Miss Trapier[9] the day after her arrival & heard thro' her of the enquiries Papa had made about the Sutton– She supposed you might come in the Catherine,[10] but I was sure our favorite Captn Berry w^{d} be preferred to all others, & I only hope he may make as good a trip home and back again as this last– and that in two or three weeks more at farthest, I shall embrace you once more. I am not sorry when it comes to the point, that you do not come by the Wilmington route– for altho' I would prefer it myself, I should not like you to run the risk of being on those railroads, which are badly constructed in Vir[gini]a & by no means safe modes of conveyance in my opinion– We had two narrow escapes which I shall tell you of when we meet– And then the hope that it will be the last sea voyage that you are to take this year at least, must console you for all the discomfort and inconveniences of shipboard. I have just [heard] from Edward to whom I wrote for a saddle. He mentions that Elizth Mason[11] was to have sailed on the 4th for Bremen and says she was looking very pretty & Sophia very well– but poor child she is suffering with her eyes just as I did & cannot see to write to me.

Thursday Eveng– I have just returned from Mrs Rotch's with a lovely bouquet of flowers she cut for me from her garden. She is a very sweet woman indeed. Her husband is recovering from the dreadful operation which he had performed in Charleston. Tell Sally that the bore Tom Francis[12] is engaged to as uninteresting a person as himself– One of the numerous family of Smith. His mother & niece, Nancy Page[13] beg to be kindly remembered to her– Dr Willing[14] has really gone after Miss T[illinghast] & it is supposed the engagement will soon be announced from Providence as there can be no possible objection on the part of her parents to one of such unexceptionable character and good fortune. I am so sorry Sophia did not catch him, but I have already someone else in my eye for her– Mrs Barclay[15] writes in rather low spirits Tom having gone to West Pt. & Susan DeLancey to Havre to join Mrs Coster[16] who is in bad health. It is very late, & I have notes of refusal to write before I go to bed, & to rise tomorrow at 6 that I may be on horseback by 7– Therefore Adieu my dearest Mamma– I shall write only once more to Charleston, & earlier in the week that you may receive it before you sail– With best love to Papa & W^{m} and all the rest, too many to enumerate here, I remain y^{r} most affect^{e} Daughter Eliza

I expect to receive my French Packages tomorrow, as Gracie & Sargent were to forward them immediately– Great anxiety is expressed by many of my fair friends, about them– several of whom take more interest in the matter than I do myself–

Private Collection

1. The Henry Middletons did not own a house in Charleston but instead rented one on Boundary Street for several years. The house was on the northwest corner of Boundary (now Calhoun) and Smith Streets, just outside the city limits on Charleston Neck. The lots were often bigger there than in the older sections of Charleston, allowing houses to be set back from the street and surrounded by gardens. Maurie D. McInnis, "The Politics of Taste: Classicism in Charleston, South Carolina, 1815–1840" (Ph.D. diss., Yale University, 1996), 112–13.

2. Sarah Sergeant was a daughter of the John Sergeants; Margaret Sergeant was her sister.

3. That is, to the Schuylkill River. Their walk was westward across land which, though central Philadelphia today, was then still largely undeveloped.

4. Mrs. Thomas Rotch was the former Susan Ridgway. Her husband died in 1840; she married Dr. John Rhea Barton, a prominent Philadelphia surgeon, in 1843.

5. Though he is mentioned in three of Eliza's letters, this person has not been identified.

6. Sidney and Henry Fisher were brothers and Fisher's first cousins. Their father, James Logan Fisher, and Fisher's father, Joshua, were brothers.

7. Of all Fisher's Quaker relatives, he loved his father's youngest sister, Esther (Aunt Hetty) Fisher (1788–1849) the most. The sewing table she gave Eliza was actually Chinese black lacquer ware decorated in gold. Aunt Hetty's sister, Hannah Fisher (Mrs. James) Smith (1777–1846) was a good person but Fisher could not stand her preaching, which Quaker women as well as men did. As a good Episcopalian, he was "mortified that an Aunt of mine, whatever her sincerity, should be giving out such stuff as an emanation from the Holy Spirit." JFF, *Recollections,* 25.

8. Emma Gadsden (d. 1841), a daughter of Thomas and Martha (Fenwick) Gadsden and granddaughter of the Revolutionary War patriot Christopher Gadsden, was a Charlestonian but lived in Philadelphia. Fisher remembered her living, earlier in the century, with Mrs. Ralph Izard and other Carolinians in a group of houses nicknamed "Carolina Row" on Spruce between Ninth and Tenth Streets. William Drayton's first wife, Ann (Gadsden) Drayton, was her sister. JFF, *Recollections,* 279.

9. Probably Mary Elizabeth Trapier, sister of Fisher's Harvard classmate, Paul Trapier of Charleston.

10. The *Sutton* and the *Catherine* were two of the coastal packets on the route between Charleston and New York. Capt. Michael Berry (ca. 1804–1862) commanded packets on this line until 1846.

11. Elizabeth (Thorndike) Mason, Sophia's widowed sister, was on her way to visit their sister Sally Ann Oelrichs in Bremen. Elizabeth soon married her brother-in-law, Theodore Oelrichs.

12. Tom Francis was Fisher's first cousin. His mother, Mrs. Francis, was the former Dorothy Willing, whose husband, Thomas W. Francis (d. 1815), was Mrs. Fisher's and Mrs. Harrison's brother.

13. Nancy Page and her sister, Maria, were Mrs. Francis's granddaughters. Their mother, Mary Francis Page, had died; their father was Dr. Robert Powell Page (1794–1849).

14. Dr. Charles Willing (1806–1887) was a Harvard classmate as well as a cousin of Fisher's. Eliza had hoped that he would fall in love with her friend Sophia Thorndike. Instead, he married Rebecca Tillinghast from Providence, Rhode Island, daughter of Joseph L .Tillinghast, member of Congress.

15. Catherine Channing (Mrs. Thomas) Barclay was a daughter of Walter Channing, a merchant in Boston who came originally from Newport. She lived in New York and had been a widow for about a year and a half. Tom was her son; Susan Delancey was probably a relative of the Barclays.

16. Matilda (Prime) Coster (1810–1849) was the daughter of Nathaniel Prime, partner of the New York banking firm Prime, Ward and King. Her husband, Gerald Coster, was also a banker.

～

To avoid getting malaria, most South Carolina Low Country planters' families who could do so usually left their plantations in the late spring and did not return until after the first frost in the fall. The Middletons, for example, always tried to leave Middleton Place in late May. Over the years they spent summers on Sullivan's Island near Charleston, in Greenville in the northwest corner of South Carolina, or at northern resorts such as Saratoga and Ballston Springs in New York and Newport, Rhode Island.

From 1833 on, though, they went regularly to Newport. At first they stayed in one of the boardinghouses that catered to an increasing number of southern as well as northern visitors. Then, in 1835 Henry Middleton bought a house which, with several additions, was able to accommodate a growing family as his children married and had children of their own.

When they left Middleton Place, the Middletons usually spent a week or two in Charleston, which was cool and considered healthy. This gave Mrs. Middleton a chance to visit with her friends and do some shopping while waiting for the boat to New York. After a few days in New York, where Mrs. Middleton arranged for servants who would spend the summer with them, she, Catherine, the servants, and at least one son to escort them, continued on by overnight steamer to Newport. Henry Middleton, with one or more of his sons, often went part of the way by railroad, stopping in Washington as he went.

To Mrs. Fisher, Philadelphia

Charleston June 6th 1839

Your welcome letter my dearest Eliza reached me on the 4th, the day after I came here– the pleasure I felt on perusing it was in some degree damped by finding it had been necessary to consult Dr Chapman. I had flattered myself that your ailments were nothing but a very slight numbness– however as the Physician is of opinion that you will soon be entirely restored by following his advice, I trust you will strictly observe his rules. Your indisposition must have been owing to fatigue & over excitement after your arrival, for the journey by your account was not fatiguing.

I am much obliged to M^r and Mrs Fisher for their politeness shewn to my acquaintances. I concluded that you would have derived much more pleasure than you seem to have done from Col. Clive's conversation– You say "he is <u>rather</u> a pleasant person"! <u>We</u> all think him superlatively so– he expressed to Miss Moore his gratitude for your polite reception of him, & found your party extremely pleasant. I hope you sang on that occasion. As to Mr Brydges he is too timid to be agreeable– He must however have moved in good society as his Father is a Baronet & has been Minister in Persia & he is himself a Naturalist. so that he cannot be quite uninformed. M^r A[llyne] Otis[1] is very fond of Col. C., W^m says. <u>He</u> has just returned from his drive into town– but without a letter from Harry which I fully expected as his name is not among the list of Passengers by the G^t Western– neither have I one from my Brother, from which I augur that his hands are still suffering from Gout. This you may be sure makes me very uneasy. Sally left the country[2] last Friday & the day after John met her. She will I believe go to Aiken although he is much averse to the separation. Your letters he has read with great pleasure, & so has Emma Smith– who came yesterday Eve^g with her Mother & Sister [Sabina] L[owndes]–[3] As she has written to you, within a few days I need not repeat what she said. Her spirits seemed very good, & she was looking rather better than she did in March though still very thin–

7th Sally & I with C[atherine] went yesterday Eve^g to see Susan in her new house, a very handsome one I think. We found her very busy making preparations for Mary's departure[4] on the 10th in the 'Catherine' a new packet, with Staterooms on Deck– Y^r Father went on board the day after we arrived & was so much pleased with it, that had it been convenient, he would have taken <u>our</u> passages in it. He cannot however (much to my regret as you may suppose) make his arrangements in so short a time. Oliver will remain only 2 days in Philad^a being impatient to return to Susan who is to go to the Beach next week– She is looking tolerably well, & the Baby very well– perfectly quiet, therefore without ailment & has a good wet nurse. À propos, on Sally's enquiring about the <u>other</u> for herself, next Octr Susan told her she was engaged, & in Decr to M^{rs} J[ulius] P[ringle].[5] This will be news perhaps for Mrs Barclay– On my return home I was sorry to find Mrs Holbrook's card,[6] as it would have given me pleasure to see her. She sent me while in the Country an excellent Book Dᴿ Keith's 'Demonstration of the truth of the Christian religion'.[7] You would like it. the evidences drawn not only from Scripture, but from Astronomy & Geology, are very striking. Wᵐ has been studying it. Mᴿ [Hugh Swinton] Leg-aré[8] called the evening after we arrived. I told him how much pleased you had been with your visit to Mʳˢ Rives. He will be at the north in August.

I sent off my letter to my Sister S[carbrough][9] on the 5ᵗʰ so that it will be in time for the Gᵗ Western, having copied the part of yours relating to the piano forte–[10] Tell me whether I did properly in desiring it shᵈ be sent by a N.Y. packet directed to the care of Messʳˢ Otis? You did not give any direction about the matter, & I recollected how you wished to have had your Trousseau sent by a N.Y. packet as they arrive so much more frequently than the Philadᵃ vessels. If I have erred, it is easy to countermand the order which can be done next month. You must know yʳ Father considers you have done imprudently in insisting the Piano should be of rosewood, because on trial the best toned may happen to be of Mahogany, & if one should be made expressly for you of rosewood, it may prove inferior in tone. Georgina [Middleton][11] called to see me & enquired particularly about you. She is going to Buncomb[12] in a day or two. Dᴿ & Mʳˢ [Mitchell C.] King[13] also are going– they have just been to see me. Miss [Harriott] Pinckney[14] & Miss [Sally] Rutledge[15] are in town but I have not yet seen them, so cannot tell you when to expect them. Your descrip-tion of the comfort & situation of Miss Hare's apartments is tempting in the highest degree, but Alas, I fear it will never be my lot to inhabit them! They are so desirable, that of course they will be taken before the Autumn– We have fortunately comparatively cool weather just now but cannot expect that it will continue. In consequence of your advice the Piano-forte is packed up to go to N.Y. a good Plan. it wants putting in order.

Sally has just returned from Mʳˢ W[illiam Bull] P[ringle]'s[16] & there saw a letter from Miss Wilson telling her that L[ady] N. had suffered dreadfully for the last 10 years from her husband's tyrannical treatment. In order to be out of his way, they are going with Mʳ & Mʳˢ Pinkerton to Sicily. the marriage is therefore deferred, for a time. Your friend Mʳˢ Ravenel[17] sailed a few days since for Greenock– her symptoms resemble Sally's she says, & it is to cure them the voyage is undertaken. I have been waiting the return of Wᵐ in hopes that I might receive a letter from Harry, & inform you of its contents but there is none. May we conclude from this omission that he is making his passage in a Packet Ship? It is so late, I must hasten to despatch this in time for the post. I shall often think of you on Sunday[18] my dearest Eliza to say nothing of the

frequency you occupy my thoughts at other times. With best regards to M^{r} & Mrs Fisher believe me Y^{r} affectionate Mother M. H. M.
Sally & all the rest send their best love to you.

PHi

1. Allyne Otis (1807–1873), son of Harrison Gray Otis, was Fisher's Harvard classmate and lifelong friend. (The name was sometimes spelled "Alleyne"; in most cases Fisher and Eliza used "Allyne.")

2. When Mrs. Middleton referred to "the country," she usually meant Middleton Place.

3. One of Emma Huger Smith's sisters, Sabina (1811–1874), married Charles Tidyman Lowndes (1808–1884). He became a planter as well as president of the Bank of Charleston.

4. Oliver Middleton was getting ready to take his ten-year-old daughter, Mary, to Philadelphia to attend Mme Grelaud's school. This was at the urging of Eliza, who felt that Mary, though a "very intelligent child," was being neglected and, besides, had a "terrible negro dialect." Although Mary's mother, Susan, had attended the same school, she was not happy about Mary's going away from home. She told Eliza, "I consider this seperation the heaviest trial I ever had." EM to JFF, January 1, 1839, MPlFdn; Susan Middleton to EMF, n.d., PHi, C/F.

5. New Yorker Jane (Lynch) Pringle (1811–1896), the daughter of Dominic Lynch, a famous wine merchant and opera lover, had recently married South Carolinian J. Julius Izard Pringle (1808–1864). A Harvard graduate and a planter, he was the son of Mary (Izard) and John Julius Pringle, Jr.

6. Harriott Pinckney Rutledge Holbrook (1802–1862), from Charleston, was the daughter of Frederick and Harriott Pinckney (Horry) Rutledge. She was by all accounts an unusually charming and well-educated person, described by Fisher as being "without the slightest pedantry or conceit." He said that "everything took a bright turn with her."

Her husband, John Edwards Holbrook, said to be "a silent man with a talent for making others talk," was a physician and professor of anatomy at the Medical College of Charleston. He was also an eminent zoologist, particularly interested in reptiles and fish. Mrs. Ravenel, *Charleston,* 476, 479.

7. Alexander Keith (1791–1880), a Scots minister, was interested in the fulfillment of biblical prophecy. His "Demonstration of the Truth of the Christian Religion" was published in 1838.

8. Charlestonian Hugh Swinton Legaré (1797–1843) was well-known as a lawyer, politician, congressman, and southern intellectual. He was a founder of the literary journal the *Southern Review;* served as U.S. chargé d'affaires in Belgium; was President Tyler's attorney general and, briefly, his secretary of state before his death in 1843. He was a leader of the Unionists in the early 1830s.

9. Mrs. Middleton's sister Anna Maria Hering (b. 1766) was married to the Hon. Jno. Lumley, who became the seventh earl of Scarbrough.

10. Henry Middleton offered to buy Eliza a piano. However, he wanted her to choose an American one and was put out when she insisted on one made by the famous

English maker Broadwood. One of her aunts helped arrange the purchase and Fisher paid for it.

11. Charlotte Georgina (Georgie) Izard (1816–1902), daughter of Ralph and Elizabeth (Middleton) Izard, married her cousin, Ralph Izard Middleton, who was the son of Alicia (Russell) and Arthur Middleton.

12. When Carolinians referred to Buncombe, they meant the area around Flat Rock, North Carolina, which was part of Buncombe County at that time. Buncombe, just north of the South Carolina border, lured many families in the summer with its cool climate and beauty.

13. Mitchell Campbell King, the son of Charleston Judge and Mrs. Mitchell King, married Elizabeth (Lizzie), daughter of Eliza's cousin John Middleton, in 1838.

14. Harriott Pinckney (1776–1866), the daughter of Charles Cotesworth and Sarah (Middleton) Pinckney, managed her own plantation on Pinckney's Island off the South Carolina coast. She, Henry Middleton, and Sally Rutledge were all first cousins (see next note).

15. Sarah (Sally) Rutledge (1782–1855) was the daughter of Edward and Henrietta (Middleton) Rutledge. She wrote a successful cookbook, *The Carolina Housewife*, which was published in 1831.

16. Mary (Alston) Pringle was Sally Middleton's aunt.

17. Mrs. John Ravenel was the former Eliza McEvers. Greenock, on the Clyde estuary, was Glasgow's port.

18. June 9 was Eliza's birthday.

⁓

To Mrs. Middleton, Charleston

Philadelphia, June 11$\underline{^{th}}$ 1839

I found your much welcome letter awaiting me on my return yesterday eveng from a pleasant expedition with M$\underline{^{rs}}$ Harrison, my dearest Mamma– Thank you for remembering my request and filling such a nice large sheet. I was so pleased to have such excellent accounts of all I love in Car$\underline{^a}$ And so happy to have a prospect of soon seeing Oliver & dear little Mary– I suppose they will be here in a week– But only think of Harry! That he should, after all our disappointments & doubts as to his coming, actually have arrived in New York 4 days ago! I did not hear of it until dinner time on Sunday, when Fisher came in & announced that M$\underline{^r}$ [Pickett?] had seen his name among the list of passengers in a sailing Vessel– I immediately wrote, begging him to come on as soon as possible, and the same afternoon rec$\underline{^d}$ a letter from him, in which he seems to hesitate between joining me here, or waiting for y$\underline{^r}$ arrival in N. Y. which he expected about the 13$\underline{^{th}}$. I had mentioned in my letter to him however that as you were to wait for the Sutton, you could not possibly be there before the 25$\underline{^{th}}$, & besought him to pass the intervening fortnight with me– Whether my entreaties may avail aught, I know not, but flatter myself, perhaps presumptuously, that he cannot prefer the society of anyone in N.Y. to mine, & that as soon as his arrangements at the Custom House are made, he will hasten to me. I therefore look for him hourly, and hope to have the happiness of embracing him this very day– I could not have heard more agreeable intelligence on my birthday and what with that, & the profitable manner in which it was spent, I enjoyed une vraie fête [*a really good birthday*]– Hearing two most excellent discourses during the day, & in the evening assembling a few pleasant people at home– Bishop de Lancey[1] gave us his farewell Sermon, which was indeed so affecting, that altho' I had heard him before but 3 or 4 times, & of course did not feel as much as the rest of the congregation whose Pastor he has been for 18 years, I could not help shedding tears at his parting address– delivered with deep feeling & in the most impressive manner– I do not wonder that they should be sorry to part with such a friend and adviser– His loss is a very severe one to the whole community– For besides being a good Preacher, he is a perfect gentleman, & one who thinks it no sin to go into society, and take part in all the innocent amusements of those committed to his charge–

On Friday I rode the Pony after a very early & light Breakfast– and liked him better than the day before. In the afternoon we drove to Germantown,[2] and paid 3 visits– To M^rs [Ann Willing] Morris,[3] a cousin of M^rs F[isher]'s, Mrs Elwyn,[4] who enquired after you particularly, and the [Benjamin] Chews,[5] Arthur's friends– Very ridiculous old people and the greatest flatterers I ever saw, but kindhearted–

The following day we went to return Mrs Pierce Butler's visit. She kept us waiting a quarter of an hour, and then made her appearance in a riding Habit & <u>coloured shirt</u>, apologizing for the delay, but pleading a headache which she intended to cure by the "Panacea of riding"– Her welcome was very cordial, and she made herself so agreeable that an hour & a half passed in her society before any of us thought of taking leave– She spoke a great deal of the dismal prospects in England, & seemed to consider a revolution there inevitable and near at hand.[6] She shewed I thought a great deal of good feeling and good sense in all she said on the subject, and gave us many anecdotes illustrating the abuse of the system of placing younger brothers in the church without the least preparation or disposition on their part– When I got up to take leave, she insisted upon running into the Garden without bonnet or gloves, to cut me some of the choicest specimens of her greenhouse– and skipped over the beds & parterres cutting the finest flowers for me, and talking so well, that I followed regardless of the broiling sun– <u>Her</u> complexion is past spoiling, and she laughed at the idea of caring for her mahogany colored skin. She pressed me to return on Monday Eveng, which she has set apart for the reception of visitors, but altho' I felt very much tempted to do so, I was afraid she might get tired of me if I so soon made her another visit, & having a good excuse for remaining at home, in the expected arrival of Harry, I thought I would defer it until next week, when I daresay she will be glad to see me as she declared that she felt a great deal better for my visit.

I had written so far when who should walk in but Harry! You may imagine my delighted surprise, and the pleasure of talking to him & hearing him talk for 3 hours– He is now gone out, but will return to dinner, and in the meantime I can just add a few words to tell you how well he is looking, altho' he thinks himself very much reduced by the voyage– a very pleasant one of 22 days– But he has written to you himself of that, and I had rather tell you what he does not I suppose mention– Of his improved health & appearance, notwithstanding his grey hairs, which I am surprised to see so numerous– I think he now rivals Oliver, & certainly has a more <u>venerable</u> air than John– He is not changed otherwise, except that he has decidedly gained flesh and ruddiness of cheek which he says was greater before he left Engl^{d}– Of course he intends to stay with me until we hear of y^{r} arrival. I am so glad I wrote to him on Sunday, for that letter induced him to come on yesterday by the late boat– and he would otherwise have waited for you in N.Y. He did not see Mrs Barclay, being very busy the two days he was in that city, & thinking he says the <u>first</u> visit was due to me– He tells me that he forwarded a letter from Uncle Oliver [Hering] to you, so that y^{r} anxieties must be removed– I am sorry to hear of poor James Campbell's death– It is a dreadful loss to his poor motherless children– What a pity that Harry did not run down to Southampton [*to see Uncle Oliver*] for a day or two before his departure– I wrote a long letter to my Aunt [*Hering*] yesterday, and begged her to have the Piano directed to the care of Otis & Mason, which I had neglected to mention to you, but which it seems you thought of yourself–

I intended giving you a description of our visit to the Woodlands,[7] a fine old house, the situation on the Schuylkill reminding me very much of Middleton Place, but Harry's arrival has put everything else out of my head, and it is now time to change my breakfast dress for dinner– I know I shall not have time to add anything more to this afterwards, and as I do not wish to detain a scrawl, the freshness of date of which will be its only merit, I will say Adieu– with best love to my dear Papa, Brothers and Sisters, I am my dearest Mamma Y^{r} most affectionate Daughter

Eliza M. Fisher

Mrs F. & M^{r} & Mrs H. always desire to be kindly remembered– and Fisher wishes to say something very respectful & affectionate which I have not time to add– I think I shall write once more to you, with a chance of your receiving it– I was delighted to meet Dr Holbrook yesterday, and find he had seen Papa well the day before he left Charleston. He was here this morng– & agrees with D^r C[hapman] that I had better <u>not</u> sing– <u>He</u> has certainly changed his note since I last consulted him. But he thinks me getting on very well, and I feel myself that I am. Pray tell M^{rs} H[olbrook] with my love I was much disappointed to find he had left her at home. I have not yet rec^d my French boxes–[8] Pray thank Emma for her letter, which I will soon answer– meanwhile she owes me another–

Private Collection

1. William H. DeLancey (1797–1865) was minister of St. Peter's Episcopal church in Philadelphia, a church with which both the Francis and Harrison families had long-standing connections. He was named Bishop of Western New York in May 1839.

2. Germantown, a separate community about five miles northwest of Philadelphia, had long been considered a pleasant and healthy place to live and soon developed into a fashionable suburb. It was incorporated into the city in 1854.

3. Ann Willing Morris (1763–1853), the daughter of Charles Willing, was a cousin of Mrs. Fisher's and Mrs. Harrison's. She was the widow of Luke Morris.

4. Elizabeth (Langdon) Elwyn was the daughter of Gov. John Langdon of New Hampshire, an old friend of George Harrison's. Her son, Dr. Alfred Elwyn (1804–1884), was particularly interested in agriculture and had a farm in Chester County, west of Philadelphia. He was a friend of Fisher's and, with him, a longtime board member of the Institution for the Blind. Alfred Elwyn married Mary Mease, Pierce (Mease) Butler's sister.

5. Benjamin Chew, Jr. (1758–1844), a lawyer, and his wife, the former Katherine Banning (1770–1855), lived at Cliveden, the Chew family's eighteenth-century estate. It was the site of the Battle of Germantown in 1777. Benjamin Chew, according to Fisher, was "from youth to age a kind and amiable man, hospitable to the stretch of his disordered fortune. An old beau in manners, he was what some called a gentleman of the old school." The Chews knew Eliza's brother, Arthur, because Arthur's first wife, Ann Van Ness, had been a schoolmate of their daughter Anne. JFF, *Recollections*, 255.

6. There was a great deal of unrest in England's manufacturing cities over the dreadful working and living conditions and lack of political representation of many industrial workers. In 1838 the Chartists began calling for such seemingly radical reforms as universal male suffrage and salaries for members of Parliament so that working people could afford to serve. At Birmingham in May 1839, they called for the use of arms to defend their liberties.

7. The Woodlands, built at the end of the eighteenth century on high ground overlooking the Schuylkill River in West Philadelphia, was one of the first American houses in the classical style. Furnished with European furniture and works of art by the Hamilton family, the house as well as the landscaped grounds, planted with a variety of trees and shrubs, were so unusual that Francis Fisher vividly recalled the impression they had made on his "youthful imagination." JFF, *Recollections*, 221.

8. Eliza's "French finery", as she called it, arrived soon after. The dresses, she told her mother, "are very handsome, but composed of such heavy silk that I should be smothered if I attempted to wear them in July & August. They will <u>keep cool</u> however & mean time I can get a foulard silk or muslin. There is nothing new in the shape of the bodices or sleeves, but they are all trimmed, either flounced, fringed or braided in the skirt– Uncle Izard has really shewed excellent taste in the selection of all the articles, and I have written him my thanks." EMF to MHM, June 18, 1839, private collection.

⁓

After much discussion about which boat they would take and worry because an outbreak of fever in Charleston might prevent them from landing in New York, the Middletons finally sailed the first week in July and arrived in New York on July 11. But, as Mrs. Middleton had said years before, "Procrastination is y^r Father's motto,"[1] so it is unlikely anyone was surprised that it took Henry Middleton several days to decide which boat they would all take to Newport. The Middletons finally arrived there on July 17 and were soon joined by Eliza and Fisher.

1. MHM to Arthur Middleton, July 8, 1832, PHi, FFP.

To Mrs. Middleton, Clinton Hotel, New York

Philadelphia – July 10$^{\underline{th}}$ 1839

My dearest Mamma,

I wrote to you by Delancey Izard,[1] who I afterwards learnt, arrived in Charleston the day after you sailed– It was by a letter of his to M^{rs} McEuen that I heard of your departure thence, I was anxiously expecting one from you, but I suppose you were too much hurried at the last to write. I now look eagerly for one from N. York, where I suppose they will allow you to land, now that the alarm about the Fever is all over– It is now a week since you sailed, and these fine Southern Breezes will have wafted you in to Port by the time this reaches N.Y. if you are not already there– Fisher has gone down to look at the NewsPapers at the Exchange that I may have the latest accounts, & I trust that he may bring me the good news I so earnestly desire– I need not tell you how much & often you have all been in my thoughts for some days past, nor how I long to be with you again. We hoped to have left this on the 17$^{\underline{th}}$, but finding that the Massachussetts goes on Tuesdays & Fridays, we are obliged to defer our departure until Friday week, the 19$^{\underline{th}}$ and intend passing immediately thro' to New Port, and if you are not ready to receive us on the 20$^{\underline{th}}$, we can easily go to Whitfield's[2] for a few days, until it is perfectly convenient for you to take us in– Indeed I think perhaps it would be better that we should remain there altogether, unless you can assure me <u>sincerely</u> that there will be room for us, now that Harry is returned–

I begged him to ask you about the arrangements for Servants– Whether in consideration for Ben[3] Papa intends trying coloured Serv$\underline{ts}$ this year– Every body here prefers them & thinks them much more respectful & manageable than the Whites, and we thought perhaps that with Kinney who is so good tempered they might agree, and if Papa consented to take Ben, our two Servants being also coloured you would only require a cook & chambermaid who might be very easily hired here or in N.Y. But of course I do not wish to interfere with any of your arrangements, and merely to know what they are & how we shall manage about our's– Murray[4] will at any rate be boarded out, and take care of the horses at the Livery Stable, but he w$\underline{d}$ be very willing to assist Ben or any one else in waiting at Table &c– But with regard to my maid Margaret– Shall I carry her on, and will there be sufficient accomodation for her in the house? She w$\underline{d}$ share a bed with any of your <u>coloured</u> women, but if you have whites altogether, and you think she w$\underline{d}$ be in the way, tell me so plainly and I will do without her entirely, or board her out also– She is a very civil & quiet creature, and would do all the chamber work in our Story, and the one above too if necessary– Pray forgive me for troubling you about this matter, but I am at a loss to know what to determine on, & beg you to tell me exactly what you wish me to do–

I suppose of course that Harry was waiting for you at the Clinton [*Hotel*]– Pray give my love to him, and say that I sh[d] have answered his letter, but did not know where to direct, as he spoke of Schooley's mountain[5] with some uncertainty– Fisher went immediately over the way to call on Sir Edward Cust,[6] but found he had gone on to Washington two days previous, and was only to pass thro' on his return– However he left his direction that he might find us out if he stopped a day– I was astonished to receive a message from M$\underline{rs}$ T. Middleton[7] yesterday afternoon, begging me to go and see her at the Marshall House–[8] I went & had from her later news of you than your last letter of the 26$\underline{th}$ gave me– She had a very pleasant & smooth passage, and so little fatigue that she seemed hardly able to believe herself 600 miles from Charleston– And in truth the climate is so much the same, that I do not wonder that she sh$\underline{d}$ think herself as far South as ever– The Thermometer does not rise higher than 80 in the house to be sure, but we have no sea breeze to cool us, and the reflection from the heated brick pavements & Houses is very great, and the atmosphere very close and sultry– Notwithstanding the heat I have been riding on Horseback 3 or 4 times a week, from 6 to 8 in the morning, or about the same hours in the afternoon– But today I thought the weather too warm, & preferred driving intending to go with M$\underline{rs}$ Harrison after dinner. They go to Longbranch[9] on the 20$\underline{th}$, and M$\underline{rs}$ F. will probably join them there in August– I have made Fisher promise to let me stay at New Port until the 15th of Sept.ᵣ & then we propose taking a jaunt to Boston and returning home by Lebanon, [*New York*] & the North River¹⁰ so as to be here on the 1ˢᵗ of Oct.ᵣ– He says that if any boat as good as the Mass.ᵗˢ leaves N.Y. on this day week he can finish his business by that time & we may either join you there & go on at the same time or wait until the day which is fixed for yᵣ departure thence & meet you on board the boat. But we do not want to stay a night in N.Y. or be at N. Port until you arrive. As soon as you are sufficiently recovered from sea sickness, pray let me know your plans, & wishes with respect to the Servants, and let me beg you not to put yourself to the slightest inconvenience on our account– Mary [Middleton] will of course accompany us, & return [*to school*] the first week in Sept.ᵣ with Fisher who is obliged to be here then on business–

I have seen a good deal of Miss [Eliza Lucas] & Mᴿˢ E[dward] Rutledge¹¹ since their arrival– I took them to drive on Monday Eveng & we were caught in the rain & obliged to wait half an hour at Laurel Hill¹² until it was over & borrow a shawl for Mᴿˢ R (who went unprovided) of the Irish Porteress. Fortunately we got in without even a sprinkling, but I shall take care how I go in Open carriages without Umbrellas & Blanket Shawls, even setting out with a broiling sun overhead in this variable climate. I have no time for more scribbling my dearest Mamma, and conclude with best love to Papa, my brother & Kitty. Write at once to Yᵣ most affectionate Daughter Eliza

Have you brought on my straw splitter? For I cannot find it among my things, & have some recollection of having given it to you to take charge of– I have at last got the straw to begin a [*bonnet*]. Fisher begs his affec.ᵗᵉ remembrances & Mᴿˢ F & Mᵣ & Mᴿˢ H. their kind regards & Compts–

Private Collection

1. Delancey Izard (1819–1849) was the son of Ralph Izard, Jr. (d. 1824), and his first wife, Elizabeth (Middleton) Izard (d. 1822). He served in the U.S. Navy until he became a planter in the 1840s.

Anne (Nancy) Izard McEuen was Delancey Izard's sister. She lived in Philadelphia and was the wife of Dr. Thomas McEuen (1799–1873), a graduate of the University of Pennsylvania. He was one of the original trustees of Girard College and active in several other Philadelphia societies.

2. Whitfield's and Potter's were the principal boardinghouses for summer visitors in Newport until larger hotels were built in the mid-1840s.

3. Ben was probably Ben Gowein, a servant who had been with the Middletons in Europe and who stayed there for some years when they left. Kinney did not go north with the Middletons in 1839, although Eliza seems to suggest that both he and Ben had been there in earlier years.

Henry Middleton's reaction to Eliza's questions is in Mrs. Middleton's letter of July 11.

4. Murray was the Fishers' manservant.

5. Schooley's Mountain was a popular resort with a mineral spring, in the hills near Hackettstown, New Jersey. It was roughly midway between New York and Philadelphia.

6. Sir Edward must have been a relative of Lady Anne Cust, wife of the Middletons' English cousin, Sir William Fowle Fowle Middleton (1784–1860).

7. EwereƩa (Barnewall) Middleton (d. 1882), originally from New York, was the second wife of Thomas Middleton (1797–1863). Thomas Middleton, who was Henry Middleton's first cousin, acted as his agent and factor in Charleston at this time. He was also a talented amateur artist.

8. The Marshall House, a hotel run by Edmund Badger, was a block away from the Fishers on Chestnut Street between Sixth and Seventh Streets.

9. Long Branch was a popular summer retreat on the New Jersey shore.

10. The Hudson River, also called the North River, was one of the prime scenic attractions in America. The Fishers' route was west across Massachusetts from Boston to the Berkshire Mountains, from there into New York state, through Lebanon to the Hudson River, and down the Hudson to New York City.

11. Eliza Lucas Rutledge (1810–1893) was Mrs. John Holbrook's sister; their parents were Frederick and Harriott (Horry) Rutledge. Mrs. Edward Rutledge, the former Rebecca Lowndes, was their sister-in-law.

12. Recently opened and reflecting a new style of cemetery, Laurel Hill was outside the city in a picturesque rural setting where visitors could meditate close to nature. It quickly became very fashionable and a place Philadelphians liked to show visitors.

∼

After years of anguish over Catherine's disturbed mental state, the Middletons seem to have agreed to seek a companion to help care for her. Elizabeth Mitchell, mentioned in the following letter, was the first woman hired in this role.

Catherine's extreme irritability had alarmed her mother as early as 1827, when at the age of fifteen she arrived in St. Petersburg from England. Rather than recovering, this talented girl, whom a friend remembered as a gentle and timid child,[1] grew angry, unpredictable, and even violent. She took a dislike to her mother and had a seemingly perverse way of putting her fingers in her ears when someone spoke to her. The doctors of the time, having never heard of schizophrenia, had nothing to offer except that Catherine's sickness came from the stomach.

Henry Middleton always insisted that Catherine should remain at home. Sometimes she was quite calm. Some people, like Mrs. Middleton's friend Sarah Pogson Smith, or her brother Arthur, could coax her into playing the piano or taking part in what was going on around her. But she remained a burden, probably an embarrassment, and certainly a source of enormous anxiety and sadness for the whole family.

1. E. Baker to EMF, April 16, 1860, PHi, BrC.

To Mrs. Fisher, Philadelphia

Clinton hotel July 11<u>th</u> [1839]

My dearest Eliza

Here we are at length, after 8 days of suffering from heat, calms & the various miseries of a sea voyage, & for the last two days the most painful apprehensions of being detained at Quarantine which kept us in fearful suspense– The Ship <u>is</u> detained, but the passengers after being examined by the Physician were allowed to proceed in a sloop to this place– You may imagine my happiness in meeting Harry & Ed<u>d</u>– the former looks very thin & not nearly as well as I was led to expect from your account of him– He put your letter into my hand which was an additional pleasure. Your Father says he shall leave this for Newport early next week– You say you cannot leave Philad<u>a</u> before next Wednesday the 16<u>th</u> whether the Massachusets will sail on that day, or on the 15<u>th</u> we do not yet know– It would be more agreeable of course to have you on board with us, so that I hope you will be able to meet us on board–

Your Father says you need make no scruple about bringing your Maid Servant with you. We shall not require her assistance, as he insisted upon bringing on an Irish Girl as housemaid & to assist in washing & besides her he has at last consented to my taking E[lizabeth] Mitchell[1] the woman Miss Moore recommended & whom he positively denied me the satisfaction of having when I ventured to request the favour– but more of this when we meet– A Cook remains to be engaged, & I suppose he will engage the same we had last summer for she has written to beg we would– bad as she is– As to Ben, y<u>r</u> Father positively declares he will not take him into his service– he will have no coloured servants of his <u>own</u>, yours he puts out of the question as you will have the direction of her yourself. He has brought on with him a White Man to serve as waiter &c, & he seems a good servant.

Who do you think was our protegée on the voyage? M<u>me</u> Cuvillier. I acted as interpreter for her, on all occasions, & we used to sit together on deck & converse when I put down my book, which of course was much more amusing to me than any thing she could say– but she is lively & obliging. I recommended her to go to the same boarding house that M<u>rs</u> P[eter] Smith[2] lives at, & dropped her there in my way this morn<u>g</u> I hope she will deliver my message to M<u>rs</u> S. & that I shall see her this Eve<u>g</u> M<u>me</u> is going to sail for Havre on the 16<u>th</u>– Miss Moore unfortunately for me is in the country. Will<u>m</u> was in the dumps during the whole passage but now seems to have regained his spirits– I must hasten to seal this as the post goes to Phil<u>a</u> at 5 o'clock with the united love of all the [family] to you & M<u>r</u> F. & with best regards to M<u>rs</u> Fisher &

Mrs Harrison & love to Mary believe me my dearest Eliza y^r Affect^{te} Mother M. H. M.

Let me hear from you frequently– Pray procure for me & bring with you five doll^s worth of best black Tea– Phila^a is famous for it & Mrs F. will be good enough to recommend you to the best store–

PHi

    1. Elizabeth Mitchell became Catherine's companion and remained with the Middletons for about a year.
    2. Sarah (Pogson) Smith came to Charleston with her family from England in the 1790s and was the widow of Judge Peter Smith. A cheerful, lively person, she was a helpful friend to Mrs. Middleton and, as she was often in Philadelphia, to Eliza as well. She was a frequent visitor at the Fishers' house.

⌢

Fisher and Eliza stayed in Newport until September, Fisher having agreed before their wedding that Eliza would be able to spend a good part of each summer with her family.

By early October, after their trip through New England visiting friends and sightseeing, the Fishers were back in Philadelphia. Eliza was counting on having her parents join them for the winter, since her father had said at the time she and Fisher were engaged that he and Mrs. Middleton might take a house in Philadelphia. Fisher, who had a pretty clear view of his father-in-law, judged—correctly, as it turned out—that this would never happen. "His ties to Carolina are too strong for this," Fisher told Uncle Harrison, "and I don't think he would be willing to trust his estate to the management of others."[1]

Fisher did, however, ask his uncle to engage rooms for the Middletons for a shorter visit, saying, "Mr. Middleton is a good deal influenced by the comforts around him. . . . In speaking to Badger you can hint to him the importance of giving his Hotel a Carolinian Reputation & as he is a Yankee & values titles you may call Mr M. 'Governor'."[2]

    1. JFF to the Harrisons, April 1, 1839, PHi, C/F.
    2. JFF to GH, September 18, 1839, PHi, BrC.

To Mrs. Middleton, Newport

[Tremont House] Boston – Septr 18$^{\underline{th}}$ 1839

My dear Mamma,

    I did not write yesterday because I was expecting to see Harry, & thought it best to defer sending a letter until I could tell you something of our plans–

I did not see him until this morning, for I was driving out in the afternoon, & he was in the Bath when I returned for a few minutes before I went to drink tea with Mrs Ritchie,[1] who was so agreeable that we stayed there until ten o'clk–

We had a very dusty and rather warm drive to Taunton [*Massachusetts*][2] on Monday– in a crowded stage coach, and could not help regretting the companions we were to have had– But indeed I thought much more of those with whom I travelled the same route just three years before, and altho' I endeavored to be cheerful, I could not succeed, & throughout the journey and since my arrival, have had a weight on my spirits which I try in vain to shake off– We were all so gay when I was last here, and enjoyed ourselves so much– with so little care for the future, and hardly any but pleasant recollections in the Past![3] But I will not sadden you by dwelling now upon what we can never cease to regret–

Papa's permission to Fisher [to] make enquiries about the rooms in Seventh S^t [*at the Marshall House,*] was very opportunely granted and the prospect of having you with me in Phil^a is very consoling, and now anticipated with some confidence. Fisher is writing today to Mr Harrison & begging him to speak to Badger on the subject & advise him to write to Papa about the terms &c– which I hope will all be satisfactorily arranged– We have almost given up our plan of going to the W[hi]te Mount^{ns} and now think of staying here until Monday and then making a tour of 5 days to the Manadnock Mount^n in New Hampshire, & down the Connecticut River as far as Springfield, & then crossing the country to Worcester and thence back here by railroad. This part of the country is said to be beautiful, & the climate much more agreeable at this season than that of The White Mountains, and I fancy we shall decide upon this plan and put it into execution, persuading the Wadsworths[4] & their party to join us if we can– as it will only take them three days out of their intended route to Hartford– and I dare say Harry will have no objection to prolong his tour with the charming and delightful Miss W[adsworth]. I have not yet seen her or Miss Harper,[5] but am going in to their Parlour when I have finished this– There are some distinguished English here at present. Col. and L[ad]y Catherine Harcourt, the daughter of Ld Liverpool & son of the Archbishop of York. They were invited to dine at Mrs Ritchie's today but declined, & proposed meeting us there in the eveng instead as their whole morng & afternoon was to be devoted to sightseeing. I am told she is an excellent nurse & a very accomplished woman.

We went yesterday morng to the Athenaeum and saw some good pictures, and in the afternoon, drove out to Cambridgeport and paid a short visit to Wash^n Allston[6] in his Studio, where he rec^d us very politely & shewed us his last picture of a noble Roman Lady, which disappointed me at first, but after-wards grew upon me so much, that I left the room reluctantly, & w$\underline{d}$ willingly have gazed longer upon the soft & meaning eyes with such a deep & dreamy expression– But after answering the Painter's questions about Uncle J. I. M[id-dleton] with whom he appeared well acquainted, we made the best of our way out of his Atelier, & left him to eat his dinner which was waiting, in an atmo-sphere that could not have been much below 90– We then dropped a card upon M$\underline{rs}$ Sparks[7] in Cambridge, & returned to Boston thro' Brighton & several other pretty little villages– The immediate vicinity of this town is certainly more highly cultivated than the environs of Phil$\underline{a}$ and the country houses larger & more numerous but they have nothing as fine as the banks of the Schuylkill & the Wissahiccon. M$\underline{r}$ [Harrison Gray] Otis has just come in to propose a drive this morng but I prefer walking, & we sh$\underline{d}$ not have time to do both, altho' M$\underline{rs}$ R[itchie] does not dine until 5– As we do not leave B[oston] for several days I hope to hear at least once from you dear Mamma– With love to Papa, W$\underline{m}$ Kitty & Mary I am Yr most affectionate Daughter Eliza

Fisher begs his kindest remembrances.

Private Collection

1. Sophia (Mrs. Andrew) Ritchie (1798–1874), the daughter of Harrison Gray and Sally (Foster) Otis, was named after her parents' close friend (and Fisher's aunt), Sophia Francis Harrison. She made several visits to the Harrisons in Philadelphia while she was growing up and was like an older sister to Fisher.

2. Their route was probably from Newport to Fall River, Massachusetts, then to Taunton and north from there to Boston.

3. Eliza had been to Boston with her sister, Maria Pringle, in 1836.

4. The Wadsworths lived in Geneseo, New York, but also had family connections to Hartford, Connecticut. Harry, along with many others, was enchanted by Miss Eliza-beth Wadsworth. In addition to her, the party may have included her brother, James, and his wife, the former Mary Wharton from Philadelphia.

5. Emily Louisa Hinton Harper (1812–1892), from Baltimore, was the daughter of former Sen. Robert Goodloe Harper (1765–1825) and his wife, Catherine (Carroll) Harper.

6. Washington Allston (1779–1843), from a prominent South Carolina family, sold the property he inherited there and went to London in 1801 to study painting with Benjamin West. After many years in Europe, he returned in 1818 to live in Boston and was by this time a well-known American painter.

7. Mrs. Jared Sparks, the former Mary Crowninshield Silsbee, had recently mar-ried Professor Sparks, historian, editor, and future president of Harvard. She was the daughter of Sen. Nathaniel Silsbee of Massachusetts. Fisher described her as a "distin-guished blue Stocking belle." JFF to Sophia Harrison, Aug. 16, 1839, PHi, BrC.

～

To Mrs. Middleton, Newport

Philadelphia, Octr 7$^{\underline{th}}$ 1839

My dearest Mamma,

As I expected I had not a moment's time yesterday to write, but I begin the first thing after breakfast this morning, fearing that if I delay at all, I shall be prevented or interrupted– Edward, who I suppose is with you, has no doubt told you how rough & disagreeable a passage we had to New York, where we did not arrive until 1/2 past ten– and of my being fortunate enough to see all the friends I cared about, on Saturday– I was sorry not to be able to induce Ned to come on with us, if only for one day, but I believe he was right to attend first to his orders, and I hope that he may yet find time to pay us a little visit– I shall not tell you anything of our evening divided with Miss Moore & Mrs Barclay, for of course he will already have forestalled all such communications– so I will merely give you an account of our reception here, the journey being always uninteresting in itself, & only rendered agreeable by pleasant companionship–

We were met by the news of the great conflagration here at Bordentown,[1] and Fisher felt some anxiety for his Uncle's property situated in the lower part of the town, which at first was represented as one scene of ruin and devastation from Water Street to Second– But fortunately it escaped and the Broadwood Piano also, the last very narrowly for both the Transportation Offices were burnt the very evening of the day it was removed thence– But to return to the fire– It was very much exaggerated, as most NewsPaper accounts are, but has been very destructive, & the loss is now estimated at 2 hundred & 50 thousand instead of two millions of dollars– As we approached the city we saw distinctly the smoke curling up at several miles distances, and the crowd was so great at the Chesnut S^{t} wharf, where they usually land, that we were taken to Dock S^{t} instead, where we found Mr Harrison's carriage waiting for us, and soon after were most affectionately greeted by M^{rs} F[isher] & M^{rs} H[arrison] who were both delighted to see us, & gave us the most cordial reception–

It was rather a relief to learn that altho' the Piano had been sent up here from the Office on a <u>common Dray</u>, wonderful to say it was not in the least injured by such rough treatment, & thanks to its being so admirably packed was not even jarred and is very little out of tune. It is a delightful Instrument, and very handsome externally, plain, but perfectly well finished, which indeed it ought to be, as it is the most expensive kind he makes– The tone is very clear & at the same time full & rich– and in short I am enchanted with it, and I have no doubt it will give great satisfaction, and be fully worth 12 hundred dollars–[2] and outlast three American Ins[trumen]ts. It was really shameful to send it on one of the roughest conveyances over the paved Streets, the [*missing*] were on the way down for it, when to M^{rs} F's horror, it appeared at the door on a dray without springs– and she dreaded to open it, thinking of course it might have been knocked to pieces– Since it has so miraculously escaped that danger, and the fire besides, I am in hopes it is guarded by some good genius within, who will preserve it from the evil influences of our changeable climate & anthracite coal, which is to be entirely discarded from the drawing room. Badger says that you may burn Liverpool Coal [*at the Marshall House*] if you prefer it, but the grates w^{d} not admit wood in sufficient quantities to give enough warmth. He promises to do every thing to make you as comfortable as possible, and appears to be very civil & obliging–

I have not yet seen many persons, for I was too much tired after unpacking on Saturday to go to Mme Grelaud's[3] in the eveng. & hear Mlle Pardi[4] play on the Harp. We are going to have that pleasure tonight, at a concert given by her and Mme Albini Vellani– a very good cantatrice I am told. We had only a few persons here last night, Mr Cole[5] among others, who came on with us from N.Y. for the pleasure of our society. He is a very good natured fellow, but not otherwise remarkable– There are a good many English here– and I find that my Boston acquaintance, Mrs Col. Shaw, has a letter for me from Col. Clive, which I have not yet seen however, as hearing that I was out of town, she did not send it– I wonder that she did not deliver it at the Tremont [*hotel in Boston,*] but perhaps did not know my name–

I presume that Harry is on the wing for N.Y. where I hope he may find the gentle dove[6] before she seeks her winter nest– Goodbye dearest Mamma, write very soon to y^{r} affectionate Daughter Eliza

Best love to Papa and the rest– I am just going to see Mme Grelaud & talk to her about Mary.

Fisher begs his best.

Private Collection

1. Bordentown, New Jersey, is on the east shore of the Delaware River, north of Philadelphia.

2. The amount $1,200 would be approximately $17,000 in 1999 dollars. Dollar conversion factor from RSahr, OrStU.

3. Mme Deborah Grelaud, a French refugee, perhaps from Haiti, who started a school for girls in the early 1800s, attracted students from the south as well as from Philadelphia. The fee was $500 a year. In 1839, the school was at 120 South Third Street.

Lucy L. Bowie, "Madame Grelaud's French School," *Maryland Historical Magazine* 39, no. 2 (June 1944).

4. Mlle Virginia Pardi (later Mme Marras) was an Italian harpist who also taught piano, harp, and singing. She lived next to the Fishers, at the Albion House on Chestnut street.

Mlle Vellani, prima donna of La Scala, had recently performed in Havana with Mlle Pardi.

5. A. Lowery Cole, an English army officer posted in Canada, was a nephew of the Earl of Enniskillen. In later correspondence he told the Fishers how much he appreciated their hospitality.

6. Elizabeth Wadsworth.

William's interest in Julia Ward was an absorbing subject of conversation in the Middleton family throughout the summer of 1839. Julia, who was the daughter of Samuel and Julia (Cutler) Ward, was then twenty and spent the summers in Newport, where her father[1] owned a house not far from the Middletons. She and Eliza were good friends who enjoyed music and shared a love of learning in general. Julia and William also saw a good deal of each other and, by the end of the summer, were talking about marriage.

Julia's mother had died when she was a little girl, so her father, a prominent New York banker, felt particularly responsible for his three young daughters. A religious man, Sam Ward did not approve of their mixing in fashionable society and was known to keep a "close watch" over Julia, who was both intelligent and charming. Fisher thought he was capable of "keep[ing] her away from a house where there are still unmarried men,"[2] and, indeed, Julia later remembered that her father, "with all his noble generosity and overweening affection, sometimes appeared to me as my jailer."[3]

When Ward fell ill and died in the fall of 1839, Julia felt guilty that she had not appreciated her father's "great kindness" and that she had sometimes disobeyed his wish to keep her out of "frivolous society."[4]

At the same time, Edward Middleton was going through something of a crisis. Twenty-nine years old and already with more than a decade of service in the navy behind him, he was so depressed at the prospect of being sent to sea again that he even thought of resigning. His father, who had been through the same thing in 1823 when Oliver resigned *his* commission after six years in the navy, was not pleased. He had done his best to establish each of his sons in a profession but was still supporting Harry as well as helping John through the difficult economic times and did not relish the thought of supporting Edward as well. Edward stayed in the navy.

1. Samuel Ward (1786–1839) was a founding partner of Prime, Ward and King, a leading banking firm in New York. In 1838 he arranged a loan of gold from the Bank of England which saved the banks of New York by allowing them to resume specie payments after the panic in 1837. It was thought that strain from that crisis led to his death in 1839.

2. JFF to Sophia Harrison, July 22, 1839, and JFF to GH, August 3, 1839, PHi, BrC.

3. Julia Ward Howe, *Reminiscences, 1819–1899* (Boston: Houghton Mifflin, 1899), 49.

4. Ibid., 53.

To Mrs. Fisher, Philadelphia

Newport Octr 11th 1839

My dearest Eliza

I had the pleasure of receiving your letter on Wednesday, & should have answered it yesterday had I seen Ed^d, or got my letter from my brother that I might have something worth communicating. This morning has brought a letter from Ed^d dated from Boston 9th ins^t to W^m– I copy it that you may the better understand his feelings poor fellow! You may imagine the pain I feel at the idea of his leaving this country for so long a period without my seeing him for a day. "I have just arrived here & reported myself for duty on board the Marion to sail on the 15th ins^t for the Brazils, I have however requested the Sec^y of the Navy[1] to revoke my orders which I have some hopes he will do. I intended to have stopped at Newport in order to see you all on my way, but thought it best to report first & then get leave to go for a day or two, which I am afraid I shall not be able to obtain, as I shall be very busy if I have the misfortune to fail in my application to be detached. I shall receive an answer from the Department on friday, & shall then inform you whether I have succeeded or not. So anxious am I to be detached that I would consent to sacrifice almost any thing to succeed." The remainder expresses his satisfaction at having seen you, & some commissions for W^m to execute for him–

Upon my expressing my regret at the destination in view, & my hope that it might be altered, your Father became very angry, & declared he would allow him nothing for his maintenance should he give up his profession & then complained of his want of ambition &c– I see no reason why Edward should not have some other appointment without being obliged to quit the Navy– we must hope he may succeed in relinquishing this disagreeable station– As soon as I know the result of his application you shall hear of it.

In the mean time it is William's intention to go to see him if he should not come this Eve^g or tomorrow, so that probably he may defer his trip to Boston until Sunday morn^g– He will I suppose go to N.Y. on Tuesday as our Neighbours [*the Wards*] are to go next Monday. Your Father also is going there but has not yet fixed upon the day. He will spend a few days there & then return to plant trees here, which will occupy him probably a week longer, so that we shall I presume not remove to N.Y. before the 28$^{\underline{th}}$.

W$^{\underline{m}}$ has just come in to tell me I am to have a visit presently from J[ulia Ward] whom he met in the town, & that her Father in consequence of the Bank affair in N.Y. will go there tomorrow. He has in some degree reconciled me to the thought of Ed$^{\underline{d}}$'s appointment for he says Rio is a healthy place, & that after remaining there some time, he may in all probability be many years at liberty to go where he likes– Should his request be granted, that is, to occupy some other station, he has the promise of Capt Gallagher[2] of the N.C. to make him his acting Lieu^t in case of his being promoted, which he has a prospect of being ere long– Cath$^{\underline{e}}$ has been taking her turn with Harry & W$^{\underline{m}}$ in reading aloud in the evenings "Concealment"[3] which is very interesting. Miss Fletcher to judge from the sentiments diffused through the work must be fully worthy of the attachment felt for her by her old admirer. He [*Harry*] is still wavering cannot make up his mind, thinks himself too old to venture upon changing his condition & thinks it would be useless to go to N.Y. for only a few days– sh$^{\underline{d}}$ the fair one remain at Baltimore for any time he w$^{\underline{d}}$ probably go there– en attendant [*meanwhile*] I believe he will stay here until we all move–

Miss W[ard] has just gone– by W[illiam]'s permission, I expressed my satisfaction at the prospect of her becoming one of the family & she cannot today make the remark of my way of receiving her which she did last week– She took a turn with us in the Garden to see the improvements going on & then sang two or three pretty airs– brought her miniature which I think a very good likeness. Y$^{\underline{r}}$ Father has given up his intention of making the lot[4] a recreation for the horses & has thrown down the fence & taken it all into the garden– so that there is a vast deal of planting going on. I must now hasten to send this off M$^{\underline{rs}}$ Pinckney[5] & M$^{\underline{rs}}$ Izard having called. Sophia [Thorndike] sends her love to you she has called twice– Miss W[ard] thinks she shall not go before Monday. With kind remembrance to M$^{\underline{r}}$ & M$^{\underline{rs}}$ Fisher & also to M$^{\underline{rs}}$ Harrison I am dearest Eliza y$^{\underline{r}}$ Affect^e Mother M. H. M.
all the party send their love–

PHi

1. James Kirke Paulding (1778–1860), New York author and politician, was secretary of the navy under President Van Buren, 1837–1841.

2. Capt. John Gallagher (d. 1842) was stationed at the New York Navy Yard in command of the U.S.S. *North Carolina*.

3. *Concealment*: a novel published anonymously in London about 1821. The author was Mary Fletcher of Edinburgh, whom Harry Middleton may have known when he studied law there, 1820–22.

4. In September 1839, Henry Middleton purchased from George Noble Jones, from Savannah, Georgia, a piece of the land Jones had recently bought adjacent to the Middletons' Newport house. On the main parcel, Jones built a Gothic cottage now known as Kingscote.

5. Elizabeth (Izard) Pinckney (1784–1862) was the wife of Col. Thomas Pinckney (1780–1842). Mrs. Izard was her daughter, Rosetta Ella, who had recently married her cousin, Ralph Stead Izard, Jr.

⌒

To Mrs. Middleton, Newport

Philadelphia – Oct 14$\underline{^{th}}$ 1839

My dearest Mamma,

I had been looking with some anxiety since Friday for a letter from you, and was therefore delighted to find that I had alarmed myself needlessly, and that you were only waiting to write that you might tell me more of Edward and his plans– I have only a few minutes ago rec$\underline{^{d}}$ y$\underline{^{rs}}$ of the 11$\underline{^{th}}$ & immediately set about answering it. I should have written much more fully last time, if I had not been convinced that Ned was with you, & would be able to tell you all I could write– I am indeed sorry that he did not stop & see you on his way to Boston, for I suppose there is little chance of his orders being revoked, or even of his having time to run on to NewPort before his departure– He told me that if he were obliged to go to Brazil, he might very possibly obtain leave to return thence after his Promotion– So that at any rate I hope we shall have him with us again before many months are past– and as you say the Station is a very healthy one– besides the master ship is a place of trust & altogether he might have fared much worse– We are all very sorry not to see him here– he is a great favorite with M$\underline{^{rs}}$ F– and at 156[1] also– They are looking forward with much pleasure to y$\underline{^{r}}$ arrival, and seem disposed to give you as warm a welcome as you could desire– For my part it is the only thing wanting to complete my happiness, for I have everything else to render me perfectly so– and cannot even complain as I did before, of not having sufficient Leisure to read & practise– as I now have all the mornings to myself for exercise & study, & the afternoons for music.

I have been quite dissipated of late– Thursday we had a very pleasant little party at home, Friday I went to a Concert, & Saturday to the Theatre– for the first time for 2 years nearly– It was Kean's[2] benefit, and the last time he was to act here, so I would not miss the opportunity– And the inducement for going was to take Mary [Middleton] who seemed rather pleased at the idea but was much more alarmed than pleased, by the cheering the governor in the next box to us, & the applause bestowed on Kean, which was really deafening– He is too vehement and rapid in his enunciation, & frequently rants too much for my taste, but I was nevertheless much affected by his acting and the play, which is deeply interesting and could not restrain my tears several times. It was the "Lady of Lyons" by Bulwer,[3] who I had no idea could write so well, and express noble & generous sentiments with so much truth & feeling– Fanny Butler who was in the opposite Box appeared to enter fully into the fictitious woes of the hero, and no doubt personified herself with the heroine, for she sobbed aloud in many parts, and I could not help wishing that she could have changed places with the miserable [*missing*] stick who represented that character–

Whether I took cold at the Theatre or yesterday at Church, where it was very warm & whence we drove home in the afternoon thro' a thunderstorm & torrents of rain, I cannot decide, but today I am confined to the house by a severe cold in the head & hoarseness <u>un</u>accompanied however by sore throat, which consoles me for the other inconveniences of salt rheum– I have ridden once on Horseback, & if the weather is favourable tomorrow and my sniffling decreased, I shall mount again. Fisher begs me to tell you with his best regards, that he sent a bill of exchange on A. & G. Ralstons of London for the amount of his debt to Broadwood [*for Eliza's piano,*] by the Packet of the 10$\underline{th}$ of which he will also send a duplicate & triplicate by the next Packet– After all the Piano is not so dear as we thought it w$\underline{d}$ be– Including every expense of freight here &c it costs one thousand and 70 dollars– which I think it is well worth– M$\underline{r}$ [Hartman] Kuhn[4] & many good judges think it the finest Instrument they ever heard, & I perfectly agree with their high opinion of its merits. I would write & thank Aunt Scarboro' for all the trouble she took about it, but if she is so much indisposed it might just worry her to receive a letter, so that I believe I will send her a message of thanks when I write to Aunt Hering– I have not rec$\underline{d}$ the letter from her, that you mention, but hope it will yet be forthcoming– Pray tell Sophia [Thorndike] I mean to write to her very soon, & that I have some very agreeable intelligence to communicate. This will irritate her bump of inquisitiveness I daresay, & therefore as I think it already duly developed, perhaps in order to maintain the just balance of her inquiring organs with the rest, you had better not say a word about it– But the fact is that M$\underline{rs}$ Fisher has proposed to Fisher, without either of us suggesting a syllable, to make arrangements upstairs so as to be able to receive S– at Xmas time, and as it was entirely her own proposal, I am sure she w$\underline{d}$ not make it without wishing to have her– And as you may suppose I am delighted to think that poor Sophia's dreary winters at N[ew] Port will be shortened by a visit to me– In little more than a fortnight I shall have the pleasure of seeing you all. How glad I shall be to shew you my comfortable and happy home– M$\underline{rs}$ F. begs me to return y$\underline{r}$ remembrances in the kindest possible manner. Pray do not delay answering this scrawl & letting me know of Edw$\underline{d}$'s movements. I am sorry that Harry has not more <u>enterprise</u>, without which of course he cannot succeed–[5] Pray give my love to him & say I am afraid by his delay he has missed his chance for some months at least– I suppose neither Papa or W$\underline{m}$ are with you, but if H[arry] remains, you will not be at a loss for companionship– With love to Kitty I am my dearest Mamma Y$\underline{r}$ affectionate Daughter Eliza

Private Collection

1. The Harrisons' house was 156 Chestnut Street, between Sixth and Seventh Streets. The Fishers', no. 170 , was in the next block, between Seventh and Eighth Streets.
2. Charles Kean (1811–1868) was an English actor, the son of the more famous tragedian Edmund Kean. This was not his last performance; he was still in town in January, advertising "positively" his last.
3. Edward G. E. L. Bulwer, Baron Lytton (1803–1873), was a popular English writer as well as politician. The Middletons read his novels *Zanoni* and *Night and Morning*. He wrote *Lady of Lyons* in 1838.
4. Hartman Kuhn (1784–1860) was a graduate and trustee of the University of Pennsylvania and a veteran of the War of 1812. He was, in Francis Fisher's opinion, a "sensible and honourable man" who made his wife, the former Ellen Lyle, "a most excellent husband." He was the son of Adam Kuhn (1741–1817), distinguished professor of medicine at the University of Pennsylvania. JFF, *Recollections,* 215.
5. The Middletons thought Harry was not energetic enough in his pursuit of Miss Wadsworth.

∼

To Mrs. Middleton, Newport

Monday – Phil$\underline{a}$ Oct$\underline{r}$ 21$\underline{st}$ 1839

It is half past nine, and I am afraid the postman has passed, without leaving a letter from you, my dearest Mamma– I am greatly disappointed, but will try & be satisfied with the hope of receiving one tomorrow– Besides my desire to hear from NewPort, I am particularly anxious to know whether poor Ned sailed or has been lucky enough to get off this time– But I must restrain my impatience, as it cannot be gratified today– D$^{\underline{r}}$ Mifflin[1] tells me he saw W$^{\underline{m}}$ in Boston last Wednesday, but M$^{\underline{r}}$ Paulding's answer had not yet been rec$^{\underline{d}}$ I trust it may be a favourable one–

When I last wrote I had a violent cold which lasted several days, but was finally cured by a long warm ride on Horseback. We had Percy Drayton[2] for a companion, and the following day (Thursday) asked Margaret Sergeant to accompany us– but the sun was so oppressively warm that I could not enjoy the ride– on Friday we had many visits to pay which occupied the greater part of the morng– and immediately after an early dinner, we drove out to the monthly exhibition of the Blind at the Institution,[3] which was really very interesting. Mary went with us & was much pleased– We saw them thread needles with their tongue, read very fluently from the book printed with raised type, answer questions in Geography by consulting a map with the Boundaries, rivers, &c raised in a similar way, and mathematical questions without any assistance at all. The least agreeable part of the exhibition was their music, which was very bad, some in the Orchestre playing well but others horribly false, which of course spoilt the whole effect– and the singing, with the exception of one voice, was execrable, much to my astonishment, for I fancied that by the loss of one sense, the others, and that of hearing especially w$^{\underline{d}}$ be much improved, and rendered more acute– This did not appear to be at all the case however, for they screeched and squalled, the women particularly, in the most excruciating manner, and I was glad enough when the Finale was announced. Perhaps their want of progress may be owing to bad instruction, for Fisher declares that they are going backward in music, and do not play & sing as well as they did last year, but certain it is that the ears of some of them, must be almost as defective as their eyes for such discord I never heard– The room was intensely hot, and I was rejoiced to escape from both these evils, a combination of which I suppose brought on the headache which sent me early to bed, and prevented my spending the eveng at Aunt H's–

Saturday it poured the whole day, & I had plenty of time for reading, practising and working–[4] M$^{\underline{rs}}$ Willing came in to Tea, and made herself very agreeable– She went to the Piano, and admired its tone extremely– & proposed singing with me. We took up Gabussi,[5] and sang about a dozen of them together very tolerably, considering that she had never seen them before, & I was so much out of practise. She was delighted with them, and took the book home with her, promising to learn them all perfectly– and also to send me some Duetts for Piano & Harp, which we intend to play for you– I told her the Harp was y$^{\underline{r}}$ favorite instrument, and that I knew you w$^{\underline{d}}$ be very much gratified to hear it again and by such a Performer, and she very obligingly promised to come down & play <u>for you</u> whenever you pleased. At the same time making particular enquiries about Papa Harry & W<u>m</u>. She says she likes <u>all</u> the Middletons and will do anything for them–

Tuesday– No letter again today– which is a greater disappointment than yesterday's– I have half a mind to <u>punish</u> you by not sending this for several days– but as I am sure your disappointment w<u>d</u> be by no means equal to my own, the <u>punishment</u> w<u>d</u> be inadequate– Indeed my dear Mamma you must not neglect me so, another week– I have now been absent from you nearly 3 weeks, and I have only rec<u>d</u> <u>one</u> letter from you– Percy Drayton told me yesterday that he had heard that Ned had got off– I hope it may be true. We had a long & delightful ride on horseback yesterday of nearly 3 hours– Up the Wissahiccon as far as Manayunk– I hope the weather will be pleasant enough for driving, when you first arrive, for I want very much to shew you some of our very pretty scenery– The woods have lost some of their beauty since these last heavy rains, but have still many varied tints, altho' the foliage is no longer so glorious as when we saw it a week ago– My little Horse behaved admirably, and never attempted to shy– We are going out to M<u>rs</u> Pierce Butler's tomorrow– I met her in the street, and she strided up and shook hands very cordially with me– She is going to the South on the 1<u>st</u> of Dec<u>r</u> & Mary Appleton[6] accompanies her. They will be in Charleston at the time of the races,[7] & return early in the spring– I went last eveng. to a very pleasant little party given to me by M<u>rs</u> R[obert] Hare–[8] I had a great many agreeable beaux to talk to, and enjoyed myself very much– They are all (the Hares I mean) intelligent and amiable, and appear disposed to be very sociable– I am frequently asked when you are coming, & every body congratulates me on the prospect of having you so near me– M<u>rs</u> N[oble] Jones[9] is to spend the winter at the Marshall House, & the Van Rensellaers also– M<u>rs</u> [Van] R[ensselaer][10] has been shamefully treated by the old Patroon, & does not like to live in such different style as her limited income must now oblige her, in Albany or New York– I am going out to see Miss Gadsden & one or two other people, and must close this scrawl. With love to all around you, I am dearest Mamma y<u>r</u> <u>neglected</u> but still affectionate Daughter Eliza

Private Collection

1. Dr. Charles Mifflin, a Philadelphian, married Mary Crowninshield of Boston and lived there.

2. Percival Drayton (1812–1865), from South Carolina, was a naval officer. He

was the son of William Drayton (who was now living in Philadelphia) and his first wife, the former Ann Gadsden. During the Civil War, Percy Drayton, like his friend Edward Middleton, remained in the U.S. Navy.

3. The Pennsylvania Institution for the Instruction of the Blind was one of Fisher's principal interests. One of its founders, he served on the board of managers until his death.

4. *Work* or *working* in a context such as this generally means needlework.

5. Vincenzo Gabussi (1800–1846) was an Italian composer and singing teacher who was living at that time in London. In addition to opera and chamber music, he composed many songs and duets.

6. Mary Appleton (who became Mrs. Robert Mackintosh) was a daughter of Boston businessman Nathan Appleton (1779–1861) and his first wife, Maria Theresa Gold (d. 1833). Appleton became very wealthy in the 1830s and 1840s as one of the original investors in the Lowell, Massachusetts, cotton mills.

7. Charleston's annual Race Week in February was the social highpoint of the year. People came from all over the Low Country for balls, parties, and a chance to see friends.

8. Harriett (Clark) Hare, originally from Providence, Rhode Island, was the wife of Dr. Robert Hare, professor of chemistry at the University of Pennsylvania.

9. Mrs. Sarah (Campbell) Jones (d. 1843), the widow of Noble W. Jones from Savannah, Georgia, spent the summers in Newport. She had two daughters, Fenwick and Mary; it was her son, George, who bought the property next to the Middletons' in Newport in 1839.

10. Cornelia (Patterson) Van Rensselaer was the second wife of Stephen Van Rensselaer III, whose family had controlled extensive lands in New York state since the Dutch settled the area in the seventeenth century. When he died in 1839, he left most of his property to his eldest sons.

～

To Mrs. Fisher, Philadelphia

Newport Octr 29$^{\underline{th}}$ [1839]

My dearest Eliza

You can have no reason to complain of my <u>neglect</u>, when you hear that I give you the earliest intelligence in my power of Edw$^{\underline{d}}$. He arrived yesterday just as we were sitting down to dine– this was you may believe a great pleasure but it was soon damped by his telling me his leave of absence was only for one day, & that the Sec$^{\underline{y}}$ of the Navy had written to say that his services on board the Marion could not be dispensed with.[1] This information he had written 4 days since, but it was only received this morning <u>after</u> his departure, for he left this at 6 o'clock with y$^{\underline{r}}$ Father who went with him as far as Providence. He appears (as I had heard from W$^{\underline{m}}$ before) more reconciled to the station, &

hopes his absence may not exceed a year. Mr Thorndike (the younger)[2] has given him several letters of introduction to his friends at Buenos Ayres which he expects to find a much pleasanter place than Rio– the Marion will probably touch at Madeira & the coast of Africa so that he cannot reach Brazil before the end of Dec^r· the vessel is quite ready to sail– that it is to do, in company with the Frig^{te} U.S. which is not quite ready, neither have the orders yet arrived for their departure. Should that be delayed until the 4th, Ed^d will try to pay us another flying visit. He begged me to give his love to you & to request you to write frequently to him. He rode out yesterday eve^g with Harry & called for a few minutes upon Miss Thorndike– he found both the M^r T's there. You have already heard from Sophia y^r Father's intention to remain here until the 4th of Novr which I begged her to communicate as she had the even^g before asked me for any message I might wish to send you, otherwise I should have returned you an answer on the same day. Our delay being unavoidable in consequence of y^r Father's planting trees, it is rather lucky that a week may be given to painting the rooms [*at the Marshall House*];[3] not that I conceive so short a time will be sufficient to dissipate the disagreeable smell. There is a kind of paint, the dead White, which is not of the glossy exterior [*kind,*] which leaves no bad smell– could you recommend it to Mr Badger? pray beg him to leave tubs of water in the rooms. The situation you mention of C[atherine]'s room is very convenient, & I promise myself great comfort there. W^m made a visit to N.Y. last week of two days– he is much annoyed at the prolongation of our stay here, & the words "Why so dull & mute fond lover" are very applicable to him at the present time.[4]

Y^r Father brought from N.Y. a very interesting book 'the Wonders of Geology' by Mantell[5] (who had been giving lectures at Brighton)– I began it, much pleased with the contents– Yesterday he put it up with a few other books for Edward. however I daresay he will get another copy & you may judge for yourself when we meet, of the merits of the work.

No letter from John since I wrote last! we may soon expect to hear of Sally's accouchement– poor soul! I hope she may recover from it speedily! Her Aunts[6] will I doubt not be attentive to her, & John being with her will be no small comfort. You may conclude from the time of our leaving this, allowing three days for remaining at N.Y. which I think quite sufficient, but which y^r Father may not; that we shall probably be in Phila^a on the 8th You are aware however of the uncertainty of his plans & movements, therefore it is best not to make sure of seeing us quite so soon. I shall write again to you my dearest Eliza before leaving this, in the mean time believe me y^r Affect^{te} Mother M. H. M.

Give my best regards to M͟r & M͟rs Fisher. Y͟r brothers send their love. Write so that I may receive y͟r letter on Sunday next–

PHi

1. Edward was to report to Boston for duty on the sloop *Marion*. It sailed for Brazil on November 10.

2. Israel Augustus Thorndike (1816–1845), called Augustus, was Sophie Thorndike's brother. He married Frances Macomb, the daughter of a sugar planter in Cuba, in 1841. The second Mr. Thorndike, mentioned later in this letter, was their father, Israel Thorndike, Jr. (1785–1867). (Sophie and Augustus's mother, Sally Otis Thorndike, had died in 1819.)

3. Mr. Badger was running behind schedule in painting and repapering the rooms the Middletons were to occupy. Catherine's room was to be near their private parlor. EMF to MHM, October 24, 1839, private collection.

4. Mrs. Middleton was quoting from a poem by Sir John Suckling (ca. 1637), but she mixed two lines. The first stanza begins: "Why so pale and wan, fond lover? / Prithee, why so pale?" The second begins: "Why so dull and mute, young sinner? / Prithee, why so mute?" *The Oxford Book of Seventeenth Century Verse*, ed. Sir Herbert Grierson and G. Bullough (London: Oxford University Press, 1958) 560.

5. Though a doctor, Gideon Algernon Mantell's (1790–1852) real passions were geology and paleontology. He published *The Wonders of Geology* in 1838.

6. Her own mother having died, Sally Middleton was particularly close to her father's half-sister, Mary (Alston) Pringle. The other aunt was Mary's sister-in-law, Emma (Pringle) Alston. Mary Alston and her brother, Charles, had married, respectively, William Bull Pringle and his sister Emma.

～

Once they left Newport, Eliza's parents and Kitty spent several weeks in Philadelphia before going on to South Carolina. This became part of their yearly travel pattern. By the time they left in December, Eliza knew that she would be having a baby in June. She was physically well but slightly anxious, and this probably added to her evident sadness at seeing her parents leave.

On this trip to the South, the Middletons went by train to Baltimore, from there by boat to Portsmouth, Virginia, then by train southwest across Virginia to Weldon, North Carolina, and then south through North Carolina to Wilmington, on the coast. Finally they took the overnight steamer to Charleston. This they considered preferable to going the whole way by sea!

To Mrs. Middleton, Charleston

Philadelphia – Thursday 19͟th Dec͟r 1839

Not having heard from you my dearest Mamma I conclude that you must have left Baltimore on Tuesday, and are by this time halfway on your road between Enfield and Wilmington, where I hope you will arrive tomorrow, and that on Saturday morng– you will be safe in Canonsboro'–¹ John & W͟ᵐ have no doubt been waiting for you there, for in a letter received this morng– from the latter he says he intends to be in town on the 20͟ᵗʰ, and the receipt of your letter announcing the change of plans would probably hasten his departure from Combahee– How very anxious I shall be to learn your safe arrival! After my entreaties to you to write immediately, I expect a few lines on Tuesday or Wednesday at farthest– and a most welcome Xmas gift they will be– I see by the Papers that some slight accident happened to the Locomotive, and that in consequence of the high wind, you crossed the river slowly & did not reach Baltimore until 5 in the afternoon. It was certainly not pleasant weather for travelling and I fear that Papa thought so too and not expecting you to brave such a tempest, did not join you on Monday eveng–² All this must remain conjecture for the present, but I shall be most happy to know facts instead, and every detail of your journey. If you were fortunate enough to procure an Extra, I don't think you could have been much fatigued by the 30 miles of staging, and I trust that everything went if not <u>smoothly</u> at least comfortably in comparison to being tossed in a berth at sea– and that you put up philosophi- cally with a few discomforts in N͟ᵒ Carolina with the reflection how much worse off you w͟ᵈ have been on board a dirty Packet Ship– I shall be much astonished if Papa does not acknowledge the truth of my oft repeated assertion, that the worst land journey (of which you had a small specimen in N͟ᵒ C͟ᵃ) is very prefer- able to a sea voyage under the most favourable circumstances–

I had a very long day after parting with you my dear Mamma– for I could fix my attention to nothing, and altho' Fisher like an amiable good soul, gave up his ride, and indeed his whole morning to read and walk with me, I hardly heard one page out of the 70 that sounded in my ears, nor answered half of the questions with which he afterwards tried to divert me– It was worse still in the eveng– at M͟ʳˢ Harrison's for I was so absent that the good old people must have observed my listlessness, which they perhaps attributed to fatigue from early rising, and therefore excused my retiring very soon– The following day I passed more profitably; after writing a long letter to Sophia, I listened with so much interest to Burnet³ that the hour for exercise came too soon, and I just took a run to Schuylkill all alone before dinner, practised afterwards & then went to the Lecture, at which I laughed a great deal at the Yankee twang and mispronunciations, without being in the least edified–⁴ We stopped at the Walns',⁵ when it was over, intending to spend the rest of the eveng– there but not finding them at home, went to M͟ʳˢ H[arrison]'s where Sally Ingersoll⁶ was delighted to meet me, and helped to make an hour pass pleasantly– Yesterday morng– Fisher was too busy to read to me, so I read to myself for 3 hours, and then trotted up with him to Dryburgh's garden[7] where I had the pleasure of seeing a beautiful bouquet cut and most tastefully arranged, and in the eveng of having it more admired than any in the room– returned home in time to sing an hour before dinner, having had the good fortune to find every body out, attended the German lesson in the afternoon, practised for nearly an hour more, and then became so much interested in Nicholas Nickleby,[8] that I could hardly put it down to dress for Mrs Coxe's[9] party– which however I enjoyed when once there, talking to several agreeable people–

It was a very handsome affair indeed, the supper and whole entertainment very elegant, and I fear that our's this eveng will be shifty in comparison. I suppose we shall have nearly 80 people in the two small rooms below and no amusement to offer them but Oysters and Ice creams and other light fare– But conversation I suppose they will come supplied with themselves, but as a great number of the bores have refused, and all the most agreeable people have accepted, I hope it will go off well. We are invited to go to the Dallas's[10] sociably[11] tomorrow eveng but I must decline sitting up a third night, dreading the effects of so much dissipation. Tell Harry that Mrs Willing came to apologize for not making her appearance tonight. If he had been here she w^d not have excused herself on the plea of her Baby's indisposition. Pray thank John[12] for his very acceptable letters from Columbia. I am indeed quite flattered that he should think of me, in the midst of his engrossing state business– Tell W^m with my love that I will answer his letter as soon as I have anything to say on the subject he is most anxious about– You can tell him of the contents of Julia's last, and I have heard nothing since except what Govr Francis[13] writes, that there is no will & that the estate [*Samuel Ward's*] is estimated over 400 thousand dollars.

And now my dearest Mamma adieu! Give my best love and Xmas congratulations and good wishes to all the dear party at M. Place and believe me as ever, Y^r most affectionate Daughter Eliza

Fisher by no means wishes to be omitted in kind messages, and begs me to add his kindest regards all round– Mrs F. begs also to be particularly remembered– She still suffers as much at night with her Rheumatism–

Private Collection

1. The Middletons' house in Charleston was in Cannonsboro, a section north of the city boundary.

2. Henry Middleton had probably stopped in Washington, D.C.

3. Gilbert Burnet (1643–1715), bishop of Salisbury under William and Mary, took

a broad view of church doctrine. His writings included "An Exposition of the 39 Articles of the Church of England."

4. The lecture may have been one of a series given at the Musical Fund Hall by "Yankee" Hill on "The Manners and Customs of the People of New England."

5. There were longstanding ties between the Walns and the Fishers. Mary (Wilcocks) Waln (1781–1841) and Mrs. Fisher were close friends, and their husbands had grown up together. Mrs. Waln's daughters, Sally (later Mrs. Benjamin Chew Wilcocks) and Mary (later Mrs. Richard Maxwell), lived with her.

6. Sally (Sarah Roberts) Ingersoll was the daughter of Quakers George and Elizabeth (Emlen) Roberts. Her husband, Harry Ingersoll (1809–1886), was the son of Charles J. and Mary (Wilcocks) Ingersoll.

7. Andrew Dryburgh, a leading Philadelphia florist, kept his garden near the Schuylkill River, at Fifth and Sassafras Streets.

8. Charles Dickens' immensely popular novel *Nicholas Nickleby* was appearing serially at that time.

9. Mrs. Daniel W. Coxe, the former Margaret Burd (d. 1845), was a cousin of Mrs. Fisher's and Mrs. Harrison's. She and her husband, who was a merchant, lived in the same block as the Fishers.

10. George Mifflin Dallas (1792–1864), a lawyer and a Democrat, served as minister to Russia in the mid-1830s and as James K. Polk's vice president, 1844–48. His wife was the former Sophia Chew Nicklin.

11. That is, informally.

12. Eliza's brother John was in his first term as a representative of Prince George Winyah district in the South Carolina state legislature in Columbia. He continued to serve until the late 1850s.

13. John Brown Francis (1791–1864) was the son of Mrs. Fisher's and Mrs. Harrison's brother, John Francis (1763–1796), who had been in business with John Brown in Providence, Rhode Island. John B. Francis was a lawyer; he served as governor of Rhode Island, 1833–1838, and as U.S. senator, 1844–45.

⌒

To Mrs. Fisher, Philadelphia

Charleston Dec.ʳ 21ˢᵗ 1839

According to my promise my dearest Eliza I lose no time in communicating to you the news of our arrival which happened this mornᵍ at 6 o'clock– We were detained on board until past 8 however– We found Willᵐ here looking very well– He had stopped at M[iddleton] P[lace] on his way from Combahee & left Sally & family there yesterday in good health– You desired me to give you every particular of our journey, to begin then with Baltimore– I arrived without fatigue at past 5 (owing to several detentions) at the Exchange [*Hotel*]– the house was crowded to excess– I was placed in a room at the top of it, & compelled to clamber up 3 p.ʳ of very high stairs to arrive at it– this drained me so violently, that I suffered exceedingly in consequence, for several days. I was obliged to go down & up stairs for breakfast & to receive the two M^{rs} & Miss Harper,[1] who all desired to be particularly remembered to you– we embarked for Portsmouth [*Virginia*] (y^{r} Father having arrived soon after us at Baltimore) at 3 o'clock, & arrived there safely on Wednesday morn^{g}, though my fatigue was so extreme, Harry & Elizth [Mitchell] were obliged to carry me upstairs. after breakfast we proceeded by the rail-car the jolting of which kept up my painful sensations– the stoppages were numberless & at length fortunately for <u>me</u> the Engine got out of the track, which caused so long a detention that the Cars arrived too late for the others which were to have carried us on at 2 o'clock, for we did not reach the starting point until 5 & then stopped at a house two miles from Weldon.

The relief of lying down on a feather bed was great, & I prudently remained on it until the next day at 12. I often thought while there, how Mrs Fisher with her notions of comfort & cleanliness would have been shocked had she been placed in such a room– The ceiling was formed of planks with beams laid across them, attached to which were cobwebs & wasp's nests innumerable! The floor raised two or three feet from the ground admitted Light, & cold air through the interstices of the planks– however I had a blazing fire, & obtained what I most wanted– rest. This airy mansion belongs to a Mr Geary Senator of the State Legis^{re} of N[orth] C[arolina]– We proceeded at 3 o'clock 2 miles to Weldon, then 30 more, & then entered the terrible Stage at 9 o'clock– I had the seat at the back to myself, & lay down on it during the 28 miles– It is impossible to describe the effect the jolting had upon me. I [ou]tlived it however, which I did not expect to do. It did not prevent me from thinking almost the whole way of you my dearest Eliza, & of the different manner in which you were passing <u>your</u> Thursday Eve^{g}–

We reentered the rail-car at about 2 o'clock in the morning, & by degrees I began to feel better. At 8 the manager told the passengers the frost was so great, we could not proceed for an hour or two & advised us to stop at a house– to take breakfast which we did, & at 1/2 past 9, reentered the Car & arrived without hindrance at Wilmington yesterday between 2 & 3– then embarked on board the N. Carolina, dined & fortunately had a very mild night for the passage. The vessel was so crowded, I could get only a cushion on the dining room bench to lie on, so that my sleep was constantly disturbed by the discomfort of my situation– my eyes feel it still—amen. Our fellow passengers were M^{rs} & Miss King on their way to <u>Cumberland Is^{d}</u> to visit Mrs Nightingale.[2] We were constantly near each other & I like them very much. They were under the care of Richard King the brother of Dr C. King y^{r} acquaintance who has just married a Miss Fisher of Philadᵃ. It was fortunate we arrived today for it began to rain as we came into the house & is a decidedly rainy day. Now, though I have told you of my sufferings, you must not imagine they are permanent– I feel nearly well & have no doubt I shall be perfectly so tomorrow–

The plan of yʳ Father is that I shall go to M.P. on Monday accompᵈ by Harry, Cathᵉ & Elizᵗʰ in a hired Carriage– the 4 horses he bought at N.Y. having all died on board the Anson!³ John will be at M.P. tomorrow (Sunday)– Wᵐ says Oliver was expected daily at Combahee– this is all I can hear from him– Pray give my best regards to Mʳˢ Fisher & Mʳˢ Harrison not forgetting Mʳ H & Mʳ F– Yʳ Father & brothers send their love to you & I am my dearest Eliza yʳ affectᵗᵉ Mother M. H. M.

P.S. Wᵐ begs you to write to him soon– do not forget to say something kind for me to my friends & acquaintances at Philadᵃ & to thank Mʳˢ Gibson for her very affectᵗᵉ note. Pray tell Mʳˢ Fisher her Tea was very much enjoyed– Elizᵗʰ unluckily dropped the jar of Strawberries on the pavement at Baltimore getting into the carriage–

PHi

1. Mrs. Harper, Sr., was Robert Goodloe Harper's widow and Emily Harper's mother. Mrs. Charles Harper, the second Mrs. Harper, was the widow of the Harpers' son Charles; she was the former Charlotte Chifelle of Charleston.

2. These were probably members of the Roswell King and Thomas Butler King families who lived on the sea islands off the coast of Georgia. Mrs. P. M. Nightingale's husband was a planter on Cumberland Island, the most southern of the Georgia coastal islands.

3. These were not the only horses that Henry Middleton bought in the North and then lost, usually as a result of a rough sea voyage to South Carolina. "I wonder he perseveres in this plan of sending horses to Carolina by sea, after such frequent losses," Emma wrote Eliza. EHS to EMF, November 16, 1840, PHi.

⌐

To Mrs. Middleton, Middleton Place

Philadelphia– Decʳ 27ᵗʰ 1839

I was so much disappointed at not hearing from you yesterday morning, my dearest Mamma, that I could not write to you– In great anxiety I sent in the evengᵍ– to the P.O. and to my delight, Murray returned with your letter of Saturday– I was overjoyed to hear that you had arrived safely, and today feel more grateful still since I have read in the morng's paper the accounts of the storm of Saturday night and of the damage done in the Charleston Harbour– How very fortunate you were to get in the preceding night and how thankful am I for your preservation and safety! But how much you must have suffered on the road in consequence of straining yourself in Baltimore! I wonder that Harry could put you up so many pair of stairs, when there were many other Hotels where you might have been better accomodated– I hope you have now entirely recovered from the effects of over fatigue there, and in the jolting stage afterward. So Mrs Butler was misinformed, and you <u>were</u> shaken over 28 miles of rough road instead of 10– and at night too! Did Papa neglect to write on for an Extra, or was there any difficulty in procuring one? You were indeed lucky to have so many hours rest, even at such an uncomfortable place as you describe <u>Senator</u> Geary's to be. But you must have been consoled by thinking that even there you were better off than at Sea– and if you had been on board the Anson! What a dreadfully rough passage they must have had to kill all the poor horses! and how very inconvenient their loss must be just now to Papa and John!

I am so fervently thankful that you were not at sea during the gale, and that altho' you suffered much from the fatigue of the journey, were feeling better, and were snugly housed on Saturday that I can hardly contain my rejoicings within the limits of moderation, and must have appeared a little out of my right mind last night at Mrs Harrison's– I chattered away at such a rate– They were delighted to learn the good news your letter contained and both begged as well as Mrs Fisher to congratulate you upon arriving at home–

I passed Xmas day very pleasantly– only I was disappointed in my hope of hearing from you– I had several very pretty presents– the prettiest from Fisher of course in the shape of a little ornamental basket for cards. Sally Waln sent me a very nice work basket de sa façon [*of her own making*] and in return I gave her the purse which Ella Butler[1] began for me– which was exceedingly admired– being of a novel form– square at one end, and with a long tassel at the other– I offered it first to Aunt Harrison but she candidly told me she would prefer a plainer one for use, and with a clasp, so I am making her one for New Year's day like that you helped me in, only blue– I gave the one which was the result of our united labour to M^rs F– and with a handsome clasp and tassel it looks very well, and she admires it extremely– I had quite as much pleasure giving Mary her Xmas presents after breakfast, as in receiving mine– M^rs F– gave her a little China Inkstand, and box full of beautiful bonbons, Fisher battledores & shuttlecocks, and I a wax doll of large size and really a sweet pretty face, who has the additional merit of opening and shutting her eyes– I thought her rather old for dolls, but when I gave her her choice she preferred one to anything else, and I thought it would teach her to sew, and <u>cultivate her af-fections</u>– and she is already very fond of it and industriously employed for [it].

Lily McEuen[2] spent the day with her, and they were very happy together and Mary is to spend Saturday with her– I took her out Sleighing on Tuesday– I enjoyed it extremely, not having been in a sleigh for 8 years, (when we made the journey hence to N.Y. in the winter of '31) and was in a perfect extacy the whole time– The snow has now melted away considerably from the middle of the Street, but the side pavements are in a shocking state of slipperiness, and one walks at the imminent risk of breaking bones– I am not allowed to <u>stir</u> without Fisher's arm,[3] and he is always ready to give up his ride for my sake. We went yesterday as far as the Tree where Penn signed the Treaty with the Indians, where there is a small monument to mark the spot looking more like a Tombstone. It is about 2 miles and a half from our house quite out of town, but I was not the least tired, altho' dreadfully draggled as it thawed on our way home and I had to wade thro' quantities of wet snow and mud–

I haven't told you what an agreeable Xmas evening we passed– We had only a few ladies to spend it with us but Miss Pardi allowed her harp to come in, and played a great deal for us, and Matilda [Willing] and I sang together, and then I sang alone, and rather better than usual for my voice is certainly improving by practise– We sang at the Grelaud's too on Saturday evening, and are going to learn some more Duetts, and a beautiful one for Harp & Piano, a selection from the Sonnambula–[4] Miss Pardi is to sing a duett from Anna Bolena with me next week. She is improving under Dorigo–[5] Sunday it snowed & stormed all day, so Fisher read me two of Barrow's[6] sermons which I liked very much, and I wrote a long letter to Uncle Izard [Middleton,] and spent the eveng– reading at home much more agreeably than if the weather had permitted our going to M<u>rs</u> Harrison's. On Monday eveng– I went to a large party at M<u>rs</u> Robert Hare's, where I would not be persuaded to dance, altho' I had several offers of partners– M<u>rs</u> [Humphrey] Atherton[7] is to give me a Ball on New Year's eve, but I am determined not to dance as it amuses me much more to look on and talk, than to join in the stupid cotillions, and I shall never waltz again–

I intended to have stopped at M<u>rs</u> Gibson's this morng– on my way to practice with Matilda Willing, and tell her of your arrival and deliver y<u>r</u> mes-sage, but the rain, a (cold dismal rain which freezes as it falls, and will make the pavements as slippery as glass) prevents me from doing both. M<u>rs</u> Fisher comes in, and begs me to tell you that I never looked better since she has known me, than I do now, indeed I am in perfect health and hope to continue so notwithstanding the cold weather, which does not affect my throat in the least– And now altho' I have much more to scribble about, I will desist in pity to your eyes and patience, & entreating a speedy answer and punctual <u>weekly</u> epistle– With best love to Papa, my brothers, Kitty and dear Sally & her little ones I am dearest Mamma Ever Y͟r affectionate Daughter Eliza

I have no further news from N.Y. tell W͟m but will write again to him whenever I have– Tell Harry M͟rs Willing wore the black Veil for him here on Thursday evening, and she desired me to tell him so and say how much she regretted him– M͟rs Pierce Butler is still detained here by her husband's illness, and will probably be so the whole winter. She is still very cordial & amiable to me, but there is no telling how soon she may change–[8]

Private Collection

1. Gabriella (Morris) Butler's husband, John, was Pierce's brother. She had connections in Charleston as well as Philadelphia, as her grandmother was Mrs. Middleton's old friend Margaret Izard Manigault.
2. Daughter of Nancy (Izard) and Thomas McEuen.
3. This, and her reluctance to dance, mentioned further on, are early indications that Eliza was pregnant.
4. Vincenzo Bellini's opera *La Sonnambula* was first performed in Philadelphia in 1835 and helped to make Italian opera popular there. *Anna Bolena* was composed by Gaetano Donizetti in 1830.
5. Dorigo, clearly a respected professional singer, is mentioned several times in Eliza's letters but has not been further identified.
6. William Barrow (1754–1836), an English churchman who wrote about divine revelation, published three volumes of his *Familiar Sermons* from 1818 to 1821.
7. Sarah (Marshall) Atherton was the wife of Humphrey Atherton (1784–1845), a lawyer. Sidney Fisher reported the ball as "very gay & pleasant with a dance on the carpet." Wainwright, *Phila. Perspective* (December 31, 1839): 93.
8. Eliza must have known that Fanny Butler had made several unflattering comments about Philadelphians in her published journal, mentioning, for example, "the Chesnut Street set," who didn't mix with anyone they did not know, "lofty pretensions without adequate foundations," and a general "want of courtesy" in the city. Even her own family thought she could be "extremely ungracious." Frances Anne Butler, *Journal* (Philadelphia: Carey, Lea & Blanchard, 1835), 1:162, 191, 151.

⁓

To Mrs. Fisher, Philadelphia

M.P. Dec͟r 29͟th 1839

My dearest Eliza

I had the pleasure of receiving your letter of the 19͟th last Tuesday when y͟r Father & W͟m joined the party here– I had come the day before, & found

Sally looking very well & the children (with the exception of Harry) fat & hearty. I ought also to except the infant, for she is very thin & delicate but has fine dark blue, prominent eyes, & will I think (if she lives) be very pretty. John arrived on the same day, & he is stouter & fatter than I ever saw him– & in good spirits.[1]

I wrote to Susan before leaving Charleston to request her to bring all the family here as soon as possible. As yet no answer has reached me– Sally saw her in Charleston, looking ill, which I am sorry to hear. I found every thing here looking as usual, dreary at this season. a hard frost had blighted the red & white Cammellias,[2] which Sally says were in full bloom when she arrived– there are many buds now of the <u>White</u>, but the excessive coldness of the weather at present, seems to destroy the prospect of their attaining their full bloom (1$\underline{st}$ They are <u>now</u> all killed by frost.) The north west wind has been blowing furiously, & gives reason to suppose you at Philad$\underline{a}$ are suffering greatly from cold. In M$\underline{rs}$ Fisher's comfortable house however you feel the cold less than you would here in this airy one. I hope the severity of the weather has not encreased her Rheumatism, which was so violent even in mild weather. I have had a comparatively slight attack of that painful disease ever since the night passed in the Norfolk Steamer. It has kept me awake several hours in the night but I think is now less painful. Major Rutledge[3] who spent two or three days with us, recommended friction as the best cure, & it has done me good. He will bring your Aunt [Rutledge] here this week to pass a few days– she is probably now on her way with E[mma] Blake[4] from Combahee– they have all taken rooms at Stewart's [*Hotel in Charleston*] for two months. M$\underline{r}$ R seems to think Emma better, but I hear that [*her sister*] Henrietta is aware of her danger. Miss [Sally] R[utledge] had left Charleston with Miss Pinckney before I arrived.

I am just returned from a walk in the sheltered part of the garden above the Spring– Your Galoches have been exceedingly serviceable to me ever since I have been here after rain, & after the thaws, which succeeded the frost. I did not see your Aunt Huger– M$\underline{rs}$ Smith & M$\underline{rs}$ Blamyer[5] called, & enquired particularly about you. the former promised to come & make me a visit when I am alone, which will probably be the case next week as Sally will leave us <u>this</u> week, & Susan's visit I suppose will not exceed a few days on account of her wishing to place the children at school. Your presents to the Children have delighted them & they all beg me to thank you for them, & often talk of Aunt Eliza– Little John begins to read, & is more attentive to his <u>studies</u> than formerly– I have Sarah again to teach French, for the short time she stays. Harry has had no attack of fever & Ague[6] for the last week, & has improved greatly in health since I came.

Your Father invited M^{rs} [Sarah Huger] Wilkinson[7] to make us a visit but I do not know when it is to take place. M^{rs} H[olbrook] too sent me word by Major Rutledge that she would come shortly. Sally seems hurt at her never having been to see her when in Charleston, particularly as at that time, Dr H. was in good health, so that she had not the excuse of his illness to keep her away. Alice Heyward[8] was very attentive to her during her illness– She is now at Stono[9] for the benefit of Russell M[iddleton]'s health, he having nearly died of Typhus fever. I have seen none of that family– H. A. [Middleton][10] again inhabits the same house [*in Charleston*] he did last year, not being able to find a larger one.

I sent to enquire after the family at Runnymede,[11] but as yet have not seen them. I expect a long letter from you by the return of y^r Father from Charleston. he intends to go there tomorrow, for which opportunity, (no other having occurred since my last letter) I am writing now. You must not count upon regularity in my letters, as you must be aware of the uncertainty of messengers being sent. You will of course give me the detail of the wedding party, & let me know I hope that you have been free from pain in the throat, & headache & that Mrs Fisher is recovering from her Rheumatism– & that M^r & Mrs Harrison are well. to all I beg to be kindly remembered, & also to Mr F. Sally & your Brothers & Father send their love & I am my dearest Eliza y^r Affect^{te} Mother M. H. M.

Sally begs me to thank you for the Apron you sent her. She admires it very much.

P.S. You desired to hear of Celia.[12] Her wrist is a little better. She, & all the servants enquired after you– the first sentence they spoke.

Jany 1st 1840– May my dearest Eliza enjoy many happy returns of the day! No means of sending this has occurred, your Father being still here. Sally & family are to leave us tomorrow, John being anxious to see after his plantation business– they will pass a week in Charleston from whence they will proceed in a lately established Steamer to Georgetown in 6 or 7 hours in the day time– this is very convenient, as they have not horses to convey their numerous family– No news yet from Oliver– You must have very severe weather at Philad^a It is colder here & has continued longer than usual– I wear my flannel jacket & my black shawl constantly in the house– you cannot therefore call me imprudent. My rheumatism is better– Sally reminded me of an old remedy which perhaps may be beneficial to Mrs Fisher. I think it has eased me– it is the fine yellow Tea paper applied to the part affected.

ScHi

1. John and Sally Middleton had five children at this time: Henry (called Harry or Hal), Sarah, John Izard, Thomas, and the new baby, Mary Helen, who was born on October 23, 1839.

2. The French botanist André Michaux is thought to have given Henry Middleton the first camellias to plant at Middleton Place in the late eighteenth century. One of the original four plants is still alive.

3. Henry Middleton Rutledge (1775–1844), son of Henrietta (Middleton) and Edward Rutledge, married Septima Sexta Middleton (1783–1865), Henry Middleton's favorite sister. They were first cousins. The Rutledges lived in Tennessee; he had been a major in the U.S. Army.

4. Emma Blake and Henrietta Rutledge were sisters and the daughters of Septima Sexta (Middleton) and Henry Middleton Rutledge. Emma Rutledge (1812–1853) married her cousin Daniel Blake, a planter on the Combahee River; his mother, Anna Louisa Middleton (Mrs. Daniel) Blake, was Henry Middleton's sister. Henrietta Rutledge (1813–1842) also married one of her cousins, Frederick Rutledge.

5. Mrs. William (Frances Pogson) Blamyer was Mrs. Sarah Pogson Smith's sister. Her husband, a Charleston lawyer, helped take care of Henry Middleton's affairs while he was in Russia.

6. A common term for malaria.

7. Sarah Huger (1818–1904), Emma Huger Smith's sister, married James Wilkinson in 1838.

8. Alice (Izard) Heyward (1802–1863) was Eliza's first cousin; her mother, Emma Philadelphia (Middleton) Izard (d. 1813) was one of Henry Middleton's sisters. Alice was the widow of Joseph Manigault Heyward (1795–1824), the son of Nathaniel and Henrietta (Manigault) Heyward.

Nathaniel Russell Middleton (1810–1890) was a planter, lawyer, treasurer of the City of Charleston in the 1850s, and president of the College of Charleston from 1858 through the Civil War. He was Alice Heyward's brother-in-law, having married her sister, Margaret Emma Izard. The latter died in 1836, leaving her husband with three small children, of whom Alice was extremely fond.

9. Stono refers to Bolton plantation, on the Stono River southwest of Charleston, which Russell Middleton inherited from his parents, Arthur and Alicia (Russell) Middleton.

10. Henry Augustus Middleton (1793–1887) was Russell Middleton's uncle and Henry Middleton's first cousin. A graduate of Harvard and the Litchfield Law School, he was a large landowner in South Carolina and in Newport. He traveled in Europe and was interested in art. He and his wife, the former Harriott Kinloch, were the parents of Mary and Lizzie, who are mentioned frequently in these letters.

11. Runnymede plantation was on the Ashley River near Middleton Place but closer to Charleston. William Bull Pringle (1800–1881) and his wife who was Sally Middleton's aunt, inherited it and were preparing to live there.

12. Celia was one of the house slaves at Middleton Place.

1840

Tell your mother that I have <u>no</u> fault to find with you & <u>entirely</u>
approve of you, and think you worthy of my nephew.

⟳

On the morning of March 12, Eliza and Fisher's first wedding anniversary, Uncle George Harrison walked the short block up Chestnut Street to the Fishers' house and delivered a speech to Eliza. Having observed her for a year, he had no fault to find with her, he said. He instructed Eliza to tell her mother that he entirely approved of her and, bestowing his highest rating, pronounced her worthy of his nephew!

Eliza's description of the scene, one of the high points of her letters, gives a wonderful sense of the old-fashioned courtliness, kindness, and direct speech for which Fisher's uncle was known and loved. Equally it shows that Eliza had—as Fisher a year before had begged his mother to believe she would—brought gaiety and affection and joy to the elderly inhabitants of 156 and 170 Chestnut Street.

Eliza and Fisher added to their happiness at the end of June when their first child was safely born. They named the baby Elizabeth Francis Fisher after Fisher's mother, and being the first infant in the Fisher and Harrison families since Fisher's own birth in 1807, she was the apple of everyone's eye. Even Mrs. Fisher adored her, temporarily overcoming her wish for a grandson.

When writing to her mother, Eliza of course was always careful to describe the baby's new teeth and all her other endearing tricks, and she also told her parents about her new life in Philadelphia, describing dinner parties and balls, Fisher's relatives and her new friends, concerts, plays, and playing her new piano at home. Eliza never meant, though, to make her letters a complete chronicle of her busy life but tried, rather, to make them as amusing, cheerful, and interesting as possible, keeping in mind that they would frequently be read or heard by several people in addition to her parents. She chose her material carefully and wrote, according to the canons of polite letter writing, about people her parents knew and not about strangers, about books and music they would enjoy but avoiding what they could not "form an idea of,"[1] and about political events they were particularly concerned with. Many important events were not mentioned at all, or—as in the case of the election of William Henry Harrison as president in 1840—only some time after they had taken place.

Mrs. Middleton's letters were very different in style and content from her daughter's. As she grew older, she gradually withdrew from most of the social contacts she had once enjoyed and for the most part saw only her old friends and family members. Reflecting this, her letters became a continuing newsletter through which she passed along news from Edward, or Harry or Arthur when they were out of the country, as well as about her husband, her children, and grandchildren in South Carolina. Indeed, she reported on the whole extended Middleton clan and their many friends.

Since they usually confined their letters to what would fit onto the four sides of a folded sheet of paper (with occasional "crossing" if they ran over) and wanted to give the recipient (who paid the postage) her money's worth, Eliza and her mother did not waste space explaining what they both already knew. Household activities, for example, fell into this category, making it difficult to form a picture of what Mrs. Middleton's domestic responsibilities were, both at Middleton Place and at Newport. Nevertheless, glimpses here and there—Mrs. Middleton sewing the layette for a new grandchild, culling recipes from a new cookbook, or sending Eliza one for "pillaw," ordering groceries in Charleston, caring for sick Negroes, hiring servants, or packing up the linen and china at the end of a summer in Newport—show that she was a busy mistress whose job was to make a complicated and continually moving household run smoothly. By contrast, Eliza had few domestic duties in the early years of her marriage, but by commenting on certain specific things—how Mrs. Fisher froze a fur piece to kill the moth eggs, a bucket of hot water left in the hall, a servant leaving early, a menu of oysters and ice cream, pads filling out the bust of a dress—she also sketched a picture of her urban household.

1. EMF to MHM, December 15, 1842, ScHi.

～

To Mrs. Middleton, Middleton Place

Philadelphia – January 3$\underline{rd}$ 1840

Two days of the new Year have already passed, and I have not yet wished you many happy returns of it my dearest Mamma, but I do it not the less heartily now, to you and all the rest of the family circle at M. Place– I hoped this morning to have heard of your being all assembled there, but there is some detention of the mails, & that alone is the cause I trust of my not hearing today. Altho' I could write with a much lighter spirit, after receiving a letter telling me of your entire recovery from the fatigues of the journey, I would not on that account delay performing my promise of despatching a weekly epistle– But attributing my disappointment entirely to the above mentioned cause, proceed to tell you of my past week's occupations and amusements. Friday and Saturday were stormy, and disagreeable days as to weather– But I employed them much more profitably than if a bright sunshine had tempted me out– We were at home and <u>alone</u> both of those evenings and passed them very pleasantly listening to reading aloud and at the Piano– Sunday I went twice to hear our excellent little Clergyman,[1] but the second time was disappointed to find a stranger in the Pulpit– Mr Campbell, the son of your former acquaintance, Miss Percy, who preached rather an eloquent discourse and reminded me excessively of Allen Smith in appearance– In the afternoon I paid a long visit to Mrs Hare in her sick chamber, which she enlivened very much by her cheerful conversation, and came home in time to receive M^r & M^rs H– and Sally Hare,[2] who I found a very agreeable addition to our family party. Monday I took Mary to spend the day with M^rs McEuen and paid her a long visit myself– talking over poor Adela [Newton]'s[3] troubles– Heaven knows what is to become of her and the Captain and his 5 helpless children– It seems the 3 elder ones can take care of themselves– at least the daughter is well married, one of the sons in a counting house doing very well, and the other, the eldest, doing very ill, in the Navy. It was his extravagance and misconduct principally, which brought on all this distress– For his Father has not only paid his debts several times, but pledged his pay in advance to save him from prison and by so doing nearly ruined himself and the rest of his family– I am told Adela behaves admirably well, and is willing to make every sacrifice and even to take in boarders, into 2 or 3 spare rooms of her house, in order to raise a little money! This is rather a degradation for an Izard to descend to, but pride must give way to dire necessity– It seems Mrs Izard[4] has been applied to for assistance, but has refused to advance the sum which they wished to borrow on good security– All her's and her sister's spare cash being already bespoken for some charitable purpose–

On Monday evening I went after the lecture to Sally Waln's, where we spent an hour pleasantly– Tuesday morning I wrote to Susan and then went and practised the Harp and Piano Duett with Mrs Willing, which will be very pretty indeed– I also paid a visit to Mrs Pierce Butler, and agreed to go and sing with her on Thursday morng– which I did, and found that we joined voices quite harmoniously together– We sang over two very fine duetts, one from the Puritani, "Suoni la Tromba,"[5] which will have a good effect, if we keep each other's courage up– The Party at Mrs Atherton's in my honour was a handsome and pleasant one– and they danced out the old year, and the new one in, very merrily, whilst I talked, much to my satisfaction to Mrs Campbell,[6] and some other agreeable people. Fisher had been suffering with one of his headaches, but insisted upon accompanying me there, and strange to say, the heat of the rooms, instead of increasing his headache, appeared to cure it for the time, but the following day he paid the penalty of his imprudence, and began the new year most miserably, suffering torments all day, and prevented from going in the eveng to Mrs Harrison's party– where, truth to say however he did not miss much– for there were none but very old or very young ladies present, except Lydia [Hare] Prime[7] & myself, and I should have been rather badly off if it had not been for her & my valuable and staunch friends her brothers Clark & Robert– To whom it is some relief to talk of books, after listening to all the uninteresting small talk which is the general tone among the good folks one meets at tea parties–

Last night we had a very <u>literary set</u> at supper at Mrs Randolph's–[8] [James Fenimore] Cooper the novelist and Charles Kean too! He is quite a gentleman in his manners, and as Mrs Butler said "very well conducted"– Her adoption of M^rs B—y's pet phrase which you thought <u>Yankee</u>, rather astonished me– I had the good fortune to be near her and Sally Waln the whole evening and Fanny [Butler] begged me to sit next to her at Supper, thereby distancing some of the gentlemen, who wanted my place, but were obliged to retire disappointed– We were very sociable and chatty together, and very little occupied with our other next neighbours, mine I had never known until he was introduced to hand me in, and hers (Matilda Willing) more inclined to devote her attention to Cooper who sat on her other side– He thought me very like <u>Arthur</u>, and spoke of the resemblance as being striking!!!

Some of the company were very much misplaced– Mr Kean between M^rs J[ohn] Butler and fat Mrs Ralston,[9] neither of them very talkative or interesting, and poor Fisher laboring hard to please good dull Mrs Randolph, whose conversational powers are not great, and hardly extend beyond a few common place observations on people and their dress– I was afraid Sidney Fisher and Cooper would quarrel, for they are both opinionated and rude, but Sally Waln succeeded in keeping the peace between them– I have been up so late for the last 3 nights that I feel quite fagged, and am determined to accept no more invitations for the present, but keep earlier hours–

Mrs Harrison is going to see Kean in Macbeth tomorrow evening, and if it were any other but Saturday, I should like very much to hear him in that, one of his best characters, they say, but I always find myself so very inattentive at church the following day, and my thoughts so apt to wander from thence back to the Theatre, that I have made a resolution to avoid if possible the painful struggle between such worldly & distracted thoughts, at a time when I ought to endeavour to have none but peaceful and serious meditations in my mind–

I have a short letter from Julia [Ward,] but it is only written to know the reason of what she calls my long silence– which she will have heard the very day she made the enquiry– As I wrote to her the previous one, explaining my neglect of ten days– She says she is quite well, very busy & in tolerable spirits, and enquires after William, who she says has not written to her Cousin for some time past– Just tell him all this, and say it is unnecessary for me to write, for this is all the letter contains–

Friday evening– Fisher interrupted me this morng to take me to go and see some beautiful specimens of the Daguerrotype– much more distinct and perfect than those we saw together and done in Paris by Daguerre himself. It is now late and I am obliged to get ready to go to M^rs H's to tea– whence I shall go to Mary Nixon's[10] if I can muster courage to face the cold– So adieu dearest Mamma with love to all at home I am Y^r most affectionate Daughter Eliza

Private Collection

1. William Henry Odenheimer (1817–1879) was assistant rector at St. Peter's Church. Soon after he was made rector in 1841, he caused a rift in his congregation by the high-church innovation of installing a cross on the church spire. Introducing daily services and weekly communion, Odenheimer made St. Peter's one of the most active parishes in the area. He became bishop of New Jersey in 1859.

2. Sarah (Sally) Hare (1802–1860) was the daughter of Sarah (Emlen) and Charles Willing Hare, Dr. Robert Hare's brother. She was a cousin of Fisher's through the Willings.

3. Adela (Izard) Newton was Nancy McEuen's, Delancey Izard's, and "Georgie" Middleton's sister. Her husband was Capt. John T. Newton, U.S. Navy.

4. Eliza Lucas (Pinckney) Izard (d. 1851) was Adela Newton's (and her siblings') stepmother. The daughter of Sarah (Middleton) and Charles Cotesworth Pinckney, she was the second wife and the widow of Ralph Izard (d. 1824). Harriott Pinckney was her sister; Henry Middleton, her first cousin.

5. The opera *I Puritani,* by Vincenzo Bellini, was first performed in 1835 in Paris.

6. Mrs. Alexander Campbell was the former Maria Dallas. George Mifflin Dallas was her brother.

7. Lydia Hare (Mrs. Frederick) Prime and her brothers, Clark and Robert, were the children of Dr. Robert and Harriett (Clark) Hare.

8. Sarah Emlen (Physick) Randolph was the wife of Dr. Jacob Randolph, a surgeon and professor at the University of Pennsylvania.

9. Probably Sarah (Clarkson) Ralston, widow of shipping merchant and philanthropist Robert Ralston.

10. Mary Nixon was the daughter of Henry Nixon, president of the Bank of North America. The Nixons were old friends of the Harrisons. John Nixon, Mary's grandfather, was remembered for reading the newly adopted Declaration of Independence to Philadelphia's citizens.

∽

Henry Middleton with his parents, Arthur and Mary Izard Middleton. Painted in England, circa 1771, by Benjamin West. Courtesy of Sandwith, Edward, and John Drinker, Middleton Place Foundation, and Frick Art Reference Library.

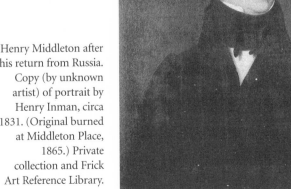

Henry Middleton after his return from Russia. Copy (by unknown artist) of portrait by Henry Inman, circa 1831. (Original burned at Middleton Place, 1865.) Private collection and Frick Art Reference Library.

Mary Helen Hering Middleton in 1831. Copy (possibly by Thomas Middleton) of portrait by Thomas Sully. (Original burned at Middleton Place, 1865.) Private collection.

Maria, Catherine, and Eliza Middleton in St. Petersburg, Russia, 1827. (Eliza is in front.) Signed "Matthes," probably the Middletons' governess, Madame Matthes. Courtesy of Eliza Cope Nolan.

Williams Middleton in St. Petersburg, circa 1828. Artist unknown. Courtesy of Historical Society of Pennsylvania.

Eliza Middleton Fisher. Possibly the portrait painted in 1840 by George Lethbridge Saunders. Courtesy of Eliza Cope Nolan.

Joshua Francis Fisher, "Fisher," before his marriage. By unknown artist, circa 1835. Private collection.

Fisher's mother, Elizabeth Powel Francis Fisher, in 1840. By George Lethbridge Saunders. Private collection.

Fisher's uncle George Harrison. By Henry Inman, 1837. Courtesy of G. H. Hart and Frick Art Reference Library.

Lily and Sophie Fisher, the Fishers' oldest daughters, in 1847, when they were seven and five years old. By Thomas Sully. Courtesy of Frances A. Bloomfield and Frick Art Reference Library.

Joshua Francis Fisher, circa 1860. Hand-tinted photograph. Courtesy of Elizabeth Francis Aub Reid.

Eliza Middleton Fisher in 1859. Photograph by Le Jeune, Paris. Courtesy of Middleton Place Foundation.

Sally Middleton at the sewing table, Middleton Place. Drawing by Williams Middleton, circa 1835. Courtesy of Middleton Place Foundation.

Capt. Edward Middleton, 1864. Courtesy of Edward Middleton Rea Collection.

Oliver Hering Middleton, 1890. Courtesy of Edward Middleton Rea Collection.

Harry Middleton, circa 1860. Courtesy of Edward Middleton Rea Collection.

Eliza Fisher's cousin and close friend Emma Huger married Joseph Allen Smith (later Izard) in 1838. Watercolor on ivory by Henry Bounetheau, 1835. (51.06.01) Courtesy of Gibbes Museum of Art/Carolina Art Association.

Sarah Pogson Smith was a friend to both Mrs. Middleton and Eliza. Watercolor on ivory by J. B. Alexander, circa 1839. (41.03.01) Courtesy of Gibbes Museum of Art/Carolina Art Association.

Eliza's friend Julia Ward was engaged briefly to Williams Middleton in 1839. She later married Samuel Gridley Howe. Engraving after drawing by Porter (no date). Courtesy of Boston Athenaeum.

Fanny Kemble, circa 1830, before her marriage to Pierce Butler. Engraving from painting by Alonzo Chappel (after Sir Thomas Lawrence). Courtesy of Boston Athenaeum.

Several friends mentioned in Eliza's letters at a party at Harrison Gray Otis's house in Boston. *Left to right:* Harrison Gray Otis, Jr., Jonathan Hunt, Meyer (unidentified), Sophia Thorndike, Henry Wadsworth Longfellow and his future wife, Fanny Appleton, Fanny Inglis (Calderon), Allyne Otis, Mary Appleton, and R. Truman. By Williams Middleton, circa 1835. Courtesy of Middleton Place Foundation.

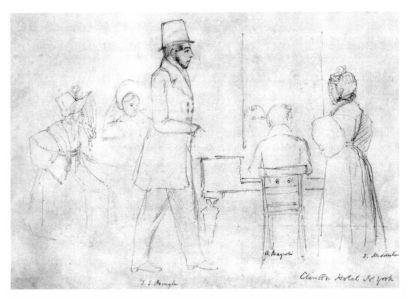

Antonio Bagioli at the piano with Eliza Middleton standing behind him. Bagioli gave Eliza singing lessons and often sent her new music from New York. J. J. (Julius) Pringle *(standing with hat)* married Jane Lynch, who was from New York. Sketch by Williams Middleton, circa 1835. Courtesy of Middleton Place Foundation.

Catherine Channing Barclay (later Mrs. Albert Sumner) and Harriott Rutledge Holbrook. Sketched at Newport by Williams Middleton, 1835. Courtesy of Middleton Place Foundation.

The Middletons always liked to sail with Capt. Michael Berry on trips between Charleston and New York. Sketch onboard the *Catherine* by Williams Middleton, circa 1835. Courtesy of Middleton Place Foundation.

To Mrs. Middleton, Middleton Place

Philadelphia Jany 15ᵗʰ 1840

I begin this evening, a day earlier than usual, to write to my dearest Mamma, because I am in a scribbling humour, & particularly happy to have had another letter yesterday from you– My anxiety was removed on Friday, by the receipt of your's of the 1ˢᵗ which was indeed most welcome after the long delay, occasioned as we conjectured by the irregularity of the mail– I was very uneasy about you all I confess, and worried myself into a head-ache, which even the arrival of a letter did not cure, and going to Mʳˢ Francis's much encreased, so that for nearly 3 whole days, I was much troubled with it– I am now perfectly well again– however, and hope that in future I shall not be kept in suspense for such a time– I am very sorry to hear that you have been suffering from rheumatism, but in yʳ last you give better accounts of it– Mʳˢ F[isher] has had less of it lately– but an attack of nervousness succeeded, which she declares much more distressing to her– both are bad enough– & she seems scarcely ever free from one or the other evil– She thanks you for your simple remedy, which at least is worth trying– I hope that you have now abandoned your habit of rising by moonlight, which certainly is a most imprudent one for a rheumatic person to indulge in, and that you wait patiently until one of your sable handmaids can kindle a cheerful fire to dress by this cold weather– I have relapsed into laziness & seldom sit down to breakfast before nine– but am hardly ever in bed until midnight, which is some excuse for tardy rising–

I am very much obliged to you for the extract from Arthur's letter– which is certainly a strange story– I do not wonder that he shᵈ dislike to remain in Madrid, attached to such a blackguard minister & heartily hope it may be the means of getting rid of Mʳ Eaton– for surely the Governᵗ will have notice of such a disgraceful transaction and recall him–¹ I have not written to Arthur, and the fact is I have now delayed it so long, that it is very awkward to break the ice & make a beginning– This alone deters me, and the fear of boring him with one of my stupid scrawls, would also be a sufficient reason to prevent me– I was just going to tell you that Mʳ Ingraham² (a friend of his here) told Fisher the other day he had late accounts from him– but your's are probably just as late– I forgot to mention in my last, that I had despatched the scarf & books to Uncle & Aunt [Hering]– Mary Nixon kindly offered to ask her cousin Captⁿ West to take charge of them, & as he made no objection & only stipulated that I should make two brown paper parcels of them, instead of sending a box, which I thought of doing, I was very glad to accept his conditions which were made because he wished to carry them on shore under each arm, & thus escape the vigilance of the Custom house officers– I hope he may be successful in his voyage, & this plan of passing them duty free particularly, as I hear the India scarf is contraband– Fisher wrote to a Mr Barclay in Liverpool, who will no doubt forward them safely to Southampton– I sent [William Cullen] Bryant's Poems to Cousin Maria Campbell, who I am sure will admire & value them– I had not time to procure the Seeds, which may be sent by another opportunity.

I am sorry to find that John & Sally have left you– but hope that Susan, and your other visitors may soon succeed them and that you may not be left alone at all– I have a letter from Sophia [Thorndike,] who is quite contented & happy at New Port– where she says they have dinner parties & evening & sleighing parties– and are very gay– Her cousin is still there, which perhaps may account for her good spirits and philosophic endurance of the once detested New Port– and she is going very soon to Boston, which is probably another sufficient reason for them– She is going to have her miniature taken by a self taught artist which I think also looks rather suspicious, but she gives no hint of any engagement, and Mrs Ritchie positively & rather indignantly denies it, to Mrs Harrison– so that I don't know what to think about it–³ S. sends her love to you–

Thursday morng– The first thing after a late breakfast I sit down to finish this to my dearest Mamma– and give her some account of M^{rs} [Hartman] Kuhn's party last night– from which I did not return until near one o'clock– I had the good fortune to be near very agreeable people, and Mr Biddle (old Nick) & that pleasantest of democrats Charles J. Ingersoll⁴ both talked a good deal to me– I had also the unexpected & rather unwelcome honour of being handed into supper by Mr Kuhn– which really made me feel quite awkward, as there were so many elderly matrons who certainly ought to have taken precedence– and I did not like to be paraded in before Mrs Sergeant & Mrs Biddle, & be obliged to take the seat of honour at the head of the table in their presence– Particularly as the party was not given to me, for they had already in the spring made a very handsome one for me– I have no doubt M^r K– wished to be very civil, but it was quite contrary to rule to distinguish in such a pointed manner the youngest married woman in company & I am afraid he has given offence & cause of jealousy by it–

A good many jokes passed about our Wedding cake– But I have forgotten to tell you that at last we have rec^d it– After 10 months delay, it is of course not quite as fresh as ever but is still in sufficiently good preservation to be sent round, and accordingly it is cut up for that purpose– It has been at the office because they say they did not know Fisher's address– so the foolish people

<u>advertised</u> for him, and many of his friends came to tell him of the NewsPaper notice which he had not seen, & they imagined meant something very impor- tant– Upon going post haste to the place indicated he was informed that the long forgotten box had been safely deposited in a store 9 months previous, and thus the mystery was soon solved–

I heard last night that the [Robert] Mackintoshes & Fanny Appleton[5] had arrived the day before and were staying at the Washington Hotel opposite– The first thing we did this morng– was to send over to invite them to meet Fanny Butler & a few others here this eveng– but they had taken their departure for Wash$^{\underline{n}}$ (where they are to spend the winter) early this morng– I have heard from M$^{\underline{rs}}$ Barclay who does not write in good spirits I think– She says it is very dull in N.Y. & seems to be left alone a good deal– She desires to be <u>affect$^{\underline{ly}}$</u> remembered to you, and <u>kindly</u> to W$^{\underline{m}}$ & <u>Harry</u> if the latter has forgotten his <u>disapproval</u> of her– I must conclude in haste with love to my dear Papa– Brothers & Kitty, and Susan if she is with you– I am ever Y$^{\underline{r}}$ most affectionate Daughter Eliza

Fisher begs to offer his best regards– There is no lack of Camellias here– I had half a dozen sent me in a bouquet last night & Fisher also presented me with a beautiful one, surrounded with exquisite flowers–

Private Collection

1. Since Mrs. Middleton's letter of the second week of January is missing, it is not clear what story Eliza was talking about. Other letters indicate, however, that Arthur, who was attached to the U.S. legation in Madrid, disapproved of John Henry Eaton, the U.S. minister to Spain (1836–40).

2. Perhaps Edward Ingraham (1793–1854), a Philadelphia lawyer and author.

3. Eliza's suspicion that Sophia Thorndike and her cousin George Herbert Thorn- dike were interested in each other was correct. They were married secretly later in the year.

4. Charles Jared Ingersoll (1782–1862) was a lawyer and a member of Congress at this time. In contrast to most of his social friends, he was a Democrat. He married Mary Wilcocks (1784–1862). Joseph Reed Ingersoll was his brother.

5. Fanny Appleton, who later married Henry Wadsworth Longfellow, and Mary (Appleton) Mackintosh were sisters and the daughters of Nathan Appleton and his first wife, Maria Theresa Gold, of Boston.

〜

To Mrs. Fisher, Philadelphia

M.P. Jany 16$^{\underline{th}}$ 1840

My dearest Eliza

I was distressed yesterday on reading your letter of 9$^{\underline{th}}$ ins^t to observe the uneasiness you felt at not hearing from me. The very day after I think you must have found by mine of 29$^{\underline{th}}$ ult$^{\underline{o}}$ & 2^d ins^t that it was not owing to my neglecting to write that you did not receive the letter– You must always make allowances for the few opportunities I have of sending to Charleston, & also for the frequent detention of the Mails– so that I beg you not to fancy any indisposition of mine or remissness to be the cause of your not regularly receiving my letters. I am now quite free from cold & Rheumatism– I wish I could say the same of Harry although he is much better today– but he has suffered exceedingly with the Influenza which has been very prevalent here as well as in Charleston– Fever, headach, and violent cough being the <u>symptoms</u>. it was distressing to witness the great depression of spirits he laboured under. Oliver who came for a day or two tried to make light of the complaint & after a few days M$^{\underline{rs}}$ Smith's arrival seemed to cheer him a little– he is now as I said above recovering & regaining his appetite. He thinks he has lost 50 lb of his weight within the last 10 days. He wishes to accompany your Father & W$^{\underline{m}}$ to Combahee– They only returned from Charleston yesterday. I have just asked the latter whether he had any commands, & he says he will write to you from Combahee.

You will be glad to know that Em$^{\underline{a}}$ Blake is much better. she walks out, that is all I can learn from Will$^{\underline{m}}$. Your Aunt [Rutledge] will not be here of course until they return from Combahee, neither will Susan be here until next month, Oliver being very busy at Edisto– he was looking very well & said that Susan was well. When we were conversing about his children he expressed as his opinion that Coosey[1] resembled <u>you</u> in character to his great delight. He considers her the most clever of his family which I have always thought the case– (You must not give a hint of this to Mary lest it should create jealousy)– he intends to place her at M$^{\underline{r}}$ Gilman's[2] who must be very well qualified to instruct & who takes only 20 scholars– it seems strange to <u>me</u> that M$^{\underline{rs}}$ G. should not assist her husband. M$^{\underline{rs}}$ [Sarah P.] Smith to whom I had sent a letter last week by W$^{\underline{m}}$ to invite her to come, met him & y$^{\underline{r}}$ Father at the Ferry on her way here on the strength of the invitation I had before given her. I need not say how much pleasure her cheerful society gives me– She begs to be particularly remembered to you– She expressed great satisfaction at the passage in your letter which I read to her on the subject of your objecting to go to the theatre on Saturday &c– If I read aright M$^{\underline{r}}$ Kirk[3] is the name of your admired Preacher– She says he is a Presbyterian & she also considers him an excellent one, though not always equally so. She was rejoiced to hear that he had drawn off so many Catholics to his Church.

I am glad to hear you have lately had so many conversations with Mrs P. Butler as you must enjoy listening to her sensible discussions on the management of children. She had expressed her opinions to me on the same subject very rationally in your drawing room– these opinions will recur to your memory one of these days perhaps– A propos, Mrs S. begs me to mention that the ancient Miss Roupell⁴ asked her, (before I arrived here) how you were after the birth of your twins which she heard had made their appearance here, where they had arrived together! This afforded Mrs S. great amusement of course– Miss R. had mixed up two different reports of you & some other young person, I presume.

For the last week we have had delightfully mild weather– the Cammellia buds again appear, & so do the violets & fragrant olive in small quantities. I had a visit yesterday from M^rs R[obert] Smith & her two daughters [*Anna and Susan*]. They enquired particularly after you, & Anna begged to be kindly remembered. The delay of their coming was owing to her having suffered much from the prevailing influenza– the young people are impatient to go to Charleston but old M^r P[ringle] is very unwilling to leave the country where he is enjoying tolerable health. R[obert] P[ringle]⁵ was one of the passengers in the Ville de Lyon. Harry met him lately riding on his way to town.

Harry was reading lately in the papers an account of a bank failure which he said Mrs Barclay must suffer from seriously– have you heard from her on the subject? I have not yet answered Miss Moore's long letter. I really have nothing to write about to one who ought to have an entertaining correspondent to reply to all her chit chat which I am utterly unable to do– Oliver says it is out of the question for him to engage a Governess while M^rs C[hisolm]⁶ lives in the same house, but he knows many people at Edisto who would be very glad to have one. How was Sophia T. when you heard from her? I have just recollected that I have not acknowledged your letter of the 3^d which Oliver brought me last Saturday, giving me an account of your literary party & other parties. I was sorry to hear that Mr F. had suffered so much from headach on the new year. that was a bad beginning.

I am expecting with anxiety a letter from my Brother, not having heard since I left Phil^a. When you are passing the Marshall house [pray] tell Mr Badger if a letter sh^d be directed to me– to his care, to send it immediately over to you, to forward to me. I delivered your message to Harry about his returning next month to Philad^a He enquired who had expressed a wish to see him. You do not say, but we may conclude the question was made by his favorite. He begs you give his compliments to her. You say Mr Cooper thought you very like Arthur– do you forget that I have often told you the outline of your faces resemble each other excepting the noses?

I do not hear of the two going to Combahee tomorrow– it will probably be the following day– I am writing this to go down by the Schooner[7] tomorrow– We cannot answer for the delays before it reaches you– let me again beg you not to be so anxious about hearing from me– you perceive I take advantage of any oppor^y to write– Give my kind regards to M^r & Mrs Fisher & M^r & Mrs Har^n Y^r Father, & Brothers send their love to you & I am my dearest Eliza y^r affect^{te} Mother M. H. M.

PHi

1. Susan Matilda (Coosey) (b. 1830) was Oliver and Susan Middleton's second child. She was born in 1830.

2. Rev. Samuel Gilman (1791–1858), originally from Massachusetts and a Harvard graduate, was the minister of the Unitarian Church in Charleston and also ran a school.

His wife, Caroline (Howard) Gilman (1794–1888), was a well-established writer as well as the editor of *Southern Rosebud,* one of the first publications for children. Among her writings were a book of poetry published in 1838 and *Recollections of a Southern Matron* two years before that.

3. Eliza had been "powerfully affected, even to tears" when she heard the evangelical preacher Edward Norris Kirk (1802–1874) in Philadelphia. "I sat in a very crowded & heated church for a whole hour listening to him, without the slightest fatigue or weariness, and regretted the close of what perhaps from a less gifted man would have been tedious." EMF to MHM, January 9, 1840, private collection.

4. Miss Polly Roupell had been a Charleston belle at the time of the Revolution.

5. Robert Pringle (1793–1860), the son of John Julius and Susannah (Reid) Pringle, lived mostly in Europe. His siblings were Edward, who married Maria Middleton; William Bull Pringle; Mrs. Robert Smith; and Mrs. Charles Alston. The *Ville de Lyon* was disabled in a storm and finally reached Bermuda, but passengers were left to get home on their own.

6. Mrs. Robert T. Chisolm was Susan Middleton's widowed mother. Miss Moore had recommended a possible governess.

7. The Middletons' schooner carried crops, letters, pianos, and anything else that needed to be transported between the Combahee plantations, Charleston, Middleton Place, and even John Middleton's plantation near Georgetown. Captain Thomas, "a most important personage altho' a man under authority himself," and his crew were all slaves. EM to JFF, January 1, 1839, MPlFdn.

∿

To Mrs. Middleton, Middleton Place

Philadelphia – Jan.ʸ 23ʳᵈ 1840

I sat by the window eagerly watching for the Postman this morning, and it appeared to me that he took a most unconscionable time to deliver the neighbour's letters– at last he rang at our bell, & I was convinced that he had one for me from my dearest Mamma, which to my great joy proved to be the case and I now sit down to thank you for it, and the pleasure it gave me– This was rather damped however by hearing of Harry's indisposition, but I was glad that you spoke of his recovery to health & spirits, in the same sentence in which you mentioned his past sufferings from Influenza– I hope the trip to Combahee & change of air have entirely restored him– You may suppose that the good accounts of your own health, rejoiced me & I only hope that you will continue to be careful of it & preserve it by prudence– I am delighted that you have so agreeable & cheerful a companion as dear Mʳˢ Smith with you– pray give her my kindest regards & love– but say that I cannot help suspecting her a little of adding <u>one</u> important trait to the scandalous report about me– altho' on consideration, even her mirth loving spirit would think too seriously to speak lightly of so terrible a visitation– so I acquit her of all but a spice of <u>malice</u> in repeating the matter & devoutly pray that the ancient spinster did not indulge in a <u>prophetic</u> strain, & knows not the <u>future</u> more truly than the <u>past</u>– for if I suspected her to be possessed of the power of the weird Sisters, I should indeed be <u>doubly</u> miserable– Of Mʳˢ Smith's own art of divination, I <u>do</u> stand somewhat in awe & particularly request her if she <u>has</u> any foreknowledge on this subject, not to distress me so long in advance by disclosing her <u>dread</u> secret– I have lately been obliged to make <u>full confession</u> to Sophia, who wrote in so congratulatory a strain, & is apparently so <u>envious</u> of what she considers my good luck, that I could not help being amused, & did not try to undeceive her– I shall have a more difficult task with <u>Emma</u> [Smith,] who I am sure will be highly shocked, and indignant at my not continuing to follow her proper and dignified conduct–[1] Alas! & would that I could! But regrets are quite unavailing now, & I must bear my hard fate with resignation– I am perfectly well, which I ought to be thankful for, and do not yet feel any of the <u>inconveniences</u> which I fear will soon <u>grow</u> around me. I walk regularly 4 or 5 miles daily, having been kept in yesterday by the rain for the first time for weeks–

I have been to no more parties since Mʳˢ Kuhn's grand affair of which I wrote to you– & do not at all regret that this week I have so much quiet & time for preparation for Confirmation– which is to take place next Sunday at our church– I have been attending Mʳ Odenheimer's weekly lectures, & reading

several books on the subject– which have given me a clear idea of the importance & necessity even, of attending to it, even after taking the Sacrament– I
applied to M͟r Odenheimer, who was quite of this opinion, & recommended
me by all means to come forward on this occasion, as the first which had ever
offered itself to me– He said it often happened that many who had not had
opportunities of being confirmed, were desirous of receiving the communion, & that of course there was no objection to admitting them to it, but that
afterwards the other & less important ordinance must not be neglected– I paid
the little Clergyman quite a long visit, (in return for one he had paid me, &
which owing to Murray's stupidity I did not receive)– and found him extremely
agreeable in conversation, and not only willing, but anxious to give me all the
advice with regard to <u>reading</u> &c that I required– His wife is a charming little
woman– very pretty & ladylike and his good feelings, & warm heartedness, will
go a great way to make one forget his defects of voice and delivery in the Pulpit–
besides his talents are unquestionable and of no common order, and I hope
we may be fortunate enough to keep him at our Church– of which there is a
good chance as his congregation are already much attached to him– They have
promised to spend an eveng– sociably with us next week, & I shall be very glad
to become better acquainted with them–

　　We had five, or at least 4 very pleasant women here last Thursday eveng–
for I do not include M͟rs J[ohn] Butler– altho' she is goodnatured & amiable–
But the others– M͟rs Pierce B[utler,] M͟rs H[arry] Ingersoll, Matilda Willing &
Sally Waln are certainly each very agreeable in their way– and were very gay &
lively– Fenwick Jones[2] was also here, but the <u>exclusives</u> took very little notice
of her, & Fanny did not know her– So it was rather awkward for me– particularly as she brought with her M͟rs M͟cLeod's overgrown boy,[3] who is said to be
clever & <u>talented</u> too, but is not much at his ease in society & very gawky and
bashful– He is gone to Savannah for his health & will be in Charleston in Feb͟y,
when I hope W͟m will find him out, and do something for him, for Fanny
Calderon's sake– He could introduce him at Aunt Huger's, where beaux in
their teens are not unwelcome[4] visitors, & to the little Middletons[5] who perhaps
may draw him out– for they say there is a great deal in him– You need not be
uneasy about not hearing from Uncle [*Oliver Hering*]– for the delay is probably
owing to the non-arrival of the "British Queen" which has now been out 22
days– & is hourly expected– I shall certainly request M͟r Badger to send any
letters to me which may be rec͟d for you at the Marshall House, & forward
them immediately– I have not said a word about that dreadful affair of the
Lexington[6] for it is too terrible to think of– & I am sure must have revived
your painful recollections, as it did mine–

I have not heard lately from Julia [Ward,] & therefore have not written again to W<u>m</u> but if I am not mistaken, he owes me a letter– You do not surely credit Bennet's[7] ridiculous report about old Sam [Ward,] the manner of his burial &c, & the small amount of his property– M<u>r</u> [Frederick] Prime thinks he has left nearly half a million but I suppose we must allow something for exaggeration, & it w<u>d</u> perhaps be his interest or his father's to have it supposed that he has a larger sum in the firm than he owned in reality–

I am glad you saw Oliver– even for two days– and that Susan will pay you the promised visit, altho' she defers it– Of course I am <u>flattered</u> at his good opinion of me & the fancied resemblance that Coosey bears me, but I do not agree with him & think Mary much quicker than she is– She is very well, & I hear very excellent accounts of her from M<u>me</u> Grelaud. Her doll is a great delight to her & fondly cherished. Adieu my dearest Mamma, With love to those around you, to whom I <u>entreat</u> you not to shew this scrawl, of which I am thoroughly ashamed, I remain Yr ever affectionate Daughter Eliza

I made a mistake of beginning at the wrong page, which I beg you to excuse as well as the numerous other faults which abound in this sheet. Fisher has had a total exemption from headache since New Year's day– which is really delightful– He begs to be affectly & respectfully remembered– M<u>rs</u> F. & M<u>r</u> & M<u>rs</u> H– always desire their best regards when I write to you & Papa & my brothers

Private Collection
All Eliza's letters between this and March 5 are missing.

1. Emma and Allen Smith did not have any children.
2. Sarah Fenwick Jones was the daughter of the Noble W. Joneses of Savannah and Newport.
3. The McLeods were relatives of Fanny Inglis Calderon and her mother.
4. Eliza first wrote "unacceptable," then replaced it with "unwelcome."
5. The "little Middletons" were Eliza's younger cousins, Elizabeth (Lizzie) and Mary Middleton, daughters of Henry Augustus and Harriott (Kinloch) Middleton. Mary (1820–1907) married William Henry Lowndes in 1842; Lizzie (1822–1903) married John Julius Pringle Smith in 1845.
6. The steamboat *Lexington* burst into flames on Long Island Sound during the night of January 13, 1840, on its way from New York to Stonington, Connecticut. Almost everyone on board was burned or drowned.
7. James Gordon Bennett was the founding editor of the *New York Herald*, whose journalistic innovations included covering financial and Wall Street news. It was therefore not surprising that he wrote about Samuel Ward, who had been a major figure in New York banking.

⁓

When Mrs. Middleton first arrived in South Carolina from England in 1799, she was delighted (as everyone always was) by the site of the house at Middleton Place, which was on high ground overlooking the Ashley River and surrounded by gardens. But "the situation," she told a friend, "deserves to have a better house built upon it." Inside, "numerous pictures" on the walls kept the house from being gloomy, but Mrs. Middleton nevertheless referred to it as an "old shackish mansion."[1]

In the ensuing forty years, or at least while the Middletons were in Russia and in the 1830s, the house apparently did not receive much attention, and by 1840 it was in need of considerable repair. The plans for improvements were ambitious, but actual progress was very slow. The shingles, for example, were not replaced until 1844.

1. MHM to Mary Stead Pinckney, November 25, [1799,] ScHi.

To Mrs. Fisher, Philadelphia

M.P. Jan.ʸ 25ᵗʰ 1840

My dearest Eliza

I came down at a quarter past 6 not long since this morn.ᵍ & can now see to write a few lines to go by the boat although they must be very uninteresting, having nothing to communicate worth your reading– no letter of yours to answer, the schooner brought neither letters or papers but a message from Mͬ T[homas] M[iddleton] that there were ten mails due from the north. Mͬˢ Smith & myself read aloud to each other, <u>she</u> in the evening. luckily for me her eyes do not suffer from it. I began by reading to her [*Mantell's*] the 'Wonders of Geology' but she would not believe any of the positive truths brought forward by the most scientific & religious men about the creation, Man being posterior to that of numberless classes of Animals which existed myriads of ages before the present state of the globe– She insists that the <u>Deluge</u> only brought about all the changes– in short I found it impossible to convince her of the contrary & sought other reading to amuse her and finished the 'Wonders' to myself.[1] You may recollect I recommended the book to you– before reading it however, let me advise you (in order to understand it better) to read Keith's 'Demonstration of the truths of the Christian religion' which explains in a most satisfactory manner the successive epochs of the different formations of the globe, in accordance with the 1ˢᵗ chap.ͬ of Genesis. Now Mͬˢ S. who recommended the book to me will not agree with <u>D</u>ͬ <u>K</u>[eith] so <u>I</u> need not expect to convince her. I ought to say there is a great deal of Dr Mantell's work (Wonders &c.) which I cannot understand.

Your Father and brothers went to Combahee on the 20$\underline{th}$. Harry was rather unwilling to go but y^r Father who was extremely anxious that he should, on promising that he would bring him back in a week, succeeded in persuading him– he will not of course return at the end of a week, & I daresay Harry's visit will be the only one he will make to that agreeable place. Before they went a ci devant Carpenter, now a landed proprietor, came here to give his opinion about a new roof to the house, & as I know you take an interest in what relates to this matter, I inform you that in two months the work is to begin– a parapet 4 feet high is to be placed round the house to conceal the high roof, the frame work of which is to remain– only new shingles– the house to be covered with Roman cement,[2] & what is of most importance the chimneys to have earthen pots over them to prevent their smoking– I hear of no internal improvements such as raising several feet, the ceiling of the drawing room, though Mr West-naer did speak of raising the window sashes by weights.

We had very cold weather the day after I wrote to you & I often thought how severely you must have felt it at Philad^a out of doors– within, you cannot feel it as much as we do here. now it is again becoming milder, though white frosts continue. Y^r Father after 3 weeks, at last tuned the piano forte & by Mrs Smith's earnest entreaties Cath^e sometimes plays, which you may suppose gives me great pleasure.[3] W^m begged me to request you to write to him. it is probable he will remain at Combahee some time after y^r Father leaves it. This is nearly the anniversary of your attack of scarlet fever– & actually, that of my dear Elea-nor's death![4] recollections sufficient to sadden a Mother– but I must console myself with the consideration that she is blest in a better world, & that my dearest Eliza is as happy in this as she can be. With the hope that her happiness may long continue, her affect^{te} Mother concludes– M. H. M.

Pray remember me affectionately to M^r & Mrs Fisher & M^r & Mrs Harrison– Mrs Smith begs to be kindly remembered to you–

P.S. (after breakfast) Mrs Smith has been reading aloud a book W^m brought on Mrs Barclay's recommendation 'A new Home, or glimpses of Western life by Mrs Mary Clavers – an actual settler' some parts of it are amusing but there is a good deal of trash in it. We wish you to enquire who this Mrs Clavers[5] is, whether a New Yorker, & what was her maiden name. Have you read a romance of real life by Miss Burney?[6] Of course it has not found its way here–

PHi

1. In this instance, Mrs. Middleton was more open-minded than her daughter about emerging scientific theories about the earth's formation and evolution. Eliza re-

fused to read Robert Chambers' *The Vestiges of the Natural History of Creation*, a book recommended by her mother, because she had heard it was "atheistical." EMF to MHM, May 8, 1845, private collection.

2. A kind of stucco.

3. After Mrs. Smith left, Mrs. Middleton told Eliza she had been "so kind during her visit in every particular, assisting me in the management of the sick Negroes, & endeavouring to manage Catherine in which she often succeeded, that I shall miss her exceedingly." MHM to EMF, February 17, 1840, ScHi.

4. Eleanor, the Middletons' second daughter, died in St. Petersburg in January 1827.

5. Mrs. Clavers was the pen name of Caroline Matilda Kirkland (1801–1864), who wrote about the rough conditions of pioneer life in Michigan. *A New Home* was published in 1839.

6. Fanny Burney (1752–1840) was a popular English novelist and diarist. She also wrote under her married name, Mme d'Arblay.

～

To Mrs. Fisher, Philadelphia

M.P. Feb$^{\underline{y}}$ 25$^{\underline{th}}$ 1840

My dearest Eliza

I sit down to write a few hurried lines before breakfast, to send by your Father who is going to Charleston. Susan & Oliver too are going– a very short visit have they made! they brought the two little Girls on Sunday & say they cannot stay longer from school, besides which Oliver is very busy in town, & M$^{\underline{rs}}$ Chisolm is to leave it on Friday– She has the care of little Olivia who I was disappointed at not seeing. Coosey & El$^{\underline{r}1}$ are both looking well & they both beg me to thank you for your presents with which they are greatly pleased. Susan is well though thin, & says she has never been so long as she has been this winter, without a Cough. She expresses great gratitude to you & also to M$^{\underline{rs}}$ Fisher & M$^{\underline{rs}}$ Harrison for their kindness to Mary– Will$^{\underline{m}}$ brought up on Sunday M$^{\underline{r}}$ M[itchell] King & another friend of his, M$^{\underline{r}}$ Manning, & returned with them yesterday– (he was to go to a ball at M$^{\underline{rs}}$ Pettigru's[2]) The former enquired of me whether you were coming this winter to Carolina. I had not time to speak with W$^{\underline{m}}$ on the subject of M$^{\underline{r}}$ Fisher's letter, he being so much occupied with his friends. He says Emma Smith will come very soon to see me– M$^{\underline{r}}$ S– only brought her to Charleston & went back immediately to his plantation, her stay therefore will be very short– Susan says she is looking very thin, but in good spirits. I hear nothing of M$^{\underline{r}}$ M$^{\underline{c}}$Leod, but told W$^{\underline{m}}$ what you wished to be done for him–

I have rec^d no letter from you since that I answered last week of the 12 & 13<u>th</u> & was very angry with myself when I recollected that I had forgotten to <u>scold</u> you for playing at Battledore– Do you not remember how I warned you against that sort of exercise? be assured it is very dangerous, so no more of it, I entreat you– & I think 4 or 5 miles walking, rather too much for you just now– <u>here</u> it would be out of the question, for the ther^r has been for the last week upwards of 70<u>°</u> during the day, so that I walk immediately after breakfast to avoid the heat of the Sun. Susan has just come down, she begs me to tell you that although I have not given her the scolding which you commissioned me to give, yet her own conscience gives it, but nothing that she could write, could express the gratitude she feels towards you for your kindness to Mary, & as she writes to <u>her</u> frequently, you hear from her of her well being. I assure her that you would be very glad to hear from her yourself, but she seems to think her letters would be superfluous.

You must not expect to hear from me regularly just now, for next week I believe there will be no opportunity for sending a letter, as your Father & brother (perhaps both) will be at Combahee & as the Schooner is gone there, for the timber necessary for the scaffolding &c–[3] there will be no chance for my forwarding a letter for perhaps a fortnight, unless some chance visitor should come. If Emma, she will most likely be here in a day or two. No news of John & his family yet, which makes me anxious on account of poor little Harry–[4] had he been well your brother would probably have gone to Charleston to be present at the races & to arrange matters at the house which is to be given up on the 9<u>th</u> of March–[5] I must now conclude with the united love of all the family to you & requesting you give mine to M^r & Mrs Fisher & kind remembrance to M^r & Mrs Harrison & believe me my dearest Eliza y^r affect^{te} Mother M. H. M.

Give my love to Sophia T. when you write– Pray tell Mary with my love that on opening the paper enclosing the bead baskets, Coosey read that the largest was a present for Sarah– this I did not know, or should have given it to her when she was here– in the Spring she will come, & then it shall be given to her.

ScHi

1. Eleanor was the third of Oliver and Susan Middleton's daughters. At this time they had Mary, who was at school in Philadelphia; Matilda (Coosey); Eleanor; and the baby, Olivia.

2. Probably Mrs. James Louis Petigru, the former Jane Amelia Postell. Petigru

(1789–1863) was one of the most successful lawyers in Charleston in the forty years before the Civil War. He was also, with Henry Middleton, a strong Unionist during the nullification controversy in the 1830s.

3. The scaffolding was to be set up to repair the house at Middleton Place.

4. He had malaria.

5. The Middletons were about to give up the house they rented on Boundary Street because the owner would not repair it. Henry Middleton proposed staying at a hotel when they were in town, an idea which was not popular with his wife. "Fancy my being placed either in Meeting or Broad St. in May or June!" she sniffed. In the end, they kept the house for several years. MHM to EMF, February 1, 1840, PHi.

Solitude and loneliness, words Mrs. Middleton used in the next letter, were characteristics of her life at Middleton Place. When Henry Middleton and William were away, either at Combahee supervising the rice plantations or in Charleston on business, she and Catherine were often the only family members at Middleton Place, and Catherine, unfortunately, was less a companion than a worry. Ten days or sometimes two weeks might pass without mail or news.

Reading was Mrs. Middleton's greatest resource, but as she grew older her eyesight grew weaker, so she always hoped Harry or one of his brothers would stay and read to her. Her children, aware of her need for company, went to Middleton Place as often as they could, and Sally and John and Oliver and Susan frequently left their children there to be with their grandmother. Visits from her old friends like Mrs. Smith or her sister-in-law, Septima Sexta Rutledge, gave Mrs. Middleton pleasure, but her comment to Eliza, "how dull our time passes here," was nevertheless understandable.[1]

1. MHM to EMF, February 23, 1844, PHi.

To Mrs. Fisher, Philadelphia

M.P. March 8th 1840

My dearest Eliza

I mentioned to you in my letter of the 24th ulto that there would probably be no opportunity of sending another for a fortnight– unluckily there has been none for my receiving one from you later than that I have already answered which makes me very anxious to hear from you. The anniversary of your marriage is fast approaching– I often think of this time twelvemonth, of all the circumstances relating to the event which has made you so happy, & although greatly as I miss your society, yet cannot but feel glad that you are not partaking of the loneliness of this place which you used so often to deplore. I had my full share of it for five days, when your Father & Brothers accompanied Susan to town– Harry was unwilling to leave me alone, but your Father <u>kindly</u> urged him to go, & he consented– On their return, I requested him not to go to Combahee, & he has remained with me for the last week. The solitude as you may suppose is not to his taste, & he is impatient to accept Oliver's invitation to spend a week with him which he will do as soon as your Father & W<u>m</u> return– We have been expecting your Aunt Huger & Emma every day for they promised to be here last week– the latter is to return to Sav<u>a</u> river on the 20<u>th</u>

Harry often expresses his wish to proceed to Philad<u>a</u> earlier than May, whether that can be accomplished I do not know. He is kind enough to read aloud to me every evening after Tea– he has chosen Boswell's life of Johnson for that purpose which I had read many years before but still find it entertaining. You may imagine how dull the evenings were without that resource, & that of M<u>rs</u> Smith's cheerful chat. In a note from her she says 'I called the other day to see Miss Roupell & we laughed over <u>her double</u> blessing. She could not remember of whom the Twin story had been told, but desired me to let Eliza know that if the Sybil <u>should be right</u>, she promises to take charge of one of the twain, & will make a pet of it– provided the Mother consents'– What think you of that?

The new moon brought us a most welcome rain, though very insufficient to fill the pond.[1] The yellow Jessamine is blooming in profusion, the Calycanthus in flower, nearly all the trees in leaf– On reading over your letter of the 19<u>th</u> & 21<u>st</u> I recollect that W<u>m</u> brought it a week ago, & that I have not yet answered it. Of course it was very interesting to me to hear of your famous party, & of everything else that you write. Just as I had written thus far, John entered the room to my great delight– he gave a good account of all his family– Hal being much better & he had left him with his Mother. He immediately put into my hands your acceptable letter of the 27<u>th</u> ult<u>o</u> & one from my brother which M<u>r</u> Fisher had been so good as to forward– John read your letter to me which gave me great pleasure 'till I heard of your being hoarse– when that is the case you ought not to sing– pray be prudent, & do not exert your voice when in that state. What you mention of M<u>r</u> [George Herbert] Thorndike appears very like being in love– You will soon know whether the attachment is mutual, I suppose–

From the account you give of your réunions, they must be very pleasant. the music always excellent– It was unlucky for W<u>m</u> that you missed speaking with M<u>r</u> Blunt.[2] I suppose it must be owing to a feeling of delicacy that Julia does not write to you, knowing now the altered state of her Father's fortune she may consider it proper to keep herself more distant from you– this however is all surmise on my part. In your former letter you mentioned the melancholy state of poor M̲̲ͬͭ March. I think with you she must be insane to perpetrate such thefts– who could ever have supposed her capable of committing acts of that kind! John heard of her through M̲̲ͬͭ J[ulius] Pringle to whom M̲̲ͬͭ Barclay had mentioned the circumstances & John & Sally went to pay her a visit– She told them M̲̲ͬͭ M. was gone to Baltimore probably to enter the Convent there.

You speak of M̲̲ͬͭ Fisher's employing two women, & sewing & cutting out herself so industriously that I guessed what kind of work you must all be engaged in, & could not help smiling as John read the passage– however he did not observe me, & made no remark. He read to Cath̲ͤ your wish to hear from her– I fear you will be disappointed– She does not seem inclined to write.

9̲̲ͭͪ I must finish this lest he should set off in haste without waiting to see his Father– The house in Bound̲ͭ St is to be retained until May– Both Harry & John think little Olivia beautiful, the flower of the flock they say– John says <u>his</u> little M[ary] H[elen] is greatly improved both in health & appearance. Sally had ridden on horseback with him twice, to my astonishment for she has often told me she could never again attempt such exercise– he says she found the rides of great service to her chest, of which she sometimes complains, & also of her side– he seems however to consider her health good. I shall make him promise to bring her here next month–

11̲̲ͭͪ I have prevailed upon John to remain until after dinner today, longer he says he cannot stay, whether his Father comes or not, as Sally was desired to send the boat for him to Georgetown on Friday next & if he should not be there, on the Sunday after– he is to begin to plant also next week. It is probable that Oliver will go to Edisto next Friday. You perceive it is not my fault that you do not receive my letters regularly once a week, as I have no means of sending to Charleston– I was on the point of finishing this, when Anne M[iddleton]³ drove Sarah [Huger] Wilkinson to the door in her poney Phaeton– <u>You</u> were of course the chief subject of our conversation– the latter recollected this day as being the anniversary of her arrival here [*for Eliza's wedding*] & said she should have written to you had not Emma appeared jealous of her being your correspondent. She will however she says write, when her Sister goes to Sav̲ͣ river. <u>She</u> has received permission it seems to remain in Charleston another week & I begged Sarah to come with her Sister to stay some days. She begged me to write you the speech M̲ͬ M[itchell] King made after being here a fortnight ago. That he was now reconciled to his grey hairs, when he found <u>you</u> no longer here– M̲̲ͬͭ <u>Lizzy</u> K[ing] is shortly to be again confined. Alice

Heyward is also at Stono & will probably come they say & see me. I begged them to tell me some Charleston news to communicate to you. Henry A. M[iddleton] is to take his family shortly to New Haven for the benefit of schools for the children, & leave them there while <u>he</u> proceeds to Italy. Miss Barclay the daughter of Ant.^y B[arclay] has eloped with Mr Bergain– This I suppose you have heard– it is news that Miss Major⁴ wrote to Sarah.

All Charleston they say is ringing with praises of M^r [Hugh Swinton] Legaré's speech⁵ of last week on the subject of the Appeal made by Mr Ball who had produced a Codicil written he said by his unfortunate brother, bequeathing him his property, in case he & his Wife should perish simultaneously in the Steamer! This presentiment appeared very improbable– there were no witnesses to attest the Codicil & Mr L. gained this Cause as well as the former Suit. Georgina [Middleton] is also at Stono & well– Harry & John joined us & walked round the garden, & we could not prevail on our visitors to stay & dine. Have you seen Mrs Gibson lately? when you do, remember me kindly to her. I must now conclude my dearest Eliza with love to M^r & Mrs Fisher & am your Affectionate Mother M. H. M.

Harry & John send their love.

ScHi

1. There had been such a long drought that the well at Middleton Place was dry. MHM to EMF, February 17, 1840, ScHi.

2. Mr. Blunt was a New Yorker who would probably have had news of Julia Ward.

3. Anne Middleton was the daughter of Arthur and Alicia (Russell) Middleton of Bolton plantation on the Stono River. Georgina Middleton, mentioned in the last paragraph, was her sister-in-law.

4. Sarah Major was Miss Sarah Moore's niece, the daughter of Jane (Moore) and Henry Major.

5. This famous case affected the Middletons' friend Mrs. Barclay. South Carolinian Hugh Ball and his wife, who was Mrs. Barclay's sister, both perished when the *Pulaski* exploded in June 1838. At issue was which of them had survived longer. If it could be shown that Mrs. Ball lived longer than her husband (which Hugh Legaré's melodramatic speech succeeded in doing), the major part of her estate would be divided between her two surviving sisters, Catherine (Channing) Barclay and Anna (Channing) Pell. Mrs. Barclay thus benefited handsomely from Mr. Legaré's victory. (She and her sister had already been awarded $80,000 in an earlier suit.) MHM to EMF, February 9, 1840, PHi.

⌒

To Mrs. Middleton, Middleton Place

Philadelphia – March 11$\underline{\text{th}}$ 1840

According to your own prediction, my dearest Mamma the hitherto regular weekly despatch from M. Place has not yet arrived– and I have been disappointed these last two days– altho' not as much so as I should have been if you had not foretold the probable delay which w$\underline{\text{d}}$ be occasioned by the absence of Papa & my brothers at Combahee– Tomorrow I shall hope to hear however & as I begin this a day before hand, may still have the pleasure of thanking you for the accustomed & ever welcome letter. Being detained at home this morng by a slight sorethroat, which I should not nurse myself for, unless I felt rather lazily disposed, and unwilling to brave rather a keen March wind, I thought I would devote to you the spare time generally dedicated to my health & exercize, and which rarely finds me sitting within doors–

Nothing worthy of note has occurred since I last wrote– I passed an hour with Mary Nixon on Friday eveng– after leaving Aunt H's– and on Saturday we had enough little girls to make up a double cotillion, who danced very merrily with Mary [Middleton] and enjoyed themselves far more than older people do at Parties– Mary was decidedly the best dancer in the room & really acquitted herself with much grace & spirit– They assembled at 6– amused themselves with caricatures &c until tea time, after which, at a little after 7 the dancing began, & they quadrilled, galopped & waltzed to their hearts content until near nine– when we gave them Ice fruit & bonbons, and sent them home as happy as little Princesses– & wishing that it could have lasted forever! Happy age! indeed, when so little delights them– I was excessively amused at the gallantry of the only two <u>beaux</u> we could find for them– The boys (M$\underline{\text{rs}}$ Montgomery's[1]) had never <u>even seen</u> dancing before, but joined in, and having good ears I suppose, got along very tolerably, and with great satisfaction to themselves, afterwards declaring they liked it very much, & never were happier in their lives! Altogether I never saw a merrier little groupe, and they parted mutually pleased with each other– I was able to retire early, and rise perfectly well & able to go twice to Church– as I wished– but only heard M$\underline{\text{r}}$ Odenheimer in the morng– as he preached elsewhere in the afternoon & we had M$\underline{\text{r}}$ Lambert as a substitute, but not at all equal to him in talent, and the power of exciting interest– In the eveng– we had besides M$\underline{\text{r}}$ & M$\underline{\text{rs}}$ H[arrison]– the McMurtries,[2] Sally Hare & half a dozen men– some of whom were agreeable, and gave an enlivening turn to the conversation– Charles Stewart[3] who came in, says Delia [Parnell] will probably be back in America in June next– and described her as perfectly happy in Ireland and having entirely won the esteem & affection of her husband's family, who think very highly of her & her talents– She no longer considers it sinful to mix in society and appears to enjoy the pleasant circle in which her lot is cast, extremely– and to have made many friends among them– Her brother is a remarkably amiable and from all I hear, excellent young man, and I hope we shall see more of him, for considering the dearth of <u>nice</u> young men, he is quite a valuable addition to our present batch of them–

I began to be so uneasy about Julia, that not hearing on Monday, I wrote her a most beseeching letter, which I think she will certainly answer immediately, and I shall probably hear tomorrow– Mrs Barclay, from whom I heard yesterday, says she was well a short time since when she called upon her at D^r [John] Francis's–⁴ So that I conclude her silence has been entirely owing to her distress at Sam's conduct, and her quitting her former home– I shall soon know– Mrs Barclay wrote me a description of the Fancy Ball,⁵ which I shall not attempt to transcribe, as it w^d take up too much time & space, & you take no particular interest in any of the people– She says William would have <u>wept</u> to see Mr Hunt⁶ in a shabby, tawdry Turkish dress suffering under the weight of a Turban loaded with jewels & Mrs Parrish's diamonds– "Having cultivated a regard for him she felt quite distressed at his frightened appearance"– She also says that Harry's friend Mrs Ray,⁷ still mourning too much for that beloved Richard, to take off black, went masqued in a [*missing*] This I think the height of affectation & absurdity– And the [*missing*] piece of pretence that could have been imagined to make herself ridiculous.

M^rs B[arclay] in speaking of some <u>foolish reports</u> in N.Y. mentions the one of her being engaged to a Mr White– and cautions me against believing what has not the <u>slightest foundation</u>. The truth is that no such report ever <u>did</u> reach me, & by her manner of telling it I doubt whether she is much annoyed at its being spoken of– altho' she protests against "liking <u>Boys</u> however handsome & well bred" and adds that she is sure his approbation of her does not extend to wishing for his wife a woman of her discreet years– She says moreover that she had determined to accompany Mr Pell⁸ to Carolina, & had even had a Trunk packed with summer wardrobe in order to pay Jane [Lynch Pringle] a visit of some weeks– when the tears of Hotty & Cath⁹ at her intended desertion made her resign her plans for their sake– I wrote a long letter to Edward on Saturday, & enclosed it to Percy Drayton, who is to sail for Rio in the Enterprize very shortly– It seems the Marion arrived there on the 8th of Jany having made a very short passage from the Coast of Africa– M^rs [William] Hunter¹⁰ who writes to her son, had not seen Edward yet– I suppose that you have got letters by the G^t Western [*from Uncle Oliver Hering*]– but they must have known of y^r being in Carolina, & therefore directed thither. I have not rec^d the letter from Aunt Hering, which she promised me–

Thursday 12th The Anniversary of my marriage! and joyfully shall we both keep it, for we have nothing but happiness to look back upon during the last year– which I only hope may be followed by others as happy and as free from care & sorrow– I need scarcely have written the former word– for certainly my cares will be encreased this present year– but as long as I have as good & affectionate a husband, and as many kind friends, I may rely on the continuance of my happiness– even altho' some troubles may be added thereto– But, dearest Mamma is it not delightful to think that the first year of matrimony which they say is the most proving of all has passed without a single cross word or look having ever been exchanged between us– or the slightest misunderstanding ever disturbing our mutual confidence in each other– I take not the least credit to myself for the preservation of peace in our ménage – for you know what an irritable & hasty temper I have– but really when one has to deal with such a heavenly temper as my dear husband's, I must have had a devilish one not to agree with him in every respect– Indeed I cannot believe that a more perfect disposition could be found any where– and I, who must have plenty of opportunities of judging, candidly confess, that I never met with his superior in that respect– or could wish it altered in the slightest degree– But perhaps it is foolish to indulge myself in these praises, just and well deserved as they are– and you will surely acknowledge them to be so as far as you know or can form an opinion–

Mr Harrison came in this morng– and with a most affectionate salute made such a flattering speech to me that I really am too modest to repeat it– He also sent you a message which I hardly dare deliver– but as he insisted that I should I suppose I cannot refuse to obey his positive commands– You must recollect that he deferred coming to a decision about my character until the year was entirely out, but he now comes to such a complimentary conclusion that if I could ever doubt his sincerity, I should be inclined to do so on the present occasion– well aware that I do not at all deserve his unqualified approbation– He gives it however in these words, which I shall try to remember exactly– "Tell your mother that I have no fault to find with you & entirely approve of you, and think you worthy of my nephew–" Which last is the highest commendation from him– For I really believe he regards Fisher as near perfection as possible– He said moreover many other things of the same kind, & nearly overwhelmed me in my modesty, and consciousness of not meriting half of what he said of me– But, as you may suppose, praise from his lips, which never speak but with sincerity, was most valuable to me– The old Lady afterwards added her's, & many affectionate things besides, and desired me to tell you, with her love, that "she is sure your mother's heart w$^{\underline{d}}$ have been gratified if you could have heard her & M$^{\underline{r}}$ Harrison speak of me at their breakfast table this morning"– I tried to express suitably my gratitude for their good opinion, but when I know how little I merit it, really I am ashamed of myself–

Adieu my dearest Mamma– I hope this may find you well & happy– but alas! I have no certainty that you are so– not having heard from you since Monday week– I ought to say that my throat was so much better last eveng that I spent it at a Quaker tea-party in Arch S$^{\underline{t}}$ to which I was invited by Fisher's Aunt M$^{\underline{rs}}$ [Hannah Fisher] Smith– They had the greatest abundance of good things, & were very kind indeed to me, & presented me with a superb bouquet of flowers– Tonight we are to have a <u>select few</u> at home to celebrate our anniversary– How I wish you and the rest of my dear M. Place friends could be of the party– Yr friend M$^{\underline{r}}$ Egerton Bridges is to be here– He called this morng– & F. invited him to return– Goodbye once more my dearest Mamma– I am as ever Y$^{\underline{r}}$ most attached & dutiful Daughter Eliza

Fisher begs me to say how happy he is today, and how much he thanks <u>you</u> for it– & for me. M$^{\underline{rs}}$ F. desires her kindest remembrances– She has been excessively nervous for several days past, but is cheered up again today, and ever anxious to contribute to our enjoyment & gratification in every way, has exerted herself & made her usual preparations for <u>company</u>– altho' there are only to be a dozen people here– But she is not satisfied unless she has everything of the best to offer her friends–

Private Collection

    1. Elizabeth Phillips (Mrs. John C.) Montgomery was the daughter of Sophia Chew Phillips (1769–1841) and granddaughter of the chief justice of Pennsylvania Benjamin Chew (1722–1810). From among her eight sons perhaps she brought James and Charles that evening. They were fourteen and twelve years old respectively.

    2. Rebecca Harrison (Mrs. James) McMurtrie was George Harrison's niece.

    3. Charles Stewart and his sister, Delia Stewart Parnell, were the children of Commodore Charles and Delia (Tudor) Stewart. Commodore Stewart (1778–1869) commanded the *Constitution* during the War of 1812 and at this time was in charge of the Philadelphia Navy Yard.

    Charles, Jr., became a lawyer and civil engineer. Delia, who was Eliza's age, married Irishman John Henry Parnell and was the mother of Charles Stewart Parnell, the champion of Irish home rule.

    4. John W. Francis, a prominent New York doctor, was Julia Ward's uncle. Sam Ward was her brother.

    5. The Henry Brevoorts had entertained about six hundred of New York's fashion-

able citizens at a costume ball on February 27. Henry Brevoort, Jr., a wealthy New York, was interested in the arts and was a friend and supporter of Washington Irving. His wife was the former Laura Carson from Charleston.

6. Jonathan Hunt, who lived in New York, was an old friend of the Middletons and of many of their friends. Mrs. Parish was probably the wife of Daniel Parish. She was a South Carolinian; he was a New York merchant who, with his brothers, specialized in the southern dry goods trade. The Parishes built a house in Newport in 1851.

7. Mrs. Mary Ray was the widow of Richard Ray. After her husband's death, she spent much of her time in Europe. Her brother-in-law, Robert Ray, a wealthy merchant, was said to have the finest house in New York. Allan Nevins, ed., *The Diary of Philip Hone, 1828–1851* (New York: Dodd, Mead & Co., 1936), 111.

8. Duncan Pell was Mrs. Barclay's brother-in-law.

9. Cath was Mrs. Barclay's daughter, Catherine; Hotty has not been identified.

10. Mary (Robinson) Hunter came from a Quaker family in New York and Newport. Her husband, William Hunter (1774–1849), also from Newport, was a lawyer who in 1840 was in Rio de Janeiro as U.S. minister to the court of Dom Pedro, emperor of Brazil. Hunter, a former senator from Rhode Island, and Henry Middleton served in Congress together.

⁓

To Mrs. Middleton, Middleton Place

Philadelphia – March 19th̲ 1840

I had not heard from you for nearly a fortnight my dearest Mamma, and was beginning to feel very fidgetty, notwithstanding my resolutions to be patient, when on Sunday eveng– Fisher went down at dusk to the P. Office and returned with two letters for me– one of which I eagerly snatched and running my eyes over it, was delighted to find that you were all perfectly well– The other was from Aunt Hering.

I have at last heard from Julia who as a sort of apology for not writing sooner, says she has been paying a visit to her friend Mary Ward[1] in Boston, of whose kindness and attentions to her she speaks with great gratitude– attributing to them her recovery to tolerable spirits, which had before been terribly depressed– She says she had passed whole days in her rocking chair, with the room darkened and her eyes half closed– The excitement of suffering was succeeded by a state of perfect apathy and indifference to everything & everybody– But the removal from scenes which had such painful associations, and change of air, restored her to a more natural and happier tone of mind and she writes in improved health & spirits. She says that her kind Uncle (I suppose the old bachelor John Ward) has consented to remain with them where they are– and she is thankful that he has, for the idea of leaving her Father's house was insupportable to her "especially as there was no occasion for such a sacrifice". So that after all, their affairs cannot be in so bad a condition as they have been represented to be, else it would surely be <u>necessary</u> for them to quit such an establishment– which cannot be maintained without much expense– But of this W<u>m</u> probably knows much more than I do, for she says she has written to him, & therefore I need not, as I have told you all that she says of herself, and the rest of the letter is addressed <u>particularly</u> to me, and treats only of <u>my</u> private affairs–

I have had quite a fright about my eyes since I last wrote. They were then slightly inflamed, & the following day became much worse– so that I went out only with a double green veil (which made people stare) and sat in darkness visible not using them at all, and for several days staying at home in the eveng– with my back to the small quantity of candle light permitted– while Fisher read constantly to me when my friends were not visiting me– The Piano was a great resource to me, for I could play in the dark– But by care & prudently abstaining from meat & butter, I have almost entirely recovered– and nothing but weakness now troubles me– I believe going to M<u>rs</u> [Thomas I.] Wharton's[2] on Tuesday eveng– did not do them much good, for she lights her house with Gas, the glare from which I found rather distressing– But as she had made her Tea party, such as it was, expressly for me, I could not avoid going– There was nobody there but M<u>rs</u> Captain Read[3] Sally Ingersoll, & Sally Waln & their own family, & we had a very quiet but rather pleasant eveng–

Yesterday afternoon I had several pleasant visitors– Mary Nixon, who I persuaded to stay, & go with me to Aunt Harrison's to tea, M<u>rs</u> Taylor of V<u>a</u>[4] & M<u>r</u> Odenheimer– between whom we had a very animated discussion on <u>Christian Liberality</u>, & how far it may be safely carried now a days, & also on the Apostolical succession of the Bishops,[5] which M<u>rs</u> T. expressed some doubts about, and M<u>r</u> O. immediately defended most warmly– It is one of his favourite doctrines, & I am afraid the good lady shocked him not a little by her doubts– He was evidently much amused at her manner of arguing and very good naturedly & patiently set her right on [some] points– I like him better every time I see him– There is so much simplicity of character, joined to such strong sense, and sound learning– which in so young a man is really astonishing– I am delighted that he has been <u>permanently</u> elected Rector of our Church– for I am sure we could not find anywhere more talent and a better heart & feelings– His independance and fearlessness in what he considers the right cause, also raises him highly in my estimation, and altho' I am inclined to think him rather too <u>strict</u> in some of his notions, that is after all erring on the right side, and is a fault which will correct itself when he is older and mixes more with his congregation– He spoke of the pleasure with which he saw Fisher at his Friday lectures and wished some more gentlemen would follow his example– I did not tell him that it was a sort of <u>compromise</u> that he [*Fisher*] proposed himself, preferring to attend them to going on Sunday afternoon, when he says he always feels drowzy, & derives no benefit from the <u>second</u> sermon– One being as much as he can well digest– Of course I do not insist upon his going against his inclination, still less because he has always been in the habit of dining with his Uncle & Aunt on Sunday, and they are disappointed if they do not see him– But he likes the Friday lectures very much, & indeed they are very admirable and instructive in the highest degree–

I wrote another letter to Edward yesterday– as Mr Hunter[6] was polite enough to propose taking one to Baltimore, whence a vessel is to sail for Rio in a few days– and the one I sent by Percy Drayton may not reach him for some time as they will be detained at Norfolk I hear– I tried to make my letter as amusing as possible, and worth going so far– but I had not much news for him– The best of course was that all our dear friends in Carolina were well by the last accounts– I was busy helping Fisher with his invitations for our Wistar party[7] which is to take place on Saturday, & folded 70 covers for him on Tuesday– I shall <u>clear out</u> & spend the eveng– with Fenwick Jones, who expects Adela [Newton] to be with her– She is coming to stay a week with her and I shall be very glad to see her– Captn Newton has obtained the appointment on board the Steam Frigate Fulton to try certain new Shot– This is a most fortunate thing, for he will now have full pay, and get along rather better it is to be hoped– Adela is trying to sell all their furniture & hire their house at Burlington[8] & intends going into cheap lodgings in the Neighborhood of Brooklyn, while he is stationed there–

I am delighted to hear that dear Sally is so well, I shall write to John in a few days– I am sorry to learn from Susan's letter to Mary that she does not intend to come on here next Summer, but to send for M– I hope she may change her mind again, for it will be a great disappointment to me not to see her and the children– My eyes are fatigued and warn me to close this scrawl and give them repose– Therefore Adieu my dearest Mamma With best love to Papa, my brothers & Kitty I remain Y^r most affectionate Daughter Eliza

P.S. My throat is quite well again– but I sing very little– Mrs Fisher is rather less nervous, & now eats <u>occasionally</u>– but still does with less food & sleep than anyone I ever knew– She is gratified by y^r kind enquiries, & always begs to be remembered– as do also M^r & Mrs Harrison who are quite well–

Private Collection

1. Mary Ward (no relation of Julia's) was the daughter of Thomas W. Ward, a Boston businessman. He was the head of Baring's American branch and treasurer of Harvard College, among other activities.

2. Mrs. Wharton was the former Arabella Griffith. Her husband, Thomas I. Wharton (1791–1856), was a prominent lawyer and jurist. Active in the American Philosophical Society and first president of the Historical Society of Pennsylvania, he also attended the Wistar Parties (see note below).

3. Mrs. George Campbell Read's husband, Captain (later Commodore) Read (1797–1862), was a longtime friend of George Harrison's and in 1840 was stationed at the Philadelphia Navy Yard. His wife was amusing, but Fisher thought her superficial and was disappointed that, though musical, she was not interested in playing music with Eliza. JFF to GH, August 3, 1839, PHi, BrC.

4. This may have been Susan Randolph (Mrs. Bennett) Taylor (b. 1782), the daughter of Edmund and Elizabeth (Nicholas) Randolph. She would have known Mrs. Fisher and Mrs. Harrison when her father was President Washington's secretary of state, 1794–95.

5. Apostolic succession refers to the belief, particular to the Roman Catholic Church, that bishops have certain powers (such as the power to ordain priests) because they are the direct successors of the apostles. Odenheimer was among the so-called High Church Episcopalians who thought likewise, thus appearing to move closer to the Catholics. Eliza later came to disapprove strongly of such High Church tendencies.

6. Charles Hunter, a naval officer, was one of the William Hunters' sons. He considered Eliza "one of the very finest & accomplished women" in Philadelphia. Edward Middleton to EMF, January 6, 1842, Edward Middleton Rea Collection.

7. Dr. Caspar Wistar invited the same group of friends to his house every Sunday evening, and after his death in 1818, the Wistar Parties continued as a men's discussion club. Membership was limited to twenty members of the American Philosophical Society, but out-of-town visitors were always invited.

8. Burlington, New Jersey, on the Delaware River north of Philadelphia.

~

To Mrs. Fisher, Philadelphia

M.P. March 23$\underline{d}$ 1840

Your letter of the 11$\underline{th}$ & 12$\underline{th}$ my dearest Eliza was exceedingly gratifying to my feelings, as it expressed the happiness you were enjoying in the kindness shown you by M$\underline{rs}$ F & M$\underline{r}$ & M$\underline{rs}$ Harrison on the Anniversary of your Marriage. It is always a source of comfort to me when I am regretting your absence, that you have married so excellent a husband, & that his family appreciate you so highly– but not more than I think you deserve. May all succeeding anniversaries be spent as happily by you as this has been! Cares, as you observe, must necessarily ensue, but let us hope, no sorrows– & that the joy experienced by the arrival of the stranger may compensate for the care it will cause you. I had fancied the 12th would be commemorated by your friends before your letter informed me of their intention. no doubt you passed a very agreeable evening– How very subject you still are to sore throat! every letter amost, mentions a slight one– You ought to be more careful of yourself. Does your Physician prescribe for you, & give you rules for avoiding the recurrence of a malady which has made you suffer so much? You had better ask his opinion, if you do, let me know what he advises.

I mentioned in my last that Harry would perhaps accompany your Father & Wm to Charleston, he was however so kind as to remain with me, & luckily their visit was a shorter one than usual, & they brought your letter & one from my Sister Scarborough– She says it gives her great pleasure to hear that you are so happily married, & in another part writes 'I am much pleased to hear that Eliza is so well satisfied with her Pianoforte, pray remember me most kindly to her'– I must rectify an error I committed in my last letter which upon Harry's enquiring what I had said about him, annoyed him exceedingly, & said it must make him pass for a fool in your opinion– I misunderstood him in thinking he wished to have news of Mrs W[illing]– it was <u>Miss</u> W[adsworth] that he requested you to mention, being anxious to know whether she is in Philada– We have heard nothing of John since he went to Waccammaw. What you write of Mary would gratify her Mother so much, that I believe I shall copy it & send it if I have time– Oliver will probably return tomorrow to his family– J. A[llen] Smith met Emma the day after she left this, & told Wm they would both try to come here for a day or two before they return to Sav[annah] river which will be next week– We have had torrents of rain lately, not sufficient as yet to fill the pond, though of the greatest benefit to planters in general– The Carpenters from Combahee[1] are preparing the timber for scaffolding which will be placed round the house next month & as the upper ceilings are to be raised a foot higher, C & I shall be compelled to sleep on the drawg room floor– The plan is to make two sleeping rooms under the new roof, & have dormant windows in them.

About 3 weeks ago Mr Dwight from Cedar Grove[2] brought three of his friends here one eveng & sent to ask permission of yr Father to walk in the garden, he met them & then invited them to take wine, & brought them in the drawing room where Harry & I were sitting, to shew them the pictures, Statues &c– which they seemed to admire– When Sarah W[ilkinson] came to see me, she asked whether I had read the account in the Courier of this place, &

who it was who had lately been here– I recollected that M͇ʳ Yaden[3] the Editor of that paper was one of the party, & when Emma came she brought with her the Article which I am keeping for your amusement. What think you of the 'live Oaks piercing the Sky'! that is one of M͇ʳ Y's flights of fancy– the whole is written in the most complimentary style & several other houses in the neighbourhood are described. I am glad you invited M͇ʳ Brydges to your party. I daresay you will meet with some of his Countrymen at Philad͇ᵃ who arrived lately in a pleasure Yacht in Charleston & went on after a few days northward, leaving the Vessel. The Captain's name is Lyon, the names of the others W͇ᵐ does not know– I have only a few minutes left to finish this for the Man is waiting to carry it to Sav[ann]a[4] & from thence to Charleston tomorrow– All here unite in love to you– Give mine to M͇ʳ & M͇ʳˢ Fisher & best regards to M͇ʳ & M͇ʳˢ Harrison & believe me my dearest Eliza, your affect͇ᵗᵉ Mother M. H. M.

PHi

1. These were slave craftsmen from the Middletons' rice plantations.
2. Dwight had bought Cedar Grove Plantation, near Middleton Place, from J. Izard Middleton, who inherited it from his mother, Mary Izard Middleton.
3. Richard Yeadon (1802–1870) was editor of the *Charleston Courier*. His article, which appeared on March 7, 1840, also mentioned the house's "elegantly furnished" interior, with walls "decorated with numerous paintings, portraits, and historical and fancy pieces, by the great masters of the divine art."
4. Sometimes referred to as "Horse Savanna," this was land west of Middleton Place and away from the Ashley River which had its own settlement of about fifty slaves and where horses and other animals were raised and kept. At Henry Middleton's death in 1846, 167 sheep, 215 hogs, 34 chickens, 2 mules, and 5 horses were being raised there. Inventory & Appraisement of the Goods & Chattels of the Hon. Henry Middleton . . . on His Plantation Called Horse Savannah, December, 1846, MPlFdn.

When Julia Ward described to Eliza in March how depressed she had been and said she had written to William,[1] she didn't tell Eliza *why* she wrote to him: she had decided to break off their relationship. William was "completely astounded" by Julia's letter but could not bring himself to answer it, feeling it "would be painful to both of us." He had to accept her decision, he told Eliza, but he deplored "most deeply the state of mind which I believe mainly dictated it; a dreadful delusion with regard to her father, & the most unwarrantable cruelty towards herself." Still, since William also mentioned "that bitterness of spirit in me which she deprecates,"[2] it seems likely that there were other reasons which led Julia to conclude that William was not the man for her to marry.

William remained single until 1849, when he married Susan Pringle Smith. Julia married Samuel Gridley Howe in 1843.

1. See EMF to MHM, March 19, 1840, private collection.
2. William Middleton to EMF, March 29, 1840, ScHi. Julia's letter to William has not been found.

To Mrs. Fisher, Philadelphia

M.P. April 1st 1840

My dearest Eliza's letter of the 19th was brought to me last Friday by Oliver & Susan, who came with the children to pay me another short visit before leaving town for Edisto the end of this week– This was a sudden resolution in consequence of the holidays being fixed for this month & she preferred staying there with Mrs C[hisolm] to remaining alone in Charleston, Oliver being obliged to see after his plantation business– She is looking better than she did, & little Olivia is a very pretty, animated babe– she walks with the assistance of her Sisters who are delighted to attend upon her, & is a great Pet of her Papa's. Mr & Mrs A[llen] Smith came last Saturday on their way to Laurel hill[1] where they went on Sunday & returned on Monday Evening, after the departure of Oliver's family– I pressed them to remain a day or two longer, but they said they had many preparations to make in Charleston as <u>they</u> were also to leave it the end of the week, therefore they proceeded thither yesterday. Emma is looking better– she begged me to remind you that you owe her a letter– You were of course the chief subject of our conversation. She was delighted to hear such good accounts of you, & much pleased to learn that Mrs Newton's affairs were improving. She had not seen Georgina. You must have seen Mrs H. A. M[iddleton] for a short time I suppose, as the family were merely to pass through Philada & have probably learnt from the Girls all the Charleston news except what relates to themselves, i.e. that Arthur Rutledge[2] & Lizzy [Middleton] are devoted to each other– I suppose they told you that Joe Huger[3] & his cousin Miss [Mary] H[uger] are engaged to be married– Emma considers it a very imprudent engagement, as neither of them have wherewith to support themselves.

I was very sorry to hear that you had been suffering so much from your Eyes. I hope they continued to mend after you finished your letter, & that you have had no return of that distressing complaint. I was disappointed at your not giving an account of your party of the 12th– I am glad poor Julia is better in health & spirits.

Sunday 5$\underline{th}$– No opportunity having offered of sending this, I have been waiting from day to day the return of your Father & W$\underline{m}$ from Combahee to afford one. They have just arrived after nearly a fortnight's absence, & the former says he will either go to Charleston tomorrow, or send. He is desirous of your Aunt Rutledge's coming here this week before the upper part of the house is dismantled– her coming will probably depend upon the state of Major R[utledge]'s health– he writes word he has had another attack of fever & Ague, which must have weakened him greatly– you know he is always thin & sallow. You will soon hear of him from the Holbrooks who are going to pass a month at Philad$\underline{a}$ which will no doubt give you great pleasure–

6$\underline{th}$ W$\underline{m}$ told me yesterday that he had written to you from Combahee & had communicated the resolution of Julia to renounce him forever– Are you not grieved that she should have formed such a determination? It proceeds from deep religious feeling & conscientiousness, & raises her still higher in my estimation when I consider the great sacrifice she makes of her own feelings towards him– he had informed me of this decision three weeks ago, but begged me not to give you the least hint of it. When I read the account she gives you of her melancholy state of mind, I could easily understand the struggle she had had with her love & duty– Her letter to W$\underline{m}$ is really affecting, & I regret exceedingly that he has lost so excellent a <u>Promise</u> who would have made such a wife as he cannot expect to find again. I urged him strongly from the first perusal of her letter, to write & endeavour to make her retract her resolution– but he would not hear of it. Harry too thought him very right to let the matter rest– You agree with <u>me</u> I daresay in thinking he ought to write & try to persuade her to relent.

Emma mentioned that her Correspondent Sarah Major had lately refused the hand of M$\underline{r}$ Blunt: that is a proof of her disinterestedness– I was sorry to learn from her that M$\underline{r}$ Beche Laurence[4] was ruined. It was settled at breakfast that y$\underline{r}$ Father & W$\underline{m}$ should go to Charleston after an early dinner– the former advised Harry to accompany them– he seemed undetermined about going, but seems so tired of this solitude, that I shall not be surprised if he makes up his mind to go. He also intends to visit Combahee next week, & proposed my inviting M$\underline{rs}$ P. Smith to come & share my solitude, which I have done; whether M$\underline{rs}$ Blamyer will spare her, is doubtful. Catherine yesterday brought me the first strawberry that has appeared– the blossoms are innumerable. The long pond after the long continued rains, is now about 2 feet deep. The scaffolding round the house is not yet fixed nor will be I suppose until next week when there will be great confusion within from moving furniture &c. Two days hence

I hope to receive two letters from my dearest Eliza, this last week not having brought me any for want of a messenger– I am y^r Affect^{te} Mother M. H. M.

Y^r Father & brothers send their love to you– pray give mine to M^r & Mrs Fisher, who I hope is better.

PHi

1. Laurel Hill, a plantation owned by Allen Smith, was several miles northwest of Middleton Place.
2. Arthur Rutledge (1817–1876) was Eliza's first cousin, the youngest son of her Aunt Septima Sexta and Henry M. Rutledge.
3. Joseph Alston Huger (1815–1895) was Emma (Huger) Smith's younger brother. He married their first cousin, Mary Esther Huger (1820–1898).
4. William Beach Lawrence (1800–1881), of New York, was a lawyer and an expert in international law. The Lawrences bought a house in Newport in the 1830s and lived there year round after 1850.

～

To Mrs. Middleton, Middleton Place

Thursday morng– Philadelphia– April 9th 1840

It is ten days since I have heard from my dearest Mamma– and the last letter is of very old date, the 23rd of March– so that I was sadly disappointed when the Postman passed this morng– without bringing me a later one and I shall look out for him very eagerly tomorrow. I told you in my last we were expecting Sophia soon–We waited dinner for her until near five on Saturday, and were disappointed– But on Monday, just as we were going to give her up, she stopped at the door, & I rushed down to welcome her– Allyne Otis did not bring her on– having staid in Boston to swallow 15 of Dr Warren's Pills[1] she says– but will follow in about a week– She is looking better than usual, notwithstanding a rather severe attack she had a fortnight ago in Boston, which Mrs Ritchie thinks was bilious, but she is persuaded was brought on by sleeping in a room in which there was a Pan of coals– & thinks she was nearly asphyxiated– She says she has lost a great deal of flesh in Boston, & calls herself very thin, but I see no great difference in her appearance, and think her looking quite <u>robust</u> for her– altho' she eats and walks as little as ever– Unfortunately the very day of her arrival, she was a good deal shocked upon walking up to Mrs Brown's (the Aunt of Mrs Thorndike who we believe is staying there) she found black crêpe on the Bell, announcing the death of poor Mary Dickey,

M<u>rs</u> T's sister,[2] a young thing of 17, who has gone off in a rapid decline– and very soon followed her brother, who died of the same disease two months ago– This of course made her feel a little nervous, & prevented her from enquiring about M<u>rs</u> T– who was to have come on to see her dying sister some days since– and we have not since been able to discover whether she arrived or not– As Miss D. is no sort of relation of Sophia's, and we had already sent out some invitations for a little musical party this eveng– in honor of her, & M<u>rs</u> C. Willing,[3] we thought it a pity to give it up– her acquaintance with the poor girl being very slight– (She has not seen her once within 4 years, when she was a mere child)– And next week being Passion week, we could not have deferred our Party until then– and w<u>d</u> perhaps have had to give it up altogether– so we consulted with Aunt Harrison, who thought it quite unnecessary to change our plans on account of this death– and as M<u>rs</u> C. Willing had consented to come tonight we could not put her off– And if M<u>rs</u> T. <u>should</u> be in town, and hear of Sophia's appearing in company, we cannot help it– We have had many refusals, but filled them up before it was too late to send out more invitations, and shall have about 20 ladies, and a majority of men– quite enough for our small room– I was to have played with M<u>rs</u> [Tom] Willing, but thinking she was in rather a capricious mood, I w<u>d</u> not count upon her– after hearing that she had sent her Harp to M<u>rs</u> Sigoigne's[4] last Friday, and after all, refused all entreaties to play–[5] To be sure she tried to justify this behaviour to me, by saying she was too dreadfully fatigued, having spent the <u>whole day</u> dancing the <u>Cachucha</u>,[6] but I did not know that she might not take up the same whim to day, and therefore have practised with Miss Pardi, on whom I can always punctually depend– It is a very difficult & brilliant duett, I am to play with her, and I am hardly <u>sure</u> of it yet, but intend perfecting myself in it before the evening–[7] She will play a piece alone, and sing also– and so will <u>perhaps</u> M<u>rs</u> Willing–

Friday morng– I could not continue my letter yesterday on account of various interruptions– and I expected confidently one from you this morng– dearest Mamma, in which I was disappointed– I hope to have better luck this afternoon– Our concert went off admirably– I was a little alarmed at the beginning of my Duett, but plucked up courage, and gained great credit & applause by it. Miss Pardi played better than I ever heard her, and sang with soul, inspired I suppose by her Innamorato–[8]

Fanny Butler sang wretchedly, her voice trembling, and her hands which she afterwards gave me to feel, <u>icy cold</u> from nervousness– but she behaved perfectly well, and was as amiable & obliging as possible– She brought with her an Englishman, by name Parker, who was terrified half out of his wits while he sang the first time but acquitted himself better the second– and gave out rather more of his voice, which was really a good one, and well managed– The poor man was also ill at ease, on account of his Frock coat, which kept him in a corner, and encreased the "national timidity" from which so many of his countrymen suffer– But being passionately fond of music, he ventured to present himself in his travelling dress, and as he enjoyed it (the music) so much, I should have been sorry if he had been kept away by a foolish ettiquette– altho' I felt for his embarrassment– He said he never heard a finer Piano anywhere than mine, and preferred it very much to both the Harps–

After a great deal of pressing on our part & fuss & I think abominable behaviour on Matilda's she vouchsafed to play, but declared that she was not at all in the humour– & certainly I have heard her shew more spirit and feeling– But yet there was enough displayed to make it very delightful, & they remained here listening to her until past midnight– So you may imagine, I was pretty well fagged, before I got into bed, as the clock struck One, & only came down to Breakfast at past nine– But as they all say it was very pleasant, and Sophia enjoyed herself extremely, I was glad that all my trouble in preparing my own share of the entertainment, & persuading Mrs W. to contribute also, was not lost. I have not told you what a pleasant visit Sophia & I had at Mrs Butler's on Tuesday– I proposed the drive to her, thinking it [would] suit her much better than trotting after me thro' the dusty streets, and she was much pleased with the reception & agreeable conversation– She gave us beautiful Flowers too, & was altogether very kind and obliging– and quite affectionate to me–

I must tell you of Fisher's gallantry– Yesterday he rode out to Dryburgh's Green House, and ordered three beautiful bouquets, which he presented to the Bride, to Sophia, & to Miss Pardi, as I had one already, and insisted upon his offering it to her as a reward for her amiability. The Azaleas of which there are now a great many, are very different from our's at the South– and much handsomer– the shape of the flower resembles very much the Rhododendron, with a delicious odour. The Hyacinths are exquisite– I suppose your's are all over–

The dinner will be on Table immediately, and I shall have no chance to add anything more after it– so Adieu, my dearest Mamma– and give my love to all around you– As ever Y^{r} affectionate and dutiful daughter Eliza

Sophia begs I will add her Love to you and Kitty– & remembrances to the rest of the family– I hope to keep her here until the week after next at least– If W^{m} is with you, pray thank him for his letter, & say I am just waiting for a letter I expect in a day or two from N.Y. that I will have something to say in my answer to him which may interest him–

Private Collection

1. John Collins Warren (1778–1856) was a founder of the Massachusetts General Hospital in Boston and professor of anatomy at the Harvard Medical School. In 1846 he was the first to use ether as anesthesia during surgery.

2. Mrs. Thorndike was Sophia's stepmother, the former Ann Thompson Dickey (1809–1893).

3. The Fishers wanted to honor Charles Willing and Rebecca Tillinghast, who were married in March.

4. Mme Anne Marie Aimée Condemine Sigoigne was one of the group of French refugees from the revolt in Santo Domingo who settled in Philadelphia in the early nineteenth century. She and her daughter, Adèle, ran a school for girls. Both were musical and played the harp and piano well.

5. Matilda Willing's unsettled behavior may perhaps be explained by the fact that her husband, Tom Willing, was in serious financial difficulty and having trouble supporting his family. In 1840 he borrowed money from George Harrison which he knew he could not repay. Uncle Harrison, for whom this was the ultimate sin, never forgave him.

6. The newly fashionable cachucha was an Andalusian dance resembling the bolero.

7. In a later letter to Edward, Mrs. Middleton indicated that the musicians who were to play and sing at a party such as this often rehearsed in the evening, before the party began. The guests were invited for nine o'clock. MHM to Edward Middleton, November 18, 1840, Edward Middleton Rea Collection.

8. Mlle Pardi was engaged to marry M. Marras, a miniaturist.

The complexities of Eliza's parents' relationship were demonstrated as the spring advanced and Mrs. Middleton tried to make definite arrangements to get to Philadelphia in time to be with Eliza when the baby came. As an astute friend had noticed, years before, Henry Middleton was often very hard on his wife even though he loved her,[1] and now, though he had promised that Mrs. Middleton would be with Eliza, he seemed to put difficulties in the way of her going.

In the end, he came round, as he always did, but to Mrs. Middleton, her husband's idiosyncrasies had become a source of frustration and anger. Since he controlled the money and made decisions about the family's travel, she could not leave South Carolina until he decided how and when she would go. Her anxiety, and Eliza's too, over whether she would get to Philadelphia in time is evident in their letters over the next weeks.

1. M. I. Manigault to Josephine duPont, September 28, 1808, Margaret Izard Manigault Collection, Hagley Museum and Library, Wilmington, Del.

To Mrs. Fisher, Philadelphia

M.P. Ap^{l} 16th 1840

My dearest Eliza

Since writing my last, I have had the pleasure of receiving your two letters of 24th March & 1^{t} of Ap^{l} brought by your Father & W^{m}. Harry remained with me after all, much as you may suppose to my satisfaction. they also brought me a letter from Arthur of Feby in which he mentions that Mr Eaton had informed several people of his recall. No intimation of it had reached Arthur, either from the Gov^{t}, or Genl Van Ness[1] & he seems to believe that some one else will be appointed to the Chargé ship [*in Madrid,*] which will be the means of enabling him to gratify his wish of returning to America, expressed in every letter he writes to me. For the last two days your Aunt & Uncle Rutledge have been here on their way to Combahee where they will stay a fortnight with Emma Blake, then go through Alabama to take their son Henry & family with them to Nashville– Maj^{r} R[utledge] looks miserably– he says however that he feels stronger than when he left Charleston & has missed the fever & Ague for the last fortnight. I hope he may recover by the continued change of air– Your Aunt is very well. She has frequently brought & sent Music to Cath^{e} who is scarcely ever satisfied with her choice & sends it back to be changed. she is sometimes two or 3 days without touching the piano forte.

We have heard nothing of Messrs DeRham & Cracroft yet.[2] their arrival is not announced in the Newspaper– so that they have probably prolonged their visits at Wash^{n} & Baltimore. W^{m} sent a message to them by young D^{r} [Lewis] Gibbes[3] (who your Father brought together with the Portrait painter Mr Osgood[4] to spend two days here) to request them to come here– they will I hope come this week, for it would be very unpleasant to them to be here next week when I shall be alone, unless Harry should consent to stay while your Father & W^{m} are at Combahee– he <u>has</u> said he could not, but the chance of those young men coming may I hope induce him to undergo another week of solitude with me– Miss Moore also sent a letter of Introduction to Captn Cadogan for Harry– he has not yet delivered it, as he is gone with the Blakes to Combahee– whether he will be here on his return is uncertain– She was very kind in writing to inform me of all the particulars she had heard from Mr Davis of Edward. She mentions having received a delightful letter from you, a particularly gratifying one, as you seem to have been so much pleased with her Nephew– By your own account Mr Fisher & yourself must have shewn them great attention. I hope your cold has passed off long ere this, & that the use of the Rose leaves for a gargle may strengthen your throat–

You enquire whether I should prefer Mrs Badger's apartments to those of
the Albion house–[5] I think the latter would suit me better than her's or the
Marshall house– I recollect Miss Hare's telling me she was obliged to provide
herself with several articles & that her own servant was obliged to wait on her
at table, add to this, that if there is no Man servant, it would not suit Harry
to be there– The Marshall house will be a very hot one in June & that to me
is a strong objection besides the smell and the narrow street, so that if your
Father should allow me to choose apartments, I would take those in the Albion,
because they are so near to you & that there must be Men to wait upon the
lodgers in that hotel– I have not yet ventured to speak on the subject to your
Father, nothing can be more uncertain than his movements, & when I told
him you were very anxious that I should accompany Harry next month, he
said, "May is a very pleasant month here" & gave me no direct answer, therefore
my dear Eliza do not flatter yourself with the hope of meeting me so soon. Of
course you will not engage rooms anywhere until it is decided when we are to
be at Philad^a.

The house in Bound[ar]y S^t is taken for another year– This is to be left
in statu quo until next winter! The carpenters have prepared the timber necessary for the roof &c & are now repairing the Stable.

Harry is much pleased to hear that Miss W[adsworth] is to be so soon at
Philad^a & often expresses a wish to be there soon. it is probable that he will
go there without me. The account you give of Miss Pardi is singular indeed! I
was surprised to read that you called Adela's husband good for nothing. I
thought he was the reverse– I suppose you have been enjoying the society of
Miss Thorndike for the last fortnight. pray give my love to her. Mrs P. Smith
writes me word that she cannot say positively when she can come here: her
nieces being at Goosecreek with their Father, she is alone with M^rs B[lamyer] &
has at present no mode of conveyance. W^m was disappointed about going to
Waccamaw.[6] Have you heard of J[ulia]'s resolution from herself? I fear the
sacrifice she has made to her duty, will make her unhappy for life, if I may
judge from the feelings you have often told me she entertained for your brother.
I am writing this to be ready for an acquaintance of W^m's to carry to town
tomorrow, a Mr Gourdine who will dine here today. Lest I should have no
time to write in the morn^g I conclude with love to M^r & Mrs Fisher & am my
dearest Eliza Y^r affect^te Mother M. H. M.

Yr. Father & Brothers & Aunt desire their love to you.
17th P.S. Mr G. did not come until today, I enquired of him whether Messrs
Audubon & De Rham had arrived. he said he had not seen the arrivals an-

nounced. Y^r Aunt will take me on Sunday to Church & wishes me to go with her to see M^{rs} A[rthur] M[iddleton] who is recovering from a severe fit of Rheumatism– 18th a ser^t is to be sent to Town this morn^g & to return I hope in the eve^g, that he may bring a letter from you. I am writing to John to beg him to come without delay–

PHi

1. John Van Ness (1770–1846), former congressman from New York, married Marcia Burns whose family owned land on which part of the District of Columbia was built. The Van Nesses were well connected in Washington social and political circles. Arthur Middleton married their only child, Ann, in 1821 and although she died within a year, he always kept in touch with her parents.

2. Miss Moore sent letters of introduction with Weston Cracroft, an Englishman, and her nephew, Henry DeRham, who were on their way to join "Audubon, the celebrated naturalist" in a tour of the South. The Fishers had entertained them in Philadelphia. "They are both very fond of rowing," Eliza told her mother, "an amusement which Wm can offer them, with the additional recommendation of Alligator shooting." Young DeRham died of fever while on the trip. EMF to MHM, March 24, 1840, private collection.

3. Lewis R. Gibbes (1810–1894), a physician and faculty member at the College of Charleston, was the son of Maria (Drayton) and Lewis L. Gibbes. His grandmother, Hester (Middleton) Drayton, and Eliza's grandfather, Arthur Middleton, were brother and sister.

4. Samuel S. Osgood (1808–1885) worked as a painter in Charleston for some time after returning in 1839 from studying at the Royal Academy in London.

5. The Albion House was next door to the Fishers. Mrs. Peters was the proprietress.

6. Waccamaw refers to the region along the Waccamaw River, which flows into the ocean near Georgetown, about sixty miles north of Charleston. South Carolina's most productive rice-growing plantations, including John Middleton's, were there.

∼

To Mrs. Middleton, Middleton Place

Philadelphia – April 23rd 1840

Many many thanks for your dear letter of the 16 & 18th dearest Mamma– which reached me yesterday & gave me as much satisfaction as usual– except one part of it, where you speak with uncertainty about coming here in May– I cannot give up the hope that Papa will fulfil his promise and permit you to accompany Harry next month and do not see what there can be to prevent your coming– I have no doubt you can be well accomodated next door, as the rooms Miss Hare had are unoccupied by <u>permanent</u> boarders– and could probably be engaged for you at some little previous notice– or you might stay at M<u>rs</u> Keagy's[1] and have private rooms, a <u>man</u> servant &c– You must have been a little surprised to receive a letter from M<u>rs</u> P. Smith dated hence– I could scarcely believe that a note which was put into my hands at Aunt Harrison's on Thursday eveng was from her– but ran over to the Marshall House to convince myself that she was there– and had much pleasure in talking over her visit to M. Place, altho' several weeks had passed since she made it. And whilst you were expecting her to repeat it, she undertook rather a longer journey–

M<u>rs</u> Holbrook is also here– she came on Saturday after being expected for 3 weeks– and I saw her for the first time on Sunday afternoon, when upon returning from Church, I found her seated in the drawing room– and gave her a most cordial greeting as you may suppose– She dined & spent the eveng with us on Monday, and quite won the heart of both the old ladies, by her agreeable manners & conversation. She is certainly a most delightful person– and I find her so not only in company but in a tête à tête walk before breakfast! Don't stare dear Mamma– I have written it and actually <u>done</u> it too! Both Monday & Tuesday morngs I was up at <u>6</u> and walked for an hour or more– But alas! on Wednesday there was a sad falling off– and today we entered the Breakfast Parlour as the clock was striking <u>10</u>– The latest hour I have ever been at our morning meal since I have lived in Phil<u>a</u>. But you will perhaps think I had some excuse when I tell you that it struck <u>One</u> before I sought my weary pillow– M<u>rs</u> Rush[2] gave Sophia & <u>me</u> a Party last night, and had the singers from the Theatre to amuse us– and as they did not make their appearance until after eleven, of course there was no getting off earlier– In the beginning of the eveng– Miss Pardi played & sang, & poor little M<u>me</u> [Maurice] d'Hauterive (the french Consul's wife) trembled & quavered thro' an air from "Robert"–[3] But was so much terrified that her voice sounded more like <u>crying</u> than singing– I really pitied the poor little thing, and was dreading M<u>rs</u> Rush's approach, seeing how <u>imperiously</u> she had carried her off to the Piano without taking any excuses– But to my infinite relief, she had the kindness to say that as the Party was for <u>me</u> (I didn't know it before) she did not intend to ask a sacrifice of me, but thought it her duty to let others amuse me, and allow me for once the privilege of listening without contributing– I really felt grateful for this consideration, and begged to assure her how sensible I was of her kindness in allowing me to play audience only– I then really began to enjoy myself– for when I have before me the horror of exhibiting, it completely spoils the pleasure of the eveng– Two things however, rather interfered with my comfort, a pain in my back, which felt nearly broken in two, & the intense heat of the crowded rooms–

Mrs Campbell said she hoped Miss Shireff[4] & Mr Wilson would give them some <u>cooling</u> airs, when they were about to sing, and they certainly were <u>refreshing</u> after poor Mme d'Hauterive's feeble attempts– They sing ballads most beautifully, & particularly well together– The harmony of their voices in an old melody without any accompaniment, was really charming. Giubilei also acquitted himself admirably in the "Largo al Factotum"[5] and I was sorry enough to leave him at the Piano, but about midnight I was so utterly exhausted that Fisher brought me away, & returned for M^{rs} H, M^{rs} F– & Sophia who were not ready to return until I had my night cap on– The night before we were at the Theatre to hear "le Postillion de Longjumeau"–[6] the music of which is pretty & gay, but not much to my taste except one or two things in it. Tonight Sophia is going to a <u>dance</u> but how they will manage even to walk a cotillion in such Heat, I cannot imagine. I intend to be in my bed at <u>nine</u>– and up again walking before breakfast with Mrs Holbrook tomorrow morng–

I am very glad that there is some chance of Arthur's return at last [*from Spain*]– Aunt Rutledge's visit must have given you great pleasure– I hope you were able to accomplish your drive to St Andrew's Church[7] on Easter Sunday– We had a very fine sermon from The Bishop[8] in the morng– and a most eloquent one on the Resurrection from Mr Odenheimer in the afternoon– Mrs Holbrook was very much pleased with him indeed, and had been prepared by Miss Rutledge to admire him– I like him better every time I hear him & trust they will elect him our Rector–

Mrs Smith spent Saturday eveng– here, and Monday also– and was delighted with Miss Pardi's playing & our duett for Harp & Piano, which I played much better than the first time– Adela [Newton] & Fenwick [Jones] were also here– The former's little girl is well again, after giving her great alarm & anxiety for ten days– The Henry A. M[iddleton]s are established at little Whitfield's [*boardinghouse in Newport*] opposite the large Factory– Poor Lizzie & Mary will find the next two months there dull enough I fancy–

I have not yet had any answer from J[ulia]. I wrote yesterday to W^m, but without having anything particular to communicate except my sympathy which is very sincere– I agree with you that if she persists in her renunciation of him, she will probably be unhappy for life– I shall be better able to judge of her <u>firmness</u> of purpose when she writes– Tell Kitty that I think she will find a new piece of Thalberg's[9] which I am learning, <u>difficult</u> enough for her– It is almost unplayable, but very beautiful and original– Sophia will stay until the end of the month. She declares that she had a pleasanter time during the quiet of last week than now that all these Parties are going on– and indeed she is hardly strong enough to sit up so late night after night– Mrs Sergeant is to give her one on Monday– and I think that will be the last at which I shall make my appearance this season– Adieu my dearest Mamma, I must go & stretch myself a little– For I am rather fagged– My love to Papa brothers Kitty & Sally when she arrives– wh. I hope will be soon– ever Y^{r} affec^{te} Eliza

Private Collection

1. Mrs. Keagy's boardinghouse was near the Fishers on Chestnut Street, between Ninth and Tenth Streets.

2. Mrs. James Rush, the former Phoebe Ann Ridgway (d. 1857), was a powerful personality and influence in Philadelphia society. One of the first to set a regular time to be "at home" to visitors, she invited talented and interesting people of all sorts to her parties, as well as the socially prominent or wealthy. She was educated in Europe while her father, Jacob Ridgway (1768–1843), a successful Philadelphia merchant and real estate investor, was U.S. consul in Antwerp.

Dr. James Rush (1786–1869) was a book lover as well as an amateur violinist. He was a son of Philadelphia physician Dr. Benjamin Rush.

3. Giacomo Meyerbeer's opera *Robert le Diable* was first performed in 1831.

4. Miss Jane Shireff was a professional singer; Mr. Wilson has not been identified. Signor Giubilei, mentioned a few sentences later, was a well-known musician in Philadelphia who gave a concert at the Musical Fund Hall a few weeks later.

5. The "Largo al factotum" is an aria from Gioacchino Rossini's opera *The Barber of Seville.*

6. *Le Postillion de Longjumeau,* a comic opera by Adolphe Charles Adam, was performed first in Paris in 1839 and quickly became popular in England and the United States.

7. St. Andrew's Church, built in 1706, is on the road between Middleton Place and Charleston. When she went to church there, Mrs. Middleton could be sure of meeting friends from the nearby plantations.

8. Henry Ustick Onderdonk (1789–1858) had been bishop of Pennsylvania since 1836 but resigned in 1844, confessing that he "habitually abused liquor." Eliza admired him as a logical preacher whose style was "pure & his enunciation very correct– a rarity in the Pulpit." EMF to MHM, January 27, 1844, PHi.

9. Sigismond Thalberg (1812–1871) was a Swiss pianist and composer.

⌒

To Mrs. Middleton, Middleton Place

Philadelphia – April 30$^{\underline{th}}$ [1840]

Good morning! my dearest Mamma– I have come down to write to you before breakfast– I won't say how <u>early</u>– But as Sophia was up at a party until near one, and afterwards packing until past two, of course I do not expect her down stairs very soon– and shall probably be able to scribble a good while before she makes her appearance– She wishes to go on tomorrow with D$\underline{r}$ Holbrook[1] to N.Y. but his movements are so uncertain, that I want to persuade her not to trust to him as an escort, but wait until Monday when there are several good opportunities– but she says she will be ready to accompany the D$\underline{r}$ who will go if his <u>Proof sheets</u> are ready– Allyne Otis will leave N.Y. on Saturday, and she <u>must</u> rest there a day or two, so she might just as well stay here until next week– But I have said as much as I could to induce her, and if she yields finally, it will have been a hardwon battle.

Here we are, at the last day of April, & tomorrow will welcome in the May– and I shall say– Mamma will <u>certainly</u> be here before the month is out– Tell Papa with my love that altho' it is a pleasant month in Carolina, it is a much pleasanter one for travelling than June, and I cannot release him from his <u>promise</u> to me last Dec$\underline{r}$. I am sure Harry will be glad to bring you on, and Miss Rutledge, who is to leave Charleston about the middle of the month will be a very agreeable companion for you also– Say to Papa too, that I hope he will not refuse now to fulfil his <u>contract</u> with me– for it was on condition that you were to return <u>early</u> in May, that he consoled me for y$\underline{r}$ absence during the winter– and indeed I shall be very unhappy & <u>nervous</u> if you delay coming on any longer– Your presence will be <u>absolutely</u> necessary the first week in June, but of course I wish to enjoy y$\underline{r}$ society a little while before that <u>terrible time</u>– and I think it will be cruel to deny me this favour– So write by return of Post, where I shall engage Lodgings for you– whether next door, or at M$\underline{rs}$ Keagy's– And I assure you there is no time to be lost about it– for if you wish to be comfortable, arrangements must be made beforehand– I am distressed to think you were making yourself so uneasy about not receiving letters from me– where they could have been, I am at a loss to imagine– But that they were punctually sent once a week is very certain– & you have no doubt long ere this been relieved from anxiety about me– I am very well again, this fine cool weather– but last week the heat was so great, that I suffered not a little in consequence, & could only walk between 7 and 8 in the morng– in the square with M$\underline{rs}$ Holbrook–

Since this delightful change, I am quite strong again, & am looking so well, that Fisher insists upon– what do you think of such <u>folly</u>? having me put on pasteboard by M$\underline{r}$ Saunders–[2] I laugh and tell him he ought to be satisfied with the prospect of the <u>little miniature</u> I shall give him in 6 weeks– (pray read that to yourself) But he will not consent to lose the opportunity of having a portrait of me by so good a Painter– His miniatures are really beautiful, and his water coloured drawings also excellent– The likenesses perfect and not <u>too</u> much flattered– and the finish admirable–[3] We are trying to persuade M$\underline{rs}$ F. to sit to him– But she declares it w$\underline{d}$ be too ridiculous to draw a "toothless old woman" & won't listen to any of our entreaties– saying she must first have her deficiencies supplied– and she does not choose to descend to posterity with her Gums all fallen in– But I don't think it is right of her to refuse to gratify so good a son– Aunt Harrison is also fixed in her determination and we try in vain all arguments to move her.

How much I have thought of this time last year, and our parting, my dear Mamma– This is the day we arrived at Richmond– and then our visit to the Rives'– It appears hardly as if a whole twelvemonth had passed over us– and happily we have nothing but pleasant events to mark it by–

Afternoon– I have been sitting with Adela Newton, who leaves town at two o'clock for Burlington [*New Jersey*] where she has a great deal to arrange before she goes on to Brooklyn, where she will pass the summer– Her little girl is well again– but very much pulled down by her illness– and no longer the rosy blooming little fatty she was a month ago– Adela looks miserably herself but is in pretty good health– I have been also paying a visit to Mrs Thorndike– who is going on to NY next week to meet her husband– She says Mrs Gilliatt[4] writes her word that nearly all the boarding Houses at New Port are already engaged– Mrs Charles Lyman[5] will be at the one Mrs Jonathan Amory occupied formerly– opposite their side garden gate– and Mrs Nathan Appleton,[6] her little daughter, and daughter in law <u>Fanny</u>, by far the most interesting member of the family, at Perry's at the Beach– Mrs Mackintosh has sailed for England, for an indefinite time– But it is likely her sister will join her there in the Autumn– Unless she loses her heart meantime– which there is not much danger of except Harry will attempt the conquest– Tell him I cannot learn anything more of Miss W$^{\underline{th}}$ and I have been so much shocked at M^{rs} W—g's speeches & behaviour, that I have not sought her much lately– & seen very little of her– She was expected at Mme Grelaud's again last Saturday, & we went thinking she w^{d} certainly bring her Harp and Dr Charles Wellesley– but she disappointed us, and we had no good music except Lizzie Grelaud's playing– For Miss Coxe's singing was the most absurd exhibition I think I ever witnessed– Mrs Sergeant's party to Sophia which was to have taken place on Monday, was deferred on account of the death of their next door neighbour Mrs Cuesta,[7] with whom they were intimate– and we have now declined it altogether as Mrs S. proposed it for an early day next week, when Sophia will be in Boston probably–

We went out to see Powelton[8] on Tuesday afternoon– and took Mrs Holbrook– It is a fine stately building– of magnificent proportions, but is at present in a very unfinished state– and the size is difficult to judge of before the walls are Plastered– 156 feet en suite [*from one end to the other*] however is palace like– and it will be the handsomest country house in America I imagine– and have a most substantial and at the same time Classical air– M^{rs} H– was much shocked at the dissatisfied & uncourtly manners of the elegant Mr Powel– who was in such a bearish mood, and appeared so discontented in the midst of his wealth, that it was really a good moral lesson– and I thought an illustration of the truth of the text– that a thankful Heart is better than much riches– We spent the eveng– at M^{rs} McEuen's after driving to the Woodlands and thereabouts for an hour– Yesterday it poured all day, and in the eveng– we had one or two people besides Aunt Harrison– Our English friend from Canada, Mr Cole– who came on from N.Y. on purpose to see us before sailing in the G^t Western– I mean to send some thing to Aunt [*Hering*] and the Bolands by him– The Books & scarf have been rec^d. Mrs Barclay writes to Fisher that Uncle had got them safely. Goodbye my dearest Mamma– I am told that Mrs Smith is below, and I have not seen her for several days– & this will be too late for the Post unless it is sent before dinner Love to all– Y^r most affectionate Eliza

Private Collection

With the exception of a letter written on May 7, no letters from Eliza between this and October 18, 1840, have been found.

1. Dr. Holbrook would have been in Philadelphia preparing his *North American Herpetology* for publication.

2. George Lethbridge Saunders (1807–1863) was an English miniaturist who painted in New York, Boston, Baltimore, Charleston, and other cities, as well as in Philadelphia, during the 1840s. Mrs. Fisher did consent to sit to him.

3. In her next letter, Eliza reported that Saunders had "had 4 sittings and standings, which are rather fatiguing, of an hour & a half, and two hours each, and will require 3 more– I think he will make a very pretty thing of it, but all I fear is that people will say, what a pity she is not as goodlooking! . . . and strange to say, he has made me look like you– I only wish he could preserve the resemblance to myself in so doing. . . . Mr Harrison says Fisher has quite enough of the original, and ought to let them have this copy of my countenance." EMF to MHM, May 7, 1840, private collection.

4. Susan (Schroeder) Gilliatt was the daughter of former Baltimore merchant Henry Schroeder and his wife, who had retired to live in Newport. Her husband, John Gilliatt, was an Englishman who invested in Newport real estate and was a warden of Newport's Trinity Church.

5. The Lymans and Amorys were Bostonians who regularly summered in Newport. Mrs. Charles Lyman was the former Susan Warren, a daughter of Dr. John C. and Susan (Mason) Warren. Mrs. Jonathan Amory was the former Hetty Sullivan (Cutler) (1772–1847); her husband had died in 1828.

6. Mrs. Appleton, the former Harriet Coffin Sumner, was Nathan Appleton's second wife. Fanny Appleton was her stepdaughter (rather than daughter-in-law).

7. Mrs. J. E. Cuesta, gentlewoman, lived at 87 South Fourth Street; the Sergeants lived at 89. Esto Cuesta, merchant, listed at the same address, was probably her son.

8. Col. John Hare Powel (1786–1856) was one of Fisher's cousins through the Willing family. He changed his name from John Powel Hare to John Hare Powel when he was adopted by his aunt, Elizabeth Willing (Mrs. Samuel) Powel. From her he inherited Powelton, a house surrounded by nearly one hundred acres on the west side of the Schuylkill River. Over the years he spent lavishly to improve it; at this time, he was adding wings to the original house.

～

To Mrs. Fisher, Philadelphia

Charleston May 31$\underline{st}$ 1840

I take up my pen my dearest Eliza with a heavy heart, because I know you will feel sadly disappointed at not seeing me arrive with your Brother, & you may judge from your own feelings what mine must be. When I wrote last, there was some chance of my arriving at Philad$\underline{a}$ by the middle of June– from the account W$\underline{m}$ brought yesterday from Capt$\underline{n}$ Berry, it is doubtful whether the [*ship*] "Cath[erin]e" may not be detained here until that time– upon hearing this, I asked your Father why I might not proceed with Harry? because in that case, I could not take care of Catherine at N.Y.– I now believe he never meant that I should be with you at the time we both so much wished to be together. I have the fullest confidence in the care M$\underline{rs}$ Fisher will take of you, an experienced Nurse is no doubt engaged for you– the exercise you have taken so regularly must be of service to you & I trust in God's mercy that you may pass safely through the painful time which will make you a happy Mother– That I might witness, & partake of your & M$\underline{r}$ & M$\underline{rs}$ Fisher's joy on this occasion, I have hitherto been anticipating with pleasure, though of course not without a mixture of anxiety, which will now be encreased by the distance between us, & the length of time I may be kept in suspense on your account. If I am not permitted to go only for a few days to see you, when I arrive at N.Y. I shall be compelled to have that happiness deferred until you join me at Newport– this is a long time to look forward to! but I must submit, having no will of my own.

Susan & Oliver dined with us yesterday– she is exceedingly thin, but does not complain of any ailment. they have not decided whether they will go this week to the beach,[1] & her going with Oliver to Philad$\underline{a}$ will depend upon whether M$\underline{rs}$ Chisolm will take charge of the Children during her absence– M$\underline{rs}$ C. is to be here on Tuesday, & then I suppose the matter will be settled, but Sus$\underline{n}$ will not be at Phil$\underline{a}$ before the end of July. an hour before dinner yesterday John arrived looking very well, having left Sally at the beach tolerably well, having occasionally pain in her Chest & shortness of breath but no cough–

Harry [*John's son*] still subject to attacks of Ague & he has determined not to let him quit the beach– I wish he would let him & Sally go to Aiken– I shall urge him to do so, & I suppose if they should both suffer from the Air of the low ground, that he will consent to their removal.

Emma called to see me a few days ago– she looked better than I expected after what I had heard– On the 4$\underline{th}$ or 5$\underline{th}$ she is to sail in the LaFayette, which she prefers to the Cath$\underline{e}$ as being more airy & having the square state room on deck which M$\underline{rs}$ T. M[iddleton] occupied formerly. I have not seen <u>her</u>. She looks miserably I hear. I have not stirred out of the Piazza since I came here. Susan has been so good as to procure for me what I wanted from the Shops– M$\underline{rs}$ Holbrook is to be here some day this week, so that I hope to see her soon, & Miss Rutledge before she goes. I am sorry all the trouble you took about looking for apartments for me has been in vain. I have a good lesson on this subject for avoiding in future to form any plans for my movements. I can however say that if you write on the 6$\underline{th}$, your letter will probably reach me, before I sail.

1$\underline{st}$ June. I stopped writing yesterday my dearest Eliza because I made sure of rec^{g2} y^r weekly despatch, 27th May, which was brought to me just now– the perusal of it makes me unhappy for it shews how distrest you were at my long absence, & I now can conceive how much more so you will be on receiving this, & being told that in spite of all your entreaties your Father will not change his determination of making me wait & go by sea! From what you say, the event is likely to occur about the middle of the month– I hoped it would not have happened before the end– God grant you may not suffer more than Mother's usually do! & that you may have all the assistance necessary– this indeed I am sure you will have– but it is a cruel thing for us to be separated at such an anxious time for a Mother. The swelling of legs is a common symptom, it is disagreeable I know from experience– You need not mind being bled, particularly as the Doctor recommends it– it is a good plan to diet yourself too– be more careful, & avoid fatiguing yourself. I am very sorry to hear that Mr Fisher has been so unwell– you add however that he was perfectly well at the time you wrote & he I hope may continue so. I am writing to M$\underline{rs}$ Smith. she too I hope will have no return of indisposition & that she will in some degree supply my place by your bedside! Oh how anxiously I shall expect a letter from her or Mr F. on my arrival at N.Y! Here is W$\underline{m}$ just come upstairs to tell me that your Father would inquire tomorrow whether the Cath$\underline{e}$ would positively sail on the 7$\underline{th}$. If not, that I might go by railroad–

3$\underline{d}$ Finding that Harry is deferring his journey from day to day, I shall send this by post, that a week may not elapse before you get it– Y^r Father saw the

Agent of the vessel who told him yesterday that it w$^{\underline{d}}$ sail on the 7$^{\underline{th}}$ so that we must try to console ourselves with the hope of my having a speedy voyage & being with you by the 13$^{\underline{th}}$. It is useless to engage rooms, as it is so uncertain when I may be in Philad$^{\underline{a}}$ As Cath$^{\underline{e}}$ is not to be there, a private parlour I shall not want. a bedroom will be all I should require, & as Harry will be with me I shall have no objection to take my meals at the public table– we need not expect that my stay there will exceed a week by which time I trust you will be quite well. I suppose there will be no difficulty in procuring a bedroom even at an hour's notice either at the Albion or Jones [*Hotel*]. Emma called again & I gave her y$^{\underline{r}}$ letter to read She says she will try to go to Phila$^{\underline{a}}$ to see you.

Y$^{\underline{r}}$ Father advised John to send for little Harry to accompany us to N.Y. & spend the summer at Newport. He is to be here on Friday. John & Sally are both very uneasy about him. the fever returns every fortnight & weakens him greatly. I wish poor Sally could remove from the beach with all my heart. the times are so hard that John says it is quite out of his power to send his family any where–[3] He believes that exercise on horseback will be the means of keeping her free from ailment & I sincerely hope it may– Poppet is the horse she rides & little Sarah rides the poney. M$^{\underline{rs}}$ Chisolm came yesterday & all the family are going on Friday to the beach. Oliver had not heard yesterday eve$^{\underline{g}}$ whether the request had been made to her of taking charge of his family, which I hope she may. If the Vessel sh$^{\underline{d}}$ be detained longer than the 8$^{\underline{th}}$ I will write again. In case I should not let me request you to beg M$^{\underline{r}}$ Fisher to write to me immediately after the event takes place & direct to the Clinton, that I may receive the news of your safety on my arrival at N.Y. With love to him & M$^{\underline{rs}}$ F. believe me my dearest Eliza y$^{\underline{r}}$ affect$^{\underline{te}}$ Mother M. H. M.

ScHi

1. In the summer, both the Oliver and the John Middletons often left their plantations to live at nearby beaches. Mrs. Middleton and Eliza were convinced that the beach near John's Georgetown plantation was unhealthy for Sally and the children and tried to find alternatives for them.

2. That is, "I was sure I would receive . . .".

3. In addition to being affected by the nationwide depression which followed the banking crisis in 1837, John had lost a great deal in a major fire on his plantation in the fall of 1838. He was so strapped financially that he disliked writing because he had "to answer so many duns and detestable business letters." John I. Middleton to MHM, September 28, 1840, PHi, C/F.

～

After more delays because of contrary winds, the *Catherine* eventually got out of Charleston harbor. The baby, Elizabeth Francis Fisher, obliged by coming two weeks later than expected, so Mrs. Middleton reached Philadelphia two days before her birth. Being near Eliza, she told Edward, "is a great comfort to both of us. I am staying at the next door & after breakfast, come every day according to M⣠Fisher's kind invitation & spend the rest of the day in her house." When the baby came, Mrs. Middleton added a postscript for Edward, saying "Eliza gave birth about half an hour since to a very fine pretty little Girl & seems as well as can be expected."[1]

Mrs. Middleton stayed in Philadelphia until the middle of July and then joined the rest of the family in Newport. There she and Eliza's father busied themselves preparing a nursery for the baby and arranging rooms to make the Fishers comfortable when they joined the Middletons later in the summer.

1. MHM to Edward Middleton, June 29, 1840, Edward Middleton Rea Collection.

To Mrs. Fisher, Philadelphia

Newport July 17ᵗʰ 1840

My dearest Eliza

It gave me great pleasure yesterday to learn that you continued to go on perfectly well. The weather has been so fine you have not been disappointed of your drive which you must have enjoyed (besides the country air) nearly as much as I have, the pure cool breezes, & the odour of the new made hay. I often think how much this climate will add to the pleasure you will feel in joining the family party. the little Lizzy too will thrive wonderfully by breathing this fine air– the heat for the last 4 or 5 days has been greater than usual the ther͏ᵗ having risen to 80º– that is cool however compared to what you have had it at Phil͏ᵃ

I was surprised on seeing Sophia to hear that she had determined to cross the Atlantic the 1ˢᵗ of Aug͏ᵗ [*to visit her sisters in Germany*]. She expressed great regret at not having it in her power to see you before leaving Boston. I urged her to go to Phil– for a day, as she was to be in N.Y. for two or 3 days, but I heard afterwards from Emma that she remained only one day there to visit her Dentist, & returned with the Smiths last Wednesday. since that, I have not seen her– the fatigue has probably prevented her walking up here. W͏ᵐ is gone to see her, & she told me she intended to write to you, therefore all that I write will probably be only a repetition of her account of herself. One thing I may propose to you, to give her a letter of introduction to C͏ᵗˢᵉ Gardanne de Vaugremont,[1] as I mentioned that should she visit Brussells Matilda would be glad to meet her, as would also Mrs Ogilvie, tho' she must have left it by this time. they would probably meet at some of the German baths however.

Of Emma I cannot give a very good account, having seen her only on the day she arrived, your brothers say she has already improved in appearance, perhaps owing to Sea bathing which she began immediately, & I sent her your old dress for that purpose as she wanted a pattern. The first visitors I had were Mrs Emery[2] accompanied by Frank Schroeder[3] both of whom made very particular enquiries about you. M^rs S[chroeder] sent me a message to beg me to go to see her, having lost some of her family, a nephew & a little Grandchild, she does not visit. I shall wait your arrival to make my calls on some of those who have been attentive to me.

Mrs Barclay was the next visitor, she too enquired after you particularly– I suppose Sophia has communicated the news of the gay Widow [*Mrs. Barclay*]'s engagement to M^r [Albert] Sumner! What a falling off from marrying a Captn of the R[oyal] N[avy] to a Cap^n of a Merchantman![4] The folly of giving herself to a man of 30, who must marry her only for her money! I really gave her credit for more sense. They pass by our house every Eve^g Arm in Arm & are the subject of great amusement to their acquaintances who describe them as appearing to understand each other upon all points. She is going next week to N.Y. for a day, & will probably bring back with her Miss [Susan] Delancey, lately returned from France. The Harpers called next, & were very sociable & Miss H. expressed a great wish to see you. Y^r brothers go frequently to visit them & drive out with Mrs C. H[arper] & Miss. The Middletons[5] came too, & brought their Mother's message that she did not visit, so that I suppose I must go to see her. Mrs Thorndike came with them. She is looking very well. Yesterday M^r T[om] Appleton[6] came to see y^r brothers. They have seen Miss [Fanny] A. only once.

Cath^e begs me to thank you for the broach which she admires exceedingly. she begs you to bring all your Music books with you. She makes many enquiries about her little niece, & seems very anxious to see you. The piano forte is better toned than those hired in former years, but of course you will find it a miserable substitute for your own. C. has just told me to request you to come sooner. Hal is not looking as well as he did when I left him at N.Y. he goes to a day school. No letter has been received from John except one to your Father just after he reached the beach, & found the family all well. I hope you have succeeded in persuading Mrs Fisher to come to Newport. pray offer her my best regards, & also to Mrs Harrison– W^m I think told you he would move into the mineral room[7] & leave you his, for your Nursery. I will try & make it convenient for the baby's reception, though I cannot pretend to make it as comfortable as the one she has in Chesnut St$^\underline{t}$. let me know whether you wish any arrangements made before you arrive. Y$^\underline{r}$ Father & Brothers send their love— pray give mine to M$^\underline{r}$ F. & believe me my dearest Eliza y$^\underline{r}$ affect$^\underline{te}$ Mother M. H. M.

I requested M$^\underline{rs}$ Fisher the morn$^\underline{g}$ I left you to beg you to bring on for me a small box of the black Tea M$^\underline{rs}$ F. had spoken of & wh$^\underline{h}$ I forgot to procure myself. Just as I was going to seal this, I was called down to receive Sophia T. She begged me to send you a great deal of love, & to say how sorry she was she could not see you before leaving America. She is going tomorrow to Boston & will sail from thence on the 30$^\underline{th}$ in the Steamer Brittania. She will write to you in a day or 2.

PHi

1. Matilda (Bétancourt) Comtesse Gardannes de Vaugremont had been a good friend of the Middletons in St. Petersburg. Mrs. Ogilvie was an English friend of Mrs. Middleton.

2. Probably Mrs. Amory.

3. Frank Schroeder was the son of Mr. and Mrs. Henry Schroeder and brother of Mrs. Gilliatt. He may once have been an admirer of Eliza's. Sidney Fisher described him as "a great Adonis and dandy. A handsome but empty headed fellow." W. E. Wilson, ed., *The Mt. Harmon Diaries of Sidney George Fisher, 1837–1850* (Wilmington: Historical Society of Delaware, 1976), 98 (May 1, 1841).

4. Catherine Barclay's first husband, Thomas Barclay (d. 1838), whose father was a Loyalist during the American Revolution, chose to serve in the British navy. Albert Sumner (1812–1856) was the younger brother of Charles Sumner, lawyer and future senator from Massachusetts. Raised eyebrows and mean remarks notwithstanding, the marriage was apparently a happy one.

5. Lizzie and Mary, daughters of the Henry Augustus Middletons.

6. Thomas Gold Appleton was the son of Nathan Appleton and his first wife, Maria Theresa Gold (d. 1833). Fanny Appleton (later Mrs. Longfellow) and Mary (Mrs. Robert) Mackintosh were his sisters.

7. This may have been where the Middletons kept a collection of minerals brought back from Russia.

⁓

Eliza and Fisher took the baby to Newport in the middle of August. They led a "very retired and quiet existence," Fisher told the Harrisons, where "every hour of the day is perfect in its way." They walked or rode to their favorite places around the island, read books and made music, saw their friends, and enjoyed the view of the sailboats on Narragansett Bay from their room in the third story of the Middletons' house.

Being parents pleased them both. "I have a comfortable rocking chair in my little dressing room," Fisher explained, "so that I can get out of the way of the baby who does not indeed often interrupt me by her screams but is apt to attract too much of my attention as a play thing– No Girl ever seemed more pleased with a doll than dear Eliza– She seems almost entirely engrossed by her little charge & makes an excellent Mother as she is good in Every other relation– She is more attached to her little Lizzie than I expected & happier in her Maternal cares than I had hoped– & I begin almost to be jealous of her attentions even to my own Child."[1]

In the middle of October, they returned to Philadelphia, stopping in New York so Eliza could see Julia Ward and do some shopping. But a fidgety baby slowed her down and she told her mother she had "determined never to unpack my trunk there for less than a week, as it is really not worth while to be so hurried & worried as I was."[2]

1. JFF to the Harrisons, August 15, 1840, PHi, BrC.
2. EMF to MHM, October 18, [1840,] private collection.

To Mrs. Middleton, Newport

Philadelphia – 21$\underline{st}$ Oct$\underline{r}$ [1840]

I joyfully opened your letter, my dearest Mamma when it was handed to me this morning, hoping that it would tell me of y$\underline{r}$ safe arrival in N.Y. but had not read many lines of it before I discovered, to my great disappointment your change of plans– & delay of another week in NewPort– I particularly regret it, as Papa's indisposition appears to be the cause– but hope that long ere this reaches you he will have entirely recovered from the fatigues of his horticultural labours– I had made so sure of your being at the Clinton yesterday morng– that I wrote on Monday, & directed my letter there, but as it will be a week old when you get it, I beg as a particular favour, that you will burn it <u>unread</u>– I therein explained why I could not write from N.Y. & took it for granted that W$\underline{m}$ had also cleared me from blame on that score– He did <u>not</u> misunderstand my message to you, for I gave to Miss Moore the commission of having y$\underline{r}$ Cloak made & not liking to trouble her about two, reserved for myself that of getting Kitty's– which I shall set about as soon as the rain permits me to leave the house– where it has detained me a close prisoner since Saturday– I had just time to go down & speak to the Furrier about the alteration of y$\underline{r}$ Cape, which he promises to have done by the end of this week– I told him to reserve part of the ends, to add to the width of y$\underline{r}$ trimming,[1] which you might, another winter, like to have round y^r Cloak– as the Pelisse² is so entirely out of fashion, & as he wanted the exact width, I opened the Parcel you entrusted to my charge in order to take it– I am sorry that I could not attend to choosing y^r satin myself in N.Y. but I had such a violent headache the last day I was there I could hardly see to choose anything & therefore left it to Miss M.

The rain has been so incessant for the last 3 or 4 days, that I have hardly seen anyone yet, but have rec^d several kind messages from various quarters– I have already told you in my last, which will not be first rec^d however that Mrs Peters, finding you were not to spend the winter here engaged her rooms to the Mifflins for the season– & we therefore took Jones' instead– which I am sure you will find very comfortable & pleasant– Fisher had engaged them for Thursday, but he has consented, since the receipt of y^r letter, to defer the engagement for a week, & they will be ready for you on the 29th or 8th if you can be here by that day– & let me know in time– They are to be sure rather farther off, but otherwise much more agreeable than those next door or Badger's–

I have been a little uneasy about the Baby, who has had ever since her arrival, the same rattling phlegm on her Chest which alarmed me that eveng– at New Port. But Mrs Waters³ who saw her the day after our arrival & Dr Chapman, whom I have since consulted, make very light of it– assuring me it is very common for young infants to be oppressed by it– & merely recommending syrups of Onions– & Ipecac–⁴ The D^r has no doubt that as soon as the weather clears she will get rid of it, & I trust she may, before it encreases & threatens Croup– of which I have the greatest horror & dread– Alas! my anxieties are now beginning– but it is foolish & wrong to dwell upon them instead of the happiness I daily enjoy in observing her improvement and growth– She is I assure you, much admired, not only by her relations, for that is of course partiality, but by impartial judges of infantile beauty, which is certainly quite distinct from other kinds– & requires perhaps the eye of a connaisseur or a Parent, to discover it– We are disappointed about the Bristol Nurse, who has determined to remain with her present employers, & intend keeping Anne, (whose manner & temper appear both much improved since she is among companions of her own colour) until we meet with a competent White woman.

Mrs F. has had quite a severe attack of Sciatica, but is convalescent– altho' she still suffers a good deal of pain at night. Pray, my dear Mamma, let it be a warning to you not to take off Flannel when there happens to be a warm change of weather for this was the cause of much suffering & you are always committing similar imprudences– I was delighted to hear of John's recovery–

thro' Sally's letter to Hal– as they have neither of them taken any notice of my numerous epistles–

It is a great pity that Harry is disappointed of his visit to the Northwest [*to see Miss Wadsworth*]– His <u>rival</u> Hugo[5] is still there I hear– Tell him his friend M<u>rs</u> W[illing] has made an energetic declaration that as her husband will do nothing to support her & the children she intends to work for them <u>all</u> herself– but whether by teaching the Harp, or the Cachucha, is not yet known– Poor thing, I pity her most sincerely– & hope her plan, whatever it is, may succeed– They have sold out in Walnut S<u>t</u> & moved to Lodgings on Washington Sq<u>re</u>. This reminds me of the De Roennes–[6] He called to see us on his way to Wash<u>n</u> and told us that M<u>me</u> has been alarmingly ill– having had a "fausse couche" [*miscarriage*] which nearly killed her– They are uncertain about spending the winter here– but I hope will be able to do so–

I suppose Papa has recollected to tell you that Jane Pringle has a daughter– now 3 weeks old– To be called Mary Izard– Cousin Sally Rutledge was to leave town today, but I suppose is prevented by this disagreeable drizzling rain, which we thought yesterday had spent itself in the torrents that fell– I fear we shall all get sick for want of exercise & wish I were joggling[7] with you in the Piazza– Tell Kitty not to be disappointed, but the socks & slippers from Ellen Baker are <u>both</u> for Baby– but she is welcome to them if she can wear them– I answered her letter, & begged her to excuse C's writing–[8]

I must now say Adieu, dearest Mamma– begging you will write again very soon– I shall direct another letter to the Clinton next Monday probably– but do not be uneasy if I sh<u>d</u> be prevented from doing so– Aunt Harrison is just come thro' the rain to see the invalid, & they both join with Fisher in kindest remembrances– My love to Papa & both Harrys as well as Kitty– & believe me as ever Y<u>r</u> most affectionate Daughter Eliza

Private Collection

1. Mrs. Middleton's trim was made of sable, which it is likely she brought from Russia. Using a home remedy to protect the fur, Mrs. Fisher "spent half an hour in combing & shaking [it] in the sun" to make sure it was free from "moths or their eggs." To make doubly sure they were gone, the trim was frozen and then sewn up, presumably in cloth. EMF to MHM, November 26, [1840,] private collection.

2. A pelisse was a long coat, with or without sleeves, which fastened down the front and often had a little cape over the shoulders.

3. Mrs. Waters was the nurse who came to take care of Eliza when her babies were born.

4. The dried root of ipecac, a South American plant, was used to make people vomit.

5. Hugh Swinton Legaré.

6. Friedrich Ludwig Baron Von Roenne was the Prussian minister to the United States; he had previously been chargé d'affaires in Philadelphia. The Von Roennes may have known the Middletons in Russia.

7. Joggling, bouncing on a long plank suspended between supports at each end, has long been a favorite amusement in South Carolina.

8. Ellen Baker was a friend in England. Eliza was asking her to excuse Catherine for not writing.

~

To Mrs. Fisher, Philadelphia

Baltimore Monday Eve^g [Nov. 23, 1840]

In compliance with your request my dearest Eliza I sit down after dinner to inform you that I have performed the journey without fatigue so far– I had a very comfortable seat in the Cars & we arrived about 1/2 past 3– Mr Q[uincy] Adams[1] was our fellow passenger– I have luckily got a room up one p^r of stairs, & there are no travellers in the public room, & if Cath^e chose to play she might take advantage of the Piano. I wish we had proceeded in the Steamer this eve^g but y^r Father would not hear of it. You are at this time nursing the dear Baby. I picture you to myself caressing her, & I see her sweet smiles– When may these pleasing visions be again realized! I must endeavour to console myself by the reflection that you are perfectly happy– that ought to reconcile me to my absence from you, but still I shall feel it most sensibly. We are to proceed tomorrow & y^r Father talks of being in Charleston on Thursday– He & Wm & Harry & Mary[2] send their love to you– pray give mine to Mr & Mrs Fisher & believe me my dearest Eliza yr affect^{te} Mother M. H. M.

Pray remember me to Mrs Harrison I hope Mr H. is quite recovered– You will send the small parcel[3] by F[rank] Huger[4] will you not? Upon second thoughts perhaps you had better send it by some other person, he being so liable to attacks of the head, he might never reach Charleston– Remember me kindly to Mrs P. Smith & tell her how disappointed I was at not meeting her– persuade her if you can to accompany Harry to Charleston–

PHi

1. The John Quincy Adamses and the Middletons were close friends when Henry Middleton served in Congress, 1815–19. Adams was secretary of state during Middleton's first years in Russia.

2. Mary Middleton did not stay in Philadelphia for a second year at Mme Grel-aud's school.

3. During the summer, Fisher had reported that Mrs. Middleton was "very feeble [and] hardly able to walk," but though there are several references in the following months to her difficulty, neither she nor Eliza described what was the matter with her. While in Philadelphia, Mrs. Middleton consulted Dr. John Kearsley Mitchell (1796–1858), a prominent physician. Mitchell sent (in the "small parcel" Mrs. Middleton mentioned) a "pad" to help her, and three years later he provided her with an abdominal supporter, but it is not clear whether this was for the same problem. JFF to the Harrisons, August 15, 1840, PHi, BrC; MHM to EMF, January 18, 1841, PHi.

4. Frank Huger (1811–1849) was Emma Huger Smith's cousin and the son of Francis Kinloch and Harriott (Pinckney) Huger. Although Emma mentioned his "fearful attacks," the nature of his disease is not known. EHS to EMF, March 1, 1841, PHi.

⟶

Harry's flirtations were, meanwhile, giving his family and friends lots to talk about. Still a bachelor at forty-three, he was first infatuated with Miss Wadsworth but hesitated; then he was intrigued by the lively and unhappily married Mrs. Willing. His mother and sister were somewhat amused at these friendships, but when a much more serious and enduring one developed with "the fair widow," Mrs. Charles Harper of Baltimore, Mrs. Middleton in particular was worried.

Despite graduating from West Point with distinction in 1815 and studying at Tapping Reeve's famous law school in Litchfield, Connecticut, Harry had no interest in either the army or the law as a career. He was interested in politics and economics and wrote various articles on those subjects, but he could not earn a living from doing that and so lived on funds provided by his father. His mother was therefore increasingly uncomfortable as his friendship with Mrs. Harper continued. "How very imprudent to encourage flirtation," she declared, when he could not afford to marry![1]

1. MHM to EMF, February 17, 1842, PHi.

To Mrs. Middleton, Middleton Place

Philadelphia – Thursday 3$\underline{\text{rd}}$ December [1840]

With great joy and thankfulness did I receive the news of your safe arrival, my dearest Mamma– Fisher had been on Sunday eveng– to enquire for letters, but I hardly dared to expect one until Monday, when he brought me y$\underline{\text{r}}$ pencilled account of the journey, and I returned thanks warmly altho' silently, to that good Providence which conducted you safely to the "Haven where you would be"– That you sh$\underline{\text{d}}$ have suffered so little from fatigue too was a subject of rejoicing, and as you had fine weather, I hope none of the party took cold, or any other disagreeable thing from the North & that you are all enjoying this delightful weather at M. Place– where I am sorry you do not find Sally & her Tribe awaiting you–

Harry appeared to be much pleased at the prospect of the fair widow's approaching visit– and does not speak of a move southward yet– so I gave the little Parcel from Dr Mitchell <u>not</u> to Frank Huger (for he was to spend an indefinite time at Washington) but to Jane Pringle, who passed thro' on her way there last eveng– and was only to remain a week with [*illegible*] Poinsett–[1] She is looking well and is perfectly restored to health– I went over to see her at M^{rs} [Daniel] Coxe's where she had dined, and was amused at the eagerness with which the good Lady and old Miss Burd offered to assist her in the nursery– knowing of course nothing of such matters–[2] Luckily I was more au fait at [*knew more about*] holding babies, and managed to quiet the poor little brat, which was sleepy & starving, and as a natural consequence screaming lustily– so notwithstanding cousin Peggy [Coxe]'s entreaties and prayers that the baby might be sent home (to the Hotel) and that Jane & I would <u>stay to Tea</u>! I sided with the <u>Mother</u>, and we marched off with the Baby leaving M^r & Mrs C. in consternation– whilst Julius [Pringle] paddled after us inveighing against Jane for rushing like a cataract thro' the street, and up stairs to her chamber–

Soon after we reached it, quiet was restored– and after administering Hive Syrup[3] to Miss Mary Izard, for she was very croupy, and if she had been <u>my</u> child I sh^d have been in a feverish state of anxiety, I brought them over to see <u>my</u> young one, who was sleeping sweetly, & looked her best– They both thought her a beauty, and I in return could say in sincerity their's was a very nice little thing indeed– fair, fat & healthy– but <u>not</u> pretty– This of course I omitted saying to them– but I could truly admire its skin, arms and hands, feet & legs, in which two latter particulars it has a decided advantage over Miss Lizzie– but <u>not</u> in feature– Of course they think it <u>perfection</u>– & no doubt in admiring mine made no comparisons disadvantageous to their own– They left me in the nursery, & Fisher had given y^r parcel to Jane before I recollected that it w^d have been better to seal it up– I afterwards sent over for it– but they were in bed, and I w^d not have travellers disturbed who were to start again early this morng– And so it is on its way to you just as D^r M[itchell] sent it here, <u>tied</u> up in paper– & I hope will reach you in about ten days–

I had a letter from Mrs Barclay[4] this morng– introducing "an excessively clever Englishman"– Mr Falconer by name– & former editor of the Westminster Review–[5] no great recommendation to F. by the way– for he is of course a rank radical. She says Jane Pringle was quite <u>fascinated</u> by him, and that <u>I</u>

no doubt who am "in the habit of looking beyond externals" will appreciate his Talents– she says he is an accomplished scholar, a political & literary man of some distinction but that nothing can be <u>less</u> impressive than his appearance, <u>more</u> impressive than his conversation– Fisher is gone out to look him up– She, M<u>rs</u> Sumner, says "I have a happy home, & when there is love there is seldom a story!" Je lui enfélicite [*I congratulate her*]–

I was at the Wedding,[6] which was dull enough, & they all appeared to feel so sad that I made great exertions to be merry– and was the life and soul of the party <u>they said</u>– On Monday M<u>rs</u> Wise received company in the morng & I suppose Fourth S<u>t</u> never was so gay before– We thought we had met all our acquaintance returning on our way there, and yet found a crowd in the Salle de réception– I tried to beg off for the eveng– but found it impossible to excuse myself– but after receiving y<u>r</u> letter went in high spirits, & amused myself amazingly well– They were all very attentive & kind to me and paid me several compts– on my dress & appearance, which joy for y<u>r</u> safe arrival had brightened up I believe– M<u>r</u> S[ergeant] begged me to tell Papa, how very much he regretted not having seen him, when he had been kind enough to call, and still more how sorry he was that he had not sooner known of his being in town– M<u>r</u> Tillinghast also enquired about Papa– and made himself very agréable to me– I am happy to say that Fisher's Wistar Party went off well, and the <u>Supper</u> was discussed with ample justice– We had Esther Binney,[7] the [Robert] Hares & one or two others here on Tuesday eveng– Baby was exhibited at Teatime, & displayed all her <u>accomplishments</u> most gracefully– She has now taken to <u>singing</u> when sung to– & it is really amusing to hear her imitations, & screams of delight–

I had been up for so many successive nights that last eveng– I ventured to refuse an invitation to Aunt H's, and staid at home to practise after Jane Pringle went away– Tonight I am obliged to go there, rather reluctantly, as F[isher] has a headache– only a slight one however– Poor M<u>rs</u> Smith has been confined to her room for many days past with a violent cough & cold– She is out today & better & begs her kindest love– She told me just now of that sad affair of the Neptune–[8] & Miss Bacon's melancholy death– which she kept from me until I had heard of y<u>r</u> arrival! This was very considerate of her, for it certainly would have encreased my apprehensions for you all– but Thank God! you have now escaped the dangers of the Sea! Would that you were never again to be exposed to them!

Fisher forwarded to you a letter which he thinks was from Edward– I hope you will tell me about it in your next– I must now say Adieu dearest Mamma with love to Papa & all the rest around you at home I am y^r most affectionate Daughter Eliza

M^r & Mrs H. are well & beg their kind rememberances as does also M^{rs} F– & Fisher his best & most respectful regards– He has paid D^r M[itchell] & I now hope that what he sent you will be useful & comfortable– Mrs Pierce Butler went [*to Europe*] in the G^t Western, & y^r letter also– I did not forget it–

Private Collection

    1. Julius Pringle's mother, Mary Izard Pringle, was widowed in 1807. In 1833 she married the diplomat and politician Joel Poinsett (1779–1851), who was secretary of war in President Van Buren's administration at this time.

    2. Miss Burd was Cousin Peggy Coxe's sister; neither had any children.

    3. Hive syrup was used to make someone vomit when they had croup.

    4. Eliza forgot Mrs. Barclay was now Mrs. Sumner; she was married at Newport in September.

    5. Thomas Falconer was editor of *The London and Westminster Review*, 1836–37. This quarterly, founded in 1824, was one of the respected English critical magazines.

    6. On November 26, Sarah Sergeant, one of the John Sergeants' daughters, married Henry Augustus Wise (1806–76). A close associate of soon-to-be President Tyler, Wise was a congressman from Virginia (and future governor of Virginia as well as minister to Brazil). He was not only proslavery, but also in favor of dueling. Although it is not explained why the wedding party was sad, it is possible the Sergeants were not entirely happy about the marriage, which was Wise's second.

    7. Esther Binney, who became a close friend of Eliza's, was a daughter of the eminent Philadelphia lawyer Horace Binney and Elizabeth (Cox) Binney.

    8. The *Neptune* was a steamship on the Charleston–New York route. No information about an accident has been found.

～

To Mrs. Middleton, Middleton Place

Thursday 10$^{\underline{th}}$ December – 1840

I had just given up all hopes of a letter from you <u>today</u> my dearest Mamma, when one was brought to me directed in your handwriting, which I eagerly seized and to my disappointment found it was only from Mary, and 10 days old! It was however of a 3 days later date than that you sent the day of y^r arrival, which is the only one I have yet received– No doubt the storm and consequent stoppage of the mails occasions this delay– but I ought not to complain of it, for I am too happy when I think that you escaped all the inconveniences of a detention & also that I had heard of your safe arrival before the roads were rendered unpassable by snow–

Several of our friends have suffered much in consequence– Mr Sergeant left this on Saturday for Baltimore and did not arrive there until <u>Monday eveng</u>– passing 3 days and two nights in the cars! & nearly starved and frozen– They made a little Tea of snow water & had <u>one</u> Teacup among all the Passengers– but luckily they procured on Sunday some assistance from the neighbouring farmers who took the women & children to their Farms, and left the men to be accomodated in the cars– After hearing this account & other similar ones, I felt truly thankful that you had all proceeded Southward as early as you did– and suffer cheerfully the privation of not receiving y^r weekly letter as soon as it is due– Mary does not say whether you were to go soon to M. Place or no– But I conclude you are lodged there safely long ere this– It is really very provoking that you are not to enjoy Sally's society during John's absence at Columbia– But I hope she will make it up to you by a long visit in the Spring–

Since I last wrote the weather has been so bad that I did not stir out for several days– but had recourse to Battledore (from which fortunately I am not <u>now</u> prohibited) for exercize– and to jumping the Baby– who loves romping dearly– She is perfectly well, but a little worried by her two lower Teeth which are <u>all but</u> through the gums– Indeed the skin <u>is</u> broken just above the point of one, which we can see distinctly– She has been a close prisoner for a week, but today there is a mild change & occasionally a gleam of sunshine & I think I shall let her take a turn in the Sleigh with Aunt H. about noon– We made an expedition to Germantown in it two days since– to see the Morris'[1] & Chews– The old gentleman [*Mr. Chew*] was more ridiculous than ever, & <u>hugged</u> both Aunt H. & Sally Hare– I fortunately kept clear of his embraces by making a timely retreat from him, having no fancy for being smothered in the Powder dust with which his coat & nether integuments are always covered– But I enjoyed the scene amazingly– altho' I was afterwards more disgusted than amused at the absurd compliments showered upon us all round– He and the old Lady both desired to be particularly remembered to you & Papa, expressing their regret that you had already left Town when they called to see you the other day– & very tender enquiries were made about Arthur who, said he, looking round at his daughter Ann, may perhaps <u>cast anchor</u> here after all! Luckily she did not overhear this delicate insinuation, for she appears to be a very nice sensible and <u>un</u>affected young woman– Marvellous that she sh^d remain so in such a family–

But enough of them– Harry and I called yesterday upon the Sergeants– The Wises are still detained by the weather– and <u>he</u> has been shivering with the Ague several times since his marriage! We also saw poor Mrs Smith, who is still suffering much with her cough– She insists upon it that she is better, and will not take the advice of a Physician– but I think her a very sick woman– and very obstinate to refuse to let me send her one– Talking of which, I persuaded poor little Mme Marras to see Dr Meigs[2] as she had been very unwell for several days & required bleeding– I tried to interest him about her, for I really do pity the poor little Soul– Her situation is bad enough under the most favourable circumstances, but wretched indeed in her case without female relation or near friends– Mrs Fisher & myself will do everything in our power for her if she remains next door– but she is uncertain whether she stays in Phil^a at all– as Marras has been advised to try his fortune at Balt[imor]e where I sh^d not encourage him to go, after Saunder's success– She has been singing with me, and given me some very pretty vocal music composed by Marras' brother–

I have just been called down to see two English (or rather <u>Irish</u>) Officers, Major Mr Goldick & Mr Maturin, with whom Harry became acquainted at Jones' & brought here to introduce that I might take them to Mrs Binney's Ball tonight– They appear very gentlemanly, and the younger one rather agreeable and delighted at the prospect of a Waltz– I am glad to shew them such good specimens of American girls as they will find the Miss Binneys– And am sure they could nowhere see any more ladylike or well educated than my favourites– Fisher is now reading aloud to me Lockhart's Life of Sir Walter Scott–[3] which is really a delightful book– I am so much pleased with "The Listener" by Miss Fry[4] which I am also reading, that when Harry goes on I must send it to you– Some of the Chapters are most excellent indeed–

Fisher says I must get ready to walk to Dryburgh's for a bouquet to wear at the Ball and it is getting so late, owing to various interruptions, that I will say Adieu– Mrs Fisher begged me to give her kindest remembrances to you– She has a <u>slight</u> nervous attack, but I am in hopes her Sleigh ride will <u>whisk</u> it away– I wrote a long letter to Edward on Sunday which a friend of Mr Hunter's was to carry to Rio Janiero– Fisher jogs me again for my delay so Goodbye with best love to Papa– Kitty & other members of the family who may be with you I am dearest Mamma, Y^r most affec^te Daughter Eliza

Robert Walsh who is just come from N.Y. says he <u>was to have</u> brought the little Picture of the Madonna from Julia [Ward] but why he did not, I did not understand– He does not believe one word of her engagement at <u>any</u> time to Kirk– but says on the contrary she was indignant at the <u>manner</u> of his offer which she <u>peremptorily</u> refused–[5]

Private Collection

1. Ann Willing Morris's daughters, Margaret (1797–1867) and Elizabeth (1795–1865), lived with her in Germantown. Elizabeth was a botanist; Margaret was elected to the Academy of Natural Science because of her original work on locusts and the Hessian fly.

2. Charles D. Meigs (1792–1869) was a leading obstetrician and professor of medicine at Jefferson Medical College, as well as the author of books on midwifery, obstetrics, and children's diseases. Like Fisher, he was a member of the American Philosophical Society and attended the Wistar Parties.

3. John Gibson Lockhart was Sir Walter Scott's son-in-law. The second edition of his immensely popular biography of Scott was published in 1839.

4. *The Listener*, by Caroline Fry (1787–1846), was so popular a second edition was printed in London in 1831.

5. Eliza and Fisher were horrified to hear rumors that Julia was engaged to Mr. Kirk, the man Eliza had heard preach so powerfully in Philadelphia the previous winter. Fisher told his aunt that "Eliza cries out against this" and that he could not bear to think that "such a woman should in a period of religious excitement sacrifice herself to such a tartuffe." JFF to Sophia Harrison, July 24, 1840, PHi, BrC.

⌒

To Mrs. Fisher, Philadelphia

Charleston Dec.ʳ 10ᵗʰ 1840

My dearest Eliza

I have delayed writing for a few days in expectation of hearing from you again– Yesterday there were five mails due from the north, so that had I written my letter would have been stopped by the way as the other mails are. Our detention so much longer than usual has been occasioned by the late arrival of the schooner to take up the baggage, provisions &c.[1] It will do that today, & tomorrow mornᵍ we are to go to M.P. Who do you think is to accompany us? It will astonish you to know that Miss [Henrietta] Drayton has at length made up her mind to make a visit to 'the dear old place' as she calls it. Her health however is so precarious that I cannot count upon her with any certainty. she says she is sure I shall repent of my urging her to make the visit, as she is frequently for weeks unable to quit her room & gives an immensity of trouble– that I can easily believe for Miss Pinckney assured me of it. She begs to occupy your room, being out of the way of noise– here is another visitor which I did not look for! Your Father has just desired me to write to her to carry her agreeable niece Louisa [Gibbes][2] with her– only fancy what a bore she will be!

Oliver & family will be with us at Xmas & John writes to say that on the 19th inst if a horse is sent to Summerville for him he will come to remain (I hope for) a week– longer I suppose he cannot, as he must be anxious to return home. Since I wrote last a letter from Sally tells me that she cannot leave Waccamaw before Feby, then she shall be <u>obliged</u> to go to Charleston. I concluded what that meant, & it was confirmed by Mrs [Robert Y.] Hayne[3] whom I met at Church– She informed me that poor Sally is to be confined about the 20th of March– poor soul! how sorry I am that her feeble frame has again to undergo another trial of that kind. She must suffer in the mean time from her usual malady, for I found 2 packages of Iceland moss[4] waiting here to be sent to her. Harry went last week with Mr C[harles] Alston[5] to Waccamaw, to her great delight no doubt. In her letter she says "I learn from a letter of Hal's that dear Eliza has no intention of coming to the south this winter– this I confess is a great disappointment to me & I am sure will be so to many others. It may however be better for the infant that they should remain quietly at Philada for the present, & I will still hope that the Spring may bring forth a new plan." She mentions nothing of her health but says that John was not well when he left her. Yr Aunt Huger however says that he seemed very well when he passed through Charleston, & I hope the Air of Columbia may have completely restored him to health.

Mary's letter to you last week served to fill up the gap in my correspondence since that time I have had the pleasure to receive Ed's letter forwarded by Mr Fisher. It is dated 25th Sepr from Rio[6] & he was then on the point of sailing for the River La Plata to join the Comm[odo]re. He seems pleased with Buenos Ayres as his letter to you shewed. Yours of the 1st Jany & mine announcing the birth of little Lizzy he recd from the hands of Miss Hunter both of which afforded him great pleasure. he says I hope you will thank Ch[arles] Hunter for his kindness in forwarding them so safely & he adds he cannot recommend a better medium for sending letters than him. When <u>you</u> see him, pray thank him for me. I shall trouble him again in a month or two, but having lately written will wait, for Arthur's arrival.

He begs to be remembered to you & to Mrs Fisher– Pray remember me also affectly to her & thank her for the trouble she took with my fur– I hope she has had no more of Rheumatism or any other complaint– Here is a note just recd from Miss Drayton saying it is quite impossible for her to go tomorrow, or indeed for some weeks, having had since we met a very severe attack, neither can her niece come. Mrs Holbrook has been to see me, & consented to pay me a short visit– last Sunday after Church she said she wd come some Saturday with the Doctor & stay till the following Monday. I hope it may be Saturday

the 19th– from Sunday the 13th until then, I shall be alone with C. & must
try to force my eyes <u>at night</u> to do their duty–

I went to see Alice [Heyward] the other day & found her in great affliction
for the loss of Mrs A[rthur] M[iddleton][7] who she said was her best friend.
She was in tears all the time I sat with her. Anne M. now lives with her. I did
not see her, as she was spending a few days with Geor[gin]a at Stono. I believe
I mentioned in my last having sent Mrs Mc Ewen's parcel the day I arrived.
Mrs T. M[iddleton] produced a Daughter on the 1st int & is doing well. I have
seen yr Aunt Huger two or three times & Sarah [Wilkinson] kindly accompanied me last week to shop for sundry articles. She said she wd Come & see me
in the country when I was alone, so I proposed to her to come next week,
particularly as her Physin had recommended change of air to her. she said however that she could not come so soon– Emma is to be in town at Xmas. Pray
tell Harry with my love that I miss his evening reading aloud exceedingly. When
is he coming? Let him bring the parcel from Dr M[itchell]. Surely he will be
here at Xmas to meet his brothers. I suppose he will call me selfish for wishing
to have him at M.P! Miss Rutledge tells me that Henrietta [Rutledge] is to be
confined in Apl or May, Emma Blake in March, & she is to accompany Mr
F[rederick] Rutge to Buncomb in Feby & stay with her sister & be confined
there herself.

I am glad to hear that your velvet cloak suits you. I have had no occasion
for my satin one. the weather is now very mild, & I shall try to walk in the
country for a qur of an hour at a time– 11th No mail yesterday– but I must
wait no longer for another letter, that of the 26th ultmo being the only one I
have recd from you, but send this off. Here is a beautiful mild morng & we
are to go [*to Middleton Place*] between 9 & 10– I believe Mary's letter informed
you that Wm was to accompany Oliver to Edisto & proceed with him to Combahee– He will then I suppose go with his Father (who will leave M.P. for Combahee on Sunday) about the 22d probably to join the Xmas party at M.P– Pray
give my love to Mrs Smith & tell her Mrs Blamyer who called to see me one
evening with one of her Daughters, is looking very well. You see her no doubt
frequently. I wish <u>I</u> could! Has the Darling any new fancies? You must tell me
all her improvements–

Your Father has purchased a pr of Carriage horses, & a very pretty riding
Mare he says– I have seen neither of them– He sends his love to you pray give
mine to Mr & Mrs Fisher & kind remembrance to Mrs Harrison & believe me
my dearest Eliza yr affectte Mother M. H. M.

I hope Mr Harrison is quite recovered– Do not expect to hear from me again
for 10 days as there will be no mode of conveying a letter to this place– I wish

when you see Mrs Hare you w^{d} give my Compl^{ts} to her, & ask her to tell you the proportions of Cammomile & Cologne water which she said she used, & found so beneficial to her eyes– P.S. y^{r} Father has just put y^{r} very welcome letter of the 3^{d} into my hands– I must conclude adieu

ScHi

1. That is, take them up the Ashley River to Middleton Place.
2. Louisa Izard Gibbes (1823–1902) was the daughter of Maria Drayton (Mrs. Lewis L.) Gibbes, Miss Drayton's sister.
3. Mrs. Hayne, the former Rebecca Motte Alston, was the second wife and widow of Robert Y. Hayne, former senator from South Carolina. He died in 1839.
4. Iceland moss, a kind of lichen, when made into a tea was recommended to cure a cough. Since Sally Middleton was often troubled by a cough, this is likely to be what she used the moss for. It was also a source of glycerol used to prevent constipation.
5. Charles Alston (b. 1796) was Sally Middleton's uncle.
6. Eliza would already have had this news: on November 26, the *Philadelphia Gazette and Commercial Intelligencer* reported that Edward's ship, the *Marion*, had arrived safely at Rio de Janeiro on September 23.
7. John Middleton wrote his mother, "You will be sorry to hear of the death of poor Mrs. Arthur M. She was an excellent person. And deserved a better fate than to be poisoned with calomel." (John I. Middleton to MHM, September 28, 1840, PHi, C/F). Calomel was used medicinally and contained mercury. Anne Middleton was Mrs. Arthur Middleton's daughter; Georgina was her daughter-in-law.

~

To Mrs. Middleton, Middleton Place

Thursday morng– 17th December 1840

I have come down stairs before breakfast to write to my dearest Mamma, hoping that afterwards I may have the pleasure of thanking you for the letter I have been expecting for ten days past– and which is still on the road, or in the hands of the Postman– I trust he will very soon deliver it to me– for this protracted delay is very annoying, and will become distressing if I am not relieved from it before long– Hitherto I have persuaded myself that the state of the snow covered railroads was the cause of my disappointment– added to which perhaps the difficulty of sending in to town without horses–

11 o'clock– I was beginning to despair of a letter from you today, when your's of the 10th & 11th was brought in, to my very great delight– It is a very satisfactory one indeed except in respect of the uncertainty of my not receiving another for ten days– but this I will not complain of whilst I am so happy to have one this morng– I am very glad you were detained in Charleston a fort-

night– for I am sure you must have found it much pleasanter there, within call of the many agreeable friends you mention having seen, than if you had been all alone in the country– I do hope that for once Mrs Holbrook will be able to perform her promise of a visit to you, and that Sarah [Wilkinson] will also exchange the air of King S^t [*in Charleston*] for that of M. Place– which no doubt w$^{\underline{d}}$ be of service to her health– Poor Sally! I pity her from my heart & yet perhaps it will not be as great a trial to her constitution as you imagine– altho' necessarily a very exhausting remedy for other complaints– I suppose Emma Blake rejoices in the same prospect, and indeed her's is one of the very few cases in which such an event may be desirable– Henrietta & herself sympathize in a most remarkable manner I think–

You are mistaken in supposing that I have seen Mrs Smith frequently– She has been much confined to the house by the cold weather & her cough, which has been very troublesome– & altho' I have called often, she seldom has come down to me, & will not let me up into her room– She was here on Saturday, & appeared much better tho' still far from well– On Tuesday I wrote to beg her to take a drive with me & baby in the country, but she sent me word she was not well enough, & yesterday I intended calling to enquire after her– but the snow-rain kept me a prisoner all day– I shall go this fine day– & hope to find her at home– & give you further accounts of her this afternoon– I don't think Miss D[rayton] would have been a very agreeable substitute for her society– but still her's would have been [better] than the solitude to which I fear you will be condemned for a week–

I have not seen Harry for two days past– but shall send after him presently to know his messages– I have not heard him speak of any intention of leaving Ph$^{\underline{a}}$ at present– but enquire several times about M^{rs} H[arper]'s long looked for visit to M^{rs} [John] B[utler]– Did you read his poetical contribution to the National Gazette of the __?[1] It is called "Boyhood" & signed H. Y. Some of the stanzas are very pretty I think– but not all in the style I should have supposed w$^{\underline{d}}$ be his, & so ladylike that I do not wonder at the Editor's mistake which I believe he led him into intentionally by using the most recherché paper, and most delicate characters– He seems to be amusing himself very well, reading to M^{rs} W[illing]– & talking to her & Mrs Campbell– to whom he devoted himself at Aunt H's on Sunday eveng– He goes to the Dallas' party to night by her invitation– and first to Miss Hare's party to the bride [*Sarah Sergeant Wise*] with us– which I fear will be something of a bore– I have been to none, since the Binney's Ball– which proved very pleasant– I had half a dozen invitations to dance, two of them very pressing– but persisted in declining– both on my own account & baby's– I do not think that her milk w$^{\underline{d}}$ have been improved by my dancing in such hot rooms and I preferred greatly talking to some agreeable people to heating myself by even walking thro' a cotillion. Matilda Willing was at the height of her happiness, waltzing [*missing*] with Mr Maturin– who seemed to enjoy himself so much that I was very glad I had carried him there– They left for Bermuda two days afterwards– He, leaving his heart with Miss Bayard,[2] with whom he became desperately smitten– There's one engagement announced, which I sh^d hardly think of mentioning, except that the young lady is a <u>cousin</u> of your's– Eliza Peters,[3] the youngest daughter of y^r friend, is engaged to a Mr Field– a young Front St Merchant, never heard of before this autumn in "<u>our circle</u>"(!) which some of the family consider a mésalliance– but as he is a worthy fellow and in <u>good business</u>, they might be well satisfied–

I have been busy hunting for Xmas presents– & at last have succeeded pretty much to my satisfaction– I wish Harry w^d go in time to carry some to the South– I want to send Kitty some Music, which perhaps she will be better inclined to play as it arrives fresh, than if she had carried it on herself– Tell her she must sometimes write me a few lines, & tell me what she wants, & I will send it by the first opportunity– I have heard of none since Jane Pringle went to Wash^n.

Fisher expects today a batch of new books from N.Y. They are principally <u>Theological</u>– in which department his Library is becoming very extensive & rich– Burnett's on the Articles & Pearson on the Creed,[4] were recommended by Mr Odenheimer– who has been twice this week to see us– not finding us the first time– Last eveng– he came thro' all the snow– conversed very agreeably indeed– & was more cheerful than I have seen him since the death of his children– He thinks Baby wonderfully improved, which indeed everybody remarks– She is now very rosy, & <u>so</u> heavy, that I assure you my arm has ached ever since I had her weight upon it for an hour during the drive to Miss Nixon's– And I should not have undertaken to play Nurse as I did at New Port so often, if I had recollected that she is now twice the size that she was when I carried her about in her little carriage– One of her lower Teeth is <u>quite</u> thro' the Gum, & the other nearly so– But altho' she <u>gnaws</u> at everything within her reach & <u>dribbles</u> copiously, there is no <u>fever</u>, or anything else to indicate that she is as Mme Guerreiro[5] said, in the "act of dentition"–

I have rec^d a letter from Sophia Thorndike from Potsdam– but of the old date of the 10th of Septr. She writes in very good spirits and appears to be enjoying herself, & not thinking of a return to this country for 18 months from that time– She was to spend the winter with Elizth & go in the Spring with her to see Sally Anne– and is hard at work studying German– which she finds rather a difficult task– She likes Theodore (E's husband) very much, & says she is very comfortably situated there in nice large & airy apartments– I enclosed Edwd's letter, & wrote a few lines to her the other day, which I sent by D^r [Robert P.] Page to London– whence he is to forward it–

Eveng– Harry has just been & begged me to tell you that he hoped to go on to Carolina before long– but that he cannot for the time as his movements do not depend altogether on himself, but on some <u>engagements</u>, the nature of which he did not explain– But he cannot be with you at Xmas– This will find you surrounded I hope by Sons & their children, and enjoying good health, I most sincerely pray– It is late & I must go up & look after Baby– so adieu my dearest Mamma, with best love to Papa, and all the other members of the family around you I remain as ever Y^r most affectionate Daughter Eliza

I spent half an hour with Mrs Smith this morng– She is better & desired her kindest regards to you– saying she w^d write some <u>intermediate</u> day, between my weekly despatch–

Private Collection

1. Eliza left a blank here. Harry's poem appeared in the *National Gazette and Literary Register* on December 10, 1840.
2. Probably the daughter of Anne (Francis) and James A. Bayard.
3. Eliza Peters, the daughter of Richard and Abby (Willing) Peters, married John W. Field. Eliza must have been teasing her mother about her cousin as the connection, through the McCalls, was remote.
4. Fisher's new books were Gilbert Burnet's *An Exposition of the 39 Articles of the Church of England* and the *Exposition of the Creed* by John Pearson (1613–1686), theologian and bishop of Chester.
5. Mme Guerreiro's husband was the Portuguese minister to Russia when the Middletons were there.

⟶

To Mrs. Fisher, Philadelphia

M.P. Decr 21st 1840

Here is indeed a fortunate arrival my dearest Eliza of your letter of the 10th which one of the [Horse] Sav[ann]a men has just brought from Charleston! I will no longer delay expressing my pleasure on reading your affectionate one of the 3^d which I had time only to acknowledge, in my last, as the carriage was waiting for me when it was put into my hands. I read it over again in the Carriage & was much pleased with the account you gave of Baby's taste for singing, it must amuse you all no doubt to listen to her attempts to imitate you. The near appearance of her teeth which the last letter mentions is quite unexpected, & most welcome news that they are coming through the gums without fever– You must have had a pleasant day with M^{rs} J[ane] P[ringle] I have just been searching for her name in the list of the Wilmington arrivals up to the 19th ins^t but see it not, so that I presume the weather has detained her at Washington. Her's was a good opportunity for sending my little parcel– I agree with you that it ought to have been sealed up. We were indeed very lucky to make our journey in such fair weather. had it been postponed until the time you mention, when Mr Sergeant travelled, it would have nearly killed me. I am glad to tell you that after being alone for 6 days John arrived yesterday to a late dinner– He is not looking as well as usual & is suffering from a severe cold & cough which however does not affect either his breast or lungs, neither has he lately had any return of fever & expects the change of air will soon remove his cough– (I am getting out of conceit of the Perryian ink stand– you see what blots my writing consists of!) He says Sally is tolerably well but used to complain of want of breath, though she has no cough– I dread the approaching confinement for the poor sufferer–

He seems delighted with little Johnny's improvement– he is fond of reading, & his great amusement is gardening– I believe I mentioned to you Oliver's wish that Sarah might stay with him & go with his girls to Mr Gilman's school. John appears to approve of the plan & I think it will make all the young party very happy– my only fear is that the obedient Sarah will learn from her cousins to say "I will", & "I wont". Oliver's family will probably be here on Thursday. John has lately rec^d a letter from y^r Uncle Izard of Octr in which he says he is in daily expectation of seeing Arthur & that he shall send by him your Jewellery–[1] I fear he [Arthur] will not pay my brother a visit.

22nd You will be glad to hear that during the 6 lonely even^{gs} I amused myself with reading "10,000 a year"[2] without injuring my eyes, which I dreaded from the smallness of the type. but by placing the lamp behind me, I avoided the glare. I agree with Mr F. that the beginning of Titmouse's history is disgusting, but that of the Aubrey family very interesting. I shall be very glad to read the "Listener" which you are kind enough to say you will send me by Harry & to keep it, as I do "10,000 a y^r" for the evenings when I am left alone. I am not likely to get the last vol. of it, as all the former were got at N.York. I have just been thinking that Mr F. would do me a great favour if he would send me by Harry the numbers of Blackwood's Mag^e containing the 3^d & 4th vol^e of the above novel, for the 3$\underline{d}$ y$\underline{r}$ Father got, has 30 pages missing! I will keep the nos. carefully, & return them to him when we meet next summer.

I liked the life of Sir W. Scott very much, but read only half as M$\underline{rs}$ Sumner had only one vol. at Newport which she lent me. I was much amused at the sentence you quote from her letter. The name of Falconer you mentioned, reminded me of a play mate of mine <u>Tom</u> F. whose name I have lately often read quoted as a very learned, scientific man. D$\underline{r}$ T. F. <u>his</u> father was an eminent physician at Bath– perhaps the grandfather of y$\underline{r}$ new acquaintance. I hope you had a pleasant party at Miss Binneys, & were not disappointed in gratifying the two Irish officers by making them admire your young friends. I am writing thus closely in order to have room to add intelligence of Susan when she comes. & I make use of the first page by crossing it to copy lines of M$\underline{rs}$ Osgood's[3] the wife of the painter who spent [...] here last spring...[4] I am anxiously expecting to hear from you and also from my brother by the "President" but hear nothing of its arrival yet– With love to Mr. and Mrs. Fisher I am my dearest Eliza Y$\underline{r}$ Affect$\underline{te}$ Mother M. H. M.

Y$\underline{r}$ father & brothers send their love. remember me to Mrs Har$\underline{n}$

PHi

1. Eliza's Uncle Izard Middleton used the money left from buying her trousseau to buy jewelry and had it ready to send by a reliable person. When Arthur finally showed up in Paris the following summer, Uncle Izard wrote to Eliza, "I can now announce to you that I have given in his charge for you a bracelet, a brooch, & a pair of Diamond drops," and concluded "with the usual excuse (If I should need it) that I have done for the best & hope that they will meet with your approbation." J. Izard Middleton to EMF, July 6, 1841, PHi, C/F.

2. *Ten Thousand a Year,* a novel by Samuel Warren published serially in *Blackwood's Edinburgh Magazine* beginning in October 1839, was the story of a young man who finds he is heir to a fortune. William Blackwood's magazine was one of the most respected British journals.

3. Mrs. Osgood, the former Frances Sargent Locke (1811–1850), had an independent career as a poet. She wrote a poem about her daughter Ellen's first tooth while her husband painted a picture of the child at the same important time. The poem began, "Your mouth is a rose bud / And in it a pearl / Lies smiling & snowy / My own little girl!"

4. The paper is torn here and several lines are incomplete.

⁓

Declining to "enumerate the bags, Pincushions, slippers & Penwipers I distributed," Eliza told her mother after Christmas she was glad "Christmas comes but once a year for altho' it is a great pleasure to <u>give</u>, & 'more blessed than to receive,' it certainly is a very troublesome thing to hunt about for appropriate presents for all ages, & the whole of last week I was occupied with searching the Shops and Fairs, which was a great waste of time—the only thing I grudge in the matter."[1]

Eliza had had a disappointment, as she made clear in the next letter, and the events which led to it illustrate the balancing act that was sometimes required to maintain harmony in the Fisher household. When they were married in 1839, Fisher promised Eliza he would try to take her back to Middleton Place for their second wedding anniversary if his mother and the Harrisons were in good health at that time; but when Fisher floated the idea in the fall of 1840, Uncle Harrison told Fisher the trip "was not to be spoken of." This was his way of indicating that Mrs. Fisher was opposed, which she frequently was to anything that took Fisher away from home. In this case, she also seems to have argued that there would be a great risk in taking the baby to South Carolina.

Fisher was caught between wanting to fulfill his promise to Eliza and trying to satisfy his mother, to whom he was genuinely devoted. To relieve his "most nervous Mother" of her anxiety, he felt required to give lengthy and repeated assurances of his attachment to his home and his "dear dear old friends." The trip was given up and Eliza was not able to go home to South Carolina until 1843.[2]

1. EMF to MHM, December 26, 1840, private collection.
2. JFF to GH, September 10, 1840, and October 5, 1840, PHi, BrC.

To Mrs. Middleton, Middleton Place

Thursday 31ˢᵗ Decʳ 1840!

I have a great feeling of regret, my dearest Mamma, in writing for the last time that date– for the past year has been one of much happiness to me, and many blessings have attended me and mine thro' its whole course. May the coming one bring with it as large a share of health & prosperity to all I love– or if these are denied us by an All Wise Being, who alone knoweth what is best for us, may He give us, his poor weak creatures, resignation and strength to bear us thro' any Trials he may see fit to visit us with– and unfailing Trust in his Mercy and goodness– The last day of the Year is always a sad one to me– For I remember with deep sorrow the many opportunities for improvement, neglected– and the many hours and days mis-spent or unprofitably wasted– But I will not trouble you with vain regrets, which only concern me & my conscience, nor tell you of the firm resolutions of doing better in future, lest they should, like others made before, be broken or remain unfulfilled– But merely express my gratitude to Heaven (in which I am sure you will join) for all the bounties which have been so profusely showered upon me, for which my heart can never be sufficiently thankful– and for which I could never swell loud enough the notes of Praise– My greatest disappointment has been to be obliged to give up my visit to Carolina this spring– let us hope we may pass the next together & look forward in the meantime to a joyful meeting at New Port in less than 6 months–

There are no applications for the <u>Francisville Lot</u> yet, and I much fear the Ward House [*in Newport*] will pass into other hands before we can afford to purchase it– as Fisher will not, of course, sacrifice property which will hereafter, in all probability, become more valuable– so that my fine projects are for the present all <u>dashed</u>–[1] Only think of poor Poppet, Fisher's trusty steed, who so often exerted himself in our service, going off in a decline, after a 3 weeks illness! We are quite grieved at his loss– but less so than we sh$^{\underline{d}}$ otherwise have been as M$^{\underline{r}}$ Harrison immediately supplied it <u>doubly</u> by giving F. one of his 2 pair– He advises F. to keep one of them, & sell the other which could not be used as a riding Horse– But I think it would be better still to sell <u>both</u>, and then suit himself and <u>me</u>, by getting two that might draw together– For even M$^{\underline{rs}}$ F– wishes me to mount again in the Spring–

I have just been called down to see Harry– who has no particular message he says– except his Love– and that he hopes to be <u>on</u> soon– This I much doubt as the Fair Widow [*Mrs. Harper*] is now in Town– and he will now divide his attentions between M$^{\underline{rs}}$ W[illing] & her– The latter <u>refused</u> to go and see M$^{\underline{rs}}$ H[arper] when he begged her to do so! a suspicious circumstance of jealous hue! Eh? I am afraid M$^{\underline{rs}}$ H. will not find Phil$^{\underline{a}}$ very amusing– For altho' there are a good many parties just now, Ella B[utler] seems to be very unpopular and to go to few–[2] They are to be at Aunt H's tomorrow, New Year's night– but are not invited (to H's great regret) to the Ball at M$^{\underline{rs}}$ Atherton's this eveng– I go to Margaret Sergeant's wedding [*to George Meade*]– and perhaps, if I am not too much fagged afterwards to wish them a happy New Year at M$^{\underline{rs}}$ A's– Tomorrow I am to dine at M$^{\underline{rs}}$ Hare's and if Baby will let me, to Aunt H's in the eveng– She is perfectly well, & the merriest little spright I ever saw– Waking me up every morng– between 5 & 6 by the <u>screams</u> of <u>Laughter</u> which issue from her crib in the next room– and attracting the notice of all passers by, during the day when she is jumping at every one in the Street from the Parlour window– where Anne regularly takes her station to exhibit and entertain her– I rather disapprove of thus encouraging her love of <u>Gadding</u>, which may perhaps grow upon her too much, if unchecked– But it is delightful to see her so easily amused–

Afternoon– I was interrupted by a visit from Esther Binney, (one of the privileged few who are not turned away, when I am really at home) and then I went up to see Mrs Smith who desires her love to you & many kind wishes besides for health & peace– She is decidedly better & was this morng– in good spirits & says she means to write to you & tell you what a lovely granddaughter you have– We went on Tuesday to hear Mr Simmons[3] (Mrs Sumner's friend) deliver a lecture on Byron– A very good one in some respects, and the recitations admirable, but I was not as highly delighted as Harry– who thought his manner excellent whereas it reminded me of a bad actor's– & his style I thought very bombastic and exaggerated– so much so, that altho' I fully intended going to hear his course on Shakespeare, I now care less about it, and am not sorry to miss the first this afternoon– F. has just gone to it after reading Wallenstein[4] with me for an hour–

He has brought me a sweet Bouquet for this eveng– and has a magnificent one for a New Year's Offering to Aunt H– I have already rec^d my two presents from him– An Almanack & a very pretty Watch stand of inlaid wood & a beautiful worked collar from M^rs F– in anticipation of tomorrow– Really she overwhelms me so with Gifts of all sorts, that what with her's & Aunt H's I need scarcely supply myself at all– and can make but a poor return to them for all they do for me– I have bought Mrs Chisolm's shawl but can hear of no opportunity by which to send it– or any thing else– which is very provoking– but I cannot tell Harry so– I was last eveng– at a little party at Sally Waln's to meet Mmes Sears and d'Hauteville–[5] and Mme Trudeau,[6] who was at New Port in the summer of '36 if you remember– She is now on her way to N. Orleans to rejoin her husb^d who is in very bad health– I heard there a report of Anna Sergeant's engagement to a Mr Gerhard–[7] a young Lawyer here of excellent character and great steadiness & industry who would they say be a very good match for her– I shall find out this eveng– the truth of the report I suppose– Fenwick Jones is really going to be married to Mr Gardiner,[8] And Mary [*Fenwick's sister*] & Mrs George J[ones] went on to Savannah together a week after the death of Mrs Savage [*Mrs. Jones' mother*] which took place suddenly some weeks ago– & was a most happy release, for the poor thing suffered agonies– Miss Harper is paying a visit to the [William Ellery] Channings[9] in Boston, & is also to spend some time with Mrs C. Lyman there, before her return to N. Port– She will not be here until the end of March, when she is to pass thro' on her way to Baltimore, where she expects to be during Lent– And now I believe I have told you all the news I could collect, & will say Adieu, as I have but an hour to practise before it will be time to make my Wedding Toilette–

So with most affectionate love to Papa, my brothers and Kitty, I am as ever my dearest Mamma Y^r devotedly attached Daughter Eliza

If Mary is with you, will you tell her I mean to write to her on Saturday & thank her for her 2 letters– It is a fortnight since I heard from you, but I am not uneasy as you warned me that you should not write for ten days.

Private Collection

1. The Fishers had discussed the possibility of buying Samuel Ward's house in Newport, and paying for it by selling property (Francisville) in Philadelphia that Fisher inherited from his grandfather Tench Francis.
2. Mrs. Harper was staying with Ella Butler.
3. William H. Simmons of Boston lectured on Byron and was going to offer a course of ten lectures on Shakespeare, commenting on all the principal plays and attempting to analyze the characters and spirit of each. Tickets were five dollars for the series, or fifty cents each. *Phila. GCI,* December 23, 1840.
4. Friedrich von Schiller (1759–1805) wrote *Wallenstein,* a historical drama, in 1798.
5. On the heels of her unfortunate (and widely discussed) marriage to a Swiss named D'Hauteville, Bostonian Ellen Sears D'Hauteville was living in Philadelphia with her mother, Mrs. David Sears, hoping the Pennsylvania courts, more than those of some other states, would favor giving her custody of her infant. The D'Hautevilles were divorced and Ellen D'Hauteville did gain custody of her child.
6. Possibly Mrs. James Trudeau, whose husband's family had longstanding connections to Louisiana. Her family lived in New York.
7. Benjamin Gerhard (1812–1864), who became an eminent lawyer, had studied under Joseph R. Ingersoll. Later he was a member of city councils and a trustee of the University of Pennsylvania.
8. Fenwick Jones married Robert Hallowell Gardiner in Newport at the end of June 1842.
9. William Ellery Channing (1780–1842) was a renowned Unitarian leader and minister of the Federal Street Church in Boston. After the mid-1830s, he was outspoken in his opposition to slavery but was able to remain friendly with southerners like the Middletons. His married his cousin, the former Ruth Gibbs; they both grew up in Newport and continued to spend their summers there.

1841

Italian women are not famous for morality, nor for good educations.

~

Arthur Middleton's sudden marriage in the spring of 1841 set tongues wagging up and down the east coast. First there were hints in his own letters, then rumors, and finally specific reports from friends who saw him in Europe: It was true! While visiting Rome on his way home from Spain, Arthur had met, and quickly married, a young girl (she was not yet twenty) with dark eyes and dark hair. She came from an old Roman family but had no fortune. Her name was Paolina Bentivoglio.

In response to this unwelcome news, Mrs. Middleton rose to her finest epistolatory heights, expressing dismay at Arthur's imprudence and wondering why he couldn't have married someone like Susan or Sally. Henry Middleton was certainly not happy about Arthur's loitering in Europe,[1] but, as the deed was done, the family made the best of the situation, rallied to give Paolina a gracious welcome—and loved her.

These were years in which Eliza was working out her roles and duties as a daughter-in-law, a mother, and a wife. In that context, her reading included, for example, *Woman's Mission,* a book that discussed how women "may obtain & exercise a <u>moral</u> influence . . . on the sterner sex."[2] At the same time, she was experimenting with ways she could use her mind and talents in meaningful ways. She read widely, continued to study Italian and German, attended lectures on English literature, and was already engaged in the "constant acts of charity" which became her habit.[3] Music was always her main interest, however. She arranged to have piano lessons, set aside regular time to practice, and took full advantage of the impressive range of musical activities Philadelphia supported at the time. Between January and May she attended five major musical performances: the first in the United States of Mozart's *Magic Flute;* his *Don Giovanni;* one of the first American performances of Bellini's opera *Norma; Zampa,* a French comic opera; and Haydn's oratorio *The Creation.* She couldn't get a seat for a sixth concert at which Haydn's "Grand Mass" was to be sung.

Both Sally and Susan had babies in the spring of 1841, and, despite her own poor health, Mrs. Middleton looked after their children while they were confined. Even when the children's "clatter" and quarreling drove her out of her own drawing room, she managed to take an interest in each child's character and development. Remembering her own experiences as a mother, Mrs. Middleton could also encourage and advise Eliza as her baby faced teething, weaning, and her first real sickness. Her psychological insight was proven when she predicted that Lizzie would be jealous of her new sister, Sophy, who was born at the end of November.

Sophy's safe arrival was a happy conclusion to the year, for 1841 had been one of death and sickness. Times continued to be hard, as Eliza and her mother mentioned more than once. The U.S. economy was in the fourth year of depression, and not only were businesses bankrupt but several states, Pennsylvania among them, had defaulted on their debts. Foreign investors, who had provided a good deal of the funding for American development in the boom years of the 1830s, lost heavily and naturally refused to invest more. As the depression lengthened, unemployment spread.

Americans, rich and poor alike, had invested in public bonds and private companies and many were now destitute. The English geologist Charles Lyell, whom the Fishers met in 1842 when he was visiting the United States, reported that "many widows and single women have lost their all, and great numbers of the poorer classes are deprived of their savings."[4] A devastating blow for many was the failure of the Bank of the United States which had operated under a Pennsylvania charter since 1836, when its federal charter expired. Having once been the symbol of financial solidity, it was forced to close in early 1841. Several of the Middletons' and Fishers' friends, such as Miss Harper, lost very large sums, leaving Fisher feeling lucky to have lost only "a few hundreds."[5]

1. JFF to GH, September 10, [1841,] PHi, BrC.
2. The book, written in 1834 by Frenchman Louis-Aimé Martin, was *De l'éducation des mères de famille, ou De la civilisation du genre humain par les femmes* [Of the education of mothers, or the civilization of mankind by women]. EMF to MHM, April 1, 1840, private collection.
3. Obituary of Mrs. Joshua Francis Fisher, *Public Ledger*, February 22, 1890.
4. Sir Charles Lyell, *Travels in North America,* quoted in John Sperling's *Great Depressions* (Glenview, Ill.: Scott, Foresman and Co., 1966), 44.
5. EMF to MHM, March 4, 1841, private collection.

To Mrs. Middleton, Middleton Place

Wednesday Evening – 6ᵗʰ January 1841

I was not mistaken in supposing that want of opportunities to Town prevented my hearing from you my dearest Mamma– but altho' I tried to convince myself that your silence was altogether owing to that, I confess my anxiety was much relieved by the receipt of yʳ last letter of the 21ˢᵗ and 27ᵗʰ inclusive, which Fisher brought me to enliven our Sunday evening circle– a very small one, on account of the dangerous illness of poor Mary Harrison–[1] She had been ill of Fever since the eveng of Miss Hare's party, a week before Xmas, but was not thought alarmingly so, by the Physician until Friday last when he advised Mrs Francis to write for her Mother– Mrs Bayard her daughter did so, but the letter arrived too late for Saturday's boat from Stonington [*Connecticut to Providence, Rhode Island*] & yesterday eveng at 10 o'clk the poor girl expired, so gently that they thought she only slept– Two hours afterwards her Mother arrived in Spruce S^{t}, and you may imagine her agony, when she found the daughter who only 3 weeks and a half before had left her in perfect health, a disfigured corpse– The most violent remedies, such as cupping, blistering and salivating had been used & on Monday Dr Mitchell had slight hopes of her recovery– altho' it seemed to me that nothing but a miracle could save her– In her lucid intervals she asked frequently for her Mother– who poor soul, until within four days had not been aware that she was seriously ill– several letters to Providence having miscarried– They now reproach themselves for not sending for her sooner– Poor Mary was delirious for several days, and the last two never closed her eyes until she fell asleep in death– But several times sang as sweetly and correctly as possible, altho' perfectly blind & <u>deaf</u>– How afflicting and solemn it must have been to hear her sing, in such a situation– Poor old Mrs Francis is worn out with watching and distress of mind– Mary was her favourite grandchild, & certainly one of the sweetest and most amiable of human beings– It must be a consolation to them all to think that her pure spirit has certainly gone to the God who gave it, and that she has no sins to answer for, but such as in His Mercy will surely be pardoned–

Thursday– We had really a gloomy day of it yesterday, dear Mamma, not only on account of our sorrow for poor Mary's untimely end, but of Fisher's indisposition– He imprudently exposed himself to the severe cold of Monday, in a Sleigh without sufficient covering, and has been suffering very much since with cold in his Face and a headache caused by the Laudanum he took to diminish the Pain– today he is better, but still unable to occupy himself– & the weather is so bad that we can none of us leave the House– We had for 4 days really Russian weather– The therm^{r} shewing 10 to 12 degrees below zero of Reamur–[2] almost constantly– But we have now a very mild change, & Torrents of rain to wash away all the Ice & snow. New Year's day was ushered in by one of the worst Snow & Hail Storms I ever saw– which put a stop to the visiting, except from some few very determined adherents to old customs–

I received two more Presents besides those I mentioned to you– A p^{r} of

French Flacons (making a very superfluous addition to the <u>six</u> already in my possession) from one of Fisher's cousins– whom I had not even been once to visit this Autumn, & a copy of M<u>rs</u> Norton's³ lately published book of Poems– some of which, particularly the Sonnets, are exquisitely beautiful– One cannot read them without having a lively interest excited for this wonderful creature, possessed of such superlative beauty & Talents, & the innocent victim of treachery (for so I am sure all unprejudiced people must pronounce her, after reading her works, & comparing them with the base calumnies of her enemies). It is now placed beyond a doubt I believe, except in the opinions of a few scandal loving folks who are ever ready to think ill of their neighbours, that it was a political intrigue got up by her husband's brother & some other designing villains, to bring discredit on L<u>d</u> Melbourne & encrease his unpopularity– and that her wretch of a husband connived at this black scheme in order to gain the price of his wife's dishonour! Can you conceive anything more vile?

I am glad you had an entertaining book to read when you were alone in the eveng– Fisher will send you the numbers of Blackwood up to the latest dates with great pleasure– But I fear there will not be an opportunity very soon– Harry does not appear at all <u>anxious</u> to leave Phil<u>a</u> at present– and when he is asked when he thinks of going South, always answers "in about a fortnight"– but as he has given precisely the same answer for weeks past, and never seems to be approaching any nearer to a definite period of departure it is I should suppose very uncertain– I cannot even find out anything of M<u>rs</u> Harper's plans– which are also very uncertain– I have never seen her but once– not having been at home when she returned my visit– and now we cannot of course have company at home⁴ & receive her and the Brides, as we intended–

I hope you have had the pleasure of Susan's society, & the dear little children to cheer you– I wrote a letter to Mary, which I hope she will soon answer, and give me an account of her visit to M. Place– I am sorry that John could not spare you more than a week– and also that he was so unwell when you wrote– It is indeed delightful to look forward to Arthur's arrival– I daresay he will be out in the next steamer– I think he will be delighted with his little niece– For she is certainly as sweet a little Picture as I ever saw– & grows in beauty every day– I am much pleased with M<u>rs</u> Osgood's lines and thank you for transcribing them– Her little teeth are indeed little pearls of price, & I think others will soon make their appearance, as her Gums look red and swollen on each side– it will be particularly fortunate if she cuts the <u>Stomach teeth</u> early I am told– She now understands her name, and also that of <u>Pussy</u> (a very nice Toy in imitation of one) which Aunt H– gave her– I have not been out of the house for 2 days, nor seen anyone but Harry who dined here day before

yesterday & then went up to Mrs Butler's– I hear he was at Aunt H's last eveng–
In great haste I must bid you Goodbye– dearest Mamma with love to Papa &
whoever besides of the family are with you– M^rs F– begs her kind remembrances to you, & Mary if she is at M. Place and F. altho' he says nothing (because asleep) w^d I am sure wish to add some thing affectionate– ever yr most
attached & dutiful child Eliza

It is reported and generally believed that Clarke Hare & Esther Binney are positively engaged, but I cannot tell– They were certainly very devoted to each other
when I last saw them.[5]

Private Collection

    1. Mary Harrison's grandmother was Mrs. Thomas Willing Francis, Mrs. Fisher's
and Mrs. Harrison's sister-in-law. Mary's mother was Elizabeth (Francis) Harrison.
When widowed, she married her cousin John Brown Francis of Providence, Rhode
Island. Her sister, Anne, was Mrs. James A. Bayard.
    2. On the Reaumur temperature scale, 80° is boiling and 0° is freezing.
    3. Caroline Norton (1808–1877), granddaughter of the playwright Richard Brin-
sley Sheridan, was a successful poet. *The Dream and Other Poems* appeared in 1840.
Her husband's suit for divorce in 1836, citing Lord Melbourne, was thought to have
been politically motivated and intended to prevent Melbourne from becoming prime
minister to young Queen Victoria.
    4. They would not entertain so soon after Mary Harrison's death.
    5. John Innes Clark Hare (1816–1905), a son of the Robert Hares, became a distin-
guished judge and professor of law at the University of Pennsylvania. In December Eliza
had noticed that he appeared "to be getting very desperately in love with Esther Binney
. . . I like them both so much that I shd be very glad to see them happy together." EMF
to MHM, December 26, 1840, private collection.

～

To Mrs. Middleton, Middleton Place

Thursday 14th January 1841

My dearest Mamma,
    I saw the Postman pass whilst we were at breakfast, and immediately ex-
pressed the wish which has been uppermost for many days past– to receive a
letter from you– whereupon Fisher made me a bet that he would bring me
one this morng– which I <u>lost</u> most joyfully, upon the fulfilment of his prediction, and my <u>forlorn</u> hope– and your's of the 6th & 7th was duly delivered to
me– and read with great pleasure. I only regretted that you had been left alone &

wish most heartily that I could share the <u>solitude</u>, the love of which M<u>me</u> Necker[1] promises to be a sign of <u>mediocrity</u> in Youth– Now I aspire to no higher rank in the scale of <u>intelligence</u> at least– for "I was born so, Mother"– and am quite convinced that no effort can raise us much higher than Nature intended we should go– but in <u>other</u> respects, I am more ambitious– & shall not content myself easily with a moral mediocrity– when I can strive after, and perhaps attain, with even more difficulty, but also greater success I hope, a more desirable excellence of <u>character</u>– rather than of mind & manners, which are all she treats of– as well as I recollect– & for the development of which, I suppose she is certainly right in saying that intercourse with "le monde" [*society*] is necessary– I do not however agree with her in her censure with regard to those of mature age– Altho' I grant that old people if they had passed a life of innocence & <u>happiness</u> ought to be "good company" for themselves– If otherwise, and how few have no sorrows to remember! cheerful society is I should say <u>one</u> of the best remedies for grief– But I will not further indulge myself with such reflexions– I am very glad that you find so much amusement in Warren's Novel [*Ten Thousand a Year*]– which I would read if I had <u>time</u>– But instead of being at a loss to dispose of my leisure hours, as you must of course be, so shut out from "human converse", I have such an <u>abundance</u> of the latter commodity that I am obliged to be the more choice in my <u>silent companions</u> and those I am at present engaged with, are too much to my taste to be abandoned for newer faces–

Fisher eagerly seized a new number of Blackwood, supposing it contained the continuation of Ten Thousand a Year, but found to his disappointment, that it did not– I have just been interrupted by a visit from Aunt H[arrison] & Sally Waln and a parcel sent by M<u>me</u> d'Hauterive from Bagioli–[2] with 10 new pieces of music in it– only 2 for the Piano– & all the rest for the voice– tell Kitty– I don't know when I shall have a chance of sending her's as Harry appears still undecided– He and Fisher dine today at M<u>r</u> Binney's– This is the first time F. has been out for a week– except once in the carriage– The pain in his face I mentioned to you did not continue severe after Thursday– but sufficient to make him fear a return of it w<u>d</u> be brought on by any exposure to the damp weather we have had almost constantly lately–

I myself have been a prisoner since Sunday– when I was imprudent enough to go out in the evening to a <u>Catholic</u> Church to hear a Grand Mass of Haydn's– which I did <u>not</u> hear however for the crowd was so great that we beat a retreat after making two attempts– the second time stumbling over the Grave stones and thro' the mud– we thought it would be like bespeaking a place in the Church Yard to remain any longer in it– Those who were more determined to jostle their way thro' & wait wedged in between the low Irish mob, were at last rewarded by hearing Dr Moriarty[3] (their great Favourite) scold them soundly for their rude behaviour which he said was most disgraceful and indeed it must have been– They broke thro' the doors of the Church, & rushed in– and he rated them well for the outrage– I have heard of several Ladies who had their Veils & Cloaks torn off & one was thrown down by a stout Patlander who snatched her Ticket from her, swearing that <u>he</u> w$^{\underline{d}}$ go in with it– You may imagine that after hearing all this the next day, I was rejoiced that Clarke Hare had proposed our timely retreat– But it was provoking to lose the <u>Music</u> which they say was fine indeed– a great many Amateurs assisting– I not only had the disappointment but encreased a slight cold, and the following day had to send for Meigs who found that it had fallen on my breast, and produced a <u>lump</u> there & Fever– he talked of bleeding one day, Leeching &c– but Soap Liniment & Logan's Plaister have <u>entirely</u> dispersed it & he paid me the last visit this morng– permitting me to go out the first clear day– When we shall have that, Heaven knows– & no one can predict from present appearances– I have not been able to see M$^{\underline{rs}}$ Harper owing to this accident– but have sent her several messages by Harry who is with her every day– They went to see Norma[4] which is got up in very superior style they say– Fisher is very anxious that I sh$^{\underline{d}}$ go and hear it– and Aunt H. proposes going early next week– Too soon after poor Mary [Harrison]'s death I think– but of course I don't breathe this– and shall probably go myself– partly to please her & F. & partly to please <u>myself</u>– M$^{\underline{rs}}$ Harper talked of going on Saturday, but M$^{\underline{rs}}$ B[utler] pressed her to stay longer, and she has consented to do so I hear– as soon as it clears I shall go and see her, and invite her for an eveng– next week–

If I were in Susan's situation I should certainly consider myself more to be <u>commiserated</u> than congratulated– But perhaps the possibility of at last gratifying Oliver with a <u>son</u> reconciles her to her lot– and really I trust she will present him with a boy instead of a 5$^{\underline{th}}$ girl– altho' they might I think have been perfectly satisfied without one– <u>I</u> am with one– <u>girl</u> I mean– & never desire another sweet and lovely as she is– and much as I love her– Even her Grandmother is quite content, and no longer sighs over her Sex– They say she is the image of me– but I see now the resemblance which struck W$^{\underline{m}}$ to poor Maria– Her hair is exactly the colour of hers and the forehead the same shape– The mouth more like Kitty's– and the hands <u>precisely</u> the same– I am glad to announce that her <u>Pins</u> are straightening, but I fear they will always be a little <u>curved</u> like Lizzie Middleton's– You go too fast, in supposing she can <u>creep</u>– Indeed such is my horror of Pins & needles, & M$^{\underline{rs}}$ Fisher's of <u>soiled Frocks</u> that I daresay she will walk first & not be allowed to go at all on <u>all fours</u>– The side Teeth are not yet thro', but beginning to worry her a little– I have her fed once a day, and twice at night, when she still continues good, & sleeps soundly–

M$\underline{rs}$ F. & the H's desire their kindest remembrances & Fisher his most respectful regards– Harry I have not seen since I rec$\underline{d}$ y$\underline{r}$ letter– But he was well yesterday & dined with us– I suppose Papa & W$\underline{m}$ have returned long ere this to M.P. Pray give them my love, as well as to Kitty– & believe me my dearest Mamma ever Y$\underline{r}$ most affectionate Daughter Eliza

I hope you have rec$\underline{d}$ the letter from Uncle [*Oliver*] F. forwarded on Friday–

Private Collection

1. Mrs. Middleton had been rereading the *Pensées et souvenirs* [Reflections and recollections] of Madame Necker, probably a cousin of the more famous Madame de Stael (Anne Louise Germaine Necker). MHM to EMF, January 6, 1841, PHi.

2. Antonio Bagioli was an Italian musician and teacher in New York. Mentioning her excellence "in his art," he had dedicated a romance to Eliza in 1835. Bagioli to EM, September 10, 1835, PHi, C/F.

3. Patrick Eugene Moriarity (1804–1875) was the pastor of St. Augustine's church in Philadelphia. An eloquent preacher, proponent of temperance, and a supporter of the Irish cause, he founded Villanova University in 1842 and was later its president.

4. The first American performance of Vincenzo Bellini's opera *Norma* was in Philadelphia on January 11, 1841. It was so popular there was "a perfect rush and crowd at the Chesnut Street theatre, to obtain seats." The principal singers, Mrs. Wood and her husband, Joseph Wood, helped bring opera to Philadelphia in the 1830s. *Phila. GCI,* January 18, 1841.

⌐⌐

To Mrs. Fisher, Philadelphia

M.P. Jan$\underline{y}$ 18$\underline{th}$ 1841

Here is a lucky chance my dearest Eliza for sending off my letter! a message at breakfast was brought me by one of the Negroes from Allen Smith now at Laurel hill, that he would call to see me on his way to Charleston today– I therefore lose no time to write & tell you how comforting your letter of the 31$\underline{st}$ (the last I have rec$\underline{d}$) of Dec$\underline{r}$ was to me in my dreary state. The sentiments of regret that you express for your waste of Time I cannot join in– According to my opinion you have spent it very profitably. Religion is the rule of your life, & when that is the case you cannot be blamed for misspending your time. I wish I had as little to accuse myself of, as you have, my dear conscientious child! It makes me very sad in this my solitude, to reflect upon the various ways in which I have all my life gone astray from the true Christian precepts. There cannot be a better Author than Blunt,[1] to convince me of my frailties, & I feel them most painfully. In your gratitude to the Father of mercies for the blessings you enjoy, I sincerely join & also for the blessing afforded me of having such a child as you, left me to compensate for the severe losses inflicted on me. Other blessings too are bestowed, that of health, & of my sons conducting themselves well– I only wish they would imitate you in making religion their study & rule of conduct. but more of this when we meet! that will not be alas! as you say for 6 months.

You will be sorry to learn that after all my expectations of seeing Susan they have not yet been fulfilled– I wrote to her a week ago to tell her how disappointed I had been in consequence, & rec$^{\underline{d}}$ a very affectionate answer, saying M$^{\underline{rs}}$ Chisolm failing to be in Charleston prevented her leaving it as she had intended. She mentions having seen a very kind letter from you to Mary for which she says she can never be too grateful, & hopes to see me in Charleston soon– this was written a week ago– I had told her I might perhaps (if y$^{\underline{r}}$ Father would take me) be there for two days, my object is to speak to D$^{\underline{r}}$ Holbrook about procuring for me a better contrived <u>Pad</u> than that D$^{\underline{r}}$ M[itchell] had made–

Now I am on the subject, I must tell you what I avoided doing before lest it should make you unhappy, that two days after I arrived in Charleston upon returning from Church I was sitting in the parlour & felt very faint– so much so, that I <u>did</u> faint– W$^{\underline{m}}$ came to my assistance, brought me pillows & blankets & I was relieved but still felt weak– he insisted upon my seeing D$^{\underline{r}}$ H[olbrook] the next day, & thinking that this indisposition might proceed from the weakness you know of, I shewed him the remedies I had got at Philad$^{\underline{a}}$. When he saw them he said there was a French Mechanic in Charleston who could make better things, but as I was expecting the little parcel, I thought it better to wait & try it. He then said that my slight attack was caused by the movement of the long journey having deranged the digestion. In a few days after I was as well as usual– & as I wrote you, I walk with the <u>assistance of</u> pasteboard! for 1/2 an hour. Still however I feel that is insufficient, & for that reason shall <u>ask leave</u> to see D$^{\underline{r}}$ H. When that may be, is still uncertain for it was a fortnight yesterday since y$^{\underline{r}}$ Father & W$^{\underline{m}}$ went to Combahee. The floods of rain that have fallen lately have made the yellow jessamine flowers bloom only in <u>one</u> part of the garden & also the Camellias & fragrant Olives– it is seldom I can, owing to the rain go out to admire them. So that there is nothing for me to do but to read all day long. My eve$^{\underline{g}}$ amusement as I told you, was a novel– I sent a list to the cir[culatin]g library for some I had seen recommended, but the only one disengaged was L[ad]y Bulwers[2] "Budget of the Bubble family". There is a vast deal of trash in it but it is written in a lively style, & one of the characters, Marmaduke Bubble is very well drawn. The heroine too, Theresa Manners is an interesting one. the <u>puns</u> are innumerable, & so are the Latin quotations. The Authoress must be a woman of extensive information, notwithstanding the account I heard, of her being one of low extraction. that may not be true however.

I cannot say that I hope you may find a riding horse to suit you, for really I fear some accident may happen to you on horseback, & you are quite well without using that mode of exercise. I am glad however that Mr Fisher's loss has been so kindly supplied, & hope that he may find his new horse as good as Poppet was– it gives me great pleasure to hear that Mrs Smith is so much better & well enough to make one of your party. Her promised letter has not yet reached me– nor any of your Jany epistles, nor any from Arthur or my Brother! if y^r Father does not come today or tomorrow, I will send Moro[3] to Charleston to bring me news. The image of your little darling is often in my mind's eye. I long to hear her laugh & see her pretty face– Y^r disapprobation of her being encouraged to love gadding by being held at the parlour window, amused me.

I think Harry might take pity on me now, & proceed homeward. There is no calculating however upon the movements of one so attracted as he is by the Belles at Philad^a Give my love to him, & also to M^r & Mrs Fisher, Mrs Smith & Mrs Harrison & believe me my dearest Eliza y^r affect^{te} Mother M. H. M.

I leave this space for any news A[llen] S[mith] may have to communicate.

<u>19th</u> <u>Charleston</u> You will be surprised to find me so soon here! A. Smith never came yesterday, but y^r Father & W^m did, between 1 & 2 oclock & business calling him here without delay, he made no objections when I explained my object to bringing me. I had the happiness to find here y^r letters of the 6th & 14th– one from Arthur of the 14th of Nov^r, one from my brother of the 29th d^o & one from Miss Moore– Think what a treat they have been to me! Everything in y^{rs} afforded me pleasure but the account of your illness, & the melancholy death of poor Miss Harrison. a dreadful shock indeed to her Mother. Her Grandmother too is much to be pitied. I remember seeing her at Mrs Fisher's in the autumn of /39 with Miss Page & her sister, when the then Miss Pardi sang with you. I regret also to hear of Mr Fisher's indisposition. You were both very imprudent in venturing out in bad, & very cold weather & I hope

your sufferings will act as a warning to both to avoid in future bad weather. Let me beg you when you feel tempted to walk out in rainy or cold weather to think of my advice & remain at home–

I like your opinion of Mme Necker's Pensée– & agree with you in thinking that cheerful society is one of the best remedies for grief. You must be anxious to know what Arthur says– at the end of his letter that he had just sent off his baggage but should have many visits to pay & letters to write & should be delayed leaving Madrid until the 21st He expected his route to be through Valencia & Barcelona & as he is desirous of seeing Marseilles Toulon & Arles, thence probably direct to Paris. He says his embarcation will depend on circumstances. he confesses the thought of a winter passage somewhat <u>dashes</u> him, the two he had made having brought him to a resolution against ever attempting a third, except as a matter of necessity. If his means hold out, he says he will make a visit of adieu to our friends in England– After this, I need not expect to see him before March–

I recommend to you a book on the management of Children by Dr A. Coombe–[4] do not read it on my recom^n but look into the 67th N^o of the West[minste]r Review & you will not be able to resist all that is said in favour of it. that review now notices briefly most of the new publications at the end. I am writing now on the 20th before breakfast that this & one to y^r Aunt Rutledge may be ready for W^m to take to the post. I suppose I shall see Emma & Susan some time today– Only little Harry has come to school here– he came by himself last week & Sarah is not to come until all the family do, next month. Oliver is at Edisto. It gives me great pleasure to hear that another Tooth has made its appearance in the mouth of your <u>little beauty</u>. Now she may be called by that name & it encreases my desire to see her improvement. No doubt Arthur will be delighted with her being very fond of children & of a very affectionate disposition. Miss Moore writes me word that Harry on the 23^d Decr mentioned his intention of leaving Philad^a 10 days after!

I must now fold this up but not before entreating you to be more careful of your health than you generally have been– With love to M^r & Mrs Fisher believe me my dearest Eliza yr Affect^{te} Mother M. H. M.
Y^r Father & W^m send their love–

PHi

1. Henry Blunt (1794–1843) was an English preacher whose ability to include human interest made his sermons very popular. Mrs. Middleton was probably reading his *Selected Sermons*.

2. Both Edward Lytton Bulwer and his wife, Lady Bulwer, the former Rosina Doyle Wheeler (1802–1882), were novelists.

3. Moro was relied on and admired as the head household slave at Middleton Place.

4. Andrew Combe (1797–1847) was a doctor noted for his straightforward approach to his patients. He believed that *The Physiological and Moral Management of Infancy* was his best book.

⌣

To Mrs. Middleton, Middleton Place

Wednesday 27$\underline{\text{th}}$ Jan$\underline{\text{y}}$ 1841

I thank you many more times than I can express for your delightful long letter, my dearest Mamma, which I had yesterday the happiness to receive– I did not at first know whether to be alarmed at y$\underline{\text{r}}$ Sudden trip to Charleston, because you never complain without a cause, or exaggerate the necessity of seeing a Physician– and as I know y$\underline{\text{r}}$ unwillingness both to consult them & to move to Town, unless <u>forced</u> to do so, I felt there must be stronger reasons for y$\underline{\text{r}}$ going there, than you chose me to understand– But on reading over y$\underline{\text{r}}$ letter, it appears to me to be written in such good spirits that you surely could not be suffering more than from the want of what I trust the Frenchman will supply in a more efficient manner than D$\underline{\text{r}}$ Mitchell– It is really most provoking after all the trouble taken, so little has yet been accomplished– but I daresay this time the contrivance will be more successful– and you will again move about, and take y$\underline{\text{r}}$ daily walks without inconvenience– and I rejoice that you so promptly carried into effect y$\underline{\text{r}}$ projected visit to D$\underline{\text{r}}$ H– but pray, dearest Mamma, be very prudent, and avoid overexertion of every sort– And so after all, you did suffer from the fatigue of the journey, enough even to make you faint away! and concealed this from me! You ought never to do so indeed, for if at any time I were to hear of y$\underline{\text{r}}$ being indisposed my mind w$\underline{\text{d}}$ soon be made up, and my Trunks packed for Carolina, and Baby is now so perfectly healthy and strong, that I sh$\underline{\text{d}}$ not hesitate on <u>her</u> account, to run on, & be with you in 4 days– I often regret now that I gave up so quietly the Southern trip in March, & yet I am perhaps wrong to think of it– and I must not indulge in vain regrets, but trust that my self denial will be rewarded by a longer holiday in the summer–

Harry has at last determined to proceed southward– and at present intends fulfilling this determination on Monday when he is to escort M$\underline{\text{rs}}$ H[arper] to Balt$\underline{\text{e}}$ He first meant to leave this on Friday (the day after the grand Harrison

Ball[1]) but consented to wait 3 days longer, to have the pleasure of accompanying her– I don't know whether she will be punctual herself– but imagine it
probable they will be off early in the week– I have not heard if H. thinks of
tarrying at Balt$^{\underline{e}}$ but infer not– from what he said just now that he should see
you very soon– I sh$^{\underline{d}}$ be very glad to change places with him– but as he w$^{\underline{d}}$
not undertake to perform the duties of mine– & even with every disposition
to do so, w$^{\underline{d}}$ be much at a loss to discharge some of them, I may as well not
propose it– He complains of want of room in his Trunks, so I will make up
a small box containing M$^{\underline{rs}}$ Chisolm's Shawl, some Music for Kitty, and the
Numbers of Blackwood, & a few other Articles for you– You will find a small
Vol. of M$^{\underline{r}}$ Odenheimer's,[2] which I think you will like if you take the trouble
to read it, & also a copy for Sally, which I beg you will give her with my love–
I have directed one to Miss Rutledge, as I promised to do, if he published them–
I have seen him several times lately– and am more and more confirmed in my
opinion of his character, & extraordinary powers of mind in one so young–
He takes the greatest interest in his little God–daughter– and I hope if she lives,
she will profit much by his good counsel and instruction–

Thursday morng– and a beautiful morng it is– We have lately had so little
sunshine, that it is quite delightful to see it once more– and I am sure I shall
enjoy a long walk today– I was greatly surprised at not having a headache, after
being nearly stunned by the Kettle Drums last night– I went to hear Norma
for the first time, & sh$^{\underline{d}}$ have been much better pleased if Aunt's box had not
been directly over the noisiest part of the Orchestre– The clash and [*missing*]
was distressingly loud– & I was fain to stop my aching ears in some parts–
particularly during the battle chorus– but on the whole I was much gratified &
some of the duetts were exquisitely sung– & the Choruses excellent– M$^{\underline{rs}}$ Wood
occasionally shewed the effects of her late illness by breaking in the upper notes,
but acquitted herself very well generally, and acted much better than I expected– They want me to go again tomorrow eveng– but I rather think I shall
decline– for I narrowly escaped being deafened– & Aunt is too much attached
to her old quarters to be induced to change them–[3]

I have not mentioned that on Tuesday eveng– we had rather a pleasant
little party here– altho' contrary to custom there were rather too few women &
a great majority of the male sex– among these were M$^{\underline{r}}$ Charles Sumner (M$^{\underline{rs}}$
Barclay's brother in law) & Prof [Henry Wadsworth] Longfellow–[4] who had
both volunteered me a visit the day previous– & brought me messages from
M$^{\underline{rs}}$ S[umner] & also from Julia [Ward] who I am sorry to find has been ill, &
still looks very delicate– This accounts for my not hearing from her– Fisher
has made me a present of all Retich's German Outlines–[5] some of them are

perfectly beautiful– Those on the "song of the Bell" the finest of all I think–
It is a great treat to study them with the originals– and they encrease greatly
my interest in the Ballads they illustrate– They are far more picturesque and
imaginative than Flaxman, but less classical–

M$\underline{rs}$ Smith was here on Tuesday eveng– & appeared freer from cough than
usual– My friend Esther was the only <u>single</u> woman in the room– but a host
in herself– She is <u>not</u> engaged to Clarke Hare– nor likely to be I imagine– which
I regret– as I think they w$\underline{d}$ suit each other admirably– Baby is just emerging
from her Bath– which she is fond of whilst in it– but the odd noises she is
making as she undergoes the process of drying & dressing, disturb me not a
little altho' they are <u>principally</u> of the good humoured sort– I am going to see
the Dioramas from Paris[6] over the way, & as I have to return home early to
dress for dinner, as we expect 2 or 3 gentlemen to meet Harry, I believe I must
conclude, promising to write by him– Pray give my best love to dear Papa, &
to W$\underline{m}$ & Kitty, and think of me as Y$\underline{r}$ most affectionate & dutiful child Eliza

Private Collection

1. To celebrate William Henry Harrison's election, the Harrison and Tyler Grand
Ball was planned for January 28. For ten dollars the Committee of Arrangement promised a "constellation of beauty, patriotism and talent," and General Harrison pictured
on his steed as decoration. *Phila. GCI*, January 27, 28, 29, 1841.

2. Reverend Odenheimer's book *The Devout Churchman's Companion* was published in 1841. He was Lizzie Fisher's godfather.

3. According to Fisher, "there was no such patron of the theatre [as Aunt Harrison,] and the second box on the left hand seemed to be hers by prescription whenever
she wished to occupy it. Tragedy, Comedy, Farce, Opera or Ballet, all attracted her."
JFF, *Recollections*, 146].

4. Sumner, the future senator from Massachusetts, and Longfellow were close
friends. They were also friends of Julia Ward's brother, Sam.

5. Moritz Retzsch was a German artist known for his outline illustrations. John
Flaxman, an English sculptor and draftsman, also did outline drawings, particularly
illustrating Greek poets and Dante.

6. The dioramas, painted by Daguerre, presented two tableaux: one of Venice and
the other of Paris. Special lighting created the illusion of movement while organ music
played in the background.

∽

To Mrs. Middleton, Middleton Place

Thursday 4$\underline{th}$ February 1841

Dear Mamma,

I cannot tell you with what unfeigned delight I welcomed another letter
from you on Monday– and the good news that you had been able to procure

what was the object of y͟r visit to town– I sincerely hope that it may prove more beneficial than former contrivances, and that its complete success may enable you to take exercise without fear of injury– I am very glad you had so good an opportunity of seeing Susan– since it seems she cannot be with you in the country– It is really provoking that the old Lady [*Mrs. Chisolm*] should not be more accomodating and give her a chance of going to M. Place particularly as the more she delays it, the greater will be the difficulty I suppose– You do not mention Kitty– but I conclude that she was with you in town– & <u>would not consent</u> to be left in the country– Tell her with my love that I hope she will practise the music I have sent her– & <u>that</u> will encourage me to supply her again, when she can play these pieces– The two for the Piano, which Bagioli sent, were so easy, that I thought she w͟d be offended at my offering them to her, & therefore sent them to Mary thinking they were quite "à sa portée" [*within her reach*]– I sent you (or rather Fisher did) <u>all</u> the numbers of Blackwood he has received– as he had read up to the story as far as it went, & he has not time at present to look at the other contents which may probably amuse you– I thought a scarf Aunt H. had on, pretty for mourning and therefore got you one like it, and a bag the chief recommendation to which is its durability, which they say is remarkable– with a <u>lining</u>, which I had not time to put in it, it will bear any wear and tear almost– Kitty forgot one of the little cravats, and left it by mistake, and the other I saw, & thinking it w͟d suit her, bought at the same time I was choosing one of <u>my</u> favourite colours (lilac and green) for myself– It appeared so uncertain that Harry w͟d decide <u>positively</u> on his departure, and so unlikely that he w͟d have room in his Trunk, that hearing of a vessel about to sail for Charleston, I thought it best to make up a box containing the few things I have mentioned, some of Mary's, and M͟rs Chisolm's shawl, which I bought for her a month ago– lest she should have no use at all of it during the cold weather– I wrote to Mary to beg her Mamma to forward to you the books &c, by the first opportunity– On second thoughts I did <u>not</u> put up The Listener– for altho' there are some good chapters in it, I did not think <u>on the whole</u> it would suit y͟r taste, or enliven your Solitude much– & Fisher decidedly objected to some passages, as being very <u>Puritanical</u>– of which more when we meet in <u>5 months</u>– You see I count the time– with hope & expectation–

I have not seen Harry since Tuesday, when he expected to leave this tomorrow– but Fisher, who dined with him yesterday at Sidney [Fisher]'s, says he spoke of going to the Ball at C. J. Ingersoll's tomorrow eveng– so that of course he has <u>again</u> deferred his departure– M͟rs H[arper] has also done so, I am told &

does not now intend going for another week– I will tell you more of Harry's plans this afternoon when I shall be able to give you his last words–

The bad weather on Monday prevented my attending M̲ᵣ Reed's lecture– so je me suis dédommagée [*I made up for it*] by going to hear D̲ᵣ Bethune[1] on Holland, the eveng afterwards– It was very interesting and amusing– particularly an account of an Amsterdam Bank, which was very applicable to that of the U.S. and the conduct of the frauds practised by the directors who "perjured their souls" by deceiving the Public with false promises and statements of its flourishing condition, whilst they were appropriating the funds for their own purposes, was so exactly a parallel case to M̲ᵣ Biddle's behaviour,[2] that the audience appeared to enjoy his covert allusions (whether designed or not I know not). There was a general murmur near us, & Old Nick himself who sat next the Lecturer on the Platform must have felt rather uncomfortable if he has any feelings or conscience– Col. Drayton says he must either be entirely devoid of either, or the best actor he ever saw in his life– for he never appears to flinch under any attacks of the sort– The whole scene reminded me strongly of Hamlet's devise to probe the conscience of the King– but it may not have been intended at all– D̲ᵣ B. gave us a piece of information which was entirely new– viz that the best living Poet is a Dutchman! His name escaped us– but he asserted it boldly– & then gave specimens, which of course lost by translation from the Dutch– but which however hardly justified his assertion– & certainly were not equal to many even below Wordsworth– who w̲ᵈ have been indignant at the preference–

Talking of Lectures, Prof. Longfellow had a high comp[limen]t paid to him unwittingly the other day when he was here– M̲ᵣ Kennedy,[3] without being aware of his presence, quoted some of his Poetry with an encomium on its merit– He, the Prof– afterwards came to M̲ʳˢ Wallace's[4] party, (on Friday eveng–) and M̲ᵣ Sumner told me he had been much gratified at the circumstance. I had some conversation with him about the Wards– He says Julia's health suffers from too much devotion to Study and that [*her sister*] Louisa is following her footsteps in the same course of unwearied application– which must sooner or later have the same effects on her constitution– He offered to take a letter for me to J. but I told him she was my debtor, & begged him to say I felt quite hurt at her neglect of me– They went off on Sunday afternoon– apparently much pleased at the attentions they rec̲ᵈ here, and the society they mingled with– I don't think M̲ᵣ S[umner] seemed much delighted with his new sister in law, & rather avoided the subject when I introduced it to him– He is very gentlemanly in his manners & appearance–

I have been keeping this open to give a later account of Harry, but as he has not come I conclude he does not intend to go tomorrow, as he told F. this morng he thought of doing– When he <u>does</u> make up his mind, which will now certainly be in a very few days, I will write again. Meanwhile adieu, dearest Mamma, I am hurried in the conclusion of this but recollect I have not said <u>one</u> word of Baby! She is, as you may infer from this very silence, perfectly well– M<u>rs</u> Drayton thinks she looks like <u>you</u>, at which I felt quite flattered, but cannot agree as to the resemblance– Love always to Papa & W<u>m</u> & to yourself from Y<u>r</u> most affectionate and dutiful child Eliza

Fisher & his Mother beg their best regards– as also M<u>r</u> & M<u>rs</u> H.

Private Collection

1. George Washington Bethune (1805–1862) was pastor of the First and Third Dutch Reformed Churches in Philadelphia.

2. As he tried to keep the Bank of the United States going in the late 1830s, Nicholas Biddle lost many of his former supporters by tightening credit and resorting to some questionable tactics, such as trying to corner the cotton market. When losses mounted, he was accused of mismanagement and wrongdoing.

3. Probably author John P. Kennedy (1795–1870) from Baltimore. In late January he was in Philadelphia to give a lecture at the Mercantile Library Association.

4. Mrs. John Bradford Wallace, the former Susan Binney (1778–1849), was remarkable, it was said, for the "noble grace of her deportment." She was the sister of Horace Binney; her husband, also a lawyer, died in 1837. Elizabeth F. Ellet, *The Queens of American Society* (New York, 1868), 263.

~

To Mrs. Fisher, Philadelphia

M.P. Feb<u>y</u> 6<u>th</u> 1841

My dearest Eliza

I grieve to inform you that yesterday with your letter of 27<u>th</u> ult. came one from my Brother announcing the melancholy news of the death of my dear & excellent Sister Gordon[1] who used to be to me in my youthful days like a Mother. He writes "Our excellent Sister expired most unexpectedly at Kingsweston on the 26<u>th</u> Dec<u>r</u> after being attacked with a Cold a few days before. Her end was tranquil & free from pain & as piously resigned as you may suppose she could be at the close of a well spent life. May we all be as well prepared for that event which to some of us cannot now be very distant." Most sincerely do I join him in this hope, & yet how painfully do I feel my own unworthiness "to meet her in a better world," the last words she spoke when we parted last, to console each other for our separation. Not a day passes without my looking forward to quit this world & yet how unfit do I feel to expect to be admitted to a better! Blunt's lectures are my daily reading & I try to profit by his excellent advice– I shall certainly read Mr Odenheimer's vol. you are so kind as to send me which I thank you for, as well as for the other books, & hope they may be brought next week by Harry– still he is so uncertain in his movements there can be no degree of certainty in looking for his coming.

A letter from Miss Moore came also yesterday by y^r Father– The purport of it is to enquire whether I will give E[lizabeth] Mitchel 20$ a month if she goes to Newport, should that be done, she advises her not to engage herself which she had intended to do, being unwell & dissatisfied with Miss Hope's place, & had gone to Miss M. to request her to find another for her– She advised her by all means to wait until my answer should arrive. I have therefore been obliged to write to say that she must not on my account decline going into service, as I cannot promise to give her those high wages, (which your Father was induced to do only because she gave him such short notice last summer that she could not leave N. York just on the eve of his quitting it, that he could not find a substitute for her to accompany Cath^e) but I should be very glad should the place she finds not exactly suit her, to take the chance of her returning to me which I earnestly hope she will. Though I did not say to Miss Moore I do to you, how unwilling I am after all that y^r Father said on the subject, to enter into any engagement with Elizth & I do not like to enter into any discussion on the case at present.[2] Miss M. asks me how I like Marg^t [Driscoll] & I have told her she is very goodnatured & willing to do any thing though she does not manage Cath^e as well as Elizth I have told you all this because you expressed a wish to have her as a nurse, but yours seems to be such a good one that perhaps you would not like to part with her– should you prefer Elizth you will of course write at once to Miss M. She says she Eth cannot expect to get any place that might now present itself at more that 10$ a month: certainly quite enough. I have not given any hint to Miss M. about you taking Elth Should you do so, we might manage in this way– let her act as Housekeeper & Cath's attendant while at Newport, & you might have <u>my</u> Marg^t for a nurse, as I am sure she w^d make a very good one. This plan is all fancy, & I w^d on no account induce you to adopt it for my convenience– consult your own & I may still be fortunate enough to find Elth disengaged at the time I want her–

<u>Sunday 7th</u> I hoped to have been permitted to send a Man with my letters to Charleston, but I am called impatient, & y^r Father will not let him go– this then will probably wait a week. What you say my dearest Eliza about coming here in case of my being indisposed, is indeed most gratifying to my feelings.

Should I be really ill at any time, I would give you notice, & hope to have the comfort of your presence. I am however well, & by wearing <u>both</u> the heavy contrivances can walk 1/2 an hour– After all, the defect of the Machine was in the shortness of the steel fastening, & that is not yet made, owing to a careless workman W<u>m</u> employed making it of the same length instead of an inch longer as he was ordered. Y<u>r</u> Father says little Harry told him the family are to be in Charleston this week. I wrote to John last week requesting him to persuade Sally to bring her two <u>indispensable</u> Women with her, & be confined here as I could not go to Charleston– I fear she will not– however she will probably as I proposed, send the three younger Children here to prevent her being fatigued with their constant demands & loud talking & being obliged to talk herself to a degree which must be very hurtful to her lungs. John mentioned that she complained a good deal of pain, which <u>he</u> imagines proceeds from Dyspepsia. She will have Susan & M<u>rs</u> J[ames] R[eid] Pringle[3] to be with her frequently & perhaps M<u>rs</u> W[illiam Bull] P[ringle] who has lately given birth to her 12<u>th</u> child.

Cath<u>e</u> expressed great pleasure at the mention you made of the music. I hope it may induce her to play for she scarcely ever now touches the piano– Pray give my love to M<u>rs</u> Smith & tell her I rejoice to hear that she is at last free from Cough. I will answer her letter soon–

8<u>th</u> In great haste as y<u>r</u> Father is sending off I must add that all my plans about Eliz<u>th</u> are frustrated. he has desired me to tell Miss Moore to offer her 15$ a month.[4] which I hope she may be glad to obtain– believe me my dearest Eliza y<u>r</u> Affect<u>te</u> Mother M. H. M.

ScHi

1. Catherine Hering (1763–1840), the oldest of Mrs. Middleton's three sisters, married John Gordon II (d. 1839). They lived in Bristol, England.

2. Elizabeth Mitchell apparently left the Middletons at the end of the summer of 1840. Margaret Driscoll, who had been suggested by Miss Moore, took her place as Catherine's companion.

3. Elizabeth (McPherson) Pringle (1783–1843) was a cousin of Sally. Her husband, James Reid Pringle (1782–1840), and William Bull Pringle were first cousins.

4. Miss Moore sent word that Elizabeth Mitchell declined to go "to such a hard place as she found her situation at Newport" for less than twenty dollars a month. She preferred "a steady place at N.Y. at 10$ a month." MHM to EMF, March 6, 1841, PHi.

～

To Mrs. Middleton, Middleton Place

Philadelphia – Wednesday 17<u>th</u> Feb<u>y</u> 1841

My dearest Mamma,

I have just sent Fisher out to walk alone, preferring to write to you by a comfortable fire, rather than go out this disagreeable damp day, with every chance of getting a wetting from the threatening clouds before going 6 squares from home– together with the risk of spoiling my new bonnet & cloak for I have of course laid aside my fine Velvet Hat & Purple Hat for plain black silk, and a grey <u>Bournouss</u>[1] trimmed with black, which will afterwards be a very suitable travelling cloak with gayer trimming. It is perhaps hardly necessary to tell you this, except that you might suppose I had omitted to pay this respect to the memory of your Sister, which to say the truth is done more for <u>your</u> sake, and as an evidence that I do not wish to accept invitations to Parties, than anything else– And altho' it is in itself an unimportant matter, people more easily understand your reasons for not going out, if they see you in mourning– You may believe me that it is no sacrifice <u>to me</u> to stay away from the Balls and Parties which are now very frequent indeed as just before the close of the gay season, people are more anxious than ever to amuse themselves, until Lent comes to put a stop to dancing and gaiety– But as I enjoy myself much more in a quiet way than in running to Balls, I am not sorry to dispense with them altogether– & have a little more time for reading and music– I took my first [*piano*] lesson from der Konig[2] on Saturday, & found him of great assistance in facilitating the difficulties of Thalberg and Henselt[3] which I am <u>determined</u> to conquer– I have not yet thanked you for your letter of the 8<u>th</u> which I was very glad indeed to receive dear Mamma– If I were to attempt to contradict you with regard to what you say in the first page of it about y<u>r</u> own unworthiness you would not I know be willing to receive praises, which however merited are never thought to be so by an humble spirit like your's– but in the sight of God this very Humility is more pleasing than aught else besides.

I have at last had a letter from Julia Ward– a very long one she had written a month ago immediately after receiving mine of Jan<u>y</u>. She gives me the whole story of the affair with Kirk– who has not behaved well at all I should judge– altho' she does not accuse him– but only wishes that "he had behaved with more delicacy and forbearance" and that she herself had with more firmness & decision– It seems that altho' never positively engaged to him, she gave him rather an uncertain answer to his proposals– which her Uncle, "perceiving the danger of her mistaking, in her excited & agitated state of mind religious sympathy, and a confused sense of duty for firm & lasting affection" desired she should reflect upon calmly for 3 weeks– and that before <u>half</u> that time had expired, after consulting her own heart & judgment, she "felt she had committed a grievous error", and one that if persisted in would utterly destroy her earthly happiness for she had never loved him– & could not marry him– She therefore wrote to him (in ten days) a very decided refusal– which it seems he did not receive– but when he called, at the expiration of the three weeks, she told him her mind very plainly, and she has had no sort of communication with him since, altho' they parted on good terms, and it was only after the receipt of her letter, that she heard any censure attached to her conduct– This is the substance of the whole story, which she gives me rather more in detail– It appears to have weighed much upon her mind, and her position must have been a very trying one– And I am afraid from her own account, & what M<u>rs</u> Prime says, she must be in a wretchedly weak state of health– The latter tells me she must be made very uncomfortable by the presence of her Uncle Richard (who is the black sheep of the family) & his vulgar wife, who were invited to stay with them, & have remained there all the winter, much to the annoyance of the poor girls who are much too refined to be pleased long with such disagreeable in[mates]. All this will perhaps interest William, & that was my principal reason for writing so much about it–

Thursday, 18<u>th</u> When I wrote last week to you, dear Mamma, I was fully persuaded that you w<u>d</u> see Harry as soon as my letter & it was not until I rec<u>d</u> a letter from him from Wash<u>n</u> that I had the least suspicion that he would stop there– Long ere this I suppose you have seen him, as he wrote me he was to leave it on Friday, & I have not heard since of any further detention– Tell him I went yesterday to see M<u>rs</u> Harper, who was looking well & said she had enjoyed herself amazingly the night before at M<u>rs</u> Kuhn's Ball– M<u>rs</u> [John] Butler was not able to go to it in consequence of a fall on the Ice which was severe enough to make her keep her bed 5 days– & be leeched & cupped– Somebody asked M<u>rs</u> H[arper] what sort of fall it was– to which she replied– "oh! she only <u>sat down violently</u>"! a very good <u>mot</u>. It is feared that there may be serious sprain of the spine– altho' M<u>rs</u> B. is not apprehensive– & talks of going to the Bachelor's Ball on Friday– which M<u>rs</u> H. says will be impossible– as she has not yet ever left her room– I was sorry to learn that Miss Gadsden has also met with a similar but much worse accident– And has been suffering extremely with the Pain in her <u>Hip</u>, which the Physicians fear is dislocated– I am going today to enquire how she is & hope to find her better– M<u>rs</u> Smith is in trouble about the death of one of her (husband's) grand-daughters– Miss Cochrane– who has had precisely the fate of poor Mary Harrison– It is singular enough that the only time I ever saw Miss C. she was speaking of the then very recent death of poor Mary, & saying how very sad it was, that a blooming young girl who came here with the brightest anticipations of happiness, should so suddenly be cut off– little thinking that she herself, then in the full enjoyment of health and amusement, was soon to meet the same melancholy fate– and die of the very same disease of the brain– Mr Harrison has had an almost miraculous escape from serious injury, by falling on the <u>wooden</u> pavement in Chesnut S^t If it had been on the stones, it w^d have gone very hard with him– as it is, he is only <u>strained</u> a little, & has neither broken bones or bruises–

I hope Sally will be able to do as you propose to her, and be with you at M. Place– but do not suppose she w^d consent to the Plan– I shall be anxious to know how she bore her journey to Town, and what is thought of her appearance by those who have not seen her for some time past– I think it most likely that Eliz^th Mitchel will immediately <u>close</u> with y^r offer of 15$ p^r month– and trust that you will have her again next Summer to save you the exertion of Housekeeping– At some future day I sh^d be delighted to have her as a Nurse but just now I could not engage her, and turn off Anne, who gives me satisfaction in the care she takes of Baby– who is very fond of her and begins to call <u>A a</u>– She also makes great exertions to crawl– but will not succeed in that, or in walking, until the warmer weather comes & enables me to disencumber her of some of her <u>nether</u> garments–

Friday– I was disappointed at not being able to send this down to the [*Post*] Office yesterday– dear Mamma– Murray being sick & John having taken his departure without leave early in the eveng, which we passed at Aunt Harrison's– where we met Sally Ingersoll who was in excellent spirits, and gave a very animated account of all the Balls & Parties at which she has been present lately– Mrs Harper is a great belle among all the young men she says, dancing every time with as much apparent pleasure as any young girl of 16. She is to stay for the two Parties next week at Mrs Coxe's & Mrs Hutchinson's[4] on <u>Shrove Tuesday</u>– the last of the season– and then (as she told me herself) goes home to play Mamma again <u>respectably</u>– Adieu dearest Mamma, I hope soon to hear from you again– and am as ever Y^r most affectionate daughter Eliza

My love if you please to Papa, brothers & Kitty– Fisher & his Mother desire their best regards– I believe I forgot to tell you that the little blue paper parcel Harry had charge of for you was from Aunt H. who sent it when she found I admired one she had herself & wanted to know where she had bought it– & begged me to ask y^r acceptance of such a trifle which she said was hardly worth offering you– and begged me to explain why she did so– Miss Gadsden[5] is rather better, but has never been able to be moved from the <u>outside</u> of the bed on which she was placed on Saturday. They think however that there is no dislocation–

Private Collection

1. A burnous was a long, hooded cloak, similar to those worn in Arab countries.
2. Eliza took piano lessons from Monsieur der Konig for several years. Wanting to "study the piano in good earnest," she arranged for him to "come every Saturday afternoon to me to put me in the way of practicing." (Eliza also spelled his name "de Connick".) EMF to MHM, February 9, 1841, private collection.
3. Adolf Henselt (1814–1889), a German, was, like Thalberg, both a composer and a pianist.
4. Mrs. Israel Pemberton Hutchinson was the former Margaretta Hare. She and her husband, who had been in business in Lisbon and U.S. consul there for many years, lived in a new house on Spruce Street, which Sidney Fisher declared was beautiful, filled with French furniture made of rosewood, mirrors, chandeliers, bronze ornaments, and had one room done in "blue and white damask & gold." Wainwright, *Phila. Perspective* (February 14, 1841): 116.
5. Eliza added a postscript (now missing because Mrs. Middleton sent it to Mrs. Rutledge) to say that Miss Gadsden had died. "I had a great deal of feeling about [her,]" she told her mother, "but her manner was so reserved, that I never dared to tell how I felt for her." EMF to MHM, February 26, 1841, private collection.

~

To Mrs. Fisher, Philadelphia

M.P. Feby 21st 1841

My dearest Eliza

Your affectionate letter of the 9th which Harry brought me the day before yesterday <u>is</u> a comfort to me as it evinces so much sympathy & religious feeling. The reflection too that my dear Sister was so well prepared to quit the world is a source of consolation. Her kindness to me & the happy months I formerly spent in her house are constantly recurring to my recollection. I find that in your letter to Harry you mention that she must have been near 80 y^{rs} of Age. She was only 77 last August– and but for that Cold she caught, might have lived many years longer. I ought not however to imagine that, as we must believe our days are numbered by the Almighty, & no caution or accident can change his decrees.

Harry brought also a letter from Arthur to his Uncle J. I. M[iddleton] who forwarded it to me at A's request, as he was called off at the time he was concluding it & had not time to write to me. It was of the 26th Decr from Marseilles.

a friend had called to shew him the curiosities of that town which he was shortly after to leave & proceed to Italy! So after all, we need not expect to see him for 3 months. The cold & rain of Paris which your uncle had complained of, induced him to remain some time longer in the southern regions, besides wishing to gratify his desire of visiting Arles & Genoa.

Oliver & W$^{\underline{m}}$ arrived just before dinner, & will set off in a few days together for Combahee– Y$^{\underline{r}}$ Father will I suppose return from thence tomorrow, & after a day or two spent here will probably go with Harry to Charleston as he [*Harry*] tells me he is determined not to share my solitude as he did last winter, & blames me for not going to Charleston– but I have good reasons for remaining here as you know.¹ W$^{\underline{m}}$ brought me a letter from John. He says that he & Sally agree in thinking it would be imprudent in her to be far from good medical or surgical aid at the time she expects to be confined, & that they intend to move to town about the 10$^{\underline{th}}$ of March. I hope that is not delaying the journey too long. I should say the voyage, for they will of course go by the Steamer. Harry has been making Cath$^{\underline{e}}$ play the Opera of Norma which he is delighted to hear. It will be lucky if he can make her practise daily. I desired her to search for the "Magic Flute"– She assures me it is not here. Pray offer my thanks to M$^{\underline{rs}}$ Harrison for the very pretty mourning Handkerchief she was so kind as to send me by Harry. When you write to Sophia Thorndike give my love to her. Her health I hope is good, as you do not mention anything to the contrary.

The rumours of a war with England make me uneasy. I cannot bear to think of it. The affair of M$^{\underline{c}}$Leod² appears to make it inevitable. Do you hear of any possible means of the matter being brought to an adjustment without involving both countries in ruin? I ask your brothers their opinions on the subject & they seem to think it can be avoided– At Philad$^{\underline{a}}$ the subject must be better understood. A war would prevent our meeting this summer I fear– At Newport we sh$^{\underline{d}}$ be exposed to the Canon of the British fleet & I suppose I sh$^{\underline{d}}$ be sent off to Spartanburgh in case of the dreadful war occuring– Phil$^{\underline{a}}$ would not be a safe residence so that I hope M$^{\underline{r}}$ Fisher would consent to carry you to Spartanburg or Greenville–³ You will smile at my anticipation of evil!

25$^{\underline{th}}$ Your Father has not yet arrived & no opportunity has yet offered for sending this to Charleston. I must beg you to mark out on the inside of your next letter the pattern of half a plain muslin Collar with a broad hem, or lining & mark the width. the sheet is large enough for half a Cape, I think, but that can be sent by another letter. 27$^{\underline{th}}$ Y$^{\underline{r}}$ Father has at length arrived having left W$^{\underline{m}}$ at Combahee. he is going tomorrow to Charleston & I suppose I must wait 5 days for your letters. two I hope may come. Harry reads to me every even$^{\underline{g}}$– sometimes Tocqueville on Democracy which I cannot say is interesting to me, & sometimes 10,000 a year which he enjoys exceedingly– it loses of course some of its interest to me, as I have already gone through it as far as Blackwood's Novr N^o goes.

You saw I suppose in the Paper that the Marion[4] had sunk in consequence of its being turned over to be repaired– I fear E^d must have lost many things by the accident, & it will probably delay his return. Harry speaks in high terms of Lizzy– he could not tell me the colour of her hair, nor whether she had more than 2 teeth. by this time I suppose she has– surely you let her creep on your nicely swept Carpets now! she can nearly stand now by the assistance of your hand can she not? I hear of no news to tell you. I believe I mentioned in a former letter that Emma Blake was not going to Buncombe. What an irreparable loss Mrs Walter B[lake][5] has sustained by the failure of the U.S. bank– 80000$!

Pray give my love to Mrs Smith. Is her health still improving? 28th Your Father & Harry send their love. Give mine to M^r & Mrs F. & believe me my dearest Eliza y^r Affect^{te} Mother M. H. M.

PHi

1. Mrs. Middleton seems to have stayed at Middleton Place because she thought it was better for Catherine to be there rather than in Charleston.
2. Alexander McLeod, a Canadian who boasted that he killed a U.S. citizen during the 1837 rebellion in Canada, was arrested in New York state. There was considerable diplomatic friction between the American and British governments until the matter was finally ended with McLeod's acquittal by a New York court in October 1841. Although Mrs. Middleton's concern may seem excessive today, she had lived through the War of 1812, when the British did attack coastal towns.
3. Spartanburg and Greenville are in the northern part of South Carolina, far from the coast. The Middletons were familiar with the area, having spent several summers there both before and after they went to Russia.
4. The *Marion* was Edward's ship.
5. Anne Izard (b. 1812) married Walter Blake in 1837. She was the daughter of Ralph S. and Hester (Middleton) Izard and inherited considerable property from them. The sum of $80,000 would be equivalent to approximately $1.3 million in 1999. Dollar conversion factor from RSahr, OrStU.

~

To Mrs. Middleton, Middleton Place

Wednesday 10th March – 1841

This snow storm comes very opportunely to make a little more leisure for me, free from interruptions, which I can devote to my dearest Mamma– Since the Baby's illness and my own indisposition,[1] kind messages and visits of inquiry have been so frequent, that the silence of the door bell is quite remarkable today– Then we have had all the bustle of receiving & unpacking the Parisian importation of Col. Powel's selection–² which M^rs F– has placed entirely at my disposal– I told her that I thought the Drawing room already sufficiently furnished with lights & ornaments– but since she was of a different opinion, & insisted upon having more, I could not do less than accept them <u>very gra-ciously</u>– as the Queen did Mrs Smith's cape!³ Joking apart– I think she has gone to an unnecessary expense– for the unpretending style of entertainment which I prefer to all others, does not require the blaze of illumination which will be made in our small room by 56 candles & 4 Lamps! The Brackets are however very tasteful & classical & the Candelabrum quite superb– but too <u>barbaric</u> in form to suit my taste altogether– The newfashioned Fender is the prettiest thing of the sort I ever saw & the <u>mute babies</u> reclining upon it, suit the state of our feeling exactly– The china is not to come until the opening of the Canal,⁴ & the <u>trash for the table</u>, as Mr Powel calls the knick-knacks, are reserved for wedding gifts & are not to be exhibited to my longing gaze before the 12th.

Thursday 11th I was unable to continue my letter yesterday, dearest Mamma– & cared less about it, as I do not intend sending it until tomorrow– I have not yet thanked you for your's of the 28th. yes– now I recollect I rec^d it before despatching my last– and one from Emma at the same time– I have since had the pleasure of hearing from John who says they were to proceed to town in a few days– So I conclude they are there by this time– I hope that you will be able to join them there– for I am sure it w^d be more agreeable to you to be with Sally, than to remain alone in the country– and as she cannot conveniently leave Charleston, I hope you may decide to spend some days at least with her there– & cannot understand why you should not allow yourself that gratification– The change of scene w^d be of service to you, & I am sure Kitty would like it– Then it seems to me it w^d be so good an opportunity for new roofing & making the proposed alterations to the House– and I daresay if you reflect upon all the inducements, you will be inclined to follow Harry's advice, & leave the solitude of M. Place for a season–

I am every moment interrupted by Miss Baby, who is seated in her wicker chair before me, and obliges me constantly to put down my pen, & pick up her playthings, which she scatters over the floor, as fast as I put them on her table– you must not imagine that she can stand, or even creep which she can only do backwards like a little crab– when I try to make her walk, she goes on the extreme tips of her toes in the <u>Ellsler style</u>–⁵ when her short clothes are put on in May, I hope she will soon learn to move about unassisted– but is at present very helpless, altho' very strong– There is no more appearance of Teeth– so that D͏ͬ Meigs was quite right in his decision that she was not feverish from that cause– She is at last allowed to leave her Nursery, after a week's imprisonment there– but only to come as far as her Grandmother's room– where I am now writing– for her cough has not yet left her– altho' in other respects she is perfectly well & very lively– It is really amusing to see her passion for that ugliest of <u>niggers</u>, Hetty–⁶ she no sooner enters, than Baby begins to jump and put her arms out to her, & when she takes her & rides her about, she actually screams with delight–

You must have seen in the Nat[ional] Gaz[ette] the announcement of Sophia Thorndike's marriage to her cousin [*George Herbert Thorndike*]– which surprized us all, as much as it must have done you– so little did I suspect it, that in several of my letters to her I mentioned some unfavourable reports I had heard about him, & thought it my duty to tell her– which I now regret, as she was already bound to him for life– He sailed in the President yesterday, and is to bring her home in a few months, when he hopes the differences between his Father & her's will be settled– This is all James Otis,⁷ who is always laconic in his epistles, tells Fisher, to whom he wrote to have the advertisement published by T[horndike]'s request– I feel rather hurt at having been kept so completely in the dark, but I suppose they had good reasons for keeping the secret so profoundly, which Sophia will explain when she next writes to me– Meanwhile we have lately heard, from a gentleman from Buenos Ayres very good accounts both of his Father & himself, which we were glad to learn– as they are a contradiction to some very disparaging rumours afloat about him, & are I trust correct–

Friday 12ͭͪ I am sure you are thinking of me today,⁸ my dearest Mamma, & I hope that long ere this your fears about me, (of which your letter of the 6ͭͪ just rec͏ͩ is full), are dispelled by the letters which I am astonished at your not having sooner received– It is extraordinary that they should have been so long on the road for I certainly wrote punctually once a week– I am very sorry indeed that you distressed yourself so much by imaginary apprehensions– which I reproach myself for having suggested by the gloomy tone of some of my letters– which I shall in future avoid– as you seem to think that the very things I described others as suffering from, had necessarily been my portion– Pray do not suppose anything of the sort likely to happen to me– for I assure you I never was in better health in my life than at this moment– The D͏ͬ has just pronounced the dear Baby to be also quite well, with the exception of a cough which he thinks very lightly of, & has prescribed syrup for– He says she

is "a very nice little thing, & seems to improve & grow every time he sees her"–
so that my <u>maternal</u> eyes do not deceive me in thinking so too–

With a new Pen, I hope to write a little more legibly, as I want to tell you
a little more about my beautiful Presents &c– In the first place, Fisher walked
out to Dryburgh's before breakfast, like a dear good fellow as he is, & brought
me the loveliest of bouquets, & the sweetest! With 4 exquisite Camellias &
plenty of delicious heliotrope &c– Then I found on my Drawing room table,
8 choice little Parisian trifles of various sorts & for various uses (It might puzzle
anyone's ingenuity to find them <u>all</u> out). We are to have here tonight– The 2
M^r^s Ingersolls,[9] Sally Waln, M^r^s Willing, Hares, Hutchinsons, and Sergeants &
Wises, who are just arrived from Wash^n^ & a few others– M^r^s Smith will come
if the weather, at present not very favourable, permits– She has just rec^d^ your
letter & thanks you for it– I am quite disappointed at not having Esther Binney–
She has a very bad cold, & fears the night exposure– M^r^s M^c^Euen too is prevented by her husband's being confined at home with the gout– I hope to hear
something of Edward from Charles Hunter who will be here– But I will not
keep this open <u>another</u> day lest you should imagine a new misfortune from
my silence– and dare not <u>scratch your eyes</u> out– so Adieu– with most affectionate love to Papa and the others I am y^r^ always devotedly attached daughter
Eliza

Your dutiful Son-in-law, wishes to be today of all others, most cordially & affectionately remembered– and indeed he deserves your best regard– if his uniform
kindness & devotion to me, & good feelings towards you & the rest of my family
entitle him to it– M^r^s F. begs me to present her very kindly & M^r^ & M^r^s H–
always wish me to do so likewise– He is better, but still kept at home by the
Lumbago–

Pray tell John with my love (if you see him) that I mean to heap coals of
fire on his head very soon– He will understand this, altho' not <u>particularly</u> well
versed in Scripture– I shall <u>first</u> write to Mary, as I know <u>little</u> people think
more of omissions.

Private Collection

1. Eliza thought worry over the baby's first real illness made her "nervous & head-
achey," but this may also have been an early indication that she was pregnant. EMF to
MHM, March 4, 1841, private collection.

2. Mrs. Fisher commissioned her cousin John Hare Powel to purchase furnishings
for the new rooms at 170 Chestnut Street while he was in Europe.

3. Mrs. Smith, who was English, sent a present to Queen Victoria, along with
verses she had composed. She received a gracious reply.

4. The china was probably shipped from New York by the Delaware and Raritan Canal, which ran across New Jersey from New Brunswick to the Delaware River, saving a long trip around the southern tip of New Jersey and up the Delaware to Philadelphia.

5. When the Viennese ballet dancer Fanny Ellsler (1811–1884) danced in New York in the early 1840s, the audience "rose in a mass, and the waves of the great animated ocean were capped by hundreds of white pocket-handkerchiefs." Philip Hone thought that in *La Tarantule* Ellsler "established her claim to be considered by far the best dancer we have ever seen in this country." Allan Nevins, ed., *The Diary of Philip Hone* (New York: Dodd, Mead & Co., 1936), 481.

6. Hetty Harvey worked for Fisher's mother for many years. In her will Mrs. Fisher provided that she should receive one hundred dollars annually and directed Fisher to increase the amount if Hetty was in need. She was buried near Mrs. Fisher in the graveyard of Trinity Oxford Church, Philadelphia.

7. James Otis, son of Harrison Gray Otis and brother of Allyne, was a businessman in New York. He was "laconic" because he suspected that Thorndike was dishonest and intended to abandon Sophia.

8. March 12 was the Fishers' wedding anniversary.

9. The two Mrs. Ingersolls were sisters-in-law: Mrs. Harry (Sally Roberts) Ingersoll and Mrs. Charles (Susan Brown) Ingersoll.

〜

Because President Van Buren took office in 1837 just as the effects of bank closings and plummeting prices hit the country, he was often blamed for the country's economic depression. As he left office in early 1841, Eliza wrote her mother that "the winter has been altogether one of the most unpleasant as regards the state of atmosphere, <u>natural, political and commercial</u> that the wise men recollect for years past. Luckily our quiet and comfort have not [been] affected, more than by the sympathy and compassion we cannot help feeling for the many distressed and seriously injured persons, whose fortunes have melted away under the sunshine of properity of 'old Nick' & other rascally speculators. We had last eveng. at Mrs. Campbell's one of the first originators of the evil, in Mr. Van Buren– who was looked at with less admiration and regard I think than formerly– altho' many of his party were present, and paid him honour due– which of course should not be withheld from even a fallen foe still more from a friend."[1]

1. EMF to MHM, March 17, 1841, private collection.

To Mrs. Middleton, Middleton Place

Thursday morng– 25th March 1841

Here am I writing to you before breakfast, my dearest Mamma, having risen an hour earlier than usual, this fine spring morning– It is delightful to have clear warm weather, after all the rain and snow of the last month– only 3 days ago there were still sleighs going about– but I hope we have now bid adieu to them until next winter– & on the doctrine of compensation (in which I for one am a believer) are entitled to a charming spring after a most disagreeable winter– In about 2 months more we may have the happiness of meeting– for I have great hopes that you may set out earlier for NewPort this year– I am going to write to the little Middletons to enquire about the Lodgings at Miss Hazard's where we might be very comfortable if we are fortunate enough to find them still disengaged– & hope to induce Mrs Fisher to spend at least part of the summer with us– as to M^{r} & M^{rs} H[arrison]– I fear it is in vain to attempt to persuade them to go further than the <u>Branch</u>.[1] You will have Arthur, & probably Edward also with you– and I wish I could hope to see dear John & Sally at the North this summer– It w^{d} be so beneficial to both– I am extremely anxious to hear of her safe accouchement, and that your fears of her being <u>caught</u> at Waccamaw have not been realized– I sincerely <u>condole</u> with Oliver on the birth of a 5th daughter–[2] and yet he may think himself lucky that it is not a 5th <u>son</u>, which w^{d} be infinitely more to be regretted in my opinion– What is the poor little girl to be called? & who or what does she look like? I have been expecting to hear these important particulars from Mary, but have heard hitherto nothing, but your brief notice of the event–

I am going to announce a <u>wonderful</u> fact, which altho' it may sound rather incredible, is nevertheless really true– and established by half a dozen witnesses at least– Pray let me ask you if any of your children were <u>smart</u> enough to talk before they were 9 months old? My baby actually says <u>Mamma</u> as plainly as I do– and for the last 3 days has been repeating this first & <u>dearest</u> word, intelligibly & <u>intelligently</u> likewise– Is not <u>that</u> precocity? I thought at first it was mere accident– but she has since repeated it with <u>evident</u> meaning <u>frequently</u>– She has on her first pair of boots too, & they assist her in crawling very much– She is at this moment enjoying a drive round the yard in her wicker carriage, amazingly– and I am just going to give her a turn myself– We think her 2 upper Teeth are coming at last, from the swollen appearance of the Gums– I wrote a long letter to Edward, day before yesterday, & sent it by a vessel which sailed yesterday for Rio– I gave him your message– but if you would like to write & will forward the letter to me, I will consult Mr Hunter about the means of despatching it to him–

We were at Eliza Peter's wedding on Saturday night– It seemed a queer day to choose, but being the birthday of Mr Field, they wished to celebrate it in that manner– There was a crowd of people one never sees elsewhere– They are noted for associating with queer acquaintances and a more common set I never met before in <u>private</u>– Poor M<u>rs</u> Peters was brought down to be <u>present</u> during the ceremony and looked like death– she had been all day in a dreadful state of agitation– This is her favourite child, & under any circumstances it would have been trying– This morng– the Bride receives company, and we are going to see her–

Friday– I returned home yesterday so much tired with hunting after a Spring Bonnet (M<u>rs</u> Fisher insisted upon carrying me to all the Milliners' in town almost) and heated by our walk thro' the hot sun, that I indulged my laziness upon the bed, in the afternoon, & rested sufficiently to walk up and see M<u>rs</u> Ewing,[3] after Tea– She has been very ill– at one time in great danger, & has never left the house for 3 months, but is looking pretty well again– & was quite cheerful, & as ladylike as usual– The Mamma (M<u>rs</u> Elwyn) was not quite so garrulous or satirical as formerly– & appears much subdued by her favourite daughter's dangerous illness– so that I found her more agreeable– & listened to her with more patience. I regret having missed seeing M<u>rs</u> Hare, who spent the eveng– at Aunt H's for the first time for months– The D<u>r</u> is in wretched health, having nearly poisoned himself with deleterious gazes [*gases*] in his Laboratory, & is ordered by his Physicians to go to Europe– He sails next week from this Port for Liverpool, young Robert accompanying him– I am going to send by the latter to Uncle Oliver [*Hering*], Bancroft's History of the U.S.[4] & some little trifles to Aunt– They are to extend their tour to Stockholm, where the D<u>r</u> wishes to see the celebrated Chemist Berzelius, with whom he is in correspondence & perhaps they may even proceed thence as far as S<u>t</u> Petersburg– I understand the Channings[5] are all coming on to stay with M<u>rs</u> Hare, soon after the D<u>r</u>'s departure–

We have delicious weather now, and I intend very soon to begin our drives into the country– and give the Baby as much fresh air as possible– One of the horses M<u>r</u> H. gave Fisher is a capital draught horse– & will no doubt be very serviceable to us– the other is to be sold for what he will fetch, as he is very inferior, & not <u>sound</u>– But Legnen & H[enry] Fisher are looking out for one for me, which Fisher can also use when I prefer driving– which I have no doubt I often shall– & at any rate don't intend to mount in town as I am more of a coward than in the "days of my youth"– & besides have more inducements to take care of my <u>precious life</u>–[6] Adieu my dearest Mamma and think of me always as Y<u>r</u> most affectionate Daughter Eliza

I have not thanked you for y<u>r</u> letter of the 15<u>th</u> dear Mamma, which I now do sincerely– I also omitted love to Papa, my brothers and Kitty– an oft repeated Phrase which cannot be much varied in expression– but will not I hope be the less acceptable because it has not novelty to recommend it– I give you on the next page the Pattern of another plain linen collar, prettier I think than the last– and recommend you to have many of them made for yourself and Kitty for they are worn universally in the morning– and are very neat– Instead of putting it on a habit shirt, just cut a piece of cotton cambric (double the shape of the collar but only half as wide), sew it to the collar and turn <u>that</u> under your cape, which is more convenient than tucking a whole handk[erchie]f in–[7]

Private Collection

1. That is, Long Branch, New Jersey.
2. Emma Middleton was born on March 4, 1841.
3. Mrs. Ewing was Mrs. Elwyn's daughter.
4. George Bancroft (1800–1891), diplomat and historian, was one of the first Americans to study at a German university. Influenced by this training, he used original sources in his ten-volume *History of the United States.* The third volume appeared in 1840.
5. The William Ellery Channings and the Robert Hares were close friends and visited each other often.
6. It is not clear whether this was Eliza's way of telling her mother she was pregnant again, or whether she had already sent a message with someone going to Charleston. Sophia Georgina Fisher was born on November 26, 1841.
7. The following notes were with the pattern:"Nothing allowed for turning in– This ought to be <u>Bias.</u> This is the width of the inside piece– If this pattern sh<u>d</u> not fit you in front you can easily alter it to suit your own dress – & make the point come out more here –" Eliza had sent the first pattern on March 4.

~

To Mrs. Fisher, Philadelphia

M.P. April 4<u>th</u> 1841

My dearest Eliza

Your letter of the 25<u>th</u> March was brought to me the day before yesterday, & gave me very great pleasure. The Baby's pronouncing 'Mama' before she was 9 months old is indeed an extraordinary circumstance & I am not surprised that it should delight you to hear her address you by that endearing name. To me it will also be a most pleasing sound, & I look forward to the month of June with the hope that we may then meet either at Philad<u>a</u> or Newport for nothing has yet been said about the mode in which we are to proceed– if by rail cars, the former must be the place of our meeting. But how could you think of living any where but in your Father's house at Newport? I could never bear the idea of losing so much of your society as your being in another house would compel me to do. M$^{\underline{rs}}$ Grant[1] told me she had engaged M$^{\underline{rs}}$ Hazard's rooms for next Summer, so that fortunately for me you have no chance of having them, and none of your Brothers could have any objection to have a good sized room for two of them. Arthur & W$^{\underline{m}}$ would willingly occupy the front room next to mine & it is very improbable that Ed$^{\underline{d}}$ should be there, if he should, he could have his bed in Harry's room. I have no doubt a comfortable bedroom could be found for M$^{\underline{rs}}$ Fisher in the houses either of Perry, or – I forget the name of the woman where M$^{\underline{rs}}$ Otis used to board, (I recoll$^{\underline{t}}$ now, Fairbanke) & if she would do me the favour to take her meals at our house it would give me great pleasure to have her as my guest– try to prevail upon her to adopt this plan, & then you will be spared the pain of separation. You must recollect Perry's where the Boston family the Codmans lodged; it was well spoken of by all the lodgers, & is very near us.

I have now a large party here.[2] Your Father brought Hal & Tom on Friday & yesterday Oliver brought little Susan & Sarah to spend two days & then return with John to Charleston, as he cannot be longer separated from Sally– he left her 3 days ago well, & able to go & see Susan & your brothers are all of opinion that she is looking well. I think the full moon tomorrow must be the day of the babe's birth–[3] She writes me word she regrets the delay, as it will necessarily shorten the time she hopes to spend here– As to Susan's coming, she says it is out of the question, as she has a white & black nurse & Oliver is to take her to Edisto next Friday where M$^{\underline{rs}}$ Chisolm & Mary & Eleanor have preceded her.

Little Johnny came up in the Wagon last week or the week before last & is quite delighted with the country, plants &c– He is the most intelligent of John's children. His knowledge of Geography is astonishing for a little fellow of 7 y$^{\underline{rs}}$ old & he knows many French words.[4] I hear him his lessons every day & am trying to teach him to write, that is rather a hopeless task, I mark the letters with a pencil, & he scratches them over with his pen. Sarah is a little taller than Susan & much prettier, they are great friends & seem to enjoy their visit here– perhaps they may stay. tomorrow Y$^{\underline{r}}$ Father & W$^{\underline{m}}$ are going to Combahee.

The pattern of the collar you sent last is as you observe a better one than the first. The [*pattern for a*] Cape will I hope come in the next letter as it is now too warm to wear silk ones.[5] The weather has been very fine for some days, & the trees are all green. as yet the insects are not troublesome, another week will of course make them so. My Brother will I am sure be very glad to become acquainted with D$^{\underline{r}}$ Hare & his Son, who can give him so many particulars about you & yours. Do be careful about trying any new horse that may be purchased for you– driving out would suit you much better, as you can take Baby with you– Emma Blake changed her plans again & went about a fortnight ago with Fred^{c} Rutledge to Buncomb. It is unlikely that D^{r} & Mrs Holbrook will perform their promise, for they frequently drive to a small Farm that Miss Pinckney gave them close to the 4 mile house.[6] they have lately built a small house upon it, & take great pleasure in laying out the grounds, & the doctor in catching reptiles no doubt amuses himself.

Oliver has just come in to say that he must go after dinner. He says in answer to your message that he is very well satisfied with the little babe being a girl, & is not disappointed at not having a son. The name is not yet decided upon. Sally begs in her note to be affectionately remembered to you. You have not mentioned Mrs Smith lately in y^{r} letters– I hope she is well. I have had the pleasure of rec^{g} another letter from my Brother of the end of Feby he did not then complain of Gout. He says "We are rejoiced to hear that Eliza & her pet are going on well. When you write tell her so." I must now conclude to be in time for Oliver– With love to M^{r} & Mrs Fisher I am my dearest Eliza y^{r} Affect^{te} Mother M. H. M.

Y^{r} Father & brothers send their love to you. remember me to M^{r} & Mrs Harrison–

PHi

1. A Bostonian, Mrs. Patrick Grant was the former Anna Mason. Mrs. David Sears and Mrs. John C. Warren were her sisters.

2. Among the grandchildren Mrs. Middleton mentions, Hal, Tom, Sarah, and Johnny were John and Sally's children; "little Susan" (Coosey) as well as Mary and Eleanor, who had gone to Edisto, were Oliver and Susan's. John said to Eliza that although the children might give their mother some trouble, "I do not think it will do her any harm, for I think she leads too quiet a life there, and has too little to amuse her." John I. Middleton to EMF, April 20, 1841, MPlFdn.

3. Mrs. Middleton always said her mother-in-law, Mary Izard Middleton, claimed that babies were born when the moon was full.

4. Mrs. Middleton had told Eliza that John "now has an excellent Overseer who will save him a great deal of fatigue & trouble, & enable him he says to attend without interruption to the education of his children– he agrees with me in the opinion that they can learn more from him than if sent to school." MHM to EMF, March 25, 1841, ScHi.

5. Eliza told her mother, "There is no alteration at all in the fashion of Capes– But they are very little worn being almost entirely superceded by high-necked dresses, which are universally worn except at Parties– This is a hot fashion for Carolina– They are generally made full in the back of the waist, & plaited from the shoulder down the front." EMF to MHM, April 1, 1841, private collection.

6. On the road north out of Charleston.

~

Four days before Eliza wrote the next letter, William Henry Harrison died unexpectedly, only a month after his inauguration as president. Vice President John Tyler succeeded Harrison and asked the members of his cabinet to continue in office. In the following months, Secretary of State Daniel Webster reached agreement with the British on the issues, including the McLeod affair, that had made war between England and the United States seem possible.

Eliza's comments were almost certainly intended to give her father and brothers, as well as her mother, a Philadelphia perspective on the events in Washington.

To Mrs. Middleton, Middleton Place

Philadelphia – April 8$\underline{th}$ 1841

I have now been ten days without receiving any tidings from you, my dearest Mamma, and begin to feel very impatient for a letter– We stopped at the [Post] Office on our way from Church, yesterday afternoon, but to my great regret there was none– I hope to be more fortunate today– if not, I shall keep this open until tomorrow– I have had a good deal to make me gloomy since I last wrote– M$\underline{rs}$ Fisher has continued very unwell– hardly leaving her bed, except for a few minutes to be present at the meals, of which she seldom partakes, & in the eveng– when she invariably feels much better– But she is herself much discouraged at the length of this attack, & it is really sad to see any one suffer so much– without being able to relieve them–

The news too from Eng$\underline{d}$ and Washington is very gloomy– but we must hope the prospect will brighten before long– and altho' the death of Harrison is certainly a national calamity, & is felt to be so particularly at this moment of anxiety– I believe no serious apprehensions of war with Eng$\underline{d}$ are entertained, and it is thought that the difficulty will be settled by the present administration who remain in office to give dignity to the old Hero's successor– The Sergeants speak very highly of Tyler– but then he is M$\underline{r}$ Wise's intimate friend– which may make them partial– If he will only follow the dying advice of his predecessor, and retain his Cabinet, all will go on well, it is hoped– & we shall not have to take refuge at Spartanburgh I trust– or witness the "abomination of desolation" which the British War Steamers might soon produce–

You will be glad to hear I daresay, what I am quite sorry to tell you– that I am about weaning dear Baby– I found that Nursing her 6 & 7 times a day weakened me so excessively, that I have had her fed oftener lately– & now my milk is diminishing so much that I cannot look forward to having enough to supply her during the summer & therefore am advised to give up nursing before the warm weather begins– that she may become accustomed to the change of food & not suffer from it in the heat of summer– so I am gradually decreasing her allowance from me– & in a few days shall probably cut her off altogether– poor little darling– I am afraid she won't love me as much– but I don't think she will be half as much distressed at the separation as I am myself– for she is perfectly satisfied with her bottle– & her Oatmeal gruel thickened with milk– which agrees perfectly with her– she eats besides a good crust of bread daily & I hope will thrive as well, when entirely removed from the breast– altho' I should have liked to keep her there until she had cut more teeth– The two upper ones are almost thro'– and can be seen, but not <u>felt</u>– And if she is early removed to a temperate climate, I am in hopes she will pass her second summer in safety– Mrs F. dreads it for her, & I really think it encreases her nervousness to <u>suspect</u> (for I w^{d} not yet <u>tell</u> her) that I mean to wean her– But as it is <u>necessity</u> & not choice which obliges me to do so she must e'en reconcile my <u>cruelty</u> to that as she best may– what consoles me much, is that <u>you</u> always weaned your's at 9 months– & certainly had healthy children– & the universality of the custom in Eng^{d} gives it some authority surely–

I have had a letter from Mme Marras– who is in great distress at the loss of her child, poor thing. It lived only 3 days– being premature– but she mourns over it, as every Mother must who is not worse than a brute– and sadly wanting in natural affection– I was sorry for Georgie [Middleton] too– but she has others to console her– I see by the Papers that the Marion is so much injured that she is probably rendered unfit for further use– and it is therefore likely her Crew will be sent home in another Vessel– whereat I shall rejoice–

I have been reading the life of Sir Humphrey Davy[1] by his Brother– which is very interesting altho' badly put together– but rendered so by the extracts from his journal & notes which are given in a very unconnected manner– The specimens of his Poetry justify the remark of Coleridge, that if he had applied himself to the cultivation of that Talent, he w^{d} have been the greatest Poet of the age as well as the greatest Philosopher– He had rare Genius and goodness combined– and his writings are very delightful to me, because full of noble thoughts– which raise him above this "mean earth" to the contemplation of higher objects, and those hopes of immortality– which were to him settled convictions– and consolations in sickness and all other trials– I find that the favourite idea he cherished of another existence is that of inhabiting other Planets, gradually attaining all knowledge & the perfection which will fit us to enjoy ourselves in the presence of infinite Wisdom, and admire the wonders of His Universe– So that <u>my</u> ideas on the same subject (which I recollect Harry was inclined to ridicule when I expressed them at New Port one starlight night) are at least those of a very great & good man– who had both Philosophy & Religion to guide him to the Truth–

Good Friday evening– I should have told you yesterday eveng how much pleasure your letter of the 4<u>th</u> which dear Fisher brought me, gave me dearest Mamma, if I had not been going to Aunt H's– I was delighted to find you had so many of the children to cheer you & gave such a good account of them– On this most Solemn day in the Christian year I have been of course entirely occupied with religious Services at Church & reading at home except when trying to interest M<u>rs</u> F. in conversation & playing with the Baby for relaxation– and a sweet plaything she really is– Her little gums were lanced this morng– as the teeth appeared to come with difficulty– M<u>rs</u> F– is rather better, & was able with F's assisting arm to go once to Church– but she is still very miserable– She is very sensible of the kindness of your offer with regard to New Port next summer– but <u>now</u> thinks she cannot possibly go so far from home– & at any rate w<u>d</u> not consent I fear to accept it– as she can seldom be induced to dine even at her Sister's– You are very good to wish me & my noisy brat as inmates, dear Mamma– but I should have many scruples in depriving my brothers of the accomodation of two good rooms– &c &c– M<u>rs</u> G[rant] is to be sure to occupy Miss Hazard's rooms– but I have not yet heard from the Middletons about Perry's & Fairbank's– As I am very tired & a little <u>headachy</u> withal– I will say Goodnight with kind love all round– Ever Y<u>r</u> most affect<u>e</u> Daughter Eliza

Fisher and his Mother beg me to add their best regards– M<u>r</u> & M<u>rs</u> H. always request me to return your kind remembrances by offering their's–

Private Collection

1. Sir Humphry Davy (1778–1829) was less distinguished for his poetry than for his pioneering work in chemistry. He invented the miner's safety lamp, isolated sodium and potassium, and did important work on the nature of chemical compounds.

～

To Mrs. Middleton, Middleton Place

Philadelphia – April 15<u>th</u> 1841

My dearest Mamma,

I have now some chance of half an hour's quiet, having had the satisfaction of putting Baby to sleep, after drawing her round the yard & singing a Lullaby–

All the servants are busy <u>cleaning up</u>– such as washing of windows, and scrubbing of paint– it is really amusing to behold– but I believe M<u>rs</u> F. thinks it can never be <u>overdone</u>– which in <u>my</u> humble opinion it <u>often</u> is– We have had horrid weather since last week– all the <u>Solemnities</u>[1] postponed in consequence of the snow storm on Monday– yesterday we had a second edition of it– but now it has cleared beautifully and we may count upon "serene skies" for some time to come– D<u>r</u> Chapman says the snow lay <u>11</u> inches deep on Monday eveng! pretty well for the season! He has certainly done M<u>rs</u> F. some good, but she still complains of being miserable every morng– however she now occupies herself & is much better, if she w<u>d</u> only think so herself– but this attack has lasted longer than usual, & she is debilitated by it– and is unwilling to stir from the house except to see M<u>r</u> Harrison– who has been quite unwell, so much so as to require bleeding– Today he is better– and I hope this fine weather will soon restore him to health– I feel infinitely better since I have had resolution to wean the baby– Since Good Friday she has not had a drop from me– and what is remarkable, has not fretted for it all– except once when I <u>tempted</u> her– rather a dangerous experiment, under which older & wiser folks are apt to yield– To my great joy she is not less fond of me, notwithstanding my <u>cruelty</u>– and cries to come to me, and cuddles me up, with her little arms hugged as closely round my neck, as affectionately as ever– But I must not fill my sheet with "fond folly"– else I could tell you of many little new ways, which are very engaging–

I had yesterday quite a treat– listening to a Spanish Lady who played on the Guitar,[2] at M<u>rs</u> Rush's in the afternoon– She has extraordinary delicacy of touch and feeling– but not quite as much <u>power</u> over the instrument as Schmidt, whose playing delighted us so much at New Port– I was delighted to hear her, however– & shall always listen with pleasure to the tones which recall memories of by gone years– & are associated with many pleasant, and some painful thoughts– This reminds me to ask you to bring on next summer the Guitar which I value as Papa's Gift– & might occasionally have an opportunity of practising upon– in my <u>Nursery</u> when I cannot leave it for the Piano– which may not be near at hand.

I am going this eveng– to hear Haydn's "Creation"[3] performed at the Musical Fund Hall– not being able to persuade M<u>rs</u> F. to accompany us– I proposed to M<u>rs</u> Smith to go– she has accepted– with pleasure she says– I made interest with <u>my friend</u> M. Meignen[4] over the way for the Tickets which are not to be bought– but of course he was charmé to oblige so good a customer as I am– I went on Sunday afternoon, for the first time in my life to a Roman Catholic Church– Having been detained until very late in the morng– at our own Church, by the number of Communicants, we could not get off early enough after dinner to return there– and Fisher preferred going to hear fine Music, which Mrs Davis[5] promised us, to hearing Dr Bethune preach– but repented of his choice afterwards– for the heat & crowd gave him a headache the following day– The fumes of the Incense too were very oppressive– & nearly overpowered me– The music was fine, but monotonous– & chanted in a very nasal twang by the principal Bass, who quite drowned the Female voices which were very sweet when heard alone– The ceremonies were associated in my mind with those of the ancient Hebrews which they no doubt resemble– & therefore were rather interesting to me– except the last– which must always be beheld with pain by every Protestant– I mean the elevation and adoration of the Host– which I had never before witnessed– It is indeed shocking to think of the perversion of the simplicity and Purity of those Precepts, which were intended to promote spirituality– & are degraded by an artful & ambitious Priesthood to a wretched Superstition– but many of these deluded creatures no doubt worship "in Spirit & in Truth"– & far be it from me to judge others– whose hearts may be (and <u>are</u> I daresay) as Pure in the sight of God as those of any who attempt to pronounce them wrong– and are themselves in error perhaps– altho' not wilfully–

Friday 16<u>th</u> Fisher brought me a letter from Emma last eveng– instead of the one I was expecting from my dear Mamma. She has been suffering again with her eyes– <u>Specks</u> floating before them– & preventing her from all occupation– This is really sad in the solitude to which she is condemned for so great a portion of the year deprived even of her husband's society & unable to read for her amusement–[6]

Mrs Fisher's Nephew, Tom Francis (Sally's fellow passenger from Havre) is very ill of Small Pox– We hear this morng that his betrothed (Miss Smith) was sent for to see him at 7 o'clk A.M. and Dr Chapman thinks his case quite desperate– He took it from <u>her</u> little Nephew an infant of a year old, whom he had the folly to take on his Lap, when he was paying a visit to his love– being aware that the disease it had was declared by Meigs to be Small Pox! There is no intercourse between our families of course, on baby's account– further than sending to enquire without entering the doors– Mrs F. wrote word to Mrs Francis– that she would, if necessary, go and help her to nurse him, & <u>remain</u> there– having no fear of it herself– but being of course fearful of communicating it to her Grandchild– But the latter w^d not hear of her going– & assured her she could do no good– but only encrease her uneasiness by going to the house– The girls (Maria & Nancy Page) have been revaccinated– but must be in great alarm I suppose– I am so anxious to keep Baby out of all danger from this frightful complaint that I do not allow her now to go into the Street, further than to Mr Harrison's– & confine her entirely to the yard– and the carriage– We drove out to Laurel Hill last afternoon, for the first time since August. The Country looks still rather <u>russet</u> than green– but I was delighted to get beyond the Pavements once more–

I have not told you of the Oratorio– It was better performed than I expected– The Instrumental part especially– Very few of the Singers were even tolerable– but on the whole, it was worth hearing– Altho' the Choruses were anything but <u>Angelic</u> or Celestial– & almost stunned us– The Music is certainly fine throughout– & parts of it are extremely beautiful– Mrs Smith was gratified by the Duetts in Paradise &c– & compensated for the trouble of going, and sitting in a crowd of 14 hundred People– I shall scribble your eyes out if I go on– so Adieu dearest Mamma– With love to all– I am as ever Y^r most affectionate Daughter Eliza

Fisher & his Mother always wish me to remember them most kindly &c

Private Collection

1. The funeral procession for President Harrison, originally planned for April 12, had to be postponed until the twentieth because of the snow storm.

2. Madame de Goñi was in Philadelphia in 1841 and again the following winter, as well as in Boston. Vincent A. Schmidt also performed in Philadelphia in the fall of 1842.

3. Haydn's oratorio, "The Creation," was performed by the Philharmonic Society.

4. Leopold Meignen (1793–1873) was a leader among Philadelphia's professional musicians as well as proprietor of a music store across the street from the Fishers. A graduate of the Paris Conservatory, he taught music theory and conducted the Musical Fund Society orchestra from 1846 to 1857.

5. Probably Mrs. Samuel Davis, wife of a wealthy planter from Natchez, Mississippi, who lived in Philadelphia at 256 Chestnut Street. Eliza's letters indicate that Mrs. Davis was Spanish. Wainwright, *Phila. Perspective,* passim; EMF to MHM, February 1, 1842, private collection.

6. In the same letter Emma told Eliza that on their plantation the flood waters were so high that Allen went "from our back door in a boat, right over banks, bridges et cetera. . . . Believe me, all women are lucky whose lots are cast in places north of the Potomac." Later, she wrote that Carolina country life had a "wonderful capacity for cutting off any exuberance of wit & spirit." EHS to EMF, April 9, 1841, and February 3, 1844, PHi.

⌣

To Mrs. Fisher, Philadelphia

M.P. Ap$\underline{l}$ 18$\underline{th}$ 1841

My dearest Eliza

For several days past I have been wishing to write to you but no opportunity has offered of sending to Town until today, which I gladly avail myself of to thank you for your letter of the 1$\underline{st}$ rec$\underline{d}$ about 10 days ago. There is I hope another in Charleston, which I have been disappointed at not receiving this morning by Coachman Abraham, who John sent here last night to bring Shoes for his Children, & neglected to send me letters & papers which I have no doubt are in Town. My astonishment was great when told by Ab$\underline{m}$ that his Mistress was still downstairs & very well– here is above a month since she expected to be confined! Your Father & W$\underline{m}$ have been at Combahee nearly a fortnight & perhaps may return before I send this off. Harry riding out a few days since, met M$\underline{r}$ A[llen] Smith's Carriage on its way to Laurel hill & the Ser$\underline{t}$ told him it was the intention of M$\underline{r}$ & M$\underline{rs}$ A. S. to be here one day this week, & that he was going to Sav$\underline{a}$ river for them– they will probably pass a day on their way, at Combahee. I shall be glad to see Emma & talk about you.

For the last fortnight the five children have been staying here. The clatter of the three boys[1] is often stunning– You know that in Carolina the drawing room is the nursery, & I am often driven out of it by their quarrelling– Susan & Sarah are comparatively quiet & well behaved, & they say their lessons to me every day very well, particularly the former– She is a very clever child. Sarah is improved in her French, as her Father teaches her & they both are desirous of acquiring information– M$\underline{r}$ Gilman's written account of Susan is exceedingly commendatory. Johnny is the cleverest of John's children, he is a great favorite of Harry's, who has nicknamed him "Professor Jack", his great delight is to ask his companions questions on Geography on which subject he is wonderfully well informed for a child of 7 y$\underline{rs}$ old– To reward him, y$\underline{r}$ Father before his departure gave him the Atlas you may remember his having purchased at Newport, with which the Child is delighted. I hear him his lessons every day, & he is improving in his French– Tom says <u>his</u> to Hal, & is a good arithmetician for a child of 5 y$\underline{rs}$ old, but cannot yet read– & he repeats what he has learnt of his Mother, very well.

I am glad you have given a letter of introduction to D$\underline{r}$ & M$\underline{r}$ R. Hare for I am sure my Brother will be much gratified in making their acquaintance & hearing their account of you. it is lucky you have so safe an opportunity of sending your presents to y$\underline{r}$ Friends. You hope Perry's house [*in Newport*] is disengaged, so do I, but not for <u>You</u>, who <u>must</u> stay with me, but for M$\underline{rs}$

Fisher, who as I before mentioned will I hope take her meals with us & have a comfortable room not far from our house. She has long ere this I trust recovered from her nervous attack. It is really a pity M^r & Mrs Harrison will not consent to spend the summer at Newport– I thought you expected Mr Otis's being there, w^d tempt him to make the excursion? The name reminds me of the late news of the President's death– it must be a great loss to many people who anticipated promotion.

I am expecting to receive in a day or two (i.e. if a Servant be sent to town) a letter from my Brother by the G^t Western– but must write to him before I receive it, or the letter will not arrive at N.Y. by the 28th the date of its departure. I shall hear in your next of several words which the dear Babe can now repeat, besides Mama & Dada– she is indeed a very forward Child & I long to witness her improvements. next week May will begin, & we may then look forward to 5 weeks bringing us together– that however depends on circumstances of which we are not yet aware. When I spoke to John about seeing him at Newport, he said, that it was out of the question to move with 6 children, so I fear you have no chance of meeting him. Susan & Oliver will probably return to Charleston next week that the Children may go to school on the 1st of May. Hal too begins on the same day– the delay of Sally's confinement will allow of her being here for only a few days, if she is to move in a month after it.

The weather has been very pleasant lately– the heat not yet oppressive, as the wind has been rather violent, & frequent rains have cooled the air. I can tell you nothing about Susan's infant except that her sister says she is healthy but has as yet no name– I must now close this as it is 2 o'clock & Ab^m is going– Y^r Father will not be here today as the time he always comes, is past. Harry sends his love to you pray give mine to M^r & Mrs Fisher & believe me my dearest Eliza y^r affect^{te} Mother M. H. M.

PHi

1. John's sons, Hal, Johnny, and Tom.

⌁

To Mrs. Middleton, Middleton Place

Thursday 22nd April 1841

It is now two weeks since I have rec^d a letter from you, my dearest Mamma, and for some days past my impatience has been encreased by frequent disappointments– and I cannot help feeling some uneasiness at this unusual silence– trying however to persuade myself that it is entirely owing to accident, & that one of y^r letters has met with the same delay which prevented y^r receiving one of <u>mine</u>– But the unwelcome thought of <u>Sickness</u> will intrude itself on my imagination notwithstanding my efforts to believe that this cannot be the reason for my not hearing– for in that case, surely one of my brothers w^d immediately write– I will not think of it, but hope to have my fears set at rest this very eveng– & meantime will quiet them as I best may– Since I wrote to you Poor Tom Francis has breathed his last– and his poor Mother is in the most indescribable state of wretchedness– His betrothed has been also in a dreadful condition– & for 3 days never closed her eyes or tasted a mouthful of food– They have since succeeded, by the aid of strong opiates, in producing sleep– but it will be very long before she regains anything like composure– <u>Her</u> grief, however, will not it is to be supposed, be <u>permanent</u>– She is very young & the <u>first</u> sorrow is more acute perhaps than even that of the Mother, who has been long schooled in affliction but <u>she</u> will never recover this loss– and is doomed to witness another of her Sons, her sole remaining one, perish also– for there is a very slender chance of Alfred's recovery– and he will probably soon return home to die– Poor Tom was perfectly resigned to his fate– & hearing that Mr Odenheimer had called to enquire after him, expressed a desire to see him– The following day, Mr O. came again and earnestly requested to be allowed to go up and comfort the sufferer– Mrs F. refused, not wishing to endanger his life, & when he pressed it, saying that he considered his duty to be at his bedside, she replied firmly that it was <u>hers</u> to prevent him from risking not only <u>his</u> life but that of his wife and child, to whom he might communicate the dreadful disease– Finding that he could not prevail upon her to permit him to go up stairs, he proposed that they sh^d unite in prayer for him there– which she of course consented to do– and it must have been some comfort to the poor fellow to know this– Mrs Francis certainly shewed her good sense & good feeling too I think– but it must have been at the expense of interfering with her Son's inclinations, a sacrifice for her to make– The interment took place the following day– for it was thought expedient to remove the corpse as soon as possible– such was the virulence of the disorder– They have taken every precaution possible– in painting, white washing & burning tar &c. Maria Page has taken the vaccine well– Nancy has not yet– but, altho' they both went up & kissed their Uncle before his death, it is to be hoped they will escape the infection.

I had the pleasure of receiving a long letter from Ed^d yesterday, of the 2nd of March, from Rio– a very late date– He writes in good spirits, but says it is nearly certain that he must remain there until the Spring or Autumn of /42– They were preparing to go to sea, & their probable destination was the river La Plata, which, next to the Delaware or Hudson, is the most welcome cruize he could make, he says– He mentions having written to you lately– and entreats us both to write often– expressing his warmest thanks for my last letter of Decr which he had rec^d. He had had the pleasure of meeting young Pringle– son of Mr Wm B. P[ringle][1] whom he found very gentlemanlike & pleasing– and who gave him news of John, & other friends in Charleston. I see that Mr Middleton has arrived at Boston by the Columbia– but fear it is not Arthur, but M^r H[enry] A[ugustus] M. who was thinking of returning Lizzie writes me word–

The Channings are all staying at Mrs Hare's– I walked up to see them after Tea last night– & spent two hours very agreeably– We cannot have a Party for them now, of course– but Mrs Fisher intends me to ask them to come & hear some music (of which they are very fond) next week– Mrs Hare wanted me to play for them last night– but her Piano was so dreadfully out of tune that I gave it up in despair after trying it in every imaginable key– & singing to it was quite out of the question. The D^r [*Channing*] was quite talkative, & I listened with deference to his Sageness– Mary is a nice girl, & a sensible one certainly– but oh! that Boston Twang![2]

Afternoon– Just this moment [I] had the happiness of hearing you were all [well] on the 18th by y^r letter dearest Mamma– Thank God! my fears were all groundless– Sally is indeed dilatory– & will have little time left to be at M. Place. I wrote to John a few days ago & directed to Georgetown, thinking he w^d still be there– You will probably receive a letter from Uncle Oliver by the Columbia– Great fears are entertained for the safety of the President, in which George Thorndike went out– If any accident sh^d have occurred– Poor Sophia![3]

Friday morng– We have been talking about New Port at breakfast, dear Mamma, & trying to persuade Mrs F. to go there– but she positively refuses to think of it, & says the only chance of her going is if M^r & M^{rs} H[arrison] consent to pass a couple of weeks there, on their way to Boston– & this is by no means probable– & will only happen if the Hotel at Longbranch should be closed this summer– in which case they may be induced to pay Mrs Ritchie a visit at her Cottage at Brooklyne–[4] which her Father has hired for her for next Summer– With regard then to Perry's– if Mrs F. still continues inexorable & you think there is really no probability of John & Sally going to New Port, and it will put my brothers to no inconvenience (Ed. appears to be out of the question, but Arthur w^d want one of the rooms we occupied probably) all these ifs considered & answered– Fisher must then decide– Of course it w^d be far more agreeable to me to be under y^r roof, particularly, as in all probability this will be the last Summer that I <u>could</u> pass there but I cannot quite give up the idea of having Mrs F. with us– altho' she insists upon it, that as she interfered with our going to the South, she will certainly not separate me from my family on this occasion–

Fisher found your Grandfather,[5] reduced in dimensions, from a <u>full length</u> to merely a bust, at an Auction Store, & immediately bought him, intending to present him to you, if you care to have him in y^r possession at New Port– He is a very good looking old gentleman– and the Portrait is no doubt accurate (as Peale's always were considered so) even to the <u>Mole</u> faithfully copied on his forehead– I fancy I see a resemblance to <u>John</u> about the Mouth– Only think of my not having even mentioned dear Baby's name! She is perfecty well, & has a 4$^{\underline{th}}$ Tooth thro'– 2 Lower, & 2 upper ones– She is very good, sitting on the floor for an hour together amusing herself with her Toys, and <u>Dolly</u>, of whom she is excessively fond– Makes no more <u>distinct</u> sounds– but creeps perfectly well, & stands with very little assistance– I am having all her short clothes made, & as soon as the weather is <u>tolerably</u> good, shall put them on– but not whilst we have rains and east winds constantly. It is the worst April ever recollected here, they say. I must not scratch any longer– so Goodbye dearest Mamma– With love to Papa, who is at home by this time I suppose, my brothers, Kitty and the dear Children one & all– Y^r most affectionate Daughter Eliza

Mrs F. joins Fisher in best regards & thanks for y^r remembrance– M^r & Mrs H. would wish me to say something kind for them if they knew of my writing. He has been quite indisposed and had a blister applied to his Chest yesterday, which relieved the pain somewhat, but he cannot be well until the weather clears up a little– It is most unseasonable–

Private Collection

1. The Pringles' son John Julius was a young naval officer.

2. After a dinner party with them, Eliza said, "I like them all in their different styles– The D$^{r's}$ is rather <u>didactic</u>, but instructive, and he gave me some new ideas in a Chapter on Education, with which he favoured me– Mary is decidedly clever, & very unaffected & pleasing, but rather infected with some of Miss Martineau's notions on the rights of women I should infer from a conversation I heard." EMF to MHM, April 29, 1841, private collection.

Harriet Martineau (1802–1876) was a friend of the Channings. In *Society in America* and *Retrospect of Western Travel,* she was critical of the position of women in the United States, saying they were taught to think of marriage as their only option. She argued that women should be allowed to participate in the political process.

3. The *President,* a new oceangoing steamship, left New York on March 11, 1841,

and disappeared in a storm. George Thorndike, whom Sophia had married, was lost along with all the other passengers.

4. Brookline, now part of the greater Boston urban area, was at that time still very rural.

5. Fisher found a portrait, painted by Charles Willson Peale, circa 1770, of Mrs. Middleton's grandfather John Inglis (1708–1775). Born in Scotland, Inglis settled in Philadelphia in the early eighteenth century; Mrs. Middleton's mother, Mary Inglis Hering, was born there in 1742.

～

To Mrs. Fisher, Philadelphia

M.P. Ap$\underline{l}$ 30$\underline{th}$ 1841

My dearest Eliza

I have had the happiness within the last two hours to receive your three letters (the last dated the 22$\underline{d}$) one from Arthur, one from Ed$\underline{d}$ (of Feb$\underline{y}$) one from my Brother, & one from my Sister S[carbrough] for all which I am most thankful, for all seem in health– but I must begin my news by informing you of Sally's safety & the birth of a little girl about 14 (born on the 18th) days ago– She wrote me a note in answer to one I had written, to say that she had been much blessed this time & had little else to complain of at present than too frequent headaches & pain in the eyes which she hoped would wear off when she is able to leave her bed. "The baby is a healthy looking little creature, & is to be christened <u>Maria</u> if she lives." Your Father & Brothers went to Charleston 4 days ago, but as I had not received letters from you for nearly 3 weeks, I thought it best to defer writing until I could receive them, & communicate the news of Sally's safety. Emma had spent a day & night here last Sunday, & from her I heard of the event having taken place, though she was ignorant of the sex of the infant having by mere chance learnt from little Prof[esso]r Gibbes who she met on the road that Sally was at last confined–

May 1$\underline{st}$ I was compelled yesterday Eve$\underline{g}$ for want of sufficient light to stop writing, Now, that the children are all in the garden I may proceed. Sally told Harry that she should not be able to come here, as John was to remain at Waccamaw until the 15$\underline{th}$ & on the 20$\underline{th}$ the family are all to go there, except Hal who is to be left at school– I still hope I may see her by going rather earlier than usual to Charleston & by their postponing for a few days their departure, but as you may suppose these arrangements cannot be made by me– Y$\underline{r}$ Father & W$\underline{m}$ are to go to Combahee in a day or two & remain there 3 weeks, so that it is very uncertain whether I shall see her– it is a great comfort however to know that she is going on well & free from any symptoms of consumption.

I think Arthur's letter of 20$\underline{th}$ & 22$\underline{d}$ March w$\underline{d}$ give you so much pleasure that I will copy it for you. " 'What on earth can Arthur be about!' has been repeated more than once, I doubt not, during the last two months– & to say the truth I am as much surprised as you can be to find myself so far from home at this time & if you tax me with heartlessness I shall not know how to acquit myself except by reminding you of that uncontrollable spirit of wandering & that absorbing admiration of the fine arts which do not exclude my better feelings (as I trust) but only keep them waiting for a moment (Indeed I thought it best to satisfy my longing at once while I could easily, than to let it remain as a germ of future unquietness–) now being tolerably satiated with sightseeing I could settle down as quietly as any one, but then I must have a family, to fix me– & must set about arranging the matter while I am in the humour.[1] Coming out of S$\underline{t}$ Peters this afternoon who should I meet but Rob$\underline{t}$ Pringle! You may suppose how much I had to say to him– & on the whole his report was highly satisfactory– if you are none of you more changed than he is it will be quite consoling– this makes up for the disappointment I felt in not meeting H. A. Mid[dleton] here from whom I expect$\underline{d}$ to get the amplest details about you all. Well! it will not now be long before I shall have the pleasure of receiving them from y$\underline{r}$ own lips– but if I sh$\underline{d}$ prolong my stay here for a few weeks longer you will not think too hardly of me, will you Mother? When I once get back again, it will probably be for good, so that I want to satiate myself once for all with sights & shows, & thus extinguish all pretext for future gadding– Au revoir my dear Mother, write immedi$\underline{y}$ & it will reach me in Paris. Give all my friends fair notice I am coming so that they may not have any pretence for treating me like a Man already dead & who ought to have been buried." With love &c

I can no longer abstain from expressing the various feelings which your letters gave rise to. M$\underline{rs}$ Fisher's severe attack grieved me exceedingly & so did the sad bereavement suffered by poor M$\underline{rs}$ Francis– She is indeed greatly to be pitied & from what you write must still be in dread of losing another son– pray let me know how she is, & whether the rest of the family have escaped the infection– You too were not well, although the other letters give a more favourable account both of yourself & M$\underline{rs}$ Fisher, & the Baby will no doubt thrive as well on the wholesome food prepared for her as from depriving you of y$\underline{r}$ nourishment. You have been well advised to wean her, & I hope will soon regain your strength & embonpoint. Try to do so that I may meet you looking & being in good health. When will that be? how can I tell– I have no voice in the matter as you know. When M$\underline{rs}$ F. is quite recovered, I hope she may be at last prevailed upon to join the party at Newport for you would all feel uncomfortable by being separated during the summer. Make no more objections about occupying the rooms you had last year. Arthur & W$^{\underline{m}}$ as I said before will be well accommodated in the one next to mine, & though I cannot help sometimes flattering myself with the hope of enjoying your & y$^{\underline{r}}$ Brother's society in a few months, yet so often have my fondest hopes been disappointed that I try to banish my airy castles– Is not the conclusion of his letter portentous? you will call me superstitious perhaps so I will say no more on the subject.

The Steamer President has probably been either destroyed by Icebergs or has stopped at some Island to obtain coals– this remains still undecided– I am glad that Arthur's voyage will be made in Summer, still a voyage is always exposed to dangers. Poor Sophia Thorndike will be in great affliction should the Steamer be lost. Emma mentioned very strange news which had been communicated through the medium of M$^{\underline{rs}}$ [Alice] Heyward rec$^{\underline{d}}$ from M$^{\underline{rs}}$ J[ames] Otis, that of an infant having made its appearance to the astonishment of the M$^{\underline{rs}}$ Ulricks [*Oelrichs*] – she says you must know all about it as it is the town talk at N.Y.! M$^{\underline{rs}}$ T[horndike] acted very wrong in not imparting the fact of her marriage to her Sisters, because she was introduced by them as <u>Miss</u> T. to their circles.

2$^{\underline{d}}$ Emma & her Sister Eliza [Huger] came yesterday with W$^{\underline{m}}$ & will spend a few days with me. M$^{\underline{r}}$ [Allen] S[mith] is gone to Sav$^{\underline{a}}$ river– You will be glad to know that she looks better than she did last week, & she begs me to give her love to you & say that you owe her a letter. I asked her for some Charles$^{\underline{n}}$ news for you, she knows of none but Alicia M[iddleton]'s[2] engagement to one of D$^{\underline{r}}$ King's Brothers– I suppose you saw the announcement in the papers of Motte M[iddleton]'s marriage to Bessy Hamilton.[3] Oliver brought Mary yesterday & he will carry her & Susan & Hal back to Charl$^{\underline{n}}$ this afternoon that they may return to their schools so that I shall have only Sarah & the 2 little boys for the next 3 weeks. Sally wishes them to remain here that they may not pass that time in idleness, as she can not hear them their lessons, & sent a message by Emma to beg me to be in Charleston in time to see her before she leaves it for Wacamaw.

I have mentioned to y$^{\underline{r}}$ Father y$^{\underline{r}}$ wish to have the Guittar brought when we go, he seems inclined to send it down by the boat tomorrow to be sent by a brig on the point of sailing for Phil$^{\underline{a}}$ I don't know its name or whether he will send it– at all events you will have it sooner or later. He & y$^{\underline{r}}$ Brothers all send their love to you pray give mine to M$^{\underline{r}}$ & M$^{\underline{rs}}$ Fisher with my best wishes for her speedy recovery & believe me my dearest Eliza y$^{\underline{r}}$ Affec$^{\underline{te}}$ Mother M. H. M.

PHi

1. Arthur's description of traveling along the French Riviera and the coast of Italy is omitted here.

2. Alicia Middleton (1824–1898), daughter of John and Mary (Burroughs) Middleton, did not marry Kirkwood King.

3. J. Motte Middleton (1817–1871) married Elizabeth Hamilton, daughter of Gen. James Hamilton. He was Alicia Middleton's brother (see above).

～

To Mrs. Middleton, Middleton Place

Thursday 6$\underline{\text{th}}$ May 1841

Altho' your letters are certainly worth two of mine, my dearest Mamma, I am not satisfied to hear from you but once a fortnight, when I write so punctually once a week– and grumble and fidget a great deal after ten days have passed over without hearing from you– There may be some irregularity in the mail since all the changes have been made in the P.O. department– and our new letter carrier is very much puzzled to find the right Houses and People– but unless I receive a letter this eveng– I shall be troubled. This is the 9$\underline{\text{th}}$ and therefore decisive day from the one on which we were vaccinated– and contrary to all expectation, I have not taken it– and Fisher has! My arm looked at first inflamed, and I was quite convinced I had the proper kind, altho' the D$\underline{\text{r}}$ was not, & he now pronounces that it was only a Spurious inflammation, which has entirely subsided– proving that I did not require re-vaccination– having originally had the disease– which Meigs is of opinion is never reproduced– On the contrary Fisher he thinks could never have had the right sort– and indeed from the first, he said his mark was too large, & looked as if there had been too much local inflamation– and he now is decidedly of opinion that he now has taken the vaccine thoroughly & properly for the first time– Only think how fortunate it is that I induced him to have it repeated! For he was of course just as liable to take the Small Pox in the natural way, as to receive the vaccine infection! I am indeed most thankful that he yielded to my entreaties, and now can almost believe that my fears were excited for the purpose of guarding him against that terrible malady– from which it w$\underline{\text{d}}$ appear from Meigs' opinion he is now securely shielded– He thinks us both entirely so– and w$\underline{\text{d}}$ have no hesitation in sending us to a Small Pox hospital he says! This however I should be extremely sorry to try– But I am rejoiced that the experiment has been made upon me, & satisfied that I need feel no further alarm, either for myself or my

Husband– or for Baby for some years– I have heard of no more cases, & the gales of the last few days have no doubt completely purified the atmosphere.

We had the Channings here <u>sociably</u> on Tuesday eveng– and M<u>rs</u> Robinson,[1] M<u>rs</u> McEuen & Miss Binney to meet them– and several agreeable Beaux– I had the Piano put in <u>perfect</u> Tune and played much to their apparent satisfaction. The D<u>r</u> is extremely fond of Music, & really seemed to enjoy it– Judge Hopkinson too was as usual very complimentary. Unfortunately Fisher had one of his bad headaches, & was unable to make his appearance– Notwithstanding which we managed to get on very well, & the eveng passed off agreeably– M<u>rs</u> & Miss Channing expressed a great desire to hear [*Mozart's*] Don Giovanni & I promised to go with them the following night if F. was well enough– and as he insisted that he was, we made up a Party, & went on Wednesday eveng– The Music, which you know is beautiful, was admirably well performed both by the Orchestre & Singers– of whom there is an unusually large number– 5 <u>good</u> ones– Miss Poole has a remarkably sweet pure voice, and some of the others are excellent– But altho' I have hardly ever been more delighted by Music, yet the whole Plot, the character of the Hero &c were so bad, & the dialogues <u>spoken</u> & not recitatived, so coarse & vulgar that I shall certainly not go to hear it again– at the Theatre– but if they give a Concert (which they expect to do) shall be delighted to listen to the Music– Miss Channing & I both agreed that our <u>disgust</u> almost predominated over our pleasure, altho' we tried to talk whenever the Music paused– The translation appears to be a particularly bad one–

Friday 7<u>th</u>! A Thousand thanks dearest Mamma for your delightful and long letter of the 2<u>nd</u>, which I was overjoyed to receive last eveng– I was very glad indeed to hear such good accounts of you all, and dear Sally particularly, and also the very name which I was in hopes she w<u>d</u> give the newborn Baby– You must really go to Town in time to see them– and then perhaps you may induce Papa to allow you to come North rather earlier too, with Harry or W<u>m</u>, if he cannot arrange his business in time to accompany you– Pray thank him for so promptly complying with my request about the Guittar– I heard M<u>me</u> Goñi again last night at a little Party at M<u>rs</u> Davis'– and she enchanted every body with the sweet Tones she brought from it– but to return to y<u>r</u> letter–

I am much obliged to you for transcribing Arthur's letter, for it amused me very much– It is very suspicious I think that he sh<u>d</u> talk in the same breath of <u>settling</u> quietly, and having a family to fix him– and being in the humour to arrange the matter! Perhaps there is some fair English woman at Rome who has won his heart– and will return home with him– I trust he is not thinking of an Italian Wife– at least with <u>Italian principles</u>– As he wishes you to write &

direct to Paris, he must expect to be still there next month, & will not sail before July I suppose– Therefore I do not advise you to look for him until August–

I am glad you had the pleasure of a visit from Emma & Eliza– I wrote to the former a few days ago– Has she decided upon New Port for next Summer? I cannot persuade Mrs F. to think of going there– unless M^r & Mrs H. will also consent to pass a week or two on their way to visit Mrs Ritchie at Brooklyne– which it is possible they may do, if the House at Longbranch is shut up– James Otis writes F. from N.Y. "I hope the young Beauty I saw at y^r house will continue to grow in grace & beauty, although more of either may not be desirable for her welfare"– There is the testimony of an impartial witness to my dear little girl's attractions– I assure you he is not her only admirer– I hope she will keep her good looks until you come for I shall really be proud to shew her to you with her brilliant complexion– I am all the time regretting that she is not called Mary Helen– for she is worthy of wearing that name indeed– & certainly resembles you– I must say Adieu, dearest Mamma, as I have 19 visits to pay with F. & must set about them– Love to all from Y^r ever affectionate Daughter Eliza

Fisher & his Mother both desire their kind regards– The latter is entirely recovered– Mr Harrison is well, & out again– Mrs Smith was at the Party last night– & I told her about y^r letter–

Private Collection
This is the last letter from Eliza in 1841, except for one written in early June during a trip up the Susquehanna and Juniata Rivers in Central Pennsylvania.

1. Perhaps Mrs. Moncure Robinson, the former Charlotte Randolph Taylor. Her husband, an engineer, was building the Philadelphia and Reading Railroad at this time.

~

To Mrs. Fisher, Philadelphia

Charleston May 30th 1841

My dearest Eliza
To my great surprise & delight y^r letter of the 26th reached me yesterday, the quickest passage I have ever known– in compliance with your request I hasten to communicate what has just been decided upon relating to poor Sally– I was greatly shocked a few days before I left the country to hear of the attack

she had had after being so unusually well for a fortnight after the birth of the child. I arrived here on the 26$\underline{th}$ & found her two Aunts sitting by her bed paying her every attention. At that time she had no fever– but it returned the day after together with severe pains in her legs & back which she thinks proceed from a cold caught a fortnight since, but Susan tells me it is a symptom of consumption among many others which affect her. Yesterday she was better, free from fever until the Eve$\underline{g}$– when D$\underline{r}$ Ogier[1] found her pulse too quick though he considered her better– She coughs very seldom & not violently– but she has had night sweats frequently, which are beginning to be less severe– I have said all I could to dissuade John from taking her to the Beach, it was out of his power to take her to Aiken, & after a few days of suspense W$\underline{m}$ yesterday proposed to your Father to take her & Sarah to Newport where he would give up his room to her, & she would be spared the trouble of having the other children to fatigue her, besides which y$\underline{r}$ Father, he says, cannot accommodate any more Ser$\underline{ts}$.[2] He will not hear of your going to a boarding house, neither will I, so I entreat you & M$\underline{r}$ F. to occupy the rooms you did last summer. It would make me very unhappy were you to abandon them, & surely you would not do so, when I beg you to be always under the same roof with me when in your power. W$\underline{m}$ can easily find a bed room near our house, & seems highly pleased with the arrangement. Think too how many intervals would occur between our meetings were you in another house, & do not deprive me of the only comfort I promise myself, that of having you at all hours near me– you must not indeed disappoint me my dear Eliza.

M$\underline{rs}$ W$\underline{m}$ Pringle is so kind as to promise to take charge of the two little girls, John will have the two younger boys at the Beach, & Hal is to remain at school with M$\underline{r}$ Coates.[3] this is the only arrangement that can be made, & I hope the sea voyage may restore the poor invalid to even a moderate share of health– perfect health she can never enjoy, & I doubt whether the air of Newport will be beneficial to a consumptive patient– I have just stopped D$\underline{r}$ Ogier on his way downstairs to ask him what he thinks of her– he is of opinion that she is better, & is glad to hear of the intended voyage, & recommends her taking a drive in the Carriage before she goes on board. <u>That</u> may not happen for a fortnight, the Allen not having yet arrived– We made a voyage in it in /39, & the cabin is not quite as close as the generality of them are, there being a Curtain to divide the two, instead of partitions. M$\underline{rs}$ Arthur Hayne[4] is to be a passenger, which I am glad of on Sally's account. M$\underline{rs}$ W[illiam] Pringle is one of the kindest women I know, & it is most fortunate that the infants will have so affectionate a protector. M$\underline{rs}$ J$\underline{s}$ R. P[ringle] & M$\underline{rs}$ C. Alston offered to take charge of Sarah but the present plan is the best, & I hope it may not be altered.

Emma Smith was here yesterday the second time since I came, & exerted herself very kindly in rubbing Sally's legs with brandy & salt,[5] & doing all she could for her. Y^r Aunt Huger came some days ago & recommended that mixture to be taken internally– it <u>is</u> said to be a cure for consumption but of course Sally w^d not venture upon taking it without medical advice. Susan comes frequently & is looking tolerably well, though thin– Livy[6] is not quite well, but Mrs Chisolm is better, & is going the end of the week to Eding's bay.[7] Susan would like to join her in two or 3 weeks, but Oliver wishes to remain here until July. He begged me, as I said I was going to write to you to tell you he had sent you a barrel of Corn Grits by the Oneco (Sloop) Cap^n Tobey– it has arrived at Philad^a. It was ground on his plantation & he thinks it will last you all the Summer. My little namesake[8] is a remarkably fine healthy child, very lively, dark eyes, but her other features like her fathers. the youngest is also very fat & large for a child of 6 weeks old but at present not pretty– Oliver's last child is not yet named.[9] I have not yet seen it, all my time having been taken up with the poor invalid.

Sarah seemed much pleased with y^r message, & with the thoughts of meeting you at Newport. Alice [Heyward] & Georgina [Middleton] called here a few days ago– the former has been exceedingly kind to Sally– Ge^a is to set out tomorrow for Buncombe. Anne M[iddleton] is engaged to be married to Mrs Dehon's[10] second son who is to take orders soon– Emma [Rutledge] Blake has another Son at Buncomb. I have heard lately from y^r Aunt Rutledge– though a very old date. She had not had a letter from you (as she did not mention it) & I therefore sent her y^r postscript which gave me the account of Miss G[adsden]'s death, which I thought w^d be a melancholy pleasure for her to read– She has been in great affliction about that event. I have not yet seen Mrs Blamyer. give my love to Mrs Smith & tell her she <u>must</u> go to Newport. It is to be hoped Mrs Fisher may accede to your proposal of joining her family there it would I am sure be of benefit to her health– with love to her & M^r F– I am my dearest Y^r affect^{te} Mother M. H. M.

Y^r Brothers & Susan & Sally send their best love to you, as does y^r Father– write soon & tell me when you expect to be at Newport.

ScHi

1. Dr. Thomas Louis Ogier (1810–1900) studied medicine in Charleston and Paris. He was Dr. Holbrook's partner.
2. Presumably additional servants would be needed if the children came too.
3. Charles Coates ran a well-known school for boys on Wentworth Street in

Charleston, where the sons of many prominent families such as the Middletons, Rutledges, and Pringles were educated.

4. Elizabeth Alston Hayne was a sister of Mrs. William Bull Pringle, Charles Alston, and Mrs. Robert Y. Hayne. She was the second wife of Arthur P. Hayne, who represented South Carolina in the Senate in the 1850s; his brother was former Sen. Robert Y. Hayne.

5. There was something of a fad for using brandy and salt for almost any ailment. It was touted as good for "reduction of inflammation of fractured limbs, the alleviation of incurable sores, in headache, toothache, inflammation in the eyes. . . etc. etc." The directions were to fill a bottle 3/4 full of brandy, add enough salt to fill the bottle, shake for 10 minutes, let the salt settle, and use without further shaking. *Phila. GCI,* January 25, 1841.

6. Livy was Oliver and Susan's daughter, Olivia. She was two years old.

7. Eding's Bay, where the Oliver Middletons and other planter families sometimes spent the summer, was on the Atlantic Ocean side of Edisto Island.

8. Sally and John's daughter, Mary Helen, was about eighteen months old.

9. The child was eventually named Emma.

10. Sarah (Russell) Dehon was the widow of Theodore Dehon, bishop of South Carolina. Their son, William (1817–1862), ordained in 1841, married his first cousin Anne Manigault Middleton. She was the daughter of Alicia (Russell) and Arthur Middleton of Bolton plantation on the Stono River.

∽

To Mrs. Fisher, Philadelphia

Charleston June 7<u>th</u> 1841

I have been disappointed for the last three days my dearest Eliza by not receiving a letter from you– perhaps you are deferring to write until your return to Philad^a which you said was to take place on the 8<u>th</u>.[1] in that case your letter will miss me for the Allen is to sail on the 9<u>th</u>. You will be happy to learn that Sally is improving daily in health & strength. She has taken three drives & finds great benefit from them. the pains in her legs & back diminish, & no fever has occurred since I last wrote. So that we must hope that by the time you meet her she will be in as good health as she was before the late attack.

A most astounding communication was made to me just before dinner– M^r W[illiam Bull] Pringle had rec^d a letter from Robt P. mentioning that Arthur had invited him to visit a Roman Genl to whose beautiful daughter he was to be married the following Sunday! Your inference then from what he wrote respecting his settling down, but it being necessary to have a family to fix him was well founded. John was of the same opinion with you. I hope however the news is not true– Italian women are not famous for morality, nor for good educations.

8$\underline{th}$ Yesterday eve$\underline{g}$ M$\underline{rs}$ W. P. came & related to me the contents of the letter– besides what I have told you, she says the young lady is of an old family but has no fortune– What imprudence of Arthur! the marriage was to have taken place the 2$\underline{d}$ of May– no name was mentioned.[2] R[obert] P[ringle] was at Florence. It will be some weeks ere Arthur's letter will reach me as he always sends them by the Havre packets– the above mentioned came by the Acadia– Susan also came yest$\underline{y}$ eve$\underline{g}$ & said Oliver would not believe the news. it is of so unpleasant a nature that I hope it may not be true. Could he have found a young woman resembling Susan & Sally in disposition & good principles I should have no objection to her. from the short acquaintance that preceded the marriage how could Arthur judge of the character of the one he has chosen? Do you remember how he used to joke about marrying a shrew, & insisting that he could succeed like a second Petruchio[3] in reforming her? I fear he will be compelled to follow that plan. You will say I always look on the dark side of every thing.

Emma & Sabina [Lowndes] were here yesterday, the former has no intention of going to the north immediately but sh$\underline{d}$ the heat disagree with M$\underline{r}$ S. in the course of the summer they may perhaps leave Charleston. Hen$\underline{a}$ R[utledge] is still very unwell at Buncomb, but rather better than she was. I believe I mentioned in my last her late confinement. The Haynes have given up their staterooms to the Coffins,[4] & intend to proceed by rail road to N.Y. perhaps you may meet them there– they are to be at the Waverley for a few days– The Children are so riotous I am every minute interrupted, & must therefore conclude with love to M$\underline{r}$ & M$\underline{rs}$ Fisher & believe me my dearest Eliza y$\underline{r}$ Affect$\underline{te}$ Mother M. H. M.

Sally & y$\underline{r}$ Father & brothers send their love– PS. I have been thinking that sh$\underline{d}$ you be at N.Y. before me you could do me a service by enquiring of Elizabeth Mit[chell] thro' Miss Moore, whether the good Cook & Housemaid I had last summer are willing to come again to remain until the end of Oct$\underline{r}$ It w$\underline{d}$ be difficult to find such good people– sh$\underline{d}$ they be in place perhaps Eliz$\underline{th}$ could recommend two others. let me find a letter from you at the Clinton. Sh$\underline{d}$ Miss M. have left N.Y. you can find Eliz$\underline{th}$ at M$\underline{r}$ Rob$\underline{t}$ Minturn's very near Miss M's residence.

ScHi

1. Eliza and Fisher had taken a trip along the Susquehanna and Juniata Rivers in central Pennsylvania.
2. In the next bulletin from Italy, Mrs. Middleton learned that "the name of the

Bride was Bentivoglio– the Father, Principe, as well as Genl." MHM to EMF, June 19, [1841,] PHi.

    3. In Shakespeare's *The Taming of the Shrew*, Petruchio sets out to tame and wed quick-tongued Kate.

    4. Thomas Aston Coffin (1795–1863), a planter on St. Helena Island, had a house in Newport. His wife, the former Harriet McPherson (1812–1852), was Sally Middleton's cousin.

〜

To Mrs. Fisher, Philadelphia

N. York June 16$\underline{th}$ 1841 <u>before breakfast</u>

Here we are my dearest Eliza! & I was delighted to have y^r letter of the 14$\underline{th}$ put into my hands yesterday a few minutes after my arrival– at first when I asked for a letter it was said there were none, & I began to fear that illness had prevented y^r writing– however the welcome letter was soon after put into my hands. Sally has improved wonderfully in health & appearance from the voyage which was comparatively a pleasant one, although for the three first days the heat was intolerable– I have reason indeed to be thankful to God for our safety & the absence of storm– The passengers too were friendly & attentive– Mrs Trapier[1] as I took leave of her asked if I had any commands for you as she is to proceed to Philad^a in a day or two, but I told her I expected you had already left it & was flattering myself I might meet you here as one of y^r former letters had given me reason to expect. Of course my wish to have you under our roof remains unchanged– <u>you must positively</u> occupy y^r rooms, so make no more objections– I can manage to keep W^m in the house too–

Elizth Mitchel has been since March in a good place at 10 $ p^r month which she prefers to living with me at 15$ which y^r Father offered. I think I shall manage very well with Marg^t as joint housekeeper with the Cook I had last year & John (the footman) has just been recommending to me an old friend of his as housemaid, so that being all of them acquainted, there is a prospect of the house affairs going on well, Blair the Washer having last year begged to be taken again into Service, & y^r Father & I agreed to her request– You are aware I suppose that he & Harry are coming on by Rail cars this week– whether they will stop at Phil^a I do not know, as they must believe you have already left it. if they should, I have been thinking you might accompany them, instead of Mr Fisher being at the trouble of taking you on to Newport & returning immediately– & by so doing, he can join you earlier perhaps than the 15$\underline{th}$ of July at Newport. I am glad to hear that Mrs F. thinks of visiting that pleasant place– by her intention of going to Longbranch, I may conclude we shall not have the pleasure of meeting M^r & Mrs H. which I am sorry for– pray make them my kind remembrance.

The day I wrote last, after sending off my letter, Sabina & Emma called before dinner bringing farther particulars relating to Arthur, which M^{rs} R[aw-lins] Lowndes had rec^d from her Sister Mrs W. Lowndes[2] who is at Rome– She says Arthur met his bride at a party at the French Ambass$^{r's}$ & when he saw her dark eyes & dark hair exclaimed, that was the style of beauty he had been wishing to have for a wife– a short time, & matters were settled– her Confessor however told the parents that marrying a Heretic w^d endanger their Daughter's salvation. The match was accordingly broken off, & She declared she w^d go into a Convent. It was then renewed, & they were married the 2^d of May, at least that was the day fixed, & M^{rs} L's letter (although Sabina forgot the date) seemed to express that the marriage had taken place. She writes in the highest terms of the beauty & accomplishments of the bride, that she has been very well educated, & that the Carolinians must prepare to receive her cordially. You will study y^r Italian, & I must try to understand her. I suppose she speaks French, otherwise the difficulty of her being understood will be great–

After breakfast– W^m begs me to give his love to you & Mr F. & to say that he will do his best, with pleasure to procure a horse, or horses for you but must first know what kind you want– y^r letter will soon inform him– As I have procured the Ser^{ts} there is nothing to detain me here, & I am begging him to enquire what day the Mass^{ts} is to go to Newp^t Y^r Father supposing he might be unwilling to leave N.Y. so soon told him he could return here after escorting us, if he wished it– He has just told me y^r Father will probably stop for a week at Washington so that you will not see him before you meet at Newport. W^m has just come in to tell me that the Mass^{tts} is not to sail before next Saturday– it is to go as far as Stonington & proceed to Newport wind & weather permit-ting, so that we must hope it may be good, for I do not like to be detained so long here even as Saturday– I must now conclude as Miss Moore is coming soon– With love to M^r & Mrs Fisher believe me my dearest Eliza y^r Affect^{te} Mother M. H. M.

Sally sends her best love to you– Write soon & come if you can, to sail in the Mass^{tts}

PHi

1. Mrs. Trapier was the former Sarah Russell Dehon, daughter of Bishop Theo-dore and Sarah (Russell) Dehon. Her husband, Rev. Paul Trapier, went north regularly to attend Episcopal church meetings.

2. Mrs. Rawlins Lowndes (d. 1883) was the former Gertrude Livingston of New York. Her sister was Mrs. William P. Lowndes; their husbands, William P. and Rawlins Lowndes, were brothers.

⌒

"Time passes [so] pleasantly & rapidly," Fisher assured his family, with "long rides every morning, a walk in the afternoon & music," that he did not miss the fashionable people who left Newport at the end of August. That summer, he and Eliza even succeeded in persuading Mrs. Fisher to pay them a visit, but "frolicking with Lizzie" was perhaps their most enjoyable occupation. Fisher described for the Harrisons how she laughed "to crack her sides" and was a "merry . . . little creature." Eliza, he reported, was "not as strong & active as she was" when she was expecting her first child, but was nevertheless well. He "had no fears for her, but that to my Mother's disappointment she may give me another girl."¹

The Middletons finally received Arthur's "somewhat tardy announcement of his marriage,"² as Eliza described it, in early July. Since he and Paolina were expected in early August, Mrs. Middleton carefully arranged the Newport house so everyone would fit in, but the anticipation was not all pleasurable. Arthur had left behind a reputation as an eccentric dandy, having appeared some years before, for example, at White Sulphur Springs, Virginia, in a "screaming check suit and a velvet shirt."³ Now word came, Mrs. Middleton told Eliza, that "Arthur's passion for dress continues– he wore a black velvet coat with the front all covered with lace & spangles– <u>this</u>, you need not speak of. W͞ᵐ predicts very serious consequences will ensue, should this ridiculous taste be adhered to in this country, & declares he anticipates his arrival with no degree of pleasure. It will make me too, very unhappy should he persist as he has hitherto done, in making himself the subject of ridicule."⁴

When Arthur and Paolina did finally appear, however, Paolina quickly won a place for herself in the family. Mrs. Middleton, who had "a fellow feeling" for Paolina because she was so far from her family and friends, described her as "a very amiable, affectionate young person– a most devoted Wife, with lively & artless manners."⁵ Eliza told Susan she was "full of vivacity and cheerfulness . . . and so affectionate withal– Her devotion to her Sposino [*new husband*] is delightful– I think you will be rather amused at the extent to which she carries it, & her obedience." She continued, "We are disappointed in her beauty, which you must not expect to find, except in her eyes & smile . . . but her manners are most agreeable."⁶

After they left Newport, the Middletons spent three weeks in Philadelphia and then continued on to Charleston at the end of November. Mrs. Middleton left Philadelphia thinking that Eliza's second child would be born in mid-December. In fact the baby took everyone by surprise by appearing three weeks early.

1. JFF to GH, September 10, [1841,] PHi, BrC; MHM to Edward Middleton, August 22, 1841, Edward Middleton Rea Collection.
2. EMF to JFF, July 8, [1841,] MPlFdn.
3. Lawrence F. Brewster, "Summer Migrations and Resorts of South Carolina Low-Country Planters," ser. 26 (Durham, N.C.: Trinity College Historical Society, 1947).
4. MHM to EMF, June 19, [1841,] PHi.
5. MHM to Edward Middleton, August 22, 1841, Edward Middleton Rea Collection; MHM to Susan Middleton, December 2, [1841,] ScHi.
6. EMF to Susan Middleton, December 13, 1841, MPlFdn.

To Mrs. Fisher, Philadelphia

Charleston Nov.͟r 28th, Sunday [1841]

My dearest Eliza

Here we are safe thank God! we arrived at about half past One– it is now nearly 3 o'clock & none of us have eaten any thing today, having had a very rough passage in the Gov.͟r Dudley. We were too sick to have any appetite & on coming to the house found it empty No servants but Peter, Elias, & Celia[1] & we are going to dine on Rice & Bacon & Eggs– this is not to be complained of, you will agree with me, as we have had no accident either in Cars or Steamer which I fully expected to happen.

You must have been glad to hear of me from M.͟rs Kuhn[2] who promised to tell you of our meeting which I was very glad had occurred as she is a pleasant woman & her Daughter a nice Girl. Miss Harper had one of her bad head achs & she could not see me [in Baltimore]. We had a good passage from Baltimore, the whole Cabin to myself & Cath.e a fortunate circumstance, for her conduct was worse than usual– at Portsmouth Maj.͟r & M.͟rs Van Ness joined the party– they had just come from Gen'l V[an Ness']s, his Uncle, & are old acquaintances of Arthur's. They had with them their youngest child & the best behaved I ever saw. She interested me being near dear little Lizzy's age. just 2 y.͟rs old– chattering very fluently induced me to enquire particularly when she began to talk, which her Mother said was at the age of 17 months so that we may hope very soon that the little Pet will begin to amuse you all with her conversation. Poor M.͟rs V[an Ness] had kept her bed 3 weeks at Washington & had a fever on the journey. the Maj.r too had last night a return of fever & Ague– they are on their way to S.t Augustine where he is stationed– She must be a New Yorker from her mode of speech, but nevertheless an amiable person–

You are nearly always in my mind dearest Eliza but I will endeavour not to fancy evils which I trust God may save you from. Mrs Fisher promised to write as soon as the event should happen & I hope she may be gratified by having a Grandson. Mrs Smith too will I hope write on the interesting subject frequently to me. When we heard that scarcely any of the servants were here I begged to be allowed to go to M.P. tomorrow– Y^{r} Father said I might go when I chose in a hired Carriage (our own & horse being in the country) but that he had business to attend to here. You who know the helplessness of C[atherine] may imagine how inconvenient it w^{d} be for me to remain here & y^{r} Father says it is not worth while to send for any more servants– he thinks it probable W^{m} may come this Eve^{g} or tomorrow but no dependance can be placed on his movements– it is a rainy day & I am not likely to see any body & it is not in my power to send this today– the Cap^{n} told me he was to return to Wilmington this eve^{g} but I cannot send this in time. Upon mentioning the plan of going tomorrow y^{r} Father now (After dinner) says that I must stay till W^{m} comes– It is nearly dark & I must conclude as I have to write an order for groceries to be brought early tomorrow morn^{g}.

Y^{r} Father & Harry send their love pray give mine to M^{r} & Mrs F. & Mrs Harrison & let me know how she & Mr H. are. I hope they are both recovering fast– I am dearest Eliza y^{r} affect^{te} Mother M. H. M.

Hal is at school, & Elias says has had an eruption. His [*Elias's*] Wife Jenny is dying poor soul– I had almost forgot to tell you that had it not been for M^{rs} F's kind present of Rusks I sh^{d} almost have starved on the road. I ate 4 for 2 days– the bread was not eatable at the inns, & all the party partook of the rusks. Mrs V. had provided herself with a basket of provisions & that was lucky for me & Cath^{e}

PHi

1. Peter, Elias and Celia were from Middleton Place but seem to have gone to the Boundary Street house in Charleston when the Middletons needed them there. Peter was the cook.

2. Perhaps the Hartman Kuhns' daughter, Mary, who married a cousin also named Hartman Kuhn.

⁓

To Mrs. Fisher, Philadelphia

Charleston Decr 2^{d} 1841

The delight & surprise I experienced yesterday my dearest Eliza in reading Mr Fisher's letter was more than I can express. And how good & kind he was to give me such early intelligence when he must have been so much agitated &

fatigued by losing his nights rest! Pray offer him my best thanks for his most welcome letter.[1] God grant you may continue to do as well as you have begun! Every thing that care & affection can bestow will I am sure contribute to your speedy recovery. The joyful event happening so much earlier than you expected, has saved me from much anxiety as I was looking forward to the middle of next month with occasional sadness. Most thankful am I to the Almighty for having spared you my dearest Child! I approve much of your making no objection to Mr Fisher's naming the Infant after Mrs Harrison. I should have advised you to do so, had I known it was his wish. It will no doubt gratify your kind Aunt, & Lizzy's 'nose will soon be put out of joint' as the old saying is. I fear Mrs Fisher has experienced a second disappointment by not having a Grandson & fancy that Lizzy will continue to be <u>her</u> Pet. I can imagine the little favorite examining her little Sister with attention & crying when she sees you nursing the infant, as I know how jealous she was, when you were occupied by anyone but herself.[2]

So the infant has a dark complexion & black hair! Lizzy had the same, therefore we may look forward to her becoming fair & having light coloured hair. I hope by the time this reaches you Mrs Waters [*the nurse*] may be with you– You have however such good women in the house that knowing all the precautions she insisted on, they may act as substitutes until she is disengaged. I suppose Paolina has been permitted to see you for a few minutes, & also Mrs Smith pray tell her with my love, that I sent the parcel to Mrs Blamyer the morn^g after I arrived, but have not seen her yet. Miss Pinckney, Mrs Izard & Miss Rutledge came to see me & the former insisted upon my using her Carriage yesterday which I did to perform some shopping, & then went to return their visit: we had a long chat about old times– they are very affectionate towards me. They enquired particularly after you– I was ignorant until I returned home of the addition to your family. they will be surprised to hear of it, & so will Sabina Lowndes who came to see me yesterday. Y^r Aunt Huger & M^{rs} T[homas] M[iddleton] came two days ago, but the other two [*Huger*] daughters have not yet made their appearance. Emma went last week to her plantation–[3]

<u>1/2 past 3</u> Y^r Father has just put into my hands Mrs P. Smith's kind & welcome letter giving me the best account of you as late as Sunday– thank her for me most gratefully. She gives a very favourable description of the baby too & what she says of Lizzy agrees with what I had fancied she felt on seeing her Mama nursing her. Little Harry's holidays have begun & he is now staying here– his Mother sent the Carriage down [*from Middleton Place*] just before dinner, that he might return in it tomorrow– She is not aware of our being

here. Moro brings word that Sally & her family are well– I proposed that Isaac should drive Harry Cath^(e) & Marg^(t) [Driscoll] & that I could also find room enough in the Carriage tomorrow but y^(r) father says there would not be room enough– I then said I might wait until the return of it, & that he could drive me & y^(r) Brother up on Sunday– he says he has not finished his business, & cannot go so soon– When I can go then is very uncertain– it is adviseable that Cath^(e) sh^(d) go, for she will not stir out of the house even to walk in the Piazza.

Arthur ought to write to inform me when to expect him that the Carriage may be sent for him, but he is such a lazy fellow about writing that he will I suppose leave it to chance to arrive in the country. Yesterday even^(g) I had the satisfaction of hearing of Susan & her family from her servant Gardenia who had just come from Edisto & said that Susan was well, two of the Children just recovering from the Chicken pox, & M^(rs) C[hisolm] rather better. I wrote this morn^(g) by her a full account of you to Susan & sent y^(r) presents, all except the Music which I [had] begged y^(r) Father to put into his trunk & he could not get it in time for her, so that Mary cannot get it until she is at M. Place where I invited Susan to join us with her family.

Friday morn^(g) Here is a week since your confinement & I trust you are by this time able to sit up & that you feel stronger than at the time of y^(r) first– M^(rs) Smith's account of you gives me reason to believe it may be so– It was too late to send this yesterday after rec^(g) her letter– it must now go after breakfast. The rains since yest^(y) afternoon have been too incessant to admit of Hal's going to M.P. today– here comes an invitation from Miss Pinckney to take Tea with her this Eve^(g). I have not accepted it, but y^(r) Father & Harry have.

I had a visit from M^(rs) C. Harper three days ago, & invited her at the request of y^(r) Father & Harry to make us one at M.P. after Xmas– She accepted it, but told H[arry] afterwards that she feared her Child w^(d) be too troublesome, he however would not listen to that excuse, & they will come I suppose. I shall write to my Brother before I leave Town to be in time for the Acadia of the 16^(th) & give him the good account of you which has made me so happy. Y^(r) Father is going to part with the old Piano forte & buy the most expensive of Chickering's here, to please Paolina. Harry advises him to hire one, but he does as he chooses you know. You may perceive by my blots, that I have not yet arranged y^(r) present the Inkstand– I hope the next letter I receive from Phil^(a) may give a good account of M^(r) & M^(rs) Harrison– pray remember me kindly to them & with love to M^(r) & M^(rs) Fisher believe me my dearest Eliza y^(r) Affect^(te) Mother M. H. M.

Y^(r) Father & Harry send their love– M^(rs) S[mith] says the infant is to be named Sophia Georgina–

PHi

1. On November 26, Arthur and Paolina dined with the Fishers, Paolina and Eliza sang together, and Eliza went to bed at 11 P.M. Sophia Georgina Fisher was born at 2:10 AM, after an "illness of less than an hour!" MHM to Susan Middleton, December 2 [1841,] ScHi.

2. Eliza told Susan that Lizzie was indeed "extremely jealous of Miss Sophia . . . but will I hope soon become reconciled to her altered position, which is only from sole to first darling– for I do not yet love the other as much– nor do I believe I ever can have exactly the same feelings towards any other child. . . Agree with me in confessing that you love most the first child, who called forth all your maternal emotions in their novelty and freshness. You must not however conclude from this, that I have none toward poor little Sophy." EMF to Susan Middleton, December 13, 1841, MPlFdn.

3. Emma Huger Smith, not knowing that the baby had already come, wrote to Eliza on December 15, "I think of you with some uneasiness, my love . . . The first must be so much the most dreaded of these terrible occasions, that my only feeling is for yr sufferings not danger. So be cheered My Child, & meet the moment womanfully– I don't know why that expression should not be as common as manfully." EHS to EMF, December 15, 1841, PHi.

～

To Mrs. Fisher, Philadelphia

M.P. Dec[r] 16th 1841

I was greatly pleased my dearest Eliza to receive your letter of the 8th two days ago, confirming the very favourable accounts I had previously had of you. It is indeed a blessing that you have passed through the dreaded event with such slight pain, & that you continue to do so well as you describe. That it happened so much earlier than was expected saved me much anxiety, for I should have been dreading to hear what you might have suffered about this time. I have now only to be thankful that all is going on so well– You were rather imprudent to write to me by candlelight for the eyes are apt to suffer during the month–[1] but I hope it has had no bad effect on them–

I left Charleston on the 8th & came up alone & found Sally looking & feeling better than she had been on her arrival– The two little Girls are the stoutest I ever saw, & remarkably lively, they are also pretty. M[ary] H[elen] extremely lively, & rather violent, but very soon pacified & is very affectionate. The boys are improved in their learning. Harry is now suffering with Erysipelas in his feet. Your little Sophy must be a great amusement to Lizzy, who by this time I hope is free from any pain in her gums– It was proposed by Will[m] just as dinner was taken off that it would be advisable to send Isaac to Charleston without delay that he might return early tomorrow before the party should set off for Combahee– I was provoked that he should not have given me earlier notice, that I might have written in time to send this– but he observed that I could send it tomorrow by the Schooner, so that you will not get this as soon as you would have done had I known of his intention– but he said he thought of it only at the moment & wished to know whether Arthur had arrived– He has remained longer at Washington than I expected. I suppose there is some gaiety going on there.

I am using the nice little Perryian Ink stand for the first time, being determined that a letter to the Donor should be written through its means. It succeeds perfectly well & prevents blotting by not filling the pen with ink more than is necessary. The weather until today has been remarkably mild & pleasant– rain has fallen this morn^g & prevented any exercise being taken– but a cold wind is now blowing, so that I suppose we shall soon have a frost: the weather while I was in Charleston was rather cold, but not severely so. The Camellias are in high beauty, & so are the fragrant Olives.

Willm for the last 10 days has been wishing to return to Combahee but y^r Father has put off going until tomorrow. There is a very worthless Overseer at Hobonny who has destroyed a large portion of Rice by his negligence & W^m is anxious that he sh^d be dismissed immediately. John has made a very good Crop. I have as yet had no answer to the letter I mentioned having written to Susan. probably next week will bring me news of her & the family– John will be here on the 18th much earlier this year than usual. You cannot imagine how busy I have been in arranging matters for the last week. The Sch[oone]r came up only yesterday & brought the old Piano forte. The plan of purchasing a new one is given up. The old one has been put in order & tuned & sounds better than it did last year. Pray give my love to Mrs Smith & tell her I was much disappointed at not seeing Mrs Blamyer. It would gratify me to hear from her again. As soon as I have some leisure I will answer her first very welcome letter– Pray thank Mr Fisher too for his of the 1st of Decr which was most acceptable. I am extremely sorry to hear of the reason which prevented Mrs Fisher from writing– the death of her good Friend Mrs Waln–[2] 17th What an affliction to her poor Daughters! Mrs F. has lost many of her friends lately. Is Miss Hare recovering? & how is M^r A[lfred] Francis? I am sorry to hear that Mr Harrison is still suffering with rheumatism.

When in Charleston I subscribed for the Qu[arterly] Rev^w[3] & found in that for last March, a very interesting Article on the Boundary question[4] which I recommend to y^r perusal. M^r H[arrison] will lend it to you. It explains very clearly that the disputed territory belongs to G^t Britain. I begged both y^r brothers to read it, but they would not. After reading the Article you will be convinced that the proofs brought forward to justify their (the English) right, are indisputable.

Isaac has just brought me a joint letter from Paolina & Arthur of the 10$^{\underline{th}}$ & they cannot on account of his business, leave Wash$^{\underline{n}}$ before the 20$^{\underline{th}}$ I must transcribe a few lines expressing her affection for you which gratify me exceedingly: "La Lasciai con molto dispiacere perche Elisa e tanto buona, che in cosi poco tempo, l'amo come un sorella e mi e costato molto di lasciarla" [*I left her with great unhappiness because Eliza is so good that even in such a short time I love her like a sister and it was very hard for me to leave her.*] She goes on to say that she had written to you & had rec^{d} y$^{\underline{r}}$ letter– So that you know how she is spending her time at Wash$^{\underline{n}}$ She expresses a wish to come on that she may be acquainted with the rest of the family. I must now finish this. Sally sends her affect$^{\underline{te}}$ regards to you & so does Sarah– Pray present mine to M$^{\underline{r}}$ & M$^{\underline{rs}}$ Fisher & M$^{\underline{rs}}$ Harrison & believe me dearest Eliza y$^{\underline{r}}$ Affect$^{\underline{te}}$ Mother M. H. M.

Write regularly <u>once a week.</u>

PHi

1. A month was the time considered necessary for complete convalescence after having a baby.

2. Mary Wilcocks (Mrs. William) Waln.

3. The *Quarterly Review* was a critical journal published in England.

4. The boundary between Maine and the Canadian province of New Brunswick had never been clearly defined. In 1838, when Canadians began lumbering on land in the Aroostook Valley claimed by the United States, tempers flared and war with England looked likely. This and other differences were settled the following year by the Webster-Ashburton Treaty.

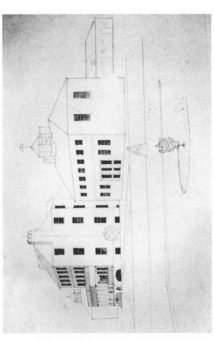

The west side of the house at Middleton Place, showing the library to the left of the house, and the "South Out House," with extra bedrooms, to the right. The stable is to the right of the circular drive. Drawing by Paolina Middleton, circa 1842. Courtesy of Middleton Place Foundation.

The east side of the house at Middleton Place, looking toward the Ashley River. The library is to the right of the house, with the stable showing behind, and across the lawn from it. Drawing by Williams Middleton, probably in the 1850s. Courtesy of Middleton Place Foundation.

Arriving in Charleston by sea. By George Cooke, 1838. I. N. Phelps Stokes Collection, Miriam and Ira D. Wallach Division of Art, Prints, and Photographs, New York Public Library, Astor, Lenox and Tilden Foundations.

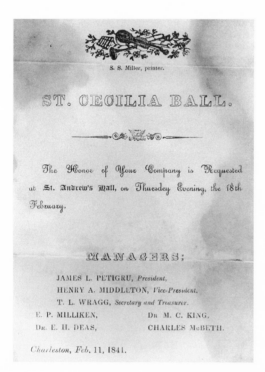

S. S. Miller, printer.

ST. CECILIA BALL.

The Honor of Your Company is Requested at St. Andrew's Hall, on Thursday Evening, the 18th February.

MANAGERS:

JAMES L. PETIGRU, *President*,
HENRY A. MIDDLETON, *Vice-President*,
T. L. WRAGG, *Secretary and Treasurer*.

| E. P. MILLIKEN, | Dr M. C. KING, |
| DR. E. H. DEAS, | CHARLES McBETH. |

Charleston, Feb. 11, 1841.

The St. Cecilia Ball was a highlight of the winter social season in Charleston. Courtesy of South Carolina Historical Society.

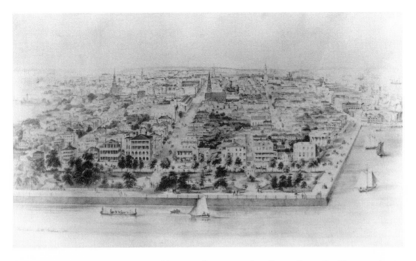

View of Charleston in 1851. Looking north up Meeting Street from the Battery, the Cooper River is to the east and the Ashley River to the west. Courtesy of South Carolina Historical Society.

St. Andrew's Church on the Ashley River Road, where Mrs. Middleton attended services when she was at Middleton Place. Watercolor on paper by Charles Fraser, 1800. (38.36.67) Courtesy of Gibbes Art Museum/Carolina Art Association.

The Fishers' house at 170 Chestnut Street (to the left of 172) was built in the early nineteenth century. By the 1840s many families had moved into newer areas further west, leaving the Fishers surrounded by stores. From *Rae's Philadelphia Panoramic Directory, 1851.* Courtesy of the Library Company of Philadelphia.

The George Harrisons' house at 156 Chestnut Street had a spacious garden behind it. From a drawing by A. Poulson. Courtesy of the Library Company of Philadelphia.

View from Fairmount reservoir, looking down at the city waterworks on the Schuylkill River (no date). Courtesy of the Library Company of Philadelphia.

The Woodlands, built in the late eighteenth century on the west side of the Schuylkill River, was decorated with European artworks and surrounded by landscaped gardens. Eliza described it as the nearest thing to Middleton Place in Philadelphia. Courtesy of the Library Company of Philadelphia.

St. Peter's Episcopal Church on Pine Street in 1829. The Fishers were members, as the Francis and Willing families had been before them. Courtesy of the Library Company of Philadelphia.

The Pennsylvania Institution for the Instruction of the Blind in 1840, of which Fisher was a founder and longtime member of the board of managers. Courtesy of the Overbrook School for the Blind and the Library Company of Philadelphia.

The Henry Middletons' house in Newport. Late nineteenth-century photograph, taken after owner James Gordon Bennett had made changes. Courtesy of Newport Historical Society (P85).

The Middletons and Fishers often took the steamer *Rhode Island* or her sister ship, the *Massachusetts,* between New York and Newport. Postcard (no date). Courtesy of Newport Historical Society (P2881).

An afternoon ride in Newport. Sketch by Williams Middleton, circa 1835.
Courtesy of Middleton Place Foundation.

Visitors arriving in Newport from the sea saw much the same sight as this, with the town rising on the hill behind the harbor. Charcoal drawing by Comte de Trobriand, circa 1854. Courtesy of the Redwood Library, Newport.

Mrs. Middleton and many other summer residents attended
Newport's Trinity Church, built in 1725. By John P. Newell, circa
1860. Courtesy of the Redwood Library, Newport.

The Ocean House opened in 1844, near the Middletons' house. Its 125 rooms
indicated Newport's increasing popularity as a summer resort. Artist unknown.
Courtesy of Newport Historical Society (P2341).

1842

We were much amused to hear Paolina declare that she
preferred Combahee to any place she had been . . . There were
so many things that interested her.

~

In 1842 Mrs. Middleton and Eliza regularly discussed the state of relations between the United States and Great Britain. They were worried that war could break out because of disputes over the northeast boundary between Maine and Canada, the McLeod affair, or England's assertion that it had the right to stop and search American ships suspected of involvement in the slave trade. Mrs. Middleton was afraid that, in case of war, the British would bombard towns along the Atlantic seaboard and incite rebellion among the slaves.

Tension was relieved when Secretary of State Daniel Webster and England's Lord Ashburton reached an amicable settlement of the boundary issue and agreed that the two countries' navies would cooperate in suppressing the African slave trade. The resulting Webster-Ashburton Treaty was ratified by the U.S. Senate in August 1842.

The national economy, meanwhile, continued to be depressed. In South Carolina, the price of rice plummeted in 1842 to half its previous value. Henry Middleton's income was so reduced that, for the first time, he had to delay payment of the annuity of $1,800, which he had promised Eliza at the time of her marriage.

In Philadelphia the streets seemed deserted, "the largest houses are shut up and to rent, there is no business, there is no money, no confidence & little hope," Fisher's cousin said.[1] Eliza's letters described widespread and continuing distress among working people as well as merchants and businessmen. When bank failures continued, Fisher lost the equivalent of more than $150,000 in the Girard Bank. Eliza balanced the gloomy tone of her letters, though, with amusing and interesting details of three prominent Englishmen who added their names to the growing list of Europeans who came to take a look at the United States: Lord Morpeth, who had recently completed six years as chief secretary for Ireland; Charles Dickens; and the geologist Charles Lyell all visited Philadelphia in 1842.

Eliza's and her mother's letters also began at this time to reflect the intellectual ferment and debate surrounding ideas and theories such as homeopathic medicine, animal magnetism, phrenology, and hydropathy.

[1] Wainwright, *Phila. Perspective* (July 15, 1842): 134.

To Mrs. Middleton, Middleton Place

Monday 10ᵗʰ January 1842

My dearest Mamma,

I observe that your letters to me always begin with acknowledgements of the receipt of mine, whereas those I write to you generally contain half a page of complaints at not hearing from you– Now surely this is pretty conclusive proof that you write seldom– for I am very ready to thank you, when I have an opportunity of doing so– but you give it rarely– However I must not forget that I <u>do</u> owe you many thanks for a half letter, recᵈ the day after I sent my last– you were then expecting a letter from Arthur announcing the day of his departure from Washington, but must have been again disappointed, for I learn from Charles Stewart, who came from thence a day or two since, that Mʳ & Mʳˢ Arthur were expected to grace with their presence the grand Ball given by M. Bodisco¹ very lately– He saw them himself (C. S. I mean) & did not hear of any intended departure, I believe– So that I much doubt whether you will see them before the <u>Race time,</u> in Charleston. And John & Sally will be so much out of patience that they will have gone to Waccamaw without seeing them I suppose.² We have all been well since I wrote– Mʳˢ F's cold is cured for the present– until some new imprudence gives her a fresh one– Lily³ has been so carefully kept in her Nursery, or only permitted to go thro' the cold passages well wrapped up, that she has had no more threats of Croup– & old Nurse Waters (who is still here, but goes away tomorrow) thinks the little cough I hear occasionally is only a common symptom of Teething– The Baby is fatter every day, & grows uncommonly fast– She was Christened at Sᵗ Peter's on Thursday, & behaved <u>beautifully</u>– merely whimpering a little at the cold water– but apparently pleased at the ceremony & looking up at the Xmas decorations, & around at the Spectators– Sophia Georgina is now irrevocably her name– & I must be satisfied with it, albeit a far less pretty one than that [*Mary Helen*] I intended for her– Mʳˢ Hare consented, with the kindest expressions about her Parents, to become her God Mother– & Mʳˢ Smith is the other– for I found that Sarah Wise had some scruples, which I did not care to try & overcome–⁴ Fisher stood himself, to solve the difficulty of providing a proper male Sponsor–

We were at Mᵐᵉ Goñi's Concert in the eveng– & heard some delightful music from Mʳ Knoop⁵ the Violoncellist– Notwithstanding the rain the room was well filled, which all the poor lady's friends must have rejoiced at– I had some misgivings about going on account of the weather but I have not suffered in consequence of waiting for the Cab– Soon after we returned home, we had an alarm about Miss Hare, whose woman came running at eleven ocl'ck to say that if Mrs F. wished to see her alive she must immediately go to her– She of course hastened there in great agitation, & found to her relief that it was only a fainting fit, which the woman in her terror at her ghastly complexion had magnified & which she was recovering from when Mrs F. got there– She had been leeched during the day for Spasms in the Throat, & was weakened also from the effects of medicine– but she has rallied again, & is now pretty much as usual– When her summons comes, I suppose it will be made in somewhat the same way, for there appears to be no doubt that the water on her Chest will rise & suffocate her– She is perfectly resigned to go– & says that she has ceased to regard Death with any fear, but will welcome him as the Harbinger of peace, whenever her Heavenly Father wills that she sh^d be removed–

Papa will be sorry to hear that Judge Hopkinson is lying at the last extremity– Fisher was at the Athenaeum when he was seized with an apoplectic Fit, and was carried up & laid in poor Mr Vaughan's bed–[6] where he was bled & blistered and in the course of an hour recovered his sensibility & was taken home– He was then perfectly himself for some hours, & expressed his willingness to die for which he told [Dr.] Chapman he was prepared– Soon afterwards he was again paralysed & his mind is now so much affected, that if he sh^d recover, his memory will be gone, & all his faculties impaired– M^r & M^rs H[arrison] are much affected at this sudden stroke– which will deprive them of one of their oldest & most agreeable friends– Only 2 days previous to his attack, he was paying them a visit, in apparently excellent health & spirits– The numerous warnings we have lately had, ought more forcibly to remind us of the injunction "Be ye also ready"– But alas! we too soon forget that it may be our turn to follow next to the Spirit-Land, & still live on disregarding the necessity of making fit preparation for the last awful hour, & that judgment which inevitably awaits every one of us–[7]

Afternoon– I sh^d like to keep this open until after the mail comes in this afternoon, so sure am I of hearing from you, dear Mamma– but my conscience does not allow me to send down twice to the P.O. thro' such vile weather, so that I must e'en send it without waiting to know if I am to receive news from the South– We heard just before dinner that poor A[lfred] Francis was rather better again– Poor fellow he cannot last more than a few days longer– & was thought so near his end two days ago that Fisher refused an invitation to dine at M^r [Richard] Rush's[8] to meet Lord Morpeth–[9] He went to M^r [Benjamin] Wilcocks[10] Dinner on Saturday when told by D^r C[hapman] that his cousin might linger for some days or even weeks but does not like to give out invitations for a dinner when he might be obliged to recall them– M^r W– had an ill assorted Party of 24– composed of D^rs lawyers & raw boys who had no other qualification than that of being his Nephews– M^r [Edward Shippen] Burd[11] will give his Lordship a <u>splendid</u> entertainment, no doubt– P[eter] McCall[12] who has seen a good deal of him, says he is remarkably pleasant & amiable– He cannot be an admirer of the fair sex, or he would hardly have reached the age of 40 without wooing– Mr Otis wrote to M^r H[arrison] by him– but the latter does <u>not</u> think it incumbent upon him to put himself out of the way to feast him–[13] & Fisher does not think it right to do it, whilst A. F[rancis] is dying– Hearing of little else than sickness & death does not put us in the humor of entertaining– which I fear will be proved by this dull letter. I will try to send something more cheering next time. But the best news I have at present is that our household is well and happy– I hope to hear the same of yours by the return of John from the Office– Adieu in haste with love to all I am y^r affection-ate daughter Eliza

Private Collection

1. In 1840, when he was over fifty, Alexander Bodisco, the Russian minister to the United States, married sixteen-year-old Harriet Brooke Williams. They were very active in Washington society.

2. Emma Smith was just as eager as John and Sally were to meet Arthur's new bride. "[I] must await February with all the patience I am Mistress of," she wrote Eliza. Exaggerating slightly, since Arthur was only forty-six, but perhaps reflecting the prevailing view in Charleston, she joked, "I'm excessively disappointed at Arthur's having gone as far as <u>fifty</u> & Rome & brought us neither a beauty or a musician; but as you speak amiably of her manners & disposition, I hope we have something to love, if not to admire, in our imported relation." EHS to EMF, December 15, 1841, PHi.

3. The Fishers now called Lizzie "Lily."

4. In reply, Mrs. Middleton asked if Mrs. Wise objected "to the little creature's learning to dance? You have heard I suppose of Mr. Trapier's telling the Miss Bowens that if he were a Bishop he would not confirm them, if they danced or went to the Theatre." MHM to EMF, January 15, 1842, ScHi.

5. Monsieur Knoop played in several cities, sometimes with Mme Goñi and some-times by himself.

6. John Vaughan, librarian of the American Philosophical Society, had recently died. He avidly sought out and introduced visitors to Philadelphia, and Fisher remem-bered meeting "distinguished travellers, or literary men from other States" in his rooms. JFF, *Recollections,* 257.

7. "Good health perhaps prevents me from thinking as much as I ought of my duties," Mrs. Middleton told Eliza. "As to thinking of death, however, not a day passes without my bringing it before my mind, & trying to reconcile myself to its approach." MHM to EMF, January 15, 1842, ScHi.

8. Richard Rush (1780–1859) was minister to Great Britain from 1817 to 1823 and was helpful to Henry Middleton in his first years as minister to Russia. As secretary of state under President Monroe, he also negotiated the Rush-Bagot Convention limit-

ing American and British naval armament on the Great Lakes. He was a son of Dr. Benjamin Rush and brother of Dr. James Rush.

9. George William Frederick Howard, Lord Morpeth, later seventh earl of Carlisle (1802–1864), had been chief secretary for Ireland from 1835 to 1841 before traveling in the United States and Canada. An abolitionist, he became an admirer of John Quincy Adams and in 1853 wrote the preface to the British edition of Harriet Beecher Stowe's *Uncle Tom's Cabin.*

Harrison Gray Otis of Boston had written a letter introducing Lord Morpeth to George Harrison. The Middletons had known him in St. Petersburg and hoped to see him in Charleston, but, Mrs. Middleton told Eliza, "this house is in so shabby & dirty a condition that I should be ashamed of his seeing it." MHM to EMF, January 7, 1842, PHi.

10. Benjamin Chew Wilcocks (1776–1845) was in the China trade for many years and had lived in Canton before returning to Philadelphia. He was an old friend of George Harrison.

11. Edward Shippen Burd's house at Ninth and Chestnut Streets was considered one of the finest houses in Philadelphia, where dinners featured "a profusion of wines and delicacies, with a great display of rich plate, china and glass." Wainwright, *Phila. Perspective* (September 23, 1841): 125.

12. Peter McCall (1809–1880), who studied law with Joseph R. Ingersoll at about the same time as Fisher, was elected mayor of Philadelphia in 1844. He later taught law at the University of Pennsylvania.

13. Mr. Otis was doubtless remembering an earlier time when the Harrisons entertained frequently and were known for their "elegant hospitality." According to Fisher, Aunt Harrison presided with grace over "four or five courses with their separate glass & porcelain." Although she herself was not "accomplished" and knew little about art or literature, for example, she was a successful hostess, he thought, because she could "listen at least with intelligence & enjoyment to clever men, & that is often all they want." JFF, *Recollections,* 247–50.

～

To Mrs. Middleton, Middleton Place

Monday morng– 17$\underline{th}$ Jan$\underline{y}$ 1842

Let me begin by thanking you for your very acceptable letter of the 8$\underline{th}$ my dear Mamma, which I meant to have answered on Saturday, but found it impossible to do– I am particularly obliged to you for telling me of your own health, and delighted to hear that it is so good, & that you are able to enjoy such long walks without fatigue– but I hope you will be prudent, dear Mamma, and not expose yourself to drafts of air, altho' the weather <u>be</u> Springlike– We have here charming weather too, but alas! no fragrant Olives, or Camellias, except what Fisher has the gallantry to bring me from Dryburgh's Greenhouse. (This Pen is too abominable, I must try another)– I have been rather indisposed since I wrote last in consequence of loss of rest, & being much disturbed at night by the <u>babies</u>– but I have now made a better arrangement, and instead of letting them be together and wake each other up, I have taken my <u>nursling</u> into my room, & have her crib close to me, into which I put her, after satisfying her <u>cravings</u>, not more than two or 3 times in the course of the night, by which means, Lily is kept quiet– in the next room, until about 6 in the morng– when I have little Sophy carried in there also, and snatch a good nap before breakfast– I seldom sleep altogether more than 5 or 6 hours, and a few days ago, was 24 hours without <u>losing consciousness</u> for a moment, but since adopting this new plan, I can get along better, & hope to do better still, when Miss Sophia out grows a certain habit of <u>grunting</u>, to which, they say, the healthiest babies are prone, but which it is difficult for me, with my wakefulness, to accustom myself to– She is a fine stout damsel, & thrives upon it amazingly– Dr Meigs has just pronounced that the Vaccine has taken, which has relieved me from much anxiety, for there is much Small Pox about town, & an infant of just her age died of it two days since, altho' it had never been out of the house–

But enough of <u>Nursery matters</u>– & let me tell you how <u>dissipated</u> I have been– staying out the other night until past 11 o'clk– at a party at Mrs Prime's– given (I suppose) to Lord Morpeth– at least he was the Lion of the eveng– & pretty well <u>stared at</u> he was– I think I never saw a more ludicrous exhibition than that of his <u>dancing</u>– and the evident delight he took in the Virginia Reel (which he himself proposed) was quite as amusing as his awkwardness– he is agreeable & sensible withal however– & I had the pleasure of asking him questions about many of our friends, in the morng– when he called, & that eveng– also– Pauline Craven[1] he saw last summer, when she was quite well, he says. When I asked him if she was <u>well married</u>– he said her husband was poor, & it was not a <u>brilliant</u> match– but upon my explaining that I meant to ask if she was happy, & her husband kind to her, he said he believed she was <u>tolerably</u> so– but you will have an opportunity of making enquiries yourself I suppose– for I daresay Papa will invite him to M. Place, & I judge from what he said of him & you, that he will accept the invitation gladly– He is gone to Wash^n, where he expects to remain about 3 weeks, & then proceeds to Car^a. He was here just one week, & asked out to dinner every day, but saw very little <u>lady society</u>– Three or four (among whom was Sally Ingersoll) went to a dinner given to him by M^r [William] Peter (the Eng. Consul) at Jones' Hotel and I confess it appears to me to have been rather an undignified proceeding on their part– savouring a little of the passion for <u>Titles</u> of which we Yankees are accused, notwithstanding our profession of republicanism–

Monday eveng– I have been so busy that really until this moment I have scarcely thought I could finish this– I ought not to keep Edward's letter from you any longer & therefore enclose it herewith– It will not be worth while to write to him again I suppose, for we shall probably hear of his arrival before a month is past– I had a mind to tell Lizzie [Middleton][2] so, last eveng– but feared the effect that so <u>joyful</u> a piece of intelligence might have on her in <u>company</u>– & therefore reserved it for a more private opportunity– She & Mary, & their Father & Mother drank tea with us en famille yesterday eveng– & M<u>rs</u> Smith came also, & was very glad to hear such good news of you– She is well, for her– but not free from cough yet– She begged me to tell you with her love, that she wrote to you ten days ago, & sent her letter by a private hand.

Mary M[iddleton] is to be married in about 2 weeks I understand–[3] In the mean time she is amusing herself very much with the devoted attentions of certain youngsters here, among whom she appears to be very popular– Indeed she complained to F[isher] of the familiarity of one of them, who came over from M<u>r</u> Burd's dinner to M<u>rs</u> Prime's party in rather an <u>exhilarated</u> state & was rather too affectionate to her– whereat Heyward Drayton[4] took great offence, & Mr. Lowndes would I suppose have challenged him– Instead of writing this stuff to you, I had better go to my baby who is squalling lustily– & this, or the "brown stout" I swallowed this morng– for lunch, has somewhat confused my poor ideas–[5] So Adieu dearest Mamma I am as ever Y<u>r</u> most affect<u>e</u> daughter Eliza

I beg my best love to Papa & the others– and Fisher & his Mother send their best regards–

Private Collection

1. The Middletons knew Pauline Craven and her parents, the Count and Countess de la Ferronays, in St. Petersburg, where the count was the French minister. Pauline became a well-known writer.

2. Lizzie Middleton and Edward were suspected of being interested in each other.

3. Mary Middleton married William Henry Lowndes (1817–1865) of South Carolina on February 8, 1842. Eliza remarked that Mary "is really a very extraordinary young woman– & her Father's own daughter." On the evening of the wedding, "at ten o'clk all the younger part of the company, (except M<u>r</u> & M<u>rs</u> L) went to a Ball at M<u>rs</u> J. Biddle's– Mary wanted to go too, but was not permitted to commit such an impropriety . . . She was very anxious to go on Mondy eveng to a party at the Whartons', & was only deterred by M<u>rs</u> M<u>c</u>Euen telling her that she w<u>d</u> be the town talk if she persisted in acting contrary to all custom." EMF to MHM, February 7, 1842, private collection.

4. Heyward Drayton was the son of Col. William and Maria (Heyward) Drayton.

5. Eliza gave up the alcohol and "returned to the Oatmeal gruel, which is after

all best for me, & the <u>Dairy</u> likewise– which, as you enquire after it, I must tell you is rather better supplied than in Lily's time." EMF to MHM, January 24, 1842, ScHi.

⌣

To Mrs. Fisher, Philadelphia

M.P. Jan.ʸ 26ᵗʰ 1842

I had yesterday my dearest Eliza the pleasure of receiving your letter of the 17ᵗʰ & at the same time one from Arthur dated Charleston where he had arrived on the mornᵍ of the 24ᵗʰ Edward's too was very welcome, & you having read it, requires no apology. You expect his arrival much sooner than he did when he wrote. Besides your anticipation, young Pringle wrote to his parents that the Marion would soon arrive, so that we may look forward to seeing Edward in a month or two. Arthur writes that Susan insisted upon his & Paolina's remaining with her, & gave them a most cordial reception. They must be much more comfortable with her than staying in Boundary Sᵗ. I learnt from your Father who returned yesterday alone, that Oliver had given him a letter for Susan informing her of Mʳˢ Chisolm being very ill– they went together last week to Edisto, & I think <u>that</u> news will make poor Susan so unhappy that she will set off for that place if she can, immediately: a great obstacle is having 5 young children– She cannot carry all of them with her, but perhaps the Miss Seabrooks her cousins may keep some of them during her absence– this is all surmise on my part– I feel very much for her, & cannot help being rather glad that the bad news has not yet reached her for this very rainy day has made your Father postpone his journey to Charleston until tomorrow. Arthur mentions his intention of staying 5 or 6 days there to see his old friends– this surprised me; but I recollected that he remained probably in order to give Paolina an opportunity of going to Church– this too is surmise–

I am sorry to find you allow the Babies to disturb your nights' rest so much as to make you ill– Why not have Lily by your bed side, instead of being so often awoke by feeding little Sophy? Anne used to keep Lily quiet by giving her the Bottle, & why should she not manage the other child in the same way? You will find that as she grows older she will become still more ravenous & you will I fear suffer increasing fatigue– cannot you change the arrangement in time? I congratulate you on the Vaccine having taken, & hope you will be spared every other anxiety on account of both the Children.

I am glad to learn that you became acquainted with Lᵈ Morpeth & obtained some news of our friends from him. <u>That</u> is what <u>I</u> should like to do, but whether he will be invited here is still unknown to me. Mr Hughes[1] is to accompany him to Charleston so that perhaps <u>he</u> may induce your Father to invite them both.

M^rs H[arper] came with Harry last Friday & makes herself very agreeable.[2] I take my short walk with her & her beau & they prolong theirs after I leave them– H. reads aloud to us every evening. I suppose she will remain a week longer to see Paolina– Another visitor is expected in a day or two– Miss Parker the daughter of H[enry] M[iddleton] P[arker][3] who you saw at Newport 3 years ago– They were crossing the ferry at Newport S.C. when their horses galloped off the boat & were drowned– the Carriage luckily was caught by the iron which is fastened (instead of a rope) from one side to the other of the Canal, & they saved that, & their baggage by the assistance of the Negroes, & went to Hobonny with your Father for a day or two on their way to some reception in the neighbourhood, & also on their way to Charleston are to stop here. A more serious accident happened the same day to Mr Elliott[4] & his Sister & son of 12 y^rs old. They imprudently sat in the carriage & the horses galloped into the canal– The which were seen just above the water when D^r DeSaussure passed by– He jumped into the canal, & your Father saw him bring out Miss E. who was under the Carriage, then her brother & his son– After a short time they were restored to their senses, & also proceeded to Hobonny from whence Willm carried them to their Mother's plantation. All their Clothes were of course in a bad condition, & required the assistance of all the negroes to bring them out of the water 40 feet deep–

You do not mention Mrs Harrison or Miss Hare. May I conclude then that they are both in a better state of health than when you last wrote? Mr Francis too I suppose is still lingering. So you really think that Lizzie in spite of all other flirtations at Philad^a still retains her attachment to E[dward]!

Harry brought me word from Charleston that John & family left it on the 17th– the operation was not performed on Sally's arm, & I believe I told you Dr H. had said it might be deferred for several months. 27th Here is a fine morn^g & I presume y^r Father will go after breakfast to Charleston. I am glad to hear that Mrs Smith was well enough to venture out in the eve^g & take tea with you– give my love to her. She has of course received my letter. After beginning to work so well, the Perryian Inkstand now scarcely sends up the ink– I often place it near the fire & it comes up slowly, but when put near me, the ink will not rise– perhaps warm weather may make it work again, though that had no effect upon the other. Harry has unscrewed the cup of the ink stand & by screwing it tightly again made the ink rise. M^rs H[arper] begs to be kindly remembered to you. Pray remember me also kindly to M^r & Mrs Fisher & M^{rs} & Mr Harrison & believe me my dearest Eliza y^r Affect^{te} Mother M H. M.

ScHi

1. Probably Christopher Hughes (1786–1849), an American diplomat who knew the Middletons and the Harrisons as well. His father-in-law, Gen. Samuel Smith of Maryland, was a close friend of George Harrison's.

2. Mrs. Middleton had not been in favor of Mrs. Harper's visit to Middleton Place because she thought it would only confirm the reports of her engagement to Harry. MHM to EMF, January 15, 1842, ScHi.

3. Henry Middleton Parker (1788–1849) was Henry Middleton's first cousin, the son of Susannah Middleton (1760–1834) and John Parker. His daughter, Emma, was probably with him.

4. William Elliott III (1788–1863), his sister, Mary Barnwell Elliott, and his son, William (1832–1867).

～

To Mrs. Middleton, Middleton Place

Tuesday 1st Feby 1842

I hailed with delight the approach of the Postman this morng– feeling quite sure that he would bring me a letter from my dearest Mamma, nor was I mistaken, for yours' of the 26th and 7th, was immediately put into my hands– and I now seize the favourable <u>sleeping time</u> of the children to thank you for it– I was very glad to learn the safe arrival of Arthur & Paolina in Charleston, & have no doubt that the illness of Mrs Chisolm w^d hasten Susan's departure to her & carry them to M. Place sooner than they at first intended– No doubt you are now enjoying their society– & before long you will be accompanying them to Charleston, so that P. will not have time to grow weary of the country– It was indeed much better that they should stay with Susan [*in Charleston,*] who I have no doubt made them perfectly comfortable– but how much distress that letter must have occasioned her– I do hope the poor old lady may yet be spared to her– for her loss will be irreparable– and Susan with her affectionate heart, will feel it deeply– If anything sh^d happen to M^{rs} C[hisolm] I may give up the hope of seeing Susan at the North next summer, which I always cherish, perhaps without much reason– So you are likely to have the house full again– & of agreeable people too–

I suppose Mr Hughes mentioned to Arthur his intention of going to Carolina– he did not to Aunt Harrison, who saw him a week ago, when he came here with M^r J[oseph R.] Ingersoll[1] and his daughter [*Mary*] from Washington– She was then quite unwell, & returned home to consult Dr Mitchell, who thought her case by no means alarming– Indeed he gave her Father great encouragement, in consequence of which he went back to Wash^n. But alas! in a few hours she became suddenly worse, & died early on Sunday morng– I heard of it in Church, & was dreadfully shocked, as any one of any feeling must have been– Her poor Father is to be greatly pitied for the loss of his only child! a most amiable, excellent young woman, who was really beloved by all her friends, & altho' neither pretty or graceful– was universally liked, and admired for her sweet disposition– Her poor Aunt too, Miss [Elizabeth] Wilcocks, is nearly beside herself with grief, and refuses to be comforted– but imagine the agony of her Father who arrived too late to see her alive– It is to be hoped that his nieces the Wilcocks[2] will now repay his great kindness to them– but they can never supply his daughter's place– and are inferior to her in everything but personal appearance– It really seems that every time I have written to you lately, something sad has occurred, & that my letters contain nothing but gloomy accounts of sickness or death– There is scarcely a family of our acquaintance out of mourning now, & in St Peter's Church almost every Pew is filled with black bonnets–

Then the Bank failures cause so much distress and uncertainty in all circles, that one hears of nothing [but] trouble of one sort or another– We must be grateful to God that sorrow & sickness have not come nearer to us– & bear cheerfully losses, which are slight in comparison to those of some of our friends– But I cannot help regretting a little the Farm at NewPort, which Fisher might have had, if Mr H. had allowed him to sell his Girard Stock last summer–[3] He now gets but one Thousand out of 6, which it was then worth, & if he had waited one day more, he w^d not even have saved that. Mr H. himself has lost 5 thousand more, & Fisher's Aunt in Arch S^t 5,000– If the other banks go, we shall all be poor together, and must learn to limit our expenses & desires, with moderation.

Wednesday morng– I could not finish this last night, for the time I had intended to devote to you, dear Mamma, was broken in upon by visitors– Lizzie M. came about dusk, & I persuaded her to stay & take tea with me, as she seemed inclined to do so & afterwards I had to fulfil my promise to go down to 156– She tells me Mary's wedding is postponed until Tuesday, & she is to proceed South the next day but one– They are all going to a Party at Letitia Jones'[4] tonight, whose invitation we could not, with any propriety accept– Lizzie says the Ball at Mrs Davis' last week was the most splendid affair she ever saw & I hear that it appeared as if all the Butchers' Bakers', confectioners',

Florists' Upholsterers' in town had contributed towards the abundance displayed on the occasion– & that the expenditures must have been lavish in the
extreme– Several hundred dollars worth of beautiful Flowers alone– The Lady
has much of the Spanish taste for magnificence & show, which is attributed
to her countrymen– Tell William that at this Carnaval time, there are very few
Parties but their very scarcity seems to make them more enjoyed– The Ather-
tons & some others are on "hospitable thoughts intent"– but as soon as Lent
begins there will be an entire cessation of gaiety, so that much as I sh$\underline{d}$ like to
have him here, I fear he w$\underline{d}$ be ennuyé à mourir [*bored to death*]– By the way,
as Paolina is "buona Catholica", she will not dare to mix in the festivities of
the race week during that strict season, I suppose– or perhaps so far from Rome,
she will venture to transgress the rules she regarded whilst there– Tell her with
my love that now she is quiet in the country, I shall look for a letter from her–
I wrote a long letter to Aunt Hering on Monday, which I had to send by a N.Y.
Packet, having forgotten that it was necessary to send it two days beforehand,
for the Boston Steamer.

You must not suppose that I continue to suffer from the want of rest I
complained of two weeks ago– Sophy's arm is now quite well, and she is an
excellent sleeper, & does not disturb me as much as Lily w$\underline{d}$ do, if I had her
with me– for she– L.– is now in the habit of waking between 3 & 4 in the
morng– & does not close her little eyes again until she takes her noonday nap–
I therefore decidedly prefer her remaining with Anne who may always go to
sleep when she does, at 7 in the eveng– whereas, I who am up until 11, like to
sleep later in the morng– & I am now getting so much accustomed to the night
nursing that I fall asleep as soon as Miss Sophy is satisfied, & after she is taken
into the Nursery in the morng– take a good nap of two hours– for their noise
seldom disturbs me now that there is a good close double door between us– &
this is the best arrangement I can make– I do not use the Bottle at all with this
Baby– but give her what she has been in the habit of taking, from her birth,
several wine glass fulls at a time of milk & water 3 or 4 times during the 24
hours– It is quite amusing to see how she gulps it down, little toper– it is much
less troublesome than the bottle, which required great attention and care to
keep it clean and my supply of milk for her is better, so that she sucks enough
without the bottle– & flourishes & fattens famously– She is actually rolling in
fat,[5] & even Sidney Fisher (no great admirer of babies generally) says she is one
of the finest children he ever saw– both her Godmothers think the same– M$\underline{rs}$
Smith often comes and plays with her, if I am out when she calls– She spent
half an hour with her yesterday, & upon my return I found her, & gave y$\underline{r}$
message– Lily dances & sings as usual but does not talk to the great disappoint-

ment of M$^{\underline{r}}$ & M$^{\underline{rs}}$ H– The latter thanks you for your kind enquiries & is getting on very well– She as well as M$^{\underline{rs}}$ F. desire their best regards, & Fisher begs me to add his likewise to all the family– With love to Papa & all my brothers & sisters I am dearest Mamma Y$^{\underline{r}}$ most affectionate daughter Eliza

Miss Hare is much better again–

Private Collection

    1. Joseph Reed Ingersoll (1786–1868), like his brother Charles, was a lawyer and a congressman (but a Whig) and later minister to England (1852–53). He married Ann Wilcocks (1781–1831), Mrs. Charles J. Ingersoll's sister.

    2. The Wilcocks nieces were Charlotte and Mary, the orphaned daughters of Samuel and Harriet (Manigault) Wilcocks.

    3. The Girard Bank, like the other Philadelphia banks, suspended paying specie more than once in the difficult years after the Panic of 1837. The bank survived, but the value of its stock fell drastically. Eliza wrote to her mother, " we must have patience, & remember that we are much better off than our neighbours– To some of whom, Ten Thousand dollars, at which sum F. calculates his Losses, is a much greater loss than to us." Ten thousand dollars would be equal to approximately $167,000 in 1999 dollars. EMF to MHM, January 24, 1842, private collection; dollar conversion factor from RSahr, OrStU.

    4. Letitia Jones (1823–43) was Noble W. Jones' half-sister; she lived with her mother on Spruce Street.

    5. Uncle Harrison dubbed her "Fattima."

~

To Mrs. Fisher, Philadelphia

M.P. Feb$^{\underline{y}}$ 17$^{\underline{th}}$ 1842

My dearest Eliza

    Harry tells me he shall perhaps go to Charleston this afternoon or tomorrow, so that I lose no time in beginning my answer to your welcome one of the 1$^{\underline{st}}$ & 2$^{\underline{d}}$. The good account you give of yourself & family is very gratifying to me. What you tell me of the sad loss M$^{\underline{r}}$ Ingersoll has lately suffered is indeed very melancholy– poor Man! he & his Sister [*in-law*] (Miss W.) can never be expected to enjoy peace of mind again– And yet such trials as those we are ordered to regard as mercies! how few even of good Christians thus afflicted can look upon them as such! I hope the two Wilcocks [*nieces*] will exert themselves to repay his kindness by affection & every attention in their power to bestow.

    I mentioned I believe in my last that M$^{\underline{rs}}$ Chisolm was better & Oliver who came here for a day last Saturday said she was to be in Charleston this week– He went on Sunday to Combahee with your Father who will return with W^m on Saturday & on the following Monday the family will go to Charleston to enjoy the gaieties of the race week– if gaieties they can be called– On the 8th Pauline, Arthur, Harry & Mrs Harper & Child went there to be present at E[liza] Huger's wedding[1] which took place on the 10th– they found it rather a dull assembly. Em^a Smith was not there being very busy at Sav^a– the party returned with the exception of Mrs H. on Saturday. Pauline made very few acquaintances, Mrs Ravenel was one– none of the Hugers could speak French & when Mrs T. M[iddleton] was asked whether she would be presented, declined, as she could not make herself understood– She has a son of about 6 weeks old. I have not yet decided upon going on Monday– it will not be worth while for only a week to pack & unpack, & it pains me to let Cath^e be exposed to visitors who will call, not to see me, but Paolina. She reads a few pages to me every morn^g of what Arthur has chosen, "She stoops to conquer"[2] of which she comprehends very little. I explain some parts, & afterwards she translates a page or two into Italian which Arthur corrects. He is very desirous that she should read, but that is not selon son goût [to her taste]. He reads aloud to me in the even^g although I assure him it worries her– he would however read to himself, so that the result would be the same– her taking a nap on the Sofa as soon as he begins. Sometimes she works your footstool, but the nap is more frequently the end of the eve^g.

Since M^rs H's departure Harry has discontinued his eve^g readings, & now retires after tea to his own room. It is only on her account that he is going to Charleston– think how imprudent to continue the flirtation when there are no <u>means</u> to allow a match to follow! I expostulate with him on the subject but in vain.

C[atherine] is just now at the Piano forte– which she very seldom touches. You will be glad to hear that Paolina endeavours to prevail upon her by coaxing to walk out, & do other things, which for me she refuses to do. P. is assisting Arthur to plant shrubs about the Garden & never leaves him while she can remain there. This day & yesterday have been cooler than usual. There was a hard frost on the 8th & afterwards very warm weather, indeed it can scarcely be called a Winter that we have had here, only occasionally some cold days. The Yellow jessamines are covered with buds many full blown, & the peach trees covered with blossoms, the willows green–

This advance of the season makes me look forward to the time when I hope to meet you & yours at Newport. At some future time M^r F[isher] may be able to purchase the Farm [at Newport,] in the mean time your two rooms will always be kept for you, which is the greatest comfort I can enjoy. You must remember too what your Father said last summer when you talked of going to a boarding house– that <u>You</u> alone should have possession of the two rooms, that his sons might find some elsewhere, but <u>you</u> must always be in our house. therefore my dear Eliza let us be together as usual, <u>if you wish to make me happy</u>. By that time Lily will chatter no doubt, which will make her much more interesting than she was last summer. I long to see little Sophy. is she becoming fairer? & does her Grandmama like her as well as she does Lily? Since you tell me how you manage them during the night, & that it suits you well, I am satisfied.

19<u>th</u> It has been determined since I wrote the above that your brothers & Paolina should go to Charleston today, in order that the latter may go to Church tomorrow. Y<u>r</u> Father & W<u>m</u> may probably arrive here soon after they are gone.

I am sorry to tell you that the good old Moro died yesterday after an illness of 5 or 6 days– Pleurisy– Arthur bled him & the Doctor attended him, but he expired & without pain. He is a great loss, for his attention to his business & his honesty can scarcely be equalled. I suppose John[3] will take his place as distributor of food &c–

It will I fear be several days ere I get your letter of the 9<u>th</u> for all the party will spend a week in Charleston. I have heard nothing of M<u>r</u> Hughes, or of any one else, so that I must look forward to a dull time, which must be passed by reading & a little work. Give my love to M<u>r</u> & M<u>rs</u> Fisher. Paolina & y<u>r</u> Brothers desire theirs to you & I am my dearest Eliza y<u>r</u> affect<u>te</u> Mother M. H. M.

PHi

1. Eliza Huger (1824–1919), Emma's youngest sister, married William Mason Smith (1818–1851). He was a factor in Charleston.

2. In addition to the play *She Stoops to Conquer,* written in the 1770s by the English poet Oliver Goldsmith, Arthur also had Paolina read and memorize lines about Italy from Byron's *Childe Harold.* MHM to EMF, February 2, 1842, PHi.

3. John was a slave at Middleton Place.

⌣

To Mrs. Middleton, Middleton Place

Thursday 3<u>rd</u> March 1842

I seem to have come round to my old day for writing, my dear Mamma, to which however I do not expect to remain quite so constant as I was last year for altho' I do not find that the second baby gives quite <u>double</u> trouble, she certainly encreases it somewhat– & the sickness of Anne has interfered a good deal with my leisure lately– Then I still continue my readings to poor Fisher–[1] his mother to be sure relieves me frequently, & they have both become interested in a new novel of Ward's (De Clifford)[2] which enables me to spend part of this afternoon in writing to you– I have listened irregularly & with "l'esprit préoccupé" [*a troubled mind,*] so that I care less about it, & indeed consider it inferior to some of his former productions– of which it appears to me to be an imitation or rather repetition– I have read aloud several of the Articles in the last London Quarterly, which I like very much– particularly that on Stephens'[3] work, which I think w$^{\underline{d}}$ tell you as much of it as you w$^{\underline{d}}$ perhaps care to know– at least as much as you might have time to read – for it certainly excites one's curiosity to read more– The review of Taylor's work (which I spoke of having read) is an excellent burlesque– but not understanding at first that irony was intended, it appeared excessively heavy & <u>flat</u>–[4]

I sent off my last letter almost immediately after receiving your's of the 19$^{\underline{th}}$, & before I had time to notice several of the subjects you mentioned– I was sorry to find that you had given up your visit to Charleston, as I think the change w$^{\underline{d}}$ have been beneficial to you, & <u>particularly</u> so to Catherine,[5] who I am sure is better for a little amusement and variety– & as to the trouble– there is nothing to be done (<u>worth doing</u>) in this world, without that– I regretted good old Moro's death– altho' I scarcely expected ever to see him again–

I received a very sad letter from Emma who is apparently much depressed by her long solitude at Sav$^{\underline{a}}$ river,[6] & disappointed at not having been able to go to town for Eliza's wedding– Her remaining on the plantation was her own choice however– she thought it her duty to be with her husband, who in addition to his difficulties, has had sickness among his people [*slaves*] to contend with– It is really a great pity that poor Emma sh$^{\underline{d}}$ be imprisoned (altho' voluntarily) in such a hole– especially as the state of her eyes prevents her from passing much time in reading– I wrote her as cheering a letter as I could compose, advising her to write verses– & if possible, undertake an <u>Epic</u>– as something which w$^{\underline{d}}$ oblige her constantly to direct her thoughts from the dreary stillness around her– She tells me that she understands Sully[7] was to go to M. Place to take Paolina's portrait, and that he was also to paint Sally for <u>me</u>– both pieces of information entirely new & agreeable to me– but I fear not very correct– Much as I should like the latter suggestion, for the present I sh$^{\underline{d}}$ not propose it– <u>times being too hard!</u> I have no answer yet from her– which I look for anxiously– as I begged her to explain her case particularly to me–

I suppose when you receive this, the pleasure seekers will have returned to the quiet of M. Place– I fear that owing to Paolina's slow progress in English,

she will not have found the parties in Charleston very amusing– Give my love
to her & beg her to persevere in her Musical studies which I hope to direct next
summer– Already we begin to think of Summer– Indeed today the weather has
been so like it, that one might have mistaken the month for that of May or
even June– I drove out with Aunt H. <u>and Lily</u> to the waterworks[8] (where I had
not been for [*missing*]) & found the sun oppressively hot– Lily is a greater
favourite than ever with the old Lady– to whom she appears attached– This
morng she w<u>d</u> not leave her, but insisted upon remaining at 156 for dinner–
She has learnt <u>one</u> new word– <u>Bowwow</u>– which she pronounces distinctly– &
I am quite delighted at hearing this addition to her vocabulary– Little Sophy
talks a great deal (in <u>her</u> language) & is extremely lively– & as good natured
as possible– M<u>rs</u> H. pronounced her <u>pretty</u> for the first time this morng– But
I do not think her so– but <u>fine</u> looking & very intelligent– What a shocking
affair is that of M<u>rs</u> H'k in New York! I am told the intrigue has been going
on four years, & that two years ago her husband warned her of the danger of
the intimacy, and remonstrated– but she never loved him I suppose– She is
gone to Charleston with T. H. her brother–

    Friday morng 4<u>th</u> – This morng I had the unexpected pleasure of receiving
your letter of last Sunday, my dearest Mamma– for which I thank you heartily–
I am glad you like the <u>exposition</u>–[9] & regret not having sent the Albions[10] by
the same good opportunity– In one of the last there is a wonderful Chapter
on Zoophytes, which I read with more interest than any Arabian Fairy tale–
There is also an account of the discovery by an English Surgeon of the manner
in which Somnambulism may be produced without any manipulations &c
which I should like to shew Arthur– & other believers in magnetic influence.[11]

    Tell William I wish he were here to go with us tonight to M<u>rs</u> Coxe's to
make the acquaintance of M<u>r</u> and M<u>rs</u> [Charles] Lyell,[12] as he w<u>d</u> enjoy much
more than either Fisher or myself their scientific conversation– for I hear the
lady is also a Geologist– Fisher has been attending his lectures, but finds them
inferior in interest to his book– his manner & method being both bad– I persuaded him to go & hear that old [*illegible*] Lardner[13] the other eveng– but he
ret<u>d</u> disappointed altho' better pleased than with Lyell– Several ladies of our
acquaintance attended his first lecture (Lardner's) whereat I marvel for I certainly w<u>d</u> never encourage such a fellow– What makes his conduct much worse
is the fact I have only lately learnt, that he was a <u>clergyman</u>– What a scandal
to religion are some of its professors– I have not seen M<u>rs</u> Smith (no association
of ideas with the latter sort) for some days– She was then recovering from a
heavy cold– I meant to call upon her today but the rain prevents my going to
her & to the lecture– The baby is just waking up & I must go to her & say

Adieu to my dearest Mamma– My best love to Papa my brothers & Sisters–
Tell Kitty I have a beautiful new Duett to send her by the first opportunity– I
am sorry I could not do so by M[ary] Lowndes. M^r & M^{rs} H are well & desire
their best regards– as does M^{rs} F– also– she is a little nervous– but says the
babies do her a great deal of good– I believe she begins to think of the separation
from them next summer– for she declares she won't go to NewPort– I am as
ever Y^r most affect^e daughter Eliza

Fisher begs me to add his kind remembrances– His eyes are not <u>inflamed</u>– but
he has not yet got over the effects of the strain brought on by reading at night &
at early Twilight– & is not able to use them yet.

Private Collection

1. Fisher had had trouble with his eyes at least since 1838. The postscript to this
letter seems to say he thought this episode had been brought on by reading at night.
Eliza told her mother he could not read anything, "so that, to keep up his spirits I exert
myself as much as possible for his amusement." EMF to MHM, February 24, 1842,
ScHi.
2. Robert Plumer Ward (1765–1846), an English politician and novelist, published *De Clifford, or the Constant Man* in 1841.
3. John Lloyd Stephens (1805–1852), an American, traveled in the Middle East
as well as in Central America, where he was an important amateur archeologist. He
wrote *Incidents of Travel in Central America, Chiapas & Yucatan* and *Incidents of Travel
in Yucatan,* which Fisher read in 1843.
4. See MHM to EMF, March 25, 1842, note 2.
5. Mrs. Middleton more than once expressed her dislike of taking Catherine to
Charleston because she would be "exposed to observation" when visitors came to call
on Paolina. MHM to EMF, January 15, 1842, ScHi.
6. Emma said Allen's "love for me led him into terrible embarassments indeed–
I trust he will work them out. You have seen John harassed by debt, & know how pleasant it looks." Allen had borrowed money to buy his plantation when the price of rice
was high, and when the price fell, he had trouble paying his debt. EHS to EMF, February
21, 1842, PHi; EM to Harry Middleton, February 15, 1838, PHi, C/F.
7. John Middleton commissioned Thomas Sully (1783–1872) to paint Mrs. Middleton's portrait in the early 1830s and had tried, without success, to persuade his father
to sit for his at the same time. He was very anxious to have Sully paint Sally. John I.
Middleton to EMF, October 12, 1841, MPlFdn.
8. Philadelphia, the first American city to provide a public water supply, by 1842
pumped water from the Schuylkill River into a reservoir on top of Fairmount, a nearby
hill. The Waterworks became a favorite spot for Philadelphians and for visitors.
9. Eliza had sent her mother a copy of Blunt's *Exposition.* Mrs. Middleton read
it every morning and said it gave her great pleasure to have the Bible "so well explained."
MHM to EMF, February 17, 1842, PHi.

10. *Albion* was a weekly magazine that often reprinted articles or extracts from English periodicals.

11. This is the first of several times Eliza and her mother discussed the merits of hypnotism. Franz Anton Mesmer (1734–1815), an Austrian physician, used hypnotism (later named mesmerism) in treating his patients. He called it "animal magnetism," believing that an occult force, or invisible fluid, emanated from his body to his patients.

In the letters, *to magnetize, magnetic sleep,* and *somnambulism* (referring to things done while asleep that are not remembered later) are all used to refer to various aspects of mesmerism.

12. Charles Lyell (1797–1875), a pioneering geologist who traveled in the United States, was considered to be among the fairest and most knowledgeable observers of nineteenth-century America. In *Geological Evidences of the Antiquity of Man* (1863) he suggested that the earth was formed by slow, continuing changes rather than all at one time. Lyell's wife was Mary Horner (d. 1873), daughter of a fellow geologist.

13. Dionysius Lardner (1793–1859), though a clergyman, was professor of natural philosophy and astronomy at the University of London and a fellow of the Royal Society. He lectured extensively in the United States in the early 1840s. Lardner's personal life was unconventional. Separated from his first wife, he lived with a married woman whom he later married after each obtained a divorce.

⌇

To Mrs. Fisher, Philadelphia

M.P. March 6$\underline{th}$ 1842

I begin this my dearest Eliza many days before I expect to have an opportunity of sending it, to tell you the pleasure your letter of the 24$\underline{th}$ Feb$\underline{y}$ gave me although the account you give of M$\underline{r}$ Fisher's eyes distresses me greatly: your next will I hope remove my apprehensions. A strain of the nerves sounds alarming, but perhaps it is only slight, & perfect rest has probably cured them. Your letter was brought by your Brothers last Thursday after dinner– your Father had returned the Monday before, & told me how many parties Paolina had been invited to. The S$\underline{t}$ Cecelia & race balls,[1] Miss Pinckney gave her a very pleasant party & supper which was attended by L$\underline{d}$ Morpeth the day before he sailed for Havanna. On that even$\underline{g}$ M$\underline{rs}$ Aiken[2] gave a grand ball which was the last she [*Paolina*] went to, for on the next day she left Charleston. Oliver gave a very handsome dinner to his Lordship & on the even$\underline{g}$ there was a small party of young people who danced: among them Sarah & her Cousins. Paolina likes L$\underline{d}$ M. very much– I regret that he could not accept your Father's invitation to come here, being obliged to go to Cuba & then to Missisipi– Your Brothers think him a dull man! W$\underline{m}$ & Harry are very desirous of inviting a number of their acquaintances– M^r & M^{rs} [William] Carson,[3] Miss Kinloch,[4] M^r & Mrs W. Lowndes[5] & one or two others– whether they will come I know not. P. likes Miss K. & says she speaks Italian well, so does Mrs Holbrook or rather Spanish, but can make herself understood. She likes Miss Pinckney & Miss Rutledge very much– perhaps I am only repeating what she will tell you herself, for when about to leave me yesterday I told her she had better write to you as she would be left so much alone at Combahee & that I did not expect to have any means of sending you a letter for several days, & she consented to do so, although she said Arthur made her spend many hours in studying English. When he told me he was going there, & should leave her here, I told them both I feared she would be very unhappy, for she is never pleased out of his sight, & has no means of amusing herself.[6] He tried to persuade her to reconcile herself to his absence but in vain, so the next morn^g (yesterday) y^r Father asked her whether she would like to accompany them & she accepted the invitation with great glee–

When Harry heard that, he said he must then remain here, for there was not accommodation for all the family at Combahee, so that only on that account has he shared my solitude for a few days, for he intends to go on horseback on Thursday to Charleston & to stay a day or two with Oliver. The party said they should return the end of the week, but I do not think they will. I have a late letter from John in which he mentions having heard from you & says that Sally continues in pretty good health & derives great benefit from Houck's Panacea. I have been writing to him & mentioned an account in the newspaper of the inhaling the tincture of Iodine as a cure for diseases of the lungs, destroying the tubercles– which is certainly very beneficial– Physicians must of course be consulted on the subject before it can be tried.

The end of your letter made me unhappy– You tell me you had desired S[ophie] T[horndike] to engage Gough's[7] rooms for you! How could you do so when you knew last year how positively your Father insisted upon your retaining your two rooms? When I read to him what you wrote, he seemed much vexed, & repeated that you had a greater right to be under his roof than any of his Sons, so that I still hope Mr Fisher will consent to your occupying them this year.[8] When I asked him what I sh^d say about the gate you wish to have in the garden, he said yes, if you wish to have it, only while Mrs Fisher remains with you at Gough's, for he thinks it is because <u>she</u> is to be at Newport, that you have engaged rooms there– <u>that</u> is the only reason he can admit for your going there. Will Mrs Fisher consent to go? I should be very happy to have her there; & if she goes, Gough's is certainly the most convenient & nearest house you could all occupy but if she does not go, why disappoint us of your accustomed presence?

Friday 11$\underline{th}$ I must now my dearest Eliza hasten to finish this, as Harry has just told me he is going this morn$\underline{g}$. He may return on Sunday & bring me y$\underline{r}$ letters, which I hope he will, but there is no depending upon his intended movements. my anxiety about M$\underline{r}$ F. is great, & I can easily conceive how unhappy the state of his eyes must make M$\underline{rs}$ F. & yourself. What do you think was the height of the ther$\underline{r}$ on the 7$\underline{th}$? 85$\underline{o}$! You probably have warm weather, but not equal to ours– Here we have it at this Season hotter than the summer at Newport. I am anxiously expecting a letter from my Brother by the Caledonia– it has had an unusually long passage–

So little Lily does not yet speak! You will be still more delighted with her when she does. Sophy must be a sweet little creature & as stout & fat by your account as little Maria, who is the stoutest & fattest child I ever saw– how extraordinary when we reflect on the delicate health of her Mother! I hope Sophia T's health is now reestablished– remember me to her when you write, & also to M$\underline{rs}$ Smith with congratulations on her Niece's marriage– I forgot in my last to thank you for the Mittens you were so kind as to send me. I found them very comfortable for two days, & then having left them on the Sofa, C[atherine] took possession of them & has worn them ever since notwithstanding the great heat of the weather.

I shall be glad to hear that Louisa[9] consents to remain with you– since she is so perfect a nurse– in that case shall you hire a white one? it w$\underline{d}$ not be agreeable to her to be under the control of an upper one I sh$\underline{d}$ think. I must now with love to M$\underline{r}$ & M$\underline{rs}$ F. beg you to believe me my dearest Eliza y$\underline{r}$ affect$\underline{te}$ Mother M. H. M.

PHi

1. The St. Cecilia Society's and Jockey Club balls were highlights of Charleston's February Race Week.

2. Harriett (Lowndes) Aiken (1812–1892) was the wife of William Aiken (1806–1887), a planter and prominent politician.

3. Caroline (Petigru) Carson was the daughter of James Louis Petigru.

4. Martha Rutledge Kinloch (b. 1818) was the daughter of Frederick and Mary (Rutledge) Kinloch. In 1844, she married Matthew Richard Singleton.

5. Probably William and Mary (Middleton) Lowndes.

6. The first time Arthur mentioned going to Combahee, Paolina "burst into tears like a young child." MHM to EMF, February 2, 1842, PHi.

7. John Goff kept a boardinghouse adjacent to the Middletons' property in Newport.

8. Fisher had said that, in view of the number of Middletons who might be at Newport, he could "not consent to crowding out any of [*Eliza's*] brothers," especially Edward, if he came home after such a long absence. Eliza had proposed making a gate from Goff's into the Middletons' garden as a shortcut to her parents' house. EMF to MHM, February 24, 1842, ScHi.

9. Louisa Darius had been Fisher's nurse when he was a child and, while she apparently had a family of her own, remained with the Fishers throughout her life. When Mrs. Fisher died in 1855, she left Louisa "$100 and half [*her*] wearing apparel." JFF, *Recollections,* 191; Will of Elizabeth Powel Fisher, February 25, 1855, PHi, BrC.

⌣

To Mrs. Middleton, Middleton Place

Philadelphia March 13th 1842

My dearest Mamma,

Instead of going to Aunt Harrison's this evening, I am determined to stay at home and write to you– as I indeed have wished to do for two days past– but for several reasons have been prevented– now, both babies are sound asleep, and after reading aloud to Fisher nearly the whole afternoon, I cannot better finish my evening than by writing to you– I hoped to have had a letter from you this eveng– but he returned with one from Aunt Hering, and you I suppose, have also one from Uncle by the Acadia–

Did you remember us yesterday? We thought a great deal of Middleton Place I assure you– & I at least hoped, that another anniversary, if we lived to see it, might be passed there– I spent it very happily here to be sure, but could not help a little heart yearning towards those among whom I was 3 years ago–[1] I had two superb bouquets full of sweets brought in to me at breakfast by my dear husband, who braved a very frosty morng– to present them early to me– He seemed yesterday to throw off all care, & was as cheerful as ever, but indeed I do not wonder that he is now frequently depressed, for he feels the privation of not being allowed to read, dreadfully– and God knows when he will again have the use of his poor eyes– They were rather better a day or two ago, but the lights last night seem to have injured them a little, & in order to avoid them at Aunt H's this evening, I have prevailed upon him to go & pass a quiet hour with his friend Mrs Hare, whilst I am writing– He insisted upon my practising with Mrs Derby[2] a couple of Gabussi duetts, yesterday & the day before, that we might sing them together last night– which we did to the apparent satisfaction of the present company– which did not amount to more than about 20 persons altogether– We had half a dozen agreeable women– & did not extend our invitations because some of our most intimate friends are in mourning, & we did not care for mere acquaintances on such an occasion– I thought of asking the Lyell's– but it was his Lecture eveng– & it w$^{\underline{d}}$ not have been worth while to have them so late as 9 o'clk. I have visited her & like her– & Fisher found him very agreeable– & heard some amusing anecdotes of his adventures at the South that eveng we passed with them at M$^{\underline{rs}}$ Dan Coxe's.

But who do you think I have had the honor of driving in company with? The <u>illustrious Boz!</u>[3] & his very quiet and simple little wife– M$^{\underline{rs}}$ Harry Ingersoll asked us to meet them sans cérémonie [*informally*] & I went expecting to be highly gratified &c &c– I confess his appearance & manners both disappointed me– nor did I find his conversation either brilliant or striking– but on the whole I rather like him– altho' he is not <u>gentlemanlike</u> looking– indeed, how should he be? But he is a fine fellow notwithstanding & if he had not so many <u>enthusiastic</u> admirers, I sh$^{\underline{d}}$ be apt to become one myself– He is anxious to see life on a Southern Plantation & I had half a mind to <u>recommend</u> him to Papa and William– but then reflected that they might both be away, & you might not find it convenient to see him, so said nothing about letters– If William should be in Charleston whilst he is there (next week) & feel inclined to do the honors of Combahee to him, he will I daresay, be infinitely obliged to him for the trouble, & perhaps may repay him richly by his conversation– But then there's the wife– you w$^{\underline{d}}$ not care <u>particularly</u> to have her meanwhile at M. Place– for altho' an amiable little person apparently, she does not seem very amusing or interesting– so I am glad I did not commit myself or you, altho' rather tempted to do so– I promised Fisher when he left me an hour ago, that I would stop at 9 o'clk & prepare for rest– of which I am sadly in want to say the truth– for my little <u>cormorant</u> awoke me <u>5</u> times last night after midnight– & I must try and make up for the want of sleep I suffered in consequence– so I will bid you goodnight! my dearest Mamma– I trust tomorrow's mail will bring me good news from you– & that I shall hear you are no longer alone– I must say Adieu with love to Papa & the rest I am Y$^{\underline{r}}$ most affectionate daughter Eliza

Monday eveng– I am quite disappointed at not receiving a letter this eveng– dear Mamma, & have only time to tell you so, and to add that we are all well, as I am going to put Lily to sleep in Louisa's absence– She has been called home by the sickness of her daughter & I am much inconvenienced by it of course–

Private Collection

1. "For my part I am so blessed in my husband & children," Eliza told her mother two weeks later, "that I often ask myself what I have done to deserve so much happi-

ness & can only endeavour to shew forth not only with my lips but in my whole life & actions my gratitude to Heaven for all the mercies I enjoy– & yet I too have <u>some</u> regrets– & certainly the separation from you & all my other dear friends in Carolina might become, if I allowed myself to dwell gloomily upon it, a source of infinite discontent." EMF to MHM, March 26, 1842, private collection.

2. Mrs. Richard C. Derby was the former Louisa Bumford (d. 1864). The Derbys were Bostonians, but also lived in Philadelphia and Newport. Though her husband was apparently not much liked, Mrs. Derby was musical and good company.

3. Charles Dickens was called Boz after his first publication, *Sketches by Boz*, about London life. He was lionized everywhere when he and his wife toured the United States in 1841–42.

~

Paolina astonished her mother-in-law by reporting, after her visit to the Middletons' rice plantations, that she liked Combahee the best of anywhere she had been in the United States. Whereas the Middleton women apparently thought Combahee isolated and boring—Eliza's reaction was, "What a dull time she must have passed during the absence of her beloved in the rice fields!"[1]—Paolina looked at the scene with a fresh eye and found much to interest her.

No record of what caught her eye has been found, but since she went to Combahee in March, she probably saw the rice fields being plowed by mules fitted with special, wide shoes to keep them from getting stuck in the mud. If she had been there a month later, she would have seen the rice being planted. She must have been amazed, as she stood near the house at Hobonny, by the vast extent of the rice fields, which stretched almost as far as she could see. The great trunks—gates made of huge beams of cypress wood that let the irrigation water from the Combahee River in and out of the ditches and canals—would have intrigued her.

Paolina probably visited the slaves' cabins set in two parallel rows, a short walk from the rice fields, and she may have been surprised, even alarmed, by the number and appearance—Eliza thought them "hideous"—of the blacks she saw.[2] The work of growing rice was done by more than 250 slaves at Hobonny and by 300 more at Newport and Old Combahee, the other two Middleton plantations nearby.

1. EMF to MHM, March 19, 1842, private collection.
2. Ibid.

To Mrs. Fisher, Philadelphia

M.P. March 25th 1842

At last my dearest Eliza I had the pleasure of receiving last Tuesday your letters of the 3d & 13th inst which to my great satisfaction gave a more favourable account of Mr Fisher's eyes, & of the happiness he enjoyed as well as yourself on the anniversary of your happy Union. May you both enjoy many more is my fervent prayer! It was unfortunate that the lights injured his eyes that evening. great care ought to be observed until they are perfectly cured– You too suffered from loss of sleep on that night, but I hope you soon recovered from the ill effects of little Sophy's wakefulness. I am glad you have been reading what interested me also, the review of Stephen's work. I have also read that of "Letters from the Baltic"[1] in the Septr N^o which my Brother & also my Sister speak highly of. I hope they may be republished here. You puzzle me by saying there is a review of Taylor's[2] work you have lately read. not in the last n^o certainly (ie Dec^r). Do you mean his management of Children, or his Physical Theory of a future life? the only review of that which I have seen is the Edin^g for April 1840– in one of the other reviews there is a short account of his work on the management of Children. This is all I know of the two works–

Arthur & Paolina have remained here longer than I expected. They will go next Monday & Harry will still remain there– Y^r Father will probably return today. What you say of Sully is not true. his high price prevents his being employed by any of our family. Your letters had been opened in Charleston, so that I hope y^r Father & W^m will make Mr Dicken's acquaintance should he have already arrived, & invite him to Combahee. I should have no objection to have Mrs D. here while Pa^a is with me; it would be very dull for her were I alone. M^r & Mrs Lyell would be much more agreeable visitors from your account of them. He of course could not lose his time in this country [*Carolina*] where there cannot be any interesting discoveries to be made in such a soil as this. Do you not attend his Lectures? They must be very instructive, although Mr F. does not approve of his manner of delivering them.

Sunday– I was interrupted last <u>friday</u> by the arrival of John with y^r Father who to my great satisfaction brought y^r letter of the 19th enclosing Edward's for which I thank you: it is a very good & affectionate one & I have a better opinion of C[harles] Hunter's judgment now, than I had before. Edward's intention of marrying as soon as he arrives here amused us all– & his brothers agreed that a Naval Officer ought not to think of taking a wife from whom he would be forced to be separated continually. I am sorry to find there is so much sickness on board the Marion: the surgeon's advice ought to be followed, although it might delay the arrival of the vessel.[3]

Y^r Father, Harry, & W^m have this minute set off for Combahee. H's motive for going is of course to be near his beloved, who is going in a day or two, to spend a month with Mrs Skirving.[4] Arthur & Paolina did not go to Charleston as I expected, but will go either tomorrow with John or Wednesday as P.

does not wish to stay there more than a day to go to Mass & make her Confession, & they are to bring two of Susan's girls with them, Mary & either Coosy or El^r. Mary said she <u>would not</u> go to Edisto with her parents because she wished to be with her new Aunt. Hal & Sarah are to spend their month's holidays at Waccamaw where John will take them the end of this week. I told him what you wrote about expecting so long, a letter from Sally– He says it is her laziness alone that prevents her writing. the swelling is on the left arm, & he thinks it a very trifling complaint & says what I am very glad to communicate that her health is better now than it has been for a length of time, which he attributes to the use she makes of the Panacea I mentioned to you. I should like to know this from Sally herself, because John cannot understand all her sufferings.

Miss Pinckney never had an intention of giving a ball it seems. W^m fancied it perhaps from what some of the Girls might have said. Miss K[inloch] regrets extremely in a very well written note in french to Paolina that she cannot accept her invitation to come here, being compelled to accompany her Mother to Combahee. P. does <u>not</u> regret it much, although she says she speaks Italian very well. I read to your Father my dearest Eliza what you wrote about your disappointment at not being able to occupy Goff's house; he desired me again to tell you that nobody but your family should occupy the two rooms in our house & that he would have no refusal– so that I flatter myself Mr Fisher will at last consent to our intreaties on that subject. The accommodation of y^r brothers may be managed by W^m & Ed^d sleeping in Harry's room & <u>he</u> can occupy the one that W^m did last summer. He– y^r Father– agrees to my proposal of removing the furniture intended for Arthur into the room & dress^g room Sally had last summer, & then I can have Cath^e as usual near me. I am very sorry to find that you are to spend the month of June in Pennsy^a instead of removing to Newport, & also of Mrs Fisher's refusal to go there– She might travel by rail cars by the way of Boston & avoid a night on board the Steamer. M^r & Mrs H. might do the same, have you ever thought of proposing that plan? It gives me great pleasure to learn that Mr Fisher's eyes are even a <u>little</u> better, they will no doubt by constant care improve daily.

À propos of eyes W^m told me that Mrs Harper [Sr.] at Baltimore had a cataract on both hers– poor unfortunate woman, I pity her sincerely! it was brought on by wetting her feet & not changing her shoes which occasioned a severe cold– You have been trying yours reading a small type you say– the subject of the "right of search" is indeed a very alarming one,[5] & your brothers think that this Goverm^t will absolutely refuse to accede to the British plan of adopting it. So that all we must hope for is that L[ord] Ashburton[6] when he finds the Amer<u>s</u> so determined to oppose his propositions may prevail upon his Goverm<u>t</u> to withdraw its resolutions– if it does not a War must inevitably ensue. I fear the British will not give up the right they so positively insist on. If they do not what will become of us! You, will be exposed to danger by remaining at Philad<u>a</u> & Newport would soon be taken. W<u>m</u> says Col<u>l</u> Perceval (an English Officer) says they will not attempt to come to the Southern States– but I think they will & make the Negroes join with them. It is really dreadful to think of such a War. [Lewis] Cass's Pamphlet is copied in the Pennsy<u>a</u> Enquirer & part of it Arthur read to me, he will read the rest I daresay. It is said that M<u>r</u> Dickens will not come to Carol<u>a</u>.

It gives me pleasure to learn that Lily is such a favorite of her Aunt, & that she gives proofs of her own attachment! So I shall not see the two little Pets or their dear Mother before July! If you all continue well until that period I ought not to complain because I have no right to expect so much happiness or such good health as I now enjoy. I told Harry what you wrote about M<u>rs</u> C[amac] he made no observations but it amused the rest of the party.[7] J[oe] Huger has a son who he has named Ar[thu]r Midd[leto]n.

My brother writes "Perhaps you may see L<u>d</u> Ashburton. Y<u>r</u> Congress must be as mad as the ruffians on the Border if they do not treat with him in the peaceable spirit in which he is sent out. I suppose he will visit his Wife's relations in Philad<u>a</u> though M<u>rs</u> Ashton" (an old friend of mine whose daughter married his son) "told me that the family did not like to mention them. Conceited fools if that be true".

M<u>rs</u> J. Butler will not be as agreeable a neighbour to us [*in Newport*] as M<u>rs</u> Sumner, who I am sorry has been disappointed of her Cottage. She may however find another though not so near us. I heard that S. Thorndike was to return to Bremen with her Sister when she returned there from her visit to the U.S. As you mention nothing of it, I suppose it is not true. Your Brothers & Paolina desire their love to you pray give mine to M<u>r</u> & M<u>rs</u> Fisher & believe me my dearest Eliza y<u>r</u> Affect<u>e</u> Mother M. H. M.

P.S. Monday Mor<u>g</u> I can add a few lines more my dearest Eliza as the trio will take an early dinner & go to Charleston afterwards. A. & P. will return on Friday when the holidays of the children begin. so that for 5 days I shall again be alone.

Yesterday eve<u>g</u> we were much amused, John especially, to hear Paolina declare that she preferred Combahee to any place she had been in the U.S. I was astonished, & asked if it were possible she could prefer it to this place– Yes, there were so many things that interested her there! I said I would tell you this, & she said there was no occasion to do so, for she would write her opinion of it herself from Charleston. I doubt whether she will find time for so doing. She was very anxious to make some Cakes like those she used to make for her little brothers & Sisters, & this mor^g she rose earlier than usual & prepared them– the receipt is a tb of flour & 1 of Sugar & Anice seed sprinkled over them– no eggs or butter– they were baked & turned out so hard it was impossible for me to eat them– however she will take them with her, though she says they have been spoilt by the baking– You must not expect to hear from me again for many days after rec^g this, for I believe there will be no means of sending to town for a fortnight.

ScHi

1. *Letters from the Shores of the Baltic,* by Elizabeth Rigby (1809–1893), appeared in 1841. She became Lady Elizabeth Eastlake when she married the painter Sir Charles Locke Eastlake in 1849.

2. Mrs. Middleton was referring to Isaac Taylor (1787–1865), an English artist and inventor as well as writer. He wrote *The Physical Theory of Another Life* in 1836. His thoughts on the management of children were probably in *Home Education,* in which he stressed ideas such as the educational importance of children's pleasures and the benefits of country life.

3. The surgeon recommended that the ship stop at every port along the route home in order to buy fresh food for the crew. Edward Middleton to EMF, January 6, 1842, Edward Middleton Rea Collection.

4. Bethia (Price) Skirving, widow of William Skirving, Jr. (1773–1805), was Mrs. C. Harper's aunt.

5. Eliza had been reading a pamphlet by Lewis Cass (1782–1866), former governor of the Michigan territory and now minister to France, in which he disputed the British government's right to stop and search any ship suspected of being involved in the slave trade. Cass, who hoped for the Democratic nomination in 1844, emphasized that American rights and freedom were at stake.

This was one of the matters Lord Ashburton discussed with Secretary of State Daniel Webster. The resulting Webster-Ashburton Treaty smoothed over but did not completely settle the question; the British intermittently boarded U.S. ships until the Civil War.

6. Alexander Baring, Lord Ashburton (1774–1848), was sent to Washington in the spring of 1842 to negotiate a settlement of disputes with the United States. He was considered an ideal choice both because he was head of Baring Brothers, a leading financial firm with American interests, and because his wife, Anne Willing Bingham, was an American.

7. Harry and Elizabeth Camac had known each other in earlier years and may have once been engaged. When Mrs. Camac was widowed in 1842, Eliza sent a message to Harry about "his old flame Mrs. Camac, whose husband has left her an annuity of 12,000$ per annum . . . given without the condition of perpetual widowhood." EMF to MHM, March 19, 1842, private collection.

⌣

To Mrs. Middleton, Middleton Place

Tuesday 12th April 1842

My dearest Mamma,

It is lucky that you forewarned me not to expect a letter for two weeks, for I should have begun to feel uneasy at not hearing, if I had not known the reason of your silence– Your last letter was such a nice long one, & so cheerful, that it ought to satisfy me for some time, & yet I am longing for another one– The day after I sent you my answer, Delia Parnell was sitting with me when a note was brought to me, as I thought from the signature, from James Pringle, but as it began very affecte^{ly} to "my dear Eliza" I looked again, & saw <u>Jane</u> and my astonishment was not much diminished, for I had no idea of her coming on at this season– She wrote to beg me to go and see her before she had shaken off the dust of Carolina from her shoes– I did so after my visitor had departed, and my <u>chickens were gone to roost,</u> and spent an hour with her in very animated conversation which, however would have been still more agreeable if Mrs Dan Coxe had not been present during the whole time– She told me a great deal about many of my friends in Carolina and mentioned having had the pleasure of making Paolina's acquaintance & seeing my brothers on the Friday previous! We could not prevail upon her to remain here the following day, altho' Julius seemed inclined to leave it to her– I thought him decidedly improved in apprearance & manners both, & certainly less dull & heavy than formerly, for which he is no doubt indebted to association with his wife– I went up to see their Baby asleep, and thought she looked like my Lily, altho' her features are larger– Jane told me they had both remarked the same resemblance– They say she can say <u>everything</u>– which I supposed means to <u>their</u> comprehension– I am inclined to feel jealous of the superior talent for talking of all the children I see of the same age– but then her <u>musical accomplishments</u> ought to be a compensation for her deficiency of speech– It is really amusing to hear her <u>singing</u>, to express her wants & make her requests–

We have all been out to Germantown this morn^g– Aunt Harrison, the two babies, Louisa & myself– and were detained there a long while in consequence of an accident which might have proved very serious– The leaders took fright at some mortar in the lane near Mrs Morris' house, & made a sudden turn to the fence, which snapped off the end of the Pole– the footman jumped off the carriage box, & secured them after a little capering about, and the pair next the driver remained perfectly quiet– Louisa was in the carriage with Lily asleep in her arms, & luckily did not scream, but sat still until they let her out safe– I did not hear of all this until sometime afterwards– but you may imagine the very idea of the danger they had escaped terrified me– I shall beg leave to decline taking the children again when the four horses are in the carriage– for I really think the leaders very vicious– or at any rate too spirited– and I was glad enough to jump out at some squares distance from home, when the approach of a grand Temperance procession with Flags flying and drums beating, alarmed them– We had a delightful drive. The country begins to look beautiful & the weather was perfectly delicious– I brought in a fragrant bouquet of Violets, jonquils & cherry blossoms– & wish you could have seen a number of sweet wild flowers they showed me to convince you that Eng$^{\underline{d}}$ is the not the <u>only</u> country where they are to be found– One little yellow flower, which grows in the woods was exquisitely sweet, like the daphne, & several I think w$^{\underline{d}}$ vie in sweetness with your favourite <u>Primroses</u>–

Fisher has a slight attack of headache this afternoon, & so I am not employed in reading to him– His eyes are so much better that he thinks he will have the use of them in another week– I <u>hope</u> so, & do not like to say to him I <u>fear</u> not, for I don't want to discourage him poor fellow! He has been very busy planting out roses &c in our little garden, & we shall soon have a very gay parterre to look out upon– We have had the Cuestas[1] & Whartons here two evengs lately, practising with me– M$^{\underline{rs}}$ F– says she is determined to encourage me to keep up my singing, that Papa may not be disappointed in the summer– but reading aloud is not very favourable to my voice– If it does not improve, I hope my <u>mind</u> will for we are very deep in the philosophy of Chalmer's[2] treatise now– which being more metaphisical than Whewell's is [*missing*] adapted to my poor comprehension– but also interesting–

I took Lizzie Middleton & Letitia Jones under my chaperonage to M$^{\underline{rs}}$ Grelaud's on Sat$^{\underline{y}}$ eveng– & altho' I expected a very dull eveng– we were agreeably disappointed, (<u>I</u> was, at least, for the others don't care for music, & therefore did not enjoy themselves probably) for M$^{\underline{me}}$ Goñi was there, & played more delightfully than ever– She is just from Boston, where she has been rather successful– but like a simple fool, lent her little earnings ($150) to that Impostor, Tasistro, who refuses to return the loan, & basely traduces her character– making up a story, about her falling in love with him &c– Poor little woman, her generosity has brought her into great trouble– She assists Knoop the violincellist at a concert he gives tomorrow night– unfortunately I have accepted an invitation to go to a Ball at M$^{\underline{rs}}$ Alsop's–[3] which will be the first I shall have attended for 15 months– It is to be a splendid affair, I hear. Even M$^{\underline{rs}}$ H. A. Middleton is going to it! He is arrived, but we have not yet seen him altho' he has been to visit us–

You may perhaps be glad to hear that M$^{\underline{rs}}$ McAlester[4] is out of danger–

we are all rejoiced at her almost miraculous recovery– They say her great composure of mind, saved her life– There has been another sudden death in our congregation– Mrs Shaw, Mrs Odenheimer's Mother, died a week ago very unexpectedly– M^rs O– was out visiting that morng– & he was at the Sergeants in the eveng– & when pressed to stay to Tea, said no, he must return home as his mother in law was not quite well– She died two hours afterward–

M^r [John Brown] Francis[5] has returned from Wash^n where he has succeeded beyond his most sanguine expectations in making the necessary arrangements with the Govern^t & says there will now be no difficulty in Rhode Is^d in all probability, & that all will go right– So that the Civil war which was anticipated is no longer to be dreaded there– nor according to the Papers, the foreign war either– & we shall I trust, meet there in health and tranquillity in about 2 months & a half more– How soon that will come!

Wednesday morng– I had the unexpected pleasure of receiving y^r letter of the 8th this morng– my dearest Mamma, & return you many thanks for it– It gave me great pleasure to hear how well you were all at such a late date– & that you were again surrounded by happy children & grandchildren to make you cheerful– I am delighted that Arthur's plan for amusing Kitty & keeping her good humoured succeeds so well– I always thought more might be done with her by kindness than any thing else–[6] Paolina's letter will never be forthcoming I fear– but don't plague her about it– She & Arthur will be coming on sooner than the rest of the family I suppose– & by railroad probably– I am curious to have the answer to my question in my last–

I must unsay what I told you of Sophia's not being a favourite for she is advancing rapidly in the good graces of all the old folks– And I don't wonder at it– for I never saw a baby more improved within the last month– She has not black eyes though– but very dark full round blue ones, with black lashes– & looks like nobody but her own sweet little self– It is impossible to be more good natured– & better both by day & night– She now regularly sleeps from about 1/2 past 7 in the eveng– till 6 the following morng– & is only taken up once at about 11 to be changed & nursed– & seldom wakes to be fed in the night– Then she takes a nap of two hours after she is bathed & generally another of one hour in the afternoon– Is she not a little piece of perfection? If she continues growing at the rate she has lately, you will scarcely be able to hold her– I nurse her 5 or 6 times in the course of the 24 hours, & 3 times she takes her allowance of three wineglass fulls of milk & water– I am quite well again, & am no more troubled with pain in the chest– Tell Mary I shall bear in mind her claims, & satisfy them as soon as I can spare an hour– My best love to her & Matty[7] and all the Uncles & Aunts who care to receive it, if they are still with you– And now I will spare your eyes, & say Adieu my dearest Mamma with the united regards of Fisher & his Mother– I am as ever Y^r affecte daughter Eliza

Poor F. had a very bad night, & is still so unwell that I have written to decline going to Mrs Alsop's ball this eveng– & am thus saved the trouble of arranging one of my _now_ rather _antiquated_ ball dresses– M^r & M^{rs} H– are as well as usual & desire kind remembrances.

Private Collection

   1. The Cuestas were probably the son and daughter-in-law of the John Sergeants' neighbor, Mrs. Cuesta, who died in 1840. Eliza made Mrs. Cuesta's acquaintance, knowing that she was a good singer.
   2. Thomas Chalmers (1780–1847) wrote about _The Adaptation of External Nature to the Moral and Intellectual Constitution of Man._ This was one of the so-called Bridgewater treatises on "the Goodness of God as manifested in the Creation" for which Francis Egerton, earl of Bridgewater (1756–1829), left money. The Fishers had also been reading William Whewell's Bridgewater treatise on _Astronomy and General Physics considered with reference to Natural Theology._
   3. The Richard Alsops lived near the Sergeants, at 93 South Fourth Street.
   4. Mrs. Charles Macalister (1806–1842) was the former Susan B. Wallace, daughter of Susan (Binney) and John Bradford Wallace (d. 1837). A day after having a baby, she became ill with what was diagnosed as varioloid, a mild form of smallpox, and died soon after. EMF to MHM, April 22, 1842, private collection.
   5. Governor Francis went to Washington to try to avert what became known as the Dorr War in Rhode Island. Many Rhode Islanders, frustrated by lack of progress in expanding the suffrage and reforming the state constitution, had voted for "The People's Constitution" to replace the old state constitution and elected Thomas Dorr as governor under its provisions. Dorr resorted to force, but his supporters were unsuccessful in taking over the state government.
   6. "Yesterday Eve^g," Mrs. Middleton told Eliza, "the young party by Arthur's advice played the game of 'What are my thoughts like,'. . . [_which he thought_] would be of service to P$^{\underline{a}}$ in accustoming her to English phrases, & he gave Cath^e great credit for the resemblances she brought forward in the answers– they were all much amused. A. & P. as I told you before have more influence over their Sister than any one. he says he understands how she ought to be treated, & I hope his plan may have a good effect." MHM to EMF, April 5, 1842, PHi.
   7. Coosey Middleton (whose name was Susan Matilda) now wished to be called Matty.

～

To Mrs. Fisher, Philadelphia

M.P. April 15$^{\underline{th}}$ 1842

   I had the pleasure my dearest Eliza to receive your letter of the 4th last Saturday– You must tell Mr Fisher I am much indebted to him for having at last consented to stay in our house. your Father too seems well pleased with his change of plans– it is very lucky indeed that Goff refused to accommodate you in the way you proposed– You need not look forward to a third baby in the house– Mrs Parnell was quite mistaken in her <u>views</u>– stoutness, is all that could have given her that wrong impression with regard to Paolina, who I have no doubt will make known to me her situation as soon as it changes.[1] She & the children & Cath^e spend most all the day in the wilderness where they have removed the long bench from the terrace, had a Swing put up, & have the pleasure of Arthur's society who in that place is making another seat with sup-ple Jack branches– they [*do needle*]work there sometimes, but their chief amusement is swinging or chatting. They have for pets two green Snakes a small Lizard, & two small Terapins.

I am delighted to learn that you are now quite free from pain, & that the baby gives you so little trouble. One subject you omitted to mention: the state of Mr Fisher's eyes– I flatter myself they are improving & that your next letter will announce their complete recovery. It will be very pleasing to me to hear Lily sing the Portuguese hymn– about her age you used to sing with Cath^e a pretty Italian air (a few bars of it) when at Georgetown. You do well to keep up your singing if it does not injure your voice which it did when you nursed Lily. I sympathise with you in your feelings in regard to Mr Harrison, & am very sorry to hear that he imagines his end approaching so soon. It is however a consolation that he can look forward to it with such composure. I hope he may yet be spared to you all for many years! I do not remember hearing you speak of M^{rs} McAlester– by this time I hope she may have recovered from the attack you mention. You have not lately mentioned Miss Hare, therefore I suppose her health is improving– & Mrs P. Smith– is she doing well? Give my love to her. Y^r Father carried the little Doctor [*Gibbes*] back to Charleston last Monday & returned yesterday, & tells me that Elias is to come here tomor-row, so that I may then receive y^r letter of the 11th.

17th The disappointment I felt my dearest Eliza by not receiving a letter from you yesterday as I fully expected, is greater that I can describe. I cannot prevent myself from fearing that illness, perhaps varioloid– may have attacked. you are never out of my thoughts, & I am haunted by a sad foreboding, notwith-standing the good advice lately received from you on the subject of distressing myself with apprehensions of evil– You are always so punctual in writing that I am sure nothing would prevent you from doing so but illness– I sometimes imagine one of the Children may be ill & <u>that</u> may have alarmed you too much to do anything but nurse & watch over them during the whole day. This is a sad state of anxiety for me which must continue several days longer– but as your Father will probably go to Combahee tomorrow, I will send towards the middle of the week to Charleston for the purpose of bringing letters that may have arrived– Elias will carry this tomorrow but not return here. I might send earlier, but might perhaps endure another disappointment should the messenger return without a letter. I cannot regard Philad^a as a healthy place– You have frequently mentioned a variety of disorders, & the Varioloid is certainly a very dangerous one. You ought not to walk about the lower parts of the town as you constantly do, for complaints must be more prevalent there, than in the upper streets. It is absurd to look forward to what may never happen but still I may <u>hope</u> that next winter you will spend here– The winter months are certainly healthy in the country– I boast not of Charleston although Miss Pinckney insists that it is the healthiest town in the world!

We have at length had showers of rain to the great benefit of the corn & pastures. There is a bad prospect for the crops– no sale for rice– & from all I can understand of the state of affairs, war seems to me inevitable. I ask Paolina what I shall say in answer to your expectation of a letter from her– She says she is so much occupied that she has not time to write but sends her love to you. In that she is joined by y^r Father & Arthur & the two Girls. Pray give my kind remembrance to M^r & Mrs Fisher & M^r & Mrs Harrison & believe me my dearest Eliza y^r Affectionate Mother M. H. M.

Your Father with his love to you, desires me to say that as Mr Fisher's eyes would be hurt by reading his letter, you must tell him that he must draw at 3 days sight upon Messrs Middleton & Wilkes for 1 thousand $, the rest, will be forthcoming shortly.[2]

PHi

1. Eliza replied, "I am quite glad that Paolina delays her encrease of family– It will be time enough for her to have such cares when she has conquered the difficulties of the English tongue, & has become more <u>americanized</u>." EMF to MHM, April 22, 1842, private collection.

2. As part of the financial arrangements made by both families when Fisher and Eliza were married, Henry Middleton undertook to give Eliza $1,800 annually, the equivalent of 6 percent interest on $30,000. However, as Mrs. Middleton mentioned, there was "no sale for rice" in the spring of 1842, and in March Henry Middleton told Fisher he would be unable to pay the money at the usual time because "the produce I had consigned to [*my factors*] with a view to the acceptance of your draft [*for Eliza's annuity*]. . . is yet unsold from the exceeding bad state of the market." John Wilkes and Thomas Middleton were in partnership as factors in Charleston at this time. HM to JFF, March 25, 1842. PHi, C/F.

To Mrs. Middleton, Middleton Place

Philadelphia 29<u>th</u> April 1842

My dearest Mamma,

Lest you should imagine that I am taken ill of <u>Varioloid</u>, or some other horrid disease because I do not send you a letter punctually, I write this morng– & have, besides, the pleasure of thanking you for your welcome letter of the 24<u>th</u> & 25<u>th</u> which gave me a great treat before breakfast, & made me relish that simple meal more than usual– This is a very ugly blot– which please excuse– & I will explain why I do not change this sheet of paper for another which I might do by going down stairs for it– You must know then that I am keeping watch over Lily to prevent her going up & down thro' the <u>cold</u> passages (for we have chilly weather again) & every time the door opens she is crazy to get out of her <u>cage</u>– This requires explanation also– but don't be alarmed as I was for a little while yesterday when I observed that she had an eruption upon her body– which upon consulting D<u>r</u> Meigs proved to be only Summer measles– her <u>second</u> attack, for you know she had one last spring– This is a very slight one, & nothing but confinement to the house & a little sweet Marjoram Tea is prescribed– altho' great <u>watchfulness</u> is also necessary to keep the little Truant out of <u>drafts</u> of air– (is it spelt so? I really forget, & have no Dictionary to consult). She is quite free from cold or cough with it– & I only wonder she has escaped so easily– particularly as I imprudently took her to drive yesterday thro' a very cold blustering wind, altho' I had remarked in the morng– that she had what I thought was merely prickly heat upon her little back– As it encreased very much in the afternoon & extended itself all over her, I sent for the D<u>r</u> who soon relieved my anxiety– I can now account for her having been a little fretful the last few days– & very restless & feverish for one or two nights– I suppose Sophy will certainly catch it too– but it is of so very mild a kind, that I do not apprehend danger for either of them– and am every day more determined to "take no thought for the morrow"– which precept does not of course imply that we are to be <u>improvident</u>– but merely that <u>anxious</u> thought (which is the sense in the original) is to be avoided, and we are to depend <u>daily</u> for all our blessings & comforts upon a good and merciful Providence–

You want me to tell you all I hear on the subject of a War with Eng<u>d</u>. If I did so, my sheet w<u>d</u> soon be filled with all the various opinions of persons who <u>know</u> nothing– The <u>general</u> impression is decidedly, that there is little danger of any extreme measure being taken, at least not for the present– & with this I am satisfied– & think that the good sense of the Peaceable party must prevail over the clamour made by such contemptible fellows as M^r [Henry] Wise. I think Mr Adams' reply[1] to him & Mr Ingersoll w^d amuse you– I read it aloud, at least part of it at Mr Harrison's in the eveng– & gained the credit from the old gent– of keeping him awake thro' it– which he said readers aloud had always failed in hitherto– Of course I do not imagine that unless the subject had been so well treated my <u>clearness</u> of enunciation would have had the desired effect– but he is always glad of an opportunity of praising me it seems–

Poor Fisher instead of recovering the use of his eyes, as he fondly hoped last week, thinks them now scarcely at all improved– I have great hopes from the change of air in to the country, which we propose to try during House Cleaning– about the middle of next month– The inducements to be a good deal out of doors will be much greater than in town & that alone will be service-able to them– We got a little tired of Chalmer's Treatise, & when about half way thro' it, gave it up for Kirby's–[2] Then we stopt to read several new Articles in the British Critic & Foreign Quart^y. The one on Dr Channing is very severe, but in F's opinion just for he abhors this new school of rationalistic transcen-dentalism which D^r C's theories lead to inevitably.

If I had time today I w^d give Arthur an account of some experiments lately made by Dr Mitchell upon patients under the influence of magnetic sleep– in which he <u>touches</u> their different Phrenological organs of Veneration, Music &c, & they immediately begin to pray– & sing psalms– & then <u>fight</u> or <u>steal,</u> as he successively touches combativeness or acquisitiveness– All this appears to us great Humbug– but we are to be invited to witness these wonderful results of the application of magnetism to Phrenology– & if "seeing is believing", which I am inclined to deny in <u>this</u> business, shall perhaps be <u>converted</u> to think that after all, men are mere <u>material machines</u> to be played upon by every adept in these mysterious sciences– The Hares are much engrossed with this subject, & startled at the exhibitions, which must be wonderful pieces of acting– many of the first Physicians, Meigs, Jackson[3] & Harris, have been present, but are very cautious in the expression of their opinions about it.

But to change the subject– I had a farewell visit from Delia Parnell who passed thro' Phil^a on her way to her embarkation in the G^t Western– & desired her kind remembrances to all my family at the South– to Papa particularly, whose many kindnesses to her, she said she never could forget– She appeared to more advantage than usual– Her heart seemed quite touched at the idea of leaving all her old friends again, & her Mother, for several years probably– She says she bore this separation better than the first & has too much <u>hope</u> to de-spond about meeting again–

I went the other day to see an old friend of yours, Mrs Madison,[4] who flattered me by saying she saw a likeness to you in me– and spoke most agreeably of Paolina, & of Arthur who seems quite a favorite of hers'– She was very gay here– went to Parties & Mrs Alsop's Ball– at which she enjoyed herself more than many young ones– Mrs Rives writes to Fisher that Wash^{n} has been induced only twice to "bustle up with unsuccessful speed" in attempting to do honor to Lord Morpeth first, & then to Ld Ashburton– She says also that he (the ambassador) & his suite all appear very amiable, & she therefore trusts under such auspices the clouds of war that are hovering in the horizon will be dissipated– I give you her <u>own</u> words on both subjects–

There is no news here, except the birth of a son to Mrs Willing– & this w^{d} be nothing very <u>new</u> but for the comments upon it which are too scandalous to be repeated much less written.[5] I will say goodnight as this had better wait for tomorrow's post <u>here</u> instead of in the Office– The hour for departure being changed to 1/2 past 2 in the afternoon– I went to see Mrs Smith this afternoon & was told she was sick– I daresay tomorrow I shall find her much better– I have begged off from spending the eveng at Miss Hare's & now the chicks are both asleep am going to solace myself at the Piano.

30$^{\underline{th}}$ Saturday– I have nothing to add except that Lily continues well notwithstanding the rash & is only a little <u>restive</u> from confinement to the nursery– Baby is perfectly well & will I hope escape infection– I must say Adieu, with love to all at home– & kind remembrances from our friends at 156 & M^{rs} F– in which Fisher unites with them, thanking you again for y^{r} solicitude about his eyes– which are better today– He read for half an hour, a good large print without fatigue– I am as ever dearest Mamma Y^{r} most affec$^{\underline{te}}$ daughter Eliza Mrs Smith was <u>out,</u> when I called this morng– so that she is of course recovered–

Private Collection

1. In the House of Representatives on April 13, Henry Wise accused England of wanting to control the Gulf of Mexico to prevent the United States from annexing Texas. If volunteers were called for to help Texas, he said, they would "flock to her standard" and "plant the lone star of the Texas banner on the proud ramparts of the Mexican capital." If this led to war with England, that would be fine.

The next day, in speaking against the right of search, Charles J. Ingersoll said the English "wanted to be the constables of the ocean." He suggested the U.S. Navy could easily burn London.

John Quincy Adams in reply accused them both of taking the idea of war very lightly "amidst professions of the most pacific spirit." If the United States went to war with Mexico and England, he suggested, it could face both invasion and an insurrection of slaves. If the South asked the North for help in such a situation, Adams reasoned, that would involve the war power; Congress would then be in charge and could declare martial law and emancipate the slaves. Congressional debates as reported in the *National Intelligencer*, April 16, 1842.

2. William Kirby (1759–1850), a minister of the Church of England, was also an entomologist. He wrote one of the Bridgewater treatises on *The Habits and Instincts of Animals* (1835).

3. Samuel Jackson (1787–1872) was professor of materia medica at the University of Pennsylvania. He was also chairman of the Philadelphia Board of Health. Thomas Harris (1784–1861), a well-known surgeon, was on the staff of the Pennsylvania Hospital for many years.

4. After former President Madison died in 1836, Dolley Madison moved back to Washington and was active almost until her death in 1849, when she was over eighty.

5. The implication is that her husband was not the father of the child.

∼

To Mrs. Middleton, Middleton Place

Monday [16th] May 1842

My dearest Mamma,

It was indeed a very agreeable surprise to me to receive your last letter of the 8th as in the previous one you had warned me not to expect another for two weeks– But I was so distressed to read the account you give me of dear Sally, that my pleasure was soon changed to pain– At the same time I recd a letter from Emma who tells me that the poor soul is again enceinte–[1] & altho' she does not give her authority, I have no doubt it comes from Mrs Wm Pringle– and is too true– Alas! what a pity that all the improvement of the last summer shd thus be thrown away! It seems to be really a sad doom, & yet the wise doctors may both be wrong, as to the effects they thought wd inevitably follow– & we must trust that her strength of constitution which has already been frequently tested in the same way, will again resist successfully– The wretched feelings you describe may be partly owing to this situation, & after the first 3 or 4 months, she will probably be relieved, temporarily at least– I dread as you do, the summer at the beach for her– but if it is an inevitable evil we must try & console ourselves with the reflection that under the circumstances she will, no doubt suffer less from the effects of the climate, than usual–

I regret much to hear of poor John's difficulties, & of the sacrifices Papa has been obliged to make–[2] If you had mentioned before his uncertainty about coming North, it wd have made me very miserable– but the engagement of the passages reassures me, & I have only to rejoice that we shall so soon meet–

The distresses of the times affect us at the North equally– and economy is the most frequently used word nowadays– How far it is carried into <u>practice</u> is another matter– but in <u>one</u> respect at least every one may now retrench– for things are sold in all the shops for almost nothing– but instead of this being a matter of congratulation– it is one for deep commiseration I think with the poor wretches who are starving in the manufactories, & the merchants who are selling at less than half the cost those goods they have imported– One hears of nothing but <u>cheap</u> goods– & no doubt many buy what they don't want, to have such bargains– I have not made many myself, because I hate to be encumbered with useless things– But I thought of you the other day, when Sally Hare told me she had bought an extremely pretty half mourning muslin for her Mother for 12 1/2 cents a Y$^{\underline{d}}$! & immediately followed her example– It is from the cargo of the Louis Philippe, but not in the least damaged– I have also supplied you with ribbons to match at an incredibly cheap rate– & tell Kitty she is not forgotten– If you have not bought her any new dresses in Charleston, you had better let me choose them here–

I am in an unfortunate predicament for lack of pens– but M$^{\underline{rs}}$ Smith has just made me only a <u>tolerable</u> one, with which I may go on without writing the same word <u>3 times</u> over as on the other page with the vile steel ones. She desires her love to you & is glad to hear you are coming in so capital a Ship as the Cath$^{\underline{e}}$ & with so good a Capt$^{\underline{n}}$ too– for I suppose Berry still commands her– We are daily disappointed about M$^{\underline{rs}}$ Holbrook's arrival– I begin to fear she will not come before we go into the Country– which we intend doing, weather permitting this day week– Fisher returned so much pleased with West Chester[3] that we have decided to go there, & as we shall be absent about ten days, I hope his eyes will benefit from the fresh air & exercize– They continue much the same– & he gave up the reading– as Chapman on his return to town disapproved of it–

There has been no further exhibition of Animal Magnetism at D$^{\underline{r}}$ Mitchell's– They talk of having another this week, & I expect an invitation– But I am sure I shall give offence by expressing my utter disbelief– for the infatuation is almost complete– Arthur's opinion seems to coincide with young Channing's who thinks it may be the <u>Will</u> of the Magnetiser operating upon his Patient, which calls forth the various emotions & sentiments he expresses in the <u>comatose</u> state. I have no opinion of D$^{\underline{r}}$ M's veracity, & think the only <u>fair</u> way of testing his experiments, is to take a person <u>wholly</u> unacquainted with Phrenology– whereas his <u>subjects</u> are crazy enthusiasts about it– & no doubt anxious to establish it as a science– which I hope they may never do–

Young Harrison Hare[4] returned unexpectedly from Rio Janeiro two days ago– but brought no news of E$\underline{d}$ except that the Marion was hourly expected there when he sailed– His Mother must be quite distressed at the occasion of his return, which is a refusal to sign a paper drawn up by Commodore Jones[5] to prevent the Midshipmen from fighting, upon oath– It seems a very arbitrary measure but may perhaps be justified upon the consideration that he lost 2 officers in a duel on a previous cruize– & wishing to preserve peace he threatened all under him to keep them close prisoners to their ships during the whole cruize if they did not consent to sign the paper– The only alternative was to resign– which several of them have done, but under the hope of being reinstated by the Sec$\underline{y}$ of the Navy– The Hares are quite troubled about it, & it seems unfortunate for the beginning. In great haste I must say Adieu– or you will wonder at not hearing– So with love to all I am as ever Your affectionate Eliza

Private Collection

1. Before Emma realized she was mistaken and that Sally was not pregnant, she had told Eliza she thought it was a "pity, that Paolina sh^d not have been the one this time. For she has no objection I hear, & poor Sally very strong ones—so it is." EHS to EMF, May 10, 1842, PHi.
2. Worried about Sally's health, Mrs. Middleton "enquired of John if he had the means of taking her to Aiken, he assured me if it were possible for him to do so he would, but it was quite out of his power– Upon hearing that I determined to ask your Father whether he could supply him with sufficient means for that purpose. When I represented to him the great risque she would incur by spending the summer on the beach he too assured me that it was utterly impossible for him to advance John any more money than he had done during the winter to keep him out of great distress. He even said that he had lately often been afraid that he sh$\underline{d}$ not be able himself to go to the north this summer. There has lately been such a low price for rice that he says he has been obliged to have it sold for less than half its value." MHM to EMF, May 8, 1842, PHi.
3. West Chester was a small town in the country west of Philadelphia. Fisher's friend, Alfred Elwyn, had a farm near there and probably recommended it as a healthy place.
4. The Robert Hares' youngest son was George Harrison Hare, named after Fisher's uncle.
5. Commodore Jacob Jones (1768–1850) had fought in the War of 1812 as well as commanded both the Mediterranean and Pacific squadrons. He lived in Delaware.

~

By the last week in May, Eliza's parents, along with Catherine, William, Paolina and Arthur had gone to Charleston. Arthur and Paolina planned to stay there until Henry Middleton had finished his business, while Mrs. Middleton and Catherine, escorted by William, were to leave for New York by sea on May 31. "You may be sure I look forward to the passage with dread," Mrs. Middleton told Eliza, "for the Thunder & lightning which happens every day will alarm me at Sea, beyond any other kind of storm."[1]

To get out of the way as Mrs. Fisher meticulously supervised the annual spring cleaning of the house in Chestnut Street, as well as to give Fisher's eyes a rest, the Fishers, meanwhile, took the children to West Chester, west of Philadelphia. Just as they were leaving, Edward arrived back from his tour of duty in South America. He had been promoted to lieutenant while he was away.

1. MHM to EMF, May 29, 1842, PHi.

To Mrs. Fisher, Philadelphia

N. York June 11$\underline{th}$ 1842

I can at length my dearest Eliza announce my arrival which occurred only yesterday Even$\underline{g}$ after a most disagreeable passage of 11 days– on the third of which we were 6 miles south of Charleston & had been near Cuba! Most thankful I am that we arrived safely & after the second day did not suffer from sea sickness. M$\underline{rs}$ R[awlins] Lowndes & M$\underline{rs}$ Coffin were agreeable fellow passengers, & supplied me with books. I was disappointed at not finding a letter from you which I requested you to send, as you must have left West Chester several days ago– I was also disappointed at not finding Ed[war]d here or even a letter from him. I wrote to him on the 30$\underline{th}$ May & directed the letter to the Post Office by W's advice– perhaps he never enquired there for one– & he may not be permitted to leave the vessel yet. In a day or two I may learn from you some account of him, as you have no doubt met soon after his arrival. I hope also soon to be informed that the change of air has as you expected had a good effect on M$\underline{r}$ Fisher's eyes & that I may soon receive you all at Newport. I have been telling W$\underline{m}$ I wished to go next Tuesday there by the Mass$\underline{tts}$. he does not approve of leaving this so soon, but as I have been so lucky as already to have engaged John, his Wife & her Sister & shall probably get Bridget,[1] there will be nothing to detain us here except procuring a Groom, which W$\underline{m}$ will not leave N.Y. without doing. Therefore I cannot say positively that we shall go next Tuesday. The DeRhams[2] have taken their passage in it, & are to spend the summer in the house the Brevoorts occupied two years ago 4 miles from Newport. Miss Moore will be with them part of the season which I am very glad to hear. She came to see me yesterday eve$\underline{g}$ half an hour after our arrival having met W$\underline{m}$ walking out. She mentioned having given a letter of introduction to you to M$\underline{r}$ Labouchere & his friend, I told her I feared you must have missed seeing them, as you must have been at the time they went to Philad$\underline{a}$ at West Chester.

If you should happen to write to S. Thorndike in a day or two, pray beg her to let Block know that we shall probably be at Newport next Wednesday & desire him to put down the Carpets clean the house &c. John has just told me that Bridget is now Cook at the Adelphi hotel, so that there is no chance of my having her. Here is a very cold day for the season. You must have the same at Philad$\underline{a}$. during the voyage we suffered at first from excess of heat & afterwards from cold brought on by a strong North wind. I must send this off now.

Here comes Marg$\underline{t}$, John's wife– She says after talking with her husband & thinking of the approaching event they deem it most prudent that she sh$\underline{d}$ remain here as she will probably be confined in July so that I shall hire a Washer at Newport. It w$\underline{d}$ as I thought be very inconvenient to have that happen there but yesterday she said the only condition that w$\underline{d}$ induce John to reenter my service would be to take her with him. If this is not sent now you will not receive it this Eve$\underline{g}$. With love to M$\underline{r}$ & M$\underline{rs}$ Fisher & kind remembrance to M$\underline{r}$ & M$\underline{rs}$ Harrison believe me my dearest Eliza y^r Affect^{te} Mother M. H. M.

PHi

1. These were servants who had gone to Newport with the Middletons in previous summers.
2. Henry Casimir DeRham (1785–1873), who immigrated from Switzerland in 1805, became a wealthy importer and served as the Swiss consul in New York. Mrs. DeRham was Miss Moore's sister. The DeRhams were the parents of Henry DeRham, who died while traveling in the south with Audubon.

⌒

The summer of 1842 started in "a succession of fogs & floods of rain."[1] The Middletons got to Newport before the end of June, but between the rain and the carriage needing to be mended, Mrs. Middleton complained that she hardly saw anyone. William went off to look for excitement in New York. By midsummer, however, there were more visitors (strangers, as the Newport natives called them) in Newport than ever before. People came, it was reported, with "the Most Splendid Carriages & Livery'd Servants—from Boston, NYork, Philadelphia &c."[2] and there was, as usual, a large group of South Carolinians—Pinckneys, Izards, Hamiltons, Coffins, and Hugers, as well as Middletons.

Mrs. Middleton and Eliza did not write much about what they and their friends did when they were in Newport since they were together for most of the summer. Fisher, however, wrote chatty letters to the Harrisons, and these help fill the gap and paint a picture of Newport summer life in the 1840s.

In addition to the regular pleasures of riding, walking, and listening to Eliza play the piano in the evening, there were parties at the Harpers' or Amorys', as well as at the Middletons', with singing and quadrilles. Or they just enjoyed "the delicious air under a full moon. Never anywhere have I known such nights as those in August at Newport," Fisher wrote.[3] They went sea bathing and made expeditions by carriage and horseback to romantic spots from which they looked out over Narragansett Bay. Friends and relatives came and went—Emma and Allen Smith, the Thorndikes, Harpers, and Joneses, the Hares, and the Channings. Some stayed in one of the Newport boardinghouses, others, like the Joneses and Harpers, were beginning to build houses of their own.

In the summer of 1842, Fisher was particularly pleased because "we have here from New York the very best band of Music I have heard in America which plays every morg & in the Eveng at some party— and once each week at a public Ball at the Masonic Hall." While protesting that he and Eliza never went anywhere, he told Uncle Harrison that there was "very gay & good society— Never was Newport so full or so dissipated," and, he continued, "a fancy Ball at Mrs. Jones on Tuesday week is to crown our festivities. We have gay people from all parts of the Union & some beauties."

Eliza added that "Everyone is talking of the Fancy Ball & all insist upon my going— but I think the costume of a bonne d'enfants [*children's nurse*] is the only suitable one for me— & think of adopting a mob cap & check apron for the occasion— Arthur will make a capital Turk & Edward will sport his magnificent Albanian Dress— Paolina of course her national costume & Fisher & Wm are still unprovided."[4]

If Eliza felt a bit tied down by the children, help at least was at hand. During the summer of 1842, Mrs. Sarah Putnam, a Bostonian recommended by Mrs. Ritchie, joined the Fishers as the children's nurse. From the start, she was "even more satisfactory" than Eliza had been led to expect in helping to bring up Lily, always a very shy child, and Sophy, who was quite the opposite.[5] Soon affectionately known as "Pum," Mrs. Putnam returned to Philadelphia with the Fishers in early October and stayed with them, caring for all six Fisher children through the 1840s and 1850s.

In the fall, the Middletons again stopped in Philadelphia for three weeks on their way back to Charleston. This time, Mrs. Middleton's children were worried about her because she had had palpitations. To relieve them she had been given "veratria", or hellebore, a medicinal herb used as a cardiac and respiratory depressant. It was also, as Mrs. Middleton's subsequent letters indicate, intensely irritating to the skin, and in one form could even be a powerful muscle and nerve poison.

1. MHM to EMF, June 19, 1842, and June 28, [1842,] PHi.
2. Catharine Engs Dennis to Mary R. Hunter, October 28, 1840, in *Newport History* 57, ser. 3, no. 195 (summer 1984): 71.
3. JFF to the Harrisons, August 15, 1840, and JFF to GH, September 10, [1841,] both PHi, BrC.
4. JFF to GH, (with note from Eliza) August 5, 1842, PHi, BrC.
5. Ibid.

To Mrs. Middleton, Charleston

Philadelphia, Thursday 17$\underline{\text{th}}$ Nov$\underline{\text{r}}$ [1842]

My dear Mamma,

I have just had the pleasure of receiving a letter from Edward, informing me of y$\underline{\text{r}}$ safe arrival, without much fatigue at Balt$\underline{\text{e}}$, & without any more symptoms of illness– This is indeed good news, & I trust in 3 or 4 days more to learn from yourself that you have borne the rest of the journey equally well. Even now whilst I am writing, I hope you are similarly occupied in announcing your arrival this morng– in Charleston– & when I hear that I shall indeed rejoice & be thankful– You were already too far South on Wednesday to feel the bad weather we had here I hope– & last night was comparatively clear–

Whilst I was on my way to the Wedding,[1] I was supposing you to be stowed away in your berth, & still thought a great deal of you all during the night– The bridal party went off very well– was less dull than such affairs generally are– & the Supper was really superb and beautiful– The Bride looked her very best & was magnificently attired. I can't say the same of the groom, who wore as usual, a <u>colored</u> neckcloth as Fisher predicted– knowing his great partiality to them. Poor fellow altho' utterly wanting in taste (for dress at least) he is a pattern in every thing else– & really a most excellent & estimable character– He is a queer one tho'– for he was just as much composed during the ceremony, & the whole evening as if he had been at an ordinary teaparty– Talking Philosophy & Politics as unconcernedly as possible– Esther behaved admirably– with the utmost dignity– & went thro' her responses without faltering– She wore my bracelet (not the one I shewed you, but a handsome one for which I exchanged it not being satisfied with the first) & thanked me very sweetly for it– Tonight they receive company & tomorrow go to Washington for 10 days, & then on their return come to our neighbourhood– I suppose there will then be a succession of Parties in their honour– & pray tell W$\underline{\text{m}}$ not to delay his coming until they are over– If he will give me timely notice I will wait, & give our's after his arrival–

Edward seems to be enjoying himself amazingly in Balt$^{\underline{e}}$ & mentions the beauty & attractions of several young ladies there, but not a word of Miss T[iffany]–[2] so I rather hope he may have got out of conceit of her– I suppose he had time to tell you of his intention of going to Wash$^{\underline{n}}$ for a week & thence to Car[olin]a. Pray when he arrives, tell him I thank him for his letter, & altho' sorry not to see him here, forgive him since I have heard his reasons for passing thro' so hurriedly– & congratulate him upon gaining the desired extension of congé [*leave*]–[3]

My writing is rather interrupted by Miss Lily's music– She is pretending to sing at the Piano to her own accompaniment, with an air & a grace truly ridiculous– She & Toty[4] are perfectly well, & with the help of new Toys sent by <u>Lala</u> bear the confinement to the house this rainy weather well. I find that M$^{\underline{rs}}$ Smith actually set off this morng– She wrote me yesterday that she heard such bad reports of the Wash$^{\underline{n}}$ way that she thought after all she sh$^{\underline{d}}$ try the Bay– How fortunate you did not take passage in the Cath$^{\underline{e}}$ which it seems had a sixteen days, very rough sail–

I hope you will tell me <u>exactly</u> how you are, my dearest Mamma, & whether the heart has been at all irregular since the application of the Veratria– I sent some to Sophia with directions how to use it, & trust she may find benefit from it– I forgot to beg you to remember me most particularly to M$^{\underline{rs}}$ Holbrook– pray do so when you see her– & also to Cousin Sally Rutledge & Cousin Alice [Heyward]– I am obliged to conclude now, as I am expected to dine at Aunt Harrison's, & must prepare accordingly– M$^{\underline{rs}}$ Fisher begs her best regards– & Fisher joins me in every affect$^{\underline{e}}$ message to all my friends– I am dear Mamma Y$^{\underline{r}}$ most affectionate daughter Eliza

I hope dear Emma did not suffer from the journey, & found her <u>beloved</u> in good health, awaiting her.

ScHi

1. This was the wedding of Esther Binney and Clark Hare.
2. Miss Tiffany was probably a daughter of Osmond Tiffany, a Baltimore merchant. Edward would have met her in Newport since the Tiffanys rented Nathaniel Amory's cottage there during the summer of 1842. The reason for the Middletons' disapproval is not clear.
3. Edward was given leave until the spring of 1843.

4. The Fishers sometimes called Sophy "Toty" when she was little. Lala has not been identified.

～

To Mrs. Middleton, Middleton Place

Philadelphia Wednesday, 23$\underline{rd}$ November [1842]

I must write a few lines this morng– to tell you how much happiness your letter of Thursday gave me, my dearest Mamma– I only received it yesterday eveng owing I believe to the stoppage of the mails by the Snow which it appears fell at the South, altho' we have seen nothing of it here– I flattered myself on Sunday eveng that I might hear from you, & on Monday my disappointment was much greater for I almost made sure of it– & I began to fear you had been detained at Weldon & were out in the Storm of Friday– I was therefore anxious all day, until Fisher brought me your letter which relieved me entirely, & sent me very joyful to Aunt H's where I announced the good news of your safe arrival– which was received there with pleasure, & congratulations came thick upon me, from many guests who came accidentally & made the eveng pass pleasantly– No doubt I was disposed to be gayer than usual, for a load seemed actually removed from my heart– & I felt as if my gratitude ought to be expressed in cheerfulness & good will to all round me– You do not mention suffering from any return of your Palpitations– so that I trust you had been free from them on the journey– but should have been much better satisfied if you had said so– however you say that you felt comfortable– which I hope means as much as the word can convey.

I wrote a short letter to Paolina yesterday, & as she wrote me that they expected to leave Washington on Thursday she will probably travel as fast as this, (which I do not intend to send today to the P. Office), & give you the latest news of herself– I am glad you had such cheerful company with you & that W$\underline{m}$ made so good a nurse– Tell him I shall depend upon his keeping his promise of returning– & shall certainly defer our Bridal party [*for Esther and Clark Hare*] until his arrival– Then when he is tired of New York gaiety we may possibly be fellow travellers to Carolina– if he will wait until Feby– but this is so very uncertain a project that you must not mention it at all out of the family– for it will depend much on the decision about the Lawsuit[1] & also on the health of all our friends here– but I have a conditional promise from Fisher & altho' he advises me not to think about it for fear of disappointment, I find the anticipation too pleasant to wish to give it up until just before the time.

I have just had a visit from Dͬ͟ Meigs (who came to lance Sophia's gums) & begged me to remind you to see Dͬ͟ Holbrook, which you know you promised me to do– Dͬ͟ M. looked at my throat, which had been a little out of order for some days, & applied the nitrate of Silver, which he thinks will cure it– with the addition of Portwine gargle– He gave me permission to go to the Concert tonight (Thursday) to hear Mͫͤ͟ Spohr Zahn[2] sing, & our old friend Schmidt on the guitar.

At one o'clock Mͫͤͩ͟ d'Hauterive & de Cuesta are to meet here & practise the "Stabat"–[3] & I have sent another copy to Mͬ͟ Fry[4] to get the Tenor part ready by next week– Franky [Schroeder] will be here shortly his mother says, & take the Bass, & I am to make Miss Brugiere's[5] acquaintance for the other Soprano– They say her voice is admirable– so that I really think we shall have an excellent Troupe– & I hope towards Christmas the performance will be perfect–

Fisher has found out that Miss Harper passed thro' Phila on Thursday last– on her way to NewPort to nurse her Mother, who has been attacked again– I suppose you have heard this from Harry's correspondent– Mͬ͟ Godly[6] mentioned it to us. He came in while we were at our dessert on Monday, & passed half an hour in the interval of going into the rail car for Burlington– where he was to spend the night at Bishop Doane's– He is to sail on Friday– & says he regrets the necessity of doing so very much– was delighted with his visit to the Rives', with whom he spent several days– He made many enquiries after you all–

Mͬ͟ Dyar & Mͬ͟ [R.] Trueman are both in town [*from Boston*] & Fisher wishes to have them here at dinner– the latter says Mͬͤ͟ Ritchie had heard from Sophia Thorndike, who was rather better, & hoping to be well enough to pay her Aunt a visit in the spring– Aunt Harrison begged me when I wrote to you, to say with her kind regards to yourself, that she had intended asking you to remember her most particularly to her three favourites, Mͬͤ͟ John (Sally), & little Mary & Sarah– & wishes you would do so for her– She is well, but Mͬ͟ H. is suffering a little with his Throat– & Mͬͤ͟ F– is extremely unwell– with a violent cold & cough, & nervous besides– She also desires her best regards to you & the rest of the family– I am so glad that dear Sally will be with you during John's absence– You & she will save poor Pauline much trouble in the choice of her Layette– & the girls must be very expeditious about making it up, or poor Bente[7] will have to be Swaddled. This day year we parted– dear Mamma. How short the time seems since then! at least all that part of it I spent with you–

Little Sophy has 3 double Teeth & another nearly thro'– Lily was threatened with Croup two nights ago, but the Syrup of Hippo was as efficacious as usual in warding it off– I must say Adieu that I may finish an article in the Edinburg [*Review*] (on M$\underline{me}$ de Sévigné & her contemporaries) which F charged me to give him on his return. It is very interesting, & I advise y$\underline{r}$ reading it– Pray give my love to Papa, my brothers & sisters, nieces & nephews & believe me Y$\underline{r}$ most affectionate daughter

Fisher with his kindest regards begs you will remind W$\underline{m}$ about a certain old chair in the garret at M. Place which he promised to <u>make over</u> to him.

ScHi

1. Fisher was worried about a lawsuit, *Sheriff vs. Charles Francis and J. Francis Fisher;* the nature of the case is not explained. Charles Francis (1771–1845), Mrs. Fisher's and Mrs. Harrison's bachelor brother, lived close to them on Sansom Street. Fisher took care of his business affairs.

2. Madame Spohr Zahn, a "finished and classical singer," was the daughter of the German violinist and composer Louis Spohr. *Phila. GCI,* November 21, 1842.

3. This is the first time Eliza mentioned her hope of singing the Stabat Mater. Palestrina, Pergolesi, and Rossini had all written such compositions, but Eliza does not say whose they hoped to perform.

4. Possibly William H. Fry, editor of the *National Gazette,* who also wrote an opera.

5. The Brugieres were refugees from Haiti who settled in Philadelphia in the early nineteenth century.

6. John Godley, an Englishman, brought a letter of introduction to the Fishers from their friend A. L. Cole. George Washington Doane (1799–1859) was Episcopal bishop of New Jersey.

7. Paolina was expecting her first child in February, and Mrs. Middleton had begun to prepare the baby's layette. Paolina and Arthur were calling their child Bente (Bentivoglio), assuming it would be a boy.

⁓

To Mrs. Fisher, Philadelphia

Charleston Novr 25$\underline{th}$ 1842

My dearest Eliza

I had the pleasure of receiving y$\underline{r}$ letter of 17th the day before yesterday & begin this that I may have time to fill the sheet before I add the news of Sally's arrival which will probably be tomorrow & then I may not have time to write anything but of her. John arrived yesterday morng by the Stage as he is obliged to leave this on Sunday for Columbia– He is looking well & says all the family are so. Oliver came last Sunday about 2 o'clock having seen the account of our arrival while travelling from Edisto & having business to do here, remained until Tuesday. He is looking uncommonly well & stout & in good spirits & gives a good account of all the family including Mrs Chisolm. We told him he must bring them all to M.P. before Xmas, which he is very willing to do, & nothing I hope will prevent their coming.

W$^{\underline{m}}$ had left this for Combahee last Saturday & neglected to give me the parcel you sent which I put under his care, the two bags for Susan & Sally & something else– I cannot recollect whether it was the two Collars for Sarah, for I cannot find them in my own trunks. I cannot remember where they were placed, however on emptying them in the country I may find them. The books are distributed except those of Johnny & Tom who will have them soon. As to the music I begged your Father to give it to Oliver to carry to his Girls but he [*Oliver*] said their Piano was in such a state they could not play on it, neither had he room for the parcel– I requested then that Cath$^{\underline{e}}$ might have the pleasure of playing it as she will not touch this piano because she has no new music. my request is however not attended to. (<u>Now</u> he has)

I saw Emma yesterday & told her I had heard from you & delivered y^{r} message to her: she begged me to give you her best love & say that she intended to write soon. I told her I had forgotten to mention her having written to you from Portsmouth which was very kind of her. She is to go to Sa[vannah] Riv^{r} this day week– She found her husband here, & he is now at Laurel hill for a day or two. I found y$^{\underline{r}}$ Aunt Huger at home yesterday & had a long chat with her. She informed me of my old friend H[enriett]a Drayton being here alone at her Sister's house– subject as usual to severe attacks. I shall go to see her this morning– I also saw Miss Pinckney, M$^{\underline{rs}}$ Izard & S. Rutledge. <u>She</u> is looking sadly dejected– they all enquired kindly after you, as did also Mrs Pinckney & her daughter.[1] Having been much occupied with purchasing articles for Paolina & the household I missed seeing several visitors among others Mrs P. Smith– I found her however at home two days ago looking well & in good spirits having had a safe voyage & journey. She begged me to mention to you that the letter you gave her for Paolina she entrusted at Baltimore to the care of a young Man who promised to deliver it. She gave me a good account of you & the Children.

She also enquired particularly about my palpitation & as you do the same I must tell you what happened four days ago, when finding a slight one about 2 o'clock (before dinner) I thought I might try the liquid which Dr Meigs desired me to moisten a rag with & rub the breast: that however gave me such pain, that I merely applied it & even <u>that</u> was painful. I was not aware of its having taken off the skin of my breast when I began to rub the ointment at night. The pain was so violent, it felt like stabbing, so that I have been compelled to discontinue the use of the ointment until my breast is quite healed, which the use of pomade divine (of which I luckily have a small quantity) contributes to do. In the meantime the palpitation is very slight & does not keep me awake at night, so that the remedy has been very efficacious. I shall not try the liquid again. W$^{\underline{m}}$ begged D$^{\underline{r}}$ Holbrook to call, which he did the day after my arrival– his questions were not very numerous but he said he would bring his Stethoscope some day, & if necessary, dry cup my breast– I told him then that we sh$^{\underline{d}}$ probably leave town in a week– he has not been here since, & perhaps it is unnecessary he should, & he said that if it were advisable to dry cup me in the country he could shew Will$^{\underline{m}}$ how to perform that easy operation. M$^{\underline{rs}}$ H. has not been to see me– the infant of M$^{\underline{rs}}$ E$^{\underline{d}}$ R[utledge] died last week of inflammation of the Lungs– to the great grief of the Mother who had been quite a different creature Miss Pinckney says during its life. I have just come in from my shopping & visit to poor H$^{\underline{a}}$ Drayton who has been suffering agonies lately, but is now a little better. The account she gives of her disease excites great commiseration. She often wishes when attacked at night by the dreadful pain that she might never again awake from her slumber– She is very well prepared to quit this world, & does not expect to remain long in it. The residence of two years at Nassau proved very beneficial to her but she had not the means to remain there longer. She is to go soon to her Sister in the country & stay there till May. She begged me to remember her kindly to you.

Just after taking off my bonnet I was called down to receive a visit from M$^{\underline{r}}$ & M$^{\underline{rs}}$ R[ussell] M[iddleton]^2 who I had called upon yesterday. She is a good looking woman & agreeable, but what a loud high toned voice! Georgina called some days ago when I was out, & is now gone to Stono. She is perfectly well & Alice I have seen twice– She is in good spirits. I have at last purchased all the articles which will be necessary for the infant. Could I have had y$^{\underline{r}}$ list it would have been more convenient. I shall be obliged to make the cambric caps at home as well as other things. I have bought lace & insertions but as to embroidery, that is not to be done– I have got 2 worked frocks & worked bodies which must be added to the cambric muslin frocks according to the pattern. It is doubtful whether Arthur will allow his child to wear Caps– he said it sh$^{\underline{d}}$ not wear shirts because the arm holes & sleeves w$^{\underline{d}}$ be too tight, & a covering tied round the neck, w$^{\underline{d}}$ answer all the purpose of a shirt!

Your Father & T. M[iddleton] say you must not address y$^{\underline{r}}$ letters to the care of the latter, because his Wife's letters are directed in that way & he was on the point of giving her yours the other day. Miss M$^{\underline{c}}$Evers found her Sister

M$\underline{rs}$ [John] Ravenel so ill she insisted upon her going with her to N.York immediately. I must not omit to tell you that Hal is within two inches as tall as his
father. Sarah too has grown very much. The schooner came yesterday but y$\underline{r}$
Father will not go to M.P. till next week: how we can find room for all the
family here I am puzzled about if Arthur & P. sh$\underline{d}$ come in a few days. Judging
from the very cold weather we have had here since the 18$\underline{th}$ ins$\underline{t}$ I have feared
you must have suffered severely from the greater degree of it at Phil$\underline{a}$ Yesterday
it became warmer & today much more so. Your little Lily's song must have
been very amusing. You must tell me how many more words she can speak as
soon as you hear them.

Saturday morn$\underline{g}$– I have been thinking you would be anxious to hear from
me as it is more than a week since my first letter & I can give you an account
of Sally when in the country– I suppose she will come in the course of the day.
I was surprised yesterday Eve$\underline{g}$ to hear Sarah play two Tunes from Norma &
"Mose in Egitto"³ very well, in very good time & I told her I w$\underline{d}$ let you know
of her progress since Feb$\underline{y}$. You must thank M$\underline{r}$ Fisher for me again for Miss
Leslie's book–⁴ I study it a little every day & find many excellent receipts &
instructions for cookery. With love to M$\underline{r}$ & M$\underline{rs}$ F. & remembrance to M$\underline{r}$ &
M$\underline{rs}$ Harrison I am my dearest Eliza y$\underline{r}$ Affect$\underline{te}$ Mother M. H. M.

PHi

1. Elizabeth Izard (Mrs. Thomas) Pinckney had two daughters: Ella (Mrs. Ralph
Stead Izard) and Elizabeth, who married Benjamin Huger.
2. Nathaniel Russell Middleton (1810–1890) was introducing his second wife,
Anna de Wolf from Bristol, Rhode Island. They were married in September 1842. Russell Middleton's first wife, Margaret Emma Izard, died in 1836, leaving three young
sons.
3. Gioacchino Rossini wrote the opera/oratorio *Mose in Egitto* [Moses in Egypt]
in 1818.
4. Eliza Leslie (1787–1858), who became widely known as the editor of *Miss Leslie's Magazine*, established her reputation when she published a best-selling cookbook,
Seventy-Five Receipts for Pastry, Cakes and Sweetmeats, in 1828.
Another clue, in addition to her using Miss Leslie's cookbook, that Mrs. Middleton
was more concerned with food production and preparation than her letters indicate,
comes from her son, John. On the back side of a letter to his mother he gave detailed
instructions for curing bacon so that, if "the meat [is] kept carefully dry no worms or
insects will attack it, even in summer." John I. Middleton to MHM, January 27, 1841,
PHi, C/F.

⌒

To Mrs. Middleton, Middleton Place

Wednesday eveng– 30$\underline{th}$ Nov$\underline{r}$ [1842]

My dearest Mamma,

I scarcely expected the good luck of a letter just a week after the last, & was therefore agreeably surprised <u>yesterday morng</u> to receive your's– of quite a late date too– with the additional lines written on <u>Saturday</u>– I suppose the Steamboat for Wilmington now leaves Charleston in the morng– or at noon– else I cannot account for receiving news in <u>less</u> than three days– for the letter which was delivered to me on Tuesday morng– must have arrived here the afternoon before! in two days & 1/2!– which is so incredibly quick, that I am inclined to think you mistook, & wrote Saturday for Friday– By this time I hope you are not only established at M. Place yourself, but that you have Sally with you, & know of the safe arrival of Arthur & Pauline– who would be likely to suffer from the cold if they are still on the road– Here we have had a snow storm all day, & the Sleighs are driving merrily thro' the streets, which will be rendered almost impassable for foot passengers, for the side pavements are covered with ice– & I fear the poor children will be imprisoned for some days.

I am delighted to hear so good an account of Oliver & his family– & of John also– but knowing the latter to be always so sanguine about Sally, I shall be better satisfied when you have seen her yourself– & can tell me of her improvement, of which too you will be better able to judge– not having seen her for so many months– I wrote yesterday, (for I ought to say that I am now continuing this on <u>Thursday</u>,) having been interrupted last night, to Mary, for I really felt ashamed of keeping her last letter to me two months unanswered– & did not wish her to suppose me utterly neglectful of it– This morng I heard from Sophia, who was rather better, & thought herself somewhat relieved by the Veratria which I sent her– she begs me to present her <u>sympathetic</u> regards to you, when I sh$\underline{d}$ write– M$\underline{rs}$ T[horndike] is better she thinks & Sally Anne very anxious that she sh$\underline{d}$ return with her to Germany in the Spring– but she has not decided to do so yet, & does not wish it mentioned–

I was sorry to hear of the suffering caused by the mere application of the Lotion & think you had better dilute it in a little water before you try it again– I hope you saw D$\underline{r}$ Holbrook again before leaving town, & made him perform the operation of cupping himself– for how could W$\underline{m}$ do it, or even learn how, at Combahee? I trust you have been able to resume the use of the Veratria, for I have great confidence in its powers– Unfortunately it seems to have lost its effect upon poor Fisher, whose eyes have been worse again for the last few days– whether from exerting them too much for he was imprudent enough to read for upwards of three hours (at different times) for some days, or whether from discontinuing the Shower Bath, which Dr Meigs disapproved of during this cold weather– agreeing with Arthur in thinking it might produce some internal inflammation or congestion by driving the blood too suddenly to the Lungs or Stomach– Chapman had on the contrary told him there would be no risk in his continuing it all thro' the winter– but he chose to consult Meigs also & as soon as I heard his opinion which coincided exactly with Arthur's I dissuaded him from taking another– The very day he left off, he was attacked by one of his headaches, from which he had been entirely free for upwards of 7 weeks, whilst he used the Shower bath daily– but it is better that he sh^d suffer occasionally from these constitutional tormentors, than from some more dangerous malady brought on by the remedy for them & the eyes it is to be hoped will recover their strength without that Hydropathy– There is a capital Lecture on this, Homoeopathy & other kindred delusions by Dr Dunglisson,[1] which has amused [us] so much, that I must try & get another copy of it to send you– & perhaps you will shew it to Arthur to whom I would recommend its perusal also– altho' I scarcely think he will be convinced of the fallacy of some of his favourite theories by ridicule–

We had rather an interesting conversation between Mr Dyar & M^r [Henry] Gilpin[2] on the subject of animal Magnetism the other day at a little dinner Fisher made for the former– Mr G. spoke of the interview between a somnambulist & a very intelligent lady, who turned out to be Miss Wightt,[3] & explained how she had deceived herself in some particulars, & in others guided (unconsciously) the sleeper, & suggested many things which she described very vaguely– & yet Miss W. persuaded herself of the resemblance to objects, which Mr G. knew well too, & w^d never have recognized–

On account of the death of poor M^{rs} T[homas Willing] Morris,[4] we have refused several invitations for parties this week– a musical one at Mrs Rush's which w^d have been quite a treat, to me, for the Seguins[5] are to sing, and one for the Bride [*Esther Binney Hare,*] at Mrs Prime's, who took the eveng– Mrs Hare had fixed on, because the latter met with a terrible accident, & has been confined ever since to her room– She tripped her foot in some pieces of carpet, & fell down a whole flight of stairs head foremost, cutting her face & bruising herself dreadfully, but most miraculously escaping without broken bones– She was of course bled immediately & put in bed, where she remained 4 days without stirring, but she is now doing very well. Mrs Prime very foolishly sent out her invitations before she knew positively of the movements of her brother, & now the party is to come off tonight, & they are not yet arrived– There are to be several next week, but our's is deferred till the week after, by

which time I hope W^m will be here– Our "Stabat" will not be ready for performance until after Xmas– The snow has interfered with our practising yesterday & today–

I am going to allow Lily the great indulgence of dining with us at Aunt
Harrison's today– & little Toty is to come in with the dessert– They are both
perfectly well, & look so sweet in their new blue frocks exactly alike, that I wish
you could see them. Mrs Fisher is much better & acknowledges it herself, which
is the best proof of it. I must now take the children while the Nurse dines– I
have so many loves to send & so little room for them, that you must imagine
them & deliver them to all the party– Adieu dearest Mamma, Your affectionate
daughter Eliza

ScHi

1. Dr. Robely Dunglison (1798–1869), an Englishman, was professor of medicine
at Jefferson Medical College, 1836–68. He was active in the American Philosophical
Society and the Institute for the Blind. Hydropathy was the treatment of diseases with
water, both by drinking it and by using it externally. Homeopathy, as developed by
Samuel Hahnemann (1755–1843), was increasingly popular as a system of treating
disease.

2. Henry Dilworth Gilpin (1801–1860), Fisher's cousin, was a lawyer. A Democrat, he was attorney for the Eastern District of Pennsylvania under President Jackson,
and briefly attorney general under President Van Buren. He was active in the Historical
Society of Pennsylvania and Girard College. He married Eliza (Sibley) Johnston in 1834.

3. Miss Ann Wight (also spelled White or Wightt) was a relative of Mrs. Van Ness's
and a former nun at the convent in Georgetown. General Van Ness continued to provide
for her after his wife's death. She became a friend of Paolina's and gave her English
lessons.

4. Caroline Maria Calvert was the daughter of George and Rosalie (Stier) Calvert
of Maryland. She married Thomas W. Morris, son of Ann Willing Morris, and died of
consumption, leaving four children.

5. Arthur and Anne Seguin, popular singers in Philadelphia and New York from
the 1830s until the 1850s, were performing Bellini's "La Sonnambula" and Rossini's
"Mose in Egitto." Eliza told her mother, "Aunt Harrison w^d I believe like me to go
three times a week with her, but I must accept some of the invitations to parties, &
cannot be running out every night." EMF to MHM, December 9, [1842,] ScHi.

∽

To Mrs. Middleton, Middleton Place

Thursday– 15th Dec^r [1842]

I was becoming very impatient & even anxious about you, my dearest
Mamma, when y^r letter partly written at M. Place was brought me, the day
before yesterday– It was two weeks exactly since I had rec^d one from you, &

altho' I had had the pleasure of receiving a letter from Pauline, with a few lines added to it from you, I was not satisfied to be so long without a well filled sheet from you– I was quite happy therefore to find that it was only the move to the country which had prevented me from hearing sooner– & glad that you had got there at last– knowing as I do, how much you prefer it to Boundary S$^{\underline{t}}$ but how sadly disappointed I was to learn that William's visit to the North, upon which I had been counting so securely, was deferred & perhaps to be given up altogether! It is really too provoking to think that the misconduct of the over-seer,[1] should interfere with so pleasant a plan– & that just as I was supposing you w$^{\underline{d}}$ tell me of the day of his departure, it sh$^{\underline{d}}$ be postponed so indefinitely– I do hope still that after installing the new overseer he may find that his presence may not be necessary for some weeks, & that he may be spared to come & see us & his New York friends until <u>planting time</u>– Meanwhile it is so very gay & pleasant here, that it is really a pity that he sh$^{\underline{d}}$ not have been in Phil$^{\underline{a}}$ to give him more agreeable impressions of our society– and Lizzie [Middleton] too– She is missing a great deal but I hope will arrive in time for M$^{\underline{rs}}$ Ridgway's[2] ball next week, which is to eclipse even M$^{\underline{rs}}$ Hutchinson's of last night– and that was extremely handsome–

But only think of my dissipation! I went on Monday to M$^{\underline{r}}$ Bohrer's[3] con-cert, & afterwards to <u>Cousin Patty's</u> (Miss Hare's) tea party– and found it (the concert I mean) so delightful that I determined not to miss the second, & there-fore, as I had previously accepted M$^{\underline{rs}}$ Hutchinson's invitation, I went over the way to the Masonic Hall at seven o'clock, listened for two hours, to the most delightful music, & returned home, finished my toilette in twenty minutes, & started for the Ball with M$^{\underline{me}}$ d'Hauterive– who had sent her carton here, & dressed in my room, & we were not the last who entered the room– I was quite excited by the delirious sounds I had been hearing, & altho' a good deal fatigued when I got home at <u>one o'clock</u>, did not regret having made such an exertion– for I never expect to hear again such tones from any instrument, as those pro-duced by Max Bohrer– They affected me even to tears, & were as full, sweet & clear as the finest voice, & I don't think the best singing, ever gave me more exquisite pleasure– Then the variety of sounds is of course much greater & his execution is marvellous, & withal so easy apparently that he does not seem to be making the slightest exertion– which was the chief or <u>only</u> defect of Knoop's playing– who evidently laboured to produce those wonderful tours de force– & wanted the soul & expression of Bohrer– but I must not "extasier" [*go into raptures*] through my whole sheet, & you must forgive my giving you a long description of what you could form no idea of, except by hearing it y$^{\underline{r}}$self– I don't know whether he will go as far South as Charleston, but if he should, it would be worth the journey to town to hear him– Rakemann[4] played a <u>monstrously</u> difficult piece, but very tiresome & monotonous– & not at all appreciable by <u>un</u>scientific ears– or even agreeable to educated ones–

I must now go & get ready for my walk– that I may dispel the effects of last night's dissipation– & on my return I must prepare for the dinner at Mr Wilcock's–[5] which is to be quite a Lord Mayor's feast of 30 people I hear– but I hope the number is exagerated– & that I shall be fortunately placed, so as to get thro' it with less ennui than might be anticipated from such a <u>tremendous</u> affair– So goodbye until tomorrow, dear Mamma–

Friday after dinner– I have left the children enjoying a good game of romps in the Parlour, & came up to finish my letter to you my dearest Mamma– The early part of the morng I was busy writing notes of invitation, & got thro' nearly 40 of them– about half the number– then I sent the children to walk, & went down to hear the Lecture at St Peter's– I afterwards paid some visits, & came home at 2 o'clock to hear Rakeman until near 3– He tells us that Bohrer is quite mortified at having so few persons at his last concert, & is determined not to give another himself– some of his friends are trying to arrange one for him– probably for <u>Thursday</u>, in which case we shall have to put off our <u>teaparty</u>– for certainly one half our guests w^{d} prefer going to listen to him to coming here– & I w^{d} rather give it up altogether, than lose the pleasure of hearing him again– I understand he thinks of going to Charleston, & wishes me to give him a letter– I have advised his delaying his visit a little– & as he intends giving Concerts in Balt. & Wash^{n}, he will scarcely reach Charleston before Feby when he will be likely to draw good audiences– You will be in town of course then, & must positively go & hear him. I need not urge Papa & my brothers to do so– for I am sure they w^{d} not miss such an opportunity–

But I must tell you of the dinner, what an agreeable surprise I had– for instead of being dull, it passed off extremely well– & M^{r} C[harles] Ingersoll who handed me in (to Clark Hare's great annoyance, for he had intimated, & I afterwards found, fully intended an offer of the same kind). Mr I. was very lively– & amused Esther & myself, between whom he sat, with his quiet humour & observations. The entertainment was very handsome & lasted 2 hours– 20 sat down to table, & many looked very tired before they rose from it, but more were well placed, & enjoyed themselves– before 9 we came away, & passed an hour at Aunt H's– where we found the [Henry] Gilpins– & Sarah G[ilpin][6] whom I always like to meet– Aunt proposed my going with her tonight to the first representation of the <u>Israelites</u>,[7] but I have been so dissipated this week that I preferred being quietly at home– particularly as I daresay it will be pretty indifferently performed– Frank Schroeder is to come in & learn some of his part of the Stabat– in which we want his aid much– M^{rs} S[chroeder] says her daughter writes her that Sophia is quite <u>revived,</u> by the veratria no doubt– I trust it continues to afford you relief also– I was very sorry to hear how much indisposed poor Mrs Smith has been & felt a great inclination to tell her so– You enquire after Mrs Francis– She is in rather better spirits but has had a severe attack of rheumatic gout– She always asks about you & Sally with interest– Pray give my love to the latter & to Pauline & Kitty, to Papa & any or all my brothers who are at M. Place! I hear Lily knocking for me, & as Betsey is gone out, I must run up & attend to her– So adieu dearest mamma I am always Y^{r} most affec^{te} Daughter Eliza

I have omitted love to the dear children & now add it– Not a word has been heard from Lizzie [Middleton]– Her mother is in a state of the most anxious expectation– I was forgetting a piece of <u>good</u> news– Rebecca McLane's engagement to Mr Hamilton of NY–⁸ the brother of John C. our acquaintance, & an excellent match for her I hear–

Pray thank Papa for sending me the fragrant olives, which have retained their delicious perfum entirely– & I hope will do so long–

ScHi

1. The overseer had been dismissed for failing "to make a good crop at Hobonny." William had to deal with other problems that season as well. Two months later Emma reported he had also "lost a good deal of rice by fire, & other accidents." MHM to EMF, December 5, 1842, PHi; EHS to EMF, February 9, 1843, PHi.

2. Elizabeth (Willing) Ridgway was a daughter of Fisher's cousin, Richard Willing. Her husband, John, was the son of Jacob Ridgway and brother of Phoebe Ann Rush and Susan Rotch (later Mrs. Barton).

3. Max Bohrer, a European violinist touring in the United States, had brought a letter of introduction to the Fishers from Allyne Otis in Boston.

4. Mr. L. Rakeman, a pianist, was introduced to Eliza by Julia Ward. "<u>You</u> will be able to convince him," Julia told Eliza, "that an American lady can play and sing perfectly, a fact which he now seems inclined to doubt." Julia Ward to EMF, April 23 [1841,] PHi, C/F.

5. This party may have been to celebrate Benjamin Chew Wilcocks' marriage to Sally Waln, which had taken place in October. Although he was sixty-five and she thirty-five, they were, his teenage niece noticed some months before, "carrying on love very desperate. He behaves very naughtily in church, pulls up his garters & ogles [her]." His relatives, the Wilcockses and the Ingersolls, were apparently not amused. Diary of Charlotte Wilcocks, April 4, 1842, PHi.

6. Fisher's cousin, Sarah Gilpin (b. 1802), was the sister of Henry and William Gilpin.

7. *The Israelites in Egypt, or the Passage of the Red Sea,* described as a scriptural opera, was performed five times in December and January.

8. Rebecca McLane, the daughter of Louis and Catherine (Milligan) McLane, married Philip Hamilton (b. 1802), who was Alexander and Elizabeth (Schuyler) Hamiltons' youngest son. John Church Hamilton was Philip's older brother.

∽

To Mrs. Fisher, Philadelphia

M.P. Dec.ʳ 17ᵗʰ 1842

My dearest Eliza

Since my last letter when I acknowledged yours of the 30ᵗʰ ult.º no other has reached me, neither has there been any opportunity of sending another, so that we are both anxiously waiting for news of each other. I often think you must be suffering severely from the intense cold which is so unusual here, & which must be infinitely greater at Philad.ª, although yʳ comfortable house must protect you within from feeling the severity of it. I hope you have not been venturing to walk, & running the risk of falling, but that you make use of M.ʳ Fisher's arm always: and that the cold has had a good effect upon Mʳˢ Fisher's ailment which I was very glad to learn had been much lessened.

On the subject of cold, I may as well mention how it has lately made me suffer (tho' slightly) because you must warn S. Thorndike about the use of the Veratria– For the last 4 or 5 days I have been feeling a great shivering & loss of appetite, & inquietude– Yesterday Arthur read in his homeopathic book the account of the effects the use of the Veratria occasioned, which agreed exactly with what I had been feeling (though slightly) & I was glad to find that the symptoms proceeded from what I could discontinue, & not from illness. The little box is now nearly empty, & Arthur advised me to leave off rubbing my breast with it, however, I am so much afraid of a return of the throbbing, that I will use it only at night, which will perhaps be 3 or 4 to come– You had better inform S. T. of the symptoms, (shivering, fever, loss of appetite & inquietude) & advise her not to use too much of the ointment– I never used a piece as large as a chinquapin nut as D.ʳ M. ordered. Did M.ʳ F. ever feel any of the symptoms above described?

I read to Arthur what you wrote on the subject of Homeopathy & Hydropathy, & have just asked him what he will answer to you ridiculing his favorite theory [*homeopathy*]– he says when you have studied medicine he will talk to you on the subject. His success in relieving several people here already, for he has been here only a week, is a good proof of the efficacy of his prescriptions.[1]

Sally came on the 8<u>th</u> & was still suffering from the effect of the Arsenic which I told you had been put into her tooth.[2] She kept her bed & her room for several days, & is even now in pain from ulcers which came on in consequence of that dangerous operation, besides its having affected her eyes & swoln her jaws. She bears all these pains with patience– & says she has been in better health for the last two months than she has been for years. Even when at the Beach that place was less hurtful to her than usual. She is looking very well, & seems to like Paolina. She [*Paolina*] too appears to appreciate her amiable disposition & to be pleased with the children– to whom she distributes bon bons, & is very sociable with Sarah– You would be surprised to hear how much progress the latter has made in Music– she is extremely fond of it too. Poor P[aolina] suffers greatly every day with pain in the back, whether she remains in the house (which we were all compelled to do during 4 or 5 days, owing to violent rain lately) or walks in the garden. John will be here next Thursday or Friday, & Oliver & Susan with some of the Children. I suppose about the same time. Ed<u>d</u> accompanied his Father to Combahee a few days since & they with Will<u>m</u> will probably be here a day or two before Xmas. It is very seldom that your 6 Brothers are in the house at the same time. I wish with all my heart you could join our party! When can <u>I</u> look forward to such a blessing!

Harry going to Charleston tomorrow gives me an opportunity of sending this & one to my Brother from whom I had the pleasure of receiving a letter of 15<u>th</u> Nov<u>r</u> last week– 18<u>th</u> I am now in great haste my dear Eliza. Harry will be off in half an hour & I have many orders to give. You will be glad to know that yesterday & today I felt no more shivering in consequence of not having rubbed myself in the morn<u>g</u>, indeed I feel quite differently now than I did some days ago. Still, I am glad that I used the Veratria for it has certainly cured the palpitation– Sally is better today & looking very well. John will be here on the 23<u>d</u> (I forgot I had mentioned that before!) The Delaware I suppose is now frozen & I shall not be able yet to send you the wild Plum jelly, but shall not forget it. I believe I mentioned how busy I have been ever since I have been in Charleston & this place with cutting out the baby linen– & other preparations for Xmas. Sally & Paolina unite in love to you. pray give mine to M<u>r</u> & M<u>rs</u> Fisher & believe me my dearest Eliza y<u>r</u> Affect<u>te</u> Mother M. H. M.

I have always forgotten to tell you that Marg<u>t</u> finding y<u>r</u> old flannel dress<u>g</u> Gown in y<u>r</u> room at Newp<u>t</u>, I told her to take it to Philad<u>a</u> & return it to you– she carried it, but forgot to give it to you, so here it is!

PHi

1. Having studied medicine in Paris, Arthur was now interested in homeopathy and was treating the slaves with homeopathic remedies.

2. Mrs. Middleton reported that Sally suffered severely "by having a tooth plugged, & filled with Arsenic to destroy the nerve: then a violent headache came on." MHM to EMF, December 5, 1842, PHi.

～

To Mrs. Middleton, Middleton Place

Philadelphia– Friday Dec.ͬ 30ᵗʰ 1842

My dearest Mamma, I have very lately written to Pauline, but I cannot, on that account prevent myself from beginning my <u>weekly</u> to you at the usual time, altho' I should have done so more cheerfully, if I had been gratified by a letter from you– which I was expecting this morning– the more anxiously because you had not been very well when you last wrote, & I have been hoping you wᵈ take the first opportunity of telling me you <u>continued</u> better– Perhaps as it was <u>Holiday time</u> for the people,[1] you did not send any of them to town– & yet I supposed they wᵈ be passing to & fro more frequently, on that account. I must <u>hope</u> to hear tomorrow– & content myself with <u>lover's food</u> until then, or perhaps even longer–

I want so much to know all about your Xmas party, & every particular of each member of it will be interesting to me– Of course Susan & her young ones will stay with you until after the new Year– & Hal & Sarah will be returning to their Schools about the same time– Tell the latter I am very glad she is so much improved in Music– & intend to send her some as a New Year's gift by Mͬˢ Sumner– who will I daresay take charge of a few little articles I wish to send by her– I am not sure when that will be, but as she has been here nearly a fortnight, & that was the time she meant to stay, I suppose she will be going early next week– & I cannot be insincere enough to press her to prolong her visit– altho' whilst here I do what I can to make it agreeable to her– You know the old Lady's strong prejudices against <u>second marriages</u> of all sorts, & this is one of the very worst cases– to be least excused I mean & yet she has been extremely amiable about it, & notwithstanding her objections to her for that reason, & others which date <u>further back</u>,[2] she has been disposed to shew her every attention, for my sake, as she knew she had claims upon me– Owing to other engagements we were not able to invite them to dine until yesterday, when we had the Middletons, Ingersolls, Sally Hare, Dͬ Elwyn & Sidney Fisher to meet them– We had proposed to the Willings (Charles & his wife) also to come, but they pleaded an engagement, & to my joy, Mͬ & Mͬˢ Wilcocks, whom Mͬˢ F. insisted upon inviting, gave the same excuse– So that we did not extend our invitations, for we knew that neither Clark Hare & Esther, nor any others of that <u>concern</u> w<u>d</u> be much inclined to make the acquaintance of M<u>r</u> & M<u>rs</u> S– The weather [was] so dreadful, that we did not send round to ask anybody for the eveng– and I was so tired by the late hour of sitting up the previous night (at M<u>rs</u> Sergeants) that I was glad there was no inducement for them to keep us up– The dinner was tolerably pleasant, even on my side, altho' I had just the seat I did not want, between M<u>r</u> S[umner] & M<u>r</u> H. A. M[iddleton]. The opposite party were quite cheerful– & the good cooking was fully appreciated–

Aunt Harrison has got over her difficulty, or disinclination to visit M<u>rs</u> S[umner] I should say, (which was natural enough from the impressions she had rec<u>d</u> thro' the Otis's &c) & intends to ask them to her New Year's party on Sunday eveng– which is to be larger & more <u>brilliant</u> than usual– She asked them to her box at the Opera on Tuesday– when I went– & took Lizzie & Harriett Huger³ also, to see Cinderella– They sang it very well but gave only about half of Rossini's Opera & introduced all the transformations of the Fairy Tale– Lizards, Rats & mice Pumpkin turned into, or rather <u>out of</u> Coach, horses & lacquies– The children were all in ecstasies, but I sh<u>d</u> have been better pleased if they had kept to the original Music & scenes, & omitted some of the Buffoonery– Tonight Aunt goes to hear Norma, but finding that M<u>rs</u> F. wished to go to the Concert the Seguins are to give tomorrow night, I preferred being at home & going tomorrow– & really I enjoy the music more when there is neither bad acting, nor all the false & flimsy representations of the Stage to distract my attention.

I had a letter from Sophia a day or two ago– giving me an excellent account of herself– She says she has been quite revived by the Veratria– & has had no bad palpitation since she used it– but I wrote immediately to give her the warning you advised– & I hope that by discontinuing it for some time she may escape any ill effect from it– D<u>r</u> Reynolds⁴ cautioned Fisher about using it for more than <u>three weeks</u>, & one may well believe that there ought to be a cessation after a certain period of so powerful a remedy– I do want very much to know that you have not found it necessary to use it again– but I must have patience. M<u>rs</u> [Israel] Thorndike's sister is dead at last– after wasting away gradually for weeks– M<u>r</u> T[horndike] was about sailing for Cuba– & Sally Anne had just gone to Boston– Sophia had not decided to go with her to Germany, but was thinking of it– She says Augustus has a boy, which measured <u>two feet & a half</u> long the day after its birth– enormous indeed– M<u>rs</u> Sumner's is a perfect <u>mammoth</u> baby– larger & heavier than my <u>little</u> Sophy, who you know, is no pigmy– The latter is imitating Lily in everything & talking nearly as plainly– They were both in a state of extasy on Sunday with their new Toys– & Lily so much in love with a large wax doll which opens and shuts her eyes, sent to her by Betty Ingersoll,[5] that she was exceedingly amiable to <u>Betty's mamma</u> yesterday–

Our practising [*for the Stabat Mater*] comes on but slowly–[6] for Miss Brugiere has been sick, & I very busy buying presents & visiting at Xmas– Franky [Schroeder] continues inexorable, & I can hear of no one to supply his place– I rather think we shall have to apply to Dorigo, unless I hear from Julia who promised to propose the part to her cousin Harry but has not yet written to me. I have been spending an hour at Aunt Harrison's this morng while the cleaning [of] rooms was going on upstairs– She was very affectionate about you, & begged me to say everything kind to you from her, & also to remember her particularly to Sally, Mary & Sarah–

Saturday morng– I heard the door bell ring whilst I was at breakfast & ran to open it, quite sure that it must be the Postman, but to my great disappointment found only Sidney Fisher, who came to invite F– to meet Mr Sumner at dinner! I am really very sad at not hearing from you my dearest Mamma, but I hope that the new year will be made happy at its commencement by bringing me good news from you– I hear that the Sumners are to start on Monday morng but how long they intend lingering on their way I know not–

Saturday afternoon– We had a pleasant ride (altho' a cold one) to Wakefield, & were very cordially welcomed there by our Uncle and Aunt–[7] who are much more courteous than Quakers are wont to be. We took little Sophy who behaved beautifully & was much admired for her good manners & healthy appearance– Fearing that Lily might not leave a good impression we left her to take a walk with her Grandmother who is very proud of carrying her to parade in Chestnut S^{t} with her velvet coat & new bonnet– She gave me a fright yesterday by swallowing a five cent piece, but as she has not suffered from it I hope there is no cause for further anxiety– altho' I fear it is counterfeit as Dr Chapman wittily remarked on a similar occasion for it has resisted the operation of a dose of castor oil hitherto– & will not probably <u>pass</u>. Mrs Sumner tells me that Cuthbert swallowed <u>three fips</u>[8] without any ill effect, which is consolatory– She offers to take my <u>small</u> parcels– I wanted to send you Fanny Calderon's book[9] which is just come out, but find it is in two rather large volumes, which she w$^{\underline{d}}$ hardly find room for in her trunk & I suppose it will soon reach Charleston. Fisher has given it to me for a new Year's present, & I daresay I shall be much amused by it– I am going to try over the music they have sent, to see whether there is any worth sending Sarah– Adieu my dearest Mamma– I wish you a very happy New Year & a score or two more– & the same, or as many more, as they please to all your party– which I suppose however will be diminished before you receive this. My best love to those who are still near you– & believe me as ever Your most affect^e daughter Eliza

ScHi

1. At Christmas, slaves were customarily given time off and the freedom to visit other plantations or go to town.

2. Mrs. Fisher's objections to Mrs. Sumner "further back" are not explained. Nor are the poor impressions about her that Mrs. Harrison had received, nor what Eliza meant by "others of that concern," mentioned later in the letter.

3. Harriet Huger (1822–1857) was the daughter of Harriott (Pinckney) and Francis Kinloch Huger. She married Alfred Ford Ravenel in 1846. Frank Huger was her brother.

4. Dr. Reynolds was an eye specialist in Boston whom Fisher had consulted the summer before.

5. Elizabeth (Betty) Ingersoll (1815–1872) was the daughter of Charles J. and Mary (Wilcocks) Ingersoll. She married Sidney Fisher in 1851.

6. Eliza was having difficulty lining up singers to sing the Stabat Mater. Not only was Miss Brugiere sick, but her old friend Frank Schroeder exasperated her with excuses about why he couldn't sing. In the end, it seemed it could not be arranged without asking two professional men singers to help, "which," Eliza said, "wd of course prevent me from assisting." EMF to MHM, January 5, 1843, ScHi.

7. Although Fisher claimed to have no love for Quakers generally, he always stayed in touch with several of his father's relatives. Among these were his uncle William Logan Fisher and his second wife, Sarah (Lindley) Fisher. Fisher admired Sarah Fisher as "a very sensible & handsome woman" and gave her the compliment of being "about the best specimen of the Quaker lady I know." The William Logan Fishers lived at Wakefield, the country house in Germantown which Fisher's grandfather built in 1799. JFF, *Recollections,* 26–27.

8. A fip was a British five-penny piece.

9. Fanny Inglis Calderon's *Life in Mexico during a Residence of Two Years in That Country,* published in 1842, was based on her experiences when her husband was Spanish ambassador to Mexico. She told Eliza her husband kept writing in the margins that she must take this or that out, so "the poor letters will be tamed down to mere milk and waterism." F. I. Calderon to EMF, October 16, 1842, PHi, C/F.

1843

[Dr. Hering] has been <u>tinkering</u> me, viz. giving me Powders
of Stamm, in plain English Tinn, which Dr. Meigs declared
will do me no more good than if I drank water out
of a Tin mug.

~

Four years after her wedding, Eliza's long wished for trip to South Carolina finally came about. Eliza's letters make it clear, however, that in 1843, as in 1840, when the question of making the trip came up the first time, Mrs. Fisher made it difficult for them to leave her. The Harrisons, as always, tactfully intervened to bring Mrs. Fisher around and to encourage Fisher and Eliza to go while they could. The timing of the trip was fortunate because a year later Eliza was pregnant again, a circumstance that would have been considered an "impediment" to travel.[1]

Taking the two little girls with them, Eliza and Fisher spent several weeks at Middleton Place so that the children were able to meet most of their cousins for the first time. The Fishers were still in South Carolina when Paolina's and Arthur's baby was born.

Fisher went with his father-in-law to visit the Middletons' rice plantations on the Combahee River and came away with a firsthand view of the risks as well as the rewards of growing rice. In telling his uncle about the fall in its price, he wrote, "Rice is sold now at about one third of what it brought four years ago." Whereas the Middletons' crop brought between $55,000 and $60,000 in 1839, it would bring only in the range of $23,000 in 1843. After paying $8,000–$10,000 to banks and to Uncle Izard in France, there would not be a great deal left to support the rest of the family. Under the circumstances, Fisher would not expect payment of Eliza's annuity.[2]

Among Americans who were searching, sometimes desperately, for ways to cure their ailments, homeopathic medicine was, by the 1840s, attracting a good deal of attention as an alternative to conventional medical treatments. This was hardly surprising. Samuel Hahnemann, the originator of the homeopathic system, rejected the harsh remedies such as purging, bleeding, blistering, and the use of toxic substances—mercury and arsenic, for example—still being used by traditionally trained doctors and instead used a variety of medicines in extremely small and dilute doses.

Whether such a system was effective was the subject of much discussion in the Middleton family. Both Arthur and his mother were fervent believers in homeopathy, and as Eliza was still bothered by the sore throat that had plagued her, off and on, since her scarlet fever, they urged her to consult a homeopathic doctor in Philadelphia, which she did despite friends who told her it was all quackery. At first she was a willing patient, but she did not get better—her brother, John, thought this was because she continued "to indulge in poisonous drugs like tea, coffee &c"[3]—and after a year, she went back to consulting her former doctors.

Mirroring the preoccupations of the country at large in their letters, Eliza and her mother discussed the merits not only of homeopathy but of mesmerism, another topic of enormous interest at the time. While Mrs. Middleton always wanted to believe the claims made for these new ideas, Eliza, in the absence of solid evidence, remained skeptical.

1. EMF to MHM, January 13, 1843, ScHi.
2. The equivalent of $55,000 in 1839 would be approximately $786,000, and $23,000 in 1843 approximately $460,000 in 1999 dollars. JFF to GH, April 5, 1843, PHi, BrC; dollar conversion factors from RSahr, OrStU.
3. John I. Middleton to EMF, August 23, 1843, MPlFdn.

To Mrs. Middleton, Middleton Place

Friday January 13th 1843

I had a most agreeable surprise on Tuesday, my dearest Mamma, for I did not expect to receive a letter from you again in less than a week since the last. Thank you most heartily for all the kind wishes it contains for me & mine, which however I should have been sure were truly felt, even if they had not been expressed– & yet am happy to have them repeated–

Every time I receive one of y^r letters I seem to be transported to M. Place, & fancy myself among you all for a time– & alas! I fear I shall have to content myself with these imaginary visits– for my fondly hoped for trip to the South, seems to become more & more improbable as the time for making it draws nearer– & the old lady is so dreadfully nervous just now, that I dare not <u>hint</u> at the subject in her presence– It is indeed provoking, for as far as I & the children are concerned, there could not be a more favourable opportunity for travelling– & another winter there <u>may</u> be another impediment, altho' at present there is not the slightest suspicion– of what you seem to apprehend for me– & I begged Mrs Sumner to assure you so– The headache & slight indisposition I mentioned was without any particular cause or consequence & merely the punishment of indulging in some of Aunt H's <u>goodies</u> at night– I am excessively thin, & they tempt me to eat more than is perhaps proper for me, hoping to fatten me up, with mush & cream &c– nothing seems to answer this purpose however– & I tell Fisher I am sure the only way to succeed, is to give me Country air– that of M.P. always agreed admirably well with me– but it appears very unlikely that I shall try it this year– Fisher would I know be glad to gratify me, but he has this plaguing law suit hanging over him– & unless it is postponed he must stay & raise funds for payment, in case he should lose it– which with M^r H's assurance there will be no difficulty in doing I hope– notwithstanding the hardtimes–

I was grieved to hear from Lizzie Middleton, that Allen Smith was sued for the payment of the Sav^{ah} plantation, & that the sale of it, & all the negroes upon it, w^d not more than pay his debt– I very much hope this may not be an altogether correct account of the matter, & that I may have more favourable information from you– but fear that these difficulties are worrying them both, & must encrease rather than diminish yearly– She [*Emma*] herself told me that he did not make enough to pay the interest upon the debt– & this must of course be ruinous, unless there is a wonderful improvement in the crops– I shall be most anxious to know, whether he is able to extricate himself with the Judge's[1] help– or if the property is to be sacrificed– What is to become of them in that case? I sh^d suppose his only chance of supporting himself w^d be to return to the North, & resume his professorship–[2] a precarious one indeed– I can now well understand why Emma has not written to me since she left Charleston– having nothing agreeable to communicate poor soul! How fortunate it is that she has no family– for altho' "children are a blessing from the Lord" they w^d greatly increase her troubles now– This sad news has quite depressed me– but I hope it may not be so bad as I apprehend–

You do not mention anything of John's affairs– which I trust are more prosperous– I was sorry to hear of poor Sarah's indisposition, which I hope is passed over– My darlings continue perfectly well– Sophy to be sure is rather restless at night– but it is only her teeth which trouble her– & wake her & her nurse up frequently– during the day she is well & lively– & every day becoming more amusing– imitating Lily in every thing– you w^d be pleased to see how loving they are to each other– kissing & hugging in the most affect^e manner– & always crying for & with one another when either gets a fall or a bruize–

You ask what new books I am reading– I have finished the first Vol. of Fanny Calderon's book which I like much & Mrs F. reads aloud to us a Swedish Novel, translated by Mary Howitt–[3] called The Neighbours– which is very pretty, & written in a very natural & amusing style– M^{rs} McEuen & Mrs Middleton both spoke so highly of it, that we were induced to get it– but it is only published in the New World, & the print is dreadfully small & pale– I am interested in a work of Taylor's,[4] on <u>Ancient Christianity</u>, which is written to shew the errors of the Oxford Divines, who w<u>d</u> follow the <u>Fathers</u> of the first centuries & appeal to their authority, equally with that of the Inspired Authors of the New Testament– who he thinks ought alone to be our guides in matters of faith– many of the pure doctrines of the gospel having very early become corrupted– <u>I</u>, like M<u>r</u> T, am <u>thoroughly</u> protestant, & w<u>d</u> reject all the superstitious <u>additions</u> to the blessed book which contains "<u>all things</u> necessary for salvation"– & is a sufficient rule of faith to the humble minded searcher after Truth– altho' of course I do not say that the <u>opinions</u> of wise & good men are to be disregarded or their instructions altogether neglected–

Saturday morng– Fisher persuaded me to leave off writing & walk out with him to the Navy Yard, & upon my return it was time to dress for a 5 o'clock dinner at M<u>rs</u> Ingersoll's (Susan's) which I found very agreeable– & was rather surprised to discover that M<u>r</u> Wilcocks, who took me in, was shrewd & even amusing occasionally, altho' his loud & boisterous manner fatigued me– M<u>r</u> Fenimore Cooper sat on my other side, & told a great many anecdotes rather pleasantly– but I could not admire his conversation which seemed to be intended for display & thought his tone overbearing & dogmatical– Fisher thinks he is much more amiable than he used to be, but agreed with me as to his manner– We had a large reinforcement of belles & beaux in the eveng– but we had ordered Aunt's carriage at 9, & therefore came away early– Tonight we are all going to hear the Seguins sing the Stabat– M<u>me</u> d'Hauterive continues so much indisposed that I don't know when we shall hope to give it here– Lizzie says the Ball at M<u>rs</u> Davis' was quite a magnificent affair, but shockingly crowded– she & her cousin Harriett [Huger] are great favourites, & extremely admired in Society– I believe I must say Adieu now, for a visit from M<u>rs</u> Harrison has just been announced, & that will probably last until <u>walking time</u>– so I shall close this with love to all with you from Y<u>r</u> most affectionate daughter Eliza

I ought to say that kind messages are always desired to be sent from M<u>rs</u> F– & M<u>r</u> & M<u>rs</u> H–

ScHi

1. Emma's father, Daniel E. Huger.

2. After he graduated from West Point in 1829 (where he stood fourth and his classmate, Robert E. Lee, second in the class), Allen Smith was assistant professor of geography, history, and ethics there for several years.

3. Mary Botham Howitt (1799–1888) translated several Scandinavian books into

English and wrote children's books. She and her husband, William, also collaborated on various writings.

The *New World* was a weekly magazine of fiction. The editors printed pirated editions of whole novels in "extras," which they could sell cheaply by using very small print.

4. Isaac Taylor, author of *Ancient Christianity* and *The Doctrines of the Oxford Tracts*, also wrote *The Physical Theory of Another Life*, mentioned in Mrs. Middleton's letter of March 25, 1842. The Oxford Divines were clergymen who supported a revival (known as the Oxford Movement) in the Church of England of practices similar to those of the Roman Catholic Church.

~

To Mrs. Fisher, Philadelphia

M.P. Jany 21st 1843

It is unusual my dearest Eliza that I should have three of your letters to answer– but so it is– those of the 30th ult^o, the 7th & the 13 & 14th inst– the last was received yesterday on the return of y^r Father, the two former two days after I had written my last, giving you news of Emma. I was really surprised to read what you mentioned relative to Mr Smith's pecuniary distress, not having heard any account of the probability of his plantation being offered for sale– As I read your letter to Sally she too seemed much astonished– but said that Emma had conversed with her on the subject of the crops being insufficient to pay off their debt, but not a word about their intention of selling the plantation– I should suppose Lizzie must have been misinformed on the matter for Mr S. has lately been building a house & Emma has been busy in purchasing furniture & making preparations for planting a shrubbery, for which I furnished several evergreens– so that you need not imagine the report is true. She begs me to tell you she would write soon after her return to Sav^h where she went yesterday–

I am very sorry to learn that you are so very thin– You say that you have only head aches & slight indispositions, therefore I hope you may soon regain your plumpness– no doubt you would soon do so, could you come here, but that desirable visit I grieve to hear cannot be accomplished this year–

Sunday– I was interrupted yesterday & as Ed^d thinks of going to Charles^n either tomorrow or Tuesday but probably tomorrow, I must avail myself of the opportunity. He will not remain here much longer, for he says he shall be at Wash^n the beginning of Feb^y & he may perhaps be ordered off soon to some distant expedition! I hope not, but it is very probable such a disagreeable sentence awaits him–[1] Your Father brought with him last Friday a very agreeable & handsome young English Officer Mr Warre who brought me a letter of introduction from Miss Moore– He has been in Canada & travelling about the different States for the last 3 years, & is to return to England in June. I asked him if he would not pass a few days in Philad^{a} on his return to N.Y. where he will go in a few days, but he said he could not, as he must hasten to the latter place– He went this morn^{g} with y^{r} Father to Combahee where he will meet W^{m} & is to spend a day or two with Arthur Blake[2] with whom he became acquainted in Charleston, & will return there shortly– A. B. has lately purchased the Estate of the late J. Middleton from his family who are in rather reduced circumstances at present. I wish you could see M^{r} W[arre]– he is as Miss M. says 'a good specimen of his country'– Y^{r} Brothers like him, & Harry seemed to take great pleasure in conversing with him. He drew this morn^{g} a sketch of the large Oak tree close to the barn & seemed to enjoy the warm weather which has been encreasing for the last week, today so warm that I have put on a muslin Gown & am sitting with the Window open, the ther^{r} up to 76°!

Poor Sally has been suffering for several days from pain (feeling like excoriation) of the eyes & is obliged to abstain from reading– in other respects she is tolerably well & has been greatly benefitted by Arthur's prescriptions– He & Paolina went to Charleston the 16th ins^{t} & the latter said she intended to write to you, therefore you cannot have felt uneasy about not hearing from me on the week after my last letter. I am anxiously expecting to hear from my dear brother, the last news from him is of the 15th of Novr. The last Steam^{r} did not bring me a letter & I am dreading to hear that he has had a severe attack of Gout or that my Sister is ill– I hope Ed^{d} may bring me a letter but if I wait for it, I shall not be able to answer it by the Steamer of the 1st of Feby this is vexatious–

It is very complaisant of Harry to read aloud to Sally & me in the even^{g} particularly as he has already read Nic^{s} Nickleby but admires it so much that he does not object to read it again. This was done in y^{r} Father & Ed^{s} absence & will I hope be repeated. 'Howitt's visits to remarkable places' interests me very much.[3] I read it when I have time in the course of the day. Mary H. is his wife, is she not? There is no chance of my seeing <u>her</u> book which you speak well of: neither can I expect to see Taylor's work (unless you should carry it to Newport) or Mme Calderon's.

I am very sorry to have so distressing an account of Mrs Fisher. By this time I hope her nervous attack has passed off– You will not give credit to Homeopathic remedies I know, but they are nevertheless very efficacious, & there is, Harry (now a convert to the system) tells me, a famous Dr Hering[4] a German pursuing with great success that practice at Philad$\underline{a}$. Could you persuade M$\underline{rs}$ F. to consult him?

I sent a message of invitation by Emma Smith to M$\underline{rs}$ Sumner & y$\underline{r}$ Father also invited her, & she said she would come with pleasure, but <u>when</u>, I do not know. Harry read aloud to S. & me nearly the whole of D$\underline{r}$ Dunglesson's pamphlet– which is entertaining, but I cannot believe the inefficacy of Homeopathy or Mesmerism– There is an account of the effects of the latter in the Spectator of Dec$\underline{r}$ 31$\underline{st}$ extracted from the London Times of 'Amputation of the thigh during the Mesmeric State without the knowledge of the patient' which is well worth your reading. I think you w$\underline{d}$ not disbelieve the effects of Mesmerism after reading the Article.

I think this warm weather will extend to Philad$\underline{a}$ & enable Vessels to pass up the Delaware. The box of Wild plums was sent to T. M[iddleton]'s & he was requested to forward it by the first opportunity. You have so often expressed a desire to know how my health is that I must not omit telling you that it is in a very good state & has been ever since the Veratria was at an end. It certainly has cured me of the throbbings which are occasionally very slight & I never felt the bad effects of it until about a month after I had begun to use it– three weeks ought to have been the time to leave it off but I was not aware of that until you told me. I have been speaking to your brothers about A. Smith's affairs, & they say there can be no truth in the account given you by L[izzie] M. on the subject.

23$\underline{d}$ Ed$\underline{d}$ has made up his mind to send a Servant to town today & to go himself on Thursday– He sends his love to you as does Sally pray give mine to M$\underline{r}$ & M$\underline{rs}$ Fisher & remembrances to M$\underline{r}$ & M$\underline{rs}$ Harrison & believe me my dearest Eliza y$\underline{r}$ Affect$\underline{te}$ Mother M. H. M.

You give a very pleasing account of the little darlings– Let me know if Lily is now able to <u>converse</u>–

PHi

1. Edward was not sent abroad again until January 1844, when he went to the Mediterranean.

2. Arthur Middleton Blake (1812–1881) was Eliza's first cousin, the son of Anna Louisa (Middleton) and Daniel Blake (1775–1834). John Middleton (1784–1826) descended from the William Middleton branch of the family. He was the father of Lizzie (Mrs. Mitchell C.) King; Alicia (who became Mrs. W. A. Sparks) and J. Motte Middleton.

3. William Howitt (1792–1879) was a popular English author in his own right, in addition to his collaborations with his wife, Mary.

4. Constantin Hering emigrated from Germany about 1830. He was the author of *A Concise View of the Rise and Progress of Homeopathic Medicine.*

⌒

To Mrs. Middleton, Middleton Place

Philadelphia – Saturday 4$\underline{th}$ Feb$\underline{y}$ 1843

It is perhaps unreasonable in me to expect a letter from you <u>regularly</u> once a week, my dearest Mamma, but I write myself so punctually that it seems rather hard that I sh$\underline{d}$ not hear as often from you– & this morng I could not help feeling disappointed when I found the Postman had <u>passed</u> our door without stopping– You were probably busy last week making preparations for your trip to town– where I suppose you now are, awaiting <u>Bentino's</u> arrival–

Now I have a <u>piece</u> of news to communicate which I hope will give you some pleasure– & perhaps if I could announce it with <u>certainty</u>, it w$\underline{d}$ be still more agreeable to you– Well then, not to keep you longer in suspense– would you be glad to hear that after all, we shall <u>probably</u> pay you a visit in Carolina? I flatter myself that you will not hear with indifference that this subject has been proposed to the consideration of our dear old Uncle & Aunt at 156, & that they immediately upon only a <u>hint</u> from Fisher, gave their acquiescence, most cheerfully, & approved <u>entirely</u> of the plan– thinking it an excellent opportunity for me to put it into execution– & most natural that I should desire to spend a few weeks with you all– & moreover believing that the journey & change of climate w$\underline{d}$ prove highly beneficial to my health, & above all to Fisher's eyes– this last consideration will I am sure go far towards reconciling his mother to parting with him– & <u>us</u> I may say– for she w$\underline{d}$ no doubt feel our absence sensibly– but her love for him has never been selfish (& what Mother's ever is?) & if she can be persuaded that he is to derive benefit from the excursion I do not doubt her being willing to make the sacrifice. We have not yet spoken to her, wishing first to obtain D$\underline{r}$ Chapman's opinion, which w$\underline{d}$ weigh much with her & being also unwilling to let her know anything of our project until it became more matured– It is only within the last 3 days that I have thought it at all practicable– But when I was urging upon F– the advantage of his making a trip to Boston, (with a view of consulting again D$\underline{r}$ Reynolds) he declared that if he went <u>anywhere</u>, he w$\underline{d}$ go to Charleston– I immediately questioned him with regard to the Law Suit, which I found w$\underline{d}$ probably not come on before <u>April</u>, & he acknowledged that he had a great desire to gratify me by taking me for <u>four</u> weeks to the South– & promised to begin by <u>sounding</u> the old people– Yesterday he did so, & found them not only willing to part with us for <u>that time</u> but ready to second him & use their influence with the old lady to give her consent– Their behaviour on this occasion was really admirable & they both declared with I am sure <u>perfect sincerity</u>, that much as they would miss us & the children, they should give their entire approbation to our departure, being fully assured of the benefit we sh<u>d</u> both derive from it– & I think no better proof of the disinterestedness of their affection could be given than their readiness to make the sacrifice in our favour– Our absence will to be sure be very short, (I speak as if the whole affair were already decided, whereas it is not so yet,) & as M<u>r</u> H. says I may never have so <u>good</u> a <u>chance</u> again, the children being both of a good age <u>&c</u>, but until all the arrangements are made I scarcely dare give myself up to the delight I shall feel if I am permitted at last to fulfil this long cherished promised visit to my native soil, & embrace my parents & the brothers & friends I have not seen for 4 long years.

Sunday eveng– I have not waited in vain, my dearest Mamma for Fisher brought me a letter from you this eveng which was so acceptable that I did not regret his having <u>waded</u> down to the Office thro' a <u>wet</u> snow which covers all the pavements after a whole day of sleet & snow– which has kept us all within doors– I cannot say that I <u>now</u> feel <u>disappointment</u> at W<u>m</u>'s determination to remain at the South since I shall probably see much more of him <u>there</u> than if he had come on– altho' I am sorry that he is disappointed– Fisher is quite delighted to hear that he will not miss his society in Carolina, & begs me to tell him that he hopes to pass a week with him at Combahee– Today our plans seem to have become much more fixed & decided– Aunt Harrison spared us the pain of <u>breaking</u> them to the old lady– & by telling her how much <u>she</u> wished us to go to Carolina for the benefit of my health (which to tell the truth is rather [better]) & F's eyes– She was much surprised and of course distressed at first to hear of our intentions– & for some hours I was almost sorry that anything had been said to her about them– however upon reflection & talking it over quietly with us, she seemed fully aware of the advantages we sh<u>d</u> both derive from our visit, & entered into my feelings very considerately– & after consulting with M<u>r</u> & M<u>rs</u> H. last night, who said everything to urge our going, she seems also determined to join them– & when I offered to give up the idea altogether, w<u>d</u> not hear of its being abandoned– D<u>r</u> Chapman with his usual dilatoriness has not yet been to give his opinion– but when he does I think it will be favourable to our <u>cause</u> & at any rate I think you can expect to see us about the 4<u>th</u> of March– unless sickness sh<u>d</u> meanwhile attack us or any one of our old friends–

You will I suppose be in Charleston at that time, where we shall like to spend 3 or 4 days– but not of course in the Boundary S$^{\underline{t}}$ House, which I know will be full to overflowing– but shall take up our quarters at a Hotel– I am afraid it will put you to inconvenience to accomodate us even at M. Place but if Sally remains there, which I <u>hope & trust</u> she will I must beg you to let us occupy two of the rooms in the South Out House,[1] where I sh$^{\underline{d}}$ <u>greatly prefer</u> being– I want you to tell me <u>candidly</u> my dear Mamma, if you have the least objection to my bringing Betsey– for I think we could do without her– particularly as you probably have some black or brown damsel who could assist the nurse to look after the Children– if you cannot well spare a girl, & w$^{\underline{d}}$ rather I sh$^{\underline{d}}$ [bring] B– I will do so– & in that case w$^{\underline{d}}$ ask for both the <u>double</u> rooms– if not the smaller middle room will be large enough for the Nurse & baby– I w$^{\underline{d}}$ scarcely have believed some days ago that I sh$^{\underline{d}}$ be writing about these arrangements! I do hope they may be carried into effect– & that I shall have the happiness of spending a month with you– I count upon having dear Sally there for at least half that time & flatter myself she will think it worth while to delay her departure to Waccamaw– tell her she promised to be at M.P. if ever I sh$^{\underline{d}}$ be fortunate enough to get there– I shall be wofully disappointed if John does not make an effort to pay us a long visit– Susan & Oliver have no excuse for not doing so– I have a letter from Mary this eveng– in which she says they are disappointed to hear from E$^{\underline{d}}$ that there is no chance of the little cousins making acquaintance this winter– I shall write tomorrow to her to contradict the assertion– which was made in consequence of the passage in one of my letters, which you say grieved you. In one short month or perhaps less I shall embrace you, I can now hope– I pray God that we may meet in health & safety, & shall resign myself & those so dear to me to this Almighty protection, who alone can save & deliver us in all perils & dangers!

I shall now say Adieu my dearest Mamma begging you to answer this as soon as possible. Fisher begs you to mention if there is any choice in the Wilmington boats[2] on which days the <u>best</u> one runs, & whether they now make the trip by night or day– If we can pass a night at Weldon? whether there is anything I can bring on for you or any one else? John is waiting to carry this down to the P. Office so once more Adieu– with love to all I am as ever Y$^{\underline{r}}$ most affectionate Eliza

I shall look for E$^{\underline{d}}$ next week– perhaps Capt$^{\underline{n}}$ Warre will be here also– I shall be glad to see him–

ScHi

1. Two smaller buildings flanked the main house at Middleton Place. To the north was the library; to the south, a building with workspace and extra bedrooms. The Mid-

dletons called it the South Out House (or simply the Out House). See illustrations following page 96.

    2. The steamboats ran between Wilmington, North Carolina, and Charleston.

∼

To Mrs. Fisher, Philadelphia

M.P. Feby 12$\underline{th}$ 1843

My dearest Eliza

I received yesterday evening the joyful intelligence of your intended visit. This was delightful, but as I went on perusing your letter your mentioning the delicate state of your health gave me great sorrow for I am sure you must be in a much worse state than you write of, & call it only a delicate state, lest it should alarm me. You have probably a Cough & pain in your throat– perhaps occasional fever! I have been continually thinking on this subject since I read your letter, & wishing that you should not delay your departure from Philad$^{\underline{a}}$ so long– the sooner you can leave that climate & enjoy this, the better will your health be, I hope– Ask Dr Chapman if he is not of that opinion– I almost dread to know what he thought of your state. I fully appreciate the kindness of M^r & M$^{\underline{rs}}$ Harrison in urging you to come here, & also M$^{\underline{rs}}$ Fisher's in entering into your feelings & complying with your wishes, though the absence of her family must be so painful to her– I wish she could accompany you. could she not be prevailed upon to do so? It would give me great pleasure to receive her, & I beg you will try & persuade her to come. The change of climate would no doubt prove beneficial to her. I hope the agitation occasioned by your plans may not have the effect of bringing on another nervous attack.

    You must have received a hurried short letter I wrote on the 9$\underline{th}$ Y^r Father says owing to W$^{\underline{m}}$'s carelessness it was not sent to the post until yesterday. He had seen Oliver in the morn^g who told him of your intended visit which has no doubt given all his family great pleasure as well as the rest, Paolina &c She was well yesterday– I have been counting the weeks in the Almanac today & think it probable that this week or next may make her a Mother. When you reflect on her being obliged to remain at least a month after the period in Charleston, you can agree to what I am going to say of the rooms you shall occupy– First, Sally says she had never any intention of going to Charleston except for a day or two on her way to Waccamaw, so that instead of your going to an hotel, come directly on to Boundary S^t in the Omnibus– I daresay I shall be out of bed ready to receive you. The rooms upstairs there will be ready for y^r reception. Three or 4 days will I hope be enough to remain in Charle^n because I am sure you will enjoy the country more. There you shall have your own room & dressing room & the room opposite the drawing room for a nursery.

As to the Out house rooms one of them in which Ed^d slept was so offensive by the dead rats, that he was compelled to keep the window open all night besides which, I cannot consent to your being in such shabby rooms. Sally is greatly delighted at the prospect of meeting you & says she will stay perhaps 10 days after y^r arrival– that will be about the time or rather sooner than Paolina will return & when she does, & Sally is gone, either P. or you can occupy Sally's two rooms upstairs– We have both been arranging this distribution of the family, which I hope will meet with your approbation. She thinks it probable that John may arrive in about 10 days, & we shall try to keep him until you arrive, but you had better come rather earlier, that you may have a better chance of enjoying their society– he cannot stay very long, as his Overseer has been (& may still be) very ill & his house is not yet ready for the reception of the family. Mr Sumner went on the 9th to Charleston & friday to Sav^a with Wm Mrs S. will probably be here a week or 10 days longer.

About Betsey's coming do exactly what you wish– You can have a very good nurse if you leave her at Phil^a– Retta who nursed Sally's children & who is now here, having married Jack. She is very attentive & good natured, & is not of much use to me, so that I should not miss her, were she to mind Lily– Her brother young Moro about a fortnight ago met with a sad accident cutting down a tree it fell on him & broke his thigh– He is however going on very well, a Surgeon luckily having set it 4 hours afterwards, & he says he is doing as well as could be expected. Retta does not mind Sally's child now & has not for the last 18 months. So that she cannot have a better occupation than that of attending to Lily.

In answer to Mr Fisher's enquiries about the Steamboats. We have made 3 passages in the Govr Dudley & one in the Wilming^n all of which were safe. I asked Mrs S. what she knew about them. She said she was in the habit of hearing her fellow lodgers preferring the Gladiator, but Harry observed that all the Steamers were alike, no accident happening & that the Captains always stopped at Smithville just on the entrance into the Ocean, if there seemed any prospect of a rough passage– that is prudent– You had better not leave Wilmington (where I am told there is a good house) should the weather be stormy, & the moon changing– the Steamers go every day & always make the voyage through the night. We arrived at Weldon about 4 o'clock P.M. had an indifferent meal, & slept there until 2 o'clock next morn^g when we were obliged to get up & enter the rail cars, & arrived at Wilmington about 3 P.M. the same day had a quiet passage & were in Charleston the next morn^g at 7 A.M. The

Almanac tells me the new Moon will be on the 1$^{\underline{st}}$ March so try to enter the Steamer before that time– I may be laughed at for believing the changes to have any effect on the weather but have observed them so often that I cannot help believing it.

How happy I should be could I look forward to your arriving in a perfect state of health! The fear of seeing you in a suffering condition takes away more than half the pleasure I anticipated. You must have suffered from the cold weather about the time you wrote, it became very cold after the heat of the previous week, when Mr Warre left us– All the fragrant olive flowers were killed & the Camelias. perhaps they may revive by the time you come & the yellow jessamines be in bloom. I cannot say when I shall be in Charleston, M$^{\underline{rs}}$ S[umner] being still here. The little green Carriage like Lily's is in Charleston for P. so that Arthur must send it for me, & if I go, Sally must keep house. I mentioned your offer of bringing what might be wanted. She begs you to bring her a box of Gardette's toothpowder–

13$^{\underline{th}}$ I wished to have sent this to Charles$^{\underline{n}}$ today but y^{r} Father who is just gone to Combahee said that the Servant should not be sent till tomorrow. I have been enquiring of M$^{\underline{rs}}$ Sumner whether she knew any thing concerning your indisposition– She said you had had a sore throat & had taken the advice of Dr Meigs who did not think you were suffering from Bronchitis. What says Dr Chapman? tell me particularly how you are & write very soon & mention the time you will leave Phil$^{\underline{a}}$ Y^{r} Father advises as I do, that you should not delay y^{r} journey but take advantage of a mild spell of weather– He says T.M[iddleton] told him he had sent the box of Wild plums but he did not tell me the name of the Vessel– I hope you have it by this time. Sally & M$^{\underline{rs}}$ Sumner desire their love to you give mine to M^{r} & M$^{\underline{rs}}$ Fisher with kind remembrance to M^{r} & M$^{\underline{rs}}$ Harrison & believe me my dearest Eliza y^{r} affect$^{\underline{te}}$ Mother M. H. M.

PHi

～

To Mrs. Middleton, Middleton Place

Philadelphia – Feb$^{\underline{y}}$ 15$^{\underline{th}}$ [1843] Wednesday

I have allowed ten days to pass over without writing to you my dearest Mamma because I wished to get an answer to my last letter before I sent you another– but as this has not yet come & it will now probably be detained on the road by the snow, I suppose it is best for me to delay no longer, particularly as I am anxious to thank you for y^{rs} of the 9$^{\underline{th}}$ which I rec$^{\underline{d}}$ this morng– By the return of Papa who took it to Charleston, you must have rec$^{\underline{d}}$ mine of the 5$^{\underline{th}}$ announcing to you our intention of paying you a visit– & I hope tomorrow or next day to hear that you <u>approve</u> of this plan– Since it has been determined upon, I have been getting so much better, that there is now little excuse for my going on the score of health– Fisher got frightened at my Cough & pain in the chest, & I believe made up his mind that I required change of air– I have now got rid of both entirely by taking care of myself, & refusing steadily to go out at night– but I am <u>shockingly</u> thin & feel persuaded that nothing will fatten & strengthen me like a spring at the south– We shall avoid the very worst month of the year (March) in this northern climate, & exchange these cold piercing winds for the vernal breezes of the most delightful season in Carolina– and then besides the pleasure I anticipate in being with you all, I expect Fisher to derive so much benefit from the journey &c that he will be fully rewarded for the trouble of taking me– He says that now he has decided to go, he can acknowledge to me that he has always looked forward to revisiting Carolina with the greatest pleasure, but did not like to talk to me on the subject for fear he sh$^{\underline{d}}$ be unable to fulfil his promise–

We both hope that Pauline will manage to introduce the little stranger very soon, for we sh$^{\underline{d}}$ be sorry to be detained in Charleston more than 3 or 4 days, & want you to be ready to accompany us to M. Place by the 9$^{\underline{th}}$ or 10$^{\underline{th}}$ of March– I suppose you will not think it necessary to stay more than a Couple of weeks with P. who has I daresay by this time sent you a summons. I trust that dear Sally will not disappoint me by leaving town as early as she intended– but will consent to remain at least a month later at M. Place. Emma writes me that she did not find her as well as the reports of her improvement in health had led her to hope– & I grieve to hear from you that she is suffering so much from her eyes– Perhaps she may find relief from a very simple remedy which Miss Grelaud, who has for years been deprived of the use of her's, has found most efficacious– & which Fisher is going to try, upon her urgent recommendation– It is elder flower water & <u>something</u> else (I forget what) but prepared in a particular way & applied to the outside of the lids & temples. He has not yet begun to use it, but intends to get a supply & take it on with him to Car$^{\underline{a}}$.

D$^{\underline{r}}$ Chapman says that constant exercize in the Country will do more for them than any prescription & highly approves of his making the journey– this appears to reconcile his Mother entirely to our departure, & since the first day or two after she was let into the secret she has regained her cheerfulness in a great degree– Then her mind has been diverted from the subject by making preparations for our musical party, which did not take place until last eveng– which was the time finally agreed upon by Miss Brugiere– We had about 60 people– a great many pretty girls, & plenty of agreeable beaux for them– & some very good music– Miss B's voice was delightful, & Mr Duggan[1] played charmingly– & after screwing my courage for an hour to the right point, I took the time when they were busily employed with the Ices & got thro' with my part of the performance very creditably– I expected to have been so frightened that the little Bird w^d have flown away– but he only fluttered becomingly as the composer intended, & flew in good time–

Everybody seemed in good spirits, & when they broke up at 1/2 after eleven a great deal was said about the pleasure of the eveng– & all appeared satisfied. The room was beautifully lighted by the brackets which were used for the first time, & all the tables being removed gave much more room than usual– I had been fancying that Ned w^d be here– & am sorry to hear he means to cut us again– but glad there is a chance of his returning to Charleston– Mr Brugiere told me last night that Julia Ward had been in Boston for some time, which accounts for her not having answered my letter of invitation– & Fanny Calderon, in a letter rec^d this morng– mentions having met her the night before at Mrs Ticknor's,[2] looking very well– she says she means to cultivate her acquaintance notwithstanding Calderon's having unblushingly confessed his having been in love with her– They intend sailing for Gibraltar in April, & settling for some time either in Seville or Madrid– but hardly expect any change in their favour to take place until the little Queen[3] attains her majority– She tells me they are to come to Phil^a & go across the mountains to see her sister Harriett before sailing– but I shall just miss seeing them & also the visit of the Oelrichs– who are expected next month– He has been astonishing the natives of Boston by appearing at the parties in a maroon coloured velvet coat! What a mistake to exhibit his fat person so conspicuously! A propos of fat people– I am very glad the Sumners have already paid their visit– as I shall be glad to see the spare room occupied by those I have more pleasure in meeting–

I hope the arrangement I proposed (of taking up my quarters in the Out House) meets y^r approbation dear Mamma, for there you will be less disturbed by the noise of the children– & nobody will be kept awake by Sophia's crying at night– which she has done lately– since she is troubled with her eye teeth– as for Lily she sleeps 12 hours consecutively & soundly– & is as stout & hearty as possible– and so indeed is Toty– how much pleasure they will have in running about the garden & playing with their little cousins–

Eveng– I had written so far & was just going to seal my letter when Ed^d made his appearance to my great surprise– He looks very well & has come only from Balt^e today– having gone on thence from Wash^n & then returned to Wash^n so that by this odd arrangement of time he is just too late for our party– which I regret. He says he means to return immediately to Charleston to be present at the next St Cecilia Ball on Tuesday– but I hope to persuade him to remain with us a few days– He does not give me later news of you than y^r letter brought me this morng, but of the town party much later & they were all well– But my letter was not yet rec^d there– & nothing known of our movements– I must now close this with love to all from Y^r ever affectionate daughter Eliza

ScHi

1. Mr. Duggan was a professional pianist in Philadelphia.
2. George Ticknor (1791–1871) was a distinguished professor of French and Spanish languages and literature at Harvard. Mrs. Ticknor was known for inviting artists, authors, scientists, and other interesting people to her parties.
3. Queen Isabella II of Spain was only thirteen when, in 1843, she was declared of age to rule.

⌇

The weather was so cold and rainy for much of the Fishers' stay at Middleton Place that Eliza and the children could not get outside for exercise. Then the whole family caught a flu that left Eliza's mother and father, Lily and Sophy, and the children's nurse, Mrs. Putnam, all with terrible coughs. Even so, the southern spring was beautiful and Fisher described woods "fragrant with the yellow jessamine" to his mother and the Harrisons. "I never saw it so beautiful & the azaleas & honeysuckles are beginning to bloom."[1]

Paolina's child, Henry Bentivoglio Van Ness Middleton, was born in mid-March, so the Fishers were able to see him before they left Charleston. According to Emma Huger Smith, Paolina seemed in greater pain after the baby's birth than during her labor, but "her Faith in Arthur [*as a physician*] equals his self-confidence."[2]

1. JFF to GH, April 5, 1843, PHi, BrC.
2. EHS to EMF, April 14, [1843,] PHi.

To Mrs. Middleton, Middleton Place

Charleston – Tuesday eveng– [April] 18th [1843]

I hardly expected to write you more than a note from hence, my dearest Mamma, but I have more to tell you than I could well compress into a note– But first let me relieve you with regard to Pauline– I found her much better than I expected, but still very weak of course– The rising between the breasts broke on Saturday, & she has since been (comparatively) free from pain– & able to nurse her baby– altho' she still does so very sparingly– The Combahee [*wet*] nurse arrived yesterday, but is only intended as a temporary substitute, as she hopes to have enough to give him herself before long– He will be very goodlooking, even handsome I think, when he fattens up a little– but is at present so thin, poor little thing, that his "elements of beauty" as M<u>rs</u> Sumner says, (by which I suppose she means, eyes, nose & mouth) are seen to great disadvantage– But I have no doubt by the time you see him (for Pauline tells me she has no thoughts of moving hence) he will have improved into a fine blooming boy–

Now I must tell you something of ourselves– We came down very comfortably in 3 hours, W<u>m</u> & I, changing offices for a time– <u>he</u> turning nurse & holding Lily in his arms during her nap, & <u>I</u> taking the reins meanwhile & driving for several miles– The Nurse [*Mrs. Putnam*] bore the journey better than I expected– but in the afternoon had so alarming an attack of spasm in the <u>Bronchia</u> (I believe it is called) that she thought herself seized with Quinsey,[1] & we sent off for D<u>r</u> Ogier, who immediately ordered leeches to be applied to her throat, & an emetic administered– These remedies have relieved her cough & the suffocating feeling, but have debilitated [her] excessively, & obliged her to keep her bed all today– He thinks her better, but talks of blistering or leeching again tomorrow, and says she cannot travel for <u>three</u> days at least– but perhaps on Friday she may be well enough– I have myself no idea that we shall set out before Saturday, & surely it w<u>d</u> not be worthwhile to do so, & be detained on the road by her illness– at some <u>charming</u> spot in North Carolina for instance– Fisher is rather disappointed, at this delay– mais que faire? [*but what can one do?*] & I for my part am not sorry to have an opportunity of seeing a little more of my Charleston friends– altho' to be sure I am rather a prisoner to the nursery– I went out this morng– for an hour or two with Emma to some shops for you & also saw Sabina [Lowndes,] & Miss Pinckney, M<u>rs</u> I[zard] & Miss R[utledge]– who all desired affect<u>e</u> remembrances to you & were concerned to hear of y<u>r</u> indisposition– I am most anxious to learn that you are quite rid of it, & have neither cough or fever & Papa authorizes me to advise you to send Jack down on Friday, to let us know how you are– So pray do so by all means, & give me very particular accounts of yourself– & of dear Sally also– Harry talks of going up to you tomorrow, but I shall make sure of sending this by the Waggon– & am now finishing it upstairs, having been called to Sophy whose cough is very troublesome– I gave her by the D<u>r</u>'s advice about 7 teaspoonfuls (at intervals) of Hippo Syrup,[2] last night, without producing the desired effect of making her vomit– & now tonight he told me to try the Squills– I hope to give you good news of her in the morning–

Mrs Smith came yesterday afternoon to see me [and] begged me to forward to you the accompanying letter to you– She talks a little of going to Eng^d in the summer, but seems very undecided yet– I hope the Calico which was only <u>sevenpence</u> & the prettiest one we saw for that price will please you– The combs were W^m's choice, & tomorrow I will go for the shoes–

We have no more letters from the north but F– wrote today to his mother to inform her of the delay– Goodnight dear Mamma– I am quite overcome by fatigue, & the want of rest of last night–

Wednesday morng– The D^r has just been & pronounced the nurse much better & says she may travel on Friday he thinks so don't fail to send Jack down to tell us how you are– The baby (Sophy I mean) coughed a good deal again last night– The Squills had no more effect than the Hippo– Today she is to remain upstairs– & the Hive syrup to be given tonight– poor monkey she is looking very pale after so much dosing but is in good spirits & humour as usual– Mrs Smith has kindly sent them each a doll of her own manufacture to amuse them on the journey– I must now close this scrawl as Michael[3] is ready– Ed^d sends his love & says he means to go with us to Norfolk & I <u>suppose</u> a little <u>farther on</u> afterwards–[4] Adieu dearest Mamma y^r affectionate daughter Eliza

Marg^t is more rational, but miserably distressed still, & most anxious to be sent home–[5] Papa says he will see about doing so tomorrow– but I cannot tell you by what vessel for no steps have yet been taken & Arthur is trying the effect of his Homeopathic medecines upon her, as Dr O. said he could do nothing more unless she were shaved & blistered on the head– Arthur thinks he can cure her. He & Pauline desire their best love to you, Sally & the children– Pray give mine to each & all & Fisher's kind regards & a kiss from each of the chicks–

ScHi
Eliza's note was addressed: (By Michael with the Waggon).

1. Quinsy was an abscess around the tonsils, producing an extremely sore throat for which there was no real cure before antibiotics.
2. Hippo syrup has not been identified. Squill was part of a bulbous herb used, among other things, as an expectorant to treat children with croup or a bad cough.
3. Michael was the wagon driver from Middleton Place.
4. Edward was apparently still interested in Miss Tiffany and thinking of going to see her in Baltimore.

5. Although the details are sketchy, Margaret Driscoll, Catherine's companion, apparently had had some sort of mental crisis. When Margaret left the Middletons later in the spring, Mrs. Middleton commented that she would be lucky if she found someone "as honest & good natured" to take her place. MHM to EMF, July 9, 1843, PHi.

⁓

To Mrs. Fisher, Philadelphia

M.P. April 26$\underline{th}$ 1843

I trust this will find my dearest Eliza & her family safely arrived at Phil$\underline{a}$ & recovering from the fatigue of the journey, & enjoying the happiness of meeting her kind Mother & Aunt & Uncle– This I often think of, trying to reconcile myself to your absence– & converse about you & the children with Sally– She begs me to thank you for the presents you sent to hers, which she considered very kind– After what you said in your note about Paolina having no intention of coming here, I was surprised to learn the day after that she would come on the 24$\underline{th}$ which she did with her infant & Marg$\underline{t}$– Her breast still continues very painful, but she can nurse her child, & although she cannot say she is better than when you left her, Arthur thinks there is no danger of the inflammation returning. The child will improve in appearance when he becomes fat but at present is miserably thin– I was glad to find Marg$\underline{t}$ had recovered from her mental malady for which Arthur deserves great credit– She behaves now just as she always did– has complained for the last two days of headache & this morning has taken a homeopathic dose which I have no doubt will soon relieve her. This cure ought I think to give you faith in homeopathy, & I hope you have consulted D$\underline{r}$ Hering & will inform me of his opinion of your complaints, & the remedies he prescribes– do not delay taking his advice I entreat you.

I had the pleasure to receive on Monday a letter from my Brother of 28$\underline{th}$ of March– but he gives a sad account of himself– the interval between that & his former letter having been past chiefly in bed. He is as incredulous as M$\underline{r}$ Fisher on the subject of Mesmerism, but having enquired of my Sister about D$\underline{r}$ Ward an acknowledged clever man who is an old acquaintance of hers, & of the circumstances I mentioned about his having by means of mesmerism amputated the leg of a Man without giving him the least pain: my Sister sent him the Pamphlet which gives the detailed account of the Mesmerian case at Wellow (n$\underline{r}$ Ollerton)– He goes on to say "But my reason tells me that there must be something kept back, which ought to explain why such things happen contrary to Nature– Why don't these Mesmerian Conjurors give proper explanations? Truth will always make its own way. concealment creates doubt"– I read this to Arthur, but he of course is so well convinced of the truth of Mesmerism that he only smiles at my Brother's want of faith in it– He as you see however, believes Dr Ward's successful experiment so well ascertained, & I have written all this, because you said that Newspaper accounts were not to be believed, & I thought it best to give you the information from its original & true source.

27th Paolina has just come in after breakfast, & says she feels better. She & Arthur & the Black Nurse occupy the 3 rooms in the Outhouse, so that there is only y^r bedroom now vacant. Whether Mrs Coffin will come is uncertain as she did not fix a day for her visit. Sally will remain 8 or 10 days longer, as John writes word that he shall not be able to be in Charleston until the 4th of May, & expressed with great regret his having missed seeing you– You must have suffered from the great heat of the weather, for on Sunday the ther^r rose to 84° & has continued ever since to rise to that height about midday– the shrubs in consequence are in bloom, ie the Fringe, the Pedisporum (wrongly spelt)[1] &c but not yet the Stewartia. Sally has been extremely interested by "the Neighbours" read aloud by Hal & some of the Girls– I cannot say the same of myself. My brother says my Sister recommends to me the perusal of 'the Jewess' by the authoress of 'Letters from the Baltic', Mrs Rigby.[2] I suppose you can procure it at Phil^a here it is not advertised.

You begged me to give an account of my health– it is now quite good, & I feel stronger– By the return of the messenger perhaps I may receive a letter from you, but I rather think it is too soon to expect one. The blue calico you last sent for C. is prettier than the other dress– She seems pleased with both. Mrs Drayton called last Saturday to return y^r visit & begged to have her Compliments sent you. You must be sorry to learn that A. Smith has lost his Lawsuit. I must now send this off– Pray give my love to M^r & Mrs Fisher with remembrances to M^r & Mrs Harrison & kisses to the Children & believe me my dearest Eliza y^r affect^te Mother M. H. M.

Sally, Paolina & all the Girls send their love to you– has the shower bath been of service to M^r F's eyes? Marg^t is quite well today.

PHi

1. That is, pittosporum.
2. *The Jewess* was written in 1846 by Elizabeth Rigby. Mrs. Middleton had read her *Letters from the Shores of the Baltic* the year before.

⌇

To Mrs. Middleton, Middleton Place

Philadelphia April 30th [1843]

I wrote you a very hurried scrawl from Balte my dearest Mamma, & promised to send something better shortly after my arrival at home– This afternoon
I have full leisure to do so– having been prevented from going to Church by
the rain– & spent the day in reading, and playing with the children for recreation– They have now betaken themselves to the Nursery to romp with Frank
[Huger,] & as Fisher has not returned from dining at his Aunt's, my time is
my own for an hour & I want to place myself "en rapport" with you–

We had rather a pleasant day coming from Balte except for the last hour
or two, when the children became restless, & the weather which was quite warm
when we started, changed suddenly– and an east wind blew so keenly on the
river that I had to confine them to the cabin– During the first part of the day
we had been quite entertained by their frolics on deck & Sophy with her usual
sociability made advances to all the passengers, & received a great deal of attention from the distinguished lover of Miss Harper (Mr Cushing)[1] who was our
"compagnon de voyage", & whose acquaintance we made at her house the
evening before– He is quite a handsome man, & rather an agreeable one, but
notwithstanding these qualifications, & his political celebrity, I don't think he
has any chance of winning the bride he is seeking– altho' Mrs C. C. H[arper]
told us that the mother & Aunt were very anxious for the match– Mme mère,[2]
was to set out for NewPort tomorrow the 1st of May– & they were to follow
in a few weeks– We heard of a great many Baltimoreans who were going there–
The T[iffany]s are not– having purchased a country seat in the neighbourhood
of B[altimore] & intending to remain there this summer–

We found Mr H's carriage waiting for us at the Wharf, and landing about
5 o'clock, drove first to their house & were received in the most affecte manner.
They are looking remarkably well, & so we thought was the old lady here– but
she says she then felt that a nervous attack was impending, & she is now suffering under it– having been on her bed all day– She attributes it partly to the
anxiety she felt about our arrival, & also to her disappointment at discovering
that Fisher's eyes are not better, & my throat still affected– The fact is, I took
cold in the Norfolk steamer, & had quite a bad sorethroat the day before yesterday– but it is now considerably better–

I suppose you will be glad to hear that I have actually had an interview
with the great Homo [*Dr. Hering*]– a most unprepossessing ill looking individ-

ual– who talked so strangely in bad English, that it required great faith in the
Science to feel much confidence in him or his prescriptions– however I mean
to take them regularly, & follow all his directions & advice à la lettre– These
to be sure are easy enough– & may be summed up in a few [words]– to gargle &
wash my throat frequently with cold water, observe a certain diet, which varies
little from my usual one for he even permits black tea & take the powders he
sent me– night & morng– He told Fisher they were "Hepar sulphurus"–³ (This
is for Arthur's satisfaction)– He did not flatter me with the prospect of a speedy
cure, but said, as I expected, that a chronic disease, which had become constitutional, w^d require time to cure it– but that he doubted not that he should
conquer it– & that in 2 or 3 weeks I sh^d probably perceive a decided change
for the better– He noted down all my symptoms very carefully– & promised
to come again on Tuesday– many of my friends here are quite amused at my
consulting this german quack, as they call him– but others have faith in him–⁴
I mean to confess it to Dr Meigs, who is coming tomorrow to see the children–
I want him to decide if Sophy has the Hooping cough– which I really believe
she has– & to have a few general directions from him with regard to it– I daresay
he will laugh at my credulity– & perhaps even be offended at my taking any
other remedies but his – mais cela m'est bien égal [*but I don't care*] & I shall
give Dr H. a fair trial–

I find that poor little Mme d'Hauterive is sinking rapidly– & no hope whatever is entertained of her recovery by the physicians who still have not informed
her husband of her danger– which I think very unjustifiable– Poor R[obert]
H[are]⁵ was so much better that they permitted his mother to be with him &
removed him to his own room– but yesterday & last night he was worse again &
from what I can learn there seems but a slender chance of his mind ever being
entirely restored– I spent an hour with his afflicted mother the day after my
arrival– she behaves like an angel about it & the patience with which she bears
this heavy sorrow is touching in the extreme– She related to me the whole affair
with Miss B[urd]– & I can now better understand from her description of poor
Robert's feelings on his subject, how he became so much interested in the girl–
who must be a mere puppet worked upon by her vixenish sister– think of their
being so heartless as to give a ball next Tuesday. I thought the invitation to us,
almost an insult under the circumstances– Their conduct is considered by all
most contemptible & shameful– & there is no doubt that the repeated & aggra-
vated mortifications they subjected him to, were the cause of the derangement
of the unfortunate youth, who was of a remarkably sensitive character– with
the highest sense of honour, and great excitability of imagination– & had reason
to believe that the girl was devoted to him– which also acted powerfully on

him– It is a sad story indeed & I am so much attached to the Hares that it makes me very mournful to think of it– Miss H[are] is pretty well– & all our other friends pretty much as we left them– Old Ridgway[6] is dead– & people exclaim M$\underline{rs}$ Rush will at last have her desire of going to Europe gratified! Which is judging her according to her own words spoken long ago–

I am most anxious to get a letter from you telling me you are all well– I hope tomorrow to have that pleasure but will now send this when the rain ceases– my best love is with you all. Y$\underline{r}$ affectionate daughter Eliza

Lily sends her love to Helen & Ria,[7] and then repeats after me quite intelligibly all the cousins by name– <u>Sarah</u>'s being the most difficult for her– & then goes over all the Aunts & Uncles in succession, not forgetting grandmama & grandpapa. She begins to cough, but does not <u>hoop</u> yet– which the nurse thinks Sophy does decidedly– She (M$\underline{rs}$ P) is much better but still rather weak– I rec$\underline{d}$ a letter from Aunt H[ering] the day after my arrival here– As usual it is without date, but I conclude is not more than 3 weeks old– I answered it immediately– announcing our safe arrival– Uncle had some symptoms of his enemy's approach, but not severe ones.

Monday morng– I thought I might as well leave this open, in case I might receive a letter from you before dispatching it– & to my great joy one was brought me while I was dressing– The account of yourself is very satisfactory– I am only sorry that you do not mention Papa's cough from which I hope however he does not suffer any longer– You have also forgotten to tell me how Sally is– I am glad you have the authority you wanted in the case of amputation– but altho' this may be well ascertained (viz– that the nerves may be rendered insensible by mesmerism) you surely do not imagine that <u>clairvoyance</u>[8] is thereby proved– or all the other wonders of Animal magnetism rendered more probable by this one <u>fact</u>– even admitting it– but I will no longer distress y$\underline{r}$ eyes by this double scrawl– So Adieu dearest Mamma, with love to each & all.

Private Collection

1. Possibly Caleb Cushing (1800–1879), who was at that time a congressman from Massachusetts. President Tyler appointed him the first American commissioner to China in 1844.

2. That is, Miss Harper's mother.

3. A homeopathic medicine, hepar sulphurus was made from the inner layer of oyster shells and used to treat complaints such as sore throats, earaches, and colds.

4. Later Eliza told her mother, "Every body here laughs at me for trying such <u>nonsense</u>– except Sally Hare– who is by the way one of my most <u>sensible</u> acquain-

tances & she has such confidence in the new treatment– that it is enough to inspire one with like faith to hear her talk about it– So that in the midst of <u>Unbelievers</u>, there is one at least to encourage me in the trial." EMF to MHM, May 10, 1843, private collection.

5. Robert Hare, Jr., had a mental breakdown, which his family and friends perceived to be due to ill treatment by Mrs. Daniel Coxe's niece Margaret Burd. Eliza's mother replied, "I am sincerely grieved for his poor Mother who you say bears her deep affliction with so much patience. My own experience can make me well understand the depth of her sorrow." MHM to EMF, May 7, 1843, PHi.

6. Jacob Ridgway left an estate of more than $3 million (in the range of $60 million in 1999 dollars), which he divided evenly between his son and two daughters. After Ridgway died, the Rushes went to live in Europe, but James Rush was unhappy away from home and they returned in 1847. Dollar conversion factor from RSahr, OrStU.

7. Helen and Ria were John and Sally's youngest daughters, Mary Helen and Maria Henrietta, who were about four and two years old respectively.

8. In this context, clairvoyance refers to any kind of beyond-normal perception (which would generally occur in a trance).

∼

To Mrs. Middleton, Middleton Place

Philadelphia– May 26<u>th</u> [1843]

I suppose I must not imagine anything is going wrong in Carolina, because I do not get news from thence, my dearest Mama, but attribute y<u>r</u> silence to the usual cause & wait patiently until at least a fortnight expires since the last favour from you was rec<u>d</u> which will be on Sunday, when I may expect one more confidently than today– I shall then know perhaps when you will be leaving Carolina, & by what conveyance– Emma I am happy to hear from M<u>r</u> Lowndes, will leave Charleston on the 1<u>st</u> of June & come this way– I am sorry she could not have been here on that day, for we are to have a famous party, a sort of "Fête Champêtre" out at Woodvale Cottage–[1] but the invitations are not given in the Widow's name, tell Harry– but in [*her sister*] M<u>rs</u> Chapman's[2] who is [to] act Hostess on the occasion, M<u>rs</u> C[amac] not appearing– as they say– Everybody says, tell y<u>r</u> brother Harry to come on– but as I think telling him, w<u>d</u> not bring him, I only repeat the observations of others– without giving my own– But I have just been writing to Ned, who I think w<u>d</u> enjoy a Ball more, & may very probably obtain leave of absence from his Ship for a few days– which he might pass more agreeably here than in Norfolk– I have heard nothing more of him than what I mentioned in my last– but have begged him to write immediately & tell me his Plans–

Fisher has been quite indisposed since I wrote to you, but is now much better, & out again, altho' I think he ought not to be this damp day, for he still coughs & yesterday was not well enough to attend the evening Party, given at the Philosophical Hall, in honour of their Hundredth anniversary– which was quite a disappoinment– but a still greater is, being obliged to refuse an invitation to dine at Mr Binney's today– if he had known he sh^d be as well today, he might have accepted, but could not on the uncertainty– We have the Warrens here [*from Boston*] – & Miss Grant & Miss Sears–^{3} They have just been spending half an hour with me, listening to my Piano– but are engaged for this eveng– & off tomorrow morng– so that they cannot accept either of my invitations to drink tea– They tell me that Fanny Appleton's engagement is really true, & that no one suspected that the Professor^4 was going to be the fortunate man– He is certainly a man of some talent, but after the publication of Hyperion, I thought she would not forgive him for his impudence– now they say there was a <u>misunderstanding</u>, & that she always liked him– The fact is, probably, that the <u>House at home</u> is not as pleasant, since the birth of the three babies– & the absence of sister & brother–^{5} both abroad– and so she decides to reward her literary lover's constancy– I hope she may not repent it–

I am glad to be able to give you better account of Robert H– He is gone to Powelton– & his Physicians entertain great hopes of his entire recovery– Poor Mme d'Hauterive too is a little better, & has been removed to Burlington [*New Jersey*] & bore the change better than they expected– but there is little hope for her– We are all going on quietly– as usual– have neither given or received Parties lately– but are to have a little one tomorrow eveng for Mrs Pierce Butler– who is looking remarkably well, & seems not sorry to be here again–^{6} She rec^d us up stairs in her bedroom, which was littered with all sorts of things– Children's toys, books, gowns, collars, &c in <u>amiable</u> confusion– but behaved very well, altho' she was rather embarrassed when she found Fisher was with us–

We are all arranged for Summer– with mats down, floors & paint scoured & scrubbed to Mrs Fisher's satisfaction–^{7} but the warm weather will not be coaxed here by the preparations made for its reception & we still have fires in the grates– You I suppose have sun enough to warm you– & perhaps more than you like– Fisher begs me to tell you that he has at last prevailed upon me to send Lily out of my room, and that he hopes now that I have nothing to disturb me that I shall get <u>fat</u> at last. I must say Adieu with love to all, or I shall be too late– Y^r affec^{te} Eliza

Private Collection

1. Woodvale Cottage belonged to Mrs. Camac. It was a large house surrounded by a sixty-acre park in North Philadelphia and known for its gardens and hothouses.

2. Emily Markoe (Mrs. George) Chapman.

3. Miss Grant and Miss Sears were nieces of Mrs. Warren.

4. Fanny Appleton was engaged to Henry Wadsworth Longfellow. He was professor of modern languages and belles lettres at Harvard, but had not yet written the poems, such as "Evangeline" and "Hiawatha," which made him famous. In "Hyperion," he modeled the heroine on Fanny Appleton.

5. Mary (Appleton) Mackintosh and Tom Appleton.

6. The Pierce Butlers had just returned from a three-year stay in England and Europe.

7. For the first time, Eliza had helped with the spring cleaning. EMF to MHM, May 17, [1843,] private collection.

∼

To Mrs. Fisher, Philadelphia

Charleston 1$\underline{st}$ June 1843

My dearest Eliza

We arrived here yesterday having had an unusually cool drive owing to a delightful change in the weather the preceding day– the ther$\underline{r}$ having been for some days previous rising from 80 to 89 so you may suppose how Paolina & myself must have enjoyed the cool change– it will not last long however for the heat is already encreasing. Susan and the three girls came to see me yesterday evening. She is well, but exceedingly thin– She says that if M$\underline{rs}$ Chisolm who is still an invalid should consent to take charge of the three younger children, she will go with Oliver & the two eldest to N.Y. by railroad to place them at M$\underline{r}$ Bolton's[1] school 20 miles from the city on the east river. You have probably seen Miss Rutledge on her way thither as she went a fortnight ago I believe, in company with Miss Lucas R[utledge] & M$\underline{rs}$ E$\underline{d}$ R[utledge] & D$\underline{r}$ Holbrook.

While at breakfast John made his appearance & brought a good account of his family. Sally had been suffering from headach but her eyes were not quite as painful as they had been. he had lately fallen against a roller of his Mill & broken one of his ribs, but made light of the accident & received relief from a homoeopathic dose. He has been curing a great number of his people by those medicines– on my asking him whether he had any message for you he sends his love & tells you he feels very shabby for not having answered your letter, which he mentioned having received in one written to Sally a month ago, as being very kind & affectionate & expressing his regret at not being able to come & see you before your departure. His family have removed to the beach only 3 miles from the plantation which they often visit in the course of the week. W$\underline{m}$ says E[mma] Smith is looking very ill, but she will leave this next Monday– I shall probably see her today.

When <u>we</u> shall go to the north is uncertain & y$\underline{r}$ Father says he cannot yet say whether we can go at any time![2] This is what I apprehended, but will not think too much about it. No vessels are going except the Sutton which is to sail today, until the end of the month, so that I must make up my mind to remain here for several weeks. Paolina is looking very well, her breast is better, & the Infant greatly improved in appearance, & can now be called little Fatty. Your brothers were amused at your account of Miss Appleton's engagement & wonder at her consenting to marry so ugly a man– You too will wonder at Miss Moore's engagement to D$\underline{r}$ Hodges[3] which Emma told W$\underline{m}$ was decided upon– What an imprudent resolution!

I am very glad to hear of young Hare's improving in health & also of M$\underline{me}$ d'Hauterive's– a sea voyage would probably effect a complete cure. I hope M$\underline{r}$ Fisher is now quite well & that you are continuing to improve in consequence of D$\underline{r}$ H[ering]'s remedies. You do not mention anything of his treatment of you in y$\underline{r}$ last letter of the 26$\underline{th}$ ult$\underline{o}$. You have done well to remove Lily from your bedside, & I have no doubt you already feel the good effects of passing y$\underline{r}$ nights undisturbed. I hope M$\underline{rs}$ Fisher is now quite well pray give my love to her & M$\underline{r}$ F– All the family desire their love to you & I am my dearest Eliza y$\underline{r}$ Affect$\underline{te}$ Mother M. H. M.
Kiss the dear Children for me & ask Lily if she still remembers me–

PHi

1. Mary and Matty (Coosey) Middleton were to go to Robert Bolton's school, the Priory, at Pelham, near New Rochelle, New York.
2. Henry Middleton may have been worried about not having enough money to take his family to Newport that year since the price of rice had fallen so low.
3. Sarah Moore married Edward Hodges, the organist of Trinity Church in New York. Although he was a worthy person and a good churchman, the Moores were not pleased. A. Nevins and M. H. Thomas, eds., *The Diary of George Templeton Strong, 1835–1875* (New York: Macmillan, 1952), 1:221.

～

To Mrs. Middleton, Charleston

Philadelphia– June 2$\underline{nd}$ 1843

My dearest Mamma,

Y$\underline{r}$ last letter came a day earlier than the expiration of the fortnight which

I had made up my mind to wait for with patience, and it was particularly welcome– We seem to be going back to Winter– for the weather is not even Spring like– & yesterday I sat shivering by the fire, & could not make up my mind to go out to the Fête Champêtre– which I do not at all regret, since I have learnt that no one followed the intention of Mrs Chapman, but thinking it too cold to go & walk over the grounds, they went 3 hours later than the hour mentioned– viz– at 8 instead of 5 & of course remained until late at night– which w^d not at all have suited me– After Fisher's departure (for W. Chester) & the letter I rec^d from Edwd telling me he could not come, I lost all inclination to go, but as Lizzie urged me very much, I made all my preparations, but when yesterday was ushered in with a keen NorthWester, I was not sorry to have the excuse of a headache, & submitted to my <u>disappointment</u> with a good grace, for it no doubt spared me a sore throat, which I sh^d <u>inevitably</u> have caught, had I ventured to expose myself at night– And since I have heard Lizzie's account of the affair, I quite rejoice at my escape– for altho' a very handsome Party, she found it very stupid, & it was at any rate, just like any other regular Ball– She says the house is beautifully fitted up, and the furniture, hangings &c, are all of the most elegant description, & she could not help thinking how <u>nice</u> it w^d be if Cousin Harry w^d come & take a fancy to establish himself there– which <u>suggestion</u> I promised her to repeat to him <u>through</u> you– She caught a glimpse of the fair Widow, who did not however make her entrée among the guests–

If this cool weather extends as far South as you are, you will be more unwilling than ever to leave the country– I can scarcely believe that June has begun– for the frost reminds one more of December & the matted floors & curtainless windows alone like summer within doors– & without the leaves appear out of season– We went out to Powelton to see poor Mrs Hare on Monday, & were quite concerned at her altered looks– She has been very unwell since she left town– & I much fear that they are occasioned also by her despondency on Robert's account– for altho' he is in some respects better, & enjoys the country, there are symptoms which are unfavourable– & they have discovered lately, by letters that he has been permitted to write to his brothers & Uncle, that he has a delusion which has continued ever since his first attack– but he had spoken of so little lately that they were in hopes he had forgotten it– Of course the fear is, that it may become <u>settled</u>, & his poor Mother seems sadly discouraged– but tries to deceive herself into the belief that he is better– Heaven grant he may be so!

I am expecting Cousin Sally [Rutledge,] who is to walk down with me to St Peter's Church, to hear the last Lecture of the course which is given this afternoon after Prayers– She will return home with me, & drink tea with us– &

I have asked the little Middletons[1] & Lily M^CEuen to meet the little Rutledges, & amuse them during our absence– Mrs Lowndes, M^rs [Edward] Rutledge & Lucas went on with Dr Holbrook the morning after their arrival here, so that I did not see them– M^rs [Noble Jones] & Miss [Mary] Jones were also their travelling companions– The latter is very much indisposed– but better than she was on the journey– but a fever which has lasted 6 weeks sounds very serious indeed– I am glad you mentioned Emma, for she has not yet written to me– I am daily looking for a letter from her telling me what day I am to expect her here– but fear that Miss Welles[2] will soon carry her off to N.Y.

I cannot ascertain from Cousin S. R. when the girls [*Mary and Matty Middleton*] will be coming on– I am really sorry they are to be so far from me– & yet I have so poor an opinion of these French schools here that I could not in conscience recommend Susan to send them to Phil^a much as I sh^d have liked to have them near me– These Boltons I am inclined to think highly of, from what I hear from various quarters– Mrs Prime has tried 3 different schools here and in N.Y. for M^r P's daughters & prefers this very much to any of them– indeed was very much pleased with their whole system of education– & their way of carrying it out also– which is not less important– They are very well educated & amiable people– who make themselves beloved by their pupils– & will inculcate not only by <u>precept</u>, but <u>example</u> the best principles– & I consider it a great advantage that the girls have plenty of wholesome country air & exercize– instead of being cooped up 6 days out of the seven in small rooms in a city–

Saturday morng– I had just got thro' with my music lesson my dear Mamma, & was taking M^rs M^CEuen, who had come to <u>assist</u> at it, to the door, when I was caught by Mrs Elwyn, who has detained me nearly an hour with her incessant <u>raraing</u>, so that I have barely time to add a few lines to this before the post goes out– Little Sophy is better today– I believe I have mentioned that she has had the mumps, & a little fever with it which made me rather uneasy– but she is now getting over it decidedly & as there is a <u>warm</u> change at last I shall send her out of doors for the first time for several days– I am in hopes I shall derive benefit from it myself– for Homoeopathy has not done much for me so far– I must send this off immediately if it is to go by today's mail. My love to Papa, Brothers & Sisters & believe me as ever Y^r most affet^e daughter Eliza

Mrs F. sends her best regards. She is much better–

Private Collection

1. The little Middletons were probably the Henry A. Middletons' youngest children, and the little Rutledges the Edward Rutledges' children. Mrs. Lowndes was probably Mary (Middleton) Lowndes.

2. Sabina E. Wells (1816–1891), Emma Huger Smith's first cousin, lived in New York. Her mother was the former Sabina Huger.

~

"I dread the thoughts of the voyage in a close cabin," Mrs. Middleton wrote from Charleston in June amid the usual discussions about which boat they would take, "& Harry does also for he is always sea sick & thinks that W$\underline{m}$ ought to be our escort as he is never sick."[1]

Once they reached Newport in the beginning of July, however, Mrs. Middleton felt better and set about finding a corner for everyone to sleep in. If Fisher "could give up his little dressing closet," she told Eliza, "I must put my cook to sleep in it for I am compelled to give the middle room for Paolina's nurse,"[2] and so it went until her children, grandchildren, and servants all had their places.

Newport's charms remained the same as always. Sometimes Eliza and Miss Harper went swimming in the ocean in the morning. Friends came to call. Henry Middleton planted trees, adding to and improving the property he enjoyed so much. There were balls and a band, musical parties, and Middleton family dinners, where Sidney Fisher reported sourly that homeopathy was the subject of "futile discussion and barren talk."[3]

Once again, in the summer of 1843, the hotels and boardinghouses were "stuffed to the roof." As William Hunter's son Thomas said, with the boat fare between New York and Newport only one dollar, it was cheaper "to keep moving than stay at home."[4] Mrs. Camac, however, was the star attraction that summer. When word spread that the young widow had been left an income of $12,000, suitors appeared from everywhere. They were said to be "as numerous as Coachmen on a wharf when a steamboat arrives," with all of them pushing and shoving to get a chance to go driving with her. "She has been driven to Purgatory [Rock] already fifty times, and on each day by a different lover– Sometimes she goes about in a gig with some favorite Jehu, and the Forlorn Hopes follow on horseback as outriders."[5]

Harry Middleton found favor at the front of this troop of admirers, which soon gave rise to rumors that he and Mrs. Camac were engaged. On the other hand, Mrs. Harper was still in the picture and at least one friend "had no doubt if the money were on her side, that she wd be preferred to her present rival."[6]

In September, the Fishers took a trip to New England. They stayed first at the Tremont House hotel in Boston while they visited the Otises and other friends. Then they made an excursion across Massachusetts to Pittsfield, explored the Berkshire Hills for a few days, and then went down the Hudson River to New York. By the beginning of October, they were back in Philadelphia.

1. MHM to EMF, June 11, 1843, PHi.
2. MHM to EMF, July 9, 1843, PHi.
3. Wainwright, *Phila. Perspective* (October 8, 1843): 141.
4. Thomas Hunter, letter of July 1843, quoted in "A Decade in Newport," *Bulletin of the Newport Historical Society* (April 1925): 16.
5. Ibid.
6. EMF to JFF, August 30, 1843, MPlFdn.

To Mrs. Middleton, Newport

Philadelphia Tuesday Oc^t 10$^{\underline{th}}$ [1843]

I had the pleasure of receiving y^r letter of the 4$^{\underline{th}}$ yesterday, my dearest Mamma, & with it the enclosed one from John which I was also very glad to read– altho' sorry to find that dear Sally was such a sufferer– I expect soon an answer myself from John, but think I shall not wait for it, but write him as I promised some account of my journey– I wrote you a few lines in N.Y. which I entrusted to Edward, who intended in a day or two to set out for NewPort– but perhaps he may have changed his mind & remained in N. Y. until Papa's arrival there– in which case he w$^{\underline{d}}$ certainly delay his visit to you, & probably send my note by post– I informed you in it that the pleasure of our expedition was somewhat lessened by our all (except Fisher) catching severe colds– The children's were of course encreased by travelling in <u>blustering</u> weather– & the necessary exposure in steamboats &c– but since our arrival at home we have been <u>nursing</u> ourselves with so much good effect, that we are able to go out again today, & enjoy this bright sunshine– I am really a <u>great deal</u> better– not only is my cold almost well, but my throat is so much stronger, that I am very much encouraged to believe, as Dr Hering assures me, that I shall in a very short time regain all the ground I have lost within the last 6 weeks by colds & <u>other</u> accidents– which of course threw me back considerably–[1] He has been <u>tinkering</u> me, viz. giving me Powders of <u>Stamm</u>, in plain English Tinn– which Dr Meigs, (whom I consulted about the children, & who enquired whether I had yet got tired of the <u>bread</u> pills) declares will do me no more good than if I drank water out of a <u>Tin Mug</u>– However I really think I have already derived benefit from them– for many of the symptoms which distressed me for some weeks past have disappeared & altho' the change of air, & mild weather may have something to do with my improvement, I am willing to give the Stamm credit too for relieving me– D^r H[ering] thinks that I shall not <u>at all</u> require a change of climate this winter– & that I shall be more likely to recover at home, surrounded by comforts, and consulting him regularly, than at the South (I mean the West Indies) among strangers, in far less comfortable quarters, [and] far from a Homoeopathic Physician– When I told him of y^r plan for me of going with my brother Arthur to Jamaica–² he said that changed the case– but still insisted that I sh^d do very well at home– & that I might easily have been relieved sooner– had I consulted a Homoeopath in Boston– I hope his opinion & my own now coinciding with his, will entirely relieve y^r anxiety on my account, my dear Mamma, and at least encourage you to look forward as I do, to my passing the winter very comfortably & without any risk of my becoming worse–

We found all our friends remarkably well– but M^{rs} F– seeing how much I & the children also were suffering with colds & coughs, became quite nervous & took to her bed, but she seems better this morng– I had yesterday a long list of visitors, who nearly all enquired of me about you, & wanted to know when you were to be here– I answered I hoped in about 2 weeks– and may it be so! Many were the enquiries made about the <u>supposed</u> engagement of my brother [*to Mrs. Camac*] – about which I very truly confessed my entire ignorance– Mrs Harper has been twice to see me– & the first time as we were quite alone, she told me of the attentions paid her by her <u>rival</u> who has had her to spend the afternoon & eveng– with her, & inviting a large party of pleasant people to meet her– she likewise told me an <u>anecdote</u> which I had heard before, with some embellishment– & which I will reserve for a <u>viva voce</u> communication, not liking to trust it to writing– Tell Harry M^{rs} H– was to leave town today & everybody is wondering what keeps him so late in the season at NewPort– I have not seen M^{rs} C[amac] but met Mrs Chapman who told me she was on her way to see me– I must say Adieu my dearest mamma & remain your affectionate E–

I am sorry that there is any doubt of Pauline's going to Boston³ for I think she w^d enjoy the visit– Give my love to her, her sposo & bambino– Pray tell me what colour Sally wished her dress to be dyed– for I cannot send it until I know– & want you to mention this when you next write– which I hope will be soon– Mrs P. Smith came yesterday to see me, & will be here again this eveng to take tea– She begged me to tell you she had decided to remain this winter in Phil^a which I was very glad to hear– Fisher has just been in to Fletcher's (The Morris House) to enquire if there were any rooms vacant– He says there will be two very good ones (which the Iturbides⁴ had when you were there) empty by the 18th (and I hope you will be here soon after that) & several others upstairs can be had–

Private Collection

1. Eliza was not well during the summer and wrote to her mother from Boston that she rested all day on the sofa in her room. "I should have enjoyed my visit more

if I had felt stronger," she told her. This, combined with her phrase "other accidents," could indicate she had a miscarriage. EMF to MHM, September 21 and September 29, 1843, ScHi.

2. Arthur seems to have thought he would go to Jamaica on business related to Hering family property there. This is the first of several references to a trip which never took place.

3. Arthur said he would not take the baby to Boston; Paolina said that in that case she would not go; Mrs. Middleton said, "How they will arrange matters, I have not yet heard." MHM to EMF, October 4, 1843, ScHi.

4. The family of Agustin de Iturbide, self-proclaimed "emperor" after Mexico's war for independence from Spain, lived in Philadelphia for many years after his death in 1824.

⌒

To Mrs. Fisher, Philadelphia

Newport Oct[r] 14th 1843

Your letter my dearest Eliza received last Even[g] was indeed most comforting– for I had been anxiously expecting to hear from you & feared that illness might have prevented your writing which I thought you would have done on arriving home– This news of yourself is much better than I expected to hear & your faith in homoeopathy has I hope increased as well as your confidence in D[r] H[ering]'s judgement. It is indeed very satisfactory to me to know that you are to remain at Philad[a] during the winter– I am sorry to hear that M[rs] Fisher suffered so much from uneasiness on your & the Children's account. She must now be happy to witness their improvement in speaking, & must not imagine that the climate of Newport brought on their violent colds. Why did you not consult D[r] H. about Lily's complaint & ask him whether Arthur's remedies for her were proper? I will give you another proof of the efficacy of homoeopathy. Paolina was very unwell yesterday & when Arthur left this for Boston at 10 in the morn[g] he advised her if she should continue so to take Nux vomica–[1] She suffered from pain in her limbs pain in her chest, fever & throwing up bile– this continued till the eve[g] & when she retired to her chamber she read the account of the Symptoms in the medical book & found that her's was an attack of bilious fever & the prescription was Camomile which she took, & though she suffered very much during the night, is now almost well. the pain in her head only remaining–

Arthur took Miss R[ebecca] Smith[2] under his protection to Boston– Y[r] Father went there the preceding day, & said he sh[d] return today but I doubt his doing so.[3] As this cannot go before Monday as the Mail leaves this at 8 o'clock in the morn^g perhaps I may be able to tell you more of his plans– when he left us he said that we were to leave this on the 18$^{\underline{th}}$ because M$^{\underline{r}}$ [George] Jones had written to M$^{\underline{r}}$ Comstock[4] to request that a Steamer should come here & take 40 passengers which would make it worth his while. His family, M$^{\underline{rs}}$ Powell's,[5] M$^{\underline{r}}$ Is$^{\underline{l}}$ Thorndike's & ours. It is to be the Naragansett, & that is the only chance we shall have of going direct to N.Y– You must have heard of the accident that happened to the Massa$^{\underline{tts}}$ on Sunday night– y$^{\underline{r}}$ Father & Ed$^{\underline{d}}$ were on board & were compelled to return to N.Y. after a very disagreeable passage of 40 miles where they anchored, & there one of the pipes exploded, so that it was with difficulty they reached N.Y. & the Mass$^{\underline{tts}}$ is now laid up.

I was glad to see Edward looking so well. We shall meet at N.Y. on thursday if we arrive there safely, & if y$^{\underline{r}}$ Father permits me to leave it on Saturday, I flatter myself you & I shall meet on that day at 3 o'clock– Harry says he will accompany me if I am allowed to go– I am glad to hear we can have rooms at the Morris house. I suppose they will be more expensive than those next door to your house– I will write on my arrival at N.Y. to let you know on what day they will be wanted. It gives me pleasure to hear that M$^{\underline{rs}}$ S[mith] will pass the winter in Phil$^{\underline{a}}$ & that I can meet her once more– pray remember me kindly to her & also to those acquaintances who were so kind as to enquire about me. M$^{\underline{rs}}$ Gardener[6] came to her brother's last week, & I went to see her– She was in better spirits than when I saw her before– She & her Sister [*Mary*] are to go to N.Y. on the 18[*th*] to remain two or 3 days while their brother is there, & then Mary is to return with M$^{\underline{rs}}$ G. to Maine– She enquired about you particularly.

15th I have just come from Church where M$^{\underline{r}}$ Vinton[7] gave a very good sermon. M$^{\underline{rs}}$ Harper [*Sr.*] gave me a seat in her Carriage, & Paolina has gone on to dine with her & Miss H. Y$^{\underline{r}}$ Father returned yesterday– To my great satisfaction he made no objection to my going to N.Y. on the 18$^{\underline{th}}$ & said he intended to go himself– but sh$^{\underline{d}}$ return here & stay at some boarding house while he should superintend the laying out of the new Garden. This will afford me a longer time I flatter myself, to remain at Phil$^{\underline{a}}$ than I expected. I gave him y$^{\underline{r}}$ letter to read & asked him whether I might go to Phil$^{\underline{a}}$ the day after I arrived at N.Y. he said I might– but perhaps he may change his mind, so that I will write to you when I arrive there. I also asked whether I might take lodgings at the Morris house which he said I might, but that it was necessary that you should enquire of M$^{\underline{r}}$ Fletcher the terms, & try to have the boarding & rooms at as small an expence as you could. If he sh$^{\underline{d}}$ charge more for the private room &

bedroom next it that M<u>me</u> Iturbide inhabited, than the back room that <u>we</u> had, I would have the latter, as it is not necessary to pay a greater sum for the front, if the back room is cheaper. Harry says he shall not stay where I do, therefore we shall only want a bed room for myself & a double bed room for Cath<u>e</u> & a Maid who y<u>r</u> Father met on board the Steamer & promised to take. She seems as if she would suit me– but more of this when we meet. Pray give my kind remembrance to M<u>r</u> & M<u>rs</u> Fisher & M<u>r</u> & M<u>rs</u> Harrison & believe me my dearest Eliza y<u>r</u> Affect<u>te</u> Mother M. H. M.

You had better write an account of the terms of the Morris house as soon as you can, that I may receive it on Thursday at the Clinton hotel– Sally told me she wished the dress to be dyed of rather a dark green colour.

PHi

1. Nux vomica (vomiting nut) contains strychnine and was used for a range of symptoms from upset stomach and cramps to dizziness and nausea.

2. Rebecca (Becky) Smith (1814–1886) was Fisher's first cousin, the daughter of his aunt, Hannah Logan (Fisher) Smith.

3. Henry Middleton had gone to Boston to buy trees for a garden on a newly purchased lot in Newport. The lot, as Mrs. Middleton described it, "takes in the large tree opposite to our house, & prevents another house being built which is a great advantage." MHM to EMF, September 29, [1843,] PHi.

4. Capt. J. J. Comstock was the captain of the steamboat *Massachusetts*.

5. Mrs. John Hare Powel was the former Julia DeVeaux (1798–1845). She came from South Carolina.

6. Fenwick (Jones) Gardiner was visiting her brother, George, whose house was next to the Middletons' in Newport.

7. Francis Vinton (d. 1872) was the rector of Newport's Trinity Church. He resigned in 1844 to become the minister of Emmanuel Church in Brooklyn, New York.

⁓

To Mrs. Middleton, Charleston

Philadelphia – Tuesday 21<u>st</u> Nov<u>r</u> [1843]

My dearest Mamma,

I had just been telling Fisher that I could not expect to hear from you until tomorrow, & he was insisting that I must have patience until <u>Thursday</u>, when yr most welcome letter was handed to me, to my great joy announcing y<u>r</u> safe arrival–¹ Most heartily did I render thanks to the great Protector for guarding you from the dangers you had passed– and surely our praises to a merciful Providence are heard & accepted– There was still another cause of gratitude in the good news of dear William's improvement– God grant it may continue! The only drawback in my pleasure was the account of poor Hal's illness– but as he must have been recovering, I suppose it will be rather a subject of congratulation that he should have been acclimated by yellow fever, if it was really that–

I hope you have not made yourself uneasy at not hearing from me dear Mamma– I meant to write yesterday but was prevented by an early visitor who staid long– & as I had appointed to pay visits with Pauline who dined & spent the afternoon with us, & accompanied us to the Opera in the eveng– I had no chance to write and do not now regret it, as I can now answer y^r letter– Pauline & Arthur arrived thro' the rain on Thursday– I had written the day before about 60 notes of invitation intending to send them on Wednesday for the next eveng– but as they came not that day– I just changed the date & had a very pleasant party on Friday eveng– owing to the shortness of the notice, there were many refusals, but we had quite enough to fill our room, about 45 of the most agreeable people we asked came & we had some very good music from Miss Julia Cox,[2] & singing, which I did not so much admire, by Mrs Chapman & Miss Hitty Cox–[3] after almost every body had gone– Mrs Pierce Butler sang an English Ballad, with a great deal of feeling– but there was as little music in it, as in most of those compositions– She made herself agreeable, & was looking well, but rather theatrically dressed– We had also Mrs H. Ingersoll, the Miss I's, M^{rs} & the Miss Wilcocks'– Bayards &c &c–[4] Mrs Wilcocks (or rather M^r) for I suppose his hospitality is superior to hers– has been polite enough to invite Arthur & Pauline to dinner, & ourselves & (I suppose) 20 others– to meet them on Thursday–

Mrs Camac is to give them a dancing party tomorrow eveng– to which I hear 60 people are asked– The only invitation I have rec^d was thro' Mrs Chapman, who told me on Friday eveng– that her sister wished me to go & meet Mrs A. M. and about half a dozen other ladies– as she has never called, or sent any other message to me, I shall not go–[5] having a very good excuse– that I have accepted no invitations for eveng– parties, & am afraid of the exposure to night air– which w^d be greater, in going out of town– I am told she was seen walking arm in arm with Harry in Chesnut S^t 2 days ago– which is here considered equivalent to an announcement of the engagement of which I have myself little doubt now– for his manner betrays great satisfaction mixed with some embarassment, when he is taxed with it– I told him the last report was that he was on his probation, which amused him much–

I have just written to announce y^r arrival to Mrs Smith & ask her to drink tea with us this eveng– & she writes me that she is not well enough to come out, having taken cold– Mrs Cuesta, Mrs Ingersoll & a few others are coming to take tea sociably– I thought of asking Mrs Chapman again but her manner & loud talking at the Theatre last night disgusted me so much, that I could not make up my mind to it– I fear Harry's refinement will often be shocked by her conduct–

Pauline & I were much pleased with the performance of I Puritani, which was better given than anything they have attempted yet– I have seen them once before in Lucia–[6] which was poor enough– I hope in y^r next you will tell me that W^{ms} has got rid of his cough entirely & has his complexion restored to its naturally healthy hue– Arthur told Dr Hering, with whom he has had two long talks, of his case & he blamed Dr Curtis[7] for his immense doses, & thought he did much harm by them–

I have just sent in to the Morris House to know if they [*Arthur and Paolina*] have any message & the answer is nothing but loves– Mr Harrison has been so much better that Dr Chapman made him drive out for the last three days– Today it rains & Fisher tells me he is not quite so well– M^{rs} F– is much as usual– perhaps rather better– They all desire kind remembrances to you in which Fisher joins–

Pray tell Papa that M^r & Mrs H. were exceedingly gratified by the kind things he said to them of their darling Nephew– & have several times spoken on the subject to me– & of the pleasure his visit gave them– My darlings are perfectly well– & beg their love to Grandmama & Grandpapa and Uncle Willin– They have been nearly all the time that I have been writing this, playing about me with the Kitchen things which are a great delight to them both– I must now say Adieu my dearest Mamma with love to all the family– & those who may care to receive it from me– I am as ever Y^r most affec^{te} daughter Eliza

Pray remind Lizzie of her promise of writing to me, & give my love to her & Mrs Holbrook– I shall expect soon to hear from Emma– I wrote on Saturday to Mary by Mr Rutledge[8] who was on his way to New Rochelle to see his daughters–

Private Collection

1. Mrs. Middleton's letter of November 25 announced the family's safe return to Charleston. They had been in Philadelphia for about a month.
2. Julia Cox was the daughter of John and Martha (Lyman) Cox and granddaugh-

ter of James Cox, the president of the Lehigh Coal and Navigation Company. In 1845 she married Thomas A. Biddle.

3. Hitty Cox (1819–1899) was the daughter of William S. and Jane Eliza (Banks) Cox. She, Julia Cox, Emily Chapman, and Elizabeth Camac were first cousins.

4. Sidney Fisher, who was also at the party, thought it "very handsome, pleasant and <u>select</u>. The elite of our society there & no snobs." Wainwright, *Phila. Perspective* (November 19, 1843): 142.

5. "The widow C. appears to be no favourite with you," John commented. John I. Middleton to EMF, November 29, 1843, MPlFdn.

6. A group of Italian singers performed *I Puritani* at the Chestnut Street Theatre. The opera *Lucia di Lammermoor* by Gaetano Donizetti was first performed in Italy in 1835.

7. Dr. Joseph T. Curtis was another homeopath, whom William had consulted in New York because he was jaundiced. Dr. Curtis treated him with sepia officinalis, the inky juice of cuttlefish. EMF to MHM, November 29, 1843, private collection.

8. Frederick Rutledge, whose wife Henrietta died in 1842, had apparently enrolled his daughters at the Priory.

⌒

To Mrs. Middleton, Middleton Place

Philadelphia – 6<u>th</u> Dec<u>r</u> [1843]

It is very pleasant to have one's expectations fully answered– and so I found it this morng– my dearest Mamma, when your welcome letter was brought in– I can hardly hope in future to hear from you as punctually– for of course the opportunities of sending from M. Place will be rarer– but you must promise me never to miss one– We are rejoiced to hear of the improvement in William's health– & also of Hal's entire recovery–[1] I rec<u>d</u> with your's a letter from John from Columbia who tells me that he left Sally better than usual– I trust you may be able to confirm this good news of her– & to mention that her eyes are mending– Fisher's continue much the same– I insist upon his disregarding appearances & wearing his blue spectacles, whenever he goes where there are gas lights which invariably distress them unless he takes this precaution. He has not yet been able to engage a reader to suit him (the little boy he tried for a week, not having strength to hold out for 2 hours at a time)– meanwhile his mother does what she can to supply the place of one in the morng– and from 4 to 6– he has 2 lectures (from D<u>r</u> Meigs & D<u>r</u> Dunglisson) to listen to– & sometimes falls asleep under– when not very entertaining–

By the use of D<u>r</u> Hering's powders and <u>prudence</u>, I got rid of the cold I mentioned in my last, & ventured on Monday to go over to the Theatre with Aunt H– and Pauline, to hear Ole Bull–[2] a most wonderful performer truly–

but altho' surprised & delighted, I was not transported & affected in the same way as by Max Bohrer– who made a much deeper impression upon me, than any Violinist ever has, or can I suppose– Last night we heard another, M. Artôt, who has also a great reputation, & deservedly no doubt– but in comparison to Bull is, I think a mere baby– yet he plays with sentiment & expression– but you heard none of those exquisite flutelike tones the other produced– & more of the bow, & that screeching & scraping which I detest– Then he had the disadvantage of being heard in contrast with Mme Cinti [Damoreau]'s³ sweet voice, more perfect in tone than any human instrument, & as flexible as art can make it– Her vocalization is truly astonishing & all her most intricate & difficult roulades, trills & cadences, are in excellent taste, and as graceful as accurate– I never have been more enchanted by any singer, not even excepting Caradori–⁴ who in style she resembles, & even surpasses in execution & finish, but not in quality of voice– which is not perhaps as silvery & clear–

I parted with Arthur & Pauline after the Concert, as they intended to start early this morng– for Washington– She is an affectionate, warm hearted creature, & I am really attached to her, & sorry that we shall not meet again for so many months– She has made many friends here– Miss [Jeannette] Hart & herself became very fond of each other, & exchanged presents of rosaries with each other– Miss H. gave her besides several other little remembrances– & appears to feel much interested in her– Pauline saw a great deal of the Scotts⁵ who are here, consulting Dr Jackson about Miss Virginia's throat– which is much affected– I believe he considers consumption likely to follow– but the Mother is not aware of this opinion– Arthur was trying to prevail upon her to try Homoeopathy– but without success–

Harry sees his old favourite frequently I hear– I have not seen him since Thursday when he dined with us, he was to have come to Aunt H's on Sunday eveng– but did not make his appearance– & last night he came to join us just after we had set out for the Concert– but missed us– I have not been able to find out how or where he is spending his time– He was not at a dinner at the Co[xes'] given to Mr Wadsworth, to which Arthur was asked, but declined accepting– We thought the omission of an invitation to H. rather singular– Arthur went up yesterday to Mrs Chapman's to try & discover how things were going on in that quarter– but had no opportunity of ascertaining–

You will be glad to hear that Mr Harrison is so much better that he came down stairs (for the first time for 6 weeks) on Sunday eveng– & is out to day notwithstanding the cold– As there is every appearance of Snow, I must go out early, & try & get thro' some of my visits, before it begins to fall– I hope Arthur & Pauline will arrive safely in Wash^n without detention– They expect to be there several weeks– but will proceed to Carolina as soon as A's business is settled– He still talks of going to Jamaica, but I think it doubtful–

Thursday, 7$\underline{th}$ I was nearly 3 hours visiting yesterday my dear Mamma, & returned home just in time for dinner & lay on the sofa all the afternoon suffering with headache which obliged me to go to bed soon after 7. It is the only <u>bad</u> one I have had for months past, & was brought on I think by taking strong Chocolate for several days– I took nothing for it but a Homoeopathic powder & today am quite free from it– It snowed all night & now lies thick upon roofs & pavements but the walking will be made still worse by the sleet which is now pattering against the window panes– and I see the people walking cautiously along the middle of the street to avoid the slippery sidewalks– I suppose I shall be a close prisoner for several days– but I can amuse myself very well within doors, with my books my music & my little girls– who grow daily more companionable– Lily is counting the days before Xmas– The greatest pleasure of which, in her estimation will be the arrival of cousin Coussee of whose kindness to her last summer, she cherishes the most grateful recollection– I must say Adieu! with love to those around you great & small I am as ever, dear Mamma, Y$\underline{r}$ affec$\underline{te}$ daughter Eliza

I saw M$\underline{rs}$ Smith 2 days ago– she was well & desired her love to you– M$\underline{rs}$ Schroeder also begged her kind regards. She has been very much indisposed with sore throat but D$\underline{r}$ Hering has relieved her, without using debilitating remedies– Arthur & he had very long interviews frequently– My throat continues improving– M$\underline{rs}$ F. has had another severe nervous attack but is up & stirring today, which is a good sign– The children are as rosy & well as possible– & very Merry– M$\underline{rs}$ F– begs her best remembrances.

Private Collection

1. Rather than yellow fever, as had originally been thought, Hal had erysipelas. He was not cured and the disease, which is now known to be a streptococcal infection, continued to plague him.

2. Ole Bull (1810–1880), a Norwegian violinist, and Joseph Artôt were two of several well-known European virtuosi who came to the United States at this time.

3. Mme Cinti Damoreau was the prima donna of the Grand Opera in Paris.

4. Mme Maria Caterina Caradori-Allan (1800–1865), a fine Italian singer, sang in England and also in the United States. Eliza, who called her "divine Caradori," sang with her in 1837 when she and the Middletons were at the same hotel in New York. EM to Harry Middleton, December 2, 1837, PHi, C/F.

5. These were Gen. and Mrs. Winfield Scott. Scott was the commanding general

of the U.S. Army at this time. Soon after this, their daughter, Virginia, entered a Catholic convent and died in 1845.

〜

To Mrs. Fisher, Philadelphia

M.P. Dec.ʳ 9ᵗʰ 1843

My dearest Eliza

I begin to write now as there will be tomorrow a means of sending this to Charleston, although were I to wait for the arrival of Sally & her family my letter would be more interesting to you, but then I know of no opportunity by which I could send a letter a week hence. I have not received one from you of a later date than the 29ᵗʰ ultᵒ which I answered before I left Charleston. We came here last Monday & found all the people tolerably well & they all enquired particularly after you: the weather has been mild, & the fragrant olives in full bloom. Wᵐ (looking much better) during the three days he staid here was all day giving directions to 3 or 4 people to arrange the flower beds at the back of the house. He then went with his Father to Combahee where they will remain until the 23ᵈ I suppose. Hal was with me until this mornᵍ when he rode down on horseback (as his Grandpapa had told him he might if he wished it) to meet his Mother at Charleston. She will probably be here next Monday with all her family & [*Oliver's daughter*] Eleanor. You may suppose how busy I have been since I came, giving work to 6 women who do not half as much as 2 whites would do in the same time. Rachel[1] for instance told me this mornᵍ that she could do no more than hem a p.ʳ of Sheets, top & bottom in a day!

Hal has been twice to Runnymede to see his young friends the Pringles. I saw Mʳˢ P. in town, & we shall be good neighbours here, particularly when Sally comes. as yet I have not made her a visit being so much occupied & now the Carriage is sent to Charleston to accommodate Sally. It gives me great pleasure to hear so good an account of your two darlings, & also of M.ʳ Harrison's recovery. You do not mention the state of M.ʳ Fisher's eyes since he has been under the advice of D.ʳ Hayes.[2] Does he find any relief from his prescriptions?

If C. will not consent to read aloud to me this Eveᵍ I must strain my poor eyes for two hours, if I can find a tolerably good print. Hal has been reading every evening but not an interesting book– a history of France by a M.ʳ Crowe[3] which M.ʳ Coates advised him to read– à propos of the latter he behaved during Hal's illness with the greatest kindness to him– gave him his own bed, & slept on a Cot in the same room, or rather sat up the greatest part of the night to attend to him. He will spend a few days here during the holidays, & also at Runnymede.

I am anxious to hear of poor Mrs Chisolm– she had been so ill during Saturday night that Eleanor told me when I met her at Church that her Mama could not go there. Monday morn^g however, W^m saw Susan in the town & she said her Mother was better. Miss Pinckney sent me a little Orange Marmalade, & a large quantity of sour Oranges which was very acceptable because I had a capital receipt for making Marm[malad]e written by Mrs P. Smith & which she used to teach me how to prepare– so when I came here, after y^r Father's depart^re I made Chloe & Eliz^th help me in the dining room to preserve them, attending exactly to every direction & intending to send you & Mrs S. some of the preserve– Unluckily it did not answer my expectation– very unlike what we used to make together– the next day I tried again another parcel, it was rather better but not good enough to send you– however I am going to send you & Mrs Fisher what you will find much better, preserved wild plumbs & jelly made by John– & I shall put a small jar of Quinces into the box, that it may not be too high for the other jars– unluckily the large jar of Quinces has been lost, having never been received at Charleston with the other boxes. I have sent to request Mr T. M. to send the box by a Phil^a vessel which I suppose can be done before the Delaware is frozen. When I know the name of the vessel by which it is sent I will inform you of it.

Sunday Morn^g– You would enjoy this beautiful day, could you walk about the grounds– What happiness that would give me! I hope your next letter will give me a better account of your throat than you mentioned in the former one & of Mrs Fisher's health improving. To her & Mr F. give my love, & kind remembrance to M^r & Mrs Harrison & believe me my dearest Eliza y^r affect^te Mother M. H. M.
Kiss the Children for me–

PHi

1. Rachel and Chloe, who is mentioned later in the letter, were house servants at Middleton Place. In another comment that indicates her perspective on running the household, Mrs. Middleton mentioned the "filthy fingers" of women who were sewing for her. MHM to EMF, January 12, 1843, PHi.
2. Dr. Isaac Hays (1796–1879), a pioneer of American ophthalmology, worked at the Pennsylvania Infirmary for Diseases of the Eye and Ear and the Wills Eye Hospital in Philadelphia.
3. Eyre Evans Crowe (1799–1868), an English journalist and novelist, wrote the first version of his *History of France* for Gardner's *Cabinet Encyclopedia* in 1830.

By the end of 1843, Fanny and Pierce Butler's marriage, which had been unhappy for many years, was past repair. Though the Butlers had been temporarily reconciled when they were in England, they were now living apart from each other, and Fanny had asked Philadelphia lawyers William Meredith and Benjamin Gerhard for advice about a legal separation. In order to be able to see her two daughters even for one hour a day, however, she had to agree to live in Pierce's house, though separate from him, and to abide by rules set by him. These included a promise that she would neither go back to acting nor advocate abolition of slavery in print, nor publish anything Pierce disapproved. All of these had been the subject of disputes between them.

Their quarrels, which Eliza and her mother mentioned from time to time in their letters, made a sad and dreary tale that ended only when they were divorced in 1849. Pierce Butler, who by then had already lost a good part of his fortune through mismanagement and gambling, was bankrupted by the financial crash of 1857. His slaves were sold at auction in March 1859 to pay his debts. Fanny supported herself very successfully by reading Shakespeare to audiences in England and the United States. The terms of the divorce allowed her to have her children with her for two months every year.

To Mrs. Middleton, Middleton Place

Philadelphia – Thursday Dec.ʳ 14ᵗʰ [1843]

It was rather an unexpected pleasure to receive your letter of the 9ᵗʰ & 10ᵗʰ this morng– my dearest Mamma, for I supposed you wᵈ not have an opportunity of sending one very soon after yʳ arrival at M. Place– Glad as I should have been to hear from you of dear Sally, I am much better pleased to look forward to good news of her, than to wait another week for a letter– By this time you are surrounded by yʳ Grand Children, who must make the house merry enough. The older ones will certainly take it by turns to read aloud to you & Sally in the evengs– which will make them pass pleasantly– How I should like to be transported into the midst of you if only for a few hours, it wᵈ be worth while to be <u>Mesmerized</u>, & sent to the Elm walk to enjoy the Fragrant Olives, for <u>of course</u> the sense of <u>smell</u> as well as sight may be miraculously <u>sharpened</u> by the will of the Operator– You, who have such faith in these (to me) incredible performances, ought to have heard Mʳˢ Smith's account of some experiments lately made at Mʳˢ Howell's– She thinks the woman, who pretended to be sent to N.Y. & a dozen other places in a few seconds, & describe

the interior of houses, people in them &c– was all the time <u>guessing</u>– occasionally she made a good hit, but more frequently went wrong– & made ludicrous
mistakes– & yet such is the love of the marvellous in mortals, that many present
were convinced, & readily found excuses for her bungling– but enough of this
trash– M<u>rs</u> Smith dined & spent the eveng– with us yesterday– & was kind
enough to read aloud to Fisher a Chapter or two of Kohl's book on Austria,[1]
which begins in a very lively & amusing manner–

Harry came in & spent an hour with us before he went to a party at M<u>rs</u>
H[enry] Fisher's– He seemed highly pleased with his entertainment the day
before at M<u>rs</u> Wilcocks'– who had a dinner of 20 for M<u>rs</u> [James] Wadsworth–
It appears to me that he enjoys himself too much in other society than that of
the Widow C. to be really her lover– and that his thoughts are too much engrossed by other charmers at these numerous parties, for one who might be
meditating on matrimony–[2] I cannot find out whether he continues his assidu-
ities auprès d'elle [*toward her*]– & people seem to be tired of talking about
them & have now a new topic & tittle tattle about M<u>r</u> & M<u>rs</u> Pierce Butler
whose squabbles have become serious enough to be known generally– I am
told by a person who is her adviser & friend that it will probably end in a
divorce– for which indeed she has applied– or rather for legal advice on the
subject– but her friends have persuaded her to keep quiet for the present– His
conduct to her has been shameful– & altho' I daresay she has her faults of
temper, it is unmanly & cruel to treat her so–[3] Even his family side with her– &
my sympathy for her was so much excited by what I heard of her unhappiness,
that I called again the other day upon her with Fisher– She returned the visit
in a few days, & had not been more than a few minutes out of the room, when
Pierce entered to my surprise– for we have not had a visit from him before since
his return. It was fortunate they had not met– which w<u>d</u> have been extremely
awkward, for they do not speak to each other.

The weather has been very cold for the last week & until yesterday I have
not been out of the house since I last wrote, except twice in the eveng– to Aunt
H's, and then M<u>rs</u> F. insisted upon my going & returning in a <u>cab</u> to prevent
the possibility of my taking cold– so that you see I am well taken care of–[4]
Today we are all going to dine there, & as it is much milder I shall take another
walk– which I yesterday enjoyed very much, after being so long shut up– &
taking the fresh air only thro' the windows– which I have several times had
open at noon, & then marched up & down with shawl and hood on, making
the children play at <u>Soldiers</u> with me– when there is much snow on the ground,
I believe this will be my best plan for exercize– My throat, which was sore for
a few days after the visiting expedition I mentioned, is now well again– & I

mean to keep it so, by avoiding exposure– & going in & out of hot rooms with my warm cloak on– Fisher's eyes were worse also for some days– owing probably to the glare from the snow, & to the heated lecture rooms he sat in for 2 hours every afternoon– Dr Hayes has now forbidden his going to them, Or Concerts, Theatres, or any crowded & lighted rooms– & I have no doubt they will continue to improve– He w^d have liked to attend Dr Lardner's course– which they say is very interesting– The scientific apparatus & experiments being remarkably so– but he must make this sacrifice, besides many others poor fellow– I pray Heaven his trial will soon be over– but the D^r does not flatter him that it will for some months yet– altho' he promises a final cure–

Not a word from Pauline yet– Mrs Fisher thanks you for y^r kind enquiries– she says she is not better, but I think she is– M^r H– continues well– The children have gone up this morng– to see Mrs Hare, who begged me to send them & poor old Miss Hamilton–^{5} who is now entirely blind of one eye– Miss Hare is in a miserable state– I think she will scarcely live thro' the winter– Miss Morris^6 is staying with her– which is a great comfort to her– Mrs Elwyn has been dangerously ill, but is thought better– Mrs Ewing arrived fortunately to help nurse her– She says she had a glimpse of you in Charleston– I must finish scribbling– but first send my best love to dear Sally & to her young ones– Fisher begs his kind remembrances to you & Sally & I am dearest Mamma Y^r most affecte daughter Eliza

Private Collection

1. Johann George Kohl, a German, was the author of a book about Russia which the Middletons had probably read. His new book was advertised in Charleston as *Austria (Vienna, Prague, etc.)*.

2. Mrs. Middleton replied, "What you write about Harry surprises me– is it possible that after all the attentions bestowed upon M^{rs} C[amac] that he should be flirting with the young Girls?" MHM to EMF, December 25, 1843, PHi.

3. "Mrs P. Butler is indeed in a pitiable state," commented Mrs. Middleton. "Were she to be separated from her husband, he would probably take her children from her– that I suppose will prevent her from obtaining a divorce, as it would make her miserable to live without them." On the other hand, when she told William about "Mr P. Butler's ill treatment of his wife, he said he was sure that she was to blame, & abused her for her oddities &c." MHM to EMF, December 25, 1843, PHi.

4. The idea of taking a cab to go less than a block seems ridiculous, but Mrs. Fisher was probably being even more protective than usual because Eliza was pregnant. The baby was due in June.

5. Miss Mary Hamilton (1771–1849) was Mrs. Hartman Kuhn's aunt.

6. Ann Willing Morris's daughter, Elizabeth.

To Mrs. Fisher, Philadelphia

Dec 17$\underline{th}$ Sunday Morn$\underline{g}$ [1843]

My dearest Eliza

As Sarah was desirous of writing to you I advised her to do so on this sheet first,[1] that I might have time to prepare my letter, should there be any chance of sending it– luckily M$\underline{r}$ R[obert] Pringle will leave Runnymede this afternoon & I will send this to him there– Sally was there yesterday & heard of this opportunity. She brought me your welcome letter of 6$\underline{th}$ Dec$\underline{r}$ last Tuesday– You enquire about her health– it is better than it was on the Beach & she is looking well but she suffers sadly from pain in her eyes, & occasional headachs, but her chest is better, & some days she feels quite well– She is only waiting for John's consent to write a particular account of her eyes & other ailments to D$\underline{r}$ Hering, for nothing that John has administered for the former has been of any benefit to them. She thinks they were injured by rubbing them with Sassafras after taking a homoeopathic dose– I am sorry to learn that M$\underline{r}$ F's eyes are not improving.

You will be pleased to hear that the Children are all well, & improved in their scholarship– Sarah particularly. She studies with great assiduity, rises at 5 o'clock at this season for that purpose by candlelight & saves her Mother much trouble by teaching Tom & by keeping him in good order– he too is much improved & is now constantly reading to his great amusement 'Masterman Ready'[2] for which Johnny requests me to tell M$\underline{r}$ Fisher he is very much obliged to him. he has grown a little, & is as usual very much devoted to his studies– he is beginning to learn Latin, & reads & translates French to me every morn$\underline{g}$ before breakfast as do also, Hal (& after breakfast) Sarah & Eleanor– The two vol$\underline{s}$ I brought "Spring & Summer Autumn & Winter" are I think extremely instructive & will be useful to Tom after he has ended his favorite book.

Hal reads aloud to us every eve$\underline{g}$ to our gratification. He is perfectly well & has had his head shaved, & wears a knitted Cap. The two little girls are as stout & fat as usual, & behave well: they both say they remember Lily & Sophy, & thank them for the Dolls they sent them. Their Mother too is very grateful to you for your presents. It is a great pleasure to her to be so near her Aunt P[ringle]. We went to see her [*at Runnymede*] the day after Sally's arrival & found her very busy arrangeing & papering her rooms– She has now 12 children with her, (the 13$\underline{th}$ is at Boston College)[3] & she is delighted with Runnymede– it is fortunate that she has left Charleston, for unfortunately the Scarlet fever there is very fatal– You will be surprised to hear that yesterday the weather was too warm for having a fire in the room even for Sally & the night was disagreeably so. I am very glad to hear that y^r cold was so soon cured by Dr H. & that you were so much pleased with the concerts you attended. Paolina is as you observe a very affectionate person, & much attached to you I have often noticed. Miss Harte is an amiable woman, & it is fortunate they have become friends.

I cannot expect from what you mention of Arthur's visit to Wash^n to see them until after Xmas– at that time Oliver will be here. You will be glad to hear that when El[eano]r came she left Mrs Chisolm better than she had been for some weeks– El^r is looking extremely well & seems to enjoy Sarah's companionship. She is a very amiable girl– You have been imprudent I find by y^r account of having fatigued yourself by numerous visits. pray be more careful of yourself & never attempt to walk on the slippery streets without holding M^r F's arm– I am sorry to have so bad an account of M^{rs} F's health but hope she is now well– With love to her & Mr F. I am my dearest Eliza y^r affect^{te} Mother M. H. M.

All here send their love to you, & pray give mine to Mrs P. Smith– with kind remembrances to M^r & Mrs Harrison & any others of my acquaintances who enquire after me. Give my love also to Mary & Matty who will have arrived by the time you receive this.

PHi

1. Sarah wrote the first part of this letter to thank her aunt for presents she sent from Philadelphia.
2. *Masterman Ready* was written by Capt. Frederick Marryat of the British Royal Navy when his children wanted a sequel to the desert island story of *The Swiss Family Robinson*.
3. That is, Harvard College.

～

To Mrs. Middleton, Middleton Place

Friday– 22nd (Dec^r) [1843]

I felt that I had omitted a duty in not writing to you yesterday, according to custom, my dearest Mamma, but I was at Church in the morng– & afterwards found myself obliged to pay some visits, which occupied my time until dinner– after which I had a visitor who sat more than an hour, when it was too late to begin a letter, as I was going to Aunt's to tea– I am now rather glad I was prevented writing, since I have today the pleasure of acknowledging y^r

welcome letter, which just told me all I wanted to know– Such good news of dear Sally & all her young ones, & as I infer, from the good spirits in which you appear to write, of yourself also– but I wish you w$^{\underline{d}}$ mention y$^{\underline{r}}$ own health sometimes–

Thank Sarah for her page, which deserves perhaps a special answer– which I cannot however promise at present, for I am particularly busy– Fisher went on Wednesday for the girls,[1] or rather he went on two days before they were to leave school, because he had business to attend to there, which w$^{\underline{d}}$ occupy him– during that time– Tomorrow we expect them, & I hope the rain will cease meanwhile, for travelling thro' it today w$^{\underline{d}}$ be very unpleasant– We have had delicious weather for 3 days, which I have enjoyed extremely after a succession of cold, wet & disagreeable days– during which I was shut up–

On Saturday night I ventured to go with Aunt H. thro' a dense fog, which afterwards turned into a drizzle, to Ole Bull's farewell Concert– which was crowded to overflowing– The excessive closeness of the room affected me– so unpleasantly, that the pleasure with which I listened to the Music was much marred– but his performance was truly surprising, & I enjoyed it as much as a sense of suffocation, which I thought w$^{\underline{d}}$ end in fainting w$^{\underline{d}}$ permit me– Notwithstanding the rain thro' which I had to walk some distance– to the carriage, I took no cold– Poor Fisher, who had been waiting in the crowd at the door for me for half an hour, (he was afraid to go in on account of his eyes) was in a perfect fever lest I sh$^{\underline{d}}$ suffer from the exposure but I did not in the least & my throat has been remarkably well for the last week– I cannot help believing that the Stamm has had its usual good effect in strengthening it– for I am certainly always better after taking <u>tin</u> but D$^{\underline{r}}$ Hering insists that it is necessary to vary, & take alternately other medecines, to prevent it from losing its good influenz– as he calls it– none of the others having the slightest, I think– I am now so much better that I hope I shall not require any further advice– & every one observes the improvement in my looks–

I hope that Sally may consult him about her eyes– Fisher now regrets that he did not give his remedies a longer trial as D$^{\underline{r}}$ Hayes' have produced no effect–[2] But I believe his <u>Farm</u> in the Country which he will probably soon be able to purchase, will supply the best cure for his eyes, in the active occupation [it will] give him out of doors– I have been very busy preparing my Xmas presents– not <u>making</u> many for I have only had time to make two or 3 little collars, but hunting them up at the Depository[3] & Church fair– the former is an excellent institution, & as I knew that many reduced ladies gain their subsistance by the sale of the articles they send there, I determined to try & get a great deal there– & provided myself with bags for the girls, & several very pretty things for others to whom I wished to give–

I have made invitations to several girls to come & spend the eveng– of Wednesday with my nieces– & hope to muster more than a dozen to dance a Cotilion to the Piano– Mrs Hare intends to have a young ladies' party while they are here, & I daresay Mrs Prime will also invite them– & perhaps Mrs Camac– whose daughter is to be here– I told Harry I meant to ask her to accompany her– but don't know if she will consent to come– He was at Aunt's 3 evengs ago, & called here whilst I was out last night– Nothing more has <u>transpired</u> on the important subject– I want very much to go & hear Mme Damoreau sing for the last time tonight, but I remember my promise to Fisher to be <u>particularly prudent</u> during his absence, & therefore keep my desires low & shall refrain from indulging them, unless it clears entirely, of which there is little chance–

Aunt H. will take the girls to see Macready[4] tomorrow night if they feel inclined to go– I was tempted to accept her invitation myself, but recollected my vows about Saturday night, and could make no exception for I know I sh^{d} be thinking of his acting all the following day– The Sumners are expected here daily– & will be asked to eat their Xmas dinner with us if they arrive in time– We hope to induce Mrs Smith to come also– She was well when I heard of her 2 days since. Poor Becky has not got off yet– being disappointed of her escort to Boston–

Not a line from Pauline– I don't know what she can be about– for I charged her to write– I must stop scribbling & go up to my chicks– Goodbye dearest Mamma– This will reach you about Monday I suppose– May you all be enjoying a very merry Christmas, is the sincere wish of Y^{r} most affect^{e} daughter Eliza

Poor Mrs Hare's heart has been cheered by very good news from Robert who had arrived in Eng^{d} & was quite well– Mrs Fisher continues much the same– she thanks you for y^{r} kind enquiries & sends her best regards– M^{r} & M^{rs} H are well & w^{d} I know return y^{r} remembrances if they knew of them–

Private Collection

1. Fisher went to bring Mary and Matty from the Priory to spend their Christmas holiday in Philadelphia.

2. Mrs. Middleton thought perhaps the reason homeopathic remedies had not helped Fisher's eyes was that he ate "tomatas" while taking the medicines. MHM to EMF, February 14, 1844, PHi.

3. The Ladies' Depository, on Chestnut Street just four blocks from the Fishers,

provided a place where women of good character but reduced circumstances could sell their handiwork for a fair price. Articles included sheets, infants' blankets, reticules, petticoats, aprons, and shirts.

4. William Macready (1793–1873) was an English actor well known for his Shakespearean roles. He first visited the United States in 1826.

⌒

To Mrs. Middleton, Middleton Place

Philadelphia – 29$\underline{^{th}}$ Dec$\underline{^r}$ 1843

The correspondance between Matilda & Sarah seems to have been kept up so constantly that there appears to be less occasion for my weekly missive my dearest Mamma– but I suppose you w$\underline{^d}$ not be satisfied if I were to make their letters an excuse for not sending mine as usual– & therefore, altho' I daresay Matilda has forestalled me in news, I shall still scribble away, & not disappoint you of y$\underline{^r}$ New Year's gift– poor tho' it be– May it find you all enjoying health & happiness– I have heard indirectly (by a letter from Susan to the girls) that Aunt Rutledge was on her way to M. Place to pass Xmas with you– and suppose you will keep her there some time afterwards–[1] Pray remember me most affectionately to her– & beg her to give my love to dear Emma [Blake] when she sees her again– I have at last heard from Pauline– she tells me she was writing to you the same day, so that I suppose there is nothing in her letter to me which she has not told you also–

I must write fast this morng– for we are going out to dine at Wakefield, & as the roads are in a bad state we shall have to set out at one to arrive there at 2 o'clk– It is to be I suppose only a family dinner, but a pretty large one– Thinking Fanny Butler, who is very intimate with them might be going, I sent this morng– to propose to her to drive out with us– but was sorry to find she was not asked today– Think of her being so kind as to offer to read to Fisher sometimes in the eveng– As I know she must have been sincere in the proposal, & she has since repeated that it w$\underline{^d}$ give her pleasure to be called upon to read aloud to him, I mean very soon to claim her promise– But since the girls' arrival I have been so occupied with plans for their amusement, that I have not been able to do so– Next week we may have a spare eveng– perhaps– but this, blindman's buff, hunt the slipper & dancing have been the order of the eveng– & I think the girls have enjoyed themselves very much– Last night they were very quiet to be sure, at M$\underline{^{rs}}$ Hutchinson's but there were so many beautiful things to see & admire, that they could not get tired of sitting still– Our little party on Wednesday night went off quite brilliantly and merrily too– there were only about 15 children, the Sergeants & Camacs having disappointed us– & themselves too I believe– the former sick, & the latter engaged– The widow sent me a very polite note of refusal, on the plea of being confined to the house by indisposition– We had several other Mammas– M͟r͟s Prime, M͟r͟s M͟cEuen &c– Lily took a nap in the afternoon that she might keep her eyes open longer at night– & was quite bright until near 9 o'clk– & excessively amused at the dancing–

She & Sophy went up to M͟r͟s Prime's on Xmas afternoon to see Emily's Xmas tree– which was very magnificent, & delighted them all– indeed the whole day was one of great excitement to the children– from the time they first opened their eyes at day dawn, & saw the Nursery decorated with Evergreens & Wreaths– there was such a mysterious awe of Kriss Kringle (who was supposed to have a hand) that they hardly dared to take down the Stockings, when they found they had actually been filled in the night– Then the opening of the Drawing room, where all the gifts were displayed on a Table, was eagerly expected, & their extasy at the toys, particularly a jumping Monkey Papa brought from N.Y. was so great, that it was amusing to behold– M͟r͟s Smith & Harry dined with us, & the whole Gilpin Family, & Uncle & Aunt came in the eveng– Fisher brought me a beautiful book from N.Y– Les Chants & Chansons populaires de la France [*French Folk Songs,*] with exquisite illustrations– they are not all perfectly proper, but prudery itself must wink at that on account of their cleverness & fun.

Saturday morng– I was obliged to leave my letter unfinished & prepare for my drive, dear Mamma, & this morng– I am much pressed for time, & can only add a few lines– We passed a pleasant day at Wakefield, & still pleasanter eveng– at M͟r͟s Hare's. The girls enjoyed themselves extremely, & are going again tonight to a juvenile party at M͟r͟s Williams'–² Susan's old acquaintance– On Monday night New Year is to be kept at Aunt Harrison's– where they are to have an unusually large party– which I hope will be gayer than the Sunday eveng– gatherings– She gave me the other day a magnificent black lace pelerine–³ just what I wanted but w͟d not be extravagant enough to buy myself– M͟r͟s F's Xmas gift was a handsome new dress– which was also acceptable as I had spent my funds & could not afford to make purchases for myself– But I must break off for Fisher is getting impatient, & as we are to have gentlemen at dinner, I must get ready for my walk & make the girls read French when we return– Wishing you all a very happy New Year (if it proves as happy as the last I shall be grateful) I am dearest Mama y͟r affectionate Eliza

Private Collection

1. Mrs. Middleton, who always enjoyed her sister-in-law's visits, reported that "long walks are taken by y^r Aunt in which Sally accompanies her & I for half an hour– She is so chatty that our time passes pleasantly with her." MHM to EMF, December 25, 1843, PHi.

2. Probably Mrs. H. Williams, whose sister-in-law, the former Christine Williams, was Mrs. Thomas Biddle.

3. A pelerine was a narrow cape, usually with long panels hanging down in front.

1844

*I beg of you, dearest Mamma, to assert y^r independence
for once.*

*But do not imagine that [Arthur] is the only one
of your brothers decidedly in favour of [annexing Texas]. All
the others are equally ardent in the cause . . . & y^r Father
perfectly <u>red hot</u>.*

～

By 1844, after five years of marriage, two little girls growing up and a third child due in June, Eliza's life was full. She was a loving and attentive mother; kept up a regular correspondence not only with her mother but also with her brothers, Emma Huger Smith, and various other friends; entertained extensively; and was a faithful parishioner of St. Peter's Church. In addition to these commitments, she also managed to preserve time for reading and for music.

Her love and knowledge of music were recognized as being "of a very high order,"[1] and it was ultimately through music that she was able best to define herself and to use her talents. She played and encouraged other amateurs to play in her own drawing room—morning, afternoon, and evening it sometimes seemed—and she also supported professional musicians who came to perform in Philadelphia. Sometimes, as in the case of the cellist Casella, her patronage was extensive and included everything from securing a doctor's services and financial help to selling tickets for concerts, arranging for publicity in the newspapers, and writing letters of introduction to friends in other cities.

Eliza had the freedom to follow her own interests because she had a nurse for the children and because Mrs. Fisher supervised every aspect of running the household. Her mother-in-law, partly because she loved to manage and did it well, and partly to protect Eliza's health, especially when she was pregnant, virtually excluded her daughter-in-law from the daily tasks of housekeeping—whether ordering meals, supervising servants, or doing the spring cleaning.

On the whole, this arrangement suited Eliza, especially early in her marriage, but there were times when she wished she had her own house. Therefore, when Fisher bought a farm in the country near Germantown in early 1844, one reason was to give Eliza a place where she was in charge, at least for the summer months. Eliza in turn hoped the farm would engage Fisher's interest and energies since he was sometimes quite depressed when his eye troubles prevented him from reading.

During 1844 the future of Texas emerged as a major political issue, particu-

larly after President Tyler authorized his secretary of state, Abel P. Upshur, to negotiate a treaty of annexation with the Republic of Texas, where Upshur was
convinced the British were about to intervene to abolish slavery. Up to that time,
even those who wanted to acquire Texas had not pushed the matter because they
knew it would revive the sectional battle over where slavery should be allowed.
In addition, many people feared that annexation would lead to war with England
or with Mexico, which had never recognized Texas's independence.

The Texas question aroused as strong and widely differing opinions among
the Middletons and the Fishers as it did in the country as a whole. It also influenced
the 1844 presidential election. Henry Clay, the Whig candidate (whom Henry
Middleton actively supported), was initially opposed to annexation but, sensing
the popular wind blowing for expansion, qualified his position as the campaign
progressed. Among the Democrats, Martin Van Buren lost the nomination to
James K. Polk, who supported not only the annexation of Texas but also the occupation of all of Oregon. Polk defeated Clay in November, although by only a small
margin of the popular vote.

1. Obituary of Mrs. Joshua Francis Fisher, *Philadelphia Public Ledger,* February
22, 1890.

To Mrs. Middleton, Middleton Place

Philadelphia – Jany 5th 1844

Altho' I shall not have much time to write this morng my dearest Mamma,
I will at least begin a letter in return for your's of the 25th & 28th which I had
the pleasure of receiving 3 days ago– & which as usual brought me good news
from all I love– except indeed the account you give me of poor Sally's eyes &
headaches– She ought to <u>live</u> in the open air, & I am glad to hear Aunt Rutledge
induced her to take long walks– riding too, would I am sure be very good for
her– I have been regretting that Fisher sent his horse into the country, for the
weather has been so fine that he might have enjoyed many rides which w^d do
him more good than the unguents & remedies he is now trying without success.
Just now he has not much time to think about his eyes however, for Mr Otis
is here, & he is constantly occupied in going about with him. We did not expect
him quite so soon, & are rather sorry he did not come either last week or next,
because as Fisher is to take the girls back on Monday he will return also, &
shorten his visit by some days in consequence– Then we had to leave him to
go to the Wedding¹ last night, to which we could not of course take him, &

yet regretted being obliged to leave him to spend a dull eveng alone at Aunt's–
Today we are to have a dinner of 12 for him, composed chiefly of his old cro-
nies– I had asked several ladies to come in the eveng– but finding that Harry
has an invitation for Mr Otis to go out to a party at Mrs Camacs' this eveng–
I have transferred my invitations for tomorrow eveng– which is rather an awkward business, and might have been avoided if Harry had not been so ridicu-
lously mysterious when I enquired about the said party yesterday– he insisted
that he knew nothing about it, altho' he evidently did– but not being able to
get anything out of him I made the invitations– which I have since retracted
not liking to interfere with Mr Otis' chance of a pleasant party– We are quite
amused at y^r enquiries about Harry's health, on which subject I am happy to
relieve y^r anxiety– The fact is that he is perfectly well, & enjoying himself without any thoughts of returning to Carolina I imagine for weeks yet– probably
when he wrote to John he may have had a slight cold– we/the girls joked him
a great deal about his <u>shamming sickness</u> as an excuse to stay here–

After dinner– We have been laughing at Harry again for complaining of
having to go out into the country this cold night– He could not persuade either
Sidney Fisher or Alleyne Otis to accompany him– the former preferring his
segars, & the latter being rather unwell– so he went alone & we thought his
<u>grumbling</u> about having to take a cold drive of 3 miles, did not look <u>loverlike</u>–
We had a very pleasant dinner– & even the girls were not tired altho' we sat
2 hours at table– They have missed their music lesson in consequence– which
I was sorry for– as they will only have one more from de Connick– I wish they
had as good a master at the Priory– where I fear their Music and French are
rather neglected– in other respects it must be an excellent school & they are
much improved–

Saturday morng– I broke off to hear the girls read French, which they had
not done all day being anxious to finish an interesting book they have read
aloud to me, a History of Jeanne d'Arc by Alexandre Dumas– & I am glad I
did not send my letter last night, since I have the pleasure today of thanking
you for y^r letter of the 1st & 2nd dearest Mamma– I am sorry I can give my Aunt
[*Rutledge*] no information of Mrs Pierse[2] about whom I have heard nothing for
2 years– The other friends she enquires about are all well– for I have met them
all within a few days– Fanny Cadwalader[3] was at Anna Sergeant's Wedding,
looking remarkably well.

It (the Wedding) was a pleasanter one than usual– At least I enjoyed myself
more than on other similar occasions– Happening to talk to agreeable people
all the eveng– The supper for 50 people was extremely handsome– and the
family in great delight at the match evidently– Anna's behaviour was very sin-

gular– during the ceremony she did not utter a syllable in answer to the Minister– but preserved what appeared to me a <u>dogged</u> silence– her lips not even moving, & only once her head nodding slightly in assent– I afterwards asked her why she made no audible response– & her answer confirmed me in the opinion that it was <u>obstinacy</u> & not agitation (as the groom flattered himself) which prevented her replying for she said <u>that</u> was not the way she wished to be married & it was against her consent &c. I suppose she meant that she wanted her own Pastor D<u>r</u> Bethune to marry her instead of Odenheimer whom she dislikes– It struck me it was a bad beginning in Matrimony– & indeed she is so queer that poor M<u>r</u> G. has I fear a poor chance of happiness–

I wish I had room left to tell you of a delightful eveng we spent on Tuesday– M<u>rs</u> Butler came to read to Fisher– but she & Harry talked more than they read, & she was so eloquent, that I listened with great interest to her arguments for the immortality of the soul until near 11 o'clk– She certainly has one which is worthy of another and higher sphere– Tonight she is coming, but not to read for I have invited several other of my most agreeable friends to give M<u>r</u> Otis a pleasant eveng– Harry whom I met just now in Chesnut St told me to say he could not go to Carolina until he rec<u>d</u> funds to proceed on his journey– He said he passed a delightful eveng out at the Cottage & stayed there until past <u>one</u> o'clock– I have written this scrawl while the girls have been practising, & the children playing about me, so that I fear you will find it full of mistakes but you will excuse them– for I have not time to correct them– Adieu! dearest Mamma I am as ever Y<u>r</u> most affect<u>e</u> daughter Eliza

I felt no ill effects from going out the other eveng– to be sure I wore long sleeves & a high chemisette, close to the throat & lined with silk to keep me as warm as a highnecked dress– M<u>rs</u> Smith is well, & is coming here tonight. M<u>rs</u> Fisher desires her best regards– she has been very unwell for a week with a bad cold & rheumatism but is now rather better– M<u>r</u> Harrison is not quite well, with a return of his old complaint–

Private Collection

1. Anna Sergeant's wedding to Benjamin Gerhard.
2. Mary (Hunter) Pierse was the William Hunters' daughter. Her husband was a British naval officer.
3. Frances (Mease) Cadwalader was the wife of Gen. George Cadwalader. John and Pierce Butler were her brothers (both having changed their name from Mease to Butler); Mary (Mrs. Alfred) Elwyn was her sister.

～

To Mrs. Fisher, Philadelphia

M.P. Jan$\underline{y}$ 9$\underline{th}$ 1844

My dearest Eliza

As your Father will probably go to Charl$\underline{n}$ tomorrow, I will answer your welcome letter of the 29th & 30th ult$\underline{o}$ to be ready for his departure– he will bring John with him I suppose on Saturday who as I mentioned in my last may perhaps go with him to Combahee– Y$\underline{r}$ Aunt R[utledge] left us on Saturday with her Son Arthur, one of the most agreeable young men I have met for many years– indeed he is so lively & well informed that Sally & I miss his society extremely– He is 6 feet 3 or 4 inches in height, & though (as I told him) he disfigures himself by a long beard, is good looking. his Mother says he has a delightful voice & sings perfectly well, but we could not prevail upon him to sing for us. Your Aunt too is a great loss to us– She is so amiable & lively & has so much conversation that you may imagine how dull our Evenings are in the parlour where we have no readers to amuse us. Y$\underline{r}$ Father sent up 3 days since a new piano forte of Chickerings, (the old one being too much out of order to be of any use) & since that C. & the two girls have been continually practising, to their great amusement & their aunt occasionally corrects their time & fingering.

Sally's eyes still are very painful, & she intends to request John again to allow her to consult D$\underline{r}$ H[ays] on the subject. her chest is much better since she has been taking homoeopathic medicines, which she does frequently & performs many cures among the negroes here. We send daily to enquire of M$\underline{rs}$ Pringle about her family–[1] the little Girl is now better, but two of the boys & M$\underline{r}$ P. are now suffering from the sore throat although M$\underline{rs}$ P. writes word to Sally that one of her sons is better today, so that I hope the disorder will not prove fatal to any of the family– She wrote word last week that all her family had taken a dose of Bella donna[2] (but their Physi$\underline{n}$ D$\underline{r}$ [E. Horry] Deas is not a Homoeopathist) & to inform me of it, as I had told M$\underline{r}$ P. when he dined here, of its wonderful effects, & of its having been prescribed as a preventive for Scarlet fever, before Homoeopathy was heard of. M$\underline{rs}$ P. forbids Sally to go near her– it would be very imprudent were she to do so, although she wishes to assist her Aunt in nursing her invalids– She begs me to give you her best love & to say it is a great treat to hear of you so frequently– We both hope that your omitting to write about your throat was not in consequence of its being painful at that time. It is always a comfort to me to hear that it is becoming better, though I must not expect to hear of its perfect cure yet.

I am very glad that M$\underline{r}$ Fisher is to enjoy the pleasure of hearing M$\underline{rs}$ P.

Butler read– it will be a great treat to you also. She no doubt feels grateful to you for your attentions, & I think you will find her a very agreeable companion as you used to do, & now may regard her more as a friend– I cannot believe she is so much to blame as W$^{\underline{m}}$ says by ruling over her husband, dining late, & ordering him always to return home at 9 o'clock & being in violent passion once by his disobeying her orders– but now, that is a trifling fault of his, compared to his present vices.[3]

You must have been very busy in preparing amusements as you describe for the Girls & little children. Xmas will always be to them a favorite season. You too have had very handsome presents which I am glad to hear of. The Girls must have quitted you with great regret. Matty insists upon Sarah's never reading her letters to any one, so that all the news of them comes from you. Your last gives no information concerning Harry's matrimonial intentions– you perhaps are as ignorant of them as myself now, but may know them ere long, as the month of March approaches. Is he now in good health? Pray give my love to him. W$^{\underline{m}}$ must not be so solitary now at Combahee as usual, having his Aunt & Cousin A[rthur] as near neighbours, who often invite him to dine.[4]

Thursday 11$^{\underline{th}}$ Yesterday, as also the two preceding days, were so rainy that y$^{\underline{r}}$ Father did not go to town– today is a fine one, & I must finish this dull scrawl. All here send their love to you– Little Maria amused us yesterday by talking of Toty, & how she used to run about with her in the drawing room– Pray give my love to M$^{\underline{r}}$ & M$^{\underline{rs}}$ Fisher & kind remembrances to M$^{\underline{r}}$ & M$^{\underline{rs}}$ Harrison & believe me my dearest Eliza y$^{\underline{r}}$ Affectionate Mother M. H. M.

Kiss the darlings for me & ask them whether they remember me– I have not yet learnt the name of the Vessel by which the sweetmeat box was sent– I hope you have by this time received it–

PHi

1. Most of the Pringles' children had scarlet fever.
2. Belladonna was a strong narcotic when taken internally. It was also a diuretic.
3. Eliza believed Fanny Butler had "never attempted to govern" her husband, "but made a mistake in not allowing herself to be more ruled by him." EMF to MHM, January 19, [1844] private collection.
4. Aunt Rutledge and Arthur were staying with Arthur's sister, Emma, and her husband, Daniel Blake, at their plantation on the Combahee River.

⌐

To Mrs. Middleton, Middleton Place

Philadelphia – Jan.ʸ 13ᵗʰ [1844] Saturday

I was disappointed this morng because I rec.ᵈ no letter from you my dearest Mamma, & yet I had thought it improbable that any would arrive, on account of the accident to the railroad between Weldon and Petersburg, or rather the infamous conduct of a wretch who revenged himself for some grudge against the proprietors by tearing up rails & woodwork for several miles– I fear this outrage will cause an interruption of the communications between us for many days– Meantime I will write as usual, altho' my scrawl may be detained on the road– but what troubles me is the idea of not hearing from you as I might otherwise have done– but patience & I may soon hear–

Fisher took the girls to N.Y. on Monday– & as none of the Boltons appeared, to the Bridge, within three miles of the Priory, where a carriage was in waiting, the next day– We parted from them with great regret– the whole household having become attached to them– indeed they are very nice girls– perfectly well behaved and amiable & I miss them very much– The children were so delighted with their kindness and exertions to amuse them, that they, at least Lily, for Sophy I confess soon forgot them, continued to mourn over their absence for some days– They luckily arrived safely at M.ʳˢ Bolton's before the snow began– which it did almost immediately after they were housed– Fisher intended remaining with Allyne Otis until the following day, but thinking the roads might become impassable if he waited many hours, he set out on Tuesday afternoon in the midst of the storm, & got here at 1/2 past 11 at night– to our great surprise and joy– We were all up, not looking for him, for Aunt H. had expressly forbidden him to travel by the night line, but as it happened, Harry, who had been reading Shakspeare to me had not left the house many minutes when F. rang at the door– and was warmly welcomed after his cold ride– He declared however that he had not suffered at all, & had had a remarkably pleasant moonlight journey notwithstanding the snow– We were doubly glad to have him at home because we had been fearing that the glare from the snow might hurt his eyes– It has been lying on the ground since Tuesday, until today but the south wind will soon melt it all away & I hope tomorrow to walk down to Church– for I have not been further than the Harrison's since Monday–

Fisher has at last been able to engage a tolerable reader, who is now beginning Alison's History of Europe[1] to him– His mother has been reading aloud to us Kohl's new book on Ireland,[2] which is very interesting, but like his other descriptions rather too minute I think– We had a great treat on Thursday eveng– As we were to be entirely alone, I wrote to beg M̲̲ͬˢ Pierce Butler to come round to us– and she came & brought with her Peter Plymley's³ letters (Sydney Smith's, which she had been recommending to F–) & Tennyson's Poems– several of which she read to us– I had no idea, judging from the poor specimens extracted in one of the reviews, which I read long ago, that they were of so high an order of poetry– One especially, "The Two Voices" was very beautiful– a logical argument on the Immortality of the soul being kept up with great interest, & clothed with most poetical imagery– She said that the conversation with Harry last week had reminded her of this Poem which is really a gem– Fanny is certainly a delightful creature– when she chooses to exert her powers of pleasing in private I mean– for her <u>company manners</u> are extremely artificial– & we all remarked to how much less advantage she appeared on Saturday eveng–when there was an evident desire to produce effect– M̲̲ͬˢ Smith said she sh̲ᵈ write you an account of her ballad &c– I was very glad on M̲ͬ Otis' account that the eveng– passed off so pleasantly– & he enjoyed himself apparently very much– & had so few opportunities of doing so during his short visit–

I rec̲ᵈ a note from Miss Moore on Monday, introducing M. Casella–⁴ an Italian performer on the Violincello of great merit, she says– I immediately thought of having a musical soirée, & he & his wife who accompanies him on the Piano, at it– our musical friends alone invited to listen– but on mentioning it to Fisher we determined only to sound the old Lady– & finding that she was rather averse to take any of the troubles of entertaining upon her just now, I gave it up– and merely proposed to dispose of some of their concert tickets– We succeeded in getting rid only of 10 & reserving 4 for ourselves & Aunt– but alas the sleet & the rain sadly spoilt my anticipated pleasure– I was all prepared to go last night, with India rubbers, shawl, cloak & bonnet actually on, and Aunt's carriage at her door, when Fisher's great anxiety lest I sh̲ᵈ take cold prevailed over my love of music & I sent to excuse myself to Aunt at the last moment– She had only meant to go on my account, & also agreed that staying within doors was best, in such very bad weather– & I was fully repaid for the sacrifice I made, by seeing Fisher's extreme satisfaction at the change of plans– He could not bear to refuse me the gratification but was miserable at the idea of my being exposed to any risk of cold– I may perhaps have another opportunity of hearing Sig̲ͬ Casella, but I fear he is too much discouraged by the empty benches last night to think of giving another Concert–

We hear that the Sumners have sailed for Charleston in the same ship which takes poor Frank Huger who is considered by his friends so ill that there is little hope of his recovery on the voyage– Emma will be very much distressed to hear this– I cannot say that I <u>much</u> regret not seeing the S's in Phil$^{\underline{a}}$ for I do not respect either the Husband or Wife altho' I cannot help having a sort of feeling for her– I have not seen Harry since Tuesday eveng– but had a message from him yesterday. I don't hear anything more of his affair– & think it must be at a standstill.

The children have escaped Influenza so far, from which almost everybody has suffered– & are both pictures of health– As for Sophy she is nearly as broad as she is long– & they both improve in intelligence & loquacity daily– Lily says her lesson to <u>Pum</u> [*Mrs. Putnam*] every morng– & can repeat several little hymns– & Sophy mimicks her in everything– I trust the scarlet fever has not travelled from Runnymede to M. Place & that you and the whole party there are well– I beg you will give my love to them all, severally, great & small, & believe me as ever my dearest Mamma Y$^{\underline{r}}$ most affect$^{\underline{e}}$ daughter Eliza

Private Collection

1. Archibald Alison (1792–1867), an Edinburgh lawyer, wrote a ten-volume *History of Europe,* which was popular in the United States as well as in England.

2. This was the same author whose book on Austria the Fishers had been reading in December 1843.

3. Sydney Smith (1771–1845), an Englishman who also wrote as "Peter Plymley," was well known for his witty and satirical writing. Fanny Butler probably showed Fisher a letter written in November 1843 , when the U.S. economy was still depressed. Smith criticized Pennsylvania for not paying back foreigners (like himself) who had invested in the state's bonds. "I never meet a Pennsylvanian at a London dinner without feeling a disposition to seize and divide him; to allot his beaver [*hat*] to one sufferer and his coat to another . . . his pocket-handkerchief to the orphan, and to comfort the widow with his silver watch." "Letter to the *London Morning Chronicle,*" quoted in John Sperling, *Great Depressions* (Glenview, Ill.: Scott, Foresman and Co., 1966), 45.

4. Augustus Caesar Casella (b. 1820), like other visiting European musicians, played in several American cities in 1844 and 1845. He dedicated a piece of music to Eliza before he returned to Europe.

∽

To Mrs. Middleton, Middleton Place

Philadelphia – Feb$^{\underline{y}}$ 3$^{\underline{rd}}$ – 1844

After an interval of 2 weeks, I received a day or two ago y$^{\underline{r}}$ letter of the 20$^{\underline{th}}$ which had been very long on the road, & today that of the 29$^{\underline{th}}$, for both of which many thanks my dearest Mamma– What you say of William's continued indisposition distresses me very much– I do wish that instead of dosing himself with drugs, the properties of which he must be wholly ignorant of, he w$\underline{d}$ go to town at once, & put himself under D$\underline{r}$ Holbrook's care– It is very evident that the Homoeopathic remedies he has been now tampering with for more than a year, have not done him much good– & he ought therefore to resort to others–[1] If he could take a Sea voyage, I sh$\underline{d}$ think that w$\underline{d}$ be of more service to him than anything else– but of course he w$\underline{d}$ not consent to that unless compelled to [for] Business, & everything else ought to give way to his health– & I now wish very much that Arthur may soon make up his mind to go to Jamaica, & induce W$\underline{m}$ to accompany him– Depend upon it that night sweats are very alarming symptoms, & he must require immediate advice– & I pray you to talk seriously to Papa about him, & endeavour to open his eyes to the danger of neglecting to seek it any longer– I trust that you will soon tell me he is persuaded to insist upon Wm's leaving Combahee, and taking the proper remedies for his illness–

I have had a terrible fright about Lily since I last wrote to you– I mentioned that we were to have a musical party on Wednesday– It was not till near one o'clk on that day that I had any suspicion of her being unwell– but as soon as I found that she was feverish, I sent down for Fisher, & we consulted together & decided to send for Meigs– who came in about half an hour, & found her very sick– The fever had encreased so rapidly that her pulse was 150, & respiration double what it ought to have been– His manner convinced me that he thought she had scarlet Fever– & you may imagine my agony at the thought– He immediately ordered Sophy out of the room, & after examining Lily thoroughly– found no eruption, but sore throat, enlarged glands & every other symptom of the dreaded disease– He had her put into a bath of warm water & vinegar twice during the afternoon & frequent <u>lavemens</u> [*enemas*] administered– These gentle remedies had so good an effect that towards night the fever had diminished greatly & her breathing became once more natural– He still however thought it was Scarlatina & Sophy slept down in her Grandmother's room to be out of the way of the infection– Indeed a room was prepared for her at Aunt H's– who wanted to have her there immediately– but as no eruption appeared we did not send her out of the house– Well, poor Lily was watched as you may suppose, with the greatest anxiety– I never left her for an instant until towards night when the fever had almost left her– I slept close to her of course, & at one o'clk in the morng– she was perfectly cool– She had the next day a slight return of feverishness, & for precaution was kept in bed all day, & took a dose of oil– which is the only medecine the D$\underline{r}$ gave her– You may well believe that I thanked him yesterday most cordially for his good & judicious treatment of her, & he laughed & made me acknowledge a Homoeopath could not have done better– He pronounced her quite well yesterday, but we kept her in the nursery until this morng– when she ate her breakfast so heartily, & seemed so anxious to come down, that I could not refuse her her liberty any longer– Have I not great reason to be thankful for this rapid recovery from what we all thought the terrible Fever? It must have been a catarrhal & gastric attack– which I can only trace to the walk she took with me 2 days before & perhaps some jelly which her grandmother gave her rather too freely–

But think what a state of agitation we were all thrown into– It made Aunt H. almost ill– & produced one of Fisher's bad headaches the following day– I rallied wonderfully, after the first shock, & was able to exert myself in a way which I did not think I sh$^{\underline{d}}$ have been capable of, under the circumstances– I prayed for strength & found it– & [many] Thanksgivings were poured from a full heart indeed. The news of the poor child's sudden illness was of course spread directly by our sending to the houses of those who were to have been at our party in the eveng– to say we could not receive them– & kind messages & notes came thickly upon us all the eveng & the next day– Thank God I could answer them cheerfully– & yesterday she was so well that I reinvited the Casellas & several others for Monday eveng– I had already done so, when I heard of poor Major Rutledge's sudden death[2] or I should not have thought of a party so soon afterwards– Indeed I hesitated, & almost decided to retract my invitations again– but then I knew what a disappointment it w$^{\underline{d}}$ be to poor Casella to lose his chance of being known, & having scholars– & thought as there was no-one here whose feelings w$^{\underline{d}}$ be hurt by it, that I w$^{\underline{d}}$ let his music be heard– Harry agreed with me, that situated as I was, it w$^{\underline{d}}$ be a pity to change the arrangements again– but I assure you I felt so much shocked at the sad news, that I regretted very much he had not mentioned it the day before, & prevented my renewing the invitations– I trust that Papa will not think me disrespectful to the memory of a person I know he so highly valued, but will understand the motives which have influenced me to act as I have done–[3] But my poor Aunt! what a dreadful blow to her it must be! A heart breaking one indeed from which she will not easily recover– Papa will I am sure feel very much for her & with her– But the visit you were anticipating will certainly not take place now– And if it does at all, you will scarcely recognize the cheerful person whose society you & Sally found so much pleasure in lately– I suppose it likely that my Aunt will give up Tennessee almost altogether & reside in future principally in Carolina with Emma Blake–

I was very sorry to hear of M$^{\underline{rs}}$ W. Pringle's loss–[4] It will give her unpleasant associations with Runnymede I fear– John's arrangement with regard to Sally is a very proper one & I am delighted to hear you are to have her with you for some time yet– I am going to write to W$\underline{m}$ as you say he is lonely at Combahee– & shall begin a letter to him this very evening– Adieu, my dearest Mamma Pray make yrself easy on my account for I am very well indeed– & my throat is better– Love to all around you & believe me as ever y$\underline{r}$ affect$\underline{e}$ daughter Eliza

PHi

1. William had been plagued by a recurring fever and night sweats. Despite his sister's advice, he stuck with homeopathy, replying, "With regard to the advice you give me on the subject of homeopathy, I must tell you that my perseverance has been too amply repaid to induce me to think for a moment of following your counsels, & I am sorry that you have not been able to meet with a like result: the fault must have been more that of the practitioners than of the practise." William Middleton to EMF, April 9, 1844, PHi, C/F.

2. "He was an excellent husband & Father," Mrs. Middleton said. MHM to EMF, February 7, 1844, PHi.

3. Eliza's father "thought it very proper that you should have your party on the day appointed– none of Major R's acquaintances were invited, & it is not probable that Mrs. R. should know any thing of it." MHM to EMF, February 14, 1844, PHi.

4. One of Mrs. Pringle's children died of scarlet fever.

⌣

Henry Middleton's last foray into politics was in support of Henry Clay's nomination as the Whig party candidate for president. Middleton was an important member of the committee to welcome Clay when he visited Charleston in early April.

William provided a description, spiced with a bit of gossip, about Clay's appearance in Charleston. It was, he told Eliza, "attended with more demonstration of welcome than has ever been exhibited for anyone except LaFayette– The affair was well got up & the Charlestonians appeared in a new light entirely– Faire fête à qui que ce soit [*giving a party for anyone who comes along*] is not their forte as you well know– On this occasion the result was chiefly to be attributed to the violent opposition of the ultra Calhounites & the clergy, among whom Fisher's friend Trapier was conspicuous as belonging to both denominations of person: a determined spirit of resistance was called forth, which made them do much more for M$\underline{r}$ C. than was at first intended. . . . on monday almost the whole population of the city attended a ball given in his honor at the great Hotel there, which was all thrown open & the piazzas enclosed, in spite of which the great crowd made it very difficult to move about."[1]

1. William Middleton to EMF, April 9, 1844, PHi,C/F.

To Mrs. Middleton, Middleton Place

Philadelphia Wednesday 21$\underline{st}$ Feb$\underline{y}$ [1844]

The Postman came so late this morng– that it was a very agreeable surprise to me to receive y$\underline{r}$ letter, for I had quite given it over for today– Many thanks for it dearest Mamma– I meant to write at any rate, this morng– but now do so with much more pleasure since I have such good news of you less than a week old– It was some comfort to hear of William's health, altho' not on the best authority– I am daily looking for an answer to my letter, which I trust may confirm the report you mention– I am so glad that Papa speaks of sending him to Europe for that w$\underline{d}$ certainly be not only highly beneficial to his health, but also to his spirits, which I think equally want reviving– I am therefore delighted at this plan, which I hope may be carried out– As to Arthur, I suppose as you say, the Jamaica expedition is abandoned– I wrote last week to Pauline by M$\underline{rs}$ Scott, begging her to give me a speedy answer– but none has yet arrived– M$\underline{r}$ Francis[1] saw A– very lately, & he did not speak of any intention of leaving Wash$\underline{n}$ at present– so that I conclude his affair with Congress is still unsettled & may drag on some time longer yet–

I read with great pleasure the complimentary letter to Papa from the Committee of the Clay Club– & his reply–[2] which was an unusually long one for him to write, but not the less interesting on that account– Harry cut them out of a Charleston Paper & sent them to me– I think the latter has no thoughts of moving his quarters at present– He at times complains of not being quite well, but looks well, & enjoys himself at all the parties– Whenever he is disengaged he comes in in the eveng & reads Shakespeare to us, on Saturday M$\underline{rs}$ Butler was a listener too– She came in late, having been detained at home by a visitor, & as she found him reading Lear, begged him to continue, which he did until ten– & we then talked until eleven– She is certainly a very good hearted person–

I begged her to write a <u>puff</u> for poor Casella, who is to give another Concert next week, & she has written to no less than <u>four</u> newspaper editors about him & will no doubt induce many to go & hear him– She is coming to hear my lesson[3] on Friday afternoon– M$\underline{rs}$ Hare begged me to allow her to be a listener & was present yesterday– & much delighted with his performance– we induced her to remain afterwards all the eveng– & found her most agreeable as usual– M$\underline{rs}$ Smith spent Monday eveng– with us, & read aloud some of Tennyson's Poems– few of which are worth reading aloud however– Those M$\underline{rs}$ Butler read being decidedly the best– M$\underline{rs}$ S– was tolerably well– & begged her love to you when I wrote– She has consented to come again this eveng, I find from M$\underline{rs}$ F– who wrote to ask her, so that I suppose she is pretty well–

I have been confined to the house some days with Influenza, which has of course affected my throat, my weak part– I do not find much relief from D^r H[ering]'s powders– which he has been plying me with in quick succession– but by avoiding the damp pavements & taking exercize up & down my south room with the windows up, I expect to be able to walk out again tomorrow– for the sun is bright, but the frost is all rising out of the ground today– & Fisher positively forbid my going down to Church this morng– but went himself in my stead– & I consoled myself by reading at home the service &c– He thanks you for y^r kind enquiries about his eyes– which are rather better again– as long as he don't use them at all– Poor Sally! I am indeed grieved to hear how much her's are troubling her– If she w^d like me to speak to Dr H. about her case, I will do so with great pleasure– altho' I have as you say lost much of my faith in the system– & indeed have promised Fisher if my throat is not relieved shortly, to consult one of the Faculty–

Owing to this cold, I have seen [very] little of Mr Harrison– who has also been an invalid– His complaint is not a dangerous one, but gives him much inconvenience & keeps him closely confined within doors– Aunt is a good deal out of spirits about him– Not that there is any cause for serious alarm– but that he does not get better– & D^r [John Rhea] Barton says that he cannot make use of such remedies as he would for a younger man– & the milder ones have hitherto failed of relieving him– I went to drive yesterday & afterwards stopped in to pay him a visit– & he told me, when Aunt was out of the room, that he did not expect to get out again until July– & perhaps never again– I am very sorry to see him so much hipped,[4] & regret that I cannot be more with him in the eveng– but when my throat is weak talking loud to him fatigues me, & Fisher will not consent to my making the exertion– besides we have had weather to imprison everybody but ducks & <u>geese</u>– as Fanny says– but after such a winter we may reasonably hope for a mild & pleasant spring– which with you has begun already no doubt–

By the bye, Fisher requested me to ask the favour of W^m when he arrives from Combahee, to take up some roots of the <u>Stewartia</u>, of the <u>Ptelea</u> & a few small Varnish Trees, which he wishes to plant out in Aunt's garden– & thinks may succeed there with plenty of sun– If the Schooner sh^d happen to be at Ashley River you might send them down & have them shipped direct from Charleston– I rec^d a small barrel of very nice grits[5] from Susan I suppose– as she mentioned to Mary she meant to send some– Pray beg Eleanor when she writes to her Mother to thank her particularly for it, for me– I am waiting for an answer to my last before I write again– M^{rs} F– desires her kindest remembrances to you– She cannot get rid of her cold as long as she is constantly committing fresh imprudences– but I hear nothing more of her nerves & take it for granted they do not trouble her– I must attend the summons to dinner & say Adieu my dearest Mamma– Ever Y^r affectionate Eliza

My best love to dear Sally and the children one and all– To Kitty also, whom you very seldom mention now– How is she getting on? We shall very soon get news of Edward I daresay– for the Delaware is daily expected from the Mediterranean & will no doubt bring letters from him–

Private Collection

1. Since John Brown Francis was a senator at this time, he would have seen Arthur in Washington. The nature of Arthur's business with Congress is not explained.

2. At the end of January, the Clay Club of Charleston unanimously resolved to make Henry Middleton an honorary member in recognition of his "consistent devotion ... to republican principles," his just sense of "the practical ability of men for the administration of government," and his regard for "the great statesman of the West as a national benefactor."

In thanking Clay's Charleston supporters on February 5, Middleton replied that "it must be a source of never failing satisfaction to me to know that my fellow citizens remember my steady devotion to republican principles." He went on to say that "my opinion (which must pass for what it may be worth) has long been made up respecting the choice left us between the available candidates [*for president*]. In all our greatest legislative difficulties on the floor of Congress, who, for thirty years past, has been among the foremost to solve them? Who has on all occasions been the unvarying friend and steady supporter of the compromises . . . upon which the glorious fabric of our Union rests? Who has been the great pacificator in our sectional conflicts?" *Charleston Courier,* February 15, 1844.

3. Casella was giving Eliza lessons in musical interpretation and style.

4. Depressed or worried.

5. Eliza apparently missed good southern cooking. "Pray dear Mamma," she wrote once, "send me in Yr next a receipt for making Pillaw [*pilaf,*] in which Peter excels I think– & which nobody understands here. Also his directions for making those nice little Corn cakes or rather biscuits." EMF to MHM, December 2, 1845, private collection.

～

To Mrs. Middleton, Middleton Place

Philadelphia – Feby 29th 1844

I have been in a state of such anxiety and nervous excitement all the morng– since I heard the dreadful news of the explosion at Washington,[1] dreading lest Arthur & Pauline might have been on board & injured, that I had not courage to take my pen until I found after reading the account of the disaster, that there was no reason to fear for their safety– We were not able to get a Newspaper giving the details of the accident & the names of the unfortunate sufferers until a short time ago when to my great relief Mrs F. ascertained the extent of the calamity– & heartrending as the description of it is, a great weight of doubts & fears was removed by the very exactness of it– For the rumors we first heard, were that several visitors, ladies & gentlemen were also severely injured– & of course my apprehensions were immediately excited– Thank God! They were unfounded– I hope dear Mamma that you will hear nothing of this terrible accident until you receive the papers announcing it– for I sh^{d} be sorry the rumour sh^{d} reach you as it did us– Pauline will feel for the grief of her friends the Gardiners– And the whole city indeed must be mourning the loss of so many distinguished men– It is too horrible to think of– but I shall find it difficult to turn my thoughts to other subjects– and selfish as it no doubt is to say so, the feeling of gratitude for the safety of those for whom I feared takes away from the unmingled horrors I sh^{d} have felt, had I first heard all the particulars–

I should not have written at all today, so completely unnerved have I been by this news– but recollecting that I had mentioned to you last week my indisposition, I thought you might magnify it in y^{r} imagination to something serious, if I did not write as usual & I am glad to be able to assure you that I am now very much better– almost well indeed– & much relieved by the anti-homoeopathic remedies I have been trying for some days– Fisher became so uneasy at the continued irritation of my throat, that on Sunday I consented to write to Dr Hering giving him very civilly his congé – & calling in Dr Jackson who gave me gargles & applications which have done me more good in 3 days, than the powders had in as many months– He says, what I all along suspected, that it is altogether a local affection requiring local applications– & fortunately the part affected is very high up, at the back of the throat behind & above the uvula– almost at the root of the nose– He agrees perfectly with Drs Holbrook & Meigs– as to the nature of the complaint– which they have all called, & Dr Hering himself agreed to call, an irritation of the mucous membrane– neither of the bronchia or Larynx, but of the Fauces–^{2} much higher up– I find that the application with a hair brush of a preparation containing a small portion of creosote, is very useful– & Dr J. says if that does not change the character of the secretions, he will try something else– I do not think any other will be necessary & fancy he has hit upon the right remedy– which you will be glad of– even altho' y^{r} favorite system may disdainfully reject all such– A propos– there was an opportunity today of sending you the box & books for the possession of which you were so anxious– Harry told me that young Pringle, Julius St Julian,[3] was to set out on his journey homewards & I reminded him of y^r request– but doubt his complying with it– for his faith in the science seems rather shaken– altho' the reason he gave for not attending to y^r wishes, was that you w^d not know how to use the medecines. Depend upon it, Sally's patients only fancy themselves sick– for if the little millionths perform such wonderful cures, why does she herself continue to suffer so much with her eyes– why were not my symptoms relieved– & why does W^m remain an invalid, notwithstanding the regular following up of the system for so many months– I have not heard from him yet– which worries me–

I spent the last eveng– at Aunt's for the first time for nearly 3 weeks– They were delighted to see me again, & both in much better spirits, for the D^r [Barton] & M^r H's own feelings assured him he was much better– & they repeated often that they were now quite satisfied that I sh^d soon get entirely well– having proper advice– M^{rs} F is delighted to have got Dr H. out of the house– & hopes you will approve of the change– which I am not so sure of [4] at first– altho' when you find that I was getting worse under the other treatment, & am now daily improving you may reluctantly consent to give it–

I have been exciting myself a great deal in Casella's favor– writing quantities of notes of recommendation for him & sending about tickets to those who came to hear him at our musical party upon whom I considered I had claims– With all my trouble I have as yet only disposed of 30 tickets but have hopes of getting off 10 more– Several persons are foolish enough to object to coming to a concert in Lent, which I really think refining upon the roman catholic strictness very absurdly– But for those who make conscientious objections I have not a word to say– only I think the abstinence to be observed is from sin, evil passions & what are vain & really frivolous amusements– but that the enjoyment of any thing so innocent as Music sh^d be condemned seems to me ridiculous and reminds me of Dr Johnson's censure of people who throw stumbling blocks in each others paths– instead of trying to make smooth the way of salvation–

Fisher is gone out this morng with Sidney F– to look at a Farm which is for sale, 9 miles from the city & 3 beyond Germantown– He has also another in view, & will not make up his mind in a hurry– unless he can suit himself. I must send this off for Mrs Smith, who sat an hour with me this morng & desired her love to you, told me the mail closed at 4– The boy must therefore be despatched before dinner– With love to Papa, Sally and all the rest, I am dearest Mamma Ever Y^r most affect^e daughter Eliza

By the bye, Fisher begged I w<u>d</u> mention to Papa that the Supplement of his Biographie Universelle [5] has arrived from France, & Pennington wishes to know what he shall do with it–

Private Collection

1. On February 28, 1844, while the USS *Princeton* was on a cruise down the Potomac River, a new gun exploded. Several people were killed, including Secretary of State Abel P. Upshur and Sen. David Gardiner, whose daughter, Julia, married President Tyler a few months later.
2. This is the narrow passage at the back of the mouth between the tonsils.
3. Julius St. Julien Pringle (1820–1890) was the son of James Reid and Elizabeth (McPherson) Pringle.
4. That is, "not so sure that you will approve, at first."
5. John Penington, at 127 S. Seventh Street, imported foreign books and was also an antiquarian bookdealer.

Henry Middleton had ordered the new edition of the multivolume *Biographie universelle, ancienne et moderne*, which aimed to include, in alphabetical order, all writers, historical personages, "savants," etc. from all periods and from all over the world.

∼

To Mrs. Middleton, Middleton Place

Philadelphia – Friday March 8<u>th</u> [1844]

I am half inclined to wait for another letter from you, dearest Mamma, which generally comes a week & a day after the last, but as it rains hard & is likely to do so all day, I shall have more time to write mine, which I can keep until tomorrow– I have not yet thanked you for yr's of the 25<u>th</u> which arrived the day after I wrote last week– & made me quite happy– as it contained such good accounts of William– He is by this time with you I suppose & I hope you find him as well as Oliver reported him. Not having rec<u>d</u> any answer to the letter I wrote him, I conclude he never rec<u>d</u> it– probably it is still lying in the Pocotaligo P.O.[1] & it is not now worth reading certainly– With your's, came a letter from Paolina, in answer to my second– not giving me much news, except that of their good health– She seems anxious to go to Carolina, but does not know when they will be able to leave Wash<u>n</u>. I have since heard, thro' M<u>r</u> Francis, that Arthur intended to set out very soon & also that he had given up his project of going to Jamaica– which is surely wise– You perhaps have heard again from them– Pauline hopes to be at M. Place before Sally's departure & seems heartily tired of the gaieties of the Capital. She wrote on the very day that the dreadful accident happened on board the Princeton & of course knew nothing of it– That will put a stop to everything like amusement for the rest of the season–

What a fortunate appointment for the South, is Mr Calhoun's![2] for he will certainly consult her interest by making terms with G^t Britain, & settling amicably the Oregon question and so yr apprehensions of war will again be removed it is to be hoped–

I expected this morng– to have rec^d a letter from Ed^d as I saw the arrival of the Delaware at Norfolk, announced yesterday–[3] perhaps he has written to you– It will be very strange if he has sent none at all– You will be glad to hear that Dr. Jackson's application has been very useful to my throat– He has contrived a handle to the brush, which enables him to poke it up very successfully– & I have not expectorated any more hard lumps for several days– He says he has cured many worse cases than mine– & laughed at the idea of its being a danger-ous disease– I daresay Arthur will consider me a backslider– but you will not allow y^r predeliction for the new system [to] prevent you from acknowledging the mistake its advocates make in rejecting all local applications– which are certainly very useful in many cases– I do not deny that the medecines may have some efficacy– but very few of them had any effect upon me certainly–

I have been writing this morng– to Mrs Harper, recommending the Casel-las to her– & begging her to speak in their favour to Miss H. also– I did not address myself to her because I thought it likely that at this season she w^d be exclusively devoted to her religion– in all its forms & ceremonies– & have little time or inclination to give to anything else– Mrs Pierce Butler has added to the obligations they owed her already, by procuring for them several letters for Balt^e which will be very useful to them no doubt– Casella says that but for her exertions & mine, his Concert w^d have been a complete failure– whereas as we put 80 dollars in his pockets– besides what he sold at the door, he was well satisfied– He had so frequently said that his wife wished to come in & make music with me, that I at last proposed their spending Tuesday eveng with me [and] asked only Mrs Butler, the Cuestas, Mütters[4] & Mrs Smith to come & listen– He played twice most divinely as usual, to my accompaniment once– I wish that you & Papa & W^m could enjoy this treat of music– for such I am sure you w^d find it– I shall miss very much the pleasure of my lessons, during his absence in Balt^e but shall renew them upon his return–

Fisher has made an offer for the Abington Farm–[5] which I hope will be accepted for he seems to have set his heart upon it– particularly since his second visit to it with Alfred Elwyn, who as well as Sydney Fisher, thinks it a very desirable one– Certainly it must be, with regard to situation, distance & neigh-

bourhood– Mrs Harrison thinks he had better not involve himself in building–
but that seems to be one of his chief objects in purchasing the land– altho' he
has no intention of beginning his operations before next Spring. If he makes
his bargain, which is to get a hundred acres for 10 thousand dollars– he will
immediately begin to plant out Trees– & busy himself with other improvements– & we shall go out early in May & stay there a couple of weeks–

Of course this year I cannot stay there during the summer [6] but shall hope
to spend part of the Autumn there, & have you at the Farm house with me. I
shall still perhaps be able to pass a month at NewPort– & another year if we
live, I shall look forward to having accomodation for you in my own house–
which Fisher is determined to have very comfortable– & well situated– If I were
disposed to take a gloomy view of everything, as Mrs F. does I might make
myself unhappy thinking of the various disadvantages attending this plan– but
I on the contrary see that there is much to be gained by it– Fisher's happiness
will be much encreased by his having active employment, which he now wants
sadly, cut off as he is from the resource of reading– Then the children will enjoy
so much the country air & liberty of running free thro' the fields & I do believe
it will suit my health better [than] the climate of New Port– in August I shall
be glad to go & breathe the cooler breezes on the cliffs & beach but with my
encreasing family the difficulties of getting there, & being accomodated there,
must also encrease– Then the growing age & infirmities of Fisher's friends will
render a separation of more than a few weeks impossible– Mr H. is very feeble &
Mrs F. is now making herself miserable at the thoughts of his going very soon–
which as he is getting better again, I do not think to be feared– Aunt's anxiety
is evidently greater than she will acknowledge– She scarcely leaves him for half
an hour & watches every movement closely– I trust that he will soon get out &
enjoy the mild weather, & feel himself again. We have a prospect of a very mild
Spring, which will be very favourable for invalids– I must say Adieu, my dearest
Mamma & as on second thoughts, I think it best to send this off today, for fear
you sh^{d} be worrying yrself about me, I will now close it, with best love to Papa,
Sally & all around you– I am as ever Y^{r} most affectionate daughter– Eliza
Mrs F. & Fisher beg me to add their kindest regards–

Private Collection

1. Pocotaligo was the nearest post office to the Combahee plantations.
2. President Tyler appointed John C. Calhoun secretary of state to replace Abel
Upshur, who was killed in the explosion on the *Princeton*.
Increasing numbers of settlers were moving into the northwest, and expansionists
were calling for the United States to take all of Oregon, despite the treaty of joint occupa-

tion with England, which had been in effect since 1818. Calhoun was opposed to anything other than a peaceful settlement of the issue, believing that in time the United States would have Oregon anyway.

Mrs. Middleton, always worried about possible war with England, had been reading the "violent speeches in Congress" about Oregon. "Mr Adams," she thought, "very properly blames the members for their rude ill bred language." MHM to EMF, March 16, 1844, PHi.

3. Edward arrived a week later. He was assigned to the ship *Lexington* in the Mediterranean squadron and expected to sail to Port Mahon in the Balearic Islands, the navy's main operating base in the Mediterranean.

4. Dr. Thomas Dent Mütter (1811–1859) was professor of surgery at Jefferson Medical College, 1841–56. Mrs. Mütter was the former Mary Alsop of Middletown, Connecticut.

5. Fisher was "determined not to run in debt, but [to] go to work very gradually, improving & adding as he finds the means." The purchase price of $10,000, which included cattle, horses, carts, plows, etc. and a house, would be equivalent to approximately $200,000 in 1999 dollars. EMF to MHM, March 15, 1844, private collection; dollar conversion factor from RSahr, OrStU.

6. She wanted to be in Philadelphia in June, when the baby was to be born.

～

To Mrs. Middleton, Middleton Place

Philadelphia – Friday – March 22$^{\underline{nd}}$ [1844]

My dearest Mamma,

Y^r letter of the 17$^{\underline{th}}$ arrived most opportunely this morng– & brought me a great deal of pleasure– I was just saying to M$^{\underline{rs}}$ F. at the breakfast table that I hoped that ring was the Postman's, as I had not heard from you for ten days– I was sorry to find that you were to lose dear Sally's society so soon– and that she was to return so early to her seclusion– which will make her summer appear longer than ever– If it is to be her fate to remain at the Beach– Is there no possibility of her coming to the North? The voyage & change of climate might perhaps restore her eyesight– & w$^{\underline{d}}$ certainly improve her health but I fear there is little hope that poor John can make arrangements to bring her on– I suppose he accompanied Papa to Combahee, altho' you do not say so– I was very glad to learn that William continued so much better– M$^{\underline{rs}}$ Harper mentioned in a letter I rec$^{\underline{d}}$ from her in answer to one I wrote introducing the Casellas to her, that she had heard from him lately– which I was rather surprised at, as I understood from you that his eyes prevented him from writing– Do not tell him however, that I was a little mortified to find that he could answer her letters & not mine– For as she is a very agreeable correspondent, it was natural he should wish not to neglect her– & very foolish in me to have any feeling about it.

I was sure, dear Mamma, that you w^d not altogether like our plan of giving up NewPort except for a month or so, at midsummer–[1] but when you consider that this year, I could not, at any rate, go there until August, & that I look forward to y^r spending the whole month of Octr with me on The Farm, you will see that you will not lose by the arrangement this year at least– and if our lives are spared for another, we hope to have better accomodation, & to induce you to spend at least a month with us on y^r way to New Port– Fisher hopes that Papa will take some interest in his planting, & give him a great many useful hints when he is laying out his grounds & gardens– Owing to this unfortunate Texas business, property in N.Y. has fallen, and he will not get the price he expected for his lots there,[2] but Mr Harrison will I have no doubt help him in his difficulties, & enable him to meet his payment on the 1st of April– and he will begin his planting moderately– & go into no unnecessary expenses until he sees his way quite clear– He has his horse again in town & means to ride out very frequently, & superintend the building of his Piazza &c– As soon as the weather moderates (for it is quite cold again) I shall drive out & suggest some alterations perhaps– but he does not want me to see the place until the Trees look a little greener & the country less bare– for fear of the first impression being unfavourable.[3] I am very sure however that I shall be satisfied, for I am determined not to put him out of conceit of it, as I encouraged him to make the purchase in the hope that this w^d conduce to his health & happiness & certainly from no selfish motives– His mother evidently disapproved of it, altho' she wisely held her tongue– or at least said little but now that the bargain is struck, & he is in for it, she begins to think it is best to put a good face on it– & says she will assist me in choosing House linen &c & furniture, of which at present we shall want but very little–

M^r & M^rs H, the latter especially, promoted F's views in every way– and see plainly that it will give them more of his society– and indeed that there are many advantages to be gain'd by our having an establishment so near them– I rejoice to say that Mr H. is decidedly better– & we now hope will be himself again in a short time– I wrote again to Pauline a few days ago, and begged her to let me know soon their plans– but if Arthur is waiting, as I am told, for the bill for the Annexation of Texas [4] to pass, you will not see them very soon– & I should think it w^d be scarcely worth while for them to go on to Carolina at all–

I should like to know what Papa's opinions on this subject are, but have little doubt that he thinks with Harry & Fisher, that it w^d have disastrous consequences– that is to say that <u>your</u> countrymen w<u>d</u> certainly go to war with us on this pretext– altho' they might not have a <u>right</u> to interfere– I most earnestly pray that such a calamity will be averted by a merciful Providence– Harry & Fisher were discussing the matter last eveng– & both seemed to agree it was much to be feared that the discontented, who form a numerous class in both countries, w<u>d</u> be eager for war, which w<u>d</u> be a popular measure.

I was interrupted by a visit from Miss Legaré [5] who came with M<u>rs</u> Schroeder– She is come to spend several weeks in Phil<u>a</u> & is quite near us in 8<u>th</u> S<u>t</u> so that as I told her I hope we shall see a good deal of her– Her eye is much better, & her health good– She is a sensible woman certainly & on her brother's account I shall be disposed to pay her all the attention in my power– M<u>rs</u> Schroeder has just returned from New Port, & says that Papa's trees are much grown, & the wall completed– She says many rooms are already taken at the new Hotel– [6] and elsewhere lodgings are engaged. I must go & get ready for my walk or it will be too late to go before dinner– The children have just returned from visiting the Sergeants, & have been much admired & praised for their good behavior M<u>rs</u> Putnam says– They beg me to give their love to you, & were going on to send it to Aunt Sally & her little children, but I told them you could not give it them– I hope you will not be left alone long– I suppose the Sumners will now be invited to pay you a visit. Adieu dearest Mamma, I am as ever Y<u>r</u> most affectionate daughter

Fisher & his Mother both beg their kindest regards– The latter is much better– My throat continues improving–

Private Collection

1. When Eliza first mentioned this, her mother replied, "But my dear Eliza you give me no small uneasiness by telling me that being more than a few weeks at Newport will be impossible! This is really a sad disappointment– I have always enjoyed that place, because you were with me– how different will be my stay there, next summer!"
Emma Huger Smith was also distressed at what she thought would be the Fishers' "abandonment" of Newport. "I'm thoroughly ashamed of my own selfishness. . . . Yet, how much yr absence must detract f[ro]m my comfort & enjoyment at Newport! The engrossing nature of yr maternal duties had, I felt, most seriously interfered with yr sympathies & intercourse with me, but I hoped & believed that in time habit wd make the discharge of those duties so much easier, that yr thoughts & affections would become sufficient for all." MHM to EMF, March 16, 1844, PHi; EHS to EMF, April 11, 1844, PHi.
2. Fisher's grandfather bought land in Hamilton County, New York, from James Fenimore Cooper's father, thinking it would increase in value and provide an inheritance for Fisher.

3. When she finally saw the farm, Eliza thought it had "capabilities" but could not yet share Mrs. Putnam's idea that it was "a little Paradise." EMF to MHM, March 29, 1844, private collection.

4. The treaty was finally defeated by the Senate in June 1844. However, just before President Tyler left office, he persuaded Congress to approve the annexation of Texas by joint resolution, which only required majority votes by the two houses rather than the two-thirds vote he had not been able to get from the Senate. Texas was admitted as a state at the end of 1845.

5. Mary Legaré Bullen, Hugh Swinton Legaré's sister, was collecting her brother's correspondence and in 1846 published two volumes of *The Writings of Hugh Swinton Legaré, Late Attorney General and Acting Secretary of State of the United States.*

6. The building of the Ocean House, which was about to open for its first season almost directly across the street from the Middletons' house, was an indication of Newport's growing summer popularity.

～

To Mrs. Middleton, Middleton Place

Philadelphia Saturday April 6ᵗʰ [1844]

I looked in vain this morng for a letter from you, my dearest Mamma, which however I ought not to have expected very confidently– for it is but a week yesterday since I recᵈ yʳ last– & I seldom hear more than once in ten days– I thought at least I shᵈ have had from Pauline the announcement of her arrival in Charleston– which Harry saw some days ago in the Papers– I had so little idea of their leaving Washington so soon, that I had just written her a note by Casella– I am however glad that you were not left long to yʳ solitude after Sally's departure– But probably Arthur may have wished to remain some days in town, in order to be present there during Mʳ Clay's visit– for which I see they were making grand preparations– & no doubt Pauline would wish to be there for other reasons– that she might attend her Church services at this solemn season– & at the joyful Festival tomorrow– So I hope they will both be suited– We have had a very sudden change of weather from a bleak & wintry East wind, to almost summer heat, the thermᵗʳ rising 60 degrees in 24 hours– It was yesterday morng & the day before quite <u>sultry</u> & I thought how you must be complaining of the heat in Carolina– but while we were in Church, a great change took place, & I was glad I had not gone there in Summer dress as I had felt tempted to do– Today it is still chilly, & there was such an appearance of rain, that I prudently determined to remain quietly at home instead of attending the funeral of Miss Telfair,[1] to which I was invited– It is not the invalid, but the elder sister who died suddenly of congestion of the lungs– giving another impressive warning, that the "race is not always to the swift, nor the battle to the strong"– for who w$\underline{d}$ have supposed that the one who has been for years so great a sufferer w$\underline{d}$ have survived her sister who was in such good health– Poor Miss Margaret is much to be pitied– She has fortunately a very good niece who may partly supply the place of her lost companion– I am very glad to say that M$\underline{r}$ Harrison has been improving for some days & has been able to walk for 3 quarters of an hour in the garden several times– He tried driving in the carriage, by D$\underline{r}$ Barton's advice, but the motion brought on a return of the pain, & he soon returned.

For some days past we have all been engrossed by one topic of conversation– which has unfortunately become the town talk, & even found its way to the Penny Papers– I mean the brutal conduct of that blackguard Schott,[2] to his poor wife, who after enduring his ill treatment in silence for years, was at last so completely worn out by it, that in terror for her life, which he has several times threatened, she applied to her father, M$\underline{r}$ Richard Willing, the brother of M$\underline{rs}$ T. Francis, your cousin, for protection and is now gone home to his house– He was much to blame for permitting her to marry such a notoriously unprincipled fellow– a gambler and everything that is bad– from whom she will now be delivered– for there is no doubt that there are ample grounds for a divorce– & luckily there are no children to interfere in the matter– The ruffian has added insults to injuries, & accuses his victim of improprieties of which no one the least acquainted with her character will believe her capable– but no doubt the scandal loving world will make the most of these accusations, altho' her innocence can be fully established– and his villainy substantially proved– But enough of this sad story, which is the exciting theme of gossip in all drawing rooms, & in more public places too just now– It was the dread of this exposure which induced the poor thing to suffer in silence so long–

I had a note from M$\underline{r}$ C[harles] Ingersoll yesterday, announcing that his wife had "added another female to the inhabitants of this planet" & "begging me to caution all those I might have any influence with against such a needless multiplication of the gentle sex in families that are boyless"– I am sorry for his disappointment, but really think people ought to be satisfied that Providence orders these things much better for us than we could for ourselves– & I mean to be content with whatever comes to me, & hope Fisher will be equally so– or at any rate resigned if he has another girl instead of a boy–

Monday eveng– I kept this open until now thinking I sh$\underline{d}$ receive a letter from you, dearest Mamma, but as it has not come yet, I fear you may imagine something untoward has occurred to prevent my writing, & will therefore not wait any longer– M$\underline{rs}$ Smith has been spending the day with me, and joins me in love to you– Harry was also here this afternoon, & begged to add his– He has published his Pamphlet,[3] & will now have no further excuse for remaining here– I look for Edward every day– & if he comes mean to give him a little party & accompany him to any he may have any opportunity of accepting, as the weather is now so fine & mild, that there will be no risk in my going out well protected at night– My throat is wonderfully better– & indeed feels today quite well– Adieu in haste with love to all I am as ever Y^{r} affecte E–

The children are quite well, & highly delighted with their Easter Eggs, of which they have each a basket full apiece– Fisher is going out again tomorrow to the Farm to plant more Trees and a hedge of the Maclura– see Nuttall's Sylvae, Plate 97–[4] The Shrubs from M. Place have not yet arrived–

Private Collection

1. Probably Mary Telfair (b. 1813) and her sister, Margaret (b. 1816), who were the daughters of Thomas and Margaret (Long) Telfair of Savannah, Georgia. Thomas Telfair (1786–1818) and Henry Middleton were in Congress at the same time.

2. When Fisher's cousin Ellen Willing became engaged to James Schott in the summer of 1839, Mrs. Fisher said, "I think her father must be truly afflicted. [Schott] has been one of our most dissipated young men of very low Connexions & I can conceive in no way an eligible match for her." Schott accused his wife of having an affair with Pierce Butler, which led to a duel between the two men in Bladensburg, Maryland. Mrs. Fisher to EMF, July 24, [1839] ScHi.

3. In his pamphlet on "The Government and Currency," Harry argued that the government could not issue paper money. His other writing included "Prospects for Disunion," in which he opposed nullification in the early 1830s; "Four Essays," which advocated free trade in 1847; and "The Economical Causes of Slavery in the United States and Obstacles to Abolition," published in London in 1857.

4. Thomas Nuttall (1786–1859), an Englishman, was an expert on North American flora. *The North American Sylva* was published 1842–49.

⌒

To Mrs. Fisher, Philadelphia

M.P. Ap^{l} 7th 1844

Here I am my dearest Eliza alone, & as you said in your last "cannot occupy myself more agreeably" than in answering that welcome letter of the 29th in which you give a good account of yourself & the invalids who are improving, & of the enjoyment you & children felt at the Farm– It must be a larger house than I expected to hear of,[1] & will no doubt be so nicely arranged by Mrs Fisher's advice, that Mr F. will not probably begin to build another for a year or two. By this time the shrubs must have been planted, & will I hope thrive. Your Lilacs ought to be in flower soon for they always are so in England in April as I well remember– today I have gathered a sprig of them for the first time this season. You must no doubt be much occupied with making preparations of different kinds, & are assisted I daresay by Mrs Putnam who you say is so delighted with the farm. but surely you might remain there until the beginning of June–[2] You however can judge better of the proper time to leave it than I can– you seemed certain that the <u>end</u> of June was the time the event would happen– You are as usual very kind in proposing that agreeable room for me to occupy–[3] but surely M^{rs} F would not approve of it, & I should be very sorry to annoy her. What you mention of Harry's intentions surprises me, having concluded by his long residence at Phil^a & the wedding not having occured in March it would not at any other time.[4] Tell him I shall be glad to see him.

I must now tell you why I am alone– Y^r Father sent Arthur & W^m here last Thursday to tell Paolina that the ball in honour of Mr Clay was not to be given that Eve^g (which by the bye Mr Trapier & the other Clergymen had been greatly incensed at)[5] because he was not to arrive in Charles^n until the 6th & leave it on the 9th so that she must return with them in order to be present at the dinner to be given today by y^r Father to Mr Clay, & the ball to be given tomorrow eve^g– this pleased Paolina, but she told me her chief motive for going was to go to Church today– so they left this yesterday after dinner & will not return till tuesday.

The Plateau, plate, & China & best wine were sent down yesterday, & there will be about 15 or 16 at the dinner– but what will surprise you W^m says y^r Father is to accompany M^r C[lay] to Church today in his own pew![6] Now all this is the <u>plan</u>, whether it will happen I must wait till Tuesday to know– & will then relate to you what I am told. Mr C. <u>may</u> be ill, as he was at Columbia which prevented his being in Ch^n at the time appointed.

Tueday Eve^g The Servt John has just returned from Char^n & informs me that the family will not return until tomorrow– As there may be no means of sending this for several days, if I neglect the opportunity which Mr Cotes who is staying at Runnymede offered me today when he made me a visit, you would perhaps be anxious to receive my letter, so I will send it to him early tomorrow morn^g– but there is nothing I can inform you about except that the dinner was given by y^r Father on Sunday[7] & the ball was attended yesterday, & today Mr Clay went up the Cooper river, which I suppose detained the family as they probably accompanied him there & tomorrow he will leave Char^n

I have not for a long time been as much gratified as I have for the last 3 days by reading over a number of the most affectionate letters from my old friends which I have kept for more than ten, twenty & thirty years– besides which a quantity of extracts I wrote at St Peters^g from a variety of books, chiefly reviews which were lent to me there. the number of notes too rec^d there, recall so many pleasing recollections! Cath^e of course never reads to me at night so I go to bed a little before 9, but rise before Sun rise– She plays nearly all the morn^g & is very quiet. The weather is now very warm, & it is probably so at Phil^a & you go frequently I suppose to the farm with Mr Fisher– Has Mrs F. been to see it? & how does she like it? How is Mrs Smith now? I daresay you will take her to see the farm– John brought me a letter from y^r Aunt Rutledge now at Combahee & says she will & Emma B[lake] also make me a visit, but when she cannot say until she sees y^r Father– she adds "remember me affect^{ly} to dear Eliza & tell her she has my best wishes for her health & happiness." Pray give my love to M^r & Mrs Fisher & Mrs Smith & believe me my dearest Eliza y^r affect^{te} Mother M. H. M.

Kiss the darlings for me– It is so dark I cannot write more. Did I tell you in my last that all John's family arrived safely at Waccamaw by the Sloop on the 31st ult^o?

PHi

1. There were five bedrooms upstairs and two sitting rooms below them. The farmer and his family had the use of four additional rooms. EMF to MHM, March 29, 1844, private collection.

2. Eliza wanted to be in Philadelphia when the new baby was born. Remembering that Sophy had arrived early and very quickly, she was "afraid of being caught in a miscalculation" if she stayed at Abington too long. EMF to MHM, March 29, 1844, private collection.

3. Eliza counted on her mother being in Philadelphia when her baby came. To make it easier for her, Eliza proposed to ask Mrs. Fisher to have her mother stay in the drawing room at 170 Chestnut Street.

4. There was gossip in Philadelphia that Mrs. Camac was "constantly seen at shops, where it is believed she is . . . preparing for her approaching marriage [*to Harry*]." Instead of marrying Harry, Mrs. Camac later committed the "folly," as Eliza termed it, of marrying her cousin William S. Cox, Jr. He was "more nearly her daughter's age than her's . . . she will certainly degrade herself, but it is nobody's business I suppose." EMF to MHM, March 29, 1844, private collection; EMF to MHM, March 10, 1845, private collection.

5. Paul Trapier objected to having a ball the night before Good Friday of Easter weekend.

6. They attended St. Michael's church, where the Middletons had owned pews since the eighteenth century. Mrs. Middleton knew her husband was not a churchgoer.

7. William told Eliza that their father "made up a dinner for [*Mr. Clay*] on Sunday, the only day on which he was disengaged, which went off remarkably well," but no more detailed account has been found. William Middleton to EMF, April 9, 1844, PHi, C/F.

~

To Mrs. Middleton, Middleton Place

Philadelphia – April 15$\underline{\text{th}}$ [1844]

I have 2 letters to thank you for, my dearest Mamma, rec$\underline{\text{d}}$ within a day or two– the 1$\underline{\text{st}}$ of a very old date, which was a great while detained on the road, & the second, finished last Tuesday, before the return of the family from town– I shall expect to have from Paolina a full account of the rejoicings in Charleston– dinner, ball &c– [*for Henry Clay*] which I was very glad to hear she was able to attend– The shrubs [*from Middleton Place*] have arrived at last– but altho' Fisher luckily had an opportunity of taking them out to the Farm this very morng– after they had been but a few hours at the wharf, I fear there is little chance of their succeeding after being a whole month out of ground– Some of the leaves on the Illicium were still fragrant however, & upon making incisions in the bark of the Varnish Trees we found they were still green– so that perhaps there may be a chance for them & at any rate we shall nurse them most carefully, & value them highly if we can coax them to flourish on our soil– Within the last week there has been the most astonishing progress made in vegetation– of all kinds– In our little yard the Pivans Japonica & Almond Trees are in full flower, & the corchoruses out too– The lilacs give promise of blooming shortly & the Lilies of the Valley also– This day 2 weeks we were shivering with cold over large fires– & today the therm$\underline{\text{r}}$ is considerably above 80– We had no such warm weather last year until June– If this heat lasts, I shall hope to get out of town by the first week in May, if the carpenters can be persuaded to finish operations by that time.

We have been extremely busy, buying furniture, crockery &c– & have now nearly completed the necessary purchases– After all M$\underline{\text{rs}}$ F– has said against our country plans, it amuses me to see how much interest she takes in the arrangements & the large contributions she is daily making to encrease our future comfort– Aunt H. is also very liberal in her gifts, & I think we shall be tolerably well supplied by the old ladies, without going to much expense ourselves– I am glad that I shall acquire <u>gradually</u> some knowledge of house-keeping for making this experiment on a small scale in the country will be an

advantage to me, & enable me hereafter to do better in town– But M^{rs} F–
evidently mistrusts my capabilities– I tell her it is not fair to prejudge me– Aunt
H. is much more disposed to appreciate my efforts– & it is quite encouraging
to hear her say that she doubts not that I shall succeed in my endeavours.

Fisher has been much excited about the Texas question– which they say
is to be decided today in the Senate– he thinks if the bill for annexation passes
the consequences will be most disastrous for the whole country, but particularly
for the South, which will be almost deserted for the richer lands, to which the
tide of emigration will be pressing onward– Then the disunion of the Northern & Southern states will follow after some years– & indeed the prospect of
this seems inevitable, & the foolish & wicked interference of the mad party at
the North must render it so eventually– I should like to know Papa's opinion
with regard to Texas– I was surprised to hear that Arthur was warmly in favour
of annexation– for what advantage can be to us to have so widely extended a
territory, & such a coast to protect, with a diminished Army & Navy, and an
accumulation of public debt? I am not much of a politician, but cannot help
taking a deep interest in this question, which is likely to affect so materially the
welfare of the whole community, & of posterity still more than ourselves–
There is some consolation in the idea that Eng^{d} will not interfere & go to war
with us at present– but the other evils (including a contest with Mexico) are
sufficient–

The children have just run in to stop the gloomy train of reflections in
which I have been indulging, & give them a more cheerful turn– They are so
merry that it does one's heart good to hear their glad voices– I am going on
Wednesday if the weather is fine, to take them out again to Abington to spend
the day, & pay a visit at Wakefield en passant – Tonight I am going to a musical
soirée to hear Mlle Borghese[1] sing– & perhaps to her concert tomorrow night–
if I can get Harry to escort me– Fisher is afraid of the gas lights. He came the
other afternoon & talked for an hour about his two widows– until I began to
change my mind & think he has still a hankering after the H– & means to
disappoint the expectations of the gossips & not marry M^{rs} C– She has thrown
off her mourning, & is dashing about in her handsome chariot, very gaily
dressed, & at last returning her visits– This was supposed to be almost equivalent to the announcement of the engagement– but he seems as far off as ever
from it I think– He says he means to go to Carolina soon. Mrs Smith dined
with us on Friday, & was well & in good spirits– I must say Adieu dearest
Mamma– for I am wanted to go over & look at China at the Shop opposite–
With love to all ever Y^{r} most affect^{e} daughter Eliza

Private Collection

1. Signorina Euphrasia Borghese, prima donna from l'Opéra Comique in Paris, was to give her "1st and Only Grand Vocal and Instrumental Concert" on April 16.

〜

To Mrs. Fisher, Philadelphia

M.P. Apr<u>l</u> 21<u>st</u> 1844

My dearest Eliza

A few minutes ago Arthur arrived from Combahee to the great comfort of Pao<u>a</u> & myself for we had been for the last week expecting the party to come, & she was weeping yesterday fearing that her husband had met with an accident when shooting. I assured her that it was according to the usual custom to say that they were to return in a week, & remain a fortnight– I must now hasten to write in time to have this taken to town as y<u>r</u> Father desired Arthur to send a servant today on account of some business respecting M<u>r</u> Clay which I have not time to ask about, but you may find in the Baltimore Papers– Y<u>r</u> Aunt Rutledge & M<u>rs</u> [Emma] Blake are to come the end of the week for a few days & W<u>m</u> will also come then. I had the pleasure of receiving your letter of the 15<u>th</u> on the return of Jack by whom I sent my last. You give a good account of your preparations for inhabiting your farm– it is indeed very kindly prepared by M<u>rs</u> Fisher & M<u>rs</u> Harrison & I think you must be anxious to be in the Country during this very hot weather– Yesterday the ther<u>r</u> rose to 89° & the nights are terribly hot. Paolina can seldom sleep well in consequence of the heat. She reads sometimes aloud to me a few pages of Prescott's Con[ques]t of Mexico[1] & we walk together in the evening– during the day she is always very busy about her Child's clothes–preparing, & her own, which of course the black Girls assist her in & she has always some patients to attend to.[2]

I have seen no papers later than the 19<u>th</u> & do not know whether the annexation of Texas has been decided upon, but it must I suppose have been, & according to your opinions on the subject it must indeed be very prejudicial to the affairs of the Southern states. I am no politician & can give no opinion of my own but if Arthur comes from his bath before I finish this, I can tell you what he thinks of it. He told me that W<u>m</u> had rec<u>d</u> a letter from Ed<u>d</u> but that it was still uncertain whether he could come here– he says the Acadia has arrived which I hope has brought me a letter from my Brother– & which I expect to receive tomorrow– one from you too I hope will come.

Here is y^r brother Arthur– he begs you not to distress yourself about Texas, & above all not to trouble yourself about the interests of the South which you may well imagine will be safe if left in the hands of her own Children– & if not interfered with by the officious kindness of our Northern brethren. Every man as the old adage hath it 'knoweth where the shoe pincheth him'– but do not imagine that he is the only one of your brothers decidedly in favour of this question, all the others are equally ardent in the cause of annexation & y^r Father perfectly <u>red hot</u>. I have not time left to give you all their reasons, but the main & absorbing reason is, the security which will be obtained for our Southern institutions, & (he says) inform Mr F. that on this subject in our part of the world, Whigs & Democrats are all united–[3]

The little Girls must now be delighted (by the time you receive this) with the country garden & the novelty of the scene– it is unlucky that the shrubs were not all in a good state. I wish you could have the Petisporum [*pittosporum*] – it is now covered with flowers, & very fragrant. we even smell it in the passage where I sit from 11 o'clock to the rest of day light, the draw^g room being so insufferably hot. in a week the Cape Jessamines will probably be in flower, if this hot weather continues. I must now conclude– Arthur & Paolina beg to send their love to you pray give mine to M^{rs} & Mr Fisher & Mrs Smith & believe me my dearest Eliza y^r Affect^{te} Mother M. H. M.

PHi

1. William H. Prescott (1796–1859) wrote the *History of the Conquest of Mexico* in 1843 and another book on the conquest of Peru four years later. Arthur Middleton, who was his classmate at Harvard, provided Prescott with information for his books and had documents copied for him in Spain.

2. Paolina was "daily occupied by preparing medicines for the Negroes: she had 10 patients yesterday & today one or two more, & succeeds perfectly well in her cures." MHM to EMF, April 17, 1844, PHi.

3. Fisher replied, "that he thinks the people of the South are very shortsighted in desiring the annexation & that what appears an immediate advantage may entail <u>consequences</u> as disastrous to them as to the whole Union– for that a war with Mexico w^d probably involve us in other difficulties with the commercial nations of Europe or a separation of the Union w^d be fatal to the security of the domestic Institutions of the South, as it w^d unquestionably be followed by a civil war." EMF to MHM, April 30, 1844, private collection.

⌒

Many of Philadelphia's new immigrants were from Ireland, and they arrived in such large numbers that in 1844 they were thought to make up about 10 percent of the population. Many of them were desperately poor, and as they were for the most part Catholics in a then predominantly Protestant city, they were not always welcomed.

In May and again in July 1844 there were serious riots, during which Catholic churches were burned, mobs went on the rampage, people were killed or hurt, and much property was damaged. Since Philadelphia did not yet have professional police or firefighting forces capable of dealing with such a situation, the state militia was called in to restore order. During the May riots, martial law was declared.

In the long run, this crisis strengthened the movement to consolidate under one city government the nearly thirty separate districts, boroughs, and townships that formed Philadelphia and to create unified police and fire departments. This was finally accomplished in 1854. In 1844, however, Philadelphians like the Fishers and their friends were horrified at what seemed a complete breakdown of authority. This, combined with the crowding and dirt of a growing city, made living in the country more appealing than ever to families like the Fishers.

To Mrs. Middleton, Middleton Place

Philadelphia – Friday May 10$\underline{\text{th}}$ 1844

I have been waiting for an opportunity of sitting down quietly to write to you, all the morng– my dearest Mamma, and at <u>one</u> o'clock, this is the first I could get– for having had the sole charge of the children myself, we first went to Aunt's garden, & staid there for nearly 2 hours– I have since given them their lunch, put Sophy to sleep, heard Lily's lesson, & have now a prospect of a quiet hour, for she is busily employed <u>sewing</u> at my side, and will be very good, only occasionally interrupting me to have her needle threaded, or hem turned down– You will judge from this how much progress in the art of <u>stitching</u> she is making– a sufficient fondness for which I wish to cultivate to make her useful & keep her out of mischief– which will be harder in Sophy's case– for she has the very spirit of it in her– & it is amusing to observe how she gets the upper hand of Lily, whenever I permit her– They require a very different treatment each of them– The one to be encouraged & the other checked– & the system of management must be adapted to the character of each–

Fisher & his Mother went out early this morng– to the Farm, to engage the services of a <u>help</u> for the Farmer's wife who is I fear inefficient, or rather with 5 children to look after, cannot be expected to have much time for cleaning up– The Carpenters are so dilatory, that we shall not probably get clear of them until the end of next week and I do not expect to move out before the 20$\underline{\text{th}}$.

I spent last Saturday there, & even M<u>rs</u> F. would have been satisfied with my bustling about to get things in order but she has determined that I shall not fatigue myself any more, & is to make all the arrangements for me next week– which offer I accept without scruple, for she is never more <u>in her element</u> than when directing &c & I confess my time will be more agreeably occupied in reading & music, than in giving orders to servt[s]– not that I w<u>d</u> object to do it, if necessary–

We have been in a state of excitement for some days past, as you will see by the papers– which give an account of the disgraceful proceedings of the mob, which has been allowed to commit the most shocking outrages unpunished–[1] There is now (since much mischief has been done) sufficient authority exerted to prevent further disturbances– but these measures ought to have been taken at first– & the delay has occasioned much bloodshed & damage– While I am writing there is a further alarm of fire– but it may prove unfounded & it is to be hoped, that the exasperated rabble will not be able to execute their threats of burning down the rest of the R. Catholic Churches– Such is the deplorable fanaticism of some of the Presbyterians that they have been heard to express the hope that every one in the city will be destroyed– may they be disappointed! Pauline's friend, Bishop Kenrick,[2] has been removed from his dangerous proximity to the Cathedral, which it was feared, would be attacked– but is now made secure by a strong guard of military– Harry visited the scene of action with Col. Bankhead[3] on Wednesday, but fortunately no firing took place while they were there– I believe today there is little fear of any further fighting–

We have attended another funeral since I wrote last– that of a person we valued much more than Miss Burd– poor Miss Roberts–[4] who died after only a few days illness– of a nervous disease of the spine– which caused her much suffering & entirely deprived her of sleep for days together– She has left her property, amounting to upwards of a hundred thousand dollars, equally divided amongst 9 Nephews & Nieces– So Sally Ingersoll gets a good slice– which is thought a <u>superfluous</u> addition to her handsome fortune– but she does [not] probably consider it so– But it seems a pity others who wanted it much more sh<u>d</u> not fare better. Poor Miss Roberts was so uniformly kind & attentive to me and my children, & had so many excellent qualities that I regret her loss– but for herself it is gain– at least so her friends must hope– for she was a Christian & had some of the virtues which distinguish true disciples in an eminent degree– never was there a more humble minded, kind hearted creature– & her Parents & best beloved brother & sister having preceded her to the grave, its terrors must have been much softened– I did not like the Quaker burial– for altho' there may be solemnity in silence– one wants a few words at least of prayer & something to lead the thoughts from the saddening external influences around to that blessed expectation which reaches far beyond into another State of existence. A more complete contrast to the pomp & ceremony of poor little Miss Burd's closing scene can scarcely be imagined–

Evening– M$\underline{rs}$ Smith has been passing the afternoon with me, & now I have just time to say Goodbye before going to Aunt's to tea– M$\underline{r}$ H. has been a good deal better for several days past, & Aunt now thinks she can leave him next week long enough to ride out to see the Farm– God grant he may continue so– I must close this in haste– With love to all I am as ever Y$\underline{r}$ affecte daughter Eliza

Private Collection

1. During the riots in the Kensington section of Philadelphia in early May, "native" Philadelphians set fire to both St. Michael's and St. Augustine's Catholic churches.

2. Francis Patrick Kenrick (1797–1863), an Irishman, became Catholic bishop of Philadelphia in 1830 and bishop of Baltimore in 1851. He encouraged free parochial schools in Philadelphia in part because he objected to the public schools' requiring Catholic children to use the Protestant Bible. Kenrick played a moderating role when the riots broke out.

3. Possibly Col. James Bankhead (d. 1856), a veteran of the wars against the Seminole Indians.

4. Elizabeth Roberts (1777–1844) was the daughter of George and Thomasine (Fox) Roberts. Her brother, George Roberts, was Sally Roberts (Mrs. Harry) Ingersoll's father. Ten days before, Eliza had described the long, effusive eulogy at Miss Margaret Burd's funeral as "in very bad taste." EMF to MHM, April 30, 1844, private collection.

⌒

As was the case in 1840 when Lily was born, Mrs. Middleton had a difficult time getting to Philadelphia to be with Eliza for the birth of her third child. In a powerful series of letters which provide the most explicit and direct expression of their true feelings in the entire correspondence, Mrs. Middleton and Eliza revealed their anger and frustration at the obstacles which prevented Mrs. Middleton from doing the most obvious and normal thing.

Henry Middleton's health, as the letters indicate, had begun to deteriorate during the spring of 1844. He probably had a small stroke in early June and, although he appeared to recover, was not completely well. This may help to explain his crossness and inconsistent behavior about Mrs. Middleton's going to Philadelphia. He was seventy-four years old.

To Mrs. Fisher, Philadelphia

M.P. May 19$\underline{th}$ 1844

I begin this my dearest Eliza very uncertain when it can be despatched, but it may be sent in a day or two without notice being given me more than half an hour of the departure of the Ser$\underline{t}$ so that I will not delay telling you of the pleasure I had on receiving y$\underline{r}$ letter of the 1$\underline{st}$ & 2$\underline{d}$ on the 12$\underline{th}$. since that, no messenger has arrived, & as I wrote you word y$\underline{r}$ Father & W$\underline{m}$ went to Combahee on the 13$\underline{th}$ & will probably return tomorrow. I was glad to learn that the Children had only a <u>slight</u> fever, & was amused to read your account of your new mode of managing them. I daresay they will soon improve in consequence of it,[1] & are at this period no doubt enjoying themselves greatly on the Farm– I was surprised to read that you were not to go there until the 13$\underline{th}$ but the delay was I suppose because the house was not ready for your reception. You do not mention whether M$\underline{rs}$ Fisher was to accompany you. She was as usual very kind in arranging matters & saving you trouble which had you persisted in might have had serious consequences. She ought to spend the fortnight with you, for she would feel very solitary if left alone in the town house, & the change of Air too would I daresay prove beneficial to her. You say that the heat at Phil$\underline{a}$ was bearable– I mentioned in my last how dreadful it was here, but for the last week it has been still greater– what do you think of the ther$\underline{r}$ rising every morn$\underline{g}$ at 8 o'clock to 80$\underline{o}$ & in the afternoon to 90$\underline{o}$! & upwards. it is the hottest weather in May that I have ever felt in Carolina– the nights too are most uncomfortable. I am wrong to complain of heat when I and the family are well– I often accuse myself of this– But what think you of Cath$\underline{e}$ insisting upon having 3 blankets on her bed & declaring that she does not feel hot. Arthur says that it is in consequence of her disease. Here is little Benti running about naked, which he does frequently in the middle of the day.

It will I am sure distress you as it does me, to know that I am not to be with you at Philad$\underline{a}$ the end of June. when I asked y$\underline{r}$ Father whether M$\underline{rs}$ Sumner's report you mentioned was as he intended,[2] he said <u>no</u>, & that I was to go with the family to Newport– & on my mentioning that I had told you he had consented to my going, to Phil$\underline{a}$ as Sally told me he had, & that I had requested you to engage a room for me next door to you, he said positively that it should not be done. So you may suppose what a disappointment this is to me! He says I am not fit to attend to you, that I should leave you in a draught of Air, instead of taking care of you & added all sorts of objections to my entreaties. It was in vain that I reminded him how short a visit you were to make at Newport & what a disappointment his refusal caused. I do not pretend to be as prudent in regard to taking care of you my dear Child as Mrs Fisher & Mrs Smith & Mrs Harrison– but the comfort of being with you I have been looking forward to, & on the denial must now endeavour to console myself & reflect that perhaps you may consent to remain with me until the middle of Octr at Newport: you used to stay until that time, & why should you not this year?

I am delighted to hear so good an account as Dr Jackson gives of your throat. The account you give of poor M^r & Mrs Burd's affliction is very distress-ing– they are indeed greatly to be pitied. There have been so many sad deaths of young people of your acquaintance that in my opinion Philad^a cannot be a healthy climate. Paolina would not believe that Miss Scott intended to enter the convent as you mentioned, but 10 days ago received a letter from her from the convent, & she told her it was her intention to remain there all her life. P. & Arthur are glad to learn so favourable an account of Miss R[ebecca] Smith. & I am glad to hear that M^{rs} S[mith] is in good spirits, that is a sign of her being in good health– will she go to Newport this summer? And Harry, what is he going to do? & will he go there? of course he has given up his intention of coming here. This will be a very busy week for me– the Schooner is here & is to carry all the baggage to Charleston y^r Father said we were to go there also this week.

Monday after Sunset– It is just as I supposed– Y^r Father & W^m came today, & he has just determined to send Jack tomorrow to Cha^n & make him return in the even^g when I hope he will bring me a letter from You. I asked him whether he had anything to say to you & whether he was going to Wash^n. He said no & seemed so annoyed at my asking him any questions that I said no more. Paolina is anxious to go to Town to see Susan & will go probably in a day or two & we shall go I suppose two days after her. I can scarcely see to write as you may perceive by my scrawl– With love to M^r & Mrs Fisher & Harry believe me my dearest Eliza y^r affect^{te} Mother M. H. M.

PHi

1. Eliza had told her mother that she and Fisher "had a serious consultation on the subject of managing them last night, & determined to be more strict with them henceforward– We began by giving them each a spanking this very morng– when they cried for nothing– & the good effects of this discipline are already visible & I hope soon to get them in good training– It is astonishing how soon the little monkies take advan-tage of any relaxation of discipline– & it is so hard to punish them when they are really sick– & consequently peevish." EMF to MHM, April 30, 1844, private collection.

2. Mrs. Sumner had reported that the Middletons were to go north earlier than usual.

∼

To Mrs. Middleton, Middleton Place

At The Farm House
Saturday afternoon May 25$\underline{th}$ [1844]

Here we are established at last, my dearest Mamma, & very comfortable, I assure you, altho' not as much so as we shall be, after getting rid of the carpenters & work people who are still about– We came out on Thursday after an early dinner, & found everything ready for us– even the beds made up, & nothing to do but <u>turn in</u> after tea– M$\underline{rs}$ F. had come out thro' the rain on Monday with Louisa & Hetty, & arranged all to her own satisfaction, & therefore you may be sure to mine–¹ Wednesday had been so cold, that M$\underline{r}$ & M$\underline{rs}$ H. put their veto upon our taking possession on that day, & it was well we waited, for the weather became very pleasant indeed the next day & the change from the carpeted town house, to the mats & bare floors, w$\underline{d}$ have been too sudden on a chilly day– We have now summer again, & a thunderstorm this afternoon has not yet cooled the air much– But I do not complain of the heat, as you might feel disposed to do, for I am sure this warm dry air suits me admirably– & my throat feels all the better for it– Fisher thinks that a <u>good hot</u> summer spent here, w$\underline{d}$ cure it entirely– I think it indeed very likely that I shall have an opportunity of trying it fairly this year– & the experiment may be worth making– I hoped M$\underline{rs}$ F. would have come out to spend the day with us, & looked forward to her visit with the more pleasure, as I expected her to bring a letter from you– She probably was too busy directing the house cleaning, or Aunt Hetty [Fisher,] with whom she was to have come, may not have been able to perform her promise– so our young chickens & green pease were prepared for them in vain–

Fisher begs I will not give you too favourable a picture of our rural retreat, lest you should form an idea of something like an English Cottage– our Farm is not so picturesque certainly– but already the results of his taste are becoming visible & there are many others which can only be accomplished with time, labour & patience– Meanwhile it is pleasant to be <u>improving</u> daily– & to imagine how differently every thing will look hereafter– The principal cause of regret is that we cannot get grass to grow in a day or a week– & it will be <u>several</u> weeks I fear, before our <u>lawn</u> assumes the appearance of one– as the ground is only now prepared to receive the seed <u>to be</u> sown. You suppose me walking about grounds– which amused us much– for we have but <u>half an acre</u> in front laid out with a few shrubs & flower beds & at the back of the house a <u>kitchen garden</u> which another year shall be transplanted elsewhere. The great advantage for Fisher is that there is so much to be done– & he may have full employment for years even around the present humble dwelling– The <u>future one</u>, which has been talked of, as to <u>be built</u>, will remain <u>in the air</u> for years to come proba- bly– for Fisher finds the expenses of repairing & enlarging this rather difficult to meet at present– & he is quite worried at being for the first time in his life in debt– He need not be however, for Mr H. will be a very patient creditor–

Sunday afternoon– As Fisher goes to town very early tomorrow morng– I must finish this for him to take or another opportuity may not occur for some days– We expect several of our friends to come & spend the day with us to be sure, but I will not count too securely upon their fulfilling their promises– Harry was to go on to Balt^c the very day we left town– to pay a short visit to Mrs Harper, who invited him to go before she left town for the Springs near Winchester, where she was to spend 4 or 5 weeks for her health– the waters being recommended by her Physician– He expected to return on Saturday, but I daresay the widow will manage to keep him longer– Next week we hope he will come & pass a day or two with us– at present we have no spare room to offer him– The very day after I wrote to Edward, I heard that his Ship had dropped down, & was to sail in about a week– His letters will still be forwarded to him & I may get an anwer I hope– but of course shall not see him before the Autumn, when they are expected to return–

After directing to M. Place, I remember that you have probably left it by this time, or will have done so when this arrives in Charleston– & y^r next will I hope tell me when you will be likely to leave Carolina– I suppose I need scarcely expect to see you in Phil^a before the 10th of next month, by which time I shall be re-established in Chesnut S^t. But altho' I shall be afraid to remain a night out here after that, I hope to come out & spend the day frequently– & to bring you with me, & send the children by the <u>Omnibus</u> which comes out twice a day– Fisher expects tomorrow to exchange his <u>pleasure carriage</u>, as the Farmer from whom he bought it called it, (who by the bye cheated him most completely in all the <u>Stock</u>) for a much lighter & nicer one– which he can more conveniently drive with <u>one</u> horse– which is at present as much as he can afford to buy– & keep besides the 5 on the farm– The one he has just bought is, it is to be hoped, a better bargain than many others in which he has been taken in– He pulled us to <u>Oxford</u> Church[2] this morng– at a good pace, notwithstand- ing the excessive heat– which reminds one of August– We were induced to go this distance to hear the Bishop who preached admirably as usual– The text,

"The Eternal Spirit" appropriate to the day– There was quite a crowded congregation for the country & a highly respectable one apparently– The old Church w<u>d</u> be quite picturesque if built of stone instead of brick– & the interior reminds me of the one at Heybridge– I must say goodnight my dearest Mamma With love to all around you I am as ever Y<u>r</u> most affectionate daughter Eliza– Fisher begs his kind regards

Private Collection

1. Eliza was of two minds about Mrs. Fisher's help. Earlier she told her mother that Mrs. Fisher "will not be satisfied unless I let her have her own way I suppose." EMF to MHM, April 30 [1844,] private collection.

2. Although it is now within the Philadelphia city limits, Trinity Oxford Church was in the country in the 1840s. Fisher and Eliza often attended church there and are buried in the church graveyard, along with several other members of the family, including Mrs. Middleton and Eliza's sister, Catherine.

Heybridge, near Maldon, Essex, was where Eliza's uncle Oliver Hering lived at the time Eliza and Catherine were in school in England.

∼

The Middletons sailed on May 31 for New York on the same ship as Lizzie Middleton and Emma Smith, carrying with them Harry's "box of summer clothes which he always sends [*to Newport*] & sends back to Charleston, in the Autumn."[1] Mrs. Middleton still did not know if she would be able to go to Philadelphia to be with Eliza.

1. MHM to EMF, May 26, 1844, PHi.

To Mrs. Middleton, Carlton Hotel, New York

Philadelphia June 12<u>th</u> [1844] Wednesday morng.

My dearest Mamma,

Harry has just brought me your letter of yesterday to read, which I have begged him to let me answer, as I indeed intended writing before I read it– He has consented to go on to N.Y. by the early line tomorrow morng & take care of Pauline & Kitty in Arthur's absence– but there is <u>one other</u> arrangement which he joins me in urging you to make– which is that instead of preparing to go to New Port tomorrow, you will pack y<u>r</u> trunk for Phil<u>a</u> & accompany Arthur here by the 5 o'clk afternoon train– Your room will be all ready for you <u>here</u>– next to mine– & I must <u>insist</u> upon your coming to me– dearest Mamma do not refuse me this request– for I have set my heart upon it & you will not I know deny me– for I shall take upon me the sole responsibility– & am very sure that Papa will forgive me for doing so– Harry agrees with me that he <u>can</u> make no objection to y<u>r</u> coming to be under the roof with me– & that he & Pauline can take very good care of Kitty– & M<u>r</u> and M<u>rs</u> Harrison, M<u>rs</u> Fisher, & Fisher & M<u>rs</u> Smith <u>all</u> give their opinion to the same effect, & approve entirely of my plan for you– So that <u>indeed</u> you must consent to gratify me this once– & yield to the united wishes & authority of so many friends– Your being in the next room to me will not put any one to the slightest inconvenience– I do not expect to have the old woman [*Mrs. Waters*] with me before the end of the month– & whenever she is called in, she will have a cot bed in my room–

I hope Arthur will be in no hurry to return from Washington– or if he should be, Harry will at any time be glad to come on for you & take you to New Port, whenever it is <u>necessary</u> for you to be there– At present it surely <u>cannot</u> be– & Pauline can very well supply y<u>r</u> place– now that you have engaged y<u>r</u> serv<u>ts</u> & made all y<u>r</u> arrangements– Every body predicts a very cool summer, & I am sure you will not suffer with the heat, unless it encreases in an extraordinary degree– So that I hope you will at least stay with me until I am safely out of my "pains & perils"– If you knew how unhappy the idea of not seeing you before <u>Sept<u>r</u></u> has made me, & how I have been <u>weeping</u> the last two days at the disappointment of not having you with me, you w<u>d</u> not hesitate to disobey orders for my sake– do not fear Papa's displeasure– for I undertake to bear the whole weight of it myself– & am perfectly convinced that he will acknowledge the reasonableness of my desire, & forgive my acting contrary to his views & consent under present circumstances– He will change them when he hears all– & I have not the least apprehension for the consequences of transgressing his commands in this instance– Nor need you have– So pray put yourself entirely under <u>my</u> command– I shall see you so soon that I will now say no more– except to add best love to Arthur, Pauline, Kitty, & Emma– We are all quite well– M<u>rs</u> F. wishes to have the corners–[1]
Ever Y<u>r</u> most affect<u>e</u> daughter Eliza

Private Collection

1. Mrs. Fisher added the following: "My d<u>r</u> Madam– I have requested our dear Eliza to leave me a small space that I might write my entreaties with hers that you consent to come to us tomorrow– Indeed I think it absolutely necessary she should have you with her & when I assure you it will afford us a real gratification to welcome you to our house I am sure you will not refuse– She has become quite nervous & this must not be suffered to increase & y<u>r</u> presence I do believe will have the happy effect of dispelling most if not all of her present anxiety– Do not hesitate d<u>r</u> M<u>rs</u> M to come to y<u>r</u> d<u>r</u> daughter & oblige yr friend E. P. Fisher."

～

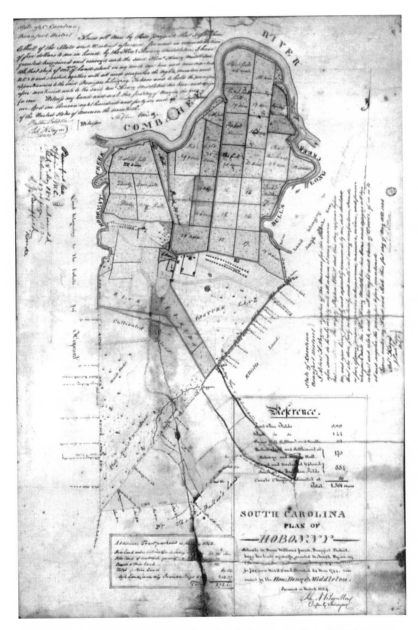

Hobonny, one of three rice-growing plantations belonging to Henry Middleton on the Combahee River, as it was in 1834. Rice fields and irrigation ditches are near the river, cultivated uplands and pasture are farther back. Two rows of slaves' cabins are behind the fields labeled 15 and 17 (acres). Courtesy of Benjamin C. Chapman.

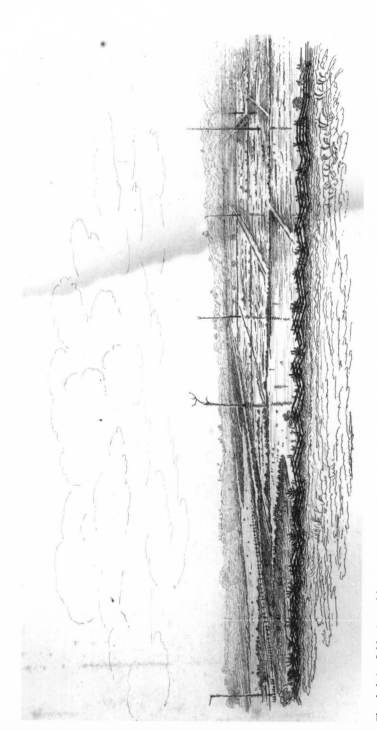

Flooded rice fields. One of few pre-1850 views illustrating rice culture. By Basil Hall, 1820s. Courtesy of the South Caroliniana Library, University of South Carolina.

"Trunks" made of cypress beams controlled water flow in and out of the rice fields at Nieuport, a Middleton plantation on the Combahee River (no date). Courtesy of the Charleston Museum.

Rice plants, irrigation canals, and the extensive fields often cultivated on large rice plantations can all be seen in this photograph of Creighton Plantation, Pon Pon River (no date). Courtesy of the Charleston Museum.

Railroad cars such as the Middletons and Fishers would have traveled in. By A. Kollner, circa 1855. Courtesy of the Library Company of Philadelphia.

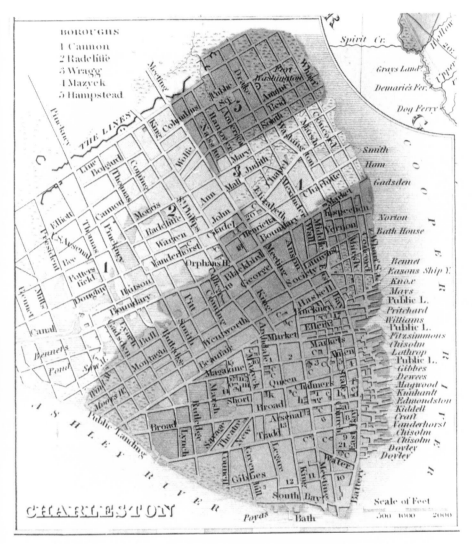

Charleston in 1841. The house occupied by the Middletons was on the northwest corner of Boundary and Smith Streets. Inset from Henry S. Tanner's map of South Carolina. Courtesy of the South Caroliniana Library, University of South Carolina.

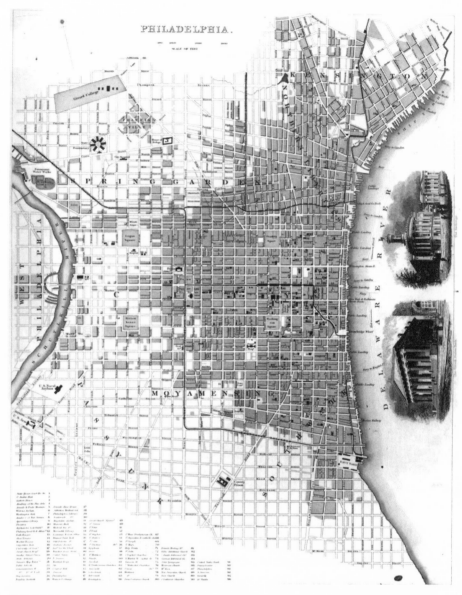

Philadelphia in 1840, showing undeveloped land near the Schuylkill River. The Fairmount Waterworks, where Eliza sometimes drove the children, is at the upper left. Courtesy of the Library Company of Philadelphia.

To Mrs. Fisher, Philadelphia

Carlton house Thursday, 11 o'clock [June 13, 1844]

My dearest Eliza

Your letter rec^d at 9 o'clock gave me so much pleasure & made me look forward to so much happiness in seeing you that I determined after thinking how much I should be scolded for disobedience &c that as you would take upon yourself the sole responsibility, & when I reflected on the kindness of Mrs Fisher in inviting me to her house, all this, & Arthur & Paolina saying that they thought I might venture to go to Phil^a I immediately began to make the necessary arrangements, speak to the Servants on the subject, & giving directions about what they were to do. I sent for Arthur to know when he intended to go to Wash^n. He said he could not until he had an answer from Genl Van Ness– and that he had been thinking about my intention of going to Phil^a & it was now his opinion that I ought not to be with you as his Father had often said to him as he did to me, I was not a proper person to attend to one in your situation, sitting with you in draughts of air, & all sorts of objections, although I reminded him that during your first confinement nothing could be said to accuse me of doing you any injury & that he ought to reflect upon the short visit you would make us at Newport– all this I mentioned to A^r. He too said I was so nervous that my feelings at the time of your confinement might have a serious effect upon you, & that I ought not to be with you particularly as your Father had positively refused my entreaties on the subject– This was indeed a sad change of opinion to give me– It affected me more than I can express, I urged the distress it w^d bring on both of us, but he still repeated your Father's orders & said that he would blame me, if you should have a worse time than with the two others, & say that it was owing to my want of care of you– that I am sure y^r Father w^d say.

And now my dearest Eliza judge from your own feeling what mine is! but do not distress yourself I entreat you– The kindest friends are near you. Mrs Fisher will I am sure be the kindest of Mothers to you, Mrs H., Mrs Smith too will do all they can to comfort & nurse you & God grant that you may soon get over the painful event! One hope comes to my mind– Y^r Father may pass through Phil^a. He may consent to my being with you when he sees how uneasy my absence makes you– if he does, I will joyfully make you the visit & beg Harry to take me to Phil^a but this is not probable.

Pray give my love to Mrs Fisher & assure her that I feel very grateful for her great kindness in offering me a room in her house where I am always so happy. A sad time I shall spend at Newport until you are there– but why do you say Sept^r? You said before you w^d be with me the beginning of August & why should you defer the visit? Let me look forward to that time, when by the blessing of God I may embrace my dearest Child! believe me y^r Affectionate Mother M. H. M.

I must tell you that it is very uncertain when Arthur can go to Wash^n. Congress is to adjourn on the 15th but he has other business to attend to there respecting Gen V. so that he does not yet know when he shall see you at Phil^a. Pray write very soon, & tell me particularly how you are.

Eve^g– I thought it best to see Harry before I sent this off & to my surprise he arrived at 2 o'clock & to my great satisfaction gave a good account of my dearest Eliza & said that he thought y^r Father might forgive me & we both talked over the matter– at last I made up my mind to go if Arthur c^d take me tomorrow– Just now we have been talking over the plan but <u>he</u> says he is sure his father will greatly disapprove of my being with you & will ask him whether he did not hear him say that I sh^d on no account be near you, as I should make you ill, & all sorts of objections which are really cruel to both of us. So again I must give up what I had hoped to be able to do.

About 1 o'clock the Ser[van]t John came to inform me that on going to the Wharf to put the baggage on board he was told that the Rhode Is^d Steamer was not to go to Newport until tomorrow, in consequence of an accident having happened to the other Steamer, it was sent yesterday to bring it in. I was very glad of the delay as it gave me time to determine about my movements– but what distressing reflections are continually passing through my mind! Pray my dearest Eliza do not be unhappy on the disappointment– You have every thing around you to make you happy– & perhaps if you sh^d see y^r Father he may consent to my going to you–

PHi

⁓

To Mrs. Middleton, Carlton Hotel, New York

Philadelphia – Friday eveng 14th [June 1844]

I have only just waited to compose myself a little after reading y^r letter of yesterday, my dearest Mamma, which has distressed me extremely, but which I can by no means allow to remain unanswered long– my first impulse was to write to Arthur, but I am really afraid I should scold him so much that I refrain from doing so, thinking that my anger, which he has excited by his unreasonable opposition w$^{\underline{d}}$ not have the effect upon him that entreaties made thro' you may– I cannot imagine what induces this sudden fear of displeasing his Father– to whom he has not always shewn this implicit obedience– I flatter myself that I have generally shewn a regard for his wishes, & I have few acts of disobedience towards him to accuse myself of– but in this instance I charge myself with the whole blame if need should be, & shall be ready to answer for it, & exonerate others entirely from any share of it.

Pray remind Arthur that we two are certainly the persons most interested in the case, & that he ought not to interfere with our happiness in so cruel a manner– I always thought him amiable & obliging but I shall have reason to change my opinion of his character, if he persists in his opposition– I have not the least doubt that I should prevail with Papa to give his consent to y$^{\underline{r}}$ coming, but unfortunately there is so much uncertainty as to his movements, that I should not know whether to write to Charleston, Wash$^{\underline{n}}$ or N.Y.– should he pass thro' Phi$^{\underline{la}}$ you may be sure I shall arrange it to my satisfaction– I am thankful at least that there is little probability of y$^{\underline{r}}$ leaving N.Y. for some days– Harry I know wished to be there some [time,] & Arthur will hardly think it worth while to go on to N.P. & return immediately– So that I trust this will find you at the Carlton, & that Arthur will consent to bring you on to me on Monday– Should he still object, just tell Harry to remember his promise to me & that I count upon his performing it– I must repeat that there is scarcely any chance of our being able to go to New Port in August– which Papa did not know, when he refused his consent to y$^{\underline{r}}$ coming to me, & which I am sure w$^{\underline{d}}$ have changed his views– Neither am I by any means sure that I shall have permission to go there at all– for it must depend upon the state of my throat &c & various other reasons & therefore y$^{\underline{r}}$ visit to me becomes of the utmost importance & it will injure my health a thousand times more to prevent than to promote it– How absurd too to say that any want of care of y$^{\underline{r}}$ part w$^{\underline{d}}$ lead to ill consequences. I do not ask you to come & nurse me, but I want the comfort of y$^{\underline{r}}$ society for the next 2 weeks, & after that the mere consciousness of y$^{\underline{r}}$ presence in my chamber will do me good– There are I know others to take good care of me, & be very kind to [me] but it is not the same thing at all as having you near me, & no one can supply a mother's place–

As to y$^{\underline{r}}$ being Nervous &c– how was it before? We are surely both as well able to go thro' the scene together now as then– & all the other objections are equally absurd & unreasonable– I can understand Papa's objecting to y$^{\underline{r}}$ going to a miserable boarding house, but it alters the case materially that you sh$^{\underline{d}}$ be under our own roof– & this I know Papa w$^{\underline{d}}$ acknowledge– In fact I am convinced that he w$^{\underline{d}}$ now retract, & could he be made aware of the various reasons I have urged & others which I have neither time nor space to write them in, he would no longer withhold his approbation of my plan– I therefore beg of you, dearest Mamma, to assert y^r independence for once, & if Arthur still refuses to accompany you, apply to Harry who, after agreeing with me in all my arguments will not draw back & side against me–

We sat up for you until past eleven last night & waited dinner for you today– & on Monday I trust shall not be again disappointed– Pray take Emma's advice– She I am sure will take my part, & perhaps exert her eloquence on her obstinate cousin to induce him to accede to our wishes– I can say no more at present than that we are all quite well– but Fisher & his Mother both think Arthur very wrong to follow his father's orders so literally & say that at least he might consent to y^r coming on with him, if he did not choose to advise yr disobedience– as I do most strongly– Pray, pray come dearest Mamma–

Private Collection

⌒

Mrs. Middleton went on, reluctantly, to Newport. Once her father got to Philadelphia, Eliza was able to arrange her mother's return, as she was sure she would be, so Mrs. Middleton turned around and went back to Philadelphia. She finally reached there on July 2, one day after Eliza had her baby. It was a girl, named Mary Helen after her grandmother. Fisher and his mother were of course disappointed at not having a boy, but Mrs. Middleton told Susan that Eliza "thinks you will agree with her that three daughters are not too many for a Mother's comfort."[1]

Thankful for Eliza's safe delivery, Emma Smith, who was in Newport, urged her to "take the pleasure of my Aunt's society, & don't let her fancy a speedy return necessary." Everyone in Newport was getting along fine, she said. "Paolina seems to keep house very nicely, & the occupation makes her happier than I ever saw her– it has a good effect even upon her health, according to her own acct–"[2]

But Mrs. Middleton stayed in the broiling summer heat of Philadelphia for only two weeks. "I am constantly thinking," she told Eliza when she got back to Newport, "of the happy days I spent with you, the kindness & hospitality of Mrs Fisher, the amusement of the children, & the healthy & improving appearance of the babe."[3]

1. MHM to Susan Middleton, July 3, 1844, ScHi.
2. EHS to EMF, July 13, 1844 , PHi.
3. MHM to EMF, July 17, 1844, PHi.

To Mrs. Middleton, Newport

Tuesday eveng– [June] 25$\underline{th}$ [1844]

After many disappointments, I have had at last the pleasure of seeing Papa & W$\underline{m}$ this afternoon, & I hasten to announce their arrival to you, dearest Mamma, & to give you the consent which I was sure Papa w$\underline{d}$ not withhold an instant– He laughed at the idea of his being <u>angry</u> at y$\underline{r}$ coming on– and I am more provoked than ever with Arthur for his interference– I told M$\underline{rs}$ Powel that I sh$\underline{d}$ give her a few lines to carry to you, & hope she will not neglect to send them up to you <u>early</u>– so that if you can come off on Thursday afternoon you may have time to make that arrangement– I am perhaps <u>counting without my host</u> for if Harry did not make any exertion to bring you from N.Y. he will be less likely to do so from New Port– but I hope for the best– & you may hear of some good escort to N.Y. whence, if Arthur has left it (which I have no means of ascertaining) W$\underline{m}$ could bring you on–

But altho' I am so anxious to see you dear Mamma, do not come unless you think you can bear the heat patiently– for it has now come on & I fear you may feel inconvenience from it– Papa looks wretchedly I think, and I am much shocked to find he has had a paralytic attack– He thinks travelling about better for him than anything else & says he will come back from N.Y. & see me, & bring you on if you choose– He says so much about my going to New Port in August, that I think I must try & get there, even if I have to leave the children out at The Farm– but God knows if I shall be well enough– if you do not come, I <u>must</u> see you before Sept$\underline{r}$.

It is past eleven, & I am so much fatigued, not having been able to lie down all day, that I must now go to bed– & send this over early tomorrow morng– to M$\underline{rs}$ Powel–

I hope to keep out of my bed until Saturday, & you <u>may</u> arrive on Friday– but you must decide whether you can bear the confinement to a sick room in July– I shall try to bear the disappointment if you decide not to come. The children are better but not quite well– I am quite <u>stout</u>– as they say– Goodnight, Fisher [has blown] out my candle– so Adieu! [*words missing*] Eliza

Private Collection

∼

After the baby, Mary Helen, was born, Eliza did not recover her strength as quickly as she had with her first two children, and her throat continued to bother

her. After a "painful struggle," she therefore agreed to accept her doctor's advice that she should not go to Newport.[1] The news that for the first time in more than ten years Eliza would not be there was a "sad disappointment" to her mother. "My dearest Eliza," she wrote, "the comfort of your society . . . has always been my chief happiness."

Eliza's absence, however, led Mrs. Middleton to send her fuller descriptions than she would normally have done of what was going on at Newport. Emma Huger Smith and her sister, Eliza, were there. So were Clark and Esther Hare and the Wilcockses from Philadelphia, the Harpers, and DeRhams. It was an added pleasure to see several people she had not seen since the years she spent in Washington.

"Crowds of boarders" filled Whitfield's and the new Ocean House hotel, although Emma reported that the lodgers did not get enough to eat at the Ocean House. "There are no pretty Girls here that I have seen," Eliza's mother said, but among the items she thought worth mentioning were dances, "constantly given at the hotels," a band, a public ball, and a new fad—the polka.[2]

1. EMF to MHM, July 20, [1844,] private collection.
2. MHM to EMF, July 25 and August 11, 1844, PHi.

To Mrs. Fisher, Philadelphia

Newport July 31$\underline{st}$ 1844

I have been much disappointed my dearest Eliza by not receiving a letter from you today having supposed that as you wrote on Sunday the 21$\underline{st}$ you would write again on the 28$\underline{th}$ according to your usual custom. You gave so favourable an account of yourself that I must not fear that illness prevents you from writing, & must anticipate the pleasure of hearing from you tomorrow, but as the post will arrive then not before 2 o'Clock (as it does every other day), there would be no time to write & answer a long letter so that it is better to begin this now, & tell you that all your acquaintances enquire about you particularly– this morn$\underline{g}$ M$\underline{rs}$ McLeod & Miss Inglis– with them came three [*McLeod*] daughters all invited by Arthur to come at 10 o'clock to teach & dance the fashionable dance the Polka which Kate M$\underline{c}$Leod was taught at Paris lately– the airs are extremely pretty, & the dance (Bohemian) something like a Waltz & Mazourka. Miss Grattan[1] also was taught, Will$\underline{m}$ & a M$\underline{r}$ Gilmor– Arthur had danced it abroad & the party amused themselves with it for an hour & half.[2] M$\underline{rs}$ M$\underline{c}$L$\underline{d}$ played the airs & so did Cath$\underline{e}$ while the former went to see whether the Calderons had arrived– they have taken a Cottage (Sher-mans) on the second Street near our house, but the C's have not come today.

Arthur Rutledge came yesterday from Boston & dined with us– he said nothing about the music that you mentioned having sent by him. he left M^r [Francis] Fogg[3] & his daughter there, & they will be here in a week. Miss R[ut-ledge] is going to Scoolly's (I know not how to spell it) Mountain[4] with her nieces. I have had a visit from M^r & Mrs Wilcocks & Miss [Mary] Waln & M^{rs} & Miss Randolph. Mr W. seemed so delighted with his child, that he brought her from the carriage to shew her to me. She is really a pretty little creature. Mrs J. Butler too & Miss Cox called yesterday, & a few even^{gs} ago M^r & M^{rs} C[lark] Hare. Emma is now looking very well, & I begged her to write to you which she said she had lately. M^r & Mrs Grattan who I have become acquainted with are very agreeable people & they are greatly pleased with the [William Mason] Smiths their fellow lodgers at Whitfield's– Poor Mary Jones is still so unhappy[5] that she never receives any visitors except her intimate friends the McLeods & Inglis'. She rides on horseback early in the morning– they say they endeavour to persuade her to associate with her acquaintances, but as yet she remains still in her own room. Miss Harper has at last arrived, not very well, but better than when she landed.

Augt 4th At length my dearest Eliza y^r letter of the 31st ult^o was brought to me yesterday Eve^g. I had been expecting to hear from you since I began this, & had not Oliver assured me you were well should have feared that were not the case– You assure me at the end of y^r letter that y^r pain in y^r back was better– but how imprudent you were to exert yourself by unpacking, as your brother says was the cause of it. I imagined from y^r saying you had been stoop-ing, that weeding & planting flowers had occasioned it– & your eyes too! you ought to be particularly careful of them & never read while lying down. I was surprised to learn that the infant was not quite well, as she seemd so healthy, but surely your milk cannot disagree with her. As long as you have no symptoms of weakness you ought to continue to nurse her– I will tell Mrs Sumner what you mention on the subject of a nurse.[6] Oliver thinks the babe very pretty. he told me you had not rec^d my letter of the 25th when he left you, which I could not account for. I hope that in future you will write as you used to do, once a week.

I read to Arthur this morn^g what you wrote about his & P's visit, & I shall shew *her* too, what you say on the subject– he cannot say at present when he can be at Phil^a– Arthur Rutledge sent the parcel of Music for Cath^e the day after he came– she is much pleased with it & thanks you for it. The two Polkas she had been playing some days before, as Miss Cottenet lent them to Arthur, who is giving lessons daily to several young girls, as are also the Miss McLeods–

Mrs Calderon arrived on Friday, & returned my visit yesterday– She is looking well, & in good spirits & enquired particularly about you, & I shall deliver y^r message to her. Mr C. is at point Comfort where the President is,[7] but will be here in a few days. Except their society & the Smiths, I know of none that it would interest you to hear about. The Harpers have all been unwell but are now better. M^rs [John Hare] Powell called with her daughter in Law some days ago I told her how much pleased I had been with her country house [*Powelton,*] but she seemed as discontented with it as usual. Mrs Lewis[8] has gone to Virginia, having heard that her Daughter was in bad health.

I read to y^r Father what you wrote enquiring after his health & begged him to tell me how he felt– he said he was better, & that is all the account he gives of himself. The four Girls are all in good health.[9] Sarah has heard lately from her Mother who is still suffering from her eyes, & is not going to Athens [*Georgia*] which I am sorry for. We read prayers together this morning, & Mary very kindly asked me whether she should read aloud to me any book I chose– They all beg to send their love to you. I must not forget to tell you that the Cassellas arrived a few days ago, & not being able to find a room at any of the hotels, went to Mrs Harpers to inform her of it, who very kindly received Mme C. into a room for that night, & since that, they are at the new hotel. Mrs H. offers her to go every day to play on the Piano in one room, & her husband in another for the Violoncello. I have not yet seen them. He called yesterday & y^r brothers received him. We have had fogs & rain for several days, which last was much wanted– You mention rain, but I suppose the dampness of your climate does not injure you as this would. I have never heard of the novel you mention.[10] I am glad to learn that the last news you had of Mr Harrison was better than the former. Pray remember me to him & Mrs H. & with love to M^r & Mrs Fisher believe me my dearest Eliza y^r Affect^te Mother

All the family send their love. Paolina has read y^r letter & begs me to tell you she will soon write to you. She thinks that Emma Smith cannot make you a visit because she never leaves N.Y. before Nov^r & you will not remain at y^r Farm I suppose so late as that month– As for my visit I cannot say when I shall be permitted to make it. Kiss the darlings for me–

Monday Morn^g– You will be glad to hear that the Cassellas are to give a Concert this Eve^g at the new hotel, all this family are going to it, & Paol^a & Willm have been recommending them to their acquaintances– Arthur has again asked the McLeods & Mme Calderon to come this morn^g to teach the Girls the Polka.

PHi

    1. Miss Grattan was the daughter of Thomas Grattan, the British consul in Boston, 1839–46. Her parents are mentioned in the next paragraph.

    2. "You would be amused to see Benti dance this popular dance," Mrs. Middleton told Eliza. "He keeps very good time, & imitates the steps wonderfully for such an infant. Lilly & Sophy would no doubt soon learn the dance." MHM to EMF, August 11, 1844, PHi.

    3. Francis B. Fogg married Arthur Rutledge's sister Mary.

    4. Schooley's Mountain in New Jersey.

    5. Mary Jones may still have been mourning her mother's death a year before.

    6. Mrs. Sumner had offered to help find a wet nurse, if one was needed, but Eliza hoped it would not be.

    7. Mr. Calderon had been appointed Spanish ambassador to the United States. President Tyler was at Old Point Comfort, near Hampton, Virginia.

    8. Mrs. Lewis, the former Eleanor (Nelly) Parke Custis (1779–1852), was Martha Washington's granddaughter. Mrs. Middleton had known her in earlier years.

    9. These were the four Middleton granddaughters who were at school at the Priory. They were spending their vacation with the Middletons in Newport.

    10. Mrs. Fisher was reading Benjamin Disraeli's new novel, *Coningsby*.

～

To Mrs. Fisher, Philadelphia

Newport Augt 22.^d 1844

    I had yesterday my dearest Eliza the pleasure of receiving your letters of the 17<u>th</u> & 18<u>th</u> which was sent direct from Phil.<u>a</u> instead of Jenkinstown, that of the 8<u>th</u> came on the 16<u>th</u>, the day after I sent my last. I thank God that my fears for you were ungrounded, & that you are rather stronger, your throat better– but still your back aches, & you are so weak as to be obliged to be on your bed every day for an hour or two– You cannot therefore call yourself <u>well</u>– but I hope Dr Meig's pills will strengthen you very soon. Nursing the Baby 4 times a day is quite as often as you ought to do. Is Whey as nourishing as Milk?[1] I never before heard of giving it to infants, but I daresay Mrs Waters was right in giving it, being so experienced in her care of children. It was good news that you were expecting Mrs Harrison, as she would not have left Mr H. if he had not been well. So Mrs Smith has not yet seen or heard from the worthless man she is expecting! I wish she could come here to enjoy this fine climate. Her visits to you will I hope improve her health, although they are so short. Miss Gilpin's visit must have been very agreeable to you, & you will now be more intimate than usual I suppose, & have another visit from her. Have you thought of her as a Godmother for little M[ary] H[elen]? when is she to be Christened & when vaccinated? I have lately seen M⁗ Hare who called here. She is looking better than she did last year. I thanked her for having forwarded my letter to Edward, & a few days after M⁗ Channing wrote to me to say that M⁗ H. would have a letter forwarded to the Mediterranean if I would send it to M⁗ C[lark] Hare–² this was very kind, & I profited by her offer, & wrote again to Edward giving a good account of you, & all the news I could collect– that was trifling enough, & what I tell you is equally so–

What do you think of William's plan which your Father consented to execute– to take away the folding doors in the drawing rooms & make only one? This has given a great deal of trouble, turned us all out of the room for the last 4 days, & when the weather becomes cold, will prevent us from making the room warmer. It has certainly improved the appearance of the room, & the ceiling has been whitewashed which as you may remember was very dirty– Elizabeth³ has been sewing the Carpet together & working over the joins, but that is not yet finished–

We have been sitting in the eve⁅g⁆ in the little library, those only who are at home, for your Brothers Arthur, H. & W. are generally out at parties, & now the subject of conversation is a fancy ball, to be given next Tuesday at the Ocean Hotel– Emma was very desirous of wearing Edward's Greek dress, but W. told her it was not proper for her, & that he intended to wear it himself. It was not to be found for some days, but luckily he found it today in Edward's trunk. Arthur is now trying on the dress he wore last summer & perhaps Paolina will be persuaded to go to the ball, although she says it would give her much trouble, & as she cannot dance she should have no pleasure there.⁴ H. & even Oliver are preparing dresses for the occasion– The general occupation is making becoming fancy dresses.⁵ I have not seen M⁗ Calderon & the M⁗ Leods since I wrote last but will deliver your message to her when I do– Emma said last Sunday she had written to you three days before. Mary begs me to give you her best love & to say that your letter when at School will be very acceptable, & all the Girls are delighted at the thoughts of being with you at Xmas, but they think the party is too large to be convenient to you & M⁗ Fisher– indeed I cannot imagine how you can conveniently receive them.

Did you write as you intended to your Aunt the end of July? Y⁗ uncle was delighted to learn of your safety & going on so well from the letter I wrote to him the day I left you at N.Y. & finishing it the next here. He thinks the farm must be a great relief to you & M⁗ F from the disturbed state of Phil⁗.⁶ I hope you told M⁗ Fisher how much obliged to her I felt on receiving her letter. pray give my love to her– She does not make you many visits– I have often enquired about Miss Page but cannot walk far enough to see her– Y^r brothers see her sometimes but are not acquainted with her though they are with Mrs Ridgeway who they admire very much– I must now finish this. All the family send their love to you & I am my dearest Eliza y^r affectionate Mother M. H. M.

Kiss the Children for me. how are M^r F's Eyes? W^m without consulting me has invited a large party for next Saturday Eve^g & supper.[7]

PHi

1. Mrs. Waters had suggested changing to whey from rice flour gruel. EMF to MHM, August 17, 1844, private collection.
2. Mrs. Hare was able to forward letters to Edward via her son, Harrison, who was also in the navy.
3. Elizabeth was Catherine's companion.
4. Paolina was expecting her second child.
5. Harry went as a brigand, and Oliver went as a domino. Sarah Middleton to Rosamund Miles Pringle, August 31, 1844, MPlFdn.
6. Uncle Oliver Hering read reports of the May and July riots in Philadelphia and wrote, "What a fright the Irish must have occasioned to [Eliza] & other peaceable inhabitants of the old quiet Quaker town. But I am glad to recollect that Kensington [*scene of the first riots*] was a long distance from Chesnut Street." MHM to EMF, June 23, 1844, PHi.
7. Mrs. Middleton overcame her annoyance with William and in her next letter to Eliza said, "Last Saturday as I told you W^m invited, & requested me & Paolina to invite above 100 people, only about 70 came however, which of course filled the rooms & they all were greatly pleased with the party– The Polka could be danced only by 6 couples because there were only 6 Gentlemen who could dance it– There were two Quadrilles & Waltzes & a vast deal of chatting, walking in the piazza, & even the Garden & soon after the Supper, 1/2 past 12, I could retire." MHM to EMF, August 29, 1844, PHi.

⌒

To Mrs. Middleton, Newport

Abington Farm Monday afternoon 26$^{\underline{th}}$ August [1844]

Altho' rather tired with all my exertions this morning, I must not lose the opportunity of perfect quiet, which does not often occur, to enable me to write to you my dearest Mamma– Aunt Harrison brought me this morng your letter of the 22$^{\underline{nd}}$ which I found a great treat as usual– for as I cannot be with you, it is at least delightful to hear pleasant news of you all– I should be quite incapable of joining in any of the gay doings which are going on around you– & do not at all regret the Fancy Ball you tell me about– the preparations for which must afford much amusement to the whole family & I suppose the girls are dressing up their Father, as they are probably not to appear themselves at it–

As to the improvement of the room, I agree with you that it will not add much to y^r comfort– & I think the alteration of the window leading into the Piazza into a door w^d have been a better arrangement, & if the object be the accomodation of the dancers they w^d probably have preferred the Piazza well lighted, to the carpeted room– As to y^r warming the room, I hope you will not stay late enough to require much fire– I begin to long for Octr that it may bring you to me–

Sometimes I flatter myself that Fisher will reward me for giving up New Port by taking me to Carolina next winter– but unfortunately the state of M^r H's health, will I fear prevent that. He was better for some days, but Aunt said this morng– he had been suffering again yesterday– His meeting with Mr Otis, who came on with Mrs Ritchie to take a final farewell of him, was a very affecting one– They were both much agitated, & found each other much altered– Being afraid of an attack of gout seizing him so far from home Mr Otis stayed only 2 days in Phil^a & Fisher just missed seeing him, to his disappointment.

Since I wrote we have had 2 more visitors– Dr Alfred Elwyn and M^r H[enry] Gilpin who each stayed a couple of days– The latter left us this morng & soon afterwards came his Sister with Aunt H– & Mrs F. who had not been out here for 4 weeks– They all spent the morng & old Mrs Morris from Germantown also made her appearance & I believe expected to have been asked to dinner, but not feeling strong enough to sit up all day, I had not the hospitality to invite her to remain– but of course we gave them all a lunch of as many good things as the Farm & town market produce– The children behaved very well, & were much caressed of course–

Lily has been in great tribulation at the idea of my going away to town without her– but is now more reconciled to my leaving her as it will be only for a day– I am going tomorrow afternoon with Fisher to see Mr H. who cannot come out to me, & is very anxious to see me & Baby– & in our little carriage there is no room for the other little girls– You have often enquired very kindly about F's eyes– & I never mention them because I have nothing favourable to say– They are much the same & he does not attempt to use them– but when the Baby sleeps Mrs Putnam reads to him– & Dr Elwyn read to him too– several amusing articles from the Reviews– The last Edin[bur]gh contains one particularly which we like very much– called The Clapham Sect–[1] giving a description of the worthies residing on or near that common– Wilberforce, Thornton, Macaulay &c all men of admirable character & the purest religious principles, which influenced their whole lives– Their zeal was sometimes without knowledge, for certainly if they had exerted themselves as much to abolish the real Slavery of their own countrymen in Eng$^{\underline{d}}$ they w$^{\underline{d}}$ have done more in the cause of Philanthropy than in writing against it in countries where it is thought so great an evil– but they were truly conscientious I believe– & now I must go & rest myself that I may feel refreshed & receive Fisher with a cheerful face when he returns from his ride– else he will be worried about me– So goodbye dearest Mamma Love to all around you from Y$^{\underline{r}}$ affecte daughter Eliza

Private Collection

1. Banker Henry Thornton, abolitionist William Wilberforce, and philanthropist and abolitionist Zachary Macaulay were among a group of prominent reformers, most of whom lived at Clapham Common near London. They were widely known for their role in bringing about the end of the slave trade and slavery in British territories.

ᕁ

To Mrs. Middleton, Newport

Philadelphia Sept$^{\underline{r}}$ 12$^{\underline{th}}$ [1844]

Having been detained here a day longer in consequence of the weather, I will not lose the opportunity of relieving y$^{\underline{r}}$ mind about me my dearest Mamma– for I am sorry to find by y$^{\underline{r}}$ last letter that you are making yrself unhappy at my indisposition– which I assure you is nothing serious, but D$^{\underline{r}}$ Meigs says entirely owing to the exhausting process of nursing– which he has so strongly urged me to discontinue, that I have taken his advice, & engaged a wetnurse he found for me– She is such a remarkably nice looking, goodhumoured person, & brings from Ireland such high recommendations, that I trust she will suit me well & make a faithful nurse for my little darling– She appears perfectly healthy, & the D$^{\underline{r}}$, after examination pronounces her <u>sound</u> in every respect, & thinks I have an excellent prospect in securing her– The only objection to her is that she has an infant of her own, 3 months old, from whom she was very reluctant to part– but she now consents to leave it under the care of her cousin– & will I hope remain several months with me– so that I shall now have a good chance of recovering my strength – by having both mind & <u>body</u> relieved– & this is all I require–

I am quite amused at y$^{\underline{r}}$ idea of sending me to Longbranch at this season– who can have put it into your head, when I was expressly forbidden to go to the sea side– I had a great deal of pleasure from Oliver's short visit, & he told me a great many particulars about you all which I was anxious to learn– Sidney Fisher too gave us much of the gossip, & to my joy announced Emma's approaching visit– I wish I could flatter myself that I sh$^{\underline{d}}$ see Papa & W$^{\underline{m}}$ before then– indeed I have a sort of feeling that they will be here by the end of this week, as Oliver said they talked of coming soon–

By the first of O$^{\underline{ctr}}$, if not earlier, I shall expect you & Kitty– & her attendant, for whom I will have a cot bed made up in her room– M$^{\underline{rs}}$ F. wrote to you yesterday– I hope you have rec$^{\underline{d}}$ her letter, & that it lessened y$^{\underline{r}}$ anxiety for me, which now my assurance that I am already better for nursing less frequently, will entirely dispel– When I have weaned altogether I hope to forget that I have a back– as for my throat, the warm weather of the last few days has been favourable to it– so enough of me–

Think of this being the 2$^{\underline{nd}}$ day since I left my dear Lily & Sophy! It seems to me a week! After dinner I was surprised to hear a loud ring at the bell, & who sh$^{\underline{d}}$ come in but Fisher, who got uneasy at M$^{\underline{rs}}$ Putnam's report to him this morng that I had a difficulty about engaging the Nurse, & fearing that I sh$^{\underline{d}}$ give up the idea of weaning, he determined to come & insist upon it. He had gone out to console the children for my absence, yesterday afternoon– & today, thinking he w$^{\underline{d}}$ have a dull time of it in the rain, with no-one to talk to but the little girls, I sent Pum out in the stage that she might amuse him by reading aloud– They all thought this a bright idea of mine, as Anne was here doing work for M$^{\underline{rs}}$ F. & undertook the charge of the baby– but he was too anxious about me to stay away– & was much relieved to find that I had been successful after all–

I have been writing to Sophia Thorndike, & feel rather tired, therefore I will now say Adieu! my dearest Mamma– with love to all around you– I am ever y$^{\underline{r}}$ most affect$^{\underline{e}}$ daughter Eliza

I cannot imagine what can have detained my last letter so long on the road– I sent it to town this day week by Clark Hare–

Private Collection

∽

To Mrs. Fisher, Philadelphia

Newport Sept$^{\underline{r}}$ 17$^{\underline{th}}$ 1844

Your letter of the 12$^{\underline{th}}$ my dearest Eliza was very consolatory as I trust you will soon regain your strength & be able to walk with Emma by whom you will receive this, as I thought if sent a day earlier by the post, there might be no means of sending it to you from Philad^a^. I am very glad you have so good a wet nurse & that the baby is so much improved as Mrs Fisher tells me, & that it has a large portion in her heart as she says, "tho' not a boy"–

It is time to answer your former letter of the 4th which was so long a time arriving. I copied exactly what you wrote about M^r^ F's Waistcoats & Pantal[oon]s & W^m^ carried it to Gould desiring him to make them without delay.[1] You do not mention in your last whether Mrs Ingersoll's child was still in the deplorable state you described–[2] it would be a happy release were she to be no more. it is indeed a blessing to have healthy children, what you are now enjoying, & will I hope always enjoy. As to the merino gown, I daresay it is quite good enough to wear in Carolina so there is no necessity about having it dyed again. I wish I could tell you when we are to leave Newport, I requested your Father to let me know his intention that it might be communicated to you–his answer was, he did not know– that I might spend 2 or 3 days with you–upon which I asked whether he intended that we should remain only so short a time at Philad^a^ "he did not know", again, & that we might go the beginning or the end of Octr there, he did not know– He went with W^m^ yesterday to N.Y. I asked him whether he intended to go to Phil^a^ but he said no, & should return here in a day or two– I presume not before Sunday when the Mass^ts^ will return– Emma can tell you more than I know of him & of all that has been going on here– I had a visit yesterday from M^r^ & M^rs^ [Sam] Ward[3] who are staying at the Ocean house. She has left her Child with her Mother at Staten Is^d^ & his Sister [*Julia*] is at Boston with her daughter who she has named Juliana Romana– her Sister is engaged to be married.

You do not mention how you found Mr Harrison, I hope better. Mrs Fisher says she is too nervous to leave home & cannot comply with your request to stay with you at the farm. If she would try some homeopathic medicines I am sure she would be benefitted by them. Arthur has been of great service to a poor Woman affected by Opthalmia who Miss Harper requested him to prescribe for– which he did 10 days ago: yesterday he repeated his visit, & she expressed great gratitude for the relief he had caused– She has been attended by physicians four years, without deriving any benefit from them– You would be glad to see how much Mrs Thorndike is improved in health & appearance which she attributes to that medicine & to the sea voyage & climate of Cuba where she intends to return this Autumn. M^r^ [George] Calvert[4] has purchased a lot beyond Mr Coffin's near Mr Hunt's– the DeRhams too have bought one, the very same that you & Mr Fisher thought of purchasing, opposite to the burnt house. but Emma can tell you of all these acquisitions & of the Party last Eve^g at Mrs Coffin's, which lasted till 12 o'clock, & then Arthur & Paolina went with the Calderons to their cottage to hear Ole Bull accompany Agripina[5], & remained there till 2 o'clock this morn^g– Arthur's reputation on the subject of homoeopathy has increased so much that a young woman just now brought a child about 5 y^{rs} old who after having a fever had become blind during the last month– he will try to cure her.

Elizth more than a fortnight ago was seized with a violent pain in her hand, Rheumatic– She applied to Arthur for cure but on the second day not finding relief, begged y^r Father to send for Dr Dunn[6] which he did, but visiting her every day & giving her quantities of medicines & leeches, she is only now rather better, & out of her bed, but not able to use her hand– Y^r brother says he is sure he could have relieved her in a much shorter time.

You must have had a very hot day yesterday as we had, but that you do not complain of, you rather think the heat improves your throat which still is painful in spite of the climate which Dr Jackson said would cure it, but if it is much better than it was here, I ought to be satisfied with your trying it. I suppose you have not written to y^r Aunt H[ering] by the St[eamer] of the 16th – I wish you had, for only think how provoking– I wrote to my brother on the 13th & sent the letter to the post the 14th thinking of course it w^d arrive in time at Boston but John brought it back saying that the mail had left this at 8 o'clock in the morn^g & the next day being Sunday there would be no other. I told Mme Calderon that you were disappointed by not hearing from her, she sent her love to you & said that she had been very much occupied by writing letters, but that she would soon write to you. Miss Harper to whom I delivered y^r message sends her love to you. She is now much better & rides on horseback– I expect to see Emma this Eve^g & will therefore finish this dull letter with love to Mrs Fisher thanking her for [her] very acceptable letter, & believe me my dearest Eliza y^r Affect^{te} Mother M. H. M.

Paolina & y^r Brothers send their love to you. 18th Emma called here yesterday eve^g my dearest Eliza & as she said she sh^d spend two days in N.Y & not be in Phil^a before next Saturday I thought it best not to give her my letter but let it take the chance of reaching you Friday, though it is uncertain whether you will send to the town on that day. I am sorry I delayed writing so long but do not follow my example this time, & write as soon as you receive this– Did you see on the 10th at 1 o'Clock two rainbows in this position?[7] W^m said it was owing to the state of some Clouds near the Sun. It lasted 20 minutes & was a very fine sight.

PHi

1. Fisher asked William to order some clothes for him at Gould's, Newport's best-known tailor, where Henry Middleton, Harry, William, Edward, and Oliver, as well as many of the Middletons' friends, all had clothes made. Fisher wished three waistcoats and three pairs of pants. The waistcoats were to be "a black ribbed silk, a Marseilles [*a reversible, cotton fabric,*] & a winter (single breasted) one– of a small pattern. The Pants– one pr. of thick black cloth, one for riding in, & one pr. of rather lighter material for country wear."

Gould's Day Book shows that the clothes, made of materials such as "double milled English wool dyed cassimere [*fancy woolen fabric,*]" "Ribbed Mohair," and "Woolen velvet," were picked up on September 17. The cost was forty-one dollars (less than Fisher had estimated); 5 percent was deducted for payment in cash. EMF to MHM, September 4, 1844, private collection; Gould Day Book, 1844–47, Newport Historical Society.

2. One of Susan Ingersoll's children was subject to convulsions and had broken her leg twice as a result.

3. After his first wife, Emily Astor, died, Julia Ward's brother, Sam, married Medora Grymes in September 1843. Julia married Samuel Gridley Howe in April 1843. Julia Romana, their first child, was born in Rome in March 1844.

4. George Henry Calvert, who was originally from Maryland, lived in Newport year-round, starting in the mid-1840s. His sister was Mrs. Thomas Willing Morris.

5. Though mentioned as a musician in Newport and Philadelphia, Agripina has not been identified.

6. Theophilus C. Dunn (b. 1800) studied medicine in Philadelphia and was a respected doctor in Newport.

7. Mrs. Middleton drew two overlapping circles to show how the rainbows had appeared.

⌒

After they left Newport in the middle of October, the Middletons went to Philadelphia to visit the Fishers, as they had done in previous years. Harry, William, and Catherine were with them. Mrs. Middleton, Catherine, and Harry went to Baltimore on November 16, where they met Eliza's father, who had been in Washington, and continued with him to Charleston.

To Mrs. Middleton, Charleston

Philadelphia – Saturday 23$\underline{rd}$ Nov$\underline{r}$ [1844]

I am indeed most grateful & happy to hear of y$\underline{r}$ arrival, my dearest Mamma, but my joy at knowing you safe in Charleston was somewhat damped by your telling me how much you had suffered from fatigue on the journey– I hope however that a few days' rest will entirely restore you to y$\underline{r}$ accustomed health and strength– I wish you had said how Papa bore the jolting– perhaps it may have been good for him, as exercize is recommended in his case, & the shocks may have been almost as beneficial as the electrifying machine[1] was– But tell me if my conjecture is correct– Certainly it w$\underline{d}$ be running a very great risk to undertake such an expedition in Paolina's situation, & I hope y$\underline{r}$ letter may induce Arthur to take her on by sea–[2] It will probably find them still in N.Y. for they have not yet come on here, altho' I rec$\underline{d}$ a message from A. by Henry Fisher, who saw him a week ago & begged him to say that they w$\underline{d}$ be in Phi$\underline{la}$ on the following Monday or Tuesday– We again waited dinner, but to no purpose– altho' Tuesday was a beautifully bright day– I shall be sorry not to see them at all of course– but think that under present circumstances the advice you give is much the safest & best to follow– unless the event has not already taken place– which I sometimes think is the only way to account for their delay–

The day you left me I did not stir out the whole day– fine as it was– but felt all the better for perfect rest & quiet– & have since been very prudent– having had indeed but 2 opportunities of walking since Sunday– every other day but Tuesday it has rained almost constantly– & today altho' it tried to clear, the clouds seem determined to have the ascendancy, or rather to descend in more rain before they leave the sky clear once more. We have been kept in some anxiety by M$\underline{r}$ [Charles] Francis' illness, which for several days was so obstinate that Fisher thought he could not get over it– He has been recovering the last 2 days, & is now quite out of danger– Nursing his Uncle in his heated room for several hours every day & frequently until late at night too, has made Fisher sick himself– he had yesterday one of his worst attacks of headache which has not quite passed away yet– Lily was in bed all day yesterday with a slight fever, probably brought on by the Custards & Sponge Cake with which her Grandmama stuffed her the day before– Today she is about again, but looks still a little languid– I never left her except for dinner yesterday, & you may imagine how completely tired out– with nursing the invalid & want of rest the previous night I was, when I could sleep soundly for 10 hours! from 8 last night till 6 this morng!

In the intervals when my attention was not required I read yesterday half a volume of Corinne–[3] with which I was delighted– for not having taken it up for years, the chief charm, eloquence of style, was as fresh as if I had never before read it– & I have not yet gone far enough to be disenchanted by the Hero's extreme weakness of character, which I remember she tries to palliate but which is wholly inexcusable & spoils all the effect of the story–

I have been exerting myself to procure a full Concert for poor Casella– who will I hope be successful on Tuesday, as he appears to be in some difficulty– & the D$^{r's}$ & nurse's bills must be paid. I have appealed therefore to the charitable feeling as well as the Musical taste of my friends– but fear that it will be as difficult to excite the one as the other– I have only been able to take one lesson with C. yet owing to the illness of M^r F[rancis] which for 2 days they thought w$^{\underline{d}}$ have a fatal termination– during which time I did not like to annoy M$^{\underline{rs}}$ F. with practising– but on Monday I shall resume the lessons–

I am writing with an abominable steel Pen, which refuses to mark on this rough paper– & I have consequently to write almost every word over again– You ask after M$^{\underline{rs}}$ Smith– I have not seen her since Tuesday when she was much affected by the death of Miss Telfair– which had just been announced to her– but she was free from neuralgia, & getting stronger–

Eveng– M$^{\underline{rs}}$ Smith has just left me, desiring her best love to you– We rejoiced together over y$^{\underline{r}}$ safe arrival & she bids me say how glad she was to hear of it– She is free from pain in her head but has a cough which prevented her from staying to spend the eveng– I am obliged to finish in haste so Adieu! my dearest Mamma, ever believe me Y$^{\underline{r}}$ most affec$^{\underline{te}}$ daughter Eliza

My best love, if you please, to Papa, my brothers & Kitty– My throat continues better & my strength improving– Fisher & his Mother both beg their kindest regards– & the children love & kisses– Baby is quite well–

Private Collection

1. Henry Middleton may have tried an electromagnetic machine, such as the one advertised by D. C. Moorhead in New York. By sending a magnetic fluid through the body, it was said to cure many ailments, among them paralysis, palpitation of the heart, and general debility. Margaret C. S. Christman, *1846: Portrait of the Nation* (Washington, D.C.: Smithsonian Institution Press for the National Portrait Gallery, 1996), 85.

2. Since Paolina's baby was due soon, Mrs. Middleton thought it would be "very imprudent" for her to travel on the rough southern railroads. MHM to EMF, November 19, 1844, PHi.

3. *Corinne*, a novel set in Italy, was written in 1807 by Anne Louise Germaine Necker, baroness de Staël-Holstein (1766–1817). Madame de Staël had been a friend of Eliza's uncle, J. Izard Middleton.

⌒

To Mrs. Fisher, Philadelphia

Charleston Novr 29$^{\underline{th}}$ 1844

My dearest Eliza

I was so busy yesterday that I had not time to answer your letter of the 23$^{\underline{d}}$ & you may imagine what pleasure I felt when the other of the 25$^{\underline{th}}$ was put into my hands about dinner time, so that I delay no longer to acknowledge both beginning before breakfast. I had been disappointed by not receiving the usual monthly letter from my brother & feared his attack of gout had prevented his writing, you may therefore conclude that it was a most agreeable surprise to me to find it enclosed in yours & was glad you had read it. his account of my Sister is much more favourable than I expected. I have in my two last letters advised him to go & live at Bath which is the most favourable residence for gouty people. Your news of Arthur's arrival at Phil$^{\underline{a}}$ & intention to proceed to Wash$^{\underline{n}}$ is as favourable, for your Father has been very angry with him for remaining so long at N.Y. & spending so much money.

We may see him & P$^{\underline{a}}$ next week, unless as you say they should stay 6 weeks at Was$^{\underline{n}}$ Gen$^{\underline{l}}$ V[an] N[ess] may perhaps invite them to do so– & it would certainly prevent great suffering & perhaps danger– Arthur too has business to perform there & P$^{\underline{a}}$ would be distrest if he were to leave her in Car$^{\underline{a}}$ soon after her confinement. I am glad to hear that your family are all well again– You must indeed have been greatly fatigued with nursing Lily. I hope she & the other two will continue in good health & give you a chance of regaining yours. All your friends here enquire particularly about you. I called yesterday even$^{\underline{g}}$ at y$^{\underline{r}}$ Aunt Huger's & saw Emma who was just going out. she begged me to tell you she would write to you soon after her arrival at her plantation to which she sets off this morn$^{\underline{g}}$. She had called to see me last week, & a few even$^{\underline{gs}}$ ago she went to M$^{\underline{r}}$ James Pringle's[1] wedding party. He has married Miss Ladson a niece or cousin of M$^{\underline{rs}}$ C. Harper.

The day we came here one of those fine large horses died, & for several days I had no chance of going out, for W$^{\underline{m}}$ went with the other two to Combahee last Sunday having been here only two days. John too remained here only 3 days– luckily a horse to match the surviving one was purchased, & a good Carriage from N.Y. that y$^{\underline{r}}$ Father had sent here gave me the means of returning visits & purchasing a quantity of Articles chiefly for country use.

Miss Rutledge & Alice Heyward called– they are both well & you will be glad to learn that M$^{\underline{r}}$ H. her father in law [2] has been so generous as to purchase for her the whole of the house in this street: you may remember that Russell M. had the half of it, but his Wife & Alice not agreeing, the latter left the house & has been during the summer at Columbia with her brother's widow– She will probably spend part of the winter with her. Miss Pinckney has lately had a severe attack of bronchitis to which she is subject but is now nearly well. She is always so attentive to me that I made her my first visit. her Sister is well. M$^{\underline{rs}}$ Holbrook never calls to see me, therefore I can tell you nothing about her.

Hal is grown quite stout, he went off yesterday as M$^{\underline{r}}$ Cotes advised him in a little vessel to Waccamaw that he might be in time to accompany his Mother & family next Tuesday in the Steamer to this place. She wishes to remain here two or three days & I believe your Father will send me & Cath$^{\underline{e}}$ to the Country on Wednes$^{\underline{y}}$ or thursday, & then send back the carriage for her to follow us the end of the week. John told me she was better now, her eyes not quite as bad as they were.

Dan$^{\underline{l}}$ Huger[3] has arrived by the Boston St$^{\underline{r}}$ & has derived the greatest benefit from Preiznitt's Water cure–[4] from being lame, he can now walk– I was sorry to hear of Miss Telfair's death– it must have greatly distrest M$^{\underline{rs}}$ Smith. it is fortunate for her that she is now free from Neuralgia. pray give my love to her & tell her M$^{\underline{rs}}$ Blamyer is looking well & improved in strength since the cool weather. It was cool when we arrived & we had fires– but for the last 3 days it is too warm for fires, & I sit in my room with the windows open. It is useless I presume to advise M$^{\underline{rs}}$ S. to apply to D$^{\underline{r}}$ Hering for a cure for her cough but I assure you that having a slight return of mine, I asked John what he would advise me to take for it– he said 'Dulcimara'[5] would soon cure it, & so it did. I took 3 or 4 globules of it, & you will laugh I daresay at my faith in homoeopathy. When you see Miss Hart pray thank her for me for the cough remedies she gave me. they were very beneficial. à propos of cures I have just read in a Liverpool paper that "Miss Martineau states in a letter to a friend, that she has been much benefitted by submitting to the mesmeric process, so much so that, after a long confinement to her room, she can now take a three mile walk with ease & pleasure."[6] You can tell this to M$^{\underline{rs}}$ Schroeder, who seems to take great interest in her. You can easily believe that the long back dated letters from my brother must afford me great pleasure by the affectionate expressions he used, & the recalling the number of events which happened during the happiest period of my life when no misfortune had occurred.

It is not proper to call those circles round the Sun rainbows, as D$^{\underline{r}}$ Gibbes said last night when I asked him if he had seen them (he is a good Astronomer). He had seen them, though not at Newport but at some place near it. He will probably be at M.P. for a few days about Xmas– I must now finish this begging you to give my love to M$^{\underline{rs}}$ & M$^{\underline{r}}$ Fisher & am my dearest Eliza y$^{\underline{r}}$ Affectionate Mother M. H. M.

I have just asked y$^{\underline{r}}$ Father what I am to tell you about his health– he says it is tolerable (he _seems_ very well) & that the motion of the rail cars did not injure him, or improve him– I began with one of y$^{\underline{r}}$ steel pens, but after a few lines could not write with it– how extraordinary it is! I had to write over the words I had tried to write.

PHi

1. James Reid Pringle, Jr. (1813–1884), son of James Reid and Elizabeth (McPherson) Pringle, married Sarah G. Ladson (1824–1877).

2. Nathaniel Heyward (1766–1851) was Alice (Izard) Heyward's father-in-law; her brother Walter's widow, Mary (Green) Izard (mentioned at the end of the sentence), had moved to Columbia after her husband died in 1835.

Alice's disagreement was with Russell Middleton's second wife, the former Anna deWolf, whose addition to the household must have changed Alice's relationship with both Russell Middleton and her three nephews. Mrs. Middleton had written to Eliza, "You know how fond she was of the three boys, & may suppose how distrest she must be to be separated from them & to live in such a detestable place as Columbia." MHM to EMF, May 26, 1844, PHi.

3. Daniel Huger was one of Emma Smith's brothers.

4. The system of "water cure" promoted by Vincent Priessnitz (1801–1851), a Silesian farmer, became fashionable in the United States and gave rise to several water-cure, or hydropathy, establishments, including one near Northampton, Massachusetts, which several of the Middleton family patronized in the late 1840s.

5. Dulcamara, made from bittersweet, had a mild narcotic effect.

6. By publicizing her belief that mesmerism had cured her, Harriet Martineau offended her doctor, who naturally insisted that mesmerism had nothing to do with her cure.

⌒

To Mrs. Middleton, Charleston

Philadelphia – Wednesday 11$\underline{th}$ Dec$\underline{r}$ 1844

I am quite disappointed at not receiving a letter from you this morng– my dearest Mamma, but will begin mine, altho' I shall probably reserve it until tomorrow, when I may have the pleasure of answering yours– which you perhaps sent by the return of the carriage from M Place– I only hope you are not waiting to announce Pauline's arrival for I find thro' M$\underline{r}$ [John] Francis that they had deferred their departure from Washington until this week– & who knows whether this delay may not oblige her to remain there several weeks? Far better w$\underline{d}$ it be to do so, than to set out on that journey at the risk of her life– as I really fear it w$\underline{d}$ be now– What madness of Arthur to expose her to such a peril within only a fortnight of the time she expects her trial! God grant her a safe end to her sufferings! This apprehension for her, causes naturally much anxiety which I shall long to have relieved by the joyful news of her being safely landed in Charleston–

I am particularly well– which I am sure you will be glad to hear– and Fisher begs me to tell you everybody remarks how well & <u>young</u> I look– I enjoyed myself so much at M<u>rs</u> Ingersoll's last week that he persuades me easily that I need not give up society altogether– & as I took no cold at all either there or at Miss Hare's, where I went to spend only a quiet eveng to be sure, but at some risk as it was very damp & had been raining all day, we have all decided that I must be very much better, & only want <u>prudent care</u> to make me as strong & well as ever I was– Of which I am sure I have <u>plenty</u> taken for if it drizzles but enough to take the starch out of a collar– I am made to drive to Aunt H's– & to the amusement of the whole company, my careful husband comes to screen me from the draft if there is but a crack of a door left open near me– He is only much more attentive than I deserve.

I have seen a good deal of M. [Jean Corneille] Gevers, the Dutch Minister– who was here last week– & was delighted with our little party & M<u>rs</u> I's. He told me much of our S<u>t</u> Peterburg friends– as he keeps up a correspondance with several ladies there– & had a letter a few weeks ago–

Thursday morng– Another disappointment today! But I will not detain this any longer, lest you sh<u>d</u> be anxious without cause– The weather is very cold, but I do not suffer from it in the least– & if you could see me I think you w<u>d</u> be pleased at the progress I have made during the last month– in strength– The baby grows handsomer & heartier– Sarah[1] says she can scarcely get along in the street for the ladies who stop her to ask whose <u>beautiful</u> baby that is– & certainly she <u>is</u> a remarkably sweet looking creature– Lily is very much improved by the Calomel,[2] which I gave her with some reluctance, but which has done wonders for her– Her appetite is now regular, & skin clear once more– Sophy is as roguish & merry as ever, & perfectly well– While on the subject of health, I may as well go thro' the family, & tell you that M<u>rs</u> F. is better than she has been for some time, M<u>r</u> Harrison much the same, & M<u>r</u> [Charles] Francis gradually recovering from the severe attack which w<u>d</u> have killed most men of his age– Fisher begs you to say to Papa, that if 2 <u>first</u> Vols of [*illegible*]'s Horace were sent to him from Penington's by mistake he can have one of them exchanged for a 2<u>nd</u> Vol. by enclosing it to John Penington, care of Carey & Hart, Phil<u>a</u>, and leaving it at Berrett's bookstore in Charleston whence it will be forwarded– & Penington will send on the 2<u>nd</u> Vol. as soon as he hears from Papa by the same channel–

I am going to send on some pretty books for the girls as Xmas presents, as I have given up all hope of having them with me this winter– The old lady has not said a syllable on the subject, & I dare not give even a hint, for fear of a return of the nerves– This is quite a disappointment to me I assure you, & I beg you will tell Sally and Susan how much pleasure it w<u>d</u> have afforded me to have them here if it had been in my power to propose it– & also to explain the reasons why it is <u>not</u>– I mean to write to Mary by the same opportunity which Mͬ Prime will give me notice of & tell her plainly how impossible it is for me (situated as I am) to do as I shͩ wish– I fear it will be a sad disappointment to them not to come on but it will indeed be scarcely a less one to me– But what can I do?

I am unwilling to close this without hearing from you, but perhaps you may be worried if you do not receive a letter from me at the usual time– I beg you to give my best love to Papa my brothers & sisters & believe me ever my dearest Mamma Yͬ most affecᵗᵉ daughter Eliza

I am very anxious to hear a great deal about dear Sally–

Private Collection

1. The wet nurse.
2. Because Lily lost her appetite and was looking yellow and thin, Dr. Chapman prescribed four grams of calomel to "clear her out & enable him to judge if she has worms which he suspects from her symptoms." Calomel, which contained mercurous chloride, was very strong medicine for a child. EMF to MHM, December 4, 1844, private collection; Mrs. Middleton's reaction is in her letter of December 14.

~

Even though his brothers had proclaimed that a naval officer should never marry since he was at sea so much of the time, Edward was lonely and hoping to find a wife.[1] He sailed for the Mediterranean in the spring of 1844 and, when he reached Naples, fell in love with a young woman named Edwardina de Normann.

Edward's letter, in which he asked his father's permission to marry Edwardina, provoked a very unfavorable reaction from his family. His parents and Eliza (and perhaps some of his brothers as well) sent off strongly worded letters trying to persuade him to give up the idea.

John Middleton opposed the marriage because "foreign women seldom like our country, and it is scarcely treating them fairly to compel their residence among us. This," he continued, "is no doubt Edward's affair. But at the same time it is to be remarked, that a silly marriage involves in its consequences, not only the parties themselves, but all of their relat[ions]." In addition, John thought it was particularly silly of Edward to "chain himself" to the navy, which he did not like, "by marrying a pauper."[2]

Why Edward's parents and Eliza disapproved so vehemently is, on the other hand, not so clear.[3] Their objections to Edwardina appear to have been related to her family background and circumstances, which were murky. Edwardina's mother, who lived in Naples, called herself the baroness de Normann—using a title that was not an English one and a surname which appeared to have been made up. The Middletons (after discarding the theory that she could be an illegitimate daughter of Caroline, the wife of George IV) eventually came to the conclusion that Edwardina's mother was more probably an illegitimate child of Edward, the duke of Kent, who was Queen Victoria's father. Regardless of their origins, Edwardina and her mother were living in Naples on very little money and in unclear circumstances. Emma Smith summed it up and said what others in the family had perhaps been thinking when she asked Eliza, "What sort of an Englishwoman do you think wd marry with a young American Lieut: & that, out of her own country, & apparently away from her own Family? Is there much to be expected f[ro]m this addition?"[4]

1. MHM to EMF, March 25, 1842, ScHi.
2. John I. Middleton to EMF, March 7, 1845, MPlFdn.
3. The correspondence between Edward and his family on the subject is missing.
4. EHS to EMF, February 20, 1845, PHi.

To Mrs. Fisher, Philadelphia

M.P. Decr 14$^{\underline{th}}$ 1844

I begin this my dearest Eliza to try whether I shall have time to finish it before the Carriage is sent down to comply with Paolina's request to use it for a week– I have been so very busy since my arrival here that I had not time to write except yesterday when I was obliged to do so, to favor Edward from whom another letter came by Sally soliciting with great feeling the same request he made in his former letter which if you remember I answered at Abington– the date of his, was about the same as that, & not having rec$^{\underline{d}}$ any of mine, he wrote on the same subject, & requested y^r Father to write to the Sec^y of the Navy to beg him to allow him a leave of absence instead of sending him to Brazil & entreated me to write immediately & to beg <u>him</u> to do so– Y^r Father said he was not acquainted with Mr Wilkins[1] but told me to write to Arthur & desire him to ask the permission but I fear the letter will not arrive in time to prevent his going there– perhaps too Arthur is a stranger to the Sec^y of the Navy–

But you will be surprised when you learn that your Father after reading the last letter & finding how devoted E$^{\underline{d}}$ was to the young girl, that he consented to his marrying her, observing that he had always been a good son. He however desired me to tell him that he could give him no money, & that as his pay was profitable, it must be sufficient to support him & his wife. This consent astonished me, because he had before so peremptorily refused it, but he seemed to feel for the poor fellow & I think you my dear Eliza would too, were you to read his letter. He must by this time be miserable on receiving my letter from Abington & will probably go to Brazil & not receive the letter I wrote to him yesterday for many months. his was dated Mahon, but Paolina's Father wrote to her that he was at Naples in Octr which place he must have left very soon after.

Y^r Father seems very well, & is going in an hour to set off for Combahee– Sally seemed in tolerable health when we met & came here with her family on the 12$^{\underline{th}}$ but yesterday was seized at dinner time with a chill & a violent head ache which has lasted all night, but is not quite as bad now, after having taken a homoeopathic dose. She sends her best love to you & thanks for all the things you have sent her & Children. She admires the Collar very much. I told her of y^r invitation to Abington which she appeared to wish could be effected, but seemed to think she could not accomplish– I am sorry to learn that dear little Lily was ill but hope she soon recovered, in spite of the Calomel– how c$^{\underline{d}}$ the doctor give her such medicine! How is M$^{\underline{rs}}$ Fisher & how is Mr Harrison? but I must give up writing for Jack has just come for any commissions & I have been interrupted sans cesse [*continually*] while I have been scribbling this– With love to M$^{\underline{rs}}$ & Mr Fisher & kisses to the children I am my dearest Eliza y^r affect$^{\underline{te}}$ Mother M. H. M.

PHi

1. William Wilkins was actually secretary of war. John Y. Mason was secretary of the navy.

~

To Mrs. Middleton, Charleston

Philadelphia Thursday eveng– 19$^{\underline{th}}$ Dec^r [1844]

I have been writing to Paolina until it is almost too late to begin a letter to you, my dearest Mamma, as I cannot finish it because I am as usual under a promise to Aunt's for the eveng– As however I begged off from the Tea, I may still have time to write a few lines before 8 o'clock and I hope it will not much signify that my letter will reach you a day later– I received your's yesterday morng– having been 2 weeks without hearing from you– except the lines you added to Paolina's letter, which you may be sure I was rejoiced to receive, but which was 6 days coming– I suppose thro' Judge Huger's remissness– How my "avant dernière" [*next to last*] came to be so long on the road I cannot understand– but you must not, really, imagine an unfortunate cause for every such detention–

I am sorry that poor Ned had been distressing himself about the separation from Miss <u>Edwardina</u> but cannot help hoping that Papa's consent to the Match may arrive too late for him to repair the mischief caused by the former letter, as it seems to me impossible that such a match should turn out well– & far better that he should grieve at a temporary disappointment than suffer from a permanent evil for so I should consider matrimony for him under the circumstances– however of course he must now decide for himself– & the best chance of his getting out of the scrape is that he will probably cross the last letter upon the Atlantic, as I see by the Report of the Sec^y of the Navy that the Fairfield[1] is to return immediately home, the St Mary's having been ordered out to relieve her– Therefore the application for change of destination is unnecessary– and by the time he reaches his native shores, the image of poor Edwardina will probably be fading from his fickle heart, if it be not already entirely effaced by that of some new fair one.

The other two subjects of your letter are Papa's good health, which it delights me to hear of as much as it grieves me to find that poor Sally was suffering so much from her head– It appears that y^r favourite system can do little for her, besides <u>amusing</u> her, for certainly you do not even pretend that it can cure or even much relieve– As for me I am more than ever convinced of its fallacy & absurdity, your dose of Dulcimara to the contrary notwithstanding & since Lily has been really so much benefitted by y^r dreaded Calomel, have a proportionate respect for Alleopathy.[2]

Friday– I have been out all the morng with the Children– visiting & hunting for Xmas presents & have just come in half an hour before dinner– which is to be later on Fisher's account as he may return from the Farm in time for it– He is put in good spirits by having at last, 12 feet of water in his Well– very precious water it is, having cost him between 4 & 5 hundred dollars! But he was determined to persevere, altho' almost despairing of success– which is now complete. The Ice House too is nearly finished, & that will contribute greatly to our comfort next summer I hope– Tell dear Sally that I can by no means give up the pleasant anticipation of having her & her little girls for companions for me and the children.

Pray when you see Oliver thank him for the sweet Potatoes he kindly remembered to send– They have been a little frosted, at least all those near the outside of the barrels, but are still, better than any I have tasted before this year– I have just written to Mary, & sent them all Xmas tokens in the shape of books– pretty illustrated editions of Poetry &c which I hope they may read with pleasure, & which will certainly be more valuable than trashy Annuals– I am very very sorry that their coming for the Holidays was out of the question– M<u>rs</u> F. never said a syllable on the subject & I did not dare to propose it– knowing that in her present nervous state it might have made her worse– & also that there were really some difficulties in the way of accomodating them as she w<u>d</u> have liked– So you must tell dear Sally & Susan how I am situated & how much pleasure it w<u>d</u> have given me to have them, if I could have invited them to my own establishment–

I am writing with a steel Pen, & with much ease as you may perceive– the secret being to use the <u>colored</u> Ink, which flows much more readily than the black– So you had better try it with your Pens– M<u>rs</u> F– begs me to tell you that she took Miss Mary Helen out visiting with her yesterday, & she was so good & looked so well that she was prodigiously admired, & pronounced decidedly the handsomest of the three– which she certainly is– but the little monkey is beginning to love her Nurse so much better than me that I am quite mortified– which I ought not to be as the preference is as yet purely <u>physical</u>, and when her <u>morale</u> is more developed, I need not fear the continuance of it– therefore as long as she continues to thrive so well with the Alderney[3] I must not let my <u>jealousy</u> get the better of me–

I have felt deeply interested in poor Fanny Butler's distresses for the last few days particularly, for her children are now altogether removed from her, and she is in extreme affliction as you may suppose– Unfortunately she has brought a good deal upon herself by her own folly, but nothing can excuse his cruel and heartless conduct toward her– She has my warmest sympathy & that of all those who know <u>all</u> the circumstances & have the least spark of good feeling– I fear the step she is about taking will only subject her to worse treatment & unnecessary humiliation,[4] but she is right to do everything & make every sacrifice for her Children, & I therefore told her that altho' I could not have <u>advised</u> her to go & live under the roof of such a man, upon such conditions, yet I honoured her for giving up <u>all</u> for her children– But alas! I fear her decision is made too late to expect any good result–

What with the scene I witnessed there yesterday & one of scarcely less violence exhibited by poor Rebecca [Smith][5] this morng I am quite unstrung– but hope that some advice to the latter may have a good effect– The other case seems irremediable but God may soften the obdurate heart, when we suppose that is impossible to do so by merely human means–

I cannot conclude my letter without begging you to give my love & hearty wishes for a merry Xmas to each one of the family party– which will be a large one I suppose by the time you receive this– Adieu! dearest Mamma, & believe me ever Y^r most affecte daughter Eliza

Private Collection

1. The Middletons seem to have had information that Edward was scheduled to return on the *Fairfield*, which was coming back after three years in the Mediterranean.
2. Homeopathists called ordinary, traditional medicine allopathy.
3. The alderney, a breed of milk-producing cow, meant the wet nurse.
4. In order to return to her husband's house so she could see her children, Fanny Butler had to agree to conditions and behavior set by him.
5. Fisher, who did not approve of his cousin, said she was a "torment" to her family and had "numerous lovers, none of whom she could make up her mind to marry." This was not the whole story, however. Various comments in Eliza's letters indicate that, although Becky was quite unstable at times, Eliza and others liked and took an interest in her. JFF, *Recollections*, 25.

⌢

To Mrs. Middleton, Middleton Place

Philadelphia Friday 27$\underline{th}$ Dec$\underline{r}$ [1844]

Altho' I have not been made happy by receiving a letter from you, my dearest Mamma, yet I begin this in hopes that before I send it tomorrow I may be able to thank you for one, which you probably have had no opportunity of sending down to Charleston until just before Xmas, upon the return of Papa & William from Combahee– and as I wish this to arrive in time to wish you all a very happy New Year, I shall not at any rate detain it after tomorrow, as you will not account for <u>my</u> silence as I do for your's–

We have had until today, most delightful Holiday weather since Monday– The Skies bright, & the sun shining brilliantly by day & the Moon brightly by night– & the whole population of the city turning out into Chesnut S^t which has been thronged so much that the crowds were pushed from the side walks into the middle of the street– all looking happy & well dressed & well behaved– So that really our quiet street looked like the Boulevards on Sunday I am told– I am glad for one that this happy season should be observed by all classes with appropriate joyousness of spirit & demeanour & that the careless & indifferent to the <u>real</u> meaning of keeping the Festival, should be reminded in <u>some</u> way, even if in no better than in parading in public, of the cause which all mankind have for rejoicing & gratitude on the day when the whole Christian Church celebrates the coming of our blessed Saviour into a world which but for His Manifestation, w^d have been lost in Sin– We had an excellent sermon at St Peter's, recommending Cheerfulness & the exercize of Hospitality & of every good feeling & I entirely approved of the whole tone of it, which I cannot always do of Mr Odenheimer's– During the Communion I as usual thought of all my absent friends, & prayed that some of them might hereafter have the comfort & peace in believing that I feel myself– and then how many subjects of devout Thanksgiving rose in my mind! & how deeply I felt my unworthiness of the blessings I enjoy– But I must not dwell too long on all this, altho' it is very near my heart–[1] I indeed little expected last Christmas that I should live to see another, & I have reason to be grateful to God that my health is so much restored, that I may now have rather more hope that my life may still be spared some years, for the sake of guiding the education of my dear little girls, to whom it may be valuable–

They, at least the two elder ones, & Lily especially, were in a state of perfect ecstacy with all that Kriss Kinkle brought them, but particularly with the contents of the <u>Stocking</u>, which was so mysteriously filled for them– They had besides a Table covered with Toys provided by their kind friends– The most curious of which was one of Mrs Smith's manufacture– really a most astonishing specimen of art & industry– in the shape of a boat a foot & a half long, very square built, (but not very substantially, of pasteboard) & meant to represent Grandpapa's Schooner from Combahee with a cargo of rice & eggs in barrels, & commanded by Captain <u>Thomas</u>, who with his mate <u>Bob</u> are most capital figures & have excited the admiration of all beholders– The funny part of it is that there is really quite a likeness to the original Thomas– unintentional of course– & the countenances & attitudes are exceedingly good–

I had several pretty Presents– one which Robert Hare brought me from Italy I am quite pleased with– It is a copy of Tasso's Inkstand at Ferrara– which he used when writing the Gerusalemme–[2] One would suppose that the warning contained in the gesture of the little Cupid whose forefinger is significantly placed on the lips, would not have been lost upon the poor poet, whose indiscretion in love nonetheless cost him so dear. Another gallant presented me with a cornet de bonbons [*cone of candies*] with the devise of a <u>full blown Rose</u> which was less acceptable than a real Rose bud picked by Fisher from our garden on Xmas morng! This will be an evidence to you of the mildness of our winter hitherto– Today however it is snowing & hailing– I must not omit to mention three very handsome presents– a new Velvet Bonnet from Aunt H. & silk dress from Mrs F. & a head dress from my husband– which were all very well-timed &

acceptable, as I had really spent so much in other ways, that I had nothing left to provide for myself– And as I am now so well fitted out, I can appropriate some of the next months' allowance to better uses than dress. All the Bills for the year are now coming in– some of them for <u>Farm</u> expenses, are pretty heavy– But it is a satisfaction to be able to pay them all– by encroaching somewhat on principal. Another year we must be much more economical– The pleasure of our Xmas was much marred by knowing that M̲ͬ Harrison was suffering more than usual– but yesterday he was better again and continues so today–

Saturday– I am again disappointed dearest Mamma, but persuade myself that the snow has interfered with the mail from the South, & that nothing else prevents my hearing– I am extremely anxious to know that poor Paolina is safe, & hope soon to have the good news about her– I am going to write a letter to Aunt Hering that it may be in time for the Packet of the 1ˢᵗ– but shall not send it until tomorrow eveng– & shall be glad to give her late accounts of you, if I hear meanwhile– I am sorry to send this without hearing from you, but if I keep it any longer you may perhaps get uneasy about me– whereas I am remarkably well– Perhaps my prudence in declining to accept invitations when the weather is bad is one reason for it– The Hoffmans are determined to have plenty of company at their house for they have regular parties once a fortnight which I have not yet attended altho' invited to go, & now here comes an invitation to dinner which I am inclined to accept, but I suppose they have gas lights & so we cannot go– I have on that account refused several at M̲ͬˢ Hare's which I much regret– Robert gave his Goddaughter a very pretty silver mug for an Xmas present. I must now close this as Mr Francis will be here at dinner & I beg you to give my best love to Papa & all around you from Y̲ͬ affect̲ᵉ daughter Eliza

Private Collection

1. Mrs. Middleton answered that she was "always gratified to hear & read your religious sentiments. . . . I wish my Sons had the same religious feelings. Harry & John seem devoid of any, which is indeed a great misfortune." MHM to EMF, January 4, 1845, PHi.

2. Torquato Tasso, a sixteenth-century Italian poet and writer of madrigals, wrote *Gerusalemma Liberata,* an epic about the liberation of Jerusalem.

1845

*The friend he has lost has been devoted to him from his very
birth, & never let him feel the want of a father.*

~

George Harrison died in July 1845. He had always encouraged, counseled,
and loved Fisher, and when Fisher brought Eliza into the family, he included her
in his many kindnesses. Fisher and Eliza relied on his good sense, loved him for
his warmth and humor, and were grateful for the many ways he had helped them
during the early years of their marriage. His death, the first among Fisher's and
Eliza's parents, naturally left a great gap in the family.

At the same time that Uncle Harrison was dying, it became more and more
clear that Henry Middleton was also a sick man. He had not recovered from his
illness in the spring of 1844, and John mentioned "a notable falling off from his
wonted health & activity."[1] The family tried not to worry Eliza, but she saw for
herself how ill her father was when he passed through Philadelphia in the spring
of 1845.

Edward, in the meantime, went ahead and married Edwardina de Normann
in Italy. Uncle Oliver Hering, apparently a believer in Edda's royal blood, mentioned "the grandeur of the connection,"[2] and Emma Huger Smith, knowing her
Aunt Middleton well, predicted that her "prejudices will luckily lend loveliness to
aught wh. England produces." As far as Henry Middleton was concerned, though,
Emma continued, "methinks the Governor's view of things is likely to be somewhat more judicious."[3]

When Edward and Edda eventually arrived in the United States, things went
better than expected. Edda was gay and affectionate and, still a teenager, got along
well with Paolina and with the older Middleton grandchildren, who were not
much younger than she was. She "enlivened" Henry Middleton's solitude when
he was not feeling well, and in his opinion—so he told his sister—Edward, as well
as Arthur, had drawn a "prize" as a wife.[4] Best of all, perhaps, Edda was considerate of Mrs. Middleton and appreciated how "very good and kind to me" her
mother-in-law was.[5]

The continuing discussions of the annexation of Texas and the control of Oregon taking place on the national scene are reflected in Eliza's and her mother's
letters. Although in mid-March Eliza thought the "war panic" over Texas and Oregon had "subsided," both issues were far from settled.[6] In his inaugural address,
President Polk restated the United States' claim to all of Oregon, while expansionists in and out of Congress took up the "54°40' or fight" chant. Polk also sent

Gen. Zachary Taylor with troops to southern Texas, where the border with Mexico was in dispute. Fears that such policies might lead to war with England, or Mexico, were therefore not unreasonable.

1. John I. Middleton to EMF, March 7, 1845, MPlFdn.
2. Edda was Edwardina's nickname. MHM to EMF, February 27, 1845, PHi.
3. EHS to EMF, February 20, 1845, PHi.
4. Septima Sexta Rutledge to HM, October 30, [1845,] MPlFdn.
5. Note from Edda at end of MHM to EMF, June 22, 1845, PHi.
6. EMF to MHM, March 17, 1845, private collection.

～

To Mrs. Middleton, Middleton Place

Philadelphia 14$\underline{th}$ Jany 1845

I meant to write yesterday & thank you for your letter of the 6$\underline{th}$ which I had the pleasure of receiving on Saturday, dearest Mamma but supposing we should have but one more day of fine weather & that I had better take advantage of that while it lasted & return some indispensable visits I waited until today believing it w$\underline{d}$ certainly snow– However we have bright skies again, notwithstanding the threats of yesterday, but I hope the delay of a single day has not caused you any uneasiness as I am quite well, and it w$\underline{d}$ be a pity you sh$\underline{d}$ think otherwise– The children too are well, considering they are well-peppered with Chicken pox– at least the baby is– Lily has very few spots out yet– & Sophy's have entirely disappeared– But poor little Helen's are rather troublesome– altho' she is not feverish– only very restless– Of course they must be kept in– which is a great pity this beautiful weather– We have not had so fine a winter since I have been in Phil$\underline{a}$, and I am always thinking it cannot continue much longer, & that we must soon expect a change for the worse– It w$\underline{d}$ be better to be sure to have some cold weather for the sake of filling the Icehouses which are still empty– and we sh$\underline{d}$ be provoked if Fisher's were to remain so after he has had the expense of building it– To judge by the mildness of the season here, you can have had no winter at all in Carolina & I find by y$\underline{r}$ letter that the flowers are all in full bloom in the garden– You were mistaken with regard to the Rose <u>bud</u>– It came <u>not</u> from the Farm, but out of our little Yard here in town– & the <u>Full blown</u> rose was only an <u>artificial</u> one, on a cornet de bonbons.

William went away [*to New York*] on Wednesday as I told you he had determined to do– but promised to return in a week or ten days–[1] so I shall look for him about Monday next– by which time the Opera will be over I believe, & I understand from Maria Murray,[2] who is here on a visit, that there are very few parties then– The one I told you I was going to have, succeeded very well– We had some very pretty music, sung by M$^{\underline{me}}$ Cuesta & M. Lafitte– & I played without getting frightened under favour of the talking noise about me– I introduced W$^{\underline{m}}$ to some of our belles, whose acquaintance he had not made before, & he seemed to enjoy himself & find them pleasant– Miss Murray appeared quite disappointed at missing W$^{\underline{m}}$. You know I used to think she had rather a penchant for him– but he never fancied her much– We had her & her little sister, Agnes here last night, & a few persons to meet them– not a party, for they are in mourning for their Uncle–

D$^{\underline{r}}$ Godon[3] told me that the Fairfield was actually on her way to this country– so that we may soon expect to see Edward– & he will miss the last letter–[4] which I do not think is <u>at all</u> to be regretted– for a most foolish match it w$^{\underline{d}}$ be certainly– and the young lady will probably console herself as soon as he does– M$^{\underline{rs}}$ Schroeder says that her son Frank writes her that E[dward] M. is engaged to a young lady half Austrian half English– & that he is to be married to her at the end of the cruize– But I told her it was very uncertain, & begged her not to speak of it to any one– nor have I mentioned it of course– hoping it might not come to pass after all– This reminds me of an equally imprudent match which is to be made here– between Mary Waln, the sister of M$^{\underline{rs}}$ Wilcocks, who has <u>nothing</u>– to a young <u>assistant</u> surgeon in the Navy[5] who has only 1 thousand $ a year to support her on– but she says it is <u>enough</u> & is determined to marry him– So she must suffer for her folly–

M$^{\underline{rs}}$ Smith was here yesterday morng– but would not come in the eveng– on account of her cough which is at times troublesome– but as long as she has no neuralgia in her head, she does not complain of anything else– She desired her best love to you, & thanks for yr kind message– She always asks me how you are, & I cannot answer very confidently, except by the tenour of y$^{\underline{r}}$ letters, which is cheerful, for you do not <u>say</u> you are well– W$^{\underline{m}}$ assures me you are looking remarkably so, which I am delighted to hear– I am sorry you were so soon to lose dear Sally– you will indeed miss her much– I shall write in due time to urge my request to herself. How unlucky that poor Susan sh$^{\underline{d}}$ be kept in Carolina next summer– but I suppose she & Oliver do not regard the <u>cause</u> of her detention an unfortunate one– I am glad she is so well in health & spirits–[6]

I am rather sad about Fisher today– He has been talking in the most desponding manner about his eyes which are <u>no</u> better, after all his patience & hope deferred– & really the trial is sometimes almost too heavy a one for him to bear– but I try to encourage him to keep a good heart about them altho' I sometimes [tru]ly despair myself of their restoration. M$^{\underline{rs}}$ Fisher seeing him so much depressed insisted upon knowing the cause & finding that he wished to engage a reader but could not at present afford to pay one, she said positively that he must at once speak to the man he had last year & she will pay the expense–

I heard the news of the birth of Paolina's little girl from Mrs Smith, who rec^d it from Mrs Blamyer several days before y^r letter arrived–7 Arthur did not write to me, altho' I had so much pressed him to do so– When you write scold him about it but give my love & congrats– I must say Adieu! With love to Papa & all around you I am my dearest Mamma Ever Y^r most affec^te daughter E–

Private Collection

1. Eliza was immensely pleased when William was able to visit Philadelphia in January. "I was delighted at the idea of his coming on," she told her mother, "not only on his own account, but as it was the best evidence of Papa's being well." EMF to MHM, January 5, 1845, private collection.

2. Maria and Agnes Murray were the daughters of James B. and Maria (Bronson) Murray of New York.

3. Probably Victor L. Godon who had recently resigned from being assistant surgeon in the navy.

4. This was the letter in which Henry Middleton gave his permission for Edward to get married.

5. Mary Waln married Dr. Richard Maxwell in April 1845.

6. "Susan mentioned to Sally & me," Mrs. Middleton reported, "that she could not go to the north next Summer as she expects to be confined in June, & will be in Charleston in May– I had observed that below her waist, she seemed rather large, but supposed it might be the effect of the bustle. She seemed quite well while she was here & begged me to send her best love to you." MHM to EMF, January 4, 1845, PHi.

7. According to Mrs. Middleton, "Paolina's troubles . . . began on new year's night at 12 & she suffered much, but is now getting on famously & is perfectly satisfied with the baby's charms & perfections." The little girl was called Angelina. MHM to EMF, January 4, 1845, PHi.

⌒

To Mrs. Middleton, Middleton Place

Philadelphia Tuesday Jany 21st [1845]

I must take advantage of the good opportunity offered by the bad weather today, to write to you today without interruption, dearest Mamma– for it is very unlikely that any one will come out thro' this snow storm to visit me– & the children, after passing the last 3 hours with me, are content to amuse themselves awhile in the Nursery– They are perfectly well again, the baby suffered very much for two or three days with the Chicken Pox– & could not sleep for more than a quarter of an hour at a time– but I am told that it is very lucky they have had it for it may keep off other diseases–

I was glad to see by this morng's paper the arrival of the Fairfield at Norfolk– & altho' there was no list of officers given, I take it for granted that Ned is on board of her– & suppose that as soon as ever he can get off, he will be with you in Carolina– Pray do not encourage him in his idea of marrying Miss Edwardina– for he will probably get over his attachment as easily as he has many others, & I cannot think that such an ill assorted match could ever be productive of happiness to him– I am sure he had much better marry Lizzie or Miss Tiffany, or even any <u>penniless</u> girl in <u>this</u> country than bring one from abroad & who comes of such a worthless race– But pray do not mention <u>my</u> name in the matter for after all I have no right whatever to give advice until it is asked & nothing but my concern for him, & the interest I feel in his future welfare would induce me to express these opinions even to you–

William is not yet returned from New York– I hoped he w$^{\underline{d}}$ arrive yesterday, as I wrote to him on Saturday telling him of 2 parties which were to take place last eveng & which I thought he w$^{\underline{d}}$ like to attend– but I suppose he prefers the Opera, which I see by the Papers is to close on Saturday next– So I daresay he may remain there as long as it continues– I was to have gone to a Musical party early last eveng– & afterwards to M$^{\underline{rs}}$ Hutchinson's to see the Polka danced– which I have only seen performed by Emma & Allen at the Farm– but Fisher was afraid to let me venture out as it was drizzling & very raw & cold– So I have missed one of my few chances, for at all the houses nearly, they now burn <u>gas</u>– which keeps us away from them–

The bad weather today will put my going to Ole Bull's farewell Concert out of the question– I hope poor Casella may have clear skies for his on Friday– He is to play a beautiful piece he has dedicated to me, which I hope to hear– but rather doubt my being permitted to go– Then there is another Concert I should like extremely to attend next week– at which the best singers of the Italian Troupe,[1] who will be here on their way to New Orleans, will appear– Altho' it is a disappointment to me to stay away when there is the strong temptation of good Music, yet I cannot help acknowledging that Fisher is quite right to prevent me from exposing myself– for I am now so very well, that it w$^{\underline{d}}$ be indeed a great pity to run the slightest risk of taking cold, & having a relapse– D$^{\underline{r}}$ Jackson thinks that if I avoid one, by extreme prudence & care, that my throat may be entirely cured next summer– I trust it may at least continue well enough to enable me to brave the New Port fogs without fear of evil consequences–

Wednesday– I am very glad that I kept my letter until today as it gives me an opportunity of thanking you for yr's of the 10th which I had the pleasure of receiving this morng– dear Mamma– I am glad to find you are well, which you must be as you speak of enjoying a walk for half an hour daily– Your solitude w^{d} not probably last much longer, & I hope that Oliver's visit was paid as he promised– 'Tis indeed a pity that Mrs W. Pringle sh^{d} still object to returning visits [*after the death of her child*] as she is so agreeable a person that you w^{d} enjoy her society– Arthur added a line at the back of yr letter to say they were all well, except the baby who was still suffering from her eyes– I am afraid they admitted too much [light] too soon– Pray when you write again to him, say that the single lines do not satisfy me & that I have been hoping to have a full account of both Mother & child from him– but shall soon write to Paolina, & beg her to report herself as it seems I have no chance of any further accounts from him– What name are they going to give the baby, <u>not</u> Marcia^2 I hope, which P. told me he thought of sometime ago–

I met Mrs Hare last night at Aunt H's, & she informed me that Edward's name was <u>not</u> in the list of officers who have arrived in the Fairfield– So that of course he has staid behind to get married– Foolish fellow! I fear he will pay dearly for his imprudence– but if there is no help for it, we must try & make the best of it– & hope that his wife may not inherit any of her Grandmother's vices– I have not mentioned the subject of course, & begged Mrs Schroeder who heard of the engagement from Frank, to keep it secret– Mrs Smith wrote me yesterday that her cough was better, I may perhaps see her today– I shall not send this until eveng– so that if W^{m} comes, I can add a few lines– You were misinformed with regard to Miss Wadsworth, she is not here, but at Genesee I believe–

Wednesday eveng– W^{m} is not come, & has not answ^{d} my letter so that I don't know exactly when to expect him– I hope however when he <u>does</u> tear himself away from N.Y. that he will still be able to spare a week here on his way South– Tell Arthur I had a visit today from his friend Mrs Commodore Morgan^3 returning the one I paid her– & she enquired very particularly about him– She appears to be a very sweet woman, & has a most beautiful boy– even handsomer than Bente I think– I must go & get ready to take tea at Aunt H's. They always ask after you in the kindest manner & desire their remembrances– M^{r} H– has been more comfortable the last week– but is very weak– Adieu dearest Mamma I am ever Y^{r} most affect^{e}

Pray give my love <u>as usual</u> to Papa, my brothers & Kitty– Tell the latter she must read aloud to you if she wants me to send her anything by W<u>m</u>. Can I execute any commission for you? Pray tell me if I can send you anything– Fisher & his Mother desire their best regards to you & the rest–

Private Collection

1. Signora Pico, prima donna, and other singers of the Italian Opera in New York were to perform on January 28 in a concert sponsored by the Musical Fund Society.
2. This would have been in honor of Arthur's first mother-in-law, Marcia (Burns) Van Ness.
3. Arthur had asked Eliza to visit Mrs. Morgan whose husband was stationed in Philadelphia. She "is I am afraid badly off for acquaintances in a place where they are not commonly fond of making new ones," he told Eliza. A few weeks later Eliza made much the same comment after she had tried to arrange a small party for the Sumners: "Many people here have an unwillingness to meet strangers or even to be introduced to them– fearing they may be expected to call on them & pay them civilities, which I am sure they need not do." Note from Arthur Middleton to EMF, in MHM to EMF, December 9, 1844, PHi; EMF to MHM, April 15, [1845,] private collection.

∽

Mrs. Middleton, Middleton Place

Philadelphia – Monday 10<u>th</u> Feb<u>y</u> 1845

Two weeks had gone by since I rec<u>d</u> y<u>r</u> last letter, dearest Mamma, & I began to feel anxious when this morng– long after the usual post hour yr's of the 3<u>rd</u> was brought me, & made me very happy– It had been long on its way– & did not contain the news of W<u>m</u>'s arrival, as I hoped it might– However it gave me the assurance that you were all well & that was great comfort indeed– Paolina added a line outside by which I was glad to find she was well– but sorry the poor baby still suffered from weak eyes– I <u>must</u> write to her, that I may get a clearer account of the matter– I hope Arthur has not been following D<u>r</u> Howe's example– & in making experiments nearly blinded his infant– some carelessness I fear there must have been, to occasion the inflammation–[1]

I have been regretting very much that y<u>r</u> letter from Abington, to Edw<u>d</u>, should ever have reached him– since it must have arrived too late to prevent his marriage, & afterwards could only give him unnecessary pain– Perhaps his plan of leaving <u>his wife</u> was only <u>prospective</u> & as he does not actually announce the important step as having <u>been taken</u>, there may be still some hope that it never will–[2] a very faint one certainly– After all the match may turn out a happy one, & I hope sincerely it may– but much doubt it–

I have just had a visit from M. Gevers who was passing thro' Phil$^{\underline{a}}$ on his way to Wash$^{\underline{n}}$– He tells me that the Calderons are in great distress at the probable loss of their brother– who saild from NY– or Boston, I don't know which, in Oct$^{\underline{r}}$ for the Havanna, whither he was escorting two young Spanish ladies who had been finishing their education with M$^{\underline{rs}}$ M$^{\underline{c}}$Leod– and the vessel in which they embarked, has never been heard of since– Altho' they have letters from the Havanna up to a very late date– He did not know the name of the young man– but as he said they mentioned he was only 25, it must be Alex$^{\underline{r}}$ [Inglis] the youngest brother, to whom they were all much attached, & a very amiable excellent fellow– The poor Mother is much to be pitied– & indeed it is dreadful for them all to be kept so long in suspense about his fate– I am glad you have so agreeable a companion as M$^{\underline{rs}}$ Sumner with you, & beg you will remember me particularly to her, if she is still with you– Pauline will I suppose soon be going to MPlace– for if Arthur means to have his claim[3] attended to this Session [*of Congress,*] he ought to be in Washgn by this time– If it be not already too late–

You enquire about M$^{\underline{rs}}$ Pierce B– She is still waiting her husband's good pleasure to return to his roof– & as he has not added another word to his instructions on the subject, nor expressed any further wish, she begins to think he does not intend her to be there at all– as she has complied with every exaction to no purpose–

She spent nearly two hours with me the other morng– & I had nearly got drawn into a discussion on Abolition with her– I told her very candidly that the only part of her conduct I could not defend was her publishing opinions which were so contrary to the interests of the man she had married–[4] knowing, as I suppose she did before she became his wife, that he had that property– She assured me that she was not aware, before her marriage of his being a Slave holder– or even owning a Southern estate– & in fact, she says that he did not at that time own any– the property having been then in the hands of his Aunts– With regard to the publication of the journal, she told me the whole Story, which w$^{\underline{d}}$ be too long to repeat now– but the only excuse for it was that she sold it to pay a debt in London, which he did not choose to pay for her– She also declared that she w$^{\underline{d}}$ not have married him, if she had known that part of his income w$^{\underline{d}}$ be derived from Slave holding– & that she had once told him, that if he could put his hand on his heart & say conscientiously that he thought himself right to hold Slaves she w$^{\underline{d}}$ never say another word on the subject– & that he replied he could <u>not</u> do so– & in her opinion it was acting against conscience which was the chief objection to it–

So far we agreed, but I told her that I believed many Southerners had a clear conscience in the matter, & thought that the condition of the labourers w$\underline{d}$ not be improved by emancipation at present– I also said that if the pictures drawn by Dickens & others of the horrible sufferings of the poor in Eng$\underline{d}$ were not greatly exaggerated, they must be infinitely worse off than the Slaves–[5] to which she answered that the immense inequality of ranks there w$\underline{d}$ also be such a bar to her happiness, that she could not live there with any peace of mind– knowing the misery & famine which it would be almost impossible to relieve & which she sh$\underline{d}$ not be able to forget, even if surrounded by plenty & Luxury– I have often thought so myself– & blessed God that my lot was cast in a land where all could make an honest living if they w$\underline{d}$ only work industriously– There are to be sure cases of want, but only where there has been intemperance or illness against which it is not so easy to provide– But, I must close my long discussion & bid you Adieu– with love to all my [*illegible*] friends near you– I am dearest Mamma ever Y$\underline{r}$ most affec^{te} daughter Eliza

M$\underline{rs}$ Smith dined with us on Friday, since when I have not seen her– She was then very well. The children are quite well– M$\underline{r}$ Harrison much as usual– M$\underline{rs}$ F. miserably nervous today– I have a cold but it is better today decidedly– So don't be uneasy–

Private Collection

1. Arthur had read Philadelphia obstetrician William Potts Dewees's *Treatise on the Physical and Medical Treatment of Children* (1836), in which Dewees recognized that "purulent ophthalmia" in babies was caused by an infection received from the mother at birth. Arthur therefore replied to Eliza, via his mother, that "you were in error in supposing that [the] Child's opthalmia was the result of want of care . . . [It] is a very serious disease & . . . has been cured by homoeopathic treatment unaided by any other resource save that of the application of three Leeches." The reference may be to Samuel Gridley Howe, Julia Ward's husband, who was in charge of The Perkins School for The Blind in Boston. MHM to EMF, March 8, 1845, PHi.

2. Edward had startled his mother by referring to his "wife" as early as October. MHM to EMF, February 2, 1845, PHi.

3. The nature of the claim is not explained but may have been related to his service in Spain.

4. A major cause of dispute between Pierce and Fanny Butler was that she published her *Journal* against her husband's wishes.

5. Mrs. Middleton agreed that "the Negroes are infinitely better fed & clothed here than the poor in England who from all accounts must be in a miserable state." MHM to EMF, February 11, 1845, PHi.

⏦

To Mrs. Fisher, Philadelphia

M. Place Feby 27th 1845

I was delighted about an hour ago my dearest Eliza to receive your letter of the 20th, the party having arrived about 1/2 past 3 o'clock Y^r Father & W^m, Arthur & P^a & the two children. The infant's Eyes are well & they have no appearance of inflammation. – interrupted by Paolina–

28th before breakfast– & I must hasten to write & either send or take this myself to Mrs W. Pringle to request her to have it taken to town by some of the family who frequently go there– I suppose you know that her eldest son married Emma Smith[1] about 3 weeks ago– Paolina has suffered from her accouchement & was ordered by the Midwife not to take long walks– (something like what Sally complained of) but Arthur can no doubt heal her–

Two letters besides yours were put into my hands– one from my brother of 27th Jany in which though he does not mention an attack of Gout his writing manifests a very trembling hand– And now who do you think the other letter came from? Edward– & in that he gives an account of his Marriage which was on the 13th of Jan^y (so that the former one in which he wrote twice 'my wife' was premature, <u>She</u> was at Naples, & he at Marseilles). He arrived at Naples on the 4th of Jany the ceremony was performed at the chapel of the British Embassy so that I presume the bride is not a R^n Cath^c. <u>She,</u> he says en passant, be it remarked was observed to have emphasized the word 'obey'– The next day they left Naples for Rome & he immediately called to see Count Bentivoglio[2] who with the C^ss gave him a hearty welcome & the next day they called to see the bride & bridegroom & the day after gave them an excellent Italian dinner– They were very much pleased with all the family, particularly with the Count, who Ed^d says "gained my heart sooner than any man I ever met with." It was with great regret, he says, that "we left them the next Evening for Civita Vecchia where we arrived the following morn^g & embarked in the Steamer for Marseilles where we arrived on the 22^d & on the same even^g for Toulon where we shall remain a few days before proceeding to Mahon–" "Unless I get my leave of Absence I shall endeavour to bring my wife home in the Lexington if I can make an exchange at the same time." He adds that if the leave of absence is obtained (which W^m says it is) he should prefer going by the way of Paris & South[hampto]n that he might see his Uncles & present his Wife to them who he is sure will enliven us all by her sprightlyness, if she fails to gain our hearts, by letting us see how much of sunshine & of shower there is in hers– She will be 18 in the month of June. was born in the Is^d of Jersey & is thought very much to resemble the Queen– this would make us suppose that her Mother was the daughter of the Duke of Kent[3] which y^r Father thinks from what he left her, is the fact.

My brother says "the intelligence of Edward's approaching Marriage has given me great pleasure not so much for the grandeur of the connection, but because I think that so good a heart as his will be likely to choose well & form a proper match"– "The daughter of the notorious Queen was removed from the tutelage of her Mother too early to be damaged by her example, & the Granddaughter seems to have been quite free from the danger of contagion" (this is a very different opinion from what you & 2 of y^r brothers give)– he says he & the old Lady will be very happy to see the bride & Bridegroom which I hope they will–

I forget the date of my last letter, but think you must have rec^d it very soon after your last was written & have known the reason why it could not be sent before. I am sorry to hear you have had a bad cough & that your throat was even slightly affected by the cold– but you assure me you are now well. A sad account of Mr Harrison! & you think his illness may be the means of preventing you from going to Newport! that indeed would be a most distressing disappointment to me– At my time of life I feel that I ought always to be near my dearest Eliza– but my own will is never granted.

W^m sent down the following shrubs & desired Mr Wilkes to have them sent to Phil^a by the first vessel & to write to Mr Fisher the name &c– 3 Illiciums– 3 Stuartias– 1 Ptilea– 5 Lagostremias–[4] 5 Varnish trees. These are all he could recollect last Eve^g– perhaps there may be more– We have here the beginning of spring– the weeping Willow now green– the yellow Jess^{ne} in bloom. All the trees & shrubs putting forth their leaves, so that the winter here has been very short. I was glad to learn that young Inglis was not lost– he wrote lately to his Mother from Cuba. How is Mrs Smith now? Has she obtained the money due to her from the W. Indies? Pray give my love to her. P[aolin]a says that Is[abell]a M[iddleton][5] has lately heard from the Priory that Sarah had been ill, but was better. She was requested not to mention it to her Mother & the boys who were told of it were desired not to write that news to their parents which would make them very unhappy. I have heard lately from Mrs Rutledge. She is now in better health & begs to be remembered to you– Miss Pinckney & family arrived at Char^n yesterday so that they have not fulfilled their promise of coming here on their way, but may perhaps come some time hence if I remind them of it which I shall do. Mrs R^h Izard has just got a daughter her 3^d Child. poor Mrs T. M[iddleton] lost her youngest boy 18 months old 3 weeks ago–

Your little girls must have been much pleased with the visit of their country companions–[6] I long to see them, but suppose they have forgotten me. Pray give my love to M$\underline{rs}$ & Mr Fisher & believe me my dearest Eliza y^r Affect$\underline{te}$ Mother M. H. M.

Y^r Father Brothers & Paolina send their love– I must hasten to go to Runnymede.

PHi

1. Emma Clara Pringle Smith, daughter of Elizabeth (Pringle) and Robert Smith, married William Alston Pringle, son of the William Bull Pringles, the Middletons' neighbors at Runnymede.
2. Paolina's father.
3. Edward, duke of Kent, was a brother of George IV and the father of Queen Victoria. While the Middletons supposed Edwardina was his granddaughter, Uncle Oliver's comments in the next paragraph imply he thought Edwardina's grandmother was Queen Caroline, wife of George IV.
4. That is, lagerstroemia.
5. Isabella Middleton was the H. A. Middletons' third daughter. She was nineteen.
6. Mr. Misch, who farmed the Fishers' land in Abington, brought his wife and little girls to spend the day in Philadelphia. EMF to MHM, February 21, 1845, private collection.

⌢

To Mrs. Middleton, Middleton Place

Philadelphia – Friday Feby 28$\underline{th}$ [1845]

As I write the date I remember with pleasure that in about 3 months more I may hope to see my dearest Mamma– for what should prevent yr coming on the end of May to pass a month with me, at the Farm on yr way to NewPort? Nothing that we can foresee at present, & as it is always best & wisest to anticipate everything agreeable, I persuade myself that as there is nothing <u>unreasonable</u> in this expectation it may very well be fulfilled– The very day after I wrote came yr letter of the 11$\underline{th}$ & 17$\underline{th}$ which relieved me from the anxiety I was beginning to feel– you are all in good health, I judge by the cheerful tone of it– altho' you do not say so– It will be the best proof to you that I am well to inform you that I was actually permitted to go to Casella's last Soirée last night![1] This was really a great treat to me as you may suppose, & quite an unexpected one too– for I had so often been disappointed by rain or bad weather, that I had made up my mind it would come again to keep me in– However it held up all the eveng notwithstanding the threats during the day, and I was able for <u>once</u> to go & enjoy myself–

Fisher just took us (Rebecca Smith accompanied me) to our seats, which we had some difficulty in obtaining, (as she came very late as usual), & then left us– not being able to stand the glare of the gas lights– I was surrounded by acquaintances, & therefore did not mind it– but for my misfortune I was placed just behind two Magpies in the shape of chattering girls, who were telling each other silly stories about susceptible young ladies falling desperately in love at <u>NewPort</u> last summer– Really if I had preferred listening to such trash to the Music which I vainly endeavoured to hear, I might have become intimately acquainted with all the circumstances of the flirtation, & might even have made a guess at the names of the parties spoken of– & who knows but Harry or W<u>m</u> may have been implicated? But what between my indignation at the impudence of the talkers, (the handsome Miss McKee, & little Miss Worell) & my despair at being thus made to miss one of the very few opportunities of hearing good music, I was not even able to console myself with the acquisition of such important <u>facts</u>– & was left only to <u>conjectures</u>– I do think it is almost <u>dishonest</u> of people to be cheating one out of one's money's worth & said something of the sort to my neighbour loud enough to be heard by the offenders who took the hint & afterwards conducted themselves with rather more propriety–

Talking of Music, what do you think of my being induced to <u>sing</u>, the other night, for the first time for years– M<u>rs</u> Elliot was here spending a sociable eveng– with the Crawfords, our country neighbours, & a few others– & put me so much "en train" [*in good spirits*] that I sang the second of several Duetts with her before I knew what I was about– I did not feel any ill effects from it however, & we are to practise together, if my voice can be coaxed back– She is a delightful musician–

M<u>r</u> Gilpin returned from Washington with the good news that Alex<u>r</u> Inglis was safe at S<u>t</u> Thomas– he wrote to his mother from thence after having beaten about for 30 days in a dismasted Ship! How happy they must be!

Do you ever see the "Living Age"[2] now? for if you do <u>not</u>, & think it worth while to pay 2 cents & 1/2 Postage, I can send you all the numbers from the beginning of Jan<u>y</u> which we have taken– They contain many very curious things– There is an article in the last Blackwood which I sh<u>d</u> like you also to read– on Mesmerism– being a review of Townshend's book–[3] written I think with great impartiality & fairness– & arguing that all the pretended miracles of Clairvoyance are unworthy of credit– but that the Comatic or Cataleptic State is certainly proved to be true– & that the operations performed upon the patient during that time are not productive of pain– the nervous sensibility being nearly, & in some cases, entirely destroyed– at least the writer seems to incline to this opinion, but has not quite made up his mind as to the <u>certainty</u>

of the paralysis of nervous sensation by mesmeric influence– which appears highly desirable at least, from the benefit which w$^{\underline{d}}$ result to poor suffering humanity, were it possible– Hood cuts up poor Miss Martineau for her letters on Mesmerism famously & her Physician has written a long letter to explain how she was cured without its aid, so the Paper states– If I could believe what M$^{\underline{r}}$ Townshend says of the improvement of sight produced by Mesmerising I sh$^{\underline{d}}$ wish poor Fisher to try it directly– I am expecting him to return from the Farm every minute– he has been away since 9 o'clk & it is now nearly 6– quite a long day– which he was to employ in working hard in the garden– If his eyes can only be restored, every sacrifice will be light, & he will cheerfully labour hard with Spade or Axe– Tell William I wish he were here to accept the invitations I receive almost daily– There are several Strangers in town for whom parties are made, notwithstanding Lent– We intend to keep the 12$^{\underline{th}}$ as usual if we are all tolerably well– M$^{\underline{r}}$ H– has been rather better the last week– & I hope will continue so– Adieu my dearest Mamma, pray give my best love to Papa, my brothers, Kitty & Pauline– M$^{\underline{rs}}$ F– & Fisher beg their kind regards to each of the party– & I am as ever Y$^{\underline{r}}$ most affectionate daughter E

The little girls are quite well but baby has taken a fresh cold which worries her a good deal– She seems almost as susceptible of the changes of temperature as myself, which I much regret– Lily & Sophy send their loves–

Private Collection

1. Eliza was pleased that she and her friends had "replenished the empty purses of the poor Casellas, wonderfully well– I have got nearly $90 for him– Mrs. Willing upwards of a hundred– Mrs. Elliott $50– and several other ladies large sums also– So they are in high spirits." Mrs. Willing, she continued, "was indefatigable, and even went to the offices of some of the gentlemen to force them into subscribing– for which she is justly censured I think– I hope that after so much trouble has been taken to collect money for Casella, that he will not squander it away." EMF to MHM, February 21, 1845, private collection.

2. *Littell's Living Age,* a weekly magazine begun in May 1844, probably interested Mrs. Middleton because the editor reprinted articles from English reviews as well as English fiction.

3. *Facts in Mesmerism, with Reasons for a Dispassionate Inquiry into It,* by Chauncy Hare Townshend (1798–1868), first published in London about 1840, was frequently reprinted in the United States.

⌒

To Mrs. Middleton, Middleton Place

Philadelphia – March 17<u>th</u> 1845

You have been very kind in writing frequently of late, dearest Mamma, & I have another letter (of the 9<u>th</u>) to thank you for, which was very acceptable– I have forgotten which day I last wrote to you, but think it must have been about a week since– & at any rate, being prevented going to Aunt's this eveng– by the rain, I feel all the inclination to scribble, particularly as I shall probably not find time to do so tomorrow– Our long projected visit to the Farm, has not taken place yet– I mean Aunt's & mine– for Fisher is backwards & forwards constantly– & indeed was on his way there today, but turned back in a snow-storm! As it is now <u>very</u> clear to the West, we hope for a fine day tomorrow, for Fisher is anxious to have Aunt's advice about his improvements &c– & after nearly 5 months absence I want to see what has been done– The work goes slowly on of course– for he cannot afford to employ more than one man to assist the gardener– M<u>r</u> H– has kindly offered to lend him what he wants, but he cannot bear to abuse his kindness–[1] and hopes now that the war panic has subsided, that he will be able to sell his Lots at a fair price– which they w<u>d</u> not bring during the agitation caused by the Texas & Oregon questions– Had he foreseen the difficulty of these sales, he w<u>d</u> never have engaged in this Farming business– for the few hundreds that it has run him into debt, have worried him more than so many thousands w<u>d</u> a Planter–

We are looking out daily for the Vessel which has on board the Shrubs from M. Place– I hope the agreeable visitors you were expecting came back with Arthur– If they did, I suppose they will have left you again ere this– I do not believe there is a word of truth in the report of S[ophia] T[horndike]'s marriage which M<u>rs</u> S[umner] retailed– I suppose it is merely a repetition of what was said last year– which she most expressly contradicted– The last account I had of her was thro' M<u>rs</u> Ritchie to whom she wrote that she was very well–

We had quite an agreeable set here on the 12<u>th</u> & some excellent singing– among other things the Old Trio of "Ma Fauchette est charmante" of which Papa is so fond, very well sung indeed– I attempted a little Gabussi duett, but got frightened at finding how little voice I had, & hardly know how I managed to get to the end of it– I had some beautiful flowers sent me & a very fine bunch from Fisher, which I am taking great care to preserve a long while– Casella offered to play for me but as there were to be several ladies present who had refused to go to his concerts, & one who actually gave a party on the night of one of them, altho' she was requested not to interfere, I did not choose them to have the gratification of hearing him–

We are going to try & get up one more concert for them, the <u>Final</u> Farewell, before they sail– which they have postponed until the 1$\underline{st}$ of May– He thinks that he shall spend part of next winter in Rome, & asked me if La Contessa [*Paolina*] w$\underline{d}$ write a letter of recommendation or two for him to her friends– I promised to prefer his request– which I hope Paolina will not refuse– as it might be of great use to him– His poor little wife is now half the time in her bed, & will scarcely survive the voyage I think– Europe is certainly the proper place for him– for he does not get proper encouragement here– and his Talents altho' great require emulation to stimulate them– A few lines expressive of the pleasure his Music gives, addressed to one of her friends whose patronage might influence the "beau monde" I shd feel very much indebted to Pauline if she w$\underline{d}$ write– and he w$\underline{d}$ be very grateful for–

I had a letter from John a few days ago, which I was very glad to receive– He says that Sally's health is better on the whole this season than the last which I rejoice to hear– & also that you are looking remarkably well– I wish he gave as good an account of Papa– Has he seen him since W$\underline{m}$ left Carolina? for it is strange that their reports of Papa vary so much– I had been flattering myself that his recovery was complete– but fear that is not the case– I do hope to pass a few weeks at least with, or rather <u>near</u> you at NewPort– for of course with the prospect of the arrival of M$\underline{r}$ & M$\underline{rs}$ Ed$\underline{wd}$ even the addition will not accomodate such a family–[2] but I can see as much of you from the Hotel opposite– If God only spares us all meanwhile which may he of his Mercy grant– Adieu Y$\underline{r}$ most affecte E

Private Collection

1. In a note which may have been written about this time, Uncle Harrison told Fisher, "I am making some fiscal arrangements. I wish you to give me the amount of your <u>proposed</u> improvements give them <u>honestly</u> & fairly, and the precise amount of the accommodation you may wish– <u>no mock modesty</u> with me I beg of you– but in all things <u>above board</u>– Say <u>Frankly</u> & <u>honestly</u> the <u>amount</u> of <u>expected</u> cost & the sum you'll require on Loan to place you at ease au sujet [*in the matter*]– let me have both." GH to JFF, n.d., PHi, Coll. 1858.

2. To accommodate an ever-expanding family, Henry Middleton was having an addition built onto the house in Newport. The Middletons had already added to the house once before in 1838.

⌣

To Mrs. Fisher, Philadelphia

M.P. March 18$\underline{th}$ 1845

My dearest Eliza

As there will be tomorrow a means of sending this to Charles$\underline{n}$ & as Paolina is not going to answer your letter until she has seen your Father, I will not delay writing although I have not yet received one since that of 28$\underline{th}$ ult$\underline{o}$ which I answered 10 days ago– but your letter to P$\underline{a}$ was very gratifying to me– She is very desirous of going to Church this week & next Monday, & also to meet Susan who will leave town with her Mother on Friday.

Arthur instead of bringing last Wednesday M$\underline{rs}$ Holbrook & Emma brought the two Miss Gilmans daughters of the Schoolmaster who is a friend of his– They are very well behaved & sensible girls & good looking, & both your brothers try to amuse them– teach them the Polka, walk out all over the grounds, exhibit in the evening the large quantity of prints of the buildings & costumes &c of the various countries & they seem to enjoy themselves– Emma S. begged Arthur not to bring M$\underline{rs}$ H[olbrook] until she herself could come, & as she expected her husband in a few days did not wish to leave town then, but I suppose she will accompany M$\underline{rs}$ H next Tuesday, when Arthur & P$\underline{a}$ will probably return here. Your Father & W$\underline{m}$ have not yet returned from Combahee– I am much obliged to you for the 4 numbers of the 'Living Age' you sent by M$\underline{rs}$ C. Harper– as I believe I told you, I wrote her an invitation to come here with Arthur but she wrote me word that she was going immediately to Savannah, as the Physician recommended for her Child, in preference to Carolina. but she says she will on her return from thence make me a visit. I have not yet read all, but the two I have, I think amusing– Arthur has taken them out of the room, therefore [I] must defer reading others till tomorrow. I never see Blackwood's Mag$\underline{e}$ but cannot help believing what Arthur has witnessed & performed by clairvoyance: In future time when it is universally practised, you may perhaps believe in it.

M$\underline{r}$ W. Pringle was here yesterday & told me that his Son (in the Navy) had received a letter from one of his Friends in the Medit$\underline{n}$ mentioning that Edward & his Wife intended to come to America in one of the Store ships from Mahon– He had not I presume money enough to enable him to make his visits as he wished, to his two Uncles [*Izard Middleton and Oliver Hering*]. We may expect to see him ere long. The Infant (for I know not yet what she is to be called, though to be christened as I mentioned to you[1]) is improving in appearance although she has an eruption on her face– She is very fat & very quiet, & Paolina is delighted by her frequent smiles. Her eyes are now well.

So Mrs Gilpin is expecting to encrease her family! I was surprised to read of it– as I was also of the marriage of S. Hare[2] which I thought would not be so soon accomplished. This is the warmest day we have had for the last week which has been unexpectedly cold– the weather as I wrote you word having been previously very warm, & we have had two days of rain, while you perhaps have had snow. the grass is now looking green which it did not before, & all the fruit trees are in blossom– I suppose the shrubs sent to you are by this time planted at Abington–

I received last week a letter from John in which he says that Sally is benefitted by being more than usual in the open air, but in her eyes he says there is no amendment, & she occasionally suffers a good deal from them: he says too that you have been so kind as to reiterate your invitation to Sally to pass next Summer with you at Abington: he assures me he fully appreciates your affectionate regard, which has always been uniform & consistent. 'A better Sister never existed.' He has I suppose told you that Sally cannot make you that visit. He is to be in Charles^{n} on the 8th of April about some business, & will come here to stay a very short time as it is a great inconvenience to be absent from home in the plantation season. He deeply regrets that Edward should have been so inconsiderate as to form such a connexion as he has. We must hope it may prove a happy match. I am anxious to know my dear Eliza that you have consented to remain with me three months at Newport, for only consider how short a time I can hope to remain in this world! and you are my greatest comfort.

I was glad to read that Lily & Sophy sent their love to me but can scarcely flatter myself that they remember me or care for me. pray give my love to them & tell them they are to be with me at Newport & amuse themselves with their little cousins. I suppose little Helen has now more teeth & will walk as Ed^{d} did at 10 months old– Pray give my love to Mrs Smith & to M^{rs} & Mr Fisher– Your Brothers & Paolina send theirs to you & I am my dearest Eliza y^{r} Affectionate Mother M. H. M.

I hope soon to have a good account of Mr Harrison– pray remember me to him & M^{rs} H.

PHi

1. The baby's names were to be Anna, Angela and Constantina. MHM to EMF, March 8, 1845, PHi.

2. Mrs. Middleton meant S. Powel, not S. Hare. Samuel Powel, John Hare Powel's son, had married Mary Johnston on March 6.

～

To Mrs. Middleton, Middleton Place

Philadelphia – March 25$\underline{th}$ 1845

Altho' I feel rather tired this afternoon, having been at the Farm all the morning, I will not delay writing to my dearest mamma, lest I sh$\underline{d}$ be prevented tomorrow– and first let me thank you for your letter of the 18$\underline{th}$ which I rec$\underline{d}$ yesterday– in which you give me good news of all the family except Papa and W$\underline{m}$ who had not returned from Combahee– I hope dear Pauline will not neglect to answer all my enquiries particularly those about Papa–

I have had a terrible fright since I last wrote & poor Little Sophy a severe lesson to teach her more caution– She is truly American in her fashion of going ahead without looking to the consequences, and stumbling over all obstacles which may chance to be in her path– & of course the scrapes she gets into are very numerous– She had not recovered from a very serious bruise on her forehead, which left her sadly disfigured (for a few days) when on Friday morng– she tripped against a bucket of hot water (not boiling fortunately) & fell, or rather sat into it– scalding herself terribly– Her screams were piercing– and the agony must have been very great– for the cotton flannel drawers soaked up the water, & could not be got off immediately– I applied as soon as possible sweet oil & Lime Water mixed– but not until M$\underline{rs}$ Putnam had rubbed her with Whiskey– which the D$\underline{r}$ says was right– He said that Turpentine w$\underline{d}$ have been still more effectual– which however I could never have had the Courage to apply– Arthur w$\underline{d}$ no doubt approve of this Homoeopathic remedy– The poor child suffered extremely for an hour after the accident occurred, and during the following day whenever the burns were dressed– They were very soon relieved by the lime water & oil, but she has been obliged to keep her bed ever since until today, when she is delighted to find she can walk once more– In the midst of her suffering when I told her that the skin was burnt off, she asked if "God would make a new skin grow on her itten egs (little legs)" and was pacified by being assured that he would– She has been wonderfully patient, altho' generally so restless and fond of romping– but until today, I have scarcely left her bedside, except to go to Church, & was amply rewarded for the pains I took to amuse her by her affection and gratitude– Her sleep at night has not been disturbed, most fortunately– tomorrow I think she will be able to have her clothes on, and run about as usual–

At last we have made our visit to the Farm– we set off a week ago (after being disappointed on account of weather about a dozen times I think) and had to return on foot, only about a mile luckily, as the wheel became loose, and it was not safe for us to proceed– As it began to snow hard soon after we returned, we did not much regret that we had not gone further– We have had very disagreeable March weather for several days, except Sunday, which was a beautiful Easter day– I had two very pretty Easter presents from Mrs Mütter & R. Smith– and the children were made happy by Easter eggs– The Trees & Shrubs arrived safe from Charleston on Thursday, and were planted yesterday– They appear to be alive all of them, and I trust will succeed after all the trouble W^m has taken– for which pray thank him for us– M^rs McEuen tells me that Mrs Izard has given Delancey I[zard] a fine Plantation with 100 workers– a very generous gift indeed! She says she hears that Lizzie is engaged to Pringle Smith– Do you know anything of it? I hear also that Delancey is paying his addresses to Susan Smith–[1] Is he likely to succeed?

Wednesday morng– I had to break off & dress for Mrs Hare's party last eveng– where I enjoyed myself very much– Tell Harry that I saw there M^rs C[amac] & her attendant Mr Cox– leaning over her with very loverlike looks– They say her sisters do not deny the engagement– Miss Julia Cox, his cousin, is going to be married to Mr T. Biddle– nephew of Mrs H. Williams'– which is said to be a very suitable match in every respect–

I was up till near one o'clock last night, for I found it so agreeable at Mrs Hare's that I allowed them to send away my Cab which I had ordered at 1/2 past 10, & remained there an hour longer– & after my return home, a serenade began which kept me up listening to it– Tonight the Grand Bachelor's Ball takes place, over the way at the Masonic Hall– & I was almost tempted to go over Cloaked & bonnetted as a Spectator in the Gallery– but don't think it will be worth while, as the Polka which w^d be the principal attraction to me will not begin 'till near midnight I am told– Several Baltimore girls have come on for it, & are staying with Miss Kuhn– & I understand that the widow Jones & her daughter from N.Y. are also expected to attend– I have got to the end of my paper & forgotten to tell you the news I hear from Mrs Schroeder who had a letter by the last Steamer from her Son Frank who tells her that M^r & M^rs Ed. Middleton had arrived at Mahon & were to sail thence for Charleston on the 10th of March in a store ship– He describes the bride, who he says is quite pretty (not beautiful) in the style of Delia Stuart with a very full bust & English appearance– He has heard her sing, & says she has a magnificent voice, but not very much cultivated– Is very lively & speaks 4 languages fluently– I am very glad to hear about the voice for Papa's sake and hope she may prove an agreeable addition to the family circle– but what folly!! FS. says that the Mother calls herself "Lady Edwardina Kent de Normann"!! The daughters name is also Edwardina, which I really think had better be changed to Dina– albeit rather an Ethiopian sound– I have many misgivings about this same match but we must hope for the best always– Adieu dearest Mamma I am as ever Y^r most affectionate daughter Eliza

Private Collection

1. Lizzie Middleton and John Julius Pringle Smith (1816–1894), son of Robert and Elizabeth (Pringle) Smith, were married on November 18, 1845. Susan Pringle Smith was J. J. Pringle Smith's sister; she married Williams Middleton in 1849.

～

To Mrs. Fisher, Philadelphia

M.P. March 31$^{\underline{st}}$ 1845

My dearest Eliza

Since my last letter was despatched I have had the pleasure to receive yours of the 10$^{\underline{th}}$ & the 17$^{\underline{th}}$ As Paolina wrote to you from Charle$^{\underline{n}}$, you must have had news every week from us–¹ there may not be another opportunity after tomorrow, therefore I will send this by W$^{\underline{m}}$ tomorrow who is to accompany the two Miss Brevoorts & M$^{\underline{r}}$ Griffin who he brought here last Saturday– They are well behaved lively Girls & M$^{\underline{r}}$ G. is an agreeable man– I suppose W$^{\underline{m}}$ told you that M$^{\underline{rs}}$ [Henry] B[revoort] & her five Daughters have been spending this winter in town with her Mother M$^{\underline{rs}}$ Carson– they are to be at Newport in the Summer. à propos of Newport, how can you think of passing only a few weeks with us, or near us? I told you I hoped you would pass 3 months in our house, & if your throat is well, what objection can you have to doing so? remember what we said on the subject– You are to occupy the room next to mine & the two additional dressing rooms now building– Ed$^{\underline{d}}$ & his Wife can occupy the room that Arthur & P$^{\underline{a}}$ did last Summer, & they must have the two upstairs, that you used to have. Cath$^{\underline{e}}$ can have Harry's until the Girls come to spend the holidays there, & then she can remove to W$^{\underline{m}}$'s room & he & Harry can sleep at any adjoining small hotel– now what objection can you or M$^{\underline{r}}$ Fisher make to that arrangement? I am sure your Father would not consent to your staying in an hotel, & it would distress me very much– think too how expensive it would be– & pray my dear Eliza consent to occupy the rooms I mention, & remain with me three months– As I said before, there can be no necessity for your being more than 2 months at Abington, for you have a good Farmer who can manage every thing there– and as to Sally being there, it is out of the question. I hope your next letter will inform me that you agree to my request. As you have heard lately from John you must know that Sally is in better health than usual, although her eyes are not improving, that is a sad injury! Have you prevailed upon Mr F. to try Mesmerism for his? it could not injure them, & <u>might</u> cure them.

Besides the two Girls, we have Mrs Coffin & her youngest boy– they came here with Arthur & P^{a} on the 25$^{\underline{th}}$– I like her very much, she is a sensible & well informed woman & I have persuaded her to stay until tomorrow– Your brothers teach the Girls the Polka in the eve^g but Mrs C. will not be their scholar, though the dancing amuses her.

This morn^g I was surprised to see Del[ance]y Izard walking with the party. When I joined them I enquired after his Sisters who he says are all well– Geor[-gin]a has been spending the winter at Stono, where he is now. He has lately been so fortunate as to receive from his Step Mother 100 Negroes & a plantation, as she had promised her husband to provide for his Son– All Step mothers would not be so generous– She & her Sister Miss Pinckney told your brothers that they could not come here. Mrs Holbrook too could not come last week & it is uncertain whether she can come at all. Emma too could not, as she was to see her Father only a day or two before going to Sav^a river– She has decided as I suppose you know, to go to Paris this summer–

The day after I wrote my last telling you it had been so warm & then cold it became much colder, & we had fires– within a few days it has been very mild, & there has been rain which improves the appearance of the grass & trees– You must have suffered from the cold, but I hope it did not affect your throat– but you say that you had so little voice that you could hardly manage to finish the song on the 12$^{\underline{th}}$. I thought of you on that Eve^g & flattered myself you were enjoying the anniversary. I suppose Pa^a informed you that Lizzie M. was engaged to be married to P[ringle] Smith– You have not in y^r two last letters mentioned <u>M^{rs}</u> P. Smith I hope she is well– do give my love to her. I am expecting to see Ed$^{\underline{d}}$ soon as the Lexington will probably soon arrive– The winds must perhaps be contrary, they have lately been very violent. The escape of the travellers in the rail Cars which you mention was indeed extraordinary–

Y^r Father went to Charl$^{\underline{n}}$ this morn^g. I was surprised that P^a wrote to you before seeing him on his return from Combahee– W^m told me he was better & he seemed so to me– he does not like to be questioned on the subject, or any other. He will return in a few days with W^m & then I presume will soon go to Combahee, unless the putting on of the new roof [*at Middleton Place*] should make them remain to superintend the work– You cannot imagine in what a state the shingles are now– so that the new ones ought to be put on without delay.

Mrs Harper told Mrs Sumner that the Calderons had taken the Observatory[2] [*in Newport*] for the family so that we shall be near neighbours. The S's are to leave Char^{n} the first week of Ap^{l} & you will see them soon, as they intend to stop about a week at Phil^{a}– Paolina sends her best love to you, pray give mine to M^{rs} & Mr Fisher & my kind remembrance to M^{r} & Mrs Harrison– believe me my dearest Eliza y^{r} affectionate Mother

Do kiss the dear Children for me.

1st April– Just as I had finished writing yesterday about Sun set D^{r} & Mrs Holbrook came. I was very glad to see them but was puzzled how to accommodate them as all the house was full & was obliged to make them have the room in the out house near the barn– The eve^{g} was passed very gaily by dancing the Polka & Laura Brevoort after 10 o'clock when I went to bed begged Arthur to magnetize her which he did but she only pretended to sleep– this morn^{g} however Mrs Coffin requested him to magnetize <u>her</u>, which he did & she actually slept for about 5 minutes when her child made a noise & awoke her– Mrs Holbrook & myself were witnesses of the success of the operation & she & the Doctor believe in magnetism.

All the party are to leave us tomorrow– Mrs H. is to go with her Mother on friday to Santee[3] & the Brevoorts to N.Y. by Rail road with the Sumners on Saturday. I was shocked to hear that poor M^{r} [Jonathan] Hunt is insane– He passed through Char^{n} a week ago, & a man was hired by his Agent to accompany him to N.Y. Poor Man! W^{m} says he has no relations there & but a few friends. W^{m} begs you to remind Mr Sidney Fisher of his promise to come here. Adieu– it is now nearly dark–

PHi

1. Eliza told her mother it was a pleasure to read Paolina's "sweet Italian, which expresses so gracefully what w^{d} sound common place in English. I read every day 4 chapters in the Italian, the morng and eveng [*church*] lessons . . . which I find the best method of studying it." EMF to MHM, April 2, 1845, private collection.
2. An observatory on the property next to the Middletons' was now rented as a house.
3. Mrs. Harriott (Horry) Rutledge, Mrs. Holbrook's mother, lived at Hampton Plantation, on the Santee River, northeast of Charleston.

~

To Mrs. Middleton, Middleton Place

Philadelphia – April 23$\underline{rd}$ 1845

My dearest Mamma,

I was much under obligation to the little D$\underline{r}$ Gibbes for carrying y$\underline{r}$ letter to town, but <u>not</u> for keeping it in his pocket for 2 days after he got there as y$\underline{r}$ date is the 11$\underline{th}$ and the Post mark the <u>14$\underline{th}$</u>– which I can only account for by supposing he had it so long in possession– in a fit of <u>abstraction</u>– while he was pursuing some of his scientific researches perhaps– I am very glad to find that you seem to have enjoyed yr gay party at M. Place and also to hear that the roof was <u>really</u> at last being renewed– You do not mention whether it was to be <u>modernized</u> at all– viz dropped lower, and made to project at the eaves– which w$\underline{d}$ certainly be a vast improvement to the appearance of the old House– Everything will be in readiness for the arrival of <u>Edward & Edwardina</u> I suppose– which you will soon announce to me– I hope poor Ned will not be ordered off to Mexico immediately– but it seems probable that the services of all officers will be in requisition soon– and the news today from England– puts the subject of <u>war</u> into one's thoughts, and into men's mouths– but I trust sincerely that the bravado of President Polk will not lead to such serious consequences– and that before the next session of Congress, peaceful measures may be devised for settling the difficulty– else NewPort would not be a safe residence– and we should all retreat in more security to the Mountains– I daresay <u>you</u> will be in a perfect fever, but hope the panic will be of short duration– What does Uncle Oliver write you about it?

The Sumners left Phil$\underline{a}$ today– He went up to Pottsville[1] with Sidney, and down into a Coal mine the descent into which he was describing to me this morng– but, I don't know how it is, altho' he certainly has tolerably good sense, there is such an intolerable <u>prosiness</u> of manner, that I cannot for the life of me prevent my attention from wandering while he is talking– They think, or at least <u>talk</u>, of building at NewPort–[2] and have taken away the plan for a country gentleman's house, which M$\underline{rs}$ Butler lent to us last year and has begged them to keep as long as they choose– We thought it on quite too magnificent a scale– but they mean to alter it to suit their convenience if they decide upon following it at all–

We had a very pleasant little Musical party on Monday eveng– M$\underline{r}$ Laffitte sang the most amusing of comic songs– M$\underline{rs}$ Elliot & M$\underline{rs}$ Cuesta also sang– and Julia Cox played two magnificent pieces, to the great admiration of every one present– As to her lover, he was in a state of ecstasy, all the eveng & seemed to have neither ears nor eyes for any one else– I had an opportunity of asking M$\underline{r}$

Sumner more about our new relation and her family– with whom he became acquainted at Naples– and he says he does not think they kept a school (as Emma had heard) and that he met the Mother constantly in the first society– "dans toutes les bonnes maisons." However as he had previously told me that he was at their house which he seemed to have forgotten the last time I asked him perhaps his account is not to be much relied upon– and he may prefer, like many of his countrymen, to say something agreeable rather than the truth–

Tell William I heard from Mrs Gilliat that Miss [Julia] de Rham was engaged, but she had forgotten the name of the gentleman– Fisher saw her in N.Y. and talked for half an hour with her at the reception at the Otis Wedding–[3] but heard nothing of her engagement– and thinks she was not in mourning– so that the report of Pres^{t} Moore's[4] death can hardly be true– or she w^{d} not have appeared so soon in such a gay scene– He says there were about 600 visitors coming in & out from 1 o'clk until 5– 200 of them invited to stay for the Collation– which was very handsome– after which they danced to a full band until 9 in the eveng– Old Mr Otis had his trunk half packed to come on to the Wedding– but not feeling very well he remained in Boston & Alleyne staid to take care of him– so that Fisher only saw Mrs Ritchie & William Otis–[5] They told him they were very uneasy about Alleyne– He is in such a dreadfully nervous state that they actually fear he will go quite crazy– but do not let this be mentioned out of the family– Fisher begged them to send him on here– which they mean to do if possible– He says poor Mr Hunt is confined in the upper part of his house in N.Y. & is at last under proper medical treatment– and as it is a case of phrenzy perhaps he may be cured– as Robert Hare was– He is really engaged to Miss [Caroline] Fleeming,[6] a daughter of Mrs Emerson of Boston– who has 30 thousand dollars now and will probably have 20 thousand more– is a remarkably intelligent well educated amiable girl– but not handsome– It is really an excellent match for Robert– the only wonder is that her Mother & friends sh^{d} permit her to marry him & yet Dr H. seems to think his son does her great honour– altho' he is evidently very much delighted at the engagement– I hope it may turn out happily, but she runs a great risk– Fisher enjoyed his visit of 3 days in N.Y. extremely– particularly the pictures he saw at Mr Lennox's and Mr Carey's–[7] He brought me a copy of Amelia's Poems[8] which I have long admired in the Newspapers, and am glad to have collected–

Thursday– I had yesterday afternoon a letter from Aunt Hering, who says that my Uncle is better since his last attack, which was a very severe one, than he has been for 3 or 4 years– but I suppose you have a letter from himself–

Aunt gives me a great deal of news about my old playmates & schoolfellows, but none that w$^{\underline{d}}$ interest you– Pray tell Harry that I have just rec$^{\underline{d}}$ a very kindly expressed invitation from M$^{\underline{rs}}$ Camac to go out & spend Saturday eveng there– but have declined it in the same Civil style– not thinking it worthwhile to run the risk of taking cold by taking the long ride out of town at night– I must say Adieu! dearest mamma & am as ever Y^r most affect^e daugher E–

Lily is much improved in manners & appearance M$^{\underline{rs}}$ Sumner thinks– She admired them all– but the baby especially– Lily begs me to give her love & tell you she spells a page of words every day– Sophy is sound asleep at my feet– I shall not wean the baby until the Autumn as she thrives so well with her nurse– and has but 2 teeth yet– She now stands nearly alone with the help of a single finger– & will very soon walk–

I intended to devote half of this large Sheet to answering dear Paolina's kind half letter which I thank her for very much– I am very sorry she was not more successful in her application– but feel as much obliged to her for making the effort as if she had been and perhaps it will not be entirely fruitless– My love to her & all the rest– M$^{\underline{r}}$ Harrison has been more indisposed for the last 2 days– suffering with rheumatism besides his other complaint– and quite nervous, which is a new symptom for him– Aunt is much out of spirits. M$^{\underline{rs}}$ F. better than usual– M$^{\underline{rs}}$ Smith is well & is coming to dine with us tomorrow– She always sends love.

Private Collection

1. About one hundred miles northwest of Philadelphia, Pottsville is on the edge of Pennsylvania's anthracite coal region.

2. The Sumners' house in Newport, which they built in 1848, is now known as Rockry Hall.

3. The James Otis' daughter, Sally, married her cousin George Theodore Lyman on April 17, 1845.

4. Nathaniel Moore, the president of Columbia College, was Miss DeRham's uncle. The report of his death was premature; he lived until 1872.

5. William Otis was a son of Harrison Gray Otis and brother of Allyne, James, and Mrs. Ritchie.

6. Miss Fleeming (or Fleming) was the daughter of Charles H. and Mary (Rotch) Fleming.

7. In 1844 James Lenox, Edward Carey, and Henry Reed commissioned painter Henry Inman to go to England and paint prominent people such as Wordsworth and Macaulay. Fisher probably saw these paintings, which were later exhibited in New York.

8. *Poems* was published under the pseudonym "Amelia." The author was Amelia Ball Coppuck Welby (1819–1852).

~

To Mrs. Middleton, Middleton Place

Philadelphia April 30$\underline{th}$ 1845

Two days ago I had the pleasure of receiving your welcome letter, my dearest Mamma, which contained news of the most agreeable kind– first that of Papa's improved health, which made me very happy– and then the favourable settlement of the Law Suit–[1] You appeared to be yourself in good health– to judge from the pleasant & cheerful tone of yr letter, and altogether it was very cheering to me– for I was rather dull & anxious about my dear little Helen– who had been suffering for 24 hours from disordered stomach & bowels, brought on by the irritation of swollen gums, and some cold taken in the last change of weather– On Friday the Therm$\underline{r}$ was in the morng upwards of 70 in the shade & in the afternoon only 45– & the consequence was of course colds– affecting all differently– M$\underline{rs}$ F. took it in her eye which has been so much inflamed that the D$\underline{r}$ ordered Leeches to be applied which she would not hear of– & a dark room & physick which are relieving her very slowly– Poor Baby has had quite a severe attack of indigestion & last evening she was so weak for want of nourishment, for she could keep nothing down, that I felt very unhappy about her– but today, thanks to D$\underline{r}$ Chapman's good care she is very much better– I was perhaps unnecessarily alarmed, & it may have been partly owing to the influence of the book I happened to be reading– a very interesting one by the bye– Lady Willoughby's Diary–[2] supposed to be written in the reign of Charles 1$\underline{st}$ – for it turns out to be a fiction, altho' it gives the impression of reality more than anything I have read– & many parts are extremely affecting– What I alluded to particularly, is the account of her child's illness & death– which touched me deeply– The devotional parts are very beautiful too, & I sympathized entirely with all her Motherly anxieties, & hopes for her children's welfare, and moral & spiritual improvement–

Thursday 1$\underline{st}$ May– I have just returned from Church this Ascension day– but heard only the service without any Sermon at S$\underline{t}$ James'– as I had not chosen to go down to S$\underline{t}$ Peter's where M$\underline{r}$ Odenheimer announced that there w$\underline{d}$ be Communion, which is quite an innovation on a week day– in accordance with Puseyite principles,[3] of which you know I do not approve– so as I cannot bear to turn my back upon the [*communion*] table, I kept away– I really think we shall another winter take a pew at Mr Neville's[4] church, as it is very unpleasant to disagree so entirely with one's Pastor on so many points– It was quite a satisfaction to me to find that such good and sensible men as M^r [William] Goddard[5] & M^r [William] Peter held the same views which I do, and agree in our admiration of Whately and Arnold–[6] I believe I told you how much delighted I was with the life & correspondence of the latter, which I will take on to NewPort if I go–

This reminds me to say in reply to yr oft repeated & kind invitations, dear Mamma, that altho' I hope to be with you there for a month or 6 weeks– it w^d be impossible for me to remain away from Fisher longer than that time for you know how utterly unable he is to amuse himself, deprived as he is of the use of his eyes, poor fellow– & his being at such a distance from Mr Harrison, even sh^d he not become any worse, for more than a week at a time is impossible– We have no hope, & the D^r gives us very little, of any material improvement in M^r H's condition– and his decline altho' slow, seems certain– It goes to my heart to hear him sometimes speak of wishing a speedy termination to his sufferings– which altho' generally not severe, are pretty constant and when he hears of a sudden death, he seems to envy it– Aunt is still wonderfully cheerful– rarely allowing her feelings to get the better of her– but those who see her, as we do, alone, observe the effort she makes in the presence of strangers–

Tell Paolina that Rebecca Smith has made quite a conquest– & one worth keeping too– if she w^d only be made to think so– A M^r [*illegible,*] the son of the old gentleman we made a voyage to Charleston with many years ago, has fallen desperately in love with her– he is very goodlooking and quite wealthy– appears to be extremely amiable & <u>she</u> thinks is intelligent– but of that I cannot yet judge– having only met him twice– once here– for we invited him on Monday eveng with a view <u>specially</u> of bringing them more together– but she is so capricious that I fear he will not press his suit– which he seems well-inclined to do, if she were to give him proper encouragement, and behave rationally– Her mind is terribly unsettled, poor thing, and Mrs Smith & I give her good advice, apparently quite in vain for she won't follow it– By the bye I have many kind messages to you from Mrs Smith who was here this morng & desired me to thank you for your kind enquiries, and to say that she hoped to go to New-Port, but could not yet positively determine to do so– She is better than usual– and doing kind & charitable actions, according to her ability, or rather far beyond it– She certainly does more in proportion to her means, than anyone I know– & receives her reward, in this life, as she will in that to come, without doubt–

My dear baby is better decidedly this eveng– The 2 upper teeth are all but thro'– I did not know how much I loved her until she was ill– Dr Chapman thinks it w^d be highly improper to wean her before the Autumn– & as Sarah behaves very well & is devoted to her, I shall keep her till Septr. Mr Harrison insists upon paying the whole expense of her wages, so that I no longer hesitate–[7] He is always doing kind & generous things, & in the most delicate manner too– Pray in y^r next, tell me if you can when you will be on, & if you will not be able to spend some time with me on Yr way to NewPort– Love to all I am Y^r affect^e daughter E

Private Collection

1. Henry Middleton sought reimbursement from the U.S. government for expenses incurred while he was in Russia. In response, the Treasury Department claimed that in 1840 he actually *owed* the government about $12,000 and initiated a suit against him for payment of that amount. Mrs. Middleton, in reporting that the lawsuit had been decided in Henry Middleton's favor, called it "a very fortunate circumstance." MHM to EMF, April 23, 1845, PHi; Robert L. Meriwether, et al., eds. *Papers of John C. Calhoun* (Columbia: University of South Carolina Press, 1959–): 8, passim.

2. The author of *So Much of the Diary of Lady Willoughby as Relates to Her Domestic History, & to the Eventful Period of the Reign of Charles the First* was Hannah Mary Rathbone (1798–1878).

3. Edward Bouverie Pusey (1800–1882) was a leader of the Oxford Movement. His followers favored practices, such as private confession and frequent communion, which the Anglican/Episcopal Church had not followed since the break with Rome in the sixteenth century.

Not all their friends agreed with Mrs. Middleton and Eliza on this issue. Mrs. McEuen, hearing Eliza discussing her opinions, was "so shocked . . . that she actually ran out of the room for fear of being convinced against her will I suppose." MHM to EMF, March 24, 1844, PHi; EMF to MHM, April 15, 1845, private collection.

4. Edward Neville was the rector of St. Philips Church at Franklin and Vine Streets.

5. William Goddard (d. 1846) was a professor, and later trustee, at Brown University in Providence, Rhode Island. His wife, the former Charlotte Ives, was a first cousin of John B. Francis. William Peter was the English consul in Philadelphia.

6. English churchmen and educators Richard Whately (1787–1863) and the future headmaster of the Rugby school, Thomas Arnold (1795–1842), were not supporters of High Church practices.

7. George Harrison had sent Eliza a note, saying, "Some Evenings past I heard, or thought I heard, something about Your alderny– When she was first spoken of I then, in mind, determined to defray the expense of her wages– The enclosed will confirm my intention, & I pray you to accept it . . . My anticipation is to prevent (hardly necessary) a too early discharge– ever Yrs– Mum." GH to EMF, n.d., PHi, BrC.

∽

To Mrs. Fisher, Philadelphia

M.P. May 3$\underline{d}$ 1845

I had the pleasure my dearest Eliza last Wednesday to receive your letters of the 15$\underline{th}$ & the 25$\underline{th}$ which y$\underline{r}$ Father & W$\underline{m}$ brought from town & was glad to find that you had been enjoying so many gay parties & were able to go to a ball– I conclude that your throat is nearly well though you never mention it, nor do you say whether you will consent to my repeated request of joining me at Newport– the beginning of July– <u>that</u> used to be the period you arrived there, & why should you not continue to be there at that time & remain with me 3 months? I told you lately how all the family might be accommodated without difficulty, & I hope your next letter will inform me that I shall have the happiness of receiving you & your family at the time mentioned. The account you give of the children is very pleasing. By this time little M.H probably walks, which must delight all the family, & Lily spells a page of words every day! pray give my love to her & tell her I am very glad to hear she is such a clever & good little girl, & that I long to see her– She will no doubt be pleased with Benti & the Infant who is as quiet & healthy as M. H. was; exceedingly fat & stout, which her Mother's large quantity of Milk contributes to support her.

I was surprised yesterday morn$\underline{g}$ by a visit of M$\underline{r}$ & M$\underline{rs}$ Julius Pringle who M$\underline{r}$ W. P[ringle] brought in his Carriage from Runnymede where they were staying for two days. M$\underline{rs}$ J. P. said she had never been in this part of the country & wished to walk about the Garden which she did with Paolina & your brothers, but begged me not to fatigue myself which I did not, the weather was extremely hot, & there were much pleasanter companions with her– She told me she was in daily expectation of seeing her brother arrive in the Lexington at Charleston– this surprised me for I thought it would go to Norfolk, & I recollected that you wrote it would go to Charleston but supposed you had been misinformed. but the reason it comes here is that it brings the body of Capt$\underline{n}$ Shubrick.[1] It is much more convenient that Ed$\underline{d}$ should land here, than be obliged to travel from Norfolk or N.Y. It is still uncertain when he may arrive & as Arthur thinks the vessel may be in Charl$\underline{n}$ in a day or two, he intends to go there tomorrow that he may receive the happy pair who however must be very much annoyed by the long voyage they have had. We think that we shall hear the Guns fire on the arrival of the Lexington as we often hear the gun at Sun set. There is no chance of knowing of it & Arthur may be detained in town a week in expectation of it. Harry & W$\underline{m}$ dined at Runnymede yesterday but Arthur excused himself as he could not dine at 3 o'clock– Harry as I told you went to Charleston on the 23^d ult^o & remained there a week, he saw Mrs Harper who is now staying with her Sister at Sullivan's Is^d where she will remain 3 weeks & cannot come to make us a visit. I was very sorry to read that President Moore was dead– what a sad affliction for poor Mrs Hodges! You seem to think it is a false report which I hope it is. W^m does not believe that Miss DeRham is engaged to be married. Poor unfortunate Mr Hunt! he ought to be taken to the Boston Asylum where Mr Robt Hare was so soon cured– I think as <u>you</u> do that <u>his</u> wife will run a great risk–

Sunday– We have this morn^g a pleasant N.W. wind, after yesterday Eve^g & the preceeding one a shower which is very much wanted– In Charl^n Mrs J. P. said water was so scarce, that it was bought. A west wind of course cannot hasten the arrival of the Lexington & I advised Arthur not to go to town today– he said he would defer his departure till tomorrow & will go with Pao^a this even^g to Runnymede & ask the schoolboys there to put this & P's letter into the post office: they always leave the country every Monday at sun rise so that the letters will be in time for the mail. The P[ringle]s are to leave Runnymede on the 8th. Y^r Father & W^m went yesterday to Combahee, this will be their last visit this spring.

Mr D^l Blake informed W^m that his infant was dead, & that his Wife was so unwell that your Aunt [Rutledge] had written to beg him to take her to England soon– it must be a very serious attack, or she would not wish to be separated from her unfortunate daughter. I am glad you mentioned Mrs Smith, for I feared she was not well. She is still afraid of being out in the evening I suppose or she would have been at your party & have conversed on the subject you mention with you & her friend Mr Peter, & have agreed with both– how strange that M^{rs} McEwen should give credit to the controversy which is so absurd!

The new roof is finished, but it is exactly like the old one, none of the improvements which you mention– the Piazza ought to have been repaired, you may remember how bad a state it was in, & is now worse but y^r Father would not allow the Carpenters to repair it, & they have left this place.[2]

You ask what your Uncle [Oliver] writes on the subject of the Oregon dispute, (which <u>I</u> dread extremely). I transcribe his short remark– 'I hope that certain pugnacious members of your Senate & house of Representatives if they have none of Quashies fears, may still have discretion enough not to run into the Lion's mouth, or try to take John Bull by the horns. On this side of the Water we think there is wisdom enough on both sides to avert such a Collision'. A war with England would be dreadful–[3] You speak of a war with Mexico, that too would be dreadful though not so dangerous as the other. I hope M^r

Harrison's health has improved since you last wrote– remember me to him & Mrs H. & give my love to M^{rs} & Mr Fisher & believe me my dearest Eliza y^{r} most Affect^{te} Mother M. H. M.

Paolina & y^{r} brothers send their love to you.

PHi

 1. Capt. Edward Rutledge Shubrick died at sea, en route to the Mediterranean, in March 1844.

 2. In April Mrs. Middleton had given additional details of the repairs that were needed to the Middleton Place house. The blinds (shutters) had been repaired, she said, but the balcony and "as you know many parts of the wainscots want repair, but whether y^{r} Father will allow them to be mended I cannot say." MHM to EMF, April 23, 1845, PHi.

 3. Mrs. Middleton thought "the dispute between this Country & England on that subject will bring on a War. The U.S. have no right to any territory beyond the Rocky Mountains. My sons will not believe that but it is perfectly attested by various treaties, between England, Spain & France." MHM to EMF, April 23, 1845, PHi.

⌁

To Mrs. Middleton, Middleton Place

Philadelphia – Friday May 16th [1845]

 I was on the point of writing to you three days ago, dearest Mamma, to prepare you for the disappointment of not seeing Edward in the Lexington, which I had just heard from Mrs Schroeder you w^{d} probably have, when the Paper containing the announcement of its arrival without him, was sent to me, & of course I knew you must already have been told the reasons of his remaining at Mahon– M^{rs} S– did not seem to know the nature of the illness which prevented their sailing in the L– but Miss Hart mentioned that Commodore Smith[1] had written to his wife that it was an <u>Hysterical</u> attack, followed by Fever, of a serious kind– but that she was much better, altho' still very weak– In a letter I rec^{d} from Emma this morng– this account is confirmed by that given her by Capt Ellison [*of the Lexington*]– & I suppose you have a letter from Edward himself– Emma thinks that unless Ned learns to control <u>Nedina</u>'s nerves she will have a <u>sobbing</u> sort of existence– & seems to suppose that this attack may have been occasioned by apprehension at the idea of coming to an unknown land & to a new family– it had before occurred to me that by some unlucky chance she had got hold of that letter from Abington in which the disapprobation of the whole family of the alliance was unanimously expressed–

which might well have produced an unpleasant effect upon her, poor Soul but it is to be hoped that Ned contrived to conceal it from her, and spare her this mortification– Instead of having a description of yr new daughter in yr next letter, as I expected, you will tell me about her illness– 'Tis really a sad beginning for the poor young thing's married life! Mrs Commodore Smith says Mahon has been remarkably unhealthy this last winter, & fevers very prevalent– so that the Climate, & <u>not</u> uneasiness of mind may have produced this–

I am sorry to say that Mr Harrison has continued more indisposed since I wrote– last night I hurried down at 7 before the children had got to bed, hoping to have an hour's chat with him, and found he had already undressed for bed, feeling quite exhausted with the pain he had been suffering from all the afternoon– He slept soundly all the time we were there, (until 10 o'clk) & had a more comfortable night than usual– indeed he rarely has much pain during the night– but suffers almost constantly in the daytime– and owing to the rheumatic pain in his head, cannot amuse himself with reading, as usual– Poor Mrs Dan Coxe is dying– She has not moved since yesterday & the D^{rs} say nothing more can be done for her– Her mind is perfectly tranquil– but her poor Husband is dreadfully afflicted– They have been a most affectionate couple for nearly 50 years– as devoted almost as Aunt & Uncle H– who are the best examples of conjugal happiness–

You may suppose with how much delight I look forward to Emma's short visit– of a few hours– she says, but I hope we may induce her to spend one day at least– She will be here probably on Monday afternoon & begs me not to ask anyone to meet her– which I could not do, at present– & so am very glad she prefers being alone with us, for the short time she remains– As the time for her departure draws near, she seems to feel very sad at the idea of having an Ocean between her & so many she loves– I will not be selfish enough to express any regret at her going– for the voyage may be of great use to her health, & I hope her travels abroad will be a source of great gratification to her– She gives me Arthur's report of all being well at M. Place a few days ago– which I am glad to hear, my last letter from you being of the 3rd. I believe I told you in one of my last letters, that Mrs Gilliat thought Papa's orders with regard to the addition to the House at NewPort had not been carried into effect– She now writes to Mrs Schroeder that the Wing is advancing rapidly, & will improve the appearance of the House greatly– Whether it will be possible for me to inhabit it, even for a few weeks, God only knows– but I will hope that our dear old Uncle's disease may not make such progress during the next 2 months as to prevent our leaving Phil^a at all– But alas! it is much to be feared that his sufferings will by that time be drawing to a close. Would that I could think otherwise!

I am most grateful for the continued health of my dear little girls– I had an alarm about Sophy who, we all thought was getting the Measles on Saturday– but the Fever passed off in a few hours– Poor George Roberts Smith's[2] second child is dying of the consequences of Measles– & the last & only remaining one very ill– He is in such a state that they have fears of his reason not being preserved– under this <u>treble</u> blow–

In glancing over this I find it such a gloomy letter that I am really sorry to send it– & beg you to forgive it & next time I will try & write on gayer subjects– The only pleasant thing I might have told you about (besides my own health & that of dear Fisher & the children) is the visit of young Rives,[3] who was full of agreeable conversation about Eng^d &c– He thinks the English are not much inclined to go to war, altho' if they are forced into it by the [*American*] occupation of Oregon, the Ministry w^d be supported unanimously by all classes, amongst whom there seems to be general detestation of Americans– Bullies, swindlers & slave dealers as they consider them– But as it is the interest of both parties to maintain peace, it is to be supposed the dispute will be settled by arbitration– I must say Adieu! my dearest Mamma & with love to Papa & the whole family circle I am ever Y^r most affecte daughter E

Private Collection

1. Commodore Joseph Smith (1790–1877) was at this time commander of the Mediterranean squadron.
2. Probably Sally Ingersoll's cousin, the son of her aunt Mary Roberts (Mrs. John J.) Smith.
3. William Cabell Rives, Jr.

⁓

To Mrs. Fisher, Philadelphia

Charleston May 24th 1845

We came here yesterday my dearest Eliza at an earlier period than usual, Arthur & family had come on the 21st– After dinner Oliver brought me a letter from my brother of the 30th ult^o in which he informs me of Ed^d's arrival. his account is so amusing that I will copy it. "To tell you of my surprise at seeing your little Sailor Barbarossa on the 27th– in spite of his red brushy beard I could not help recognizing my friend Edward, when he presented himself in front of my easy chair–¹ He had arrived late during the previous night from Havre & taken a Bed at an hotel at the bottom of the town where he left his Wife– As soon as my Old Lady could get a Carriage she went with Ed$^{\underline{d}}$ to be introduced to Edwardina & to bring her here, & here we have them snug & hope to keep them for some time. I need not tell you how delighted we are at having our favorite Boy with us again & how highly pleased we are with his merry little Wife. He might well say to you that she would keep y$^{\underline{r}}$ house alive, for she is all good humour drollery & fun, without a particle of Art or affectation about her. Of course she is as well domesticated with us as if she had been our inmate all her life"– He adds "do not fancy that the Gout is afflicting me– I am in good health." Thank God for that! and think how kind he is, writing to me only a fortnight after his former letter, had he not I should have been in suspense about Ed$^{\underline{d}}$ for he has not written– my brother did not know when he would leave him, but I conclude he is now in the Great Western which will probably arrive the last day of this month at N.Y.

When <u>we</u> shall arrive there, or when we shall sail from hence I cannot tell you– I have been begging W$^{\underline{m}}$ to ask y$^{\underline{r}}$ Father to allow us to go in the Ship Char$^{\underline{n}}$ which is to sail either the 28$^{\underline{th}}$ or 29. if he refuses, we may perhaps be detained here a month, for I observe no vessel mentioned in the Newspaper ready to sail & all the good ones have just left this place. I asked y$^{\underline{r}}$ Father just now if I should tell you when you might expect to see him at Phil$^{\underline{a}}$, he said he did not know.

I received y$^{\underline{r}}$ letter of the 16 & 17$^{\underline{th}}$ two days after I wrote my last & thought it best not to answer it until I came here, that I might give you some news, which luckily I have been able to do, & W$^{\underline{m}}$ has just told me that y$^{\underline{r}}$ Father has consented to our going next week in the Charl$^{\underline{n}}$ & he is this morn$^{\underline{g}}$ going to engage births for us, & Arthur's family. Your letter did indeed contain sad information– poor M$^{\underline{rs}}$ D. Coxe! I regret the loss of such a good woman– M$^{\underline{r}}$ Harrison too is in a deplorable state, & must make you all very unhappy but thank God! you & your family were all well– & I cannot reconcile myself to the idea of your not being with me at Newp$^{\underline{t}}$ which you still seem uncertain about. I rec$^{\underline{d}}$ also with your last, a letter from Ed$^{\underline{d}}$ when at Mahon, mentioning his Wife's illness, & his intention of going to Paris & South[ampto]n– Emma must have given you news of them & you must have seen her a day earlier than you expected.

I hope as you do, that the dispute between England & the US. may be settled by Arbitration & that M$^{\underline{r}}$ Calhoun may be sent as an Arbiter, for his opinion on the subject (which Harry read to me in the Newspaper) is much more reasonable than those of other people. I cannot bear to think of war against England– what would become of us all!

Susan is to come & see me this morn^g but I must not wait for her as W^m is going presently & will take this– She is to be confined next month & Paolina says she is well though thinner than she was– She says too that as Arthur is going to Wash^n soon, he on his way to Newport after his visit there, can take you with him– that is a good plan is it not? if Mr F. should be unable at that time of leaving Mr H. The boys came last Even^g to see us, Johnny is improving in appearance fatter & taller, & they have good news from their parents– John will be here about the end of the month. I do not know exactly whether Arthur will go with us by Sea, Paolina hopes he will & he certainly ought to accompany her for he can go to Wash^n from N.Y. She & y^r Brothers send their love to you, pray give mine to M^{rs} & Mr Fisher & believe me my dearest Eliza y^r affect^{te} Mother–

PHi

1. Both Mrs. Middleton and Eliza also had red hair.

∼

To Mrs. Fisher, Philadelphia

Clinton Hotel June 5th [1845]

My dearest Eliza

We arrived here this morn^g between 5 & 6 but were obliged to remain until 7 in the Ship as there was so much to be done with the packages. as soon as we came to this house we heard that Ed^d was at the Carlton & I immediately sent a message to him to come here which he did about 10 o'clock with his Wife who is a very good looking girl– perhaps you would not call her pretty– She is very affectionate & Paolina is delighted with her– They staid so long (tho' I begged them to dine with us) that I have scarcely time to write this to tell you how delighted I was to receive y^r letter of the 25th May the day before I left Charl^n telling me that you w^d come to Newport as soon as I was established there, <u>that</u> I hope I shall be next week– John (the Ser^t) came this morn^g. he says he will go with me, but his Wife having now 2 Child^n cannot, as she is not well. I begged him to find me a woman or two, one a washer the other a housemaid & if he does, I might go next Saturday the 7th & I desired Elizth to try & find the same cook (her friend) who we had last year. Should I be lucky enough to find all these, nothing need detain me here– Ed$\underline{d}$ will accompany me, as Harry who came with us wishes to remain here for some time– Arthur will probably come on by railcars, stopping at Wash$\underline{n}$. Y$\underline{r}$ Father & W$\underline{m}$ too will I suppose come on by that way. I have the greatest pleasure in anticipating your long wished for visit my dear Eliza but how short it will be! 3 or 4 weeks![1] However I am thankful that I can see you even for so short a time. I [*am glad to*] hear that M$\underline{r}$ Harrison is better & that M$\underline{r}$ Fisher will be able to bring you on to N$\underline{t}$ as soon as possible– I will write to you again when there & fear I shall be detained here till next Tuesday when the R$\underline{de}$ Is$\underline{d}$ goes again. E$\underline{d}$ tells me he has heard from you & you from him– I think you will like y$\underline{r}$ new Sister– I must now finish this with love to M$\underline{rs}$ & M$\underline{r}$ F. & am my dearest Eliza y$\underline{r}$ affect$\underline{te}$ Mother M. H. M.

PHi

1. At this point, Eliza thought she could go to Newport in July. She was afraid that Uncle Harrison would be too sick for her to leave if she waited until August.

⌒

Fisher's uncle Charles Francis died in early June. He "breathed his last quietly and without a struggle," Eliza told her mother. "Poor old gentleman he had long been tired of life."[1] Fisher had helped to take care of his uncle's business affairs for several years and therefore already knew the contents of his will.

1. EMF to MHM, June 11, 1845, private collection.

To Mrs. Middleton, Newport

Philadelphia – Sunday eveng– June 15$\underline{th}$ [1845]

I received your letter of Wednesday, yesterday morning, my dearest Mamma, but did not answer it immediately as I knew no boat w$\underline{d}$ leave N.Y. today, and that I might therefore just as well wait– as your anxiety about not hearing from me must have been relieved by the receipt of my letter of Wedy– I meant to have written again on Friday, but was so busy that I really had not half an hour to spare– then I thought too I w$\underline{d}$ wait until the opening of the Will, and give you an account of it– There was no change made in the last one except that of adding 2 thousand dollars to John Francis'[1] legacy– making it 5 instead of 3– & even that, Fisher thought, & told his Uncle several times, was too little to leave him– however he would not give him more– He leaves his sister Mrs Fisher 20 thousand, and all his furniture & personal property, and the whole of the residue of his estate, which when expenses & taxes are deducted, will be about 22 or 3 thousand dollars, to Fisher– which will give us an additional income of about 12 hundred dollars–² M^{rs} F– has given us as much of the Furniture as we want for the Farm which is just now very acceptable– & will make us quite comfortable out there– Wishing to keep my mind as calm & spirits as cheerful as possible whilst attending upon our poor sufferer, I did not go over to Sansom S^{t} until after the funeral, as I feared the effect which the sight of death might produce upon my nerves– & felt that I sh^{d} require all their strength to carry me thro' the scenes I cannot help anticipating we are soon to witness–

Most fortunately the information of Mr Francis' death did not agitate Mr Harrison– he merely remarked "So poor Charles has got the start of me"– and was not at all depressed in consequence– For 2 or 3 days since I wrote he was improving slightly in strength, we flattered ourselves– but last eveng & today he has had much more pain, and the weakness is visibly increased– It is impossible, as I wrote you on Wednesday, for me to leave him in this critical state & even if I could reconcile myself to being away from his dying bed, I could not desert poor Fisher now that he requires all my efforts to cheer him– Poor fellow, his spirits are sadly depressed, and it surely is my duty to stand by him in his hour of trial– Much as I long then to be with you, my dearest Mamma, I cannot think at present of going on to NewPort– but trust that I may some weeks hence have the happiness of passing some time under the roof with you– at any rate I will hope so–

We have had intensely hot weather which was rather uncomfortable to be sure, but agreed perfectly well with my throat however– today there is a great change, and it is very cool tonight– I feel more anxious it sh^{d} remain so for poor Aunt's sake than even the children's– for the heat exhausts the little strength which anxiety & fatigue have left her– but as she said this morng– she has hitherto been mercifully supported, & she will not now lose her confidence in divine aid–

Nothing yet from the travellers– I now begin to look for them daily– Pray when you see Fanny Calderon give my best love to her & thank her for her kind letter– which I am really not in spirits to answer just now & therefore beg you to explain how I am situated for 4 or 5 hours every day in a sick room, watching a poor sufferer, & of course on my return home too sad & weary to do anything but attend to the children– whose bright faces & happy voices are our greatest solace– They are quite well, dear little things– & I hope will continue so– next week I shall probably send them out to the Farm– Adieu dearest Mamma, with love to all I am ever Y^{r} most affect^{e} daughter Eliza

Private Collection

    1. This was John B. Francis, Charles Francis' and Mrs. Fisher's nephew. Both left him money.
    2. The sum $22,000 in 1845 would be approximately $440,000 in 1999 dollars, and $1,200 would be approximately $24,000. Dollar conversion factor from RSahr, OrStU.

～

    When Mrs. Middleton arrived in Newport, along with Kitty, Paolina, Edda, William, Harry, Edward, and the servants, she found workmen still plastering and painting the rooms of the new addition and the rest of the house in disorder. The drawing room was full of pieces of wood instead of furniture, and she couldn't even sleep in her own room because the door had been taken off.

To Mrs. Fisher, Philadelphia

Newport June 18th 1845

    I had been for the last few days expecting to hear from my dearest Eliza & at last an hour since her letter brought by M^{r} D[eVeaux] Powel has been put into my hands. I sympathise sincerely with you & the family with the grief you are all suffering, which will I fear soon increase, as there seems to be no prospect of cure of poor Mr Harrison's malady. The decease of Mr Francis must have caused much sorrow, though as you observe far less distressing than that which you fear will soon follow. The Will is very acceptable at this time, as you have sometimes mentioned Mr F. being obliged to pay larger sums than he could at that time afford. No letter from Arthur later than the 4th has been received, which prevents us from knowing the movements from Charles^{n}.

    I have slept for the last 4 nights in my own room the door being fixed, & that in the next room will soon be finished but when the drawing room will be in a state to inhabit is very uncertain. We have had visits from the Sumners, Harpers, Calderons, Joneses (even Mary), Thorndike[s] & Calvert[s,] & Mrs Johnson[1] & her unmarried Daughter all enquiring particularly about you– Yesterday even^{g} Pa^{a} Ed^{d} & Edda went to a party at Mrs Sumners where there was singing & waltzing– Edda sang without any accompaniment. Agripina sang, but the former does not approve of her voice. A letter has come today to Ed^{d} allowing him a leave of Absence for only 6 months, 3 being over, so that he can only remain here until Sept[r]– a great disappointment, for he believed he should have a year's leave of absence. He went immediately after my reading to him M[r] Fisher's message, to Gould[2] & carried the letter that he might particularly explain the articles, & when he returned said that G. would send them to Phil[a] next week.

The more I am acquainted with Edda the more I become attached to her, she is so affectionate & respectful to me, & as I mentioned before a very affectionate wife & to Paolina like a Sister. They are always laughing together which is lucky for the latter, as she is so anxious to hear from Arthur. Harry went to N.Y. last friday but hoped to return in a week. The Garden is now very pretty, filled with flowers & shrubs. The Sycamores are all dead– those I am told all over the island also dead. The De Rhams will be here in a week who I shall be glad to see– M[rs] Grant's cottage is finished but she has not come yet. I have brought your 4 numbers of the 'living Age' that I might return them to you– when you come pray bring some more, & the Peerage book, as I want to remember some names which I have forgotten. I have not since I came here had much time to read, altho' every morn[g] before breakfast the book of Sermons M[r] Fisher gave me occupy my time– they are a very good selection & I often wish to converse with you on the subject of some of them & also on the prophecies in the Bible– but when can we meet! From what you write, I fear a later time than I flattered myself we should see each other– You say the hot weather agrees perfectly well with your throat– I comforted myself with the belief that your throat was quite well. has it been worse during the winter, or what has occasioned any pain in it?

The weather here is so very cool that I have put on one of my winter gowns. I hope the Boston St[eame]r will bring a favourable account of the Oregon question being likely to be settled instead of involving both countries into a War. what a misfortune that would be for all of us! What do the Philadelphians expect on that subject? M[r] Calhoun gives the best opinion about it than any any other I have read, though of course I know very little of other speeches & writings. All your Brothers insist that Oregon belongs to the U.S. I have read from the London Times that it was positively (at least the greatest part of it) ceded by Spain to England many years ago.

I sent John [*the servant*] to enquire after Miss Hare, she says she is not well, & in bed but will try & come to see me tomorrow, & that she left you & your family well. M[rs] Jones is going today on the way to Niagara– I must now bid adieu to my dearest Eliza & am her Affectionate Mother M. H. M.

Ed[d] & Paolina send their best love to you– Pray give mine to M[rs] & M[r] Fisher & M[rs] Smith, & best regards to M[r] & M[rs] Harrison. Mr & M[rs] Stockton[3] of Phil[a] who were fellow passengers of Ed^d in the G^t West^n are spending their summer here– do you know them?

PHi
Except for two (dated June 22 and September 15), no further letters have been found from Mrs. Middleton in 1845.

1. Perhaps Mrs. Johnston, whose daughter, Mary, had recently married Samuel Powel.
2. Fisher had again ordered clothes from Gould, the Newport tailor. The two pairs of pantaloons in the order were made larger in the waist and hips, as Fisher had grown "stouter." EMF to MHM, [June 16, 1845,] private collection.
3. Probably Commodore Robert F. Stockton (1795–1866), U.S. Navy, and his wife, the former Harriet Maria Potter of Charleston. Stockton helped to take California during the Mexican War. He was also president of the Delaware and Raritan Canal Company and later a U.S. senator.

∼

To Mrs. Middleton, Newport

Philadelphia Friday 20$^{\underline{th}}$ June [1845]

This morning I rec^d your letter of the 18$^{\underline{th}}$, my dearest Mamma, and hasten to reply to it, because it is important to send my answer in time for the boat tomorrow– Papa was with me when I received it, and I read aloud to him whatever I thought would interest him– I was much shocked to hear from Arthur two days ago, how very ill he had been in Charleston a fortnight since, which you never even hinted at to me– perhaps it was as well not to mention his extreme illness, for even now it makes me very unhappy to think of the danger he was in– particularly as I do not consider it by any means past, & see plainly that he is still suffering very much– & may have another similar attack at any moment– W$^{\underline{m}}$ assures me that the D$^{\underline{rs}}$ think there is less probability of its occurring again for some months– but the disease is evidently hanging about him & it makes me very sad to think how little I can be with him–

I could not persuade him to remain later than 12 o'clk today, altho' he only arrived yesterday afternoon– but he talked of returning shortly to see me– W$^{\underline{m}}$ is looking remarkably well, I am glad to see– Tell Paolina I think her Sposo also looking very young & handsome– He was here only one afternoon– & in a great hurry I put into my Bonnet box, some things which I thought might be useful to Pauline & Kitty– and a muslin shawl which I beg Edda to accept– I had just bought it from a reduced lady to whom it belonged– but never intended to wear it myself– as you know I never wear <u>pink</u>– & always meant to offer it to one of my sisters– Pauline will perhaps smile at my sending her a dress– which I hope she will not disdain– for I thought it remarkably pretty & had only had it on 2 or 3 times– She will see that I had not even time to take out the <u>pads</u> in front, which she will certainly not require– but I could not appear without, in my present <u>lean</u> condition– The other dress which I thought would suit Kitty, I have never even <u>tried on</u>– for it came home from the dress maker's after I went into mourning– & if there had been time, I should have had the trimming in front altered, & made narrower– Pauline must accept one of the scarfs, if she thinks it worth accepting, & give the other to C[atherine]– I meant the collars & Pelerines for you & Catherine– & the bonnet for the latter– if large enough– I will try & find some more of the ribbon to match & send it on– so that you may add a row or two to the front– The white gauze ribbon came off a bonnet, and I thought you might trim a cap with it–

Mr Harrison has been more comfortable, the last 2 days, but takes scarcely any nourishment, & does not wish to take anything to prolong his life– He told me today when I urged him to do so that he did not desire a life of pain– & altho' the parting from us w^d be painful, as it <u>must</u> come, it was better it sh^d be soon over– His great dread appears to be that he should wear out the strength of his poor wife– & for <u>her</u> sake, he fears to linger– It is impossible to be more composed at the prospect of death– and if he had only faith in a Redeemer I should say that nothing more could be desired for him– he has however conso- lation in his Religious belief, & has several times expressed his entire conviction that he is going to happiness, & shall meet us all again– Surely if goodness meets its reward hereafter he ought to be rewarded for a more excellent man or a nobler-hearted one, never breathed–

I am very sorry, in reading over yr letter, to find that I have forgotten to send you on some more <u>Living Ages</u>, as I intended by W^m. I will do so by the first opportunity however– I like the selections in them very much, & have scarcely ever time to read anything else besides my daily bread of heaven– The children remain quite well– thank God! I think of leaving them all at the Farm, when I go on to NewPort to see you– next month perhaps– but my plans must still be very uncertain–

We have cool weather again & I hope it may continue so– I think of going out to the Farm with Fisher tomorrow, if Mr H. should not be worse mean- while– Pray remember me kindly to all those who are kind [enough] to enquire after me– & give my love to my Sisters & brothers– I am my dearest Mamma Yr affect daughter Eliza

I have just had a visit from <u>Miss Wightt</u> who begged me to give her love to Pauline– She is quite <u>rejuvenated</u>, and as usual as fine as silks lace & embroidery & even <u>flowers</u> can make her– very bad taste for such an old spinster methinks–

Private Collection

～

To Mrs. Middleton, Newport

Philadelphia July 7<u>th</u> [1845]

I wrote you on Friday, my dearest Mamma, that our dear Uncle's sufferings had encreased very much within the past 2 days– They were at last terminated by death on Sunday (yesterday) morng at 1/2 past one, A.M. I witnessed the closing scene during which our poor Aunt sustained herself with wonderful composure– She watched with intense anxiety every gasp, & when all was over, shed no tear for many hours– but allowed herself to be put to bed, where she sank to rest, completely worn out by the fatigue & sleeplessness of so many days & nights– She was during the day relieved several times by weeping, & was much calmer than we had hoped for– but now that the excitement has subsided, she begins to realize her loss, which she will feel more deeply every day of her remaining life–

Poor Fisher has been dreadfully agitated– and his bursts of grief have quite overcome my resolutions of fortitude, poor fellow it is his first great sorrow, & I, who have felt before the bitterness of losing one beloved, could most sincerely feel for him & with him in his affliction– which is no common one– for the friend he has lost has been devoted to him from his very birth– & never let him feel the want of a father– A most tender one he has proved himself on every occasion– & extended to me & my children the love & affection he bore to Fisher– Never can I forget his kindness & generosity– & the deep & thoughtful interest ever manifested towards me & mine– and to my latest hour I shall look back with gratitude upon his often repeated expressions of affection for me of which I well know I was unworthy– I send you the day's papers which contain notices of his character, which I think you & Papa will read with satisfaction– They are well deserved, & not the less gratifying to her feelings– She talks constantly about him, & thus unburthens her sorrowful heart– The Funeral is to take place tomorrow morng– soon after sunrise– & <u>no</u> written or published invitations are sent– These are his own written directions left to Fisher & M<u>r</u>

White–[1] as he wished to avoid all parade & ostentatious display– and to be attended to the Grave only by a few of those he loved–[2]

M^{rs} F– saw all the last offices performed for him & then went to bed with a raging headache for the rest of the day– She is now much better & unusually free from nervous feelings– strange to say– Mine have been somewhat shattered, as you may well suppose for it is the first deathbed I ever witnessed– except indeed poor little Mary Helen's–[3] when she passed away with scarcely a struggle to that Heaven whence her pure little spirit had come only a short time before– He too will be received there if ever mortal man may expect a reward for goodness–

I have written so awkwardly over this sheet without thinking, that I must now enclose it–[4] but this will give me an opportunity of telling you about the children– for whom I sh^{d} have had no room on the other– They are much better, but Sophy's appetite has not returned– this afternoon at 3 o'clk I sent them out to Gray's Ferry to get some cooler air– than they could find in this hot city– I hope that in about ten days or a fortnight at farthest we may all go out to the Farm– but we have not yet dared to mention the subject to Aunt– but wait for an opportunity of introducing it– I must now hastily close this with best love to Papa & all my brothers & sisters– Aunt has just come in, and begs her love to you also– she feels refreshed by her afternoon's nap she has just been taking– but she is sadly changed poor soul! & looks at least 80– Once more Adieu! dearest Mamma I am as ever Y^{r} most affect^{e} daughter Eliza Mrs Fisher is staying here, and will remain ten days at least.[5]

Private Collection

1. William White (1810–1858) was Uncle Harrison's lawyer. He was the grandson of George Harrison's friend and brother-in-law, Bishop William White.

2. George Harrison had also made his wishes clear to his wife at least as early as 1839, when he wrote, "I pray of you not the least Funeral parade– an Interment late in the Evening– or very early in morng– No Invitations– or Ultra mourning dress– calmly & quietly, let all be done." Memorandum, GH to Sophia Harrison, January 1839, private collection.

3. John and Sally Middleton's daughter, Mary Helen, was five years old when she died in 1837. Two years later, the Middletons gave the same name to their next daughter.

4. Having written over most of the space usually left for the address, she added another sheet of paper.

5. Eliza was writing from the Harrisons' house.

～

To Mrs. Middleton, Newport

Philadelphia – Thursday July 10th [1845]

As I have more leisure this afternoon than I may probably have tomorrow, I wish to employ it in writing to you my dearest Mamma– I rec^d yesterday your note of the previous day which was delivered much earlier after date than they generally are– very soon after you wrote it you must have rec^d mine of Monday announcing the death of our kind good Uncle– Altho' we had so long expected it, and endeavoured to prepare our minds for the blow, it was not the less severe– and will be felt more every day by poor Aunt– who was at first so composed– She has been much more agitated since the Funeral– & of course now that his remains are removed to the Grave she feels more desolate than ever– but still commands herself better than I could have supposed it possible for her to do– Poor Fisher has been terribly overcome– & agitation of mind brought on one of his worst attacks on Tuesday, after he had seen all that was left of his best friend deposited in the Tomb– I was really quite alarmed about him– for he fancied that he was going to have an Apoplectic fit– which idea got possession of me and banished sleep from my eyelids for the third night– however his unpleasant symptoms were removed by quiet and gentle reme-dies, & today he felt well enough to go and spend the day at the Farm–

Last night I was disturbed by the poor little baby– who had a severe attack of Colic– but I made up for want of rest in the night by sleeping until near 9 this morng– Helen seems quite herself again, but poor Sophy is very complain-ing and has lost her appetite– They all spent the day out at the Farm yester-day– & on Tuesday or Wedn^y of next week I hope to take them there to stay! We yesterday spoke to Aunt on the subject of her going out with us– and at first she w^d not hear of it– but after some time we ventured to introduce it again– & thought she listened with less reluctance– altho' she still said that she could not leave town except to ride out & see us for a day. I think when she finds that Fisher and his Mother cannot be induced to leave her, she will consent to go out & stay a few weeks in the country– One objection which she makes is that she will have so much business to attend to– for she is sole Executrix, & will have a very large estate to settle– but Mr H. has left his affairs in such admirable order that she will not have the trouble she imagines & there will be no occasion for her to pay the Legacies, which are very numerous, for many months unless she pleases–[1]

She has told us 3 the contents of the Will, which is not to be regularly opened until next week– we have known the general outline of it for some time past– & are perfectly satisfied– He had at first, some years ago left her everything– but she afterwards begged him to provide for his own family, so that hereafter she might have no trouble about it herself– and I hope they will be satisfied, for he has not forgotten any of them, and has divided nearly a hundred thousand dollars amongst them and that too, after giving them during his life upwards of 70 thousand at different times– I never heard of a more generous creature– & his giving so liberally was the more meritorious, as he did it, not from affection, but a sense of duty to the children of a sister– to whom he was tenderly attached– He liked M^{rs} M^{c}M[urtrie] better than the others– but as Aunt said yesterday, the _parings_ of Fisher's nails were more precious to him than anything belonging to her– Now this must be in the strictest confidence, for of course we do not wish to excite ill feeling or jealousy– & everything has been done to prevent it– He has made no difference between us & them in the Will except that he gives to us both with strong expressions of affection, and nothing of the sort to any others– & his private injunctions to my Aunt with regard to what they always intended sh^{d} be Fisher's will very soon be complied with– for she means to make her Will immediately– do not breathe this except to Papa– for at present we sh^{d} not like it to be spoken of– mum.

My plans still remain uncertain until we get her to decide about leaving town– if she will do so within a fortnight or 3 weeks, I will leave the older children with her in the country, and run on & pass 2 or 3 weeks with you at NewPort– but if not I do not see how I can leave Fisher at all– I trust she will yield for his sake, if not for that of her own health, which w^{d}, I am sure, be much benefitted by the change– We must wait & have patience–

Lily is leaning over me, & begs me to send her love to Grandmama– She is become a very good girl, & is a great comfort to her Mamma, & poor Aunt, who is perfectly devoted to her– I must say Adieu dearest Mamma with love to Papa & the rest I am ever Y^{r} most affectionate daughter Eliza

I had almost forgotten to say that Fisher requests Edward to be at the trouble of enquiring of Gould whether he has sent on the box of clothes he ordered for him 3 weeks ago– for he has not yet seen or heard anything of them– and w^{d} like to know if his Orders have been attended to– Once more please do not mention the contents of the 3rd page–

Private Collection

1. George Harrison left legacies to most of the children and grandchildren of his sister, Mary, wife of Bishop William White, and of his brother, Matthias, who was Rebecca McMurtrie's father. He excluded one or two nephews, however, whom he consid-

ered unworthy. Fisher was still dealing with these legacies after Sophia Harrison's death in 1851; several of the legatees had apparently expected to be given much more than they received.

Uncle Harrison left the rest of his estate to his wife. It was understood that after her death, Fisher would inherit everything.

～

After Uncle Harrison's death in early July, Eliza postponed her visit to Newport until August. As she had "perfect confidence" in Mrs. Putnam's and Louisa's abilities, she decided to leave Lily and Sophy with them at the farm and to take the baby and Sarah, the wet nurse, with her to Newport. She spent a month there with her family and returned at the end of August. "Oh! how much I missed that cordial greeting from our dear old Uncle," she wrote to her mother, "who always welcomed us so heartily on our return home."[1]

1. EMF to MHM, July 22 [1845] and [August 29, 1845,] private collection.

To Mrs. Middleton, Newport

Meadowbank Farm–[1] Friday 5$\underline{th}$ Sept$\underline{r}$ [1845]

I am sorry to write again without having heard from you, my dearest Mamma– but will not put off writing until I hear as I cannot receive a letter for 2 days more– & this must go to town with Fisher tomorrow– He went over to the Post Office before breakfast, but returned empty handed– and is now taking a long walk with Miss Gilpin for which I did not feel quite strong enough, & therefore preferred staying at home to chat with you– I scribbled off a few lines in great haste last week to announce my safe arrival [in Philadelphia]. The next morng I came out here and found my darlings had been so anxious to see me that they had walked early to the Turnpike to meet me– but came back disappointed for we were detained in town & did not get here for 2 hours after they had been expecting us– They looked pale and rather thinner both of them– but appear to be in perfect health, & will regain their roses & plumpness I hope now that the heat is over– for we have such delicious weather, that I think even you would enjoy it, & not require the therm$\underline{r}$ to be lower than 65 at breakfast– I hope Papa may be tempted by this cool change to come on & bring the girls with him–[2] and in this expectation I am having their rooms prepared today for them– All the three children are above me in their new Garret Nursery– M$\underline{rs}$ Putnam having preferred taking charge of them together– but I haven't yet told you the good news that little Helen is fairly weaned– and her Nurse actually gone– in search of another place– I proposed to her to remain here until Oct$\underline{r}$ but she preferred going to town to consult D$\underline{r}$ Meigs upon the propriety of undertaking to nurse another baby– which I had no idea she w^d have strength to do for she felt so very unwell the day after her return here, that she begged me to let the child be weaned at once– 2 days afterwards however she began to feel so much better & stronger that she thought, as her milk had not at all diminished she w^d try & continue nursing during the next winter– which it is most desirable for her to do if her strength holds out– but I wrote to Meigs to beg him to examine particularly into her case & advise her what to do–

Little Nell[3] has borne her privation wonderfully well, & is improved already in appearance– perhaps Arthur may suppose his medecines begin to shew their effect, but indeed I must confess my incredulity on that subject– and attribute the happy change to the difference of diet &c– & not to homoeopathy– I wish you could have seen her joy when she first saw her little sisters– they were in a perfect extasy of delight too– and the first night Lily came back half a dozen times after saying good night to hug her dear Mamma– & evidently felt her happiness deeply– She and Sophy beg their best love to you, Grandpapa & all Aunts Uncles & cousins–

Fisher returned from town on Tuesday quite out of spirits, for he left his Mother suffering from a slight attack of Gout in her foot– but yesterday we rec^d a letter saying she had got over it– & was able to hobble down to Aunt's. 5 o'clock– An hour ago just as we were setting out upon our drive the carriage from town drove up with Mrs Fisher & M^rs [Henry Gilpin] & Mr Wm Gilpin[4] in it– they had taken an early dinner & come out to spend the eveng with us & M^rs F– put into my hands your most acceptable letter of the 3rd for which many thanks dearest Mamma– I am very sorry to hear of Pauline's ailment– & also that only the elder girls will be here– for I hoped Papa w^d bring them all– & then take back the 2 younger ones to school by the 15th– Mrs Fisher's foot still pains her & requires an easy shoe– I must say Goodbye in haste, as they are waiting for me downstairs– & Mrs F. will have this put in the Office this eveng–

With love to Papa & all the rest I am always Y^r most affecte daughter Eliza

Has Edward received his orders yet? & when may I expect to see him & Edda? The children were delighted with their dolls tell the latter– and have called them both after her 2 names–

Private Collection

1. From this time on, the farm was called Meadowbank.
2. The Middleton granddaughters who were at the Boltons' school in New Rochelle were again spending their vacation in Newport.
3. This was the baby's nickname.

4. William Gilpin (1813–1894) was Sarah and Henry Gilpin's younger brother. He went with John C. Fremont to the Pacific coast in 1843, fought in the Mexican War, and in 1861 became the first governor of the Colorado Territory.

⁓

To Mrs. Middleton, Newport

Meadowbank Farm Saturday 13$\underline{th}$ Sept$\underline{r}$ [1845]

Fisher brought me y^r welcome letter of the 10$\underline{th}$ yesterday morning, my dearest Mamma, but I did not answer it then thinking there w$\underline{d}$ be no opportunity to town before Monday– but if my letter had been ready, he might have taken it this morng– for he went in unexpectedly, in consequence of a note rec$\underline{d}$ from his Mother announcing the arrival in town of the Rives'– whom he hopes to bring here to dinner– En attendant [*meanwhile*] I take advantage of a half hour's leisure to scribble a few lines– I have been quite disappointed that the girls were not all permitted to come on– but hope that the 2 elder ones at least will be here on Tuesday or Wedn$\underline{y}$ and that both Papa & W$\underline{m}$ will accompany them– for our Virginia friends [*the Rives*] will not be here more than 2 or 3 days & we shall have 3 spare rooms after their departure– I went to town with Miss Gilpin & F– on Thursday to see the old ladies and found them both well– M$\underline{rs}$ F's gout having disappeared without giving her much trouble– and M$\underline{rs}$ H, altho' still in wretched spirits having rather improved in strength I think since I had seen her– They talked of paying us a visit today, but w$\underline{d}$ have been prevented by this East Wind even if M$\underline{r}$ & M$\underline{rs}$ R. had not arrived– I daresay you have quite a storm at New Port– & find fires necessary–

We are just making preparations to begin them, and have our Carpets down which add greatly to our comfort– The children have all managed to take colds, which I hope will not be very severe– I am perfectly well– and quite able to take an hour's walk over hill and dale– we had a delightful one last eveng– thro' a part of the country I had never seen before– & had some very pleasant scrambles thro' the woods while Miss G– was with us– You w$\underline{d}$ be astonished at the variety of wild flowers we found– many of them sweet too– and some beautiful–

We had a visit from Fanny Butler on Tuesday– I had written to her by her request to tell her of my return home, and she fixed her own time to come out & dine– I was very glad she did so, for it may be the last time we shall meet, as she is going away very soon– Just as I, and all her friends expected she w$\underline{d}$ be, she is driven out of the country by the outrageous behaviour of P[ierce] &

the whole B[utler] family who are leagued together to make her miserable & deprive her of her children– Poor thing she is much to be commiserated– Miss G– & I wept at the tale she told us of her sufferings and wrongs– I do not mean to say she has acted <u>wisely</u>– but all the heart and the good qualities are on her side, & the faults she can be <u>justly</u> charged with are want of prudence & temper and a woman of her temperament could not be expected to bear patiently the provocations & trials she has had heaped upon her for many years– Her remaining here can no longer be of any use to her children, and by returning to Eng<u>d</u> she can make herself useful to her Father, whose health is bad, & who writes to urge her to go to him– He thinks of wintering at Rome, and that will be a more agreeable residence to Fanny, as her associations with life in London are very painful since her last visit–

Tuesday– I have been waiting ever since Saturday for an opportunity to town– my dearest Mamma– I hope you are not making Yrself uneasy at not hearing from me– Today we expect M<u>r</u> & M<u>rs</u> H. Gilpin & Rob<u>t</u> Hare & his bride to dinner– We had not intended them to come together, but they both happened to fix upon the same day, which I rather regret as they will not be particularly congenial I fear– but as they are all sensible people I daresay they will make themselves agreeable to each other– The Rives' did <u>not</u> come out with F. on Sat<u>y</u> for M<u>r</u> R. was lame, & they left town early on Monday morng– I had a farewell visit from poor Fanny B. on Sunday– She was to leave Phil<u>a</u> the next morng– and had not been permitted to see her children to take leave of them– My heart ached for the poor Soul as she spoke of her sad fate– Surely the crime these people are guilty of who <u>force</u> her away will be fearfully visited upon them & to falsehood they add cruelty– but I will not speak of their conduct– [it] is too base–

I have just finished a letter to John & must now prepare to receive my guests– Tomorrow I shall go to town where I hope to meet Papa, the girls & W<u>m</u> & bring them back with me– Adieu dearest Mamma Y<u>r</u> affecte daughter Eliza

Love to all around you– The children are well & beg their love– I was grieved to hear of poor Edda's sore throat– It is lucky that I left New Port before the Epidemic prevailed, for I sh<u>d</u> certainly have been one of the victims of Sorethroat– whereas here mine is in tolerable good order– Adieu! once more dear Mamma–

Private Collection
The date of this letter has been corrected to Saturday, September 13, from September 15.

∽

At the end of September, William took Oliver's daughters, Mary and Matilda, from Newport to visit the Fishers at their farm. Whereas the younger girls, Sarah and Eleanor, went directly back to school at the Priory, Mary and Matilda were not returning to the school and were going instead to meet their father in Philadelphia. Eliza took them to be fitted at the dressmaker as well as to look at musical instruments. Their grandmother Chisolm had given each of them $900 for a harp and a piano.

Before they left Newport, the rest of the family—hoping to persuade them to stay longer—had told the girls the Fishers' farm was dull and uninteresting. Matilda was therefore pleasantly surprised to find when she got there that the farm was neat and clean. Aunt Eliza, she told her mother, was an excellent housekeeper, which she supposed was thanks to Mrs. Fisher's instruction.[1]

Mrs. Middleton, too, was able to enjoy the fall weather with Eliza and the children at the Fishers' farm after she left Newport, and then stayed in Philadelphia for a week or so longer before starting back to Charleston. This was a journey which was increasingly difficult for her. As she had already told Edward several years before, "Travelling & sailing backward & forward every year is very fatiguing to me."[2]

1. Matilda Middleton to Susan Middleton, October 1, 1845, ScHi.
2. MHM to Edward Middleton, August 22, 1841, Edward Middleton Rea Collection.

To Mrs. Middleton, Charleston

Philadelphia – Nov[r] 20th [1845]

I should have been much disappointed at not hearing from you this morng– my dearest Mamma if I had not heard from M[rs] Gilpin who saw Harry in Balt[e] on <u>Friday</u> that he was to meet you the next day in Petersburg– where of course you must have passed a whole day to rest– & I trust therefore that making the journey so leisurely you and Papa suffered from much less fatigue than usual– The worst part of it to be sure was to come afterwards– but you must have been much better able to bear the jolting on the Railroad after having a comfortable night's rest at Petersburg– but I hope to have a good account of you all this eveng– as even if you did not reach Charleston till Monday morng– your letter w[d] have time to travel back to me in 3 whole days– Most anxiously do I expect its arrival you may be sure, & before this time tomorrow I shall <u>certainly</u> be relieved from suspense.

You must have had the loveliest weather for the whole journey– Here it has been perfect– and I need not say how often I looked up to the bright moon, gratefully hoping she was lighting you safely on your way– On Tuesday I went with Aunt H. to spend the morning at the Farm, where Fisher was busily employed directing the planting of his Pear Trees from Boston– & some he added to the list here– He also helped to put in some dozen shade & ornamental Trees in the circle & near the house– & remained there 2 whole days working hard– The result of all his labours will <u>tell</u> next Spring– and the <u>garden</u> will then be less difficult to find we hope– meanwhile it is a great amusement to poor Fisher to improve it–

Neither Arthur & Pauline nor William have yet made their appearance & I have not had a line from them, & have not written, because I was in daily expectation of seeing them– M<u>r</u> Gilpin says they are looking for them also at Gen<u>l</u> Van Ness' [*in Washington, D.C.*]– You will be glad to hear that he says he heard <u>nothing</u> of War at the seat of Government– & agreed with M<u>r</u> Coxe last night that there was little chance of it now– since the President appears inclined to retract his pretensions to the <u>whole</u> [*Oregon*] Territory– and his Organ, the <u>Union</u>, speaks of <u>dividing</u> our claims with the British– so that there is every probability of a peaceful termination of the business– unless a difficulty about California sh<u>d</u> arise– The <u>Oregon</u> question we may consider in a fair way of being amicably settled– So pray do not disturb yourself any further on the subject–

Friday morng– I was terribly disappointed at not hearing from you last night dear Mamma, & proportionately delighted this morng by the letter I had so earnestly longed for– I cannot understand why you <u>returned</u> to Goldsboro'[1] after going as far as Wilmington [*North Carolina*]– for surely, if there could be found there no accomodation for the night, it w<u>d</u> have been better to pass it in the cars, than jolt back over so many miles of road– and return the following day over the same distance of 60 or 70 miles– is it not? Pray explain how and why this was to me– but you are safely lodged & suffered less from fatigue, & that ought to satisfy me–

I hope when you go to Middleton Place you will take possession of the chamber opposite the Drawing room– for it will save you from much unnecessary labour of climbing stairs– which will not hurt Edda's young legs– Tell her with my love she must not permit you to mount up so high– & she is so amiable & affectionate that I know she will be anxious for any arrangement that will suit <u>your</u> convenience best– I shall be very glad to receive her promised letter– with an account of the Wedding[2] & her <u>first impressions</u> of Carolina– which she must give truly–

I do not think it likely you will see Arthur & Paolina much before Xmas altho' I know, as I have already told you, nothing of their movements– but am daily watching for their arrival when the cars come in from N.Y. I daresay they will spend a week here & 2 more in Washⁿ– Mrs Smith is pretty well, she will be most pleased to hear so good an account of you– Mrs Fisher's nervous attack is passing off & M^{rs} H– as well as usual– Fisher has taken D^r McEuen out to the Farm to spend the day with him– I wish he c^d have had a more agreeable companion but he expressed a desire to go, & of course Fisher asked him– You will be sorry to hear that poor Mrs Bayard (Mrs Francis' daughter) is in great distress at the prospect of losing her eldest daughter Mrs Schermerhorn,[3] who is dangerously ill in N.Y. of nervous fever & not expected to recover– She has 2 <u>Homoeopathic</u> D^{rs} attending her– Her Uncle, Ed^{wd} Bayard & another– It w^d be very very sad for her parents to lose her for she is their <u>Idol</u>, & really an intelligent fine young woman– The Husband is devoted to her too– but he w^d console himself I daresay but the poor Father & Mother much less easily– Mr Wilcocks is very low– & many think is going to die– He has an aversion to every kind of nourishment, & absolutely rejects all that is offered him– With all his faults, he was a kind hearted generous creature & I am really sorry to hear of his deplorable condition– I must not cross any more, & say Adieu dearest Mamma With best love to Papa & all my brothers & sisters I am ever Y^r most affec^{te} daughter Eliza

Pray do not be uneasy about my throat, for it is tolerably well– & why sh^d I try a remedy for a disease (Bronchitis) which I never had? You are really fond of quackery to take Newspaper recommendations to be worth any thing–

Private Collection

1. Goldsboro, North Carolina, is between Enfield and Wilmington on the railroad line. The letter in which Mrs. Middleton described their journey to Charleston is missing.
2. Probably Lizzie Middleton's marriage to John Julius Pringle Smith.
3. Ellen Bayard married Augustus Van Cortlandt Schermerhorn of New York.

～

To Mrs. Middleton, Middleton Place

Philadelphia Wednesday 17th Dec^r [1845]

I have not written within a week to you my dearest Mamma because I wrote to answer Edda's letter & also to announce to her Edward's arrival here– and therefore delayed for a few days thanking you for the letter which arrived by mail the following day– I hope soon to hear that poor Edda bears her trial more calmly–[1] I understand that Commodore Read expects to sail sometime next month– so that it w$^{\underline{d}}$ hardly have been worth while for her to make the journey to Boston– Two of our acquaintances will be in the Cumberland– D$^{\underline{r}}$ Maxwell, who married Mary Waln– & her brother, W$^{\underline{m}}$ Waln who is to be Secretary to the Commodore– The first is said to be rather an agreeable nice person, but we know him very slightly– the other is an indifferent fellow I believe, but I am glad he has got the appointment, for M$^{\underline{rs}}$ Wilcocks w$^{\underline{d}}$ have had to support him here, & she could ill afford it–

I have been hoping to receive the letter which W$^{\underline{m}}$ half-promised to write me on his arrival– but I suppose he had not time to do so, & perhaps he went off immediately to Combahee with Papa– Still not a word from Arthur– I imagine they will stay out to the end of the year in N.Y. & perhaps begin the new one by coming on– They would find Phil$^{\underline{a}}$ very dull to be sure– for since M$^{\underline{rs}}$ [John Hare] Powel's death,[2] the few parties which were intended in honour of young M$^{\underline{rs}}$ [Robert] Hare & M$^{\underline{rs}}$ S[am] Powel have of course been given up– Neuralgia, of which she died, appears to have become quite prevalent– poor M$^{\underline{rs}}$ Montgomery (Miss Philips) has been a dreadful sufferer with it– but is now recovering– She told me today that she had endured such agony for 6 weeks, that she w$^{\underline{d}}$ have preferred bringing a child into the world every day during that time to undergoing the torture occasioned by Neuralgia in the Bowels– so you may imagine how severe the pain must have been– M$^{\underline{rs}}$ Powel's case is considered a very extraordinary one, for the Physicians have never before known of one in which it attacked the heart–

I wrote the other day to Sarah to tell her & Eleanor how sorry I was to find that the old lady had no intention of inviting them to spend their Holidays here– I had been hoping she might, but as the time drew so near & not a hint was given I was reluctantly forced to conclude she did not mean to ask them– which I assure you is a great disappointment to me– for I required their visit to cheer me up a little after all the sad things which have damped me lately– but of course, I dare not propose it to her in her nervous state, & it only makes me regret the more that she had not consented to live with Aunt H– when I could very easily have arranged it to my satisfaction. However I am perhaps wrong to wish her out of the house– for she certainly tries to be very kind, & saves me a vast deal of trouble in the housekeeping line– but when I am deprived of the pleasure which seems so natural of having my friends & relations to stay with me, I cannot help wishing I could have my own way a little more, & be mistress of my own house– Then I look forward to the Spring when I shall be at liberty to do as I choose at the Farm– but that does not console me for the disappointment with regard to the dear girls– which I am truly sorry for–

You ask about Mrs Butler– I have not yet sent her the <u>challenge</u>[3] which she required from me before she w^{d} write but intend to do so now in a few days– I understand she is gone to Italy with her father for the winter and the story which is going the rounds of the Newspapers about her going on the Stage again, is as <u>true</u> as such authority generally is– I am obliged to finish this stupid scrawl in a hurry for it is tea time, & I am expected at Aunt H's as usual– & after shopping & visiting all the morng– I am wretchedly dull, & w^{d} much prefer spending the eveng at home at the Piano–

We are going to try & make the children happy at Xmas with a <u>Tree a l'Allemande</u> [*in the German style*] as you remember seeing them arranged at Mme de Giese's–[4] Dear Sally is I suppose with you– Pray give me a very particular account of her & the children– Fisher's eyes are rather improved by the Veratria & he still wavers about going on to N.Y. I am <u>quite</u> well– my throat decidedly better– for which thank God! & for many other things besides– In haste I must say goodbye dearest Mamma & with love to all I am Y^{r} most affect^{e} daughter Eliza

The children are well and send their love– They are counting the days before Christmas with impatience– Mrs Smith was here today, but I missed her– Mrs Drayton desired me to present her kind regards to you. The Col. is as well as usual–

Private Collection

1. Edward Middleton had been ordered to Boston, where the frigate *Cumberland* was preparing to sail in early 1846. Edda was pregnant and very upset at Edward's absence.
2. Julia DeVeaux Powel died on December 8, 1845.
3. The nature of Mrs. Butler's challenge is not mentioned.
4. The baronne de Gise was a friend of Eleanor and Maria Middleton's in St. Petersburg.

～

To Mrs. Middleton, Middleton Place

Philadelphia– Decr 26th 1845

I snatched your letter off my breakfast plate with great delight this morng– my dearest Mamma– for as I had been 2 weeks without any tidings of any of you, I was very impatient to hear you may well suppose– and thankful was I to find that accident alone had prevented your writing sooner– You never mention yourself but I hope were as well as usual & the account you gave of Papa was quite encouraging–

I thought of you all a great deal yesterday– and pictured to myself the family party round the dinner table– Our's was very small– for we had but 2 additions to our own party of 5– (the 2 older children at table–) young Mr Rives, & Robert Hare who was asked to meet him– poor Mrs Smith was not able to come out at all– for she had so much encreased her cough, that she was afraid to venture thro' the wet streets– I went to see her today & found her better, but still quite unwell– but taking nothing but a little horhound candy which I daresay however will relieve her <u>quite</u> as much as the Homoeopathic remedies you say Sally was still persevering in– I am very sorry to hear of her cough– you do not speak of her eyes– probably because you had nothing favourable to say– and do mention the children <u>particularly</u> in your next– which you forgot to do–

Mine have been in perfect ecstasies for the last 48 hours– the presents began to come on Christmas Eve– and they have now enough to last them a year I think– Fisher took a vast deal of trouble, in arranging a Tree, and erecting round it a sort of <u>canopy</u>, ornamented with Christmas wreaths of Holly, fir &c– you will perhaps imagine that <u>Lily</u> has attempted to draw this sketch[1] which I only put in to give the children some idea of the <u>front</u> view– the whole affair reaches to the Drawing room ceiling & is covered with Toys, Bonbons, baskets &c– underneath the Tree all sorts of animals are grazing upon <u>Moss</u>, meant to represent grass & in front there is a <u>pond</u> with Geese, Swans, & sheep in wax– Then the table is set out with Dolls, books boxes &c &c– The whole forming a very pretty coup d'oeil [*sight,*] when lighted up–

The children assembled at about 5 o'clk yesterday afternoon, & then the mysterious Veil which had covered it all day was removed– & they flocked round to admire– to the number of 16– after they had <u>gazed their fill</u> of wonder I struck up a dance on the Piano– & they figured away– or rather little Marie d'Hauterive did– for the others looked on at her performance in surprise & delight and could with difficulty be persuaded to join her– she went thro' all the attitudes & steps of the Polka, Cachucha &c– The Sergeants & Miss Hart who came with their nephews & niece, were highly amused at this exhibition– which was really one of extraordinary grace for such a baby– After the dance, they played at Hunt the Slipper– then ate Ice cream &c– & afterwards I distributed all the little presents from the Tree & each went away in great satisfaction with 2 or 3 toys a piece– This morng– I dressed up the Tree afresh for Lily &

Sophy– and nothing more is to be taken off until after New Year– as we thought it pretty enough to reserve it until then– & meantime perhaps Bente may arrive & have the benefit of some of the Toys– I sent Pauline a message by young Mr Rives who went this morng to N.Y. & promised to see her & deliver it– I do hope she has the girls from N. Rochelle with her, as I could not follow my inclination for inviting them– & I conclude their parents w^d not object to their spending a few days with her– during the Holidays–

I am reading a most interesting book by M. Monod– it is called– "Lucile, ou la lecture de la Bible"–^{2} and treats the subject in a masterly style– answering in familiar dialogue all the <u>objections</u> raised by the pupils of Rousseau & other sceptics against the whole plan of Revelation– The tone of the writer is so excellent, & his zeal is so well tempered by charity that he touches the heart while he convinces the understanding– & I cannot help wishing while I am reading it, that some of my <u>unbelieving brethren</u> would give it a fair & candid consideration which w^d I feel sure open the way to their receiving the <u>truth</u> in all its beauty & sublimity–

I am very sorry to hear of poor Edda's indisposition– What does she hear from Edward? for I do not expect him to find time to write to me– I do not feel by any means certain of war– altho' I confess there may <u>now</u> be some ground for alarm– but they won't go beyond the <u>brink</u>– unless G^t Britain sh^d suddenly <u>tip them over</u>– We must hope she will keep quiet & bear the provocations they have certainly been guilty of–^{3} I must send this off in haste with love to Papa and <u>all round</u>, I am dearest Mamma Y^r ever affect^e daughter Eliza

Private Collection

1. Eliza drew a rough sketch of the tree under its canopy.
2. Adolphe Monod (1802–1856) published *Lucile, ou la lecture de la Bible* in 1841.
3. Since Mrs. Middleton's letter is missing, it is not clear to what this passage refers.

1846

*[I] was afraid of telling you of [your father's] indisposition lest
it should make you unhappy. . . . William thinks he had better
remain near Dr. Ogier until he is quite free from the attacks
which occurred lately every other day.*

*The Americans are so rude & so inclined to make War [over
Oregon] that I fear it cannot be avoided.*

⁓

"When we left Charleston [*your father*] had returned to M. Place– I thought
him looking no worse than he did last Autumn; indeed better, in so far as he was
<u>paler</u>, without being thinner."[1] With such notes, Emma Smith as well as William
and Paolina kept Eliza informed about her father's health in the first months of
1846. Henry Middleton spent most of that time in Charleston in order to be near
his doctor, and was only able to go to Middleton Place once or twice. One of his
sons was always with him.

Reading these signals clearly, Eliza wanted to go to South Carolina to see her
father but could not get there. The reason was almost certainly that she was pregnant with her fourth child.

Her mother gave no sign, at least to Eliza, that she knew he was dying. When
the doctors declared in March that he should leave Carolina before the heat, Mrs.
Middleton tried to make preparations to move the whole family to Newport while
waiting, as she always had, for her husband to decide how and when they would
go. Despite the talk of Newport, however, it was clear by early May that for Henry
Middleton travel was out of the question. He died on June 14.

Meanwhile, the United States had been moving toward war with Mexico.
Eliza's earlier premonition that Ned might be sent to Mexico turned out to be
true.[2] His ship reached Vera Cruz in March 1846, fighting broke out in April, and
by mid-May Congress had declared war. Edward was granted a furlough but did
not reach home until after his father died and Edda had had their baby.

In the winter of 1846, with both the British and the American governments
by then anxious to settle the Oregon dispute, President Polk sent Louis McLane
to London to negotiate. The resulting treaty dividing Oregon at the forty-ninth
parallel was signed on June 15, the day after Henry Middleton died.

1. EHS to EMF, April 2, 1846, PHi.
2. EMF to MHM, April 23, 1845, private collection.

To Mrs. Middleton, Middleton Place

Philadelphia Jany 2nd 1846

Your letter of the 27th was a most acceptable New Year's arrival, my dearest Mamma, and made me enjoy the congratulations for the day much more than if I had not received such good news from home– I am anxious to send my heartiest wishes for the happy return of this and many other seasons to you & all the rest of the family, and also to give poor Edda rather better news than she heard from her husband– Commodore [George] Read told Aunt Harrison only 3 days ago, just before his departure for Boston, that he expected to be absent only 2 years– & you may therefore assure Edda that she is misinformed with regard to the length of Edwd's absence– as the Comm^re of course must know his own orders– & I think she ought to be still more cheered by the probability which is now so much encreased of Peace being maintained with Eng^d–[1] I daresay you are still incredulous on this subject, but I am more firmly convinced than ever by the opinion of many sensible and farseeing persons that the negociations will be renewed and arranged amicably– notwithstanding the blustering of certain demagogues and bullies in Congress– Already the prospect is brightening, and I think ere very long all apprehensions of war will be removed–

I am astonished that you had not received the letter from Aunt Hering which I enclosed to you ten days ago– By this time however you will have had explained to you the cause of Uncle's silence– The next Steamer will no doubt bring you one from himself– I wrote a long letter to Fanny Butler by the last, and had no time to answer Aunt's– I was very glad to be able to give her very favourable accounts of her children from M. Picot,[2] whom I went to make enquiries of respecting them– He found the oldest extremely unmanageable at first, but he has now got her into pretty good order by shewing great firmness & good sense– Sally Ingersoll, who spent an eveng– at Aunt H's lately, told me that her cousin Miss Fox,[3] had had a long & very pleasant letter from Fanny, who had been received in the kindest manner by all her friends in England, and was then staying in the country with some of them– The News Paper reports about her intention of returning to the Stage are of course untrue–

But I must tell you something of New Year's day– In the first place my good husband rose early to go out and order me a beautiful bunch of flowers which I rec^d before breakfast as usual– As I had been of late often to church on week days, I determined to stay at home & receive my friends, whom I have very seldom an opportunity of seeing at home– We had many visitors, who all admired the Xmas tree, which I had dressed up again for the occasion, and which we decided to pull down in the afternoon, as it was beginning to fade, and the children were getting anxious to take possession of the Toys which remained upon it– We dined at Aunt's to meet M͏ʳ J. B. Francis, who arrived the day before & cheered her at the time we feared w͏ᵈ have been particularly saddened by former associations–⁴ In the eveng– several agreeable people dropped in to see her & she appeared to suffer less than we had apprehended–

I had a letter from Sarah yesterday which was really beautifully written & remarkably well expressed– She says it w͏ᵈ have given them great pleasure to have spent some days at the Carlton with their Uncle & Aunt [*Arthur and Paolina*]– but as they did not expect them she fears it might put them to inconvenience, and therefore thinks it best to remain at New Rochelle– It is really an evidence of great delicacy on the part of the girls to come to that conclusion for I have no doubt they longed ardently to follow my suggestion, which it is most extraordinary that Arthur & Pauline⁵ did not propose to them during the Holidays when it might so easily have been arranged– for some of the Boltons are constantly coming to N.Y. and I regret more than ever that it was not in <u>my</u> power to invite them here– as they must sensibly feel the neglect of their Aunt P. who has never even written them a line– Now that New Year is past we may I suppose expect them on here– & they may think it worth while to stay for M͏ʳˢ Camac's Fancy Ball on the 13͏ᵗʰ.

What dreadful accounts I see in the Papers of the Famine in the upper parts of S. Carolina, in Spartanburgh particularly– I hope they may be exaggerated, but it must be productive of great misery among the population who depend upon the corn crops for their support– I hope they have not failed also in the low Country– Tell Harry we hail from <u>Abington</u>– <u>don</u> is the English termination I believe– I must say Adieu! dearest Mamma, with love to all I am ever Y͏ʳ most affecte daughter Eliza

Lily has been amusing herself with her slate for the last hour. M͏ʳˢ Smith dined here on New Year's Eve & spent the eveng– with us at Aunt's– Her cold & cough were much better.

I am glad to hear better accounts of dear Sally but sorry you are so soon to lose her– I shall certainly write to her when she returns to Waccamaw– It is remarkable that with all your wonderful Homoeopathic remedies & Water cures poor Edda continues to suffer so much with headaches– Surely it ought not to be permitted–

Private Collection

1. Calhoun had spoken out against the firebrands in Congress, saying that war over Oregon was not an acceptable means of settling the disagreement with England.

President Polk, after a belligerent address in which he recommended that the United States withdraw from the treaty of joint occupation of Oregon, then let it be known that negotiations with England were still possible.

2. Frenchman Charles Picot and his wife ran a school for young ladies in Philadelphia. The Butlers' daughters were Sarah (Sally) (b. 1835) and Frances (Fan) (b. 1838).

3. Mary Dickinson Fox (1807–1895) lived with her brother, Charles, at Champlost, on the north side of Philadelphia near the Harry Ingersolls. She was the daughter of George and Mary (Dickinson) Fox.

4. The Harrisons had always given a party for their friends on New Year's Day.

5. The Middletons gradually shifted from Paolina to Pauline.

⌒

To Mrs. Middleton, Middleton Place

Philadelphia Jany 9th 1846

I had this morng– the pleasure of receiving your letter of the 4th my dearest Mamma, for which I immediately sit down to thank you– I am sorry you were making yourself unhappy about Uncle Oliver, whose attack however severe must have passed off entirely by this time– and I doubt not the next Steamer will bring you a letter from him confirming this good news– I wish you had mentioned Papa's health, which I have begged you always to do, and also to speak of your own– pray do not forget my request– You must enjoy the mild weather in the garden, where I suppose the Camellias have ventured to bloom again– Our country looks very desolate– not a leaf of any kind is to be seen on any tree or Shrub– but our little grass plot in front is still green at the Farm– where I spent last Tuesday with Fisher–

Our Gardener says that in digging round the roots of Trees which were to be removed he found the frost had penetrated 14 inches underground– but the day we were there it was all rising up, and the walks were terribly muddy– to Lily's great discomfort– for she accompanied me and was quite horrified at the dirt she brought in with her– Her dislike to dirt is an inheritance, and she carries it so far that I sometimes cannot help laughing at the resemblance I perceive in this and some other points of character to her Grandmother– She is however very fond of books– which the old lady never was I believe and really has now learnt to read almost perfectly– She also spells very well words of 3 or 4 syllables out of the book– and I hear her every day a little French lesson– which she begins to take a great interest in– Little Sophy is much less inclined to study– but reads a little every day in the first Vol. of little tales in 3 letters– & makes out much better than she did at Abington– You expect to hear of Helen's talking– but she has not yet advanced beyond the 2 or 3 words

she could say when you went away– altho' she understands everything perfectly, and has a great many pretty little ways– She is growing fatter every day– &
the only trouble her teeth seem to give her now is at night, when she is often
restless, and keeps poor Pum awake by the hour–

You have not described the appearance of Sally's children– which I am
anxious to hear about– Is little Helen as pretty as ever, and are they both as
well behaved & good humoured? Poor Sally's eyes are not likely to get well
by Homeopathic treatment, and I think she had better let me send her some
<u>Aconitine</u>,[1] which Fisher thinks is really going to cure him at last– He has to
be sure only tried it for a few days, but if it proves as beneficial as he hopes it
will, I w$^{\underline{d}}$ strongly advise her trying it also– It is the <u>crack remedy</u> which D$^{\underline{r}}$
Elliot[2] has used so successfully and the other Physicians are now beginning to
follow his example– but use it rather more cautiously than he does. His patient
Mary Jones has I believe sailed for Savannah with the Gardiners– who passed
thro' Phil$^{\underline{a}}$ the other day, and came to see me but I was out unfortunately–
Arthur & Pauline will receive a message from me tomorrow by M$^{\underline{r}}$ Francis
who went this afternoon to N.Y. & intended to go to the Carlton & tell them
how much disappointed I was not to have seen them yet– Every morng I fancy
they are going to arrive in the afternoon– but really I begin now to think they
will remain in New York all the winter– If they sh$^{\underline{d}}$ come on I shall have an
opportunity of sending you "Lucile"– which I am sure you will like to read–

I do indeed wish I could run on & pay you a visit for a few weeks dear
Mamma but situated as we are it is impossible at present– & as to my leaving
my Husband and children– of course that is out of the question– I must look
forward to the month of <u>May</u>, which I trust will bring you all to Phil$^{\underline{a}}$. On
Edda's account it will be necessary for you to come as early as that– I am glad
to hear she keeps up her spirits better poor child– I understand from M$^{\underline{rs}}$
Wilcocks that the Cumberland will probably be detained several weeks longer
at Boston to get in her Crew– I had nearly forgotten to tell you what an agreeable <u>eveng</u> at home we had on Wednesday– & that the <u>Practising</u> went off so
well that we determined to renew it every week– M$^{\underline{r}}$ Laffitte sang admirably
at first sight the music of Ernani[3] which I like much better than I did at first–
and he & M$^{\underline{rs}}$ Cuesta & Frank Shroeder sang several trios very well together–
We had only 2 or 3 listeners & do not intend to encrease their number– I
enjoyed the music so much that it kept me awake nearly all night which I hope
it will not when I hear more of it– Fisher is waiting with Overcoat on & Hat
in hand to take me to Aunts'– where M$^{\underline{rs}}$ Commodore Stewart is to meet me,
so that I must in haste conclude with love to all– Y$^{\underline{r}}$ most affectionate Eliza

Private Collection

1. Aconitine, made from wild aconite, could have side effects such as distorted vision and difficulty in speaking.

2. Samuel Elliot was a New York oculist. His remedies were said to be violent and his bills high. William Elliott to Ann Elliott, September 3, 1847, in Beverly Scafidel, "The Letters of William Elliott" (Ph.D. diss., University of South Carolina, 1978), 527.

3. Giuseppe Verdi's opera *Ernani* was first performed in 1844. Frank Schroeder introduced Eliza to Verdi's music, saying that it was in "an entirely new style." EMF to MHM, November 24, 1845, private collection.

⁓

To Mrs. Middleton, Middleton Place

Philadelphia – Jany 16$^{\underline{th}}$ [1846]

At last I have the pleasure of announcing to you the long expected arrival of Arthur & Pauline, my dearest Mamma– which you will I am sure be glad to learn, as in about 2 weeks more you will probably see them in Carolina– They have been here since Monday & will only make out the rest of the week and proceed to Washington next Monday, and the following week to Charleston– I thought it probable I should receive a letter from you this morng & was not disappointed– & quite delighted to read Edda's well filled half-sheet enclosed in your's– which to be sure was rather short– but you gave none but good news– and it was most acceptable– Thank dear Edda most heartily for her affectionate lines which are very expressive of her sad feelings at her husband's departure– I have looked in the papers for the sailing of the Cumberland, but have not yet seen it announced, altho' she <u>dropped down</u> in the stream some days ago– I am very glad to hear the Commodore has appointed him [*Edward*] Flag Lieut. but am sure he owes this favour to his own merit exclusively, and not to any friendship which the Comm$^{\underline{re}}$ [*George Read*] feels for <u>me</u>– altho' we are on good terms– and he is particularly attached to Aunt H– which of course w$^{\underline{d}}$ not have influenced him unless he had found out Ned's good qualities–

Pauline has just come in, so that I must finish this hastily as I am going to dine out at M$^{\underline{rs}}$ Hare's– P. looks remarkably well, altho' she is suffering from a bad cold in the head– Arthur is half the day enveloped in Wet Sheets or bathing in cold water, but the other half feels so fresh & strong, and has so excellent an appetite that one cannot understand the necessity of his undergoing all these operations– he rides this hobby to death as usual–[1] & talks of little else– Cold

water now entirely supersedes with him the use of all drugs– even Homoeopathic ones– & he imagines it is to cure every ill that flesh is heir to– and tries
to convince every body of its efficacy– which I do not at all doubt in many
cases– but not in all–

We had quite a pleasant little Réunion on Wednesday eveng & a great deal
of good music– Pauline has been taking singing lessons of Bagioli who has
certainly improved her style– But I must not forget to tell you of the Brilliant
Fancy Ball[2] which they attended on Tuesday eveng– Arthur wore Fisher's dress
of Sir Christopher Walton– altered to fit him and it was remarkably becoming & handsome– & Pauline at the tenth hour literally, made up her mind to
go as I recommended, as a Sybil with a Turban & red Shawl draped round
her Shoulders & was much admired– Harry's two widows (the Mistress of the
Revels & M^rs W[illiams])[3] both looked particularly well in Costumes of the
16th Century & the latter enquired of Arthur when he was coming on. She
seemed to have reason to expect his return to Phil^a soon– M^r C[ox] was close
to the lady of the house all the eveng & excited remark by his devoted attentions– There were between 2 & 3 hundred persons present & many magnificent
dresses– We saw about a dozen of them at Aunt H's– where as many came in
to exhibit themselves to her– among others Matilda Willing, who wore a French
Cauchoise dress[4] of the reign of Louis quinze– & looked very well in it–
Arthur & Pauline are going to night (Saturday) to hear her play on the Harp
at Susan Ingersoll's– who invited them expressly for that purpose– but on account of Mr Wilcock's recent death, cannot have anything of a party–

I should be delighted to go & listen to her Music, but as I have not for 3
years past invited M^rs W[illing] to our House, I do not think it right to go &
meet her in that sociable way unless I could make up my mind to renew our
former intercourse, which I cannot– disapproving as I do so decidedly of her
manners & conversation & whole course of conduct– I do not pretend to judge
of her innocence or guilt of action for I have no opportunity or desire to enter
into any enquiry upon that subject– but of her tone & language I can & ought
to judge– & they are not according to my taste. Still I return her visits, not
wishing to quarrel with her, & am civil when we meet– but as to seeking her
society, with the opinion I have of her loose principles, I cannot do it– M^rs F.
disagrees with me, & wishes me to go tonight– & invite her here– but altho'
I should of course make no objection to her doing so, I must be permitted to
act as I think consistently in this & other matters–

I have, as you will perceive detained this letter until today (Saturday) because I found it impossible to finish it yesterday– as immediately after Pauline
left me, I had to dress for Mrs Hare's dinner– which I found very agreeable.

I must now conclude in haste that I may be prepared for A. & P. who are coming to spend the day with us– Pray give my best love to Papa, my brothers & Sisters– & believe me, dearest Mamma As ever Y^r most affect^e Daughter Eliza

Mrs Smith dined with us 3 days since, & was better than usual– Poor Miss Hare is quite sick, & I fear will not get over this attack– for altho' she is not in immediate danger– she is much reduced by keeping her bed for ten days– Mrs F. is of course very anxious about her & is herself suffering from a severe cold– Mrs H. is much as usual– on the whole better in spirits I think– Fisher is well & the children also–

Private Collection

    1. Wrapping patients in wet sheets for substantial periods of time was one of the essentials of a cure through hydropathy, Arthur's most recent enthusiasm.
    2. Mrs. Camac gave the ball and was Mistress of the Revels.
    3. Harry had been visiting Mrs. Williams regularly for over a year.
    4. A style worn by a woman of the "pays de Caux" in the north of Normandy. She probably wore a full, gathered skirt, a shawl, and a high, conical hat covered by lace at the top.

⌐

To Mrs. Fisher, Philadelphia

M.P. Jany 18th 1846

    I had my dearest Eliza the pleasure of receiving your letter of the 9th on the 15th thanks to Mrs Pringle who sends so frequently to town & her servants call at our house there, for letters & papers– This is of great consequence to Edda who expects daily to hear from Edward: she has lately been very much afflicted by not hearing from him for nearly a week & feared that he was ill– I too feared that was the reason, but Sally said it was probable he was on his way to Charleston as Edda had mentioned to him that his Father was not well. It will be a fortnight tomorrow since he [*Henry Middleton*] went there, as I mentioned to you, but was afraid of telling you of his indisposition lest it should make you unhappy– We have now heard from Johnny who saw him in the parlour last friday that he was much better & Willm frequently writes a line or two to Edda to inform her that he is better, so that you must not make yourself uneasy by supposing he is still suffering.
    It is the same sort of nervous complaint with which he was attacked last May & I omitted to write to you on the subject until his health was improving &

mention it now lest you might hear from some of your acquaintances that he is not well. It is uncertain when he will return as W^m̲ thinks he had better remain near D^r̲ Ogier until he is quite free from the attacks which occurred lately every other day, but during the last week I believe he has escaped them. I try to make Edda believe that Ed^d̲ has sailed, but she says she is sure he would not without writing to her, & tho' I do not tell her that he is probably ill, yet I fear that is the only reason that prevents him from writing poor fellow! The climate of Boston must be at this season very injurious to him– perhaps M^r̲s̲ Read may have heard from the Com^r̲e̲ some account of him, if she has, do let me know of it.

You ask me dear Eliza about my health, it is thank God! as good as ever. I am very glad to hear that M^r̲ Fisher's eyes are improving– I read to Sally what you wrote about them, & she begs me to thank you for proposing to send her some Aconitine, but she thinks her eyes are in a much worse state than M^r̲ F's– & that perhaps that application might be injurious. They are frequently very painful– reading two days since a letter from Hal twice, caused great pain, & she is obliged to avoid exerting them except by hearing Tommy & the little Girls their lessons, which I tell her I would do if she would allow me, but she says that gives her less trouble than other trials of them. You ask whether Helen is as pretty as ever? She is I think, & good tempered & affectionate, as is also little Maria, both very obedient to their Mother, & devoted to Edda who is very kind to them, & also to the boys– She has been writing to Hal, who when here was greatly pleased with her. I wish Sally could have advice from some Occulist, D^r̲ Elliot I daresay could cure her eyes, but she has no chance of seeing him. Arthur may perhaps give her some good advice when he comes, which I hope he will in a week or 10 days– Sally will remain until the end of the month as John was so much occupied at his plantation that he wrote he should not be able to leave it as soon as he had expected. Oliver staid only a few days in Charl^n̲ & will probably be there with his family this week.

This week will be an important one for the Hibernia will bring news from England which I suppose will make Congress decide upon War [*over Oregon*]– the Members seem so determined upon it. You must have lately read the speeches they make on the subject– Hannegan[1] & many others make me fear there is no chance of avoiding war– & what a terrible one it will be! I am also looking forward for a letter from my dear brother, but not without fear.

Johnny came yesterday with M^r̲ Cotes to M^r̲ Pringle's, & Sally went there & brought him here, after dinner she will take him there & he will go with two Pringle boys tomorrow before Sun rise to Charl^n̲ by this means I can send my letter. Sally is to dine with her Aunt tomorrow– they meet frequently & M^r̲s̲

P. is now in better health & spirits– She was very ill last summer. I am glad to hear you have weekly singing parties to amuse you– do you sing yourself? & you were kept awake nearly all night by the enjoyment of it! I hope it may not prevent you from sleeping again– And Lily is learning French! You are bringing her up very famously, & she, indeed all the children must make you very happy.

Here is good news just arrived by old Abraham who was sent to Charl$^{\underline{n}}$ yesterday for letters for Edda– He says your Father is much better, & that if the weather sh$^{\underline{d}}$ be good tomorrow, he & your brothers will be here– so that you must not make yourself uneasy about him. Edda has at last received a letter from Ed$^{\underline{d}}$ who has not been ill. He is now in the Sound & the vessel will not sail till the 1$^{\underline{st}}$ Feb$^{\underline{y}}$– She is now quite delighted– sends her best love to you as does Sally, & Johnny begs to send his love– They are going in a few minutes to conduct him to Runnymede for the pleasure of a drive so I must seal this– Pray give my love to M$^{\underline{rs}}$ & M$^{\underline{r}}$ Fisher & M$^{\underline{rs}}$ Harrison & M$^{\underline{rs}}$ Smith who I hope is now well & believe me my dearest Eliza y$^{\underline{r}}$ affectionate Mother M. H. M. Give my love also to the little girls.

PHi

1. Edward Hannegan (1807–1859), senator from Indiana, introduced resolutions saying that the United States owned all of Oregon to the 54°40' line, and that to surrender any part of it would be to abandon the country's honor. Mrs. Middleton was glad that Calhoun "opposed his absurd speeches & I hope he has more influence than several of the other warlike members."

Still worried a month later, she told Eliza, "the Amer[ican]s are so rude & so inclined to make War that I fear it cannot be avoided." MHM to EMF, January 11 and February 23, 1846, PHi.

∼

To Mrs. Middleton, Middleton Place

Philadelphia Saturday – Jan$^{\underline{y}}$ 24th [1846]

I am quite out of humour with the Southern mail for not bringing me a letter from you my dearest Mamma, but on the other hand the Northern mail has brought us this morning such excellent news that I am partly consoled for my disappointment– Who would have believed that the Peel ministry w$^{\underline{d}}$ have been reinstated so soon,[1] and that the Message of the President would have produced no angry feeling in England? And yet this is the news brought by the

Hibernia, to our very great joy & comfort– I really now congratulate you dearest Mamma upon the Pacific aspect of affairs– which just as they appeared to be at the worst, (for we apprehended much from the change of ministry & Lord Palmerston's well known belligerent dispositions) have taken such an unexpected & happy turn, & now seem really to promise the fairest termination of all difficulties– For my part I no longer regard War as probable– altho' Fisher still doubts the result of so much <u>mischief making</u> in Congress by the Western members– I must say that during the last week matters seemed to be growing worse daily & I began to be seriously apprehensive that the <u>storm cloud</u> would burst over us, & your fears be realized– Now my confidence has returned that Peace & Justice will prevail, & all be settled to the satisfaction of the <u>moderate</u> on both sides– & this I trust will be your conviction when you have read the last accounts– So think no more of <u>Spartanburgh</u>, dear Mamma, but make up y^r mind that we shall meet happily in the merry month of May– I shall be anxious to hear from you of Uncle Oliver's continued improvement– which I hope he has been able to assure you of himself–

Arthur & Pauline left this for Washington on Monday, where they talked of staying only a week– but I shall know more of their movements when I receive the letter she promised to write to me from thence– They enjoyed the little party at Mrs Ingersoll's I mentioned they were going to– & M^{rs} W's music of course– but I did not regret having come to the conclusion of staying away–

We had a violent storm on Wednesday, of snow & hail, which kept all our musicians at home so that the few friends who ventured out to see us heard only my Piano– which I regretted the more as they had made the sacrifice of coming thro' such bad weather– Today we have a little dinner of ten of the most agreeable young men we could think of to meet young Rives and Harrison Ritchie–² who is spending a few days here on his way to Wash^n– The old lady <u>detests</u> dinners, and therefore gives me the head of the Table– I on the contrary expect to enjoy much pleasant conversation & shall not be at all <u>put out</u> if every thing does not go on in the smoothest manner– The two elder children will go & dine with Aunt H. who loves to have them– & they will be glad to get out after being shut up by the Snow & Ice for 3 days– The Sleighs are still flying thro' the Streets, but this will be the last day probably that we shall hear the pleasant noise of their Bells– for it is moderating every hour and thawing rapidly– Tell Harry that his friend Miss Emily Kuhn is engaged to the Mr Harrison of Balt^e who was attentive to her 2 summers ago at New Port– People are surprised for he is in very bad health and is poor– but she is herself very sickly and perhaps sympathizes with him on that account– It is wondered how a gentleman with <u>one lung</u> could make himself heard by a <u>deaf</u> lady– but perhaps he <u>wrote</u> his addresses to her– They are to be married very soon I understand– What a sad thing is William Wadsworth's[3] attack of Apoplexy, which they say he cannot survive! he had only been married a few weeks to a very charming person– Miss Austin– I pity the poor Sister, who was devoted to him, almost as much as the "mourning bride"– for she will be left quite desolate, & Mrs W. returns to her brothers & Father–

My dear Baby comes in to claim my attention– She is the rosiest & fattest of the three now– altho' the others look very well– & are much improved by <u>Curls</u>– as Pauline will tell you– She will also give you a very good account of my healthy appearance which everyone remarks– thanks I believe to my cold Water bath– I have been sitting still all the morng & must now go & take a little exercize or I shall not be able to enjoy my dinner at all. I suppose the Cumberland will now sail immediately as they were only waiting the arrival of the English Steamer– dear Edda must keep a stout heart, & I am sure you will all try & comfort her– With love to her, dear Sally, Kitty, my brothers & Papa I am dear Mamma as ever Y^r most affec^{te} daughter Eliza

Private Collection

  1. Sir Robert Peel (1788–1850) was prime minister until November 1845. When Lord John Russell was unable to form a new government, partly because of disagreement over including the anti-American Lord Palmerston, Peel became prime minister again and was able to reach agreement on the Oregon treaty.
  Eliza referred to Polk's message to Congress recommending withdrawal from the treaty of joint occupation of Oregon.
  2. Harrison Ritchie (1825–1894), Sophia (Otis) Ritchie's son, had recently graduated from Harvard.
  3. William was the brother of James and Elizabeth Wadsworth.

⁓

To Mrs. Fisher, Philadelphia

M.P. Feby 1st 1846

My dearest Eliza

As Johnny is to be in Town early tomorrow mor^g I must give him this by dinner time, as he will go to Runnymede directly after, & Mrs Pringle will let him accompany her sons tomorrow. Your letter of the 24th I had the pleasure to receive Friday Eve^g from John who we had been expecting, as also y^r Father for several days, but he came alone, & although he said his Father was much better, the Doctor thinks he ought not leave Town yet. He also brought me a note from Paolina who had arrived on Thursday morn^g with all her family. She says nothing of coming here, as I suppose Arthur wishes to enjoy some of the gaieties which may take place this month– Edda is so kind that she will not leave me until they come, although she has been invited by Susan to stay with her & the Girls [*in Charleston,*] which she wishes to do, that she may have there a Music Master, & be superintended by Mary & Matty. Harry intended (John says) to return here, but cannot determine I suppose to quit M^{rs} H[arper] to whom he pays visits twice a day. After her resolution communicated to you 3 y^{rs} ago, is it not strange that they should continue so intimate?^{X} [1]

I was indeed rejoiced to find at last by the news brought by the Hibernia that peace would probably continue with England, which the U.S. ought to be thankful for, as Mexico has declared War against them.[2] Ed^d writes to Edda that the Cumberland may perhaps sail to Mexico– that is more to be feared than his going to Africa, although I do not make that observation to <u>her</u>– He might be in danger of fighting with the Mexicans, which I hope he may escape.

I am much obliged to you my dear Eliza for sending me Lucile & the 7 numbers of the Living Age, which will amuse me very much, & which I will take good care of. Yesterday I had time to read when alone only 24 pages of Lucile, which seems as you say an excellent work. I read as much as I can to Sally after dinner (as before, she is occupied with the Children, & taking long walks with Edda) the Memoirs of Lady Hester Stanhope,[3] which amuses her extremely. What an extraordinary creature she was! Have you read the book? it would astonish you to read the account the Doctor gives of her.

I am rejoiced to hear that you are so well, & <u>look</u>ing so well, & that the Children too are in such good health, in this last letter you do not mention Mr Fisher's eyes, I hope they continue to improve. Did Arthur shew you a book he has lent to John & which he read aloud to me yesterday, "Hydriatics or Manual of the Water cure, especially as practised by Vincent Priessnitz"–[4] He read accounts of its having cured affections of the Eyes & inflammation of the Lungs, in short of every disease– I think you would like it, as there is much advice given about the treatment of young Children– You had better procure it, a small book.

You would be pleased as Sally observed to see the White Camellias in full bloom. the Weather is now warm– Johnny brought me a small twig of the weeping willow, the leaves just opening– those near the river are beginning to look green something unusual at so early a season & having had so cold a winter– however I daresay we shall have more cold weather soon– Yours must now be much warmer than it has been. I am afraid Susan cannot come here, as she cannot I suppose bring all her Children in her Carriage, & cannot leave any of them in Town as M̲ʳ̲s̲ Chisolm is not there. still in very bad health at Edisto. M̲ʳ Sidney F[isher] will I suppose soon be here, though you have not told me when he is to leave Phil̲ᵃ. M̲ʳ Wadworth's death is indeed a melancholy event.

You mention M̲ʳ Rives– do not believe what he told you, I am sure it is not true, for the person he mentioned is visited by many respectable people & I have heard more about her than when we were talking on the subject. After taking my walk I must now conclude– Sally & Edda & John send their love to you– Give mine to M̲ʳ̲s̲ & M̲ʳ Fisher & M̲ʳ̲s̲ Harrison & M̲ʳ̲s̲ Smith, & believe me my dearest Eliza your Affect̲ᵗ̲e̲ Mother M. H. M.

give my love to the Children–

PHi

1. The "x" directed Eliza to a note: "Take no notice of this, as y̲ʳ letter may be opened by y̲ʳ brother in Town."

2. Mrs. Middleton may have referred to the Mexican government's refusal to receive Polk's envoy, John Slidell, which, in diplomatic terms, was an unfriendly act. War had not yet been declared.

3. Lady Hester Stanhope (1776–1839), William Pitt's unconventional niece, left England to travel in the Middle East and died in poverty in Lebanon. The *Memoirs of Lady Hester Stanhope as Related by Herself in Conversations with Her Physician* were published in 1845.

4. This book by Francis Graeter was published in New York in 1842. Harry, as well as Arthur, had caught the water cure mania and according to Emma Smith, was in Charleston, "dividing his time between M̲ʳ̲s̲ H[arper] & wet sheets." The following week, Eliza responded that, "As to my treating my children in that way, I should not dare to try experiments upon them until the system has been more fully tested." EHS to EMF, April 2, 1846, PHi; EMF to MHM, February 7, 1846, private collection.

⌣

To Mrs. Fisher, Philadelphia

M.P. Feb̲ʸ 14̲ᵗ̲h̲ 1846

To my great surprise my dearest Eliza Will̲ᵐ yesterday came into the drawing room having brought your Father at last from town, & informed me that he was much better, which he seemed to be when he came in a few minutes after & had a good appetite at dinner– While at the table Arthur & family arrived & I supposed they would remain here until May, but a few minutes since, Paolina told me they should return tomorrow afternoon with Edda & stay a week there which is the Race week, & attend Susan's ball next Monday– Harry was to have come today but the weather is so bad that he cannot come on horseback. Such a violent rain & wind is unusual– You I suppose have the same, which I fear may be injurious to you & the children. I was very glad to learn yesterday by your letter of the 7<u>th</u> ins<u>t</u> that they were recovering from their late attack [*of croup and colds,*] & hope dear little Helen may not suffer from cutting her teeth. Sally & family left town only yesterday, which was a very fine day, but today I suppose they will be compelled to remain at some Inn on their way to Wac[camaw] for the rain would prevent their ending their journey in such bad weather.

I allowed Paolina & Wil<u>m</u> to read your letter to me that they might understand the falsehood of the reports about Harry & Will<u>m</u>. I am sorry poor R[ebecca] Smith is so little to be depended upon–[1] M<u>rs</u> Harper, P<u>a</u> says, will go to Savannah soon & on her return to Ch<u>n</u> will remain until May. her Child is greatly improved. Will<u>m</u> begs me to tell you that he requests you to send as soon as is convenient the roots that are in your town Garden that M<u>r</u> Fisher told him have very sweet flowers & spring up without difficulty. He does not know the name, but says M<u>r</u> F. can understand what he wants.

Sunday– We are to have an early dinner, & the party will leave us at 3 o'clock the day being fine. Harry will probably come. Edda told me she forgot to mention that Paolina intends to write soon to you & now sends her love– Give mine to M<u>rs</u> & M<u>r</u> Fisher M<u>rs</u> Harrison & M<u>rs</u> Smith & believe me my dearest Eliza Y<u>r</u> affect<u>te</u> Mother M. H. M.

Cath<u>e</u> sends her love & thanks for the Collars you have sent her. This is a short letter but Edda must have told you everything worth hearing. give my love to the Children– Y<u>r</u> Father is better today.

PHi

1. Rebecca Smith had repeated some gossip about Mrs. Harper, William, and Harry, which Eliza regretted having repeated. "It will be a lesson to me," she wrote, "in future never to credit anything at second hand– for much mischief is generally the consequence." EMF to MHM, February 7, 1846, private collection.

⌇

Mrs. Middleton, Middleton Place

Philadelphia, Feb<u>y</u> 24<u>th</u> [1846]

I sent you a message by Edda, which I hope you have received, my dearest Mamma, as it will account to you for not hearing from me quite as punctually as usual– She had twice written & I had not answered her kind letters, & therefore addressed myself to her at the end of the week. I will now no longer delay thanking you for your <u>very short</u> half letter, which was however satisfactory as far as it went. We had the storm you mention, only a much colder edition of it– a heavy snow, which still lies in the streets several inches thick– but it has become so much milder that I hope we shall have soon a rain to wash it away– This morng was beautiful, and the children enjoyed a long walk, which they have seldom lately had an opportunity of doing, the pavements having been in so slippery & sloppy a state– I have however been kept in very little by weather, and when every one else has been confined by severe colds & Influenzas, I escape, really to my own surprise, for I have never been freer from them than this winter & now consider myself a hearty woman at last– I even resisted the alternate effect of intense heat at Meyer's Concert[1] & the cold damp night air into which we emerged afterwards– which some months ago w$\underline{d}$ certainly I think have given me cold– My expectations altho' very highly raised, were even surpassed by his performance– which is really the most marvellous transformation of a Piano into a whole Orchestre by a single pair of hands, that I could have imagined possible– So much delighted was I by his almost miraculous power, that I intend going to hear him again tomorrow night, notwithstanding he has chosen Ash Wednesday, which I regret for his own sake, as many will I think be deterred from going on that account, Episcopalians as well as Catholics, but as I am sure I should not be spending the eveng– more profitably by being at Aunt's, where gossip (<u>not</u> scandal) is the order of the eveng, I may as well have the gratification of listening to good music which does not <u>weaken</u> religious feelings if it does not promote them–

Our practisings are to be in future on Thursdays instead of Wednesday evengs & this week we do not intend asking any listeners, as we are going thro' a new Opera, & want to have it to ourselves– Last week we had half a dozen ladies besides those who come habitually– who were much pleased with the selection we made– but I was so much shocked at hearing of the death of M$\underline{r}$ [William] Goddard, just before they came, that I could not shake off the sadness this news caused– He is a dreadful loss to his family, to whom he was tenderly attached, and altho' I have [no doubt] he was well prepared, & therefore the suddenness of his death is not to be regretted on his own account, yet [to] them it must have been horrible to see him snatched away from the midst of them, when a few moments before he was apparently in as good health as usual. M$\underline{r}$ Francis while writing about it, encloses a scrap from a New Port paper announcing the death of W$\underline{m}$ Lewis, [*missing*] former serv$\underline{t}$ who went off in a drunken fit I suppose. No loss to any one I fancy– & a relief to his wife– whom he maltreated abominably I understand–

Tuesday eveng– The children have been with me all the afternoon, and I must now close this hastily, hoping to have something better worth sending next week– My best love to dear Papa & all my Brothers & Sisters– Pauline will I suppose be quite ready to return to M. Place after Lent begins– if she has been persuaded to outstay her week in town– I hope poor Edda has enjoyed herself with the girls– you must miss her though, very much– Adieu! again dearest Mamma– & believe me Y^r most affectionate daughter Eliza

Tell W$^{\underline{m}}$, Sidney [Fisher] still seems very uncertain about going to Carolina, altho' he has not yet quite given up the hope, he says, of getting off–

Private Collection
This is Eliza's last letter.

1. Leopold de Meyer was one of the several European musicians who toured the United States in the 1840s.

～

To Mrs. Fisher, Philadelphia

M.P. March 21$^{\underline{st}}$ 1846

With great pleasure my dearest Eliza your letter of the 13$^{\underline{th}}$ was yesterday given to me by your Father who I had been expecting several days previous & it is nearly a fortnight since I have heard from you. I thought it better not to write until I should see him & give you a good account of him which I can now do, & send this tomorrow when Arthur intends to go to Town.

I am delighted to hear how much you have enjoyed yourself on the anniversary of an event which has contributed so much to your happiness & for which I am so thankful.[1] Your children are indeed a great blessing & will I hope be a continual comfort to you. I was greatly surprised, & uneasy when I first read that you had intended to come to Carolina this Spring, for I was afraid you had a bad cough & threatened as you had been three years since with a serious illness, but I afterwards supposed that your reason for coming here was to see your Father whose illness had made you so desirous of being near him: this I hope was the cause of your intention, for when I have learnt from your Brothers how well you looked, & y^r letters have so often informed me that you were now better than you had been for a long time, I may believe that you really have been, & continue to be in good health. I wish I could look forward to the pleasure of seeing you my dear Eliza in two months! If you would meet me at Newport it would indeed be a great comfort, but we cannot go to Phil$^{\underline{a}}$ as you seem to think we shall. Your Father perhaps may go there by the rail cars, though I should think the journey would be more fatiguing to him than a Sea voyage which you know is the mode of conveyance for me & the rest of the family to N.York– Rail Cars too would be much too dangerous for Edda in her situation. She is still staying with Susan, the Girls entreating her to remain with them. I am surprised to learn that she has not yet heard from Edward, as it is now a month since he left Boston, & the Vessel might have arrived at Mexico in a fortnight. The winds may probably have been adverse– they have been very tempestuous during the last month, but I hope they have not injured the Ship.

It was indeed unlucky that your Duett was so improperly accompanied by Miss La Roche– is she a French girl? M$^{\underline{rs}}$ Smith gives me a very agreeable & amusing description of your party & of a number of other subjects, by which she seems to be as usual in good spirits & I hope in good health– pray give my love to her & thanks for her lively letter & tell her that I hope she will spend the summer at Newport which would give me great pleasure. She might have lodging at the Ocean house so near us. She thinks England & America will be peaceable, I hope so, but the Oregon queston is not yet settled. When the next Steamer arrives the affair will probably be so. I am very glad to learn that D$^{\underline{r}}$ Jackson is recovering.

I asked A$^{\underline{r}}$ this morn$^{\underline{g}}$ whether he should go to Ch$^{\underline{n}}$ tomorrow. he said not until Monday or Tuesday if his Father sh$^{\underline{d}}$ go on Monday, so that this will not arrive as soon as I expected. He has had no account from Wash$^{\underline{n}}$ of any Legacy being left him by G$^{\underline{l}}$ Van Ness.[2] Miss Wight wrote only to inform Paolina of his illness & Death. She will indeed be in a sad state if he has not provided for her. The Penn$^{\underline{a}}$ Inquirer mentions a Will that he has made, & that is all we know about it.

I read your message to Cath$^{\underline{e}}$. She is behaving as usual– hems many yards for P$^{\underline{a}}$ & practices frequently, which is fortunate. Yesterday & today are Spring weather the Yellow jessamines are now in full bloom. Harry expresses great indignation at my not inviting M$^{\underline{rs}}$ H[arper] to come here, i.e. not <u>writing</u> an invitation, for I <u>did</u> invite her to make me a visit when at Baltimore & she agreed to do so– but H. says that when he spoke to her about coming here, she said she could not, so that I thought it was useless to write to her on the subject. She is going in a few days to Savanna, & will soon return & remain in

Ch$^{\underline{n}}$ untill the begin$^{\underline{g}}$ of May. Will$^{\underline{m}}$ went to Combahee a few days since & will return next week–

Sunday– You will be glad to hear that your Father seems very well today, & as you must be anxious to receive my letter which I have not been able to send before will send it after dinner to M$^{\underline{rs}}$ Pringle requesting her to have it put into the Post tomorrow when her Sons go early to town. Pa$^{\underline{a}}$ sends her best love to you– give mine to M$^{\underline{rs}}$ & M$^{\underline{r}}$ Fisher & M$^{\underline{rs}}$ Harrison not forgetting the dear little Girls & believe me my dearest Eliza y$^{\underline{r}}$ Affect$^{\underline{te}}$ Mother M. H. M.

PHi

    1. March 12 was the Fishers' wedding anniversary.
    2. A legacy from General Van Ness would have been very helpful since Arthur was not employed.

~

To Mrs. Fisher, Philadelphia

M.P. March 29$^{\underline{th}}$ 1846

My dearest Eliza's letter of the 23$^{\underline{d}}$ I had yesterday afternoon the pleasure to receive by Arthur who returned from town after having spent there three days & who informed me that his Father was still better & intended to come here either Monday or Tuesday & bring with him Edda & the two Girls. Harry too will come I presume as M$^{\underline{rs}}$ H[arper] is gone to Savannah. W$^{\underline{m}}$ had not returned from Combahee but will no doubt by that time. It was a great disappointment to me not to get a letter from my dear Brother by the Hibernia who must have been unable to write from another attack of Gout as he never fails to do so when able– Had you heard from your Aunt, you would have informed me of it: a month will therefore elapse before I can hear from him, or of him.

The news you give me of yourself although it causes a disappointment of not having you with me at Newport as long as I expected,[1] still affords me the happy expectation of meeting you at N.Y. & taking you with me to N$^{\underline{t}}$ which will indeed be a great comfort, & bringing Lily there is a good plan, & I hope you will remain longer than you say. As to my being with you during your confinement, that does not of course depend upon my will, but your Father's. And most fervently do I hope that your next will prove as safe as the former have been. You seem to expect another Daughter, but to please M$^{\underline{rs}}$ Fisher it had better be a Son. I agree with you in your opinion of the death of M$^{\underline{rs}}$ Ingersoll's unfortunate Child being a great blessing. it must be a consolation to her that she has been so devoted to her, endeavouring to relieve her from her sad state.

Your letter was read to Arthur & Pᵃ. They both think it probable that Govʳ V. N.² has destroyed his Brother's will. Paᵃ received yesterday a long letter from Miss Wight in which she says that the Will is not yet found, but that the Genˡ had often told her that he would provide for her (as you have been told)–

April 5ᵗʰ No opportunity my dearest Eliza have I had for sending this to town, but fortunately yesterday Willᵐ came & brought me your letter of the 28ᵗʰ ultᵒ. his Father he said was better & would come here on Tuesday, & he will leave us tomorrow, & soon after go to Combahee. He also brought me a letter from my Brother of the 1ˢᵗ of March by Ste[ame]r which I ought to have received 10 days since, & told you how disappointed I was about not getting it. Thank God! he says I may consider him convalescent, in fact very well, with only the usual exception of the weakness of his lower joints, & some small inflammation of his legs– That I think a dangerous symptom, for dropsy always brings on swelled legs, but I hope it is only in consequence of Gout in them. My Sister too is in good health.

You will be glad to hear that Edda (who arrived last Tuesday with Mary & Matilda) received yesterday a letter dated 4ᵗʰ March from Edward from Vera Cruze, a most affectionate one. He was to remain there 6 weeks but did not know what was to be the destination of the Cumberland: he is very anxious to procure a furlough & be with her soon– that is very uncertain. She is subject to pains in her back but has just come in to tell me she is going to accompany Paolina to the long pond where she is to bathe (walking up & down in it forty minutes). What think you of such a plan? She is drest as when walking, & the water does not reach higher than her waist– Arthur when the weather is not rainy, bathes in it every day & receives he says great benefit from it. Luckily there are as yet no Alligators in it.³

I am delighted my dear Eliza that we shall meet at N.Y. & that you will remain with me at Newport until the first week in June– Do not imagine that it will be any inconvenience to me to prepare your rooms– Which would you prefer? the new front room close to mine, or the old room upstairs. The other new room also next to mine, I must have prepared for Edda as she will have a nurse, & I must be near her instead of climbing upstairs. I intend to write to Mʳˢ Sumner, (now at Newport from whom I received a note yesterday) to request her to tell Block that we shall probably be there the middle of May, & explain to him the manner I wish to prepare the rooms. I hope you have no objection to the front room, if you have, the same room you occupied downstairs last summer can be made ready for you– tell me which you will have. I shall also enquire of Mrs S. whether there is a good Midwife at Newport, if there is not, D^{r} [David] King is a much better Phys^{n} than Dr Dunn. Willm said yesterday that we should leave Car^{a} in 3 weeks, which surprised me, but tant mieux! I hope the Ship Charleston will take us on, the best I ever was in, or the N.Y. which is of the same quality– Y^{r} Father is to go on by the rail cars so that you will see him & accompany him I hope to Newport, as Mr Fisher can only take you away from us. You never mention now the state of his eyes– I hope they are better.

I gave A^{r} & P^{a} y^{r} letter to read & they are both of the same opinion in regard to that wicked man–[4] They are going to Char^{n} in a few days to pass Good Friday & Easter Sunday & return next week– The account you give me of the Oregon question being soon settled is indeed a most agreeable intelligence. Emma Smith is now at Sav^{a} & Mrs Harper is to make her a visit– She declined coming here as she should not return until the beginning of May when she should be very busy, & we on the eve of departure. Edda sends her best love to you & begs me to enclose the little Lilac garland. Paol^{a} too sends her best love as do y^{r} brothers– I am my dearest Eliza y^{r} affectionate Mother M. H. M.

PHi
There are no letters between this and Mrs. Middleton's of May 13.

1. Eliza's letter of March 23 is missing, but she must have explained that she could not be in Newport for the whole summer because her baby was due in early August.
2. Cornelius Van Ness was a former governor of Vermont.
3. Matty Middleton described her Uncle Arthur amusing himself in the Long Pond, and "only think," she wrote her mother, "of his having induced Aunt Pauline to accompany him on these aquatic tours." She also reported that Arthur read *The Tempest* and *Twelfth Night* aloud to them. Matilda Middleton to Susan Middleton, April 8, 1846, ScHi.
4. The reference is not clear; Mrs. Middleton may have meant Governor Van Ness.

∽

To Mrs. Fisher, Philadelphia

Charleston May 13$\underline{th}$ 1846

Although I have written only 5 days since my dearest Eliza you may be anxious to have later accounts of our intentions– first I can tell you that your Father is better than when I last wrote– Last Sunday he told W^{m} he ought to engage Staterooms for the family in the Ship Ch[arlesto]n which he had visited the preceding day & was to decide on Monday whether we should be passengers– this seeming the decision & that sailing on the 16$\underline{th}$ would not be too late for Edda, I was delighted to anticipate the happiness of meeting you soon– but alas! how soon were my hopes frustrated! Edda had walked with Arthur & seemed very well when she came in at tea time on Sunday, but a few minutes after, she went into her room & sent for Pao$\underline{a}$ who remaining there some time, & then coming down & begging W$\underline{m}$ to send for D$\underline{r}$ Ogier to see Edda, I was alarmed & went to see her & learn what was her complaint– It was the same that she had at Mahon– she was suffering with pains in the head & the back & was delirious. When D$\underline{r}$ O. came, he prescribed remedies for her, Laudanum &c & even advised her attendants to bind up her head with a wet cloth. I remained some time with her, but Arthur who was there told me I could be of no service to her, & had better go to bed. P$\underline{a}$ however sat up the whole night with her & told me the hysterics lasted until 1 o'clock– She after that became better & slept constantly remaining in her bed all Monday– Yesterday she got up, & in the even$\underline{g}$ felt so well that she went into the parlour. D$\underline{r}$ Ogier said she must not go in the vessel for she might be on board 10 days & should such an attack occur as she had just suffered from, it would be very dangerous. W$\underline{m}$ went to the ship & said we could not go in it– There, ended my hopes.

Edda when we were talking on the subject was so kind as to say that she could easily go to N.Y. by the rail cars, for she could not bear to think of my being prevented on her account to meet you, that I <u>must</u> go on with Harry who has offered to accompany me– I asked D$\underline{r}$ O. yesterday whether he thought it would be safe for her to do so? he said it would not– Pa$\underline{a}$ as I believe I mentioned to you, says she will stay with Edda during her confinement & that I can go to the north– <u>that</u> does not depend upon <u>me</u>, & unless your Father when well enough to leave this should consent to my going with him which I ought to do, & be with him at Newport, I shall be compelled to remain here until July. These circumstances ought to prevent my ever in future looking forward to any events I wish to happen, which I often do & cannot resist, but this last disappointment ought to cure me of my folly.

John is still here, which gives us all pleasure, but poor Sally must be in a forlorn state without him, as she cannot read & has no near neighbours. Susan comes frequently to see us, she is thin, & P$\underline{a}$ says is not well, though she did not tell me she had any complaint. I have not been to see her boy yet who is now well, he has lately been ill from cutting his teeth.[1]

Emma has been to see us twice since I last wrote. she said she had not yet written to you, so that it was lucky I told you of her intention of not leaving Ch$\underline{n}$ before June. You will early in that month go to Abington I suppose. I have no notion of the engagement you mention of W$\underline{m}$ to one of the pretty girls.

When I asked him about it, he would not give me any information on the subject. Cath's arm is now well– she cannot practice for the Piano is packed up & we know not whether it will be taken out & used while we stay here. It gives me pleasure to find this climate cooler at this season than I have ever found it & as yet no mosquitos, which is very extraordinary– in the country there were, & sand flies also–

I must now send this away– All the family send their love to you.[2] Give mine to M^rs & Mr Fisher, Mrs Harrison & Mrs Smith & believe me my dearest Eliza y^r Affect^te Mother M. H. M.

PHi

1. Oliver and Susan's sixth child and first boy, Oliver Hering Middleton, Jr., had been born the summer before on July 17, 1845.
2. In her last letter, written a week later, Mrs.Middleton said to Eliza, "I am afraid all the unhappiness you have felt about . . . y^r Father will injure you though (thank God!) you say . . . that you are in perfectly good health." MHM to EMF, May 20, 1846, PHi.

～

"On me devolves the melancholy duty of informing you that our poor Father breathed his last this morning at 4 o'clock," John wrote Eliza on June 14, 1846. "His condition (more particularly as regards the nervous malady from which he had so long suffered) was such," John explained, "as to make us pray for his release. He could scarcely be said to be alive to us when I reached town on 5th May, & he has only lingered and languished ever since. We take the remains of our beloved parent to Middleton Place on Wednesday morning next."[1]

Announcing Henry Middleton's death the next day, a Charleston newspaper recalled his "good sense and sound judgment" as well as his "political integrity." In his private capacity, the writer remembered him as "a polished gentleman with [a] high sense of honor . . . [and a blend of] suavity and dignity which rendered his social qualities highly attractive to all who had with him the pleasures of private intercourse." The City Council passed a resolution honoring him, summoned the militia regiments, and on June 16 gave South Carolina's former governor a funeral with the highest military honors.[2]

Emma Huger Smith, who left immediately for Philadelphia to be with Eliza, said her father "looked so stately & noble afterwards, that I could scarcely realize that the Spirit was gone, & that he was to command no more."[3]

While Henry Middleton was slowly sinking, Edda's baby, a boy named Edward, was born in Charleston on June 6. After her husband's death, Mrs. Middleton went to Philadelphia rather than Newport, so she could be with Eliza when her fourth child was born.

1. John I. Middleton to EMF, June 14, 1846, PHi, C/F.
2. *Charleston News* and *Charleston Courier,* June 15, 1846.
3. EHS to EMF, June 16, 1846, PHi.

Epilogue

Eliza's fourth child, born in the summer of 1846 after her father died, was a boy. He was named George Harrison Fisher but lived only a few months. Eliza and Fisher had three more children in the next years: first Maria Middleton, then a second son also named after George Harrison, and last, Henry Middleton, born in 1851. Emma Huger Smith, as direct as ever, scolded Eliza about her last pregnancy, reminding her that she needed all her strength "for the Family you have already, without wasting it on additions so little required."[1]

Mrs. Middleton chose to live primarily in Philadelphia after her husband died. Eliza hoped to have her mother live with her at 170 Chestnut Street, but the house was too small to accommodate both Mrs. Middleton and Mrs. Fisher as well as the Fishers and their children. To Eliza's "unfeigned sorrow,"[2] Mrs. Fisher showed no interest in easing the situation by moving down the street to live with her sister, so Mrs. Middleton settled in a suite of rooms nearby, continuing for two or three more years to go to Newport in the summer. She became increasingly infirm, however, and died in the spring of 1850, when she was almost seventy-nine. Fisher sent the news of her death to Arthur, who was in Europe, saying, "It was not my good fortune to know her till age and sorrows had made great changes in her, but I always greatly admired the gentleness and sweetness of her disposition, her purity and kindness of heart, her refined and dignified manners."[3]

Aunt Harrison died the following year. She had always been Fisher's "devoted friend," and he and Eliza missed "all the daily and unremitting attentions

---

1. EHS to EMF, November 11, 1850, PHi.
2. EMF to Arthur Middleton, December 17, 1846, PHi, C/F.
3. JFF to Arthur Middleton, May 27, 1850, MPlFdn.

and kindnesses" she gave them.[4] Mrs. Fisher, the last of the older generation, followed her sister in 1855. She of course left virtually everything she owned to Fisher, with the exception of a few small legacies to her grandchildren, the poor communicants of St. Peter's Church, and Hetty Harvey and Louisa Darius, her longtime servants. In a tribute to her daughter-in-law, she also left Eliza a significant legacy. "I give, devise and bequeathe to my dear daughter Eliza M. Fisher," her will stated, "thirty thousand dollars as an Evidence of my affectionate approbation."[5]

After Mrs. Fisher died, Fisher and Eliza moved down the street to the Harrisons' old house, which Fisher had inherited when Aunt Harrison died and which he had always loved. After only a year, though, it was so damaged by a fire next door that they had to move out, and from then on, the Fishers' city residence was at 919 Walnut Street.

Fisher by then was a wealthy man, having inherited the bulk of George Harrison's estate. Estimated at $400,000 in 1845,[6] this inheritance enabled Fisher to pursue his dream of building a country house and, with the advice of the landscape designer, Andrew Jackson Downing, he chose a site near their farmhouse in Abington. "Alverthorpe," a large Italian-style villa designed by the architect John Notman, was the emotional center of the Fisher family from the early 1850s until Eliza's death in 1890.

The settlement of Henry Middleton's estate after he died in 1846 was protracted and complicated, and it disrupted the Middleton children's hitherto cordial relationships. Although Eliza's father owned Middleton Place, the house in Newport, the three rice plantations on the Combahee River, and several hundred slaves, he also had debts on the order of $250,000, the equivalent of approximately $5 million today.[7] He was fully aware of this and stipulated in his will that half of the annual income from his estate was to be set aside to pay these debts. In addition, Eliza was to receive the $30,000 that had been promised to her when she was married.

By 1860, to all intents and purposes, everything, except Eliza's "portion," had been paid off. This had been accomplished, however, by distributing only a minimum amount of income to all the Middleton children except Kitty. She lived from 1846 on with a family near Philadelphia and was always provided for, either from her father's estate or, during and after the Civil War, by Fisher.

---

4. EMF to Susan Middleton, April 4, 1851, ScHi.

5. Will of Elizabeth Powel Fisher, February 25, 1855, PHi, BrC. In 1999 dollars, $30,000 would be approximately $600,000. Conversion factor from RSahr, OrStU.

6. The $400,000 left by George Harrison when he died in 1845 would be the equivalent of approximately $8 million in 1999 dollars. Conversion factor from RSahr, OrStU.

7. Dollar conversion factor from RSahr, OrStU.

The policy of making only minimal distributions probably did not cause undue hardship for Eliza, Oliver, and John, who each had other resources, or for Williams,[8] since he had been given Middleton Place. It did, however, distress Arthur, Harry, and Edward considerably. Both Harry and Arthur, who had Paolina and the children to support, had depended on funds from their father during his lifetime and had expected to receive a good income from their share of his estate after his death. Although Edward lived on his salary, he wanted to leave the navy and could not afford to do so unless he had another source of income.

Complicating this even more, Henry Middleton divided his properties unequally between his six sons, with Williams receiving both Middleton Place and a large share of the Combahee plantations. Although the brothers agreed among themselves to a more equitable division within days of their father's death, this issue of fair distribution of the estate was a source of misunderstanding and anger among all the children until well after the Civil War.

With the possibility of war approaching, Eliza went to Charleston in April 1861 to see her family. The guns firing on Fort Sumter, which she heard before she left to return north, guaranteed that the Middletons would be divided against themselves. Her three brothers in South Carolina supported the Confederacy. John, who had become a very successful rice planter known for his modern agricultural techniques, signed the Ordinance of Secession, as did Williams. John and Sally's sons, Johnny and Tom, served in the Confederate army. So also did Oliver and Susan's boy, Oliver; he was killed in 1864.

Edward Middleton, on the other hand, remained in the U.S. Navy. "I did not resign my commission," he explained later, "because I considered myself bound by my oath of allegiance to the United States and to defend the Constitution." He retired as a rear admiral in 1876.[9]

As the war went on, Eliza defended her brothers in the South, and Fisher, who in any case thought the Lincoln administration was incompetent, supported his wife. He was criticized in Philadelphia for being pro-southern, but his position was probably much more complex than it appeared. He reminded his son, for example, to remember that his uncles were honorable men, even if they were mistaken.[10] With their children growing up amid friends with very

8. By this time all correspondence seems to refer to Williams, his given name, rather than William.

9. Harry, who had married an English woman, Ellen Goggin, in 1858, was in Europe during the Civil War. Arthur had died in Europe in 1853. His son, Benti, returned to the United States and fought for the Confederacy. Statement by Edward Middleton, (n. d.), Southern Historical Collection, University of North Carolina.

10. JFF to George H. Fisher, February 26, 1862, MPlFdn.

pro-Union sentiments, and knowing at the same time that their southern family and friends were suffering, Fisher and Eliza waited out the war in anguish.

At Middleton Place, the house was burned by Union troops in the last days of the war; books, papers, paintings—all were thrown out of the library and either burned or taken. At the Combahee plantations, rice, buildings, and animals were destroyed. And although their properties were not as damaged, John and Oliver, as well as Williams, were completely impoverished.

Fisher and Eliza helped many of their relatives and friends during and after the war. Fisher paid the fees at the Pennsylvania Hospital for a young Middleton cousin because the boy's parents could not send money to the North. He sent contributions to Dorothea Dix to help care for wounded Confederate prisoners. Eliza even tried to send cotton through the Union blockade of Charleston to be sold in Europe for the widowed Paolina, who was hard-pressed for money. Their help continued after the war and included paying the taxes to prevent Middleton Place from being sold.

Fisher, at the end of the war, was "a man prematurely old and disheartened by the events he had just lived through."[11] He died in 1873, before he was seventy, and was remembered for his "intelligence and characteristic earnestness,"[12] and as a "gentleman of much culture and refinement . . . generous and warmhearted, devoted to his friends, ever ready with kind word and deed."[13]

Eliza died in 1890, when she was seventy-five. Only Oliver and Kitty, of all her siblings, outlived her. Letters poured in from people who felt honored by her friendship. "I never left her presence without feeling that if I were not improved . . . it was my own fault," one wrote; she would be missed by the poor, "whose wants she relieved," said another. "I was a stranger . . . and [she] treated me with such kindness and had such patience with my ignorance and inexperience," wrote yet another. One of Lily Fisher's friends recalled "all the childish pleasures your mother promoted for you all & all your friends."[14]

By the time Eliza died, few of the people she and her mother had known and enjoyed half a century earlier were still alive, and the outlook and style of life they shared had long since changed. Fortunately, Eliza saved both her mother's letters and her own so that their correspondence, which captured so much of their spirit and lives, still exists for succeeding generations.

11. JFF, *Recollections*, x.
12. Annual Report of the Pennsylvania Institution for the Blind, 1873, Archives of the Overbrook School for the Blind.
13. Obituary of JFF, *Philadelphia Age*, January 22, 1873.
14. Various friends to Elizabeth Fisher (Mrs. Robert P.) Kane, February–April 1890, private collection.

Selected Bibliography

The many reference works to which I am greatly indebted, including genealogies, census records, and biographical, literary, and musical dictionaries, are not listed unless they are quoted directly.

PRINCIPAL MANUSCRIPT SOURCES

Historical Society of Pennsylvania, Philadelphia:
>   Cadwalader Collection, J. Francis Fisher Section, contains many Middleton and Fisher family papers, including nearly all of Mary Hering Middleton's letters to Eliza Fisher and a handful of Eliza's letters to her mother. Emma Huger Smith's letters to Eliza Fisher are in this collection.
>   Brinton Coxe Collection contains Fisher and Harrison family papers.
>   Fisher Family Papers, 1681–1955, contains Middleton and Fisher family papers.
>   Joshua Francis Fisher Papers (Collection #1858).

Middleton Place Foundation, Charleston: Middleton family papers.

Private collections, including Edward Middleton Rea Collection: Middleton and Fisher family papers.

South Carolina Historical Society, Charleston: Middleton family papers in several collections, including approximately forty letters between Eliza Fisher and Mary Hering Middleton.

Southern Historical Collection, University of North Carolina, Chapel Hill: Edward Middleton Papers; Nathaniel Russell Middleton Papers.

Single manuscripts, in various collections, are cited in the notes.

SELECTED SECONDARY SOURCES

Adams, John Quincy. *Diary, 1794–1845*. Edited by Allan Nevins. New York and London: Longmans, Green & Co., 1929.

Albion, Robert G. *The Rise of New York Port (1815–1860)*. Hamden, Conn.: Archon Books, 1961.

———. *Square Riggers on Schedule*. Princeton: Princeton University Press, 1938.

Basch, Norma. *In the Eyes of the Law: Women, Marriage, and Property in 19th Century New York*. Ithaca: Cornell University Press, 1982.

Baym, Nina. *American Women Writers and the Work of History, 1790–1860*. New Brunswick, N.J.: Rutgers University Press, 1995.

Bell, Malcolm, Jr. *Major Butler's Legacy: Five Generations of a Slaveholding Family*. Athens, Ga.: University of Georgia Press, 1987.

Biddle, Edward, and Mantle Fielding. *The Life and Works of Thomas Sully*. Philadelphia: Wickersham Press, 1921.

Bleser, Carol, ed. *The Hammonds of Redcliffe*. New York: Oxford University Press, 1981.

———, ed. *In Joy and Sorrow: Women, Family and Marriage in the Victorian South, 1830–1900*. New York: Oxford University Press, 1991.

———, ed. *Secret and Sacred: The Diaries of James Henry Hammond, a Southern Slaveholder*. New York: Oxford University Press, 1988.

Blumin, Stuart M. *The Emergence of the Middle Class: Social Experience in the American City, 1760–1900*. Cambridge and New York: Cambridge University Press, 1989.

Bowie, Lucy Leigh. "Madame Grelaud's French School." *Maryland Historical Magazine* 39, no. 2 (June 1944).

Boyd, Julian P., ed. *The Papers of Thomas Jefferson*. Vol. 16. Princeton: Princeton University Press, 1961.

Brady, Patricia. *George Washington's Beautiful Nelly, The Letters of Eleanor Parke Custis Lewis to Elizabeth Bordley Gibson, 1794–1851*. Columbia: University of South Carolina Press, 1991.

Brewster, Lawrence Fay. "Summer Migrations and Resorts of South Carolina Low-Country Planters." *Historical Papers of the Trinity College Historical Society*, series 26. Durham: Duke University Press, 1947.

Bushman, Richard L. *The Refinement of America*. New York: Alfred A. Knopf, 1992.

Butler, Frances Anne. *Journal*. 2 vols. Philadelphia: Carey, Lea & Blanchard, 1835.

Callcott, Margaret Law, ed. *Mistress of Riversdale: The Plantation Letters of Rosalie Stier Calvert, 1795–1821*. Baltimore: Johns Hopkins University Press, 1991.

Carpenter, Frank. "Paradise Held: William Ellery Channing and the Legacy of Oakland." *Newport History* 65, pt. 3 (1994).

Christman, Margaret. *Portrait of the Nation*. Washington, D.C: Smithsonian Institution Press for the National Portrait Gallery, 1996.

Clifford, Deborah Pickman. *Mine Eyes Have Seen the Glory: A Biography of Julia Ward Howe*. Boston: Little, Brown & Co., 1978.

Clinton, Catherine. *The Plantation Mistress: Women's World in the Old South*. New York: Pantheon Books, 1982.

Coclanis, Peter A. *Shadow of a Dream: Economic Life and Death in the South Carolina Low Country, 1670–1920*. New York: Oxford University Press, 1989.

Conrad, Susan Phinney. *Perish the Thought: Intellectual Women in Romantic America, 1830–1860*. New York: Oxford University Press, 1976.

Cott, Nancy F. *The Bonds of Womanhood: "Woman's Sphere" in New England, 1780–1835*. New Haven: Yale University Press, 1977.

Cutler, William W., III, and Howard Gillette, Jr. *The Divided Metropolis: Social and*

Spatial Dimensions of Philadelphia, 1800–1975. Westport, Conn.: Greenwood Press, 1980.

Davidson, Cathy N. *Revolution and the Word: Rise of the Novel in America.* New York: Oxford University Press, 1986.

Davidson, Chalmers Gaston. *The Last Foray: The South Carolina Planters of 1860: A Sociological Study.* Columbia: University of South Carolina Press, 1987.

Dennis, Catharine Engs. " 'My Much Loved Friend': Mrs. Dennis to Mrs. Hunter, 1838." *Newport History* 57, pt. 1 (winter 1984).

———. "All the Ton at My China Store & I Love to Talk." *Newport History* 57, pt. 3 (summer 1984).

Dewees, William P. *Treatise on the Physical and Medical Treatment of Children.* Philadelphia: Carey, Lea and Blanchard, 1836.

Easterby, J. H. *The South Carolina Rice Plantation as Revealed in the Papers of Robert F. W. Alston.* Chicago: University of Chicago Press, 1945.

Edgar, Walter. *South Carolina: A History.* Columbia: University of South Carolina Press, 1998.

Ellet, Elizabeth. *The Queens of American Society.* New York: Charles Scribner, 1868.

Elliott, Maud Howe. *Uncle Sam Ward and His Circle.* New York: Macmillan, 1938.

Faust, Drew Gilpin. *James Henry Hammond and the Old South: A Design for Mastery.* Baton Rouge: Louisiana State University Press, 1982.

Feldberg, Michael. *The Philadelphia Riots of 1844.* Westport, Conn.: Greenwood Press, 1975.

Fisher, Joshua Francis. *Recollections of Joshua Francis Fisher Written in 1864.* Arranged by Sophia Cadwalader. Boston: privately printed, 1929.

Fisher, Sidney George. *Mt. Harmon Diaries, 1837–1850.* Edited by W. Emerson Wilson. Wilmington, Del.: Historical Society of Delaware, 1976.

Floan, Howard R. *The South in Northern Eyes, 1831–1861.* Austin: University of Texas Press, 1958.

Fogel, Robert William, and Stanley L. Engerman. *Time on the Cross: The Economics of Negro Slavery.* Boston: Little, Brown & Co., 1974.

Foner, Philip S. *Business and Slavery: The New York Merchants and the Irrepressible Conflict.* Chapel Hill: University of North Carolina Press, 1941.

Fox-Genovese, Elizabeth. *Within the Plantation Household: Black and White Women of the Old South.* Chapel Hill: University of North Carolina Press, 1988.

Freehling, William W. *Prelude to Civil War: The Nullification Controversy in South Carolina, 1816–1836.* New York: Harper & Row, 1965.

Gerson, Robert A. *Music in Philadelphia.* Westport, Conn.: Greenwood Press, 1970.

Goldman, Perry M., and James S. Young, eds. *The United States Congressional Directories.* New York: Columbia University Press, 1973.

Grant, Mary H. *Private Woman, Public Person: An Account of the Life of Julia Ward Howe from 1819 to 1868.* Brooklyn, N.Y.: Carlson Publishing, 1994.

Hinding, Andrea, ed. *Women's History Sources: A Guide to Archives and Manuscript Collections in the U.S.* 2 vols. New York: Bowker, 1979.

Hone, Philip. *Diary, 1828–1851.* Edited by Allan Nevins. New York: Dodd, Mead & Co., 1936.

Howe, Julia Ward. *Reminiscences, 1819–1899.* Boston: Houghton Mifflin, 1899.

Hunter, Miss Anna F. "A Decade of Newport As Seen by Two Wandering Sons." *Bulletin of the Newport Historical Society* 53 (April 1925).

Jabour, Anya. "'Grown Girls, Highly Cultivated': Female Education in an Antebellum Southern Family." *Journal of Southern History* 64, no. 1 (February 1998).

Johnson, Michael P. "Planters and Patriarchy: Charleston, 1800–1860." *Journal of Southern History* 46, no. 1 (February 1980).

Joyner, Charles. *Down by the Riverside: A South Carolina Slave Community.* Urbana and Chicago: University of Illinois Press, 1984.

Kasson, John F. *Rudeness and Civility: Manners in 19th Century America.* New York: Hill and Wang, 1991.

Kerber, Linda K. *Women of the Republic: Intellect and Ideology in Revolutionary America.* Chapel Hill: University of North Carolina, 1980.

Klein, Rachel N. *Unification of a Slave State: The Rise of the Planter Class in the South Carolina Backcountry, 1760–1808.* Chapel Hill: University of North Carolina, 1990.

Littlefield, Daniel C. *Rice and Slaves: Ethnicity and the Slave Trade in South Carolina.* Baton Rouge: Louisiana State University Press, 1981.

Low, Betty-Bright P. "Of Muslins and Merveilleuses: Excerpts from the Letters of Josephine duPont and Margaret Manigault." *Winterthur Portfolio 9.* Charlottesville: University Press of Virginia, 1974.

———. "The Youth of 1812: More Excerpts from the Letters of Josephine duPont and Margaret Manigault." *Winterthur Portfolio 11.* Charlottesville: University Press of Virginia, 1976.

Lyell, Charles. *Travels in North America in the Years 1841–2, with Geological Observations on the United States, Canada and Nova Scotia.* 2 vols. New York: Wiley and Putnam, 1845.

Lystra, Karen. *Searching the Heart: Women, Men and Romantic Love in Nineteenth-Century America.* New York: Oxford University Press, 1989.

Lytle, Sarah. "Thomas Middleton: At Ease with the Arts in Charleston." In *Art in the Lives of South Carolinians,* edited by David Moltke-Hansen. Charleston: Carolina Art Association, 1979.

Madeira, Louis C. *Music in Philadelphia and the Musical Fund Society.* Edited by Philip H. Goepp. Philadelphia: 1896. Reprint, New York: DaCapo Press, 1973.

Manigault, Harriet. *The Diary of Harriet Manigault, 1813–1816.* Colonial Dames of America. Rockland, Maine: Maine Coast Printers, 1976.

Mason, George Champlin. *Reminiscences of Newport.* Newport, R.I.: Chas. E. Hammett, 1884.

McComb, Charles F., ed. *Letterbook of Mrs. Mary Stead Pinckney.* New York: Grolier Club, 1946.

Meriwether, Robert L., ed. *The Papers of John C. Calhoun.* Vol. 8, 1823–1824. Edited by W. Edwin Hemphill. Columbia: University of South Carolina Press, 1959– .

Middleton, Alicia Hopton. *Life in Carolina and New England during the 19th Century.* Bristol, R.I.: privately printed, 1929.

Miller, William Lee. *Arguing about Slavery: The Great Battle in the U.S. Congress.* New York: Alfred A. Knopf, 1996.

Morison, Samuel Eliot. *Harrison Gray Otis, 1765–1848: The Urbane Federalist.* Boston: Houghton Mifflin, 1969.

———. *The Life and Letters of Harrison Gray Otis, Federalist: 1765–1848.* 2 vols. Boston: Houghton Mifflin, 1913.

Munroe, John A. *Louis McLane: Federalist and Jacksonian.* New Brunswick, N.J.: Rutgers University Press, 1973.

Myers, Robert Manson. *The Children of Pride: A True Story of Georgia and the Civil War.* New Haven: Yale University Press, 1972.

O'Brien, Michael, and David Moltke-Hansen, eds. *Intellectual Life in Antebellum Charleston.* Knoxville: University of Tennessee Press, 1986.

Pease, William H., and Jane H. Pease. *James Louis Petigru: Southern Conservative, Southern Dissenter.* Athens: University of Georgia Press, 1995.

———. *The Web of Progress: Private Values and Public Styles in Boston and Charleston, 1828–1843.* Athens: University of Georgia, 1991.

Perry, Benjamin F. *Reminiscences of Public Men.* Vol. 3. Spartanburg, S.C.: The Reprint Co., 1980.

Pessen, Edward. *Riches, Class and Power before the Civil War.* Lexington, Mass.: D. C. Heath, 1973.

Ravenel, Mrs. St. Julien. *Charleston: The Place and the People.* New York: Macmillan, 1906.

Reinier, Jacqueline S. "Rearing the Republican Child: Attitudes and Practices in Post-Revolutionary Philadelphia." *William and Mary Quarterly,* ser. 3, vol. 39 (January 1982).

Rippy, J. Fred. *Joel R. Poinsett, Versatile American.* Durham: Duke University Press, 1935.

Rogers, George C., Jr. *Evolution of a Federalist: William Loughton Smith of Charleston (1758–1812).* Columbia: University of South Carolina Press, 1962.

Rosengarten, Theodore. *Tombee: Portrait of a Cotton Planter with the Plantation Journal of Thomas B. Chaplin (1822–1890).* New York: Morrow, 1986.

Rothman, Ellen K. *Hands and Hearts: A History of Courtship in America.* New York: Basic Books, 1984.

Salmon, Marylynn. *Women and the Law of Property in Early America.* Chapel Hill: University of North Carolina Press, 1986.

Sargent, Nathan. *Public Men and Events from the Commencement of Mr. Monroe's Administration in 1817 to the Close of Mr. Fillmore's Administration in 1853.* Philadelphia: Lippincott, 1875.

Saul, Norman E. *Distant Friends: The United States and Russia, 1763–1867.* Lawrence: University Press of Kansas, 1991.

Scharf, J. Thomas, and Thompson Westcott. *The History of Philadelphia.* 3 vols. Philadelphia: L. H. Everts & Co., 1884.

Schwaab, Eugene Lincoln, ed. *Travels in the Old South.* 2 vols. Lexington: University of Kentucky Press, 1973.

Scott, Anne Firor. *Making the Invisible Woman Visible.* Urbana: University of Illinois Press, 1984.

———. *The Southern Lady: From Pedestal to Politics, 1830–1930.* Chicago: University of Chicago Press, 1970.

Sears, John F. *Sacred Places: American Tourist Attractions in the 19th Century.* New York: Oxford University Press, 1989.

Smith, Daniel Blake. *Inside the Great House: Planter Family Life in 18th Century Chesapeake Society*. Ithaca and London: Cornell University Press, 1980.

Smith, Margaret Bayard. *The First Forty Years of Washington Society*. Edited by Gaillard Hunt. New York: Chas. Scribner & Sons, 1906.

Smith, Thelma M. "Feminism in Philadelphia, 1790–1850." *Pennsylvania Magazine of History and Biography* 68 (July 1944).

Smith-Rosenberg, Carroll. "The Female World of Love and Ritual: Relations between Women in Nineteenth Century America." In *Feminism and History*, edited by Joan Wallach Scott. Oxford and New York: Oxford University Press, 1996.

———. "Beauty, the Beast and the Militant Woman: A Case Study in Sex Roles and Social Stress in Jacksonian America." In *A Heritage of Her Own: Toward a New Social History of American Women*, edited by Nancy F. Cott and Elizabeth H. Pleck. New York: Simon & Schuster, 1979.

Sperling, John. *Great Depressions: 1837–1844, 1893–1898, 1929–1939*. Glenview, Ill.: Scott, Foresman & Co., 1966.

Strong, George Templeton. *Diary, 1835–1875*. Edited by Allan Nevins and Milton Halsey Thomas. 4 vols. New York: Macmillan, 1952.

Trapier, Paul. *Autobiography of the Rev. Paul Trapier*. Charleston: Dalcho Historical Society, 1952.

Wainwright, Nicholas B., ed. *A Philadelphia Perspective: The Diary of Sidney George Fisher Covering the Years 1834–1871*. Philadelphia: Historical Society of Pennsylvania, 1967.

———. "Samuel Breck's Diary." *Pennsylvania Magazine of History and Biography* (October 1978 and January 1979).

Watson, John Fanning. *Annals of Philadelphia and Pennsylvania in the Olden Time* . . . 3 vols. Philadelphia: E. S. Stuart, 1898.

Weigley, Russell F., et al., eds. *Philadelphia: A 300–Year History*. New York: W. W. Norton & Co., 1982.

Wheeler, Mary Bary, and Genon Hickerson Neblett. *Chosen Exile: Life and Times of Septima Sexta Middleton Rutledge*. Gadsden, Ala.: Rutledge Co., 1980.

Wister, Fanny Kemble, ed. *Fanny: The American Kemble*. Tallahassee, Fla.: South Pass Press, 1972.

Wood, Gordon S. *The Radicalism of the American Revolution*. New York: Alfred A. Knopf, 1992.

Yates, Gayle Graham. *Harriet Martineau on Women*. New Brunswick, N.J.: Rutgers University Press, 1985.

Dissertations

Bergquist, Harold E., Jr. "Russian-American Relations, 1820–1830: The Diplomacy of Henry Middleton, American Minister at St. Petersburg." Ph.D. diss., Boston University, 1970.

Hurst, Harold Whee. "The Elite Class of Newport, Rhode Island, 1830–1860." Ph.D. diss., New York University, 1975.

Kilbride, Daniel P. "Philadelphia and the Southern Elite: Class, Kinship and Culture in Antebellum America." Ph.D. diss., University of Florida, 1997.

Lane, George Winston, Jr. "The Middletons of 18th Century South Carolina: A Colonial Dynasty, 1678–1787." Ph.D. diss., Emory University, 1990.

McInnis, Maurie Dee. "The Politics of Taste: Classicism in Charleston, South Carolina, 1815–1840." Ph.D. diss., Yale University, 1996.

Scafidel, Beverly. "The Letters of William Elliott." Ph.D. diss., University of South Carolina, 1978.

NEWSPAPERS

Charleston Courier
National Gazette and Literary Register
National Intelligencer
The Pennsylvanian
Philadelphia Gazette and Commercial Intelligencer
Philadelphia Public Ledger

INTERNET

Sahr, Robert. "Consumer Price Index (CPI) Conversion Factors to Convert to 1999 Dollars (Preliminary)." Political Science Department, Oregon State University, Corvallis, Ore., 97331–6206 (www.orst.edu/dept/polsci/fac/sahr/sahr.htm).

Index